Polygamous families in contemporary society

We dedicate this book to the members of the plural families who participated in the project. Their openness, sincerity, and friendship will always be remembered and appreciated.

Polygamous families in contemporary society

Irwin Altman
The University of Utah

Joseph Ginat
University of Haifa

CAMBRIDGE
UNIVERSITY PRESS

Published by the Press Syndicate of the University of Cambridge
The Pitt Building, Trumpington Street, Cambridge CB2 1RP
40 West 20th Street, New York, NY 10011–4211, USA
10 Stamford Road, Oakleigh, Melbourne 3166, Australia

© Irwin Altman & Joseph Ginat, 1996

First published 1996

Printed in the United States of America

Library of Congress Cataloging-in-Publication Data
Altman, Irwin.
Polygamous families in contemporary society / Irwin Altman, Joseph
Ginat.
    p. cm.
Includes bibliographical references and index.
ISBN 0-521-56169-8. – ISBN 0-521-56731-9 (pbk.)
1. Polygamy – United States – History. 2. Mormon Church – United
States – History. 3. Mormon families – United States – History.
I. Ginat, J. II. Title.
HQ981.A45   1996
306.84'23 – dc20   95–46687
                                                                 CIP

A catalog record for this book is available from the British Library.

ISBN 0–521–56169–8 hardback
ISBN 0–521–56731–9 paperback

Contents

Foreword

This volume is the work of research scientists of uncommon talents and experience. Irwin Altman, the senior author, is a social-environmental psychologist of international reputation, the author and editor of numerous books and specialized research papers, and the recipient of many scholarly honors. Joseph Ginat, an anthropologist, has published extensively and is well known for his work on Israeli-Arab family, political, and cultural relations. Together they have produced a remarkable volume of research that is at once objective and sympathetic. They have achieved an understanding of their subject while observing it from the outside and at the same time experiencing it almost intimately from the inside. The degree of confidence and trust established with the men and women whom they studied – at times yielding surprising disclosures – is a testament to the honesty and integrity of the authors as well as the humanity of their participants.

Much that has been written about Mormonism and the Mormon people has been seriously flawed by the bias of its authors. If not apologetic or propagandistic, it has been pejorative or judgmental. For more than a century from the Mormon beginnings in the 1830s, attempts to treat the Mormons, their history, beliefs, and practices, dispassionately and without prejudice were few and far between. This was especially true of Mormon polygamy, which was practiced secretly in the early years but flourished openly after 1852 until its official church prohibition in 1890 and 1904. Yet despite the church interdiction and legal proscription by both state and national laws, polygamy thrives today in various enclaves of dissident Mormons that have no affiliation with the mainline Church of Jesus Christ of Latter-day Saints.

Altman and Ginat are not the first serious scholars to give attention to Mormon polygamy, but their subject is not the history of the institution or its past character. Rather the contemporary practice of polygamy is what concerns them, specifically the familial relationships involved. Their extensive observation and analysis of human relations and their general research into sociopsychological problems have provided them with insights, perspectives, and methods that make their work distinctive and give it exceptional value.

There are scholarly accounts of the demographics of Mormon polygamy, such as those of Stanley Ivins and George Smith, to say nothing of the extensive materials in church histories or the excellent historical study by Richard S. Van Wagoner, *Mormon Polygamy: A History.* And in his *Religion and Sexuality,* Lawrence Foster has provided a valuable comparative sociological analysis. But where these studies are about *polygamy,* the Altman–Ginat work is an intimate study of *polygamists,* their attitudes and behavior in their familial relations. This work has more in common with *A Mormon Mother* by Annie Clark Tanner, the classic true story of a polygamous wife, or the firsthand accounts of life in polygamous families that can be gleaned from the pioneer journals of both men and women. It has some affinities with the anecdotal information provided by journals and interviews with children and other relatives of polygamists found in Kimball Young's *Isn't One Wife Enough?* But these are accounts of polygamy as it was practiced in the past under circumstances quite different from those of the present. Altman and Ginat study the present and treat their subject as a living institution that thrives despite its conflict with the civil law and with the will of a church that had hoped to stamp polygamy out – to say nothing of the moral pressures from a society fully committed to monogamy.

The authors' objectives and research methodology, as well as their techniques for ensuring their informants' anonymity, are spelled out in their introduction, but there is nothing stilted or labored about the study. The family groups appear in undisguised relations and their members as candid and sincere individuals – no mean accomplishment in a scholarly study into such a humanly sensitive field. It is one thing to examine the past as a historian; it is quite another to understand and appreciate the living present as a scientist or social philosopher. This work has all the color and excitement of a good novel, combining the sensitivity of the artist and the sane, reliable information of the scientist.

This volume is not only a rich vein of information for students of the social and psychological factors in human relations, lively reading for the lay person, and a pool of inspiration for fiction and drama. It is also a valuable source for future historians of religion, morality, and social institutions. Here one can enter into a surprising and fascinating world that is little understood, defies conventional Western morality, and is therefore usually kept at least semisecret and out-of-bounds not only for the general public but also for the serious student.

Sterling M. McMurrin

Preface and acknowledgments

Our work on this book began quite coincidentally and accidentally. In 1986 Gloria and Irwin Altman were in Israel attending a conference, having also previously arranged to spend some social time with Dalia and Joseph Ginat. The Ginats and Altmans had been casual acquaintances in Utah in the 1970s, during the time that Joseph was completing his Ph.D. in anthropology and Irwin was a faculty member in psychology at the University of Utah. Over the course of many social occasions when the Ginats hosted the Altmans in Israel, we decided to collaborate on a study of family life among Mormon fundamentalists who espoused and practiced polygamy. During his years in Utah, Joseph had become acquainted with members of fundamentalist groups, many of whom he and Dalia visited in their homes and communities, and several of whom spent time with the Ginats in Israel.

We originally planned a small-scale study of relationships between husbands and wives, and between wives, in modern plural families. But once begun, the project grew and grew, our interest and commitment mounted, our relationships with fundamentalist families deepened, and the work expanded into a decade-long effort. This book is the story of what we learned and also reflects the intellectual perspectives, collegiality, and close personal relationships of the Altmans and Ginats with one another, and with the families who participated in the work.

There are several reasons for studying polygamous families in contemporary society. First, as a social-environmental psychologist, and an anthropologist, we are interested in family and close interpersonal relationships among friends, lovers, partners, and spouses – how these relationships are managed; how they play out in the context of family and kin, neighbors and communities; and how they vary and are similar across cultures.

Second, our work on close relationships is guided by a transactional philosophical perspective, which emphasizes sensitivity to the holistic nature of interpersonal bonds, the importance of social and physical settings and influences on relationships, the dynamic and changing character of close affiliations, and the need to study close bonds throughout their life history. A transactional perspective seemed to be an appropriate framework for studying contemporary plural family life.

Third, we live in an age of diverse and newly emerging forms of family and close personal relationships, many of which are not well understood by scholars or citizens alike. With high rates of divorce, the single-marriage nuclear family is less prevalent than ever before. Instead, we see serial marriages, blended families with partners and children from earlier marriages, single-parent households (usually headed by women), same-gender relationships openly functioning as families, new immigrant groups living in extended family arrangements, elderly group living, and so on.

Mormon fundamentalists practicing polygamy represent still another type of family lifestyle now on the scene in contemporary society. Although polygamy is illegal and has been renounced by the main Mormon church since 1890, there are somewhere between 20,000 and 50,000 members of Mormon fundamentalist families in the western United States, Mexico, and Canada who condone and practice polygamy in accordance with 19th-century Mormon religious beliefs. Indeed, a growing number of fundamentalists continue the practice in spite of a history of hostility and condemnation by American society, and in the face of legislation and potential prosecution by local, state, and federal governments.

In the long run we wish to understand how close relationships in all their diversity, including polygamous bonds, are similar and different from one another. What makes for their success or failure? What are their dynamics? In particular, polygamous relationships among Mormon fundamentalists have some unique challenges that may shed light on features of close relationships in general. As contemporary Americans, Mormon fundamentalists, many of whom are converts to the fundamental religious belief system, hold fast to the ideal of each husband–wife dyad being a special and distinctive relationship. But they also believe that the whole plural family – all wives and the husband – should be a unified communal family. Our question is how do they achieve a viable interplay of these seemingly contradictory *dyadic* and *communal* ideals? Thus we wish to explore their successes and failures in the face of pressures from society as a whole, and the lack of experience of many participants with plural family life. We also examine how they cope with their challenging lifestyle in many aspects of day-to-day living – such as courting, weddings, adjustment to a new marriage, living arrangements, decorating practices, management of budgets and resources, and celebrations.

To our knowledge this is the first broad analysis of psychological and anthropological aspects of life in modern Mormon plural families. Although there are several analyses of plural family life among 19th-century

Mormons and a number of historical, journalistic, and partial analyses of contemporary fundamentalism, we believe that the present work provides a unique perspective on life in modern plural families.

This book is based on interviews and observations of plural families and fundamentalist communities from 1987 to 1992. During those years we worked collaboratively with about 100 members of approximately two dozen families over the course of some 200 interviews and observations. Our participants were members of two large groups of fundamentalists, one centered in a rural town and region and the other headquartered in and around a large metropolitan area. To place our analysis in context, we have also drawn on archival and ethnographic material describing polygamy in other world cultures and among 19th-century Mormons.

The book is organized as follows: chapter 1 presents an overview of the religious underpinnings of present-day Mormon fundamentalists, followed by our conceptual approach and goals. The first section of the book describes the history of the Mormon religion, its early practice of polygamy, and the eventual rejection of plural marriages by the Mormon church (chapter 2); the rise of fundamentalism and the renewed practice of polygamy in this century (chapter 3); and the groups and communities with whom we worked (chapter 4).

The second section of the book (chapters 5–9) presents the results of our interviews and observations on the *early phases of close relationships* in modern plural families, including the decision to add a new wife to a family, courtship, weddings, honeymoons, and initial adjustments by wives and husbands to a new marriage.

The next sections, on *physical environments* of plural marriages (chapters 10–12), examines living and housing arrangements in polygamous families and the psychological attachments of husbands and wives to their homes (including how they decorate dwellings, establish territories, manage privacy, and so on).

We then portray a few aspects of *everyday life* in plural families in chapters 13–15, including the ways husbands "rotate" among their wives and families, and how families manage their budgets and resources and celebrate birthdays, anniversaries, and holidays.

Chapters 16–19 address *social-emotional relationships* between wives, husbands and wives, and parents and children. Here we provide detailed case examples of established, emerging, and dysfunctional plural families.

Chapter 20 summarizes our work, and reflects on the future of contemporary Mormon plural families.

Appendix A presents our research methodology. Appendix B describes demographic features of our participants and families and of 19th-century Mormon polygamous families.

This work could not have been completed without the assistance, encouragement, and contributions of many people and organizations. To all of them we offer our thanks and appreciation.

Most of all we are grateful to the men, women, and family members who invited us into their homes and communities, who were always gracious and sincere, and who offered us a glimpse into their lives. And we appreciate the support of church and community leaders who made us welcome at a variety of functions in their communities. We will forever remember the goodwill and friendship of all our participants, and we dedicate this book to them.

We also extend our thanks to the many colleagues and anonymous reviewers who commented on earlier drafts of the manuscript or on briefer articles and presentations of this work in other settings. They are too numerous to mention by name, but their advice and support are gratefully acknowledged. We are also indebted to four members of the fundamentalist groups with whom we worked for their careful review of the manuscript. A special word of thanks goes to Philip McBride, Bryn Mawr College, for his comments and expressions of encouragement. We are also grateful to Sterling M. McMurrin for his eloquent and gracious foreword to this book.

As always, our universities and colleagues supported us in many ways. The University of Utah provided financial assistance during earlier phases of the project, and the University Teaching Committee and the university generously granted Irwin Altman a faculty fellowship and sabbatical leave to complete the book. The College of Social and Behavioral Science and Dean Donna Gelfand, and the Department of Psychology and Chairperson Charles Shimp, always provided tangible and intangible support, encouragement, and understanding over the many years of the project. We also extend our thanks to the Jewish-Arab Center at the University of Haifa, and to the University of Haifa Research Authorities, whose assistance and support made it possible for Joseph Ginat to undertake the project.

We were privileged to work with Angela Newman, University of Utah. With extraordinary patience, competence, and goodwill, Angela typed many thousands of pages of field notes, data summaries, and draft manuscript – often from mumbled dictation and nearly illegible scribblings. Without her energy and commitment this project would have been stalled at many critical junctures.

We are also indebted to the Cambridge University Press staff. Our special thanks go to Julia Hough, our editor. At every decision point, her advice and judgment were not only impeccable but always presented with an unusual combination of forthrightness, grace, and civility. We appreciate very much our professional and personal relationship with Julia. Paul Dreifus and the staff at Cambridge were also a pleasure to work with. We especially acknowledge the assistance of Janis Bolster, production editor, and Vicky Macintyre for her thorough editing of the manuscript.

To our wives, Gloria and Dalia, we express our love, respect, and appreciation, as we have throughout our lives together. They were with us at every point in this work – participating in many trips, visits, and meetings at our and participants' homes, displaying insights into various aspects of the work, and being accepting and open minded about a different lifestyle.

As social scientists our goal was to describe and understand a unique family lifestyle now on the contemporary scene – and one that will surely continue into the future – and to advance research and theory on close relationships. We approached the task as scholars, intending neither to advocate nor condemn plural family life, and we have tried to present a forthright and balanced analysis. At the same time, we also hope that the ideas and content of the book are useful to the members and families of the fundamentalist groups we studied – by perhaps presenting them with another perspective on the lifestyle they choose to live, identifying the complexities and challenges many families face, and opening up for discussion alternative modes of coping with facets of their everyday lives. Thus we hope that our work has direct and tangible value for those who gave so much to it.

Finally, we aspire to the possibility that our research will help the "world" understand better the motivations, challenges, and complexities of family life in the groups we studied. We live in a time of great change and diversity in lifestyles and, although we each must live according to our own values and beliefs, it is also important to have some understanding of why and how others choose to live. In learning about the lifestyle of others we have an opportunity to avoid, or at least reduce, the animosities, hatreds, and divisiveness that can be so destructive among people who live differently and who often misunderstand one another. Indeed, through knowledge and understanding our very diversity may enrich and enlarge our worldview as a society and civilization.

Permission has generously been granted to quote from the following copyrighted works:

"Changed faces: The official LDS position on polygamy, 1890–1900," by M. S. Bradley. *Sunstone* 75 (1990): 26–33. By permission of *Sunstone*.

"The women of fundamentalism: Short Creek, 1953," by M. S. Bradley. *Dialogue* 23 (1990): 15–27. By permission of the Dialogue Foundation.

Kidnapped from that land: The government raids on the Short Creek polygamists, by M. S. Bradley. Copyright 1993. By permission of the publishers, University of Utah Press.

"Divorce among Mormon polygamists: Extent and explanations," by E. E. Campbell and B. L. Campbell. *Utah Historical Quarterly* 46 (1978): 4–23. By permission of the Utah Historical Society.

"The persecutions begin: Defining cohabitation in 1885," by K. Driggs. *Dialogue: A Journal of Mormon Thought* 21 (1988): 109–125. By permission of the Dialogue Foundation.

"Emmeline B. Wells," by P. R. Eaton-Gadsby and J. R. Dushku. In V. Burgess-Olson (ed.), *Sister saints* (pp. 457–478). Copyright 1978. By permission of V. Burgess.

"Effects of polygamy on Mormon women," by J. L. Embry. *Frontiers* 3 (1984): 56–61. By permission of *Frontiers: A Journal of Women's Studies,* University of New Mexico.

Mormon polygamous families: Life in the principle, by J. L. Embry. Copyright 1987. By permission of University of Utah Press.

"Situated action: An emerging paradigm," by G. P. Ginsburg. In L. Wheeler (ed.), *Review of personality and social psychology* (pp. 295–325). Copyright © 1980. By permission of Sage Publications, Inc.

"Plural wives," by S. S. Goodson. In C. L. Bushman (ed.), *Mormon sisters: Women in early Utah* (pp. 89–111). Copyright 1976. By permission of Claudia Bushman.

"Feminist implications of Mormon polygamy," by J. Iversen. *Feminist Studies* 10 (1984): 505–522. By permission of *Feminist Studies.*

"Notes on Mormon polygamy," by S. S. Ivins. *Western Humanities Review* 10 (1956): 229–239. By Permission of *Western Humanities Review,* University of Utah.

Polygamist's wife, by M. Merrill. Copyright 1975. By permission of Olympus Publishing Company.

Mormon enigma: Emma Hale Smith, by L. K. Newell and V. T. Avery. Copyright 1984. By permission of Doubleday, a division of Bantam Doubleday Dell Publishing Group, Inc.

" 'Wait till your mothers get home': Assessing the rights of polygamists as custodial and adoptive parents," by R. M. Otto. *Utah Law Review* 4 (1991): 881–931. By permission of the *Utah Law Review.*

"Mormon haters," by C. H. Sheldon. In C. L. Bushman (ed.), *Mormon sisters: Women in early Utah* (pp. 113–131). Copyright 1976. By permission of Claudia Bushman.

"Women as heads of houses: The organization of production and the role of women among pastoral Maasai in Kenya," by A. Talle. *Ethnos* 1–2 (1987): 50–80. By permission of Scandinavian University Press.

Mormon polygamy: A history, by R. S. Van Wagoner. Second edition, copyright 1989. By permission of Signature Books.

Patriarchs and politics: The plight of the Mormon woman, by M. Warnski. Copyright 1978. By permission of McGraw-Hill.

Isn't one wife enough? by K. Young. Copyright 1954 by Henry Holt & Co. By permission of Henry Holt & Co.

Irwin Altman
Joseph Ginat

1

Introduction

Harry, now in his 60s, had been away from home on a business trip for several days. After a long drive he arrived at the family compound and was greeted by an excited group of about 20 of his 65 children and two of his five wives. Soon thereafter the other wives and more of his children came to see him. He and his children and wives greeted one another warmly, especially since it was the weekend of the monthly family reunion and meetings. Everyone was expected home that weekend, including Harry's 37 sons and 28 daughters and their families and more than 300 grandchildren and great-grandchildren.

William and his three wives – Carlyn, Danielle, and Alayna – have begun to achieve their dream of a home of their own in which they and their 12 children can live as a united family, in accordance with their religious beliefs. All converts to Mormon fundamentalism, they have struggled for years, living in rented apartments, basements of homes, and, during one hard winter, in a tent. In spite of ever-present economic strains, they finally began building their own home in a semirural area near Metropolitan City. The family has been in difficult financial straits, so construction goes slowly, they try to grow some of their own food, and they find whatever work they can in a tight economy. Admitting that they don't have much experience in plural family life, they also experiment with different living arrangements and ways to relate to one another, raise their children, and meet their religious beliefs.

Lauren, the second wife, finally quit her marriage to Fred after eight years of struggling to work things out with Fred and Elaine, the first wife in their polygamous family. She claims that Fred favored Elaine almost from the beginning of her marriage and that Elaine also didn't treat her very well. Lauren felt like a second-class person and didn't have enough time with Fred to develop their marriage; Fred gave Elaine nicer furnishings for her home and even told Lauren that he preferred Elaine to her. Elaine made things worse by demeaning Lauren, flaunting her relationship with Fred, and not supporting her as a co-wife. It finally became too stressful for Lauren, so she requested and was granted a "release" (divorce) from the marriage by the religious leader of their church.

The Sunday church service was attended by 600 to 800 people. Following several announcements, the singing of hymns, and a sacrament service, the 80-year-old religious leader, who is husband to eight wives and father of 43 children, delivered a sermon on the evils and decline of morals in the modern world and the need for members of the congregation to attend to their religious roots in 19th-century Mormonism and in the teachings of the biblical prophets. Other male elders spoke of the importance of fathers and husbands as religious and family patriarchs and the need for congregants to follow men as holders of the priesthood. Some speakers also called for appreciation and respect for wives and mothers, who are, one man said, "jewels in the crowns of their husbands."

The people and polygamy

These vignettes are a glimpse into the story of this book, which deals with close relationships between a husband and his wives and between wives in contemporary polygamous families.

Who are these people and why do they believe in and practice polygamy? Surprising as it may seem, approximately 20,000 to 50,000 Americans are currently members of Mormon fundamentalist religious groups and believe in the principle of plural marriage, or polygamy. To be more precise, they practice and subscribe to a particular form of polygamy, termed *polygyny*, which involves a husband and two or more wives.

The families in the vignettes are members of organized fundamentalist religious communities who claim to follow the theological dictates of 19th-century Mormonism, officially known as the Church of Jesus Christ of Latter-day Saints (LDS Church). A uniquely American version of Christianity, the LDS religion was founded in the early 1800s in the northeastern United States by Joseph Smith, a charismatic and inspirational leader. As described in chapter 2 early Mormonism was one of several conservative counterreactions to emerging liberal values of the late 17th and early 18th centuries. In their opposition to greater freedom of choice of marital partners, women's rights, easier divorces, abortions, and a general rise in individual rights, several conservative religious movements of the times, including Mormonism, called for the reestablishment of strong families, orderly community and religious structures, strict gender roles with women assuming traditional domestic and child-rearing responsibilities, and the

ubordination of women to male patriarchal leadership. Under Joseph
mith, who claimed to have received from an angel a scripture describing
he history and religion of an ancient people – the Book of Mormon – the
ew Church of Jesus Christ of Latter-day Saints attracted a number of
ollowers. After years of migration and relocation, and then Joseph Smith's
ssassination, the Mormons emigrated to Utah in 1847 under the leader-
hip of Brigham Young and established a combined religious and secular
ociety, which flourishes to this day.

The practice of plural marriage, or polygyny, evolved under Joseph
mith over a period of several years as one aspect of early Mormon the-
logy. Several principles of this theology were linked to the idea of plural
narriage. A key principle was that a stable and orderly family life depends
n part on a husband or father functioning as a religious and social leader.
his dictum was traced to the biblical patriarchs, who were empowered
vith religious priesthood roles and who presided over polygynous families
vith multiple wives and many children. Another principle pertained to mar-
iage and life in the hereafter: a religiously "righteous" man and his wife
r wives could live as a "king" and "queen(s)" in the hereafter in their
wn heavenly universe, surrounded by their progeny. Because women could
ot enter the priesthood, an idea reflected in the Old Testament, their only
ntry to a heavenly state in the hereafter was through their husband. And
ecause only religiously righteous men, who are in a minority in the world,
nay live in an exalted state in the hereafter, women were encouraged to
narry such men, even in a polygynous mode, in order to achieve the prom-
se of a heavenly existence in the afterlife. Original Mormon doctrine also
ostulated that marriages in the civil system were for "time" only, that is,
n earthly life; marriages performed by religious leaders were for "time and
ternity," extending into the hereafter forever. This doctrine therefore made
t possible for polygynous marriages to be performed within the church and
hereby to bypass the civil system and avoid direct confrontation between
ecular and religious principles. These principles continue to be strongly
eld today by Mormon fundamentalists.

It was, and still is, also important for a fundamentalist husband and his
vives to have many children. This responsibility stems from their belief in
premortal existence and the need for premortal souls to pass through
arthly existence before entering the hereafter and to act in righteous ways
n earth.

Mormon religious doctrine of the 19th century and today is far richer
han that described here, as will become evident in subsequent chapters.
he crucial point to note for the time being is that modern fundamentalists
elieve in and practice plural marriage in accordance with the tenets of
arly Mormonism, even though the main LDS Church, now numbering

some nine million members worldwide, began denouncing the practice c
polygyny in 1890. Although subscribing to many of the same theologica
principles as fundamentalists, the main LDS Church vigorously and un
equivocally rejects the practice of polygyny, does not recognize fundamen
talists as Mormons, excommunicates any of its members who are affiliate
with fundamentalist groups, and has actively assisted and condoned th
actions of civil authorities against fundamentalists who practice plural mar
riage. And because fundamentalists consider themselves to be the "true
followers of Joseph Smith and original church theology, they are an em
barrassment and irritant to the main LDS Church.

Why fundamentalists believe in and practice polygyny is straightfor
ward. They believe themselves to be following Mormon religious doctrine
And they hold to the practice in spite of the fact that bigamy (a perso
having two or more spouses) and cohabitation-habitation (a person livin
with two or more members of the opposite sex) are felonies in the crimina
code of Utah and that polygamy is explicitly banned in that state's consti
tution. Furthermore, fundamentalists continue to practice plural marriag
in the face of rejection and criticism by American society, and in spite c
the possibility of arrest, prosecution, and the loss of their jobs when the
are found out to be engaged in plural marriages. With strength and fervor
they hold fast to the conviction that they are following the true path o
Mormon theology.

Contemporary fundamentalist polygyny

Studying husband–wife and wife–wife relationships in contemporary po
lygynous families is consistent with our long-standing research interest i
close interpersonal relationships. Over the years we have examined hov
close relationships form, progress from casual to intimate bonds, and some
times deteriorate and break up; how close relationships are played out i
various settings such as homes, public places, and elsewhere; and wha
factors make for their success or failure (see, e.g., Altman, 1975, 1990
Altman and Chemers, 1989; Altman and Taylor, 1973). In addition, th
study of close relationships is a rich and expanding topic, especially on th
contemporary scene.

Relationships in modern times

We live in an era of plural, diverse, and heterogeneous beliefs and values
cultural subgroups, and lifestyles – all of which are likely to intensify i

he coming decades as a result of changes in the demographic and social
andscape of America and the Western world. Centrifugal and pluralistic
orces abound in the wake of geopolitical changes that are altering the
haracter of once stable nation-states. The effect of these changes is com-
ounded by large-scale migrations; present and projected shifting demo-
raphics within nations, including the United States; an expanding global
conomy, which is tying the fate of people around the world together; and
he potential for war and terrorism in the hands of small or unstable
ations and ideological groups.

Accompanying these broad social changes is an increasing diversity of
ypes of close interpersonal relationships and family forms. The stereotyp-
cal ideal of the nuclear family of a mother, father, and their children that
ervaded American and Western society in the first decades of the 20th
entury had given way to acceptance, or at least acknowledgment, of the
act that the social landscape is now populated by a great diversity of close
elationships and family types: single-parent families, usually headed by
vomen; blended families in which a woman and man bring children from
revious relationships into a new family; cohabiting couples; same-sex re-
ationships; cohabitation parenting in which unmarried couple members
gree to have children and share responsibility but do not live together
Kilbride, 1994); elderly people living in group situations; older children
vho are divorced returning with children to live with their parents; unique
ultural and ethnic family structures; families in homeless shelters or other
ransient circumstances; immigrant populations with family members sep-
rated for periods of time; and others. To this diversity we add the rela-
ively small number of fundamentalist Mormons who believe in and live in
 plural family structure.[1]

We are interested in this array of close relationships and family struc-
ures as scholars and citizens. As scholars, we believe it is important to
tudy and understand these relationships in and of themselves – to see how
hey work, their underlying dynamics, their similarities and differences, and
actors associated with their viability and well-being. So the opportunity to
ain some understanding of life in plural families is consistent with our
cholarly goals.

But we also have an interest as citizens of a changing world in which it
s inevitable that people with varied lifestyles will come into contact, and
ven clash over differences in values and beliefs, including how they live in
amilies and close relationships. We accept the reality that these diverse
elationship forms are here to stay. Thus it is more important than ever
efore to promote mutual tolerance, if not genuine acceptance of those
ifferences. If we can penetrate the superficial and often inaccurate stere-
types about others who live differently from us, then we may be able to

achieve a greater degree of social unity, peace, and goodwill amidst th
diversity and plurality that will be with us for decades to come.

Managing relationships in plural families

Given the uniqueness of polygyny in American and Western society, w
anticipated that managing relationships between a husband and his wive
and between the wives would be enormously challenging for reasons botl
external and internal to such relationships. External pressures stem fron
the general hostility of American society to polygyny; internal challenge
arise from the dynamics of husband–wife and wife–wife relationships o
plural marriages.

External pressures

External social pressures with which contemporary polygynous familie
must contend are associated with society's antipathy toward plural mar
riage. Tolerant as many Americans have become of alternative forms o
relationships – such as blended families, single-parent families, cohabitin;
couples, same-gender relationships – the idea of polygynous marriages con
tinues to be beyond the boundary of acceptability in American society. Th
idea of several women married to a man in a patriarchal family structur
raises the hackles of many civil and women's rights activists, and probabl
of most Americans, whether of liberal or conservative stance. A polygynou
family structure and its apparent gender inequities are simply unacceptabl
to many contemporary Americans. External pressures and rejection b
American society, not to mention the strong opposition of the main Mor
mon Church to polygyny, are surely large obstacles for fundamentalists
Imagine the difficulty of managing a complex set of husband–wife anc
wife–wife relationships in the face of condemnation by American society
and by the very religious organization with which one is historically anc
theologically linked. Participants are fearful about publicly stating that they
are a plural wife or polygynous husband to the school system, to co
workers, or to the many people with whom they come into contact in daily
life. How does one cope with plural family life in the face of queries, re
actions of amazement, and explicit or implicit criticism of one's marita
relationship? How does one meet the challenge of maintaining a healthy
set of family relationships in the face of reinforcement of a monogamou:
value system in television, movies, and printed media? For us, one task i:
to understand how, in the face of these external challenges, members o:

polygynous relationships cope with their situation to achieve some level of viability.

Internal dyadic challenges

All close relationships – monogamous or otherwise – also face an incredible number of internal challenges. Monogamous partners must figure out how to relate to one another in a variety of life domains and cope with the inevitable changes in their joint life connected with raising children, working or pursuing careers, aging and health problems, and experiencing day-to-day conflicts and tensions. Self-help books, newspaper advice columns, divorce rates, and the frequency of marital counseling all attest to the challenges faced by contemporary Americans and others around the world as they attempt to achieve viable and satisfying close relationships.

But these statements refer to monogamous relationships, usually between a man and a woman. In the American value system a husband–wife couple is joined by a sacred bond, and the partners ideally have a unique, distinctive, intimate, and love-based relationship. Furthermore, this idealized image is reinforced by literature, the law, and the media and in everyday life. The fact is, however, that fundamentalists hold to the same value system. They also believe that husband–wife relationships should be based on love and that dyadic bonds between a husband and wife should be intimate, unique, and special. They also believe that every husband–wife couple in a plural family should have its own distinctive character and should satisfy the ideal of love and intimacy. How is this possible for polygynous partners amidst all the other challenges involved in developing a viable relationship? Imagine being a woman whose husband has one or more other wives, all having to share him while seeking their own unique, special, intimate, and loving relationship with the same man. How can this be achieved? What does a wife think on seeing her husband in an intimate and close relationship with another woman on a regular basis? What does she feel knowing that her husband is having sex and sleeping with another woman with whom she herself has regular contact (and with whom she may even be sharing living quarters)? What is it like for an older wife to see her husband marry a younger and seemingly more attractive woman? And how does a young new wife feel when she sees her husband and an established wife in a smooth and easy flowing relationship with one another, while she struggles to develop her own relationship with her husband? What stresses does a new wife face living in the home of an established wife and being unable to meet the American ideal of creating and managing her own home for herself and her husband? Conversely, what is it like for an established wife to have a new wife live with her, intrude on her routines, and be intimate with her husband in her home? The stresses and challenges facing wives in polygynous families magnify manyfold the ordinary problems faced in monogamous relationships. But what about the challenges facing husbands in plural marriages? What is it like managing multiple intimate, special, and unique relationships with more than one woman at the same time? How is it possible to have distinctive emotional, love-based ties to more than one woman at a time? How should a man behave toward each wife in the presence of other wives and still ideally achieve a special relationship with each one? How should a husband apportion his time between his wives and families? How is it possible to simultaneously deal with the day-to-day life and emotional issues of each wife and family? How can a husband resolve with each wife his and their personality differences and cope with their mutual interpersonal emotions, needs, and stresses that are inevitably part of married life? Where should a husband live from day to day? How can he be available for family crises and needs?

Internal communal challenges

Achieving viable multiple *dyadic* relationships between a husband and wives in plural families is surely a complicated matter. But there is yet another major challenge. Members of contemporary polygynous families believe that they should also strive to become a unified, cohesive, and integrated *communal* family unit. That is, religious values and cultural norms call for wives to love, support, and nurture one another. They are also expected to support each other's relationship with the husband. And husbands are expected to be fair to, to love, and to honor all wives. Of course, these idealized communal values are not always achieved in practice, in the same way that cultural ideals for monogamous marriages are not always realized.

Taken together, participants in modern plural families subscribe to the American view that each marital relationship in a family – a *dyad* – should be special, unique, intimate, and individualized. At the same time, they seek a unified, cohesive *communal* family structure in which all participants support, nurture, and function as a cohesive family unit.

In the following chapters we explore the interplay of dyadic and communal relationships in various aspects of polygynous life: the decision to add a wife to a family, courting practices, weddings, adjustment to and by new wives, relationships between husbands and wives, rotation of husbands among families, home management, living arrangements, attachments to home by husbands and wives, celebrations, conflict resolution, and other topics. Managing dyadic and communal relationships in plural families is an extraordinary balancing act requiring enormous energy, attention, and patience by family members. Other polygynous cultures sometimes face the same challenges but may over decades and centuries have developed norms and practices for managing family relationships. However, Mormon polygyny involves a relatively new culture, with few firm traditions and little guidance available to its practitioners. It is, in other words, an emergent culture "in search of itself," one that is striving to develop formal and informal mechanisms by which its members can achieve viable relationships in plural families. And the problem is magnified by the fact that many husbands and wives are converts, meaning that they grew up or lived in monogamous families and only joined the fundamentalist movement as adults or when their parents joined. Thus many men and women in plural families have had little or no prior personal experience with this lifestyle.

This cultural group presents an unusual opportunity to study close relationships in families struggling to develop a viable polygynous lifestyle amidst a variety of internal and external pressures and in the context of relatively little personal experience or cultural guidelines. *The central conceptual question addressed throughout this book is how do contemporary polygynous families cope with the challenge of simultaneously achieving viable dyadic and communal relationships?* Or, how does each husband–wife dyad develop and sustain a constructive marital relationship in the context of other husband–wife pairs, while simultaneously working toward a healthy set of communal relations between wives and within the family as a whole? To answer this question we will tap into a variety of aspects of plural family life, to examine how individuals, couples, and families achieve a viable interplay of dyadic and communal relationships, the successes, stresses, and failures they experience, and the trial and error steps they take to manage their unique and complex lifestyle.[2]

Studying close relationships through a transactional lens

To study close relationships in polygynous families we adopted a strategy that has guided our work for many years. It is based on the "worldviews" or approaches to knowledge described by the philosophers John Dewey and Arthur Bentley (1949) and Stephen Pepper (1942, 1967). In our synthesis and extension of their ideas we identified four worldviews that apply to psychological phenomena: *trait, interactional, organismic, and transactional* (Altman and Rogoff, 1987).[3] Our research is guided primarily by the transactional perspective, particularly the following principles:

1. Close personal relationships are embedded in and inseparable from other *social contexts*, including family and kin; friends and co-workers; *physical settings* of homes, workplaces, and public environments; and broad *historical and cultural contexts*. Social, physical, cultural, and historical contexts affect, define, reflect, and are integral to the nature and dynamics of close relationships.
2. Close personal relationships are holistic social units; they can be profitably studied in terms of patterns of behaviors that fit together like a "symphony."
3. Close relationships involve "dialectic" oppositional processes.
4. Close relationships are dynamic. They evolve and change over their history.
5. A transactional perspective is broadly based in its research strategy and approach to knowledge.

1. Close relationships are "contextual." As just mentioned, close relationships are embedded in and inseparable from cultural and historical contexts, social contexts, and physical environmental settings. The contextual nature of close relationships, which is a primary concern of our approach, is too often ignored by scholars and participants in relationships. The fact is that close relationships do not exist apart from the various contexts in which they are embedded. Those contexts affect and give meaning to close relationships. Couples and couple members relate to, are influenced by, negotiate with, and often must take into account family, kin, friends, co-workers, and other *social contexts*. For example, families in a variety of cultures, including that of Mormon polygynists, often play key roles in courtship, weddings, and early stages of relationship formation through interfamily negotiations, gift exchanges, and wedding rituals. Furthermore, couples may be bonded and responsible to families and kin in different ways throughout their marital history. The couple is therefore partly defined by these *social contexts,* and is inseparable from them, and they constitute a crucial part of the "meaning" and definition of a relationship. Thus it is just as important to understand the ways in which dyads are embedded in a variety of social contexts as it is to understand the internal dynamics of close relationships – feelings, actions, and dealings of couple members with one another.

Husband–wife couples in plural families must develop and manage each dyadic relationship in the social context of multiple dyadic relationships and of communal relationships between wives. To achieve viability, each couple unit, each wife, and the husband must relate to other wives and couples in a constructive fashion. Thus the very meaning and functioning of each dyadic pair is inseparable from the social context of other husband–

wife pairs and of the relationship of the husband and of all wives to one another. Close relationships are also embedded in *physical environments.* They occur in places and involve objects and things that may have special significance to couples. For example, couples may return periodically to favorite private places – a park, restaurant, beach, or vacation spot – that memorialize their relationship. Or homes may symbolize the close bond between couple members. Treasured objects, decorating styles, photographs, and special furnishings reflect the personalities and values of couple members. Thus homes and the things in them define to couple members and to the world who they are and what they value and symbolize the dyad as a social unit. Places and things may also reflect the social contexts of couple members in relation to family, kin, and others. Photographs and family memorabilia, awards and trophies, and gifts from others are tangible symbols of the social contexts of couples.

To gain some sense of the physical contexts of dyadic and communal relationships in Mormon polygynous families, we examined living arrangements, household management by wives, psychological attachments of husbands and wives to homes (decorating, privacy regulation, territorial control over homes), rotation of husbands among wives and homes, gift giving and other aspects of celebrations, and management of the husband's clothing and possessions.

Close relationships are not only embedded in immediate and proximal social and physical contexts; they are also linked to broad *cultural and historical contexts.* Norms about how to court, establish a home, raise children, manage gender relationships, and many other facets of day-to-day life are often aligned with broad cultural norms and historical trends. For example, even though polygyny has long been renounced by the main Mormon Church, contemporary fundamentalists rely on the religious values of the 19th-century LDS Church to justify their present-day practice of plural marriage. They do this in the face of more than 150 years of condemnation, prosecution, arrests, and other actions by American society at large and by the main Mormon Church. That history of beliefs, practices, and perceived persecutions against them and their forebears is deeply ingrained in the minds of contemporary fundamentalists and is reflected in their family life and community norms and practices.

Since the lifestyle of modern fundamentalists cannot be fully appreciated without some sense of their historical and cultural milieu, chapters 2 and 3 summarize the history of the LDS religion and culture, with particular attention to the practice of polygyny. Chapter 4 describes community life in the two fundamentalist groups with whom we worked. The remainder of the book deals with dyadic and communal aspects of life in a sample of polygynous families.

2. *Close personal relationships are holistic social units.* The transactional perspective ideally seeks to comprehend holistic social units such as couples, families, and groups by studying complex patterns of behavior occurring in everyday life.[4]

Close relationships are like a symphony, ballet, or baseball game in that they display complex but coherent patterns of activity. Each involves a set of participants who are working toward a common goal, assume different but coordinated roles, and function as an integrated unit. The concept of a "behavior setting" has been introduced to portray activities that occur in everyday life in homes, stores, schools, and elsewhere (Barker, 1968; Wicker, 1982, 1987). In behavior settings, such as symphony performances and baseball games, actors are positioned in various locations and assume various roles to play out elaborate patterns of behavior in relation to one another; these patterns ideally yield a smooth and holistic flow of events. Or, different sections and instruments of a symphony orchestra do different things at different times, move in and out of the flow, contribute to the whole in unique ways, but also function as an integrated and coherent unity. Similarly, in a baseball game team members do different things and have different responsibilities, yet relate to one another in an organized way, such that their mutual actions are contingent on and sensitive to one another and to the flow of events. It would be impossible to fully understand a symphony or baseball game by focusing only on a violinist or second baseman, or by attending to only one type of action by a participant, say, a violinist playing a solo or a second baseman fielding a grounder in the third inning. To appreciate a "whole" symphony or baseball game, one must be sensitive to the actions of a variety of participants as they relate to one another. Thus the complex interplay, connectedness, and mutuality of people, activities, and setting give shape to the whole.

In the case of interpersonal bonds, it is important to examine broad repertoires of behavior – both verbal and nonverbal – in order to identify patterns of interaction between participants. In verbal interaction, patterns can be seen in the intensity and inflection of the partners' speech, the interruptions, the silences, pauses, and varying speech rates. People also interact in nonverbal ways – gesturing, moving their arms, bodies, and legs, smiling, gazing, making head movements, and the like. Furthermore, people use the physical environment in social interaction, moving closer together or further apart, shaping homes to reflect their separate and joint identities, and using public and private places to symbolize aspects of their relationship. Consequently, people bring a vast repertoire of actions to close relationships, often developing complex and unique patterns of interaction that apply uniquely to a particular social bond.

The kinds of husband–wife and wife–wife interactions we studied included courtship, weddings and adjustment to a new wife entering a family, living arrangements, location of a husband's clothing, place attachment by husbands and wives to homes, celebrations, conflict resolution, and the rotation of a husband among his families. In keeping with our overall strategy, we tapped into a broad repertoire of actions, behaviors, and life domains in order to grasp the holistic patterning of dyadic and communal relationships in polygynous families.

3. Close relationships involve "dialectic" or oppositional processes. The idea of dialectics extends back in human history for thousands of years and applies to a variety of world cultures. Three key ideas underlie our approach to dialectics and that of others: namely, opposition, the holistic unity of opposites, and stability or change.[5]

The pivotal role of opposition in the world was first defined by Ancient Greek and Chinese dialectic philosophers, who conceived of the world as composed of oppositional processes or forces, such as cold and hot, fire and water, harmony and conflict, good and evil, and an upper world and an underworld. These oppositional processes are pitted against one another in a never-ending interplay. Some ancient Chinese philosophers treated Yin and Yang forces as fundamental oppositions. Yin, or "female," forces, exhibit passivity, dependence, nurturance, and receptivity; Yang forces are dominant, active, creative, aggressive and represent "male" qualities. The idea that opposition underlies human functioning appears in a variety of philosophical, religious, anthropological, and psychological analyses. For example, the religious and cosmological beliefs of many cultures contain opposites such as God and the devil, an upper world of Heaven and an underworld of Hell, or related manifestations of good and evil. Opposition is also a fundamental concept of some Western philosophies and political theories, from Aristotle and Plato to Hegel, Kant, Marx, and others. It is also present in theories about human social and psychological processes. For example, the *id* and *superego* of Freud's personality theory are in dialectic opposition, with the id symbolizing primitive urges of self-gratification and the superego representing countervailing societal restrictions on individual behavior. Similarly, Jung postulated the presence of *animus,* or male qualities, and *anima,* or female qualities, in every personality, with corresponding features such as activity versus passivity and aggressiveness versus altruism.

Since dialectic polarities are also part of a unified whole, they give meaning to and partly define one another. Thus conflict implies and partly defines its opposite, harmony; the idea of yin "female" forces in ancient Chinese philosophy implies and gives meaning to the idea of "male" yang forces. Oppositions are therefore inseparable qualities of a holistic unity. Dialectic oppositions also exhibit stability and change. For example, harmony and conflict in a close relationship vary in relative strength from time to time, with one or the other being stronger in different circumstances. It is the dynamic interplay of dialectic oppositions that is associated with the flow, growth, and deterioration of close relationships. Some dialectical theories posit that oppositional processes progress toward ideal and more "advanced" states; others believe that oppositional dynamics are endless and are not directed toward any ultimate point.

The concept of oppositional processes guides our analysis of husband–wife and wife–wife relationships in modern plural families. As already pointed out, husbands and wives in the groups we investigated have to cope with the demands of establishing and maintaining multiple distinctive *dyadic* marriage relationships in the face of the opposite ideal, namely, to have positive *communal* relationships between wives and in the family as a whole. That is, the more each couple seeks a distinctive, unique, and special dyadic character, the more they are likely to minimize the communal nature of the plural family. And the more family members work to achieve a unified communal family, the more they probably deemphasize specific dyadic relationships. Dyadic and communal relationships are therefore somewhat contradictory and in opposition to one another. In order to be viable, plural families must figure out how to achieve an acceptable unity and balance of dyadic and communal oppositions, they must cope with inevitable changes in the "strength" and demands of either side of this opposition as their life circumstances change, and they must forever strive to work out a reasonable interplay of these seemingly contradictory goals. Because circumstances change, their task is unending, and the problem of how to manage dyadic and communal oppositions is an ever-present one. Our goal is to see how they address these dialectical oppositions in a variety of everyday life activities, their successes and failures in achieving a rapprochement between dyadic and communal ideals, and the strategies they use as their family lives evolve in new directions.

4. Close relationships are dynamic; they evolve and change over their history. As partners progress from being acquaintances to friends to lovers to parents to middle-aged partners and thereon, their interactions and feelings vary in level and quality of affection, intimacy, commitment, conflict, and alienation. Changes in relationships take place for many reasons: partners' feelings and experiences with one another, health, economics, the presence or absence of children, relationships with other family members, work, and professions. In short, change is an intrinsic and inseparable aspect of close relationships.

As pointed out in some of our work, changes in close relationships can be of a linear or cyclical nature (Werner, Altman, and Oxley, 1985; Werner and Baxter, 1994; Werner and Haggard, 1985). Some examples of linear changes are progressive and cumulating shifts in intimacy and information exchange and transitions in relationships (courtship, the incorporation of children in a family, moving from one home to another, and the like). Linear changes may entail the past, present, and future. Partners often incorporate their individual and joint past histories, as well as those of other relatives and friends, as an aspect of their mutual bond – in the form of stories, recollections, photographs, and objects. Participants also plan and forecast their future life, homes, family life, and jobs, thereby bringing hypothetical future events into their present lives. And, of course, the present is a central aspect of relationships as people live and relate to one another in their everyday lives.

Linear change in close relationships also has a temporal quality emanating from the scale or duration of events. A courtship may be very brief or very long; a celebration may be perfunctory or extended; a relationship may become more intimate either gradually or quickly; and interpersonal conflict may transpire over short or protracted periods. We tried to be sensitive to linear temporal issues in polygynous families by examining various phases of relationships, such as courtship, weddings, adjustments to family growth, husband–wife and wife–wife relationships as family life progressed, and changes in living arrangements. Wherever possible, we tried to learn about past-present-future orientations. For example, we probed the similarity of one courtship in a family to earlier ones, the ways in which decorations in homes reflected the past (e.g., links to ancestors, parents, and others), and idealized future forms of living arrangements.

Cyclical change pertains to recurring activities and events that may be repeated daily, weekly, monthly, annually, or on some other regular basis. Partners in a close relationship may come together and separate on a regular basis as they work; eat at favorite restaurants; celebrate anniversaries, birthdays, and holidays; or visit relatives on a daily, weekly, or other basis. In addition, cyclical events may focus on the past, the present, or the future, or combinations of these. Thus yearly birthday or anniversary celebrations often make past features of a relationship salient, highlight the present bond, and may even project toward future celebrations and continuity of the relationship.

Cyclical changes also vary in scale or duration. Some events are relatively brief, such as the recurring daily routines of partners eating together, separating for part of the day, returning home, and spending time together.

Other cyclical events occur over a longer period: Christmas celebrations, for example, may last several days or a week. Another aspect of cyclical scale involves the interval between recurring events. Some events, such as birthdays, recur infrequently. Others, such as daily routines, have shorter time intervals between repetitions.[6]

To capture these various aspects of cyclical processes in polygynous families, we studied frequently occurring events, such as daily household management by wives; activities with longer time intervals between repetitions, such as a husband's periodic visits to his families and wives; and events of infrequent recurrence, such as celebrations of holidays, birthdays, and anniversaries. Some events (e.g., daily cycles of home management) were of short duration, whereas others (e.g., holiday celebrations over a period of several days) were longer.

5. *A transactional perspective is broadly based in its research strategy and approach to knowledge.* Put simply, a transactional perspective calls for a pragmatic approach to research methodology that says: let the problem or phenomenon guide the selection of research tools. Do not impose a favorite method onto a phenomenon when it may not "fit." Study a phenomenon using tools that allow the phenomenon to "speak in its own language"; don't force the phenomenon into a predetermined research procedure or measurement format (Altman and Rogoff, 1987).

In accordance with this philosophy, we decided that the best way to understand dyadic and communal processes in polygynous families was to immerse ourselves as best we could in the lives of our participants. We visited their homes, participated in community activities, did open-ended interviews, and observed homes and communities.

We did not use formal surveys, highly structured interviews with fixed responses, or other restrictive techniques. As discussed in appendix A, we adopted a free-flowing strategy because we wanted to be open to topics that emerged spontaneously, as well as to those we had planned to study. Moreover, we believed that highly structured interviews or questionnaires would inhibit the participants, who were often reserved and hesitant to discuss their lives with others.

Our research approach also included historical and cross-cultural analyses of polygynous family life. We consulted archival sources, newspaper and magazine articles, autobiographies, and other writings on the theology and history of this unique American religion. Relying on ethnographic reports by anthropologists, we also examined husband–wife and wife–wife relations in cultures around the world that have historically practiced polygyny.

Our original observational and interview data, material on the history

ıd theology of the 19th-century Mormon movement, and information
ıgarding polygyny in other cultures provide a broad perspective with
hich to understand contemporary fundamentalist polygyny. An appreci-
ıion of the social, cultural, religious, and historical roots of Mormon fun-
ımentalism may help to minimize uninformed judgments and inaccurate
ereotypes about this most unusual American lifestyle.

Our transactional strategy also reflects a distinctive scientific and philo-
ıphical approach to knowledge (Altman and Rogoff, 1987). Our goal is
ı describe and understand the pattern and flow of psychological processes.
7e are less concerned with identifying specific antecedent–consequent re-
ıtionships (A causes or leads to B) and more with searching for patterns
ı relationships between variables – much as one pieces together the parts
ı a jigsaw puzzle. A transactional approach to knowledge is analogous to
ımprehending a symphony, ballet, sculpture or piece of art, the whole of
hich may consist of many aspects, none of which "causes" any other.
ather, they exist as aspects of a unified whole that unfolds in a coherent
ıw. Ginsburg (1980, p. 307) put it well:

> [One tries] to identify relationships among component parts and processes
> – but none of the components is "caused" by the prior occurrence of another
> component; and even more important, none of the components "caused"
> the action or act of which they are components. The identity of the com-
> ponents is a functional identity which derives from the larger unit of which
> they are components, such as the act which the component actions are in
> the process of producing.

ummary

ontemporary Mormon polygynous families offer a great opportunity to
ıudy the development and management of close personal relationships. In
ıe present work, we are especially interested in the unique nature of re-
ıtionships between husbands and wives and between wives in plural fam-
ıes, and in the methods used to ensure that such complex sets of
ılationships remain viable in the face of little cultural guidance or personal
ıperience with polygynous relationships.

Polygyny is also of interest in the context of present-day American so-
ety, which features a diversity of close relationship forms, including single
ırents, blended families, cohabiting couples, and same-gender relation-
ıips. Polygynous relationships add to the spectrum of that diversity. Stud-
ng these varied forms of interpersonal bonds is important not only for
ıholarly reasons but also for the well-being of those who choose to live
ı any of these "here-to-stay" lifestyles.

Our philosophical approach to close relationships is a "transactiona
one. That is to say, we emphasize social, physical, cultural, and historic
contexts of relationships; a holistic perspective; a dialectic perspective (
dyadic (husband–wife) and communal (wife–wife) processes in polygyno
families; and a broad methodological and philosophical perspective f(
studying close relationships.

In keeping with our transactional world view, the next chapters sur
marize the social, cultural, historical, and theological contexts of plur
family life in the 19th and 20th centuries. We then turn to the main top
of the volume – dyadic and communal processes in contemporary plur
families.

Historical background

The chapters in this section are a prelude to our study of the day-to-day life of contemporary Mormon plural families. They provide the historical and religious contexts in which contemporary plural families are embedded. The more than 160-year history of the Mormon religion, the rise and fall of the practice of polygyny in the 19th century, and its revival in the fundamentalist movement of the 20th century are ever present in the minds of today's practitioners of plural marriage. Thus the relationships between husbands and wives and between wives in present-day Mormon plural families cannot be fully understood without some knowledge of the historical events underlying their beliefs and practices.

Chapter 2 summarizes the early years of Mormon history and religion, especially the emergence of polygyny as a theological doctrine, the eventual settlement of the Mormons in Utah after years of migration, and the practice of polygyny up until 1890, when the LDS Church renounced the practice as a result of enormous legislative pressure from the U.S. government and the desire of the Mormons to achieve statehood.

Chapter 3 tells the story of the revival and growth of modern fundamentalism in the 20th century up to the present, in spite of arrests, raids, and prosecution by civil authorities, and overt opposition and renunciation by the main LDS Church.

Chapter 4 introduces the people and groups with whom we worked over the past several years. We describe the rural and urban communities in which participants live, aspects of the religious and social structure of their communities, and personal and demographic information about individuals and families.

Mormon history, 1830–1890: The early years

The Mormon religion is relatively young, having been established only in 1830. Yet it has a rich and complicated history. One of several Christian religious movements arising in the United States in the 1800s, the Church of Jesus Christ of Latter-day Saints has grown and prospered over the years. Its present membership exceeds nine million, and Mormonism is now a worldwide religion with a large following in Canada, Mexico, and Latin America and growing numbers in Europe, Asia, and Africa. The international headquarters of the LDS Church is in Salt Lake City, Utah, and there are many members in Utah and surrounding states. There are also many Mormons in California and other western states.

The historical backdrop of the early 1800s

A host of factors contributed to the rise of religious movements in America in the early 1800s. In some respects, the era was similar to the 1960s and 1970s, which were turbulent years for America's established values and traditions. The divisiveness of the early 1800s resulted in many conservative countermovements, Mormonism among them, aimed at restoring "traditional values" and establishing greater stability in society.

Another striking feature of American and other Western societies of the late 1700s and early 1800s was a growing emphasis on individual autonomy and freedom (Coontz, 1988; Hawes and Nybakken, 1991; Kern, 1981; Rothman, 1984). More people embraced the idea of romantic love, sexual freedom, and the freedom to choose one's marital partner. Divorce laws were also relaxed, women grew more independent, and birth control, abortions, prostitution, and pornography became more prevalent. At the same time, religious and familial control over individuals weakened, partly as a result of Western society's increasing urbanization. As work shifted from agriculture to industry, a middle class emerged that was ready to

challenge the established social hierarchy, and the legal system began
acknowledge individual rights.

Spilling out from this cauldron of social upheaval were a variety of co
servative religious or quasi-religious utopian countermovements that soug
to reestablish traditional "family values." They called on women to stay
home, be subordinate to men, rear children, display modesty and gentili
and view marriage and sex as instruments of procreation (Coontz, 198
Kern, 1981). These groups also stressed moral behavior, adherence to 1
ligious values, stable families, and responsibility and loyalty to commu
ties. Many groups believed that the path to a viable society lay in stal
family structures under a male patriarchal system.

Establishing the Mormon religion

Mormonism had its origins in this social, cultural, and religious turbulen

> Into this light came Joseph Smith, the 24 year old New York farmer w
> founded a religion based on his translation of a set of gold plates deliver
> by an angel. The Book of Mormon, a record of God's dealings with the pi
> Columbian ancestors of the American Indian, not only explained the H
> brew origins of the Indian but established America as a chosen land destin
> to receive the fullness of the everlasting gospel. Written in King James E
> glish, Smith's translation sounded biblical, but its location and concept
> framework were American. The Book of Mormon gave America a sacr
> past and a millennial future. It became the keystone of a new Americ
> religion. (Van Wagoner, 1989, p. 1)

Joseph Smith was born in 1805 in Vermont and later lived in Palmyr
a town in upper New York State. Although his family was poor and 1
was not highly educated, Joseph Smith was literate and aware of the re
gious turmoil of the era. In his first teen years Smith had a series of religio
visions, the first of which revealed God and Jesus Christ to him as he w
praying in a wooded area. Although criticized and ridiculed for recounti
this vision, he persisted in reporting it and thinking about religious issue
His second vision occurred a few years later in 1823, when he was 18 yea
old: an angel, Moroni, appeared before Joseph and told him of gold leav
or "plates" on which he and his father, the prophet Mormon, had inscrib
the history of an ancient people who had lived in the Americas (Arringt
and Bitton, 1979). According to LDS teachings, Joseph Smith was giv
the plates three years later, along with two transparent stones found wi
them that enabled him to "translate" their ancient script. Smith's transl
tion of the golden plate became known as the Book of Mormon. He is sa

have spent some time on this work, dictating the material to a scribe
om behind a curtain. Several scribes and friends reported seeing the plates
1d attested to the translation process, although there have been criticisms
1d alternative explanations for the existence of the Book of Mormon (in-
1ding allegations that Smith obtained a copy of a novel depicting the
story of an ancient people or that he fabricated the material directly).
The Book of Mormon recounts events beginning about 600 B.C., when
group of Hebrews traveled to the American continent in the face of the
1pending Babylonian conquest of the Holy Land. Over the course of the
2xt centuries they grew in numbers and built cities and temples but then
2lit into two warring groups. According to the Book of Mormon, Christ
1me to the Americas following his crucifixion and instituted a period of
2ace and tranquility, which eventually gave way again to conflict and
2heaval and the destruction of one group. The angel Moroni was the last
-ophet of the defeated group. He hid the record of his people, written on
2lden plates, until such time as a righteous man appeared in "the latter
1ys" to restore the gospel and divinity of Christ. According to Mormon
2ctrine, that man was Joseph Smith (Arrington and Bitton, 1979).
Joseph Smith first talked about establishing a new religion in about
329. It was around this time that Smith and a friend were "visited" by
2hn the Baptist in a wood, and he and others began to engage in mutual
1ptisms. Smith and a few followers established the new religion in Fayette,
ew York, in the spring of 1830.

Believing the church to be a restoration of all blessings, powers, and ecclesiastical authority given by Jesus Christ, they [Joseph Smith and a few fol-
lowers] named themselves "latter day" saints as opposed to the "former
day" saints of biblical times. . . .
   When the people questioned who would be their leader . . . Joseph announced that the Lord had revealed that he himself should be called "a seer,
a translator, a prophet, an apostle of Jesus Christ". From this time Joseph
was called "the prophet." (Newell and Avery, 1984, p. 31)

he years in Ohio, Missouri, and Illinois: 1831–1846

2tween 1831 and 1838 the Mormons established communities in Kirtland,
hio, and in Independence, Liberty, and Far West, Missouri. As their num-
2rs grew, the fledgling group assumed a strong role in local economics
1d politics, so much so that conflicts and controversies arose in each place
2tween Mormons and non-Mormons. One basis of tension was Mormon
1igious doctrine, including the belief that Smith was a prophet of God
1d the implication that Mormonism was the "true" latter-day religion.

Rumors that Joseph and his key associates were practicing polygyny adde
to the hostility of non-Mormons.

Mormons were also accused of engaging in land speculation, theft, coun
terfeiting, and other illegal acts (Arrington and Bitton, 1979). A bank tha
Joseph Smith organized in Ohio was said to have issued notes withou
sufficient funds and reserves. When the bank failed, Smith was beaten
tarred, and feathered by angry non-Mormons. The Mormons also delve
into politics and were accused of aspiring to control local, state, and eve
national offices (Arrington and Bitton, 1979). In Missouri their antislaver
views riled the local citizenry (Newell and Avery, 1984), and there wer
some armed conflicts with secular authorities. Following raids and retal
ations on both sides, the governor issued an order to "exterminate" th
Mormons. Smith and his key supporters were captured, jailed, and sen
tenced to death. Recognizing that they had little hope of a future in Mis
souri, Joseph Smith directed Brigham Young, his eventual successor, t
move the Mormons eastward to Illinois. Smith escaped from prison in 183
and fled to the new settlement in Illinois.

In spite of these difficulties, the Mormons laid a strong religious foun
dation during the Ohio and Missouri years. Joseph Smith compiled hi
revelations and writings, established a school to teach his followers, orga
nized a leadership quorum of 12 apostles, constructed a "temple," estab
lished a press, and published the "Doctrine and Covenants," an importan
theological statement, as well as a book of hymns (Newell and Avery
1984).

The consensus of historians and writers seems to be that Joseph Smit
first entertained the idea of plural marriage, at least intellectually, as earl
as 1831 or 1832 and that he practiced some form of polygyny during th
middle and late 1830s in Kirtland, Ohio. However, it has been suggeste
that Joseph Smith thought about and eventually practiced polygyny onl
gradually, and not in an all-at-once, preordained fashion (Foster, 1981,
Through his knowledge of the Old Testament and his "translation" of th
Book of Mormon Smith was certainly aware that the biblical patriarch
beginning with Abraham, had practiced polygyny. Abraham's wife Sarah
unable to bear children, encouraged him to marry their servant Hagar ii
order to carry on the family line. Sarah then miraculously gave birth ti
Isaac in her later years. In his search for a religious system that woul
enhance family organization and produce an orderly social structure, Smit
saw polygyny as a lifestyle that righteous men, under God's guidance, coul
adopt because it was like that of the biblical patriarchs. As Smith inter
preted them, selected passages of the Book of Mormon allowed for th
possibility that "alternative" family structures might be called for some day
At the same time, the Book of Mormon denounced inappropriate sexua

elationships, especially concubinage, "fornication and whoredom." It has een suggested that

> the deeper roots of his theology lay in his interpretation of the Old Testament. His concept of the kingdom of God paralleled Israelite theocracy. . . . Smith's theology of marriage and family too may have drawn on ancient Israelite traditions. Like the biblical patriarchs of old, Mormon males empowered with priesthood were entitled to receive divine guidance in family matters. Women, on the other hand, were denied both priesthood and hierarchic position. This Old Testament focus evidently also drew Smith to the idea of biblical polygamy as part of the "restitution of all things." (Van Wagoner, 1989, p. 3)

Although Joseph Smith appears to have engaged in some form of plural arriage during the Ohio and Missouri era, it is not clear that there were formal" marriage ceremonies or that he had many such relationships. And hatever occurred was done in considerable secrecy. It was not until the lormons migrated to Nauvoo, Illinois, in 1839 that plural marriages were omewhat more openly practiced.

Especially important during the Ohio and Missouri days is the fact that mith and his followers had gravitated toward a theological conception of arriage that provided the seedbed for polygyny. First, they distinguished etween marriages for "time" (those that were binding while a husband nd wife were on earth but were not carried forth into the hereafter), and arriages that were "for time and eternity" (those that would go on after eath and in the hereafter). Second, they portrayed marriage as a religious icrament and posited that only marriages performed by Mormon religious aders would last through time and eternity. In so bypassing the civil sys-m the Mormons set the stage for their claim that polygynous marriages ere acts of God.

It was in Nauvoo, meaning "city beautiful" (Newell and Avery, 1984), at the Mormons developed a politically, economically, and religiously itegrated community during the years 1839–1846. It was also during the auvoo period that Joseph Smith was assassinated and that the Mormons ibsequently began their final exodus to Utah. Nauvoo grew rapidly and rospered after the Mormons arrived; by 1844 it had a population of about 0,000, which made it the state's second largest city, next to Chicago (Arngton and Bitton, 1979). The Mormons built a large temple in Nauvoo, stablished businesses, factories, and an agricultural base there; and orgaized a militia under the command of Joseph Smith (who was appointed eutenant general by the governor of Illinois). They also continued to pub-sh the Book of Mormon and other theological works. Joseph Smith ex-erienced several religious revelations in this period. Furthermore, he

encouraged missionary activity to other countries and wrote theologica
statements regarding the relationship of people to God, the eternal potentia
of individuals, baptisms for the dead, and endowment ceremonies.
But the seeds of conflict and upheaval also grew in this new locatior
partly because of the increasingly visible practice of plural marriage b
Smith and some of his closest associates. Made an issue by enemies withi
and outside the church, plural marriage contributed in large measure to th
hostilities and violence that eventually resulted in the demise of the Nauvo
community and the exodus to Utah. There were also political crises. Fo
example, following an assassination attempt against the governor of Mis
souri, with some believing that the Mormons were responsible for the at
tack, the Missourians attempted to arrest Joseph Smith. On the basis o
agreements between the two states, the governor of Illinois agreed to issu
an arrest warrant for Joseph Smith, but Smith evaded it and became a
fugitive for several months. He finally appeared for trial but was free
because of insufficient information.

Animosities came to a head in the spring of 1844, when Mormon dis
sidents published a newspaper that denounced the sex lives and plural mar
riage practices of church leaders and criticized Smith's domination o
Nauvoo's political system. The Nauvoo city council, which was under th
church's control, stated that the newspaper was libelous and endangere
the social well-being of the community. Its members then arranged to hav
the newspaper office raided and its printing press destroyed. Anti-Mormon
were outraged and filed charges against Joseph Smith and other leader
accusing them of inciting a riot. Following legal maneuvering, flight fron
arresting authorities, and negotiations with the governor, Joseph Smith al
lowed himself to be jailed under the protection of public security forces
However, Joseph and his brother Hyrum were assassinated by a group o
men who forcibly gained entry, apparently after the security forces aban
doned their positions.

As for the issue of polygyny, its religious rationale lay not only in the
principles noted previously but also in the theological idea of Smith calle
"spiritual wifery," developed by other sects during the early 1800s. Smit
stated that a man and woman could bond in a "spiritual" way as husban
and wife. Since civil marriages were judged by the Mormons to be invali
or only for "time" on earth, a man and a woman could engage in spiritua
marriages under church sponsorship in anticipation of a life together in th
hereafter. Another justification for plural marriage was that women neede
to be married or sealed to "worthy" or "righteous" men in order to gai
a proper place in heaven. One result of the evolving doctrine of spiritua
wifery was that Joseph and his followers not only had plural wives bu
even "spiritually" married the wives of other men. This action gave rise to

polygynous and polyandrous relationships (i.e., in which a woman has more than one husband).

But it was Joseph Smith's revelation on July 12, 1843, that put the capstone on plural marriage (Newell and Avery, 1984; Van Wagoner, 1989). Some say that the revelation was designed, in part, to win over Joseph's wife, Emma Smith, who was opposed to plural marriage. The revelation pointed out polygynous practices of Old Testament patriarchs and made clear the distinction between marriages for time and marriages for eternity; thus it condoned plural marriages on theological grounds and instructed Emma to obey the principle or suffer serious consequences:

> Under the "law of the priesthood" a man "cannot commit adultery with that that belongeth to him and to no one else. And if he have ten virgins given unto him by this law, he cannot commit adultery, for they belong to him. . . . If any man have a wife . . . and he teaches unto her the law of my priesthood, as pertaining to these things, then shall she believe and administer unto him, or she shall be destroyed, saith the Lord your God." (Newell and Avery, 1984, p. 153)

The revelation also emphasized that a righteous man was one who would have many children and would thereby achieve a godlike status in the hereafter, where he would administer a patriarchal "universe" surrounded by his wives, children, and family:

> Those persons sealed under this new law were advised that they would come forth in the first resurrection and, in the life after death, would inherit thrones, kingdoms, principalities, powers, and dominion. . . .
> Smith explained that God was an exalted man and that mortal existence was a testing ground for men to begin progress toward exalted Godhood. Salvation became a family affair revolving around a husband whose plural wives and children were sealed to him for eternity under the "new and everlasting covenant." (Van Wagoner, 1989, p. 56)

The stereotypes of men and women implicit in the revelation and in other writings of the era further rationalized the practice of polygyny. Women, on the one hand, were portrayed as being dependent on men; their proper sphere was in the home, raising children, and their sex drives were expected to weaken at "midlife." Men, on the other hand were believed to have strong and "inexhaustible" sexual needs. Women were also thought to be "endowed with monogamic tendencies and men with polygamic ones" (Hardy, 1992, p. 87). This mingling of social stereotypes and religious theology was a common justification for polygyny during the Nauvoo era.

Some commentators believe that the revelation crystallized years of thought and deliberation and was a response to immediate pressures in

Nauvoo. It has also been suggested that the concerns of his brother Hyrum, his wife Emma, and the rampant rumors and confusion among followers may have precipitated Joseph Smith's declaration (Van Wagoner, 1989; Newell and Avery, 1984).[1] The revelation of 1843 became *the* crucial statement for the practice and rationale for polygyny among Mormons in the remainder of the 19th century, although it was only disclosed to key leaders at the time. It was not until 1852, five years after the Mormons had settled in Utah, that Brigham Young openly declared the revelation to be the doctrine and practice of the church.

While secretly engaging in plural marriage in Illinois, Smith and his close associates publicly denounced the practice. Yet he also tested the waters in sermons. When one statement on the subject was criticized by his followers, Smith preached another sermon indicating that plural marriage was not to be practiced now but would be at some point in the future. So, while denouncing plural marriages, Joseph Smith planted the seeds and foundation of polygyny and even practiced it secretly (Newell and Avery, 1984). And he advised his close associates to not let anyone, including their wives, know that they were engaging in plural marriage.

Apparently Joseph Smith himself was ambivalent about plural marriage, fearing that he might be committing adultery or that he might be rationalizing his own personal impulses rather than following the word of God (Foster, 1981). Key followers also resisted his teachings and the pressure to engage in plural marriages. Some verged on apostasy, others were emotionally upset, some threatened Smith if he forced them to participate in plural marriages. Even Brigham Young, his loyal lieutenant and eventual leader of the church (and years later a proponent of polygyny), stated on first hearing of Smith's revelation: "I was not desirous of shrinking from my duty . . . but it was the first time in my life that I desired the grave" (Goodson, 1976, p. 90).

This resistance of even the most devoted followers was understandable, given the long-standing American and Christian heritage of monogamy. Moreover, plural marriages were illegal, they would require men to support multiple families, and in Smith's teaching they implied that civil marriages were not binding in the hereafter. Yet many eventually gave in, believing that if they did not do so they would be jeopardizing their salvation in the hereafter. Furthermore, their willingness to engage in plural marriage became a test of their loyalty to Joseph Smith and to the teachings of the church. Once having yielded, they took a crucial step toward total commitment to the group and further separation from the larger society. Since only about 30 of the church's top leaders had reportedly engaged in plural marriages by the time of Smith's death, the practice at this time was still quite limited (Foster, 1991).[2]

On the whole, events in Nauvoo solidified the Mormons into a coherent social and religious community, laid down principles of secular communal organization, and set forth religious doctrine regarding marriage and polygyny. At the same time, these very successes contained the seeds of internal divisiveness and external hostility that eventually led to the flight from Illinois to Utah.

The exodus and settlement in Utah

The new leader following Joseph Smith's death, Brigham Young, found himself faced with further conflict between Mormons and non-Mormons – in the form of raids, killings, and the destruction of property. In 1845 the Illinois legislature repealed the Nauvoo city charter and filed legal charges against church leaders. Brigham Young and others decided that they would have to leave Nauvoo. As in other cases, their religious, economic, political and social influence in the community, as well as increasing evidence of plural marriage practices, forced the Mormons to flee.

This time they sought an isolated place where they could exert religious and secular control. That place was to be in Utah, in the Rocky Mountains. But it would be a hard and long trek of more than 1,200 miles across hostile country, and it was not until July 1847 that the first group reached Utah, a year and a half after they began the exodus from Nauvoo.

In many ways Brigham Young resembled Joshua of the Old Testament, just as Joseph Smith did Moses. Like Moses, Joseph was the visionary who led his followers from community to community in the "desert." Like Joshua, Brigham Young finally brought the people to "the promised land," where they settled permanently.

In the winter of 1845–1846 large numbers of Mormons began a trek across Iowa, facing severe weather and supply shortages and carrying whatever possessions they could in wagons and handcarts. By late spring 500 wagons had reached Council Bluffs, Iowa. During the summer of 1846 there were 15,000 people, 3,000 wagons, 30,000 head of cattle, and numerous sheep, horses, and mules on the road out of Nauvoo (Arrington and Bitton, 1979).

After wintering over in Omaha, Nebraska, in 1846–1847, Brigham Young led a party of 143 men, 3 women, and 2 children in 73 wagons to Utah. Crossing the plains and making their way through the canyons and passes of the Rocky Mountains, they entered the Salt Lake Valley three months later, in July 1847.

The advance party immediately began to plant crops, construct a small dam and irrigation system, and build a settlement. Brigham Young and

some of the party then departed eastward in order to guide others to th
new land of "Zion." As a result of Young's personal determination and
organizational genius, encampments and temporary settlements sprang up
along the trail to Utah, and a systematic plan was in place for those to
come. Immigrants were organized into groups of 10s, 50s, and 100s, with
a hierarchy of leaders at each level. They planted crops along the route so
that successive groups could survive, established a mail service, and orga
nized supply schedules. Their extensive organization and coordination laid
a firm foundation for things to come. To this day the Mormon church and
community reflect a hierarchically organized, social, religious, and eco
nomic system with strong leadership at every level and a pragmatic, task
oriented approach to secular and religious affairs.

Thereafter a steady stream of people made the trek to Utah. They came
in wagons or pulled handcarts across the plains and through the mountains
By 1848 some 2,500 people had made the journey to Utah, and the flow
continued throughout the century. The first settlers struggled to survive in
its harsh high-desert environment. They cleared fields, planted crops, and
built primitive dams. But the soil and weather worked against them, and
the first crops were meager. And in 1848 their crops began to be decimated
by hordes of crickets. Unable to control the crickets, so the story goes, the
pioneers fell to their knees in desperation and prayed for divine interven
tion. As if by heavenly assistance, it is told, waves of sea gulls came from
the great Salt Lake in the west and devoured the crickets. In commemo
ration of this event, a large sculpture, the Seagull monument, is located on
Temple Square in the center of Salt Lake City.

By the first winter the new settlers had established a small settlement
built a protective wall around it, prepared fields for spring planting, and
constructed a number of log dwellings. Over time Brigham Young's orga
nizational talents were applied broadly. For example, he drew up guideline
for the design of the city specifying the size of lots and blocks, street widths
the siting of houses on lots, and the location of shops. Present-day Sal
Lake City reflects many aspects of his original design. In addition, Young
put in place an infrastructure that included a legal system, public works
projects, means for regulating land and resources, allocations of farm plots
to citizens, taxes, minting gold coins, and a provisional government for the
hoped-for "State of Deseret" (Arrington and Bitton, 1979).

The community was also organized into church "wards," or congrega
tions, of several hundred people, each presided over by a "bishop" (lay
minister). Wards were responsible for building schools, roads, and fences
as well as conducting religious services and activities. The bishop was to
be a minister, judge, tithe collector, and agricultural supervisor. Importan
religious buildings were to be at the center of the city. For the first few

years the central meeting place was a bowery made of brush, rough logs, and dirt; later the settlers worshipped in an adobe building. Eventually they constructed a large tabernacle. The most sacred building, the Temple, took 40 years to build, with granite rock hauled from the mountains 20 miles away.

The design of the city placed the Temple at the 0–0 coordinates of a Cartesian system. All locations and streets in the city were defined in terms of their distance and direction from the Temple. The city blocks were laid out in a north–south and east–west configuration, and the result was a highly ordered and predictable system. The symbolism of a religious site at the literal center of the city contrasts with the design of Washington, D.C., where the U.S. Capitol is at the center of the city, to emphasize the importance of representative government. Clearly, the guiding principle of the new Mormon settlement was a religious one.

The organization of the new community reflected an orderly, cooperative, and unified society over which the Mormons would have complete control. Religion would thus be intertwined with secular life. Like other social experiments of the era – such as the Shaker and Oneida communities – this one fostered cooperation, communality, order, and social responsibility, in contrast to the individualism prevalent elsewhere in early 19th-century American society. These and related values are important to mainstream and fundamentalist Mormons to this day.

One purpose of this cooperative, hierarchical, and secular-religious society was to avoid the problems experienced in Ohio, Missouri, and Illinois. If the Mormons could control politics, economics, religion, and other facets of life at the outset, in a place where no one else had lived, then eventual conflict with non-Mormons might be minimized, and the pioneers might be able to practice their religion free from persecution, conflict, and competition.

The early settlers also hoped to establish LDS communities over a large area in the western United States. For the next half century they "colonized" far and wide, establishing one outpost after another in all directions – in Utah, Idaho, Wyoming, New Mexico, Arizona, Nevada, Colorado, and as far west as San Bernardino, California. When the federal government put pressure on the Mormons for practicing polygyny, they also established colonies in Canada and Mexico.

By the last decade of the 19th century membership in the LDS Church had grown considerably, partly as a result of the immigration of more than 85,000 European converts, primarily from Great Britain and the Scandinavian countries (Arrington and Bitton, 1979). By 1880 the population of Utah Territory was 144,000 (79% Mormon); by 1900, shortly after statehood, the population was 277,000 (65% Mormon) (May, 1992).

With their numbers increasing, Brigham Young attempted to create a self-sustaining church-controlled economy. He was very blunt and forceful on this point, stating that the Mormon community needed to grow and manufacture every necessity in order to be independent and free of "the gentile world" and its profane practices and lifestyle (Arrington and Bitton 1979). To achieve this goal, the Mormon pioneers developed factories, farms and dairies, foundries and iron works, machine shops, textile mills, and coal mines. Many communities followed a "United Order" principle according to which collective economic activities were to promote Christian unity and harmony, care for all members, foster a simple and hardworking lifestyle, and, above all, maintain church control over everyday life. Not all programs succeeded, but communal bonding and loyalty, in contrast to the individualistic values of the era, were a strong norm.

Mormon culture continues to be highly communal, with a church welfare system to care for the needy, individual volunteerism on behalf of the community, assistance to neighbors in times of crisis, and loyalty to the local church ward and its members. At the same time, perhaps as a result of the early spirit of self-sufficiency, Mormons are active business people, adhere to a work ethic, are entrepreneurial, and have a sense of special purpose and distinctiveness as a group. The Mormon Church itself is heavily engaged in a variety of major business and industrial ventures, has significant television and radio interests, and owns rich grazing, farm, and dairy lands around the world. Utah's state symbol, the beehive, a model of industriousness and hard work, characterizes well the ethos of both the pioneering years and the modern era. Furthermore, the church is constantly building new temples and church buildings worldwide, as its membership grows beyond the present nine million people. Some 40,000 missionaries (mostly young males) proselytize in the United States and abroad, financially supporting themselves for up to two years as they advance the work of the church.

During the early days of Brigham Young's 30-year tenure, polygyny occurred on a small scale. However, in 1852, five years after arriving in Utah, the Mormon church publicly pronounced polygyny to be official church doctrine. This announcement may have been withheld until 1852 because the Mormons wished to firmly establish their settlement in Utah or to have a legitimate governmental status – although it failed to achieve statehood in 1849, Utah became a territory in 1850 (Foster, 1981). Moreover, with federal authorities increasingly on the scene, it no longer made sense to hide the fact of plural marriages. The church leadership may also have gone public in order to foster cohesion and the acceptance of plural marriage among Mormons themselves, many of whom were still ambivalent about the practice (Foster, 1981).

The rise and fall of polygyny

Following the 1852 announcement, the Mormon settlers engaged vigorously in plural marriages: "No period of Mormon history demonstrated a devotion to polygamous duty more than the two-year period from 1856 to 1857, known as the Mormon Reformation. This movement . . . stressed cleanliness, confession, repentance, self-sufficiency – and plural marriage. . . . During this two-year period, sixty-five percent more polygamous marriages were contracted than at any other two-year period in Mormon history" (Van Wagoner, 1989, p. 92). Men, especially leaders, and women were pressured to enter plural marriages. Sometimes the pressure was blatant: those who refused would no longer be assured of a proper place in the hereafter. Even so, many resisted or were ambivalent about polygyny, as noted in subsequent chapters, and expressed dismay, dissatisfaction, and unhappiness with plural family life and plural marriages. Yet there also were many strong supporters.

At the same time, the Mormons were arousing hostility nationwide because of their polygyny, political rebelliousness, alleged acts against non-Mormons, and suspected support of Indians against the federal government. When in the late 1850s President James Buchanan ordered federal troops to "invade" Utah, the Mormons responded with guerrilla attacks. After negotiations, federal troops peaceably entered Salt Lake City, and a period of relative tranquillity followed. Although the Mormons supported the United States in the Civil War and hoped their loyalty would be rewarded with statehood, their petition in 1862 was denied.

Then came another blow: some members of the federal government began proposing legislation to outlaw polygyny and restrict Mormon political independence. The first piece of legislation, the Morrill Act, was passed by Congress in 1862 and was signed by President Abraham Lincoln. After several other legislative initiatives over the next two decades, along with court cases and the closing of loopholes, the Edmunds/Tucker Act of 1887 struck at the heart of plural marriage practices. It also affected Mormon political control in Utah and citizens' rights. Intervening legislation attempted to eradicate plural marriages by preventing polygynists from acting as judges, officials, or jury members in cases involving plural marriage; barring polygynists from holding political office; depriving wives of the right not to testify against their husbands; confiscating properties of those evading prosecution for being polygynists; barring polygynists from becoming naturalized citizens, extending federal control over all criminal, civil, and chancery court cases; and placing the offices of the territorial attorney general and marshall under federal authority (Arrington and Bitton, 1979; Otto, 1991; Van Wagoner, 1989).

At the same time, the noose was tightening in the political arena and in the courts. Persons of such stature as Presidents James Buchanan, Abraham Lincoln and Ulysses S. Grant spoke out against the Mormon practice of polygyny. Furthermore, Grant replaced Brigham Young with a new territorial governor of Utah and appointed a chief justice of the territorial court who immediately indicted Young on charges of cohabitation. Although the case was rejected by the U.S. Supreme Court on procedural irregularities, Grant continued to encourage congressional legislation against the Mormons (Van Wagoner, 1989). Like their predecessors, Presidents Rutherford B. Hayes, James A. Garfield, and Chester A. Arthur railed against plural marriage, even in political campaigns, an inaugural address, and a State of the Union address (Embry, 1987; Van Wagoner, 1989).

Despite the mounting political and legislative pressure, the Mormons remained confident of their right to practice polygyny under the religious freedom provisions of the U.S. Constitution (Van Wagoner, 1989). With the federal government's concurrence, the Mormons decided to test anti-polygyny laws in a legal case involving George Reynolds, secretary to Brigham Young and a practitioner of plural marriage. In 1879 the U.S. Supreme Court upheld lower-court convictions of Reynolds (Arrington and Bitton, 1979; Embry, 1987; Otto, 1991; Van Wagoner, 1984). The Supreme Court concluded that people could freely "believe" in certain religious principles, such as plural marriage, but that they were not necessarily free to "act" upon their beliefs, especially if those beliefs were in conflict with social principles and laws, or if they contributed to social "disorder" and upheaval – which the Court judged to be the case with plural marriages (Dyer, 1977).[3]

Obviously disappointed by the Reynolds decision, the Mormon leaders nevertheless reaffirmed their beliefs in plural marriage. The new church president, John Taylor, publicly denounced the Reynolds decision and encouraged the faithful to continue practicing plural marriage:

> [Taylor] defiantly argued from the pulpit that "the people of the rest of the country are our enemies" and "we must not yield to them. . . . When they enact tyrannical laws, forbidding us the free exercise of our religion, we cannot submit. God is greater than the United States. And when the Government conflicts with Heaven, we will be ranged under the banner of Heaven and against the government. . . . Polygamy is a divine institution. It has been handed down direct from God. The United States cannot abolish it. No nation on earth can prevent it, nor all the nations of the earth combined. I defy the United States. I will obey God." (Van Wagoner, 1989, p. 113)[4]

In spite of Taylor's defiance, the full force of federal legislation finally came down on the Mormons in the Edmunds Act of 1882 and the Edmunds/

Tucker Law of 1887 (Anderson, 1957; Arrington and Bitton, 1979; Foster, 1981; Otto, 1991; Van Wagoner, 1989). The Edmunds legislation made plural marriage and cohabitation criminal acts and barred polygynists from jury service, political office, or service as election officials. In addition, elections in Utah were placed under presidential authority, and only men who took an oath that they did not cohabit with more than one woman were permitted to vote. Federal agents began arresting polygynists on "cohab hunts" and offered rewards for information about participants in plural marriages or cohabitation (Van Wagoner, 1989). Those arrested were tried before non-Mormon judges and non-Mormon juries.

Polygynous men were forced "underground." They visited their plural families secretly, split up the living arrangements and locations of their families, sometimes left wives and children to fend for themselves, and were constantly on the move as they fled the authorities. Even church leaders, including the president, went into hiding. Within a few years more than 1,000 men had been convicted and imprisoned for practicing polygyny or cohabitation.

To evade the authorities, some plural families settled in remote regions of Arizona, Nevada, Wyoming, and Colorado. Others moved to Mexico and Canada, where laws prohibiting polygyny were not enforced. More than 3,000 settled in Mexico over the course of a decade (Van Wagoner, 1989). There still are Mormon fundamentalist communities in both Mexico and Canada.

With unrelenting pressure, the federal government and Congress forged new legislation – the Edmunds/Tucker Act of 1887 – to close some of the loopholes of the Edmunds Act. Most important, this new legislation came down hard on the Mormon church as an institution:

> Wives could be forced to testify against husbands, and . . . children of plural marriages would be disinherited. Female suffrage was abolished, and a test oath was administered which disenfranchised all polygamists and prohibited them from jury service or political office. (Van Wagoner, 1989, p. 133)

The Act further required that all marriages in Utah be certified with the territorial probate court, including the name of the official presiding at the ceremony and the marital status of the parties. Moreover, the Act required all prospective male voters in the territory to take an oath swearing that they did not practice or encourage others to practice polygamy. . . .

The stiffest provisions . . . were reserved for the Mormon church. The Act invalidated the corporation of the Church of Jesus Christ of Latter-day Saints and authorized proceedings to have any church property and buildings not used exclusively for religious purposes escheat to the United States. Finally, the Act dissolved the Perpetual Immigration Fund Company, which made loans to needy Mormons who desired to immigrate to Utah and dictated that the Fund's property and assets escheat to the federal government. (Otto, 1991, p. 894)

Three years later, in the spring of 1890, the U.S. Supreme Court upheld by a bare majority the constitutionality of the government's right to seize the Mormon Church's financial holdings. This followed an earlier decision by the Court authorizing the government to disenfranchise Mormons under the terms of the Edmunds/Tucker Act (Arrington and Bitton, 1979). These judicial decisions not only endorsed punitive actions against individual Mormons but threatened the Mormon Church as a religious, economic, social, and political system. The church would lose its financial base, its leaders and members would be disenfranchised, and there was no further recourse through the courts or legislative channels. The future seemed grim. But with the death of President John Taylor in 1889, a firm and unbending advocate of polygyny, the stage was set for the Mormon Church to make its first pronouncement against plural marriage.

As it became more and more apparent that the church's power was being stripped away, the newly elected president, Wilford Woodruff, stated openly that he would not authorize new plural marriages, even though he continued to do so secretly (Van Wagoner, 1989). In 1890 church leaders and U.S. government officials discussed the renunciation of polygyny in exchange for potential statehood for Utah and possible relief from the new laws. Following these "carrot-and-stick" discussions, Wilford Woodruff issued the Manifesto of 1890, which stated in part:

> Inasmuch as laws have been enacted by Congress forbidding plural marriages, which laws have been pronounced constitutional by the court of last resort, I hereby declare my intention to submit to those laws, and to use my influence with members of the Church over which I preside to have them do likewise. There is nothing in my teachings to the Church or in those of my associates . . . which can be reasonably construed to inculcate or encourage polygamy; and when any Elder of the Church has used language which appeared to convey any such teaching, he has been promptly reproved. And I now publicly declare that my advice to the Latter-day Saints is to refrain from contracting any marriage forbidden by the law of the land. (Otto, 1991, p. 895)

By complying with the "law of the land" the manifesto enabled the church to protect its assets. The manifesto also prompted the government to reduce its arrests and prosecutions of polygynists, and eventually it gave amnesty to those in plural marriages. Furthermore, the manifesto enabled the formation of a provisional state government in 1894. Statehood was achieved in 1896, but the Utah Constitution contained a provision forever prohibiting polygamous or plural marriages.

Although most Mormons accepted the manifesto as the word of their prophet, some resisted or were upset and confused (Arrington and Bitton, 1979). After all, church members had been taught for four decades that practicing plural marriage enhanced their opportunity to achieve a proper heavenly status. How could polygyny be tossed aside so readily? A number of Woodruff's contemporaries and later scholars reasoned that the manifesto was a political statement, offered up to preserve the very existence of the church in the face of enormous pressure by the federal government. Many contemporary fundamentalists continue to hold that view, thereby partly justifying their continuation of plural marriages.

Further evidence of the manifesto's political purpose is the fact that other church authorities at the time did not sign the document, its opening statements departed from customary format, no penalties were introduced for disobeying the manifesto, and the document did not say that polygyny was "wrong," only that it should not be practiced because of secular laws (Van Wagoner, 1989). It is also the case that some members of the church's leadership were absent when the document was approved and that the manifesto did not say anything about the legitimacy of earlier plural marriages (Woodruff later stated that the manifesto only applied to future marriages and that past marriages were valid and acceptable). In addition, Woodruff's plea to the Mormon conference to support the manifesto was couched in pragmatic and secular terms rather than theological terms. He noted, for example, "It is not wisdom for us to make war on sixty-five million people. . . . This is in the hands of the Lord and he will govern and control it" (Van Wagoner, 1989, p. 145).

Following the manifesto the number of church-authorized plural marriages declined but did not cease (Hardy, 1992; Quinn, 1985; Van Wagoner, 1989). Records indicate that those wishing to engage in polygyny were advised by church authorities to go to Mexico to consummate marriages. All the while, church leaders were publicly speaking against plural marriages (Cannon, 1983).[5] For the next several years the situation was mixed, with some church leaders publicly condemning plural marriages but practicing it themselves and authorizing the marriages of others.

On the national scene, anger mounted over the ongoing cases of polygyny in the face of church leaders' public statements to the contrary; some even pressed for a U.S. constitutional amendment forbidding plural marriage and polygynous cohabitation. Matters came to a head in 1904 when Reed Smoot, an apostle of the Mormon Church but a monogamist, was elected U.S. senator from Utah. Smoot's seating as senator was challenged, and the matter was taken up in three years of hearings and investigation (Van Wagoner, 1989). Not only did all of the old issues come out during the hearings, but the president of the church at the time, Joseph F. Smith was found to be a practicing polygynist who had also approved some plural marriages while publicly stating that the church no longer condoned or encouraged them (Cannon, 1983). Smoot was eventually confirmed by the U.S. Senate, but not before further pressure led the church to pronounce, in the Manifesto of 1904:

> Inasmuch as there are numerous reports . . . that plural marriages have been entered into contrary to the official declaration of President Woodruff, of September 26, 1890, I Joseph F. Smith, . . . do hereby affirm and declare that no such marriages have been solemnized with the sanction, consent, or knowledge of the Church of Jesus Christ of Latter-day Saints. . . . If any officer or member of the church shall assume to solemnize or enter into any such marriage he will be deemed in transgression against the church, and will be liable to be . . . excommunicated therefrom. (Van Wagoner, 1989, p. 168)

Although stronger than the 1890 statement, the Manifesto of 1904 contained several ambiguities: it did not forbid plural marriages outside the United States; it did not deal precisely with unlawful cohabitation; and it was not presented as a theological revelation. In 1907, however, the Mormon Church made public a document affirming the separation of church and state, the loyalty of the church and its members to the United States and its laws, and the rejection of polygyny as a violation of both civil and church law (Van Wagoner, 1989). Subsequently, church leaders who married new plural wives were removed from ecclesiastical positions; some were also excommunicated if they continued to openly advocate plural marriage.

As the Mormon Church became more and more opposed to plural marriage, a core group of fundamentalists continued to hold firmly that plural marriages were theologically justified, and they called for continuation of the practice. Thus conflict over plural marriage shifted from the LDS Church versus the United States to the LDS Church versus fundamentalists committed to plural marriage and other theological practices. The story of that conflict and the rise of fundamentalist Mormons in the 20th century is taken up in chapter 3.

Some facts and figures about 19th-century Mormon polygyny

Although appendix B provides the details of Mormon polygyny, it is useful here to consider a few of the basic facts about plural marriages in the pioneer era: how many men practiced polygyny, how many wives they had, and so on. By and large, it appears that relatively few Mormon men engaged in polygyny, and of those who did, most had only two wives. These data are quite consistent with practices in other polygynous cultures, described in the technical note at the end of this chapter. According to an analysis of 6,000 pioneer families (Ivins, 1956), 15–20% of Utah Mormon families were polygynous at one time or another, although the numbers vary from decade to decade. In 1856–1857, for example, the number of plural marriages skyrocketed; as noted earlier, this was a period of religious fervor known as the Mormon reformation (Ivins, 1956; Van Wagoner, 1989).

Of 1,800 other pioneer cases about 67% of the men practicing polygyny had only two wives, 20% had three wives, and less than 10% had four or more wives (Ivins, 1956; see also Smith and Kunz, 1976). At the same time, some men, especially church leaders, had many wives and children. Brigham Young allegedly had 27 wives, was "sealed" to twice that many living women and to at least 150 other women who had previously died (Ivins, 1956). Heber Kimball, a church leader close to Brigham Young, had 43 wives and 65 children (Van Wagoner, 1989). Three other church leaders had 11, 10, and 19 wives, respectively (Goodson, 1976), and Joseph Smith's early associates who practiced polygyny had an average of 5.1 wives (Faux, 1983).

The partners in some of these marriages were older women and widows seeking security and support. Brigham Young, for example, married several of Joseph Smith's widows following his assassination. This practice originated in part in the biblical teaching that a man should marry his brother's widows in order to care for them. Many of these marriages were "for time only," whereas the woman's marriage to her original husband was "for eternity."

In summary, only a small proportion of Mormon families practiced polygyny in the pioneer era. The average was perhaps 20%, with variations over the years and across geographical regions. Furthermore, most plural families had only two wives, with many fewer having three or more wives. These data are consistent with those of other polygynous cultures, as is the fact that it was primarily church leaders and other select men who were the predominant practitioners of plural marriage and who had larger numbers of plural wives.

TECHNICAL NOTE

Polygyny is a common form of family structure in many non-Western cultures, especially traditional and low-technology cultures. Plural marriage has also been practiced from time to time in Western Christian history by royalty, small religious sects, and others.

Polygyny around the world

The most comprehensive data on polygyny in world cultures can be found in the Human Relations Area Files (HRAF). Initiated several decades ago by the anthropologist George Murdock (1967, 1981), the HRAF comprises a vast array of coded ethnographic information on 1,264 world cultures.

Number of cultures practicing polygyny

In a sample of cultures from the HRAF (Murdock, 1967), 77% (193/250) practiced some form of polygyny, 17% (43/250) were monogamous, and 1% (2/250) practiced polyandry (a few others could not be classified). Another sample from the HRAF pool (see Murdock's *Atlas of World Cultures,* 1981) contains information from 563 cultures in six regions of the world. When we tabulated these data, we found that 78% of the cultures practiced polygyny, less than 1% practiced polyandry, and 21% were strictly monogamous. Thus polygyny appears to be common practice among world cultures.

It should be noted that a great deal of HRAF information pertains to traditional, isolated, low-technology cultures, often with small populations. Also, the practice of plural marriage has changed in some cultures as a result of urbanization, technological development, and political upheavals. Nevertheless, even if considered only historically, polygyny is or has been an accepted and frequently practiced marital form in many world cultures.

Incidence of polygyny within cultures

How many marriages in a specific culture are polygynous? In a sample of more than 200 societies in the HRAF, monogamous marriages are more frequent than plural marriages in societies that practice polygyny (Murdock, 1967). Furthermore, plural marriages usually involve older, wealthier, or high-status men.[6] Furthermore, other studies show that only a relatively small proportion of men in polygynous cultures marry more than one wife – often fewer than 10% and usually no more than 25–35%.[7] So although polygyny is not uncommon, its incidence within cultures is relatively infrequent. These rates of polygyny are comparable to those among 19th-century Mormons reported earlier.

Number of wives in polygynous families

Although figures vary across cultures, most polygynous marriages involve two wives. Marital data for 1966–1977 from 15 African countries, for example, show that the average plural family there had 2.0–2.5 wives, with many fewer marriages involving three or more wives (Welch and Glick, 1981). These figures are consistent with those for sub-Saharan African cultures, which reportedly have an average of 1.5 wives in polygynous families (Dorjahn, 1959). Note, too, that it is customary for Negev Bedouin men in Israel to have two wives, although Muslim law allows them to have up to four wives (Marx, 1987).[8] These data are also consistent with 19th-century Mormon pioneer polygynous families, as discussed earlier.

As also mentioned earlier, the practice of plural marriage may be changing in some cultures as a result of urbanization, greater access to the mass media, migrations, political upheaval, and technology. For example, plural marriages among members of two African cultures have decreased in urban versus rural areas (Clignet, 1970), although this pattern does not occur in all cultures (Clignet and Sween, 1981). Furthermore, women's participation in polygyny among the Yoruba in Niger, Africa, appears to depend on several factors (Ware, 1979). For example, older, educated, Christian women seem less likely to be plural wives than uneducated Moslem women of all ages.

Polygyny in Judeo-Christian history

Plural marriage has also been part of the history of Judeo-Christian cultures, as recounted in the Old Testament. As already noted, Abraham, the father of the monotheistic Judeo-Christian religious heritage, married Hagar, a servant, at the urging of his wife Sarah, so that he could have an ancestral line. The practice of polygyny continued for generations among later Jewish biblical prophets and kings. Some European Jews practiced plural marriage well into the Middle Ages (Kilbride, 1994). Furthermore, polygyny has occurred sporadically over the centuries of Christian history (Cairncross, 1974). Even though the Catholic Church frowned on the practice beginning in the 7th century, it was occasionally sanctioned by religious leaders. In the 8th century, for example, Pope Gregory II permitted some men to have more than one wife, and a 15th-century pope permitted a Spanish king to marry a second wife.

In the absence of specific prohibitions in the New Testament, religious leaders at one or another time advocated plural marriage on moral and religious grounds. One Calvinist preacher of the early Renaissance argued that polygyny was a legitimate practice in certain circumstances, for example, when one received a call from God or when "special" men were required to help increase the population (Cairncross, 1974). And throughout the Middle Ages, religious leaders, royalty, or small sects advocated or practiced polygyny in the name of God and the biblical patriarchs. Sometimes self-appointed "righteous" men felt obligated to spread their "seed" in order to follow the biblical dictum that people should multiply and populate the earth.

During the Protestant Reformation of the 1500s, a time of political, social, and religious upheaval in western Europe, polygyny was openly advocated in some quarters – usually under the banner of religious values regarding family structure, gender roles, and biblical heritage (Cairncross, 1974). Another factor that probably contributed to the practice was the high death rate among males as a result of wars and disease.

In 1534 polygyny was advocated as a religious virtue by a radical Anabaptist Protestant sect in the city of Munster, Germany. Led by John of Leyden, a charismatic individual, this group practiced polygyny for a year or so, with the biblical patriarchs as role models, and with John preaching that he and others were ordered by God to increase the population, and avoid "wasting semen" (Cairncross, 1974). But all of this came to an end when the town was conquered by supporters of Christian monogamy.

This short experiment was not the last case of polygyny among Protestant groups. Some theologians of the era, including Martin Luther, succumbed to pressure from political and other elites desiring to practice polygyny in order to retain their support and ensure the success of the Reformation. Polygyny was also occasionally practiced with religious approval in some communities following the end of the Thirty Years' War in 1648. Owing to the decimation of the adult male population during this lengthy conflict, Christian theologians authorized men to have two wives over the following 10-year period in order to replace the male population. Husbands were also instructed by these theologians "to observe seemly behavior, to make proper provisions for both wives, . . . to avoid ill feeling between them" (Cairncross, 1974, p. 74).

Ultimately, however, Christian religions rejected plural marriages. For example, the Catholic Church absolutely rejected polygyny in the 16th century and has maintained that stance ever since (even though polygyny continues to be practiced today in a variety of Christian and Catholic groups in some African countries). Polygyny was also advocated by the poet John Milton in the 1600s and by Napoleon later on (as a way of increasing the labor pool in the French colonies – but not in France itself!). Even Adolf Hitler considered a proposal for men to engage in "stable conjugal relations" with more than one woman in order to restore the male population lost in World War I (Cairncross, 1974).

Thus, although 19th- and 20th-century Mormon polygyny is widely considered an anomaly, the fact is that the idea and practice of plural marriage have a long history in Christianity, albeit on a relatively small scale. In many cases the rationale for practicing polygyny was similar to the dictum of fundamentalist Mormon theology, namely, that certain men should "multiply and populate the earth." Almost every Christian polygynous group, including Mormons, has also condoned polygyny on the basis of biblical practices.

3

Contemporary fundamentalist movements

The present chapter traces the history of Mormon fundamentalism from the Manifesto of 1890 to the present time. Although the Mormon Church denounced plural marriages in increasingly stronger terms over this period, a small band of fundamentalists held fast, continued to follow what they believed to be the true tenets of the religion, and coalesced into a formal organization in the late 1920s. From then on the movement developed into the several groups that are active today. The events described next are rooted in the minds of modern fundamentalists and help to explain their religious faith and commitment to plural family life.

Beginnings: 1890–1929

As federal and civil opposition to plural marriages mounted in the years prior to the Manifesto of 1890, the president of the Mormon Church, John Taylor, became a fugitive because of his advocacy of the practice. In 1886 Taylor had a religious experience that fundamentalists recount as a testimonial to their belief in plural marriage (see Driggs, 1990; Bradley 1993; Van Wagoner, 1989). While in hiding from federal agents, Taylor was guarded by several young men, including Lorin Woolley (who years later founded the modern fundamentalist organization). One night, Woolley heard voices conversing in Taylor's room, when he was presumably alone. The next morning Taylor told his bodyguards that during the night he had been visited by Joseph Smith and Jesus Christ, who had instructed him to hold fast to the principle and practice of plural marriage, despite the growing pressure not to do so. Taylor then had a revelation from God confirming the validity of the principle of plural marriage. After describing the visitation to the guards and church leaders, John Taylor "set apart" several men, including Lorin Woolley and his father John Woolley, and gave them the power to perform plural marriages and other priestly functions and to authorize others to do so (Bradlee and Van Atta, 1981).

Between these events and 1929, the U.S. government and the Mormon Church came down hard on polygynists. The number of plural marriages declined, polygynists were gradually cut off from the main Mormon Church, and church leaders who continued to participate in or approve of plural marriages were punished. John Taylor's son, a church apostle, was stripped of his position and eventually excommunicated because he held fast to the principle of plural marriage.

Nevertheless, a small group of diehards kept the fundamentalist spirit alive. In 1912 Lorin Woolley made his first *public* statement regarding the 1886 visitation by Joseph Smith and Jesus Christ to John Taylor. For many people, Woolley's statement affirmed the "validity" of plural marriages in the face of the 20-year campaign by the Mormon Church to stamp out the practice. For many believers, this statement also signified that Woolley had special religious authority that he could pass on to others (Van Wagoner, 1989; personal communication from an elder in a present-day group). Woolley's statement was published in 1929 when he, the only living survivor of those granted special religious authority by John Taylor in 1886, became the leader of a formal organization of fundamentalists and ordained several men to serve as apostles (Van Wagoner, 1989). The modern fundamentalist movement was born.

Growth and schisms: 1930 to early 1950s

During the next decades the fundamentalist movement established an organizational structure and became increasingly visible. At the same time, internal conflict and disagreement mounted, eventually resulting in a permanent schism and separate fundamentalist groups. During this period the main Mormon Church was especially hostile toward fundamentalists, encouraging arrests and legal actions against those practicing plural marriage. For the fundamentalists, then, these were years of both growth and struggle.

Led by John Y. Barlow in the middle 1930s until his death in 1949, the fundamentalist group established communities Salt Lake City, Utah, and in an isolated town, Short Creek, on the Utah–Arizona border, which was hundreds of miles from the eye of the government and the church. As Mormon church and civil legal pressures mounted, plural families migrated to Short Creek, and the town became a haven and center of their activities (Baer, 1988; Bradley, 1993; Van Wagoner, 1989; Young, 1954).[1] By 1935 Short Creek had about 20 homes and 200 people (half of whom were not part of the fundamentalist movement), a combination store and gas station, a post office, lumber mill, and a one-room schoolhouse (Bradley, 1993).

John Y. Barlow, the new prophet, moved to the community, establishing it as one center of the fledgling fundamentalist movement. At the same time, Joseph Musser, then a senior apostle, and his followers remained in Salt Lake City, Utah, which helped set the stage for an eventual split in the movement.

In 1942 the fundamentalists in Short Creek established a tax-free co-operative association, the United Effort Plan (UEP) (Bradley, 1993; Young, 1954). The UEP put into practice the 19th-century Mormon ideal of a unified community having ownership of the land, and with everyone working cooperatively, and sharing in achievements of the group. The UEP is still in effect and controls a great deal of land in the adjoining communities of Colorado City, Arizona, and Hildale, Utah (the present name of the former Short Creek community). Residents may apply to the governing board (church and community leaders) for permission to build a home on a parcel of land, are tenants at will, and are only expected to assist with tax payments, albeit voluntarily. The UEP also controls agricultural land in the community, which members may work for wages, with profits going to a trust for the benefit of the community.

The Short Creek and Salt Lake communities of the movement grew throughout the 1940s, with John Y. Barlow appointing new members to the governing council, several of whom were his allies. One of these men, LeRoy Johnson, eventually became prophet of the rural group following its split from the Musser-led group in the early 1950s. The movement also continued to face serious opposition from the Mormon Church and civil authorities. In the 1930s church president Heber Grant not only denounced and excommunicated practitioners of plural marriage, but he stated that the LDS Church would assist legal authorities in criminal prosecutions of polygynists (Bradley, 1990; Van Wagoner, 1989). And during Grant's presidency the church published what came to be known as the Final Manifesto – which both condemned polygyny and denied the validity of John Taylor's 1886 revelation advocating plural marriages. In addition, church members were required to sign an ecclesiastical "loyalty oath" denouncing polygyny. Those refusing to do so were excommunicated. Church authorities also encouraged members to report people attending fundamentalist meetings, urged public libraries to exclude fundamentalist writings from their holdings, and requested postal authorities to prohibit mailings of fundamentalist literature (Van Wagoner, 1989). In addition, church relief support for poor polygynous families was withheld, and children of polygynous parents were denied baptism until they were old enough to repudiate their parents' practices (Van Wagoner, 1989).

During the 1930s and 1940s a variety of legislative, criminal, and civil actions were directed at the growing fundamentalist movement. This should not be surprising, given the powerful influence of the LDS Church in the Utah legislature, as well as its influence in neighboring states. In 1935 Utah made "cohabitation" a criminal felony. Chapter 112 (Section 103-51-2) of the Utah penal code states: "If any person cohabits with more than one person of the opposite sex, such a person is guilty of a felony." Although vague and ambiguous, this law was invoked in several polygyny cases in the 1930s and 1940s. And in 1973 the Utah legislature included the following statute in Chapter 7 of the Criminal Code, Section 76-7-101, "Offenses against the family":

> 1) A person is guilty of bigamy when, knowing he has a husband or wife or knowing the other person has a husband or wife, he purports to marry another person or cohabits with another person.
> 2) Bigamy is a felony of the third degree.
> 3) It shall be a defense to bigamy that the accused reasonably believed he and the other person were legally eligible to marry.

The Constitution of Utah, 1896 (Article 3), also contains the following prohibition against polygamy, although the preceding criminal code statutes are the only ones under which polygamy can be prosecuted: "Perfect toleration of religious sentiment is guaranteed. No inhabitant of this state shall ever be molested in person or property on account of his or her mode of religious worship; but polygamous or plural marriages are forever prohibited."

Using the 1935 legislation on cohabitation, authorities in Utah and Arizona (the latter acting in accordance with their laws) took several actions against fundamentalists. One such action was a raid on the Short Creek community in 1935 by Arizona authorities, who arrested three men (including John Y. Barlow) and three of their wives on charges of cohabitation (Bradlee and Van Atta, 1981; Bradley, 1993; Driggs, 1990). Charges against Barlow were dismissed, but the other two men were convicted of cohabitation and imprisoned for almost a year. Two of the women's cases were dismissed, and the third woman received a suspended sentence (Bradley, 1993). Several other criminal charges were filed against polygynists over the next several years.

In 1944 a coordinated strike force of federal agents and Utah, Arizona, and Idaho authorities arrested about 46 men and women in various locales on charges of cohabitation, criminal conspiracy, mailing obscene literature, and white slavery (Bradley, 1993; Van Wagoner, 1989). The 1944 raid was precipitated by a number of factors, including the increasing size of the fundamentalist movement, their outspoken views about plural marriage, and the publication of their magazine, *Truth*. This magazine, published since 1935 and edited by Joseph Musser, openly criticized the Mormon

Church and cited articles and tracts of 19th-century Mormon leaders advocating plural marriage. *Truth* may have been such an irritant to the main Mormon Church that it, and the increasing numbers and visibility of the fundamentalist movement, may have precipitated the 1944 raid (Van Wagoner, 1989).[2] The raid made national news, including a pictorial display in *Life* magazine showing children, wives, and husbands in plural families and identifying them by name. The Mormon Church publicly stated that it condemned plural marriages, excommunicated practitioners, and had assisted state and federal authorities in the arrests (Van Wagoner, 1989).

Although charges of kidnapping, conspiracy, and the use of the mails for obscene purposes were not upheld, the U.S. Supreme Court affirmed convictions based on the Mann Act (transportation of women across state boundaries for immoral purposes) (Bradley, 1993; Van Wagoner, 1989). Several cohabitation convictions under the Utah criminal code were also supported on appeal. Fifteen men who were imprisoned were subsequently paroled when they agreed to live only with their legal wives and not attend meetings advocating plural marriage (Van Wagoner, 1989). In spite of the 1944 raid and convictions, *Truth* continued to be published until 1956, the fundamentalist movement grew, and its adherents remained steadfast in their beliefs concerning plural marriage.

During this period a split based on religious doctrinal differences also took place within the movement – between the rural Short Creek group and the Salt Lake group led by Joseph Musser, who had become leader when John Y. Barlow died in 1949. Thereafter, Musser suffered the first of a series of strokes that led a number of council members, especially those affiliated with the Short Creek group, to question his religious views and rationality and his ability to lead (Bronson, n.d.). The conflict came to a head when Musser appointed Rulon Allred to the council in 1950. Allred, a naturopathic physician, had cared for Musser, was his personal friend, and had acted on behalf of Musser in church affairs. The Short Creek group rebelled at this appointment, stating that Musser was intellectually incompetent and had come under the inappropriate influence of Allred (Bradlee and Van Atta, 1981; Bronson, n.d.). But Musser stood his ground and in the face of sustained revolt formed a new council, with Allred as the senior member and heir apparent to the leadership (Bradlee and Van Atta, 1981; Bronson, n.d.; Van Wagoner, 1989).[3]

Only a handful of council members remained loyal to Musser.[4] The others joined the dissidents, and the Short Creek group eventually set up its own council to govern the newly named Fundamentalist Church of Jesus Christ of Latter-day Saints. Following a short period of interim leadership in the early 1950s, Leroy Johnson became prophet of the Short Creek movement and led it until 1986, when he died at the age of 98.

Upon Joseph Musser's death in 1954, Rulon Allred became prophet and led the urban group until 1977, when he was assassinated by members of a new dissident group, the LeBarons.

The modern era: 1950s–1990s

The Fundamentalist Church of Jesus Christ of Latter-day Saints (Colorado City, Arizona, and Hildale, Utah)

The modern era began with a traumatic raid on the Short Creek community in 1953. That raid is still imprinted on the minds of fundamentalists, especially those from the original Short Creek community, in much the same way that Valley Forge and the Boston Massacre during the American Revolution are fixed in the minds of Americans. In many respects, the raid became a rallying symbol for fundamentalists, gave them a clear sense of identity, and even brought them some attention and sympathy from the broader secular world. (Full accounts of the raid can be found in Bradlee and Van Atta, 1981; Bradley, 1990; Bronson, n.d.; Dyer, 1977; Van Wagoner, 1989; Young, 1954. For a comprehensive description of the incident, see especially Bradley, 1993.)

The raid was conducted by the state of Arizona with the implicit, if not explicit, support of the Utah authorities and the Mormon Church. Under the political and social control of the fundamentalists, the Short Creek community was undoubtedly a powerful presence and irritant to the civil authorities and the Mormon Church. The town did not just house a handful of "invisible" polygynists: by the early 1950s it had reached a population of 400. Cattlemen in the area complained that their grazing fees were being used to educate children of polygynists (Bradley, 1993; Van Wagoner, 1989), and welfare workers in Arizona reported increasing numbers of women in plural families applying for support (Bradlee and Van Atta, 1981; Bradley, 1993). Moreover, some wives seeking welfare were below the legal marriageable age of 18, and a number were even below 16, the age at which parental consent for marriage was required (Bradlee and Van Atta, 1981).

As a result, the Arizona authorities decided to "stamp out" the practice of plural marriage in the Short Creek community. First, they secretly appropriated $10,000 to hire a private detective agency to probe events in the town. Rumor had it that the Mormon Church had guaranteed $100,000 to the state of Arizona if it took action against the Short Creek polygynists. Mormon bishops in Phoenix and Mesa surveyed their members to identify homes in which women and children from the Short Creek comnunity could be housed after the raid. The Arizona legislature subsequently ppropriated $50,000 to plan the raid a year in advance (Bradlee and Van \tta, 1981; Bradley, 1993; Van Wagoner, 1989).

The raid on Short Creek, which was apparently reported in the Salt Lake ιewspapers in advance of the event, took place on Sunday, July 26, 1953.[5] That morning the governor of Arizona, Howard Pyle, made a lengthy radio ιnnouncement:

> Before dawn today the state of Arizona began and now has substantially concluded a momentous police action against insurrection within her own borders. Arizona has mobilized and used its total police power to protect the lives and future of 263 children. They are the product and the victims of the foulest conspiracy you could possibly imagine.
>
> More than 120 peace officers moved into Short Creek. . . . They have arrested almost the entire population of a community dedicated to the production of white slaves who are without hope of escaping this degrading slavery from the moment of their birth. (*Arizona Republic,* July 27, 1953) (Bradley, 1993, p. 208)

Here is how the raid progressed:

> At 4:00 AM . . . heavily armed law enforcement officers arrived at the Short Creek community square, car sirens wailing, red lights flashing, spotlights glaring. The posse was accompanied by national guardsmen, the Arizona Attorney General, superior and juvenile court judges, policewomen, nurses, doctors, twenty-five carloads of newspapermen, and twelve liquor control agents. They expected to find the community sleeping. Instead they found most members of the colony grouped around the city flagpole singing "America" while the American flag was being hoisted. (Van Wagoner, 1989, p. 194)

> Men, women and children [were] standing behind the picket fence that encircled the schoolhouse. They had assembled an hour earlier, dressed and well groomed, to sing while they waited. . . . [T]he music was intermittently broken by nervous gasps, tears, and whispers moving through the crowd like waves upon water.
>
> When Sheriff Fred Porter climbed out of the lead car, Leroy Johnson [the prophet], wearing a clean white shirt, necktie, dark pants, and dark blue suspenders, stepped forward with quiet dignity to meet him. He told Sheriff Porter that they had run for the last time and were going to stand and shed their blood if necessary. (Bradley, 1993, p. 130)

The raid was no surprise to the community. Observers had been stationed эn the outskirts of town the night before and shot off a stick of dynamite ιs a warning when the authorities were visible in the distance.

The authorities searched homes, confiscated literature and some personal ιffects, arrested a number of men, and placed some women and many

children under the state's protective custody (Van Wagoner, 1989). Although the numbers of men, women, and children reported to be involved
in subsequent events vary (see Bradley, 1990, 1993; Driggs, 1990; Dyer,
1977; Van Wagoner, 1989; Young, 1954), it appears that arrest warrants
were filed for about three dozen men and more than 80 women (Bradley,
1993). A number of the men arrested were charged with several offenses,
including cohabitation, conspiracy to conduct unlawful cohabitation, and
misuse of public property, such as the schools. All of the accused men were
eventually set free, partly because the Arizona State legislature had no criminal statutes to implement the state constitution's anti-polygamy clause
(Bradley, 1993). Others were granted probation and suspended sentences
after plea-bargaining on one charge or another (Bradlee and Van Atta,
1981; Bradley, 1993).

Some women and children were released and returned home. Other children were placed in foster homes in Arizona partly on grounds of parental
neglect. Some mothers and children lived in foster homes for several years
after the raid. Some mothers were also pressed to give up their children for
adoption. After protracted legal battles over violations of due process by
the Arizona authorities, children and mothers were released and returned
to the Short Creek community (for the details of these events see Bradley,
1990, 1993; Driggs, 1990; Dyer, 1977; Van Wagoner, 1989).[6]

Despite the trauma of the 1953 raid, the Short Creek fundamentalists
maintained political and social control over the town and continued to
practice plural marriage much as they had done before. The community
grew on both the Arizona and Utah sides of the border, and within a few
years the adjoining communities were named Colorado City, Arizona, and
Hildale, Utah. Although socially unified and spatially contiguous, the two
towns maintain separate educational and social services associated with
each state.

Ever since the raid, there have been only sporadic legal activities by
either Utah or Arizona authorities against the Colorado City and Hildale
communities and against fundamentalists in other geographical regions.
More recently, legal actions have been initiated in respect to polygynists
holding public positions, adoption rights of polygynous families, and the
like. However, most cases have been directed at individuals, not communities at large. Moreover, these cases do not charge individuals with cohabitation or polygyny but focus on derivative issues. Thus the authorities
have taken little concerted action against fundamentalists since the late
1950s.

The Colorado City and Hildale group of fundamentalists has grown
steadily over the past 40 years. Members live in surrounding communities
in the region, there is a sizable contingent living in Salt Lake City, Utah,

and a small group resides in British Columbia, Canada. From the estimates of others and discussions with group members, we judge that there are approximately 4,000 to 5,000 members in Colorado City and Hildale (as does Bradley, 1993), a few thousand members in Salt Lake City, and a small number in other communities, for a total membership of 8,000 to 10,000.

The Colorado City and Hildale communities have been politically controlled by members of the fundamentalist church, as have the schools and other services. And the United Effort Plan described earlier maintains ownership and control over a great deal of residential and agricultural land in the town and surrounding area (the majority of homes in the community are reportedly occupied by members of the UEP; see Bradley, 1993). With its continued expansion, the community has attracted businesses and created employment. A small factory is owned by a community leader, a cooperative supermarket has been established, and there is a town cafeteria. In the 1980s the community built a large meetinghouse named after LeRoy Johnson. This center – used for church services, dances, plays, high school graduations, and other events – is an elaborate 42,000-square-foot structure that was built entirely with volunteer labor and materials. Today the town boasts of an airport (that was cited as Arizona Airport of the Year), a restaurant that moved from Salt Lake City, a motel, a small factory that manufactures fireplace logs, new shops, a radio station, and other amenities (see *Arizona Highways,* August 1994).

The community has also established its own university, Barlow University, in honor of prophet John Y. Barlow. Administered by his son Louis Barlow, a leading member of the community, the university began offering two-year certificate and degree programs in 1990. Its catalog states that the curriculum "is directed primarily to provide education for members of the Fundamentalist Church of Jesus Christ of Latter-day Saints" (p. 1) and to offer programs "to educate, refine, and elevate the whole man. . . . in Arts . . . , Sciences . . . , Foundations/theology, and Learned Professions" (p. 10).

With little fear of being prosecuted for practicing plural marriage, the community is now less secretive about its activities. Selected residents have participated in media interviews about aspects of their lifestyle, including a PBS documentary aired on the anniversary of the 1890 Manifesto. Openness to outsiders is controlled, however, and a handful of community leaders (especially the current mayor, Dan Barlow, another son of John Y. Barlow and one of the lookouts in the 1953 raid) serve as community spokespersons.

There have been no arrests for cohabitation or polygyny in recent years by Utah or Arizona authorities, and none seem likely in the foreseeable future. Indeed, present-day officials have stated publicly that they will not initiate charges against polygynists because no significant harm to the community is being perpetrated, there are too many polygynists to prosecute, and there are more important legal and criminal matters to attend to.

However, legal action does occur occasionally in cases where issues are more narrowly defined. For example, the state of Arizona brought charges to dismiss Sam Barlow, also a son of John Y. Barlow, as a law officer in the community, on the grounds of his admitted plural marriages in violation of the state constitution. Barlow claimed that his religious freedom to practice plural marriage was guaranteed by the Constitution of the United States and that there was no enforcing statute to implement the anti-polygamy provision of the state constitution. In May 1992 the Arizona Law Enforcement Officer Advisory Council ruled that Barlow's decertification as a law officer should be dismissed because "there has never been ... any determination that polygamy is a practice inconsistent with the peace and safety of the state. Barlow's violation of the Constitution and his oath due to his religious beliefs [do] not violate the public trust" (*Deseret News,* May 17, 1992).

Now and then civil suits are also linked to polygynous marriages. In the early 1990s, for example, a former member of the community filed a suit in an adoption case. The defendants, a Hildale–Colorado City family, had informally adopted the children (from a former marriage) of a plural wife who died shortly after marrying into the family. The sister of the deceased woman, who had left the fundamentalist group, charged that she was the appropriate guardian of the children. The Utah Supreme Court eventually ruled that an adoption judgment should be based on the well-being of the child and other traditional criteria, not on the practice of plural marriage alone. A similar judgment was made in 1987 by the Utah Supreme Court in a custody case involving the breakup of a polygynous family (Driggs, 1991).

As these cases show, most contemporary legal actions involving the Colorado and Hildale fundamentalists are focused on specific issues, not on the practice of polygyny as a crime in and of itself. A similar pattern prevails among other fundamentalist groups. Without a strong legal basis, there is little likelihood of massive arrests and raids in the near future. Furthermore, large numbers of people are now practicing polygyny, the group is essentially a peaceful one, and the LDS Church does not want to be the center of attention or to publicize the existence of the fundamentalist movement. And the legal authorities have more important matters to address.

Although there is an unstated "peace" between the Hildale–Colorado City fundamentalists and the LDS Church and secular government, a social and legal rift has developed within the community. Following prophet Leroy Johnson's death in 1986, a group of dissidents, some of whom were long-time members of the community, claimed title to a share of the land and resources controlled by the United Effort Plan. According to one source, the assessed value of the UEP land, based on community tax rolls, is about $17 million (Bitton, 1987), although some report the figure to be as high as $65 million (*Deseret News,* December 12–13, 1994).

The dissident group has established a neighboring polygynous community in the region and filed a lawsuit claiming some portion of the UEP resources as rightfully theirs. It has also charged inappropriate evictions of members from UEP land, unlawful omission of the group as beneficiaries of the trust, misuse and management of funds by the governing body, and violation of the UEP's original charter. The law suit, initiated in 1987, is still in the courts.

As of this writing the Colorado City and Hildale community and the Fundamentalist Church of Jesus Christ of Latter-day Saints are reasonably well off, growing, and extending their influence into other communities in the region.

The Apostolic United Brethren: the Musser–Allred group

Following the schism in the early 1950s, Rulon Allred, the protégé of Joseph Musser, assumed leadership of the urban group of fundamentalists, named the Apostolic United Brethren (AUB). His brother, Owen, has led the group since Rulon's death in 1977.

Under Rulon Allred's stewardship, the AUB stabilized and grew steadily between 1954 and 1977 (Bradlee and Van Atta, 1981; Solomon, 1984; Van Wagoner, 1989). A naturopathic physician, Allred was the son of a prominent polygynist and politician who had violated the Manifesto of 1890 and fled to Mexico after marrying a second wife. Although as a young man Rulon Allred had denounced plural marriage, he eventually accepted the principle and was excommunicated from the Mormon Church. Arrested and convicted in 1944 in one of the major raids, Allred served time in jail but was released when he and others promised not to advocate or practice plural marriage again (Bradlee and Van Atta, 1981). Unable to avoid doing so, however, Allred fled to Mexico, subsequently returned and turned himself in to the authorities, and was soon released again. During the prosecutions in the 1940s and 1950s, Allred kept his families separated, moved them frequently, sometimes to other states, and was on the run himself for months at a time. According to his daughter Dorothy (Solomon, 1984), Allred and others were spied on during these years, when the Mormon

Church allegedly infiltrated the group and helped the authorities identify and track down fundamentalists.

An older member of the AUB told us that the group grew slowly during the early years of Allred's leadership, largely as a result of births rather than incoming converts. In the 1970s, however, converts began joining the group, and growth accelerated. We were told that many members of the LDS Church joined the fundamentalists because they resented the 1978 revelation calling for the admission of Blacks to the main Mormon Church priesthood – a role that had been previously prohibited because of the belief that Blacks carried a biblical curse. To this day, fundamentalists denounce the 1978 revelation.

Rulon Allred was described to us as a bright, educated, distinguished, and charismatic individual, a forceful speaker, and a kind and gentle man. Under his and his brother Owen's leadership the group has grown from a small contingent to somewhere between 1,000 and 1,500 families, and 6,000 to 10,000 members.[7]

In 1961 the AUB bought land and established a community in a Rocky Mountain state (Bronson, n.d.). The community of 70 to 75 families and 600 to 700 people is called a United Order cooperative, since all work and resources are shared, and it thereby fulfills early church doctrine. The group also has a communal group of about 300 people in a neighboring country. And a small AUB contingent of about 25 families and 100 to 150 people reportedly resides in southern Utah. This group lives in a larger town and is not a separate community. In addition, the AUB recently founded a small community of less than 100 people in north-central Utah. There is also a small cohort in Great Britain. The AUB has a large meetinghouse near Salt Lake City, which is used for church services, meetings, recreational activities, and educational programs. In addition, it has land holdings for farming and ranching.

Rulon Allred's leadership ended in 1977, when he was assassinated by members of the dissident LeBaron group (Bradlee and Van Atta, 1981; see also Van Wagoner, 1989). The events that eventually led to this act began in the 1920s with the claim by Alma LeBaron, an excommunicated polygynist, that the mantle of church leadership had been passed to him from the church's founder, Joseph Smith. LeBaron's sons, raised in Mexico, believed their father to be the rightful leader and, although they were members of the Allred group, continued to hold to their sense of special mission. Following Allred's failed attempts to ensure their loyalty, the LeBarons established their own fundamentalist church in 1955. Under the leadership of Ervil LeBaron, the group soon claimed a membership of more than 500. But in 1972 Ervil was convicted of complicity in his brother's death, presumably because of the conflict between them over leadership of their group

(Bradlee and Van Atta, 1981). Upon his release from prison, the violence within the LeBaron group was reignited and Ervil LeBaron was arrested again in 1976, but this time he was released for lack of evidence.

For years LeBaron had been attempting to convince Rulon Allred that he, Ervil, was the "true" leader of fundamentalism. LeBaron had even physically threatened Allred in letters, phone calls, and various other forms. According to a member of the group, Allred ignored these intimidations as the rantings of a man from a family with a history of emotional instability. In 1977 Rena Chynoweth, a young wife of Ervil LeBaron, and Ramona Marston, a stepdaughter, entered Rulon Allred's medical office and shot him to death. In 1979 four principals in the case, including Rena Chynoweth, were tried and found innocent. LeBaron was arrested in Mexico that same year, brought to trial in the United States in 1980, and found guilty of conspiring to kill Rulon Allred and his own rival brother. LeBaron died in prison in 1981.

Thereafter, rival factions in the LeBaron family continued on a path of violence, with mutual assassinations extending into the late 1980s. As of this writing, however, the LeBaron group has not been too visible, and it no longer seems to be a significant presence in the fundamentalist movement.[8]

Allred was succeeded by his brother Owen, a long-standing member of the governing council and a key adviser to Rulon. The AUB has grown steadily under his leadership, by virtue of new converts and a high birth rate. The AUB runs a children's summer camp, operates its own elementary school (children receive credit in the public educational system by passing appropriate tests), and offers a variety of social and educational events for their community.

The AUB's relations with the civil authorities and the Mormon Church are similar to those of the Colorado City and Hildale fundamentalists. There have been no large-scale arrests or raids for engaging in plural marriages since the 1950s. Like other groups of fundamentalists, however, they have had to deal with internal conflicts and separatist movements. One of these other movements has been led by Alex Joseph, an outspoken, charismatic, and flamboyant man who is mayor of a town he established in southern Utah. Alex Joseph and his wives appear occasionally on local and national media and at present claim little religious affiliation with Mormonism. Originally a convert to the LDS Church, Joseph was a member of the Allred group for a few years but then in 1970 established his own church, the Church of Jesus Christ in Solemn Assembly, as a result of a falling out with Allred over financial matters (Van Wagoner, 1989). Alex Joseph openly criticized the AUB and Allred in the press, so much so that he became a suspect in the murder of Allred. Denying such charges in a

TV interview, he openly (and correctly) accused Ervil LeBaron's group of the crime (Bradlee and Van Atta, 1981). Alex Joseph continues to practice polygyny openly, manages the town he established, and freely discusses his lifestyle in the media.[9]

Other fundamentalists

Several fundamentalist groups formed over the years have remained small or faded away, whereas others have survived and even prospered. One of these successful groups, the Latter-day Church of Christ or the Davis County Cooperative Society, was organized by Eldon Kingston in 1935 and today is said to have more than 500 members and assets in excess of $50 million (Baer, 1988; Bradlee and Van Atta, 1981; Van Wagoner 1989).[10] Not easily penetrated by outsiders, the Kingston group "presently owns over thirty businesses in Utah, as well as several farms, a 300 acre dairy farm . . . , a thousand-acre farm . . . , and a large cattle ranch. . . . Their largest operation is a coal mine" (Van Wagoner, 1989, p. 202). The Kingston group claims that it no longer practices polygyny. However, several members were excommunicated from the Mormon Church in the early 1960s for engaging in polygynous cohabitation (Van Wagoner, 1989).

Recently, some independent practitioners of plural marriage, along with members of several small groups, have been embroiled in civil or criminal court cases. In one such case, two brothers raised as Mormons, Ron and Dan Lafferty, were excommunicated for advocating and forming a small group practicing plural marriage. In 1984, following a "revelation" from God, they murdered their sister-in-law and her baby because she spoke out against plural marriage. Convicted of murder, one Lafferty was sentenced to life imprisonment and the other to death (Van Wagoner, 1989).

Another criminal case involved the Singer–Swapp plural family, residents of a small town 40 miles from Salt Lake City. In the 1970s the Singers withdrew their children from the public school system to give them a home-based education, but the authorities contested the removal of the children from the educational system. In the meantime, Singer married a second wife with children (while she was still legally married to someone else). As legal battles ensued, tensions mounted, and in 1979 Singer was killed by law officers serving him with an arrest warrant. Although Singer was shot in the back, the lawmen claimed that he had threatened them with a gun.

Sometime later, a young man, Adam Swapp, married two daughters of John and Vicky Singer. In 1988, still angry with the authorities about John Singer's death and his perception of the LDS Church's treatment of the family, Swapp bombed the Mormon chapel in a nearby town, later claiming that he acted in accordance with divine advice. The authorities, suspecting the Swapp–Singer group, obtained arrest warrants and placed the family compound under siege. After 13 days the lawmen decided to move in and capture the alleged perpetrators. In the ensuing gun battle, Swapp was wounded, a police officer was killed, and the family surrendered. Adam Swapp was sentenced to a long jail sentence for violating state and federal laws, and other family members received varying prison terms (for details see Van Wagoner, 1989).

In yet another case, Royston Potter, a police officer in a town in the Salt Lake City area, was fired in 1982 when it was discovered that he had two wives and had been practicing plural marriage as an independent Mormon fundamentalist (he had been raised as a Jehovah's Witness, converted to Catholicism, and eventually converted to Mormonism before becoming a fundamentalist Mormon). In reaction to the firing, Potter filed a civil suit claiming that under the First Amendment of the U.S. Constitution, his religious freedom had been violated (Van Wagoner, 1989). Potter lost his case, and subsequent appeals to higher courts were denied.

In a different type of case, Arvin Shreeve was arrested in 1992 in Ogden, Utah, on charges of sexual child abuse and related offenses. An alleged independent polygynist, Shreeve and members of his family were charged with forcing female minors to engage in sex with one another and with adult women and with making pornographic movies of women and young girls. Shreeve and some of his wives were found guilty of several charges.

The present situation

If the past 25 years are any guide to the future, cohabitation and polygyny are unlikely to precipitate mass raids and arrests similar to those of the 1930s to the 1950s. At the same time, we can expect to see occasional legal actions against individuals accused of committing specific crimes or civil suits involving individuals or groups of fundamentalists. Although plural marriage may be associated with such cases and may make them more newsworthy, issues of polygyny and cohabitation will probably not be the central focus of legal issues.

As of this writing, the LDS Church seems to have adopted a "hands-off" attitude toward fundamentalists, generally ignores them, and has not openly encouraged the authorities to act against them. The church has not made many public pronouncements recently regarding plural marriage, has not condemned the practice of specific groups, and has not commented on civil and criminal suits involving fundamentalists. Discussions about polygyny, even regarding its practice in pioneer days, are now rare in the Mormon Church: "The concept of plural marriage is not part of the oral or written traditions of the modern day public Church. Except for descendants of pioneer polygamists with a sense of history, polygamy is as foreign to the contemporary Mormon as it might be to someone outside the Church. For some it is barely part of their mythic past" (Bradley, 1990, p. 32).

Furthermore, the legal and civil authorities have not made any arrests for polygyny or cohabitation for years. Indeed, the civil authorities have publicly stated that they have no intention to level formal charges against fundamentalists. For example, a front-page headline in the *Salt Lake Tribune* on August 6, 1991, read: "Law Looks Other Way If Polygamy Is Only Crime." According to the attorney general of the state of Utah, "Unless it is associated with child abuse, welfare fraud or any other illegal act, polygamy for its own sake has not been a crime susceptible of successful prosecution and uses up an awful lot of resources." To this, County Attorney David Yocum added: "If we are going after illegal cohabitation we'd have to line them all up – the older people living together, young couples, even homosexual couples living together – all violate the bigamy/cohabitation law. People don't make complaints about polygamists or cohabitation, so we don't investigate, don't file charges. Cohabitation is pretty difficult to prove." (*Deseret News,* September 11–12, 1991).

In 1991 a commission to revise the Utah State Constitution proposed that statements banning polygamy be removed on the grounds that the language was archaic, few other states had such a prohibition, and existing laws regarding bigamy would suffice. But a prominent member of the commission countered: "Outside of Utah, I am worried some may latch on to it, saying 'What are those crazy Mormons in Utah doing now?' The national press could have a field day. Some outside the state see us in a strange light, the Singers, polygamy, Hoffman, that kind of thing. My opinion is, the less said about it (polygamy), the better" (*Deseret News,* September 11–12, 1991).

Interestingly, a 1992 Canadian court concluded that a law banning plural marriage violated constitutional guarantees of religious freedom. The case involved a small group in British Columbia who are affiliated with the fundamentalists of Hildale, Utah, and Colorado City, Arizona. Not surprisingly, a leader of the Fundamentalist Church of Jesus Christ of Latter-day Saints heralded the decision as a step toward eventual legalization of polygyny in the United States (*Salt Lake Tribune,* June 16, 1992).

Although fundamentalists nowadays are not especially fearful of being prosecuted for practicing polygyny or cohabitation, they are still wary and do not flagrantly display their beliefs or lifestyle. Older members of these groups recall vividly earlier raids and arrests, fleeing from the authorities, hiding their families, and suffering actions against them by the LDS Church.

everal participants told us that they actively avoid letting co-workers or business associates know that they are fundamentalists or that they practice plural marriage, especially if others are members of the LDS Church. At the same time, several fundamentalists said that they no longer hide their or their children's identity from the school system and permit all children to register under the father's name. (In earlier years, children often used their mother's last name in order to hide their family status.) And some families told us that their neighbors were fully aware of their plural marriage status but were still friendly toward them.

Another small indicator of their present sense of security is the occasional obituary notice of the death of a fundamentalist. Part of a 1989 obituary in a Salt Lake City newspaper stated: "He was a father of a numerous posterity, consisting of 7 wives and 56 children. He has 340 grandchildren and 70 great grandchildren. He was preceded in death by two of his wives and 7 of his children." The obituary also named his siblings, details of his life history, and the location and time of funeral services. Clearly, there was no attempt to hide much about this man, his family, and the group to which he belonged.

Another obituary in 1994 noted that the deceased and his first wife had "entered the Law of Celestial marriage" with his second wife, and that he later married a third wife. It also mentioned that "his commitment to this law sent him to prison twice; in 1945 and again in 1959. However, he remained firm in his beliefs. . . . Six of his sons served their country, two of them while he was in prison for living his religion." The remainder of the notice named his 11 sons and 19 daughters and their spouses, and an accompanying article noted that some of them had entered into plural marriage. The obituary also listed the time and place of funeral services.

The fact that fundamentalists participate in local conferences, appear on television (sometimes with their wives and children), and are interviewed by newspapers and magazines, often without hiding their identity, attests to their sense of security about not being prosecuted. Some who have appeared in the media are independents; some seem to be publicity seekers. Representatives of major groups have also participated in interviews and other public events. For example, leaders of the Allred and Colorado City–Hildale groups occasionally accept interviews in which they explain their beliefs and lifestyle. Such appearances are low key and dignified, do not criticize the LDS Church, and emphasize the morality and good citizenship of fundamentalist members. When an independent polygynist was arrested and charged with sexual abuse of children, Owen Allred, leader of the Apostolic United Brethren, was interviewed in the *Salt Lake Tribune* (1992); the headline stated: "Polygamist fears Ogden sect's notoriety will taint the image of other groups." He said:

It has absolutely nothing to do with us. I don't know anything about th man who is the head of it, or anything. When these things come up, we a all categorized in the same way and are lumped together with groups li the LeBarons that have a reputation for crime and violence. We've neve caused any trouble to anybody anywhere. We uphold and sustain the lav of the land (except when those laws conflict with religious beliefs).

The foreseeable future

In all likelihood, the present "truce" between the Mormon Church, th civil authorities, and fundamentalist polygynous groups will continue. Thu the membership of the fundamentalist movement is also likely to continu on its path of recent growth. At the same time, we anticipate that schism and conflict among fundamentalists will arise as new groups or separati movements come to the surface, as new leaders emerge from within c outside, and as small independent groups and individuals make known tha they are practitioners of plural marriage. This has been the pattern withi Mormonism and fundamentalist movements throughout their history, an there is no reason to expect otherwise in the future.[11] Indeed, Mormo religious values of free agency and the idea that personal revelations fro God and religious figures can theoretically come to anyone increase th possibility of future schisms. Now and then, other individuals will no doub claim that they have been chosen by divine revelation as the "One an Mighty" who is to bring the word of God on earth. If they convince other of their revealed role, then a new group will be formed, sometimes in op position to other fundamentalist groups.

In other words, the fundamentalist Mormon movement, including it practice of plural marriage, is here to stay. It is embedded in a long histor on the American scene, its members believe strongly in their religion an way of life, they are aware of and even proud of their distinctiveness i American society, and have held fast to their beliefs in the face of pressure criticism, and persecution by the larger society. Their numbers will increas by virtue of internal birth rates and conversions, existing groups will grow schisms will occur, and new groups will form.

With this historical and contemporary background in hand, we are nov ready to address the main issue of the book – husbands and wives in pres ent-day Mormon fundamentalist plural families. We begin with a descrip tion of the people with whom we worked and the communities in whicl they live.

4

The people and their communities

The participants in our study live in two communities, which for purposes of their anonymity we describe in an incomplete or ambiguous way. We also present a profile giving participants' ages at marriage, number of wives and children in families, occupations, and other biographical information; and we describe geographical features, locations, historical roots, and religious, secular, and social activities in somewhat general terms. Because the backgrounds and values of many present-day fundamentalist communities are similar, they may easily be mistaken one for another. Readers are therefore advised not to leap to conclusions about the identities of people or groups.

The role of communities in the lives of fundamentalists

Individual, interpersonal, and family dynamics are embedded in, affected by, played out, and inseparable from the norms, values, customs, and practices of their larger communities and cultures. This is a central axiom of the transactional perspective described in chapter 1. And it applies to people and families in contemporary fundamentalist groups. Because they are rejected by the mainstream Mormon Church and by American society at large, fundamentalists are highly dependent on their co-religionists, leaders, and communities for social and emotional support, and even for their economic well-being. Such support can be quite strong and positive. At the same time, fundamentalist communities often demand loyalty, strict adherence to norms and values, and allegiance to their leaders. Many individuals and families accept these conditions because fundamentalist groups promise cohesive and orderly community life involving shared values, mutual assistance, moral behavior, and clear-cut rules of social and religious behavior. In addition, some fundamentalist groups are geographically isolated, with the result that their communities have even greater influence on religious, social, political, and economic aspects of life. Furthermore, some

members are converts who fervently desire to be woven into the social an
religious fabric of their new faith, and who may separate themselves from
people in their past lives, including families.

The powerful influence of fundamentalist Mormon communities is per
sonified in their patriarchal leadership. Their principal leader is sometime
called a prophet and is believed to be a direct agent of God. In addition
larger fundamentalist groups often have a council of elders who assist th
religious leader in managing the theological affairs of the group (and ofte
their social and secular affairs as well). The prophet or leader may prescrib
appropriate behavior for group members, teach religious doctrine, manag
the financial affairs of the group, engage in decisions about church activi
ties, counsel congregants, resolve conflicts in families, approve or arrang
marriages, and grant divorces. To one degree or another, members of fun
damentalist church councils also participate in these activities.

Although the religious hierarchy and the social norms of modern polyg
ynous Mormon communities play an important role in the lives of thei
people and families, their authority is not absolute. Individual personalities
ambitions, and economic and social status contribute to a diversity of life
styles within the fundamentalist credo. Furthermore, communities differ i
the extent to which they control various aspects of day-to-day life. Fo
example, the rural community in which we worked has very powerfu
norms to which members and families are expected to subscribe. We de
scribe it as *ultraconservative*. Although the urban community also ha
strong community norms, they are less comprehensive and forceful; w
characterize this group of fundamentalists as *conservative*.

The rural community of Redrock: The United
Fundamentalist Church

Most of the 5,000 people living in the town of Redrock belong to th
United Fundamentalist Church (the fictitious name we will use for thi
group). A contingent of about 2,000 members of the group live in the mai
city in the region, Metropolitan City, some 300 miles to the north. Other
live in small towns in the region of Redrock. And several hundred member
live in a country adjacent to the United States. We could not determine th
exact number of members of the United Fundamentalist Church but esti
mate a total membership of 8,000 to 10,000 on the basis of statements o
participants and figures cited in published sources.

The Redrock community is in an isolated rural area in the Rocky Moun
tains of the western United States. The land in this region is high-mountai
desert, with stark and beautiful red sandstone formations. Although th

community is accessible by paved roads, it is not on a major travel route. Traffic through the town is light, and people in the area usually have a specific reason for being there. As a result, strangers and visitors to the community stand out; although treated politely by residents, they quickly sense that they are outsiders. The closest larger towns, with hospitals and other facilities, are about one to two hours' driving distance away.

The Redrock community was established in the first part of the 20th century as a haven for Mormon polygynous families who believed that they could freely pursue their religious beliefs in an isolated setting (perhaps much like the pioneer Mormons of the 19th century who came to Utah because of its isolation). From a handful of families in its early years and a few hundred people around midcentury, the community grew to its present size. The town now has elementary schools and a high school, supermarket, cafeteria, small clinic, visiting dental services, a small factory, gas stations, and other services.

As noted in previous chapters, 19th-century Mormon pioneers and contemporary fundamentalists subscribed to a United Order ideal that called on everyone to work and share resources in a communal system. So it is in Redrock. Considerable land in and around the community is owned by the United Fundamentalist Church, to whom it was given by the original founders and others who later joined the group. The land is managed by the Cooperative Alliance Agency (CAA), a church-controlled corporation whose assets are estimated to be worth many millions of dollars.

The CAA is a major player in business, agriculture, and real estate in the community. For example, a family who wishes to build a home on community land must receive approval from the CAA. If approved, the family may build a home without any rental charges. But they do not own the land; rather, they are "tenants at will" and can be evicted at any time. This means that the CAA has considerable power over residents. They must also agree not to hold a mortgage on their homes and to build only when they have the cash to do so. As a result, many residents build their homes gradually and add on to them only as family resources permit. Thus a family might start with a basement or first floor, and live in it or in an adjacent trailer until there is enough money to construct the next story of the home. It is also customary for friends and family members to help build each other's homes, in keeping with the strong norm of cooperation and mutual support.

The CAA grants plots to individuals for farming and itself maintains large agricultural lands on which members of the community work for salaries and wages. Furthermore, the supermarket in the community is owned and operated by the CAA. The CAA also owns a fee-free residential facility for the elderly and for group members temporarily without a home.

The CAA rents the land on which a public school is located to the state. Finally, the CAA contributes to a variety of community projects and services from its investments, gifts, and profits. Through its multifaceted activities, the CAA is a visible symbol of the powerful role of the church in the everyday lives of individuals and families.

The United Fundamentalist Church also exerts significant control over the public school system and town government. Most of the teaching and administrative staff of one school are members of the church and residents of the community. (This is less the case in another school.) And the town's civil officials are members of influential church families. The church also plays an important part in the social and public life of the community. Social events, including a community dance every few weeks, are run by the church, are held in the church meetinghouse, and include a blend of religious and social activities. In addition, civic activities, such as town improvement projects, are often initiated and supported by the church. As our participants explained, the church hierarchy plays an important role in the lives of individual families. Not only does the prophet arrange many marriages, but there is a strict dress code for children and adults alike, and people are expected to volunteer for community and church projects. The church also provides many benevolent services. For example, it cares for indigent elderly members of the community in a group home, and a senior member of the church, "Uncle James," functions as community problem solver for those in need. Acting on behalf of the prophet and the religious council, he provides financial assistance to those in distress, guides families through an equitable distribution of their resources to wives who become widowed, and is always on call to help resolve other problems. Uncle James is also the "social director" of the community. He organizes community-wide events, including social dances and Sunday evening entertainment in the church meetinghouse.

In essence, the Redrock community is almost a theocracy. Its church and religious affairs, civil government, education, public services, work and business, and home and social life are all intertwined with and strongly influenced by the United Fundamentalist Church and its Cooperative Alliance Agency.

The urban community of Metropolitan City: The Church of Latter-day Apostles

The Church of Latter-day Apostles (a fictitious name) has grown over the years to a present membership of approximately 6,000 to 10,000 follow-

s.[1] And they are growing steadily by virtue of a high birth rate and in-
oming converts.

In contrast to the rural group, most members of the Church of Latter-
ay Apostles are not concentrated in a single community. Approximately
alf of the congregants reside in the general vicinity of Metropolitan City,
e largest urban center in the region, but they are not heavily concentrated
 any one area. A number of families live in a semirural area and in small
wns adjacent to Metropolitan City; others live in suburban settings
ound the region.

Most members do not live on church land. Although the church owns
me residential and commercial property, families in and around Metro-
litan City rent or buy their own homes. Also in contrast to people of
edrock, only a few members of the Church of Latter-day Apostles work
r the church administration and school or on agricultural land. Most
ople have jobs in private companies and public organizations or operate
eir own businesses. Although they pay a tithing to the church, they retain
eir earnings and run their families independently.

The Church of Latter-day Apostles also has several satellite communities
 the region, elsewhere in the state, in a neighboring state, and in a nearby
untry. The largest satellite community is in a rural and isolated area in
other state. At the time of our research, the 600–800 residents of this
mmunity lived on land owned by the church. The community was es-
blished a few decades ago as a United Order settlement in accordance
ith long-standing Mormon religious and social values. This is a place
here members strive to live and work in a communal spirit and where all
pects of day-to-day life reflect their religious beliefs. Such a community
 impossible to maintain in the dispersed urban setting, so this town is a
mbol of the group's adherence to religious values. Residents cooperate
 working the community farm, caring for livestock, and operating a small
iry. The community has a general store, gas station, school, fire depart-
ent, and town council. Like members of the rural Redrock group, resi-
nts may build a home on church-owned land without paying rent or
suming a mortgage. Some residents work in the community; others com-
ute to work in a larger town some miles away. Earnings are turned over
 the religious leader of the community, who then allocates money on a
rmula basis according to family size.

Because the religious and civil leadership are essentially one and the same,
e community is tightly under the church's control. At one time, for exam-
e, the community's religious leader decided that no one would celebrate
iristmas, because he felt that it was a commercialized, non-Christian pagan
liday. The celebration was renewed several years later when a new reli-

gious leader was appointed by the main church. In earlier years, the who community also celebrated the regular visit of the leader of the church with dance and religious meetings. According to a former member of the com munity, there were regular observances of the leader's birthday, Josep Smith's birthday, Mormon Pioneer Day (July 24), and other such occasion These celebrations involved everyone in town and included any of several a tivities – a baseball game, pet shows, a barbecue, and speeches by elders. T community encompasses all aspects of life – day-to-day living, work and t home, and religious and social life. With many church services, religion meetings, social dances, and holiday celebrations, the town is a world un itself and more or less independent of the larger culture. At the same tim visits, movement of church members into and out of the town, and involv ment by the religious leader and elders of the larger group help the comm nity remain tightly linked to the parent church.

Another small group of families lives in a community in a neighborin country. The members of this community are citizens of that country, a though they are accountable to the main church. The community also o erates on a United Order principle, according to which the land an facilities are owned by the Church of Latter-day Apostles and the resider share in its operation and resources.

Another small group of members lives in a large town of several thou sand people, most of whom are members of the main LDS Church. The do not pattern their lives after a United Order model but work in the tov and in the surrounding region as separate families and individuals.

A new satellite community has recently been established in a small tow some distance from the Metropolitan City area in which the main grou is located. (Two clusters of families in other locations have also joined t Church of Latter-day Apostles because of recent policies by the main LE Church that they felt were too "liberal.")

The church's religious and secular affairs are managed by the leader an a council of church elders. Because members in the urban region live dispersed neighborhoods and areas, support themselves privately, and ov or rent their dwellings, they function somewhat independently of th church on a day-to-day basis. (This is not the case, obviously, for membe of the Church of Latter-day Apostles who live in its United Order satelli communities; their lives are very closely intertwined with the church.)

"Conservatives" and "ultraconservatives"

There are major social and doctrinal differences between the urban Chur of Latter-day Apostles and the rural United Fundamentalist Church. A

ough they share the same general theological beliefs and Mormon heri-
ge, including the rationale for and practice of plural marriage, the urban
oup is "conservative" and the rural group "ultra-conservative" in their
cial and religious norms and practices. The rural community, on the one
nd, encourages people to subscribe closely to church rules and requests,
d individuals achieve stature and recognition through community service
d conformity. The urban community, on the other hand, offers individ-
ls somewhat more freedom of action, a more flexible set of religious and
cial activities, and a less structured atmosphere. Again, these differences
e only relative, because both groups call for a high degree of loyalty to
urch doctrine and social norms.

Several factors probably contribute to the ultraconservative and conser-
tive stances of the rural and urban fundamentalists. Historically, the
oups have had leaders with different personalities and conceptions of the
propriate norms and values for their respective groups. The location and
embership of the groups may also contribute to their differences. Because
e rural group is in an isolated region and many of its members live in
e Redrock community, the church is able to exercise tight control over
any aspects of everyday life. In addition, they tend to attract few converts
om the outside and instead are expanding primarily through internal
rths. As a result, contact with the outside world is fairly restricted. As
ted earlier, the church's control over many aspects of the economy, land,
griculture, and public services further encourages members to conform to
oup norms.

In contrast, the urban group's membership is increasing by virtue of new
nverts, as well as internal births. Converts bring in new ideas and add a
versity of perspectives to religious and social values. Because members
ve and work in a variety of settings, often amid the population at large
and around Metropolitan City, they have more exposure than rural fun-
mentalists to different lifestyles and viewpoints. Many members of the
ban group also use public service systems – including schools – which
obably add to their experiences and views. In general, therefore, many
ban fundamentalists relate to a larger slice of American culture on a daily
sis, which probably contributes to their somewhat less conservative ap-
oach to dress and clothing, church services, social events, youth activities,
d the like.

he ultraconservative United Fundamentalist Church

Dress and clothing. Members of the rural Redrock community follow
very strict dress code that emphasizes modesty. Women and girls wear

high-necked, long-sleeved dresses that fall well below the knee. These a
"pioneer-style" dresses with large collars and wide sweeping skirts and a
often brightly colored. We never saw women or girls wearing pants or jea
(sometimes young girls wear pants under their dresses), shorts, high hee
elaborate jewelry, lipstick, or makeup. Their neatly groomed hairdos a
also unique and reminiscent of an earlier period in American histor
Women and girls alike wear their hair in tight braids or buns with lar
waves and dips, and not a hair is out of place. We rarely saw women
girls wearing loose flowing hair (we were told that such styles are immode
and sexually provocative and thus frowned upon). A key theme in fema
dress is modesty – not flaunting or showing too much bare skin on t
arms, legs, or body. Tight-fitting clothing is also taboo. The community
women and girls are always clean and neat, take pride in their clothin
and spend a great deal of time grooming, especially creating elaborate ai
varied hairdos.[2]

Men and boys also follow a conservative dress code, although it is le
dramatic and distinctive than that of women and girls. Usually we
groomed, men and boys always wear long-sleeve shirts (for modesty v
were told). Their dress is often western style: cowboy shirts, trousers, ai
boots, with vests or suits on formal occasions. Their clothing is usual
subdued, with white or light-colored plain shirts. Men and boys do n
wear shorts, sandals, tank-top shirts, or clothing that exposes too much
their bodies. Modesty and conservative styles are the norm for men's ai
boys clothing, much as they are for women and girls. Hairstyles, too, a
usually simple. Short, combed hair is the norm; we never saw any man
boy with long, shaggy, or disheveled hair, pony tails, shaved heads,
otherwise. In general, women's and girl's clothing seemed to be much mo
varied, colorful, and stylish than that of men and boys.

Church services. Although religious values are similar in Redrock ar
the Metropolitan City communities, differences can be seen in the flow ai
atmosphere of church services. Sunday services of the United Fundamei
talist Church are held in an elegant building that also serves as a communi
center for dances, social events, high school graduation, and other activitie
All the materials and labor used to construct the building were donated b
members of the community. The quality of materials and workmanship
superb, and the structure and its facilities are a source of great pride i
everyone. A large organ and stage for church services stand at one end
the main hall, which has a seating capacity of 3,000 to 4,000 people. A
the other end is a stage for plays and theatrical events. Behind the stage v
saw a complex electronic system for lighting, sets, and various theat
needs. An elaborate roller system for storing thousands of folding chairs

ider the stage. Columns and woodworking around the main hall are elab-
ate in detail and workmanship, as are the ceilings and floors. The floors
e tiled in an attractive design, the lighting is sophisticated, and the ma-
rials and artisanship everywhere are excellent. The walls of the halls out-
de the main meeting room are covered with high-grade marble slabs that
ere recovered from a government building being renovated in another
ate. The marble was hauled to the community by volunteers in several
uck shipments. The building also contains a large modern kitchen, an
aborate funeral viewing room, and meeting rooms and offices.

We were taken on tours of the building on two occasions by a son of a
articipant in our project who works full time as the center's construction
id building manager. An entourage of about 30, mostly young people and
ildren, followed along. Everyone was extremely proud of the building,
id they were pleased as we marveled at the dedication of the volunteers
ho donated materials and worked on it. In response to our praise, some-
ie quoted from a community elder who had said: "We want careful,
ucated and skilled people to build this building, but we also want it done
ith inspiration." It seemed to us that they had indeed succeeded in both
spects. The meetinghouse is a tangible symbol of the loyalty and bonding
people to their church and community. It also reflects the ability of the
urch to mobilize group members on a voluntary basis for such a mo-
entous task.

Church services are held every Sunday afternoon. When we attended,
e hall was quite full, with congregants of all ages. In contrast to the
rvices in the urban group, the atmosphere and flow of events was formal
id serious at all times.

The service was conducted by the prophet, who introduced each speaker
id activity. Seated on the stage with the prophet were the religious leaders
the community and a choir of about 100 men and women. The service
nsisted of a series of speeches by community leaders, prayers, songs by the
oir and congregation, and a sermon by the prophet. The more than half
zen speakers were all men, and they spoke about religion, morality, sup-
rt for the prophet, and loyalty to the community. A few speakers empha-
zed that community members should be loyal and steadfast in the face of
cent legal actions by a group of dissidents who were challenging aspects of
e Cooperative Alliance Agency's control over community land and re-
urces. One speaker criticized the dissidents and called on the congregation
"keep the spirit of God" and be alert and ready to oppose the adversaries.
iother man said the "old ship Zion" was under attack, and "we have a big
ght and we must fight them. Everyone knows what to do. Do it."

A second theme in several speeches centered on supporting the prophet
id obeying his teachings and leadership. One speaker stated, "We must

be obedient to Uncle John, our prophet. If we are obedient and show o
confidence in him, then he will be able to show his confidence in us
Another speaker said, "Don't find fault with the prophet. There must be
oneness with the prophet – it is for our own good." Still another state
"The Lord gave us a good leader." (We suspect that there were sever
reasons for these themes: customary emphasis on the patriarchal structu
of the church, the threats by dissidents, and the relative newness of t
present prophet and his low-key personality, in contrast to that of the d
ceased former prophet, who had been a commanding and charismatic fi
ure.)

Several speeches also stressed the patriarchal structure of families, t
roles of men and women and boys and girls, and the importance of meetii
one's religious responsibilities. In the words of one speaker, "Man is t
head of women, boys should be ready to assume their responsibilities
men and fathers, . . . girls should be sweet and kind to their mothers." T
ward the end of the service the prophet delivered a sermon that quot
extensively from a speech by Brigham Young.

At the end of the service, hundreds of people formed a line, walked on
the stage, and shook hands with the religious leaders and the prophet.
general, the service was formal, only dealt with serious topics, and as a
ready mentioned, the main participants were church and community lea
ers, all of whom were male. The service therefore reflected a "conservativ
atmosphere. It had little of the informality and varied program of the urb
group's Sunday church service.

Sunday evening entertainment. That evening we attended a social pr
gram in the meetinghouse. It reminded us of an old-time "amateur hour
with community members entertaining one another and displaying the
talents in music, songs, and readings. The meeting was led by Uncle Jame
the elder who runs many community activities. We were invited to sit o
the stage with him and other community leaders. The program that u
folded combined religious and moral teachings with entertainment and pa
ticipation by community members, including women and girls, and peop
of all ages. The atmosphere was pleasant and relaxed, in contrast to t
more serious and somber tone of the afternoon church service.

The program began with a benediction and a song by the audience.
woman then spoke on righteous living, and a man then sang a song. Ne:
a teenage girl read an essay she had written on the topic "My Mother
Mean." The girl's mother was "mean" because she insisted that her ch
dren eat and behave properly, go to bed at a decent time, be truthful, ai
work hard. It was a humorous presentation that showed the mother w
enforcing all of the community's values.

A piano and accordion duo next played what they called "all-time favorites," which were songs such as "Silvery Moon," "Remember Me," and
others. Several songs were from the early part of the 20th century. A
woman then spoke seriously about the ways in which people influence others directly and indirectly, and their responsibilities to others. This was
followed by two girls singing an operatic aria with piano accompaniment.
A group of girls from one family then sang the old song "Let a Smile Be
your Umbrella on a Rainy Afternoon."

The next presentation, a very serious talk by a man, emphasized obe-
dience to the prophet. The speaker quoted from Brigham Young and other
prophets and kept repeating the phrase, "If you love the prophet then
mind' him." Each of us then spoke briefly about our research project and
recent political events in Israel.

Toward the end of the program, Uncle James asked the men and boys
present to help pitch hay in preparation for automatic bailing by the com-
munity-owned machine. As soon as he asked for volunteers, about 20
young men stood up. Uncle James expressed his appreciation and told them
where to assemble the next morning.

At the end of the meeting, audience members lined up below the stage,
came up in turn, and shook the hands of everyone on the platform, including us. They were polite and pleasant and thanked us for attending the
event and sharing our thoughts with them.

In general, the meeting gave us a feeling of being transformed in time
to an earlier era in rural America. The songs were "safe" popular tunes of
the 1920s and 1930s, and the talks emphasized traditional themes of loyalty, responsibility, moral behavior, and basic principles and values. Although the several hundred people in the audience seemed to enjoy
themselves, they were quite reserved. Few people laughed out loud or
cheered any of the performances, there was never any applause, and although very attentive, people were generally nonexpressive.

The evening's entertainment brought community members together for
a shared social event whose tone contrasted with the serious atmosphere
of the afternoon church service. And the event gave boys and girls and men
and women an opportunity to make public presentations, whereas during
the church service only men of high status spoke. Finally, the program was
a blend of religious and social content, with some of the entertainment
material drawn from an earlier period in American history, one in which
life seemed simpler and rested on rock-solid moral values.

The social dance. About twice a month on a weekend evening the religious leadership sponsors a social dance in the church meetinghouse in
Redrock. The dance brings together many age groups, is a way for young

people to socialize in a controlled setting, and is a colorful event enjoy
by all members of the community.

The dance is held in the main hall of the meetinghouse, which is clear
of chairs for the event. About 400 to 600 people of all ages participate
in the dances we attended, although most were young people, includi
boys and girls of 13 years and older (children do not attend the dance un
they are about 13; there are dances for young children in which they lea
how to dance and behave in social situations).

Everyone was dressed up – women and girls in attractive pioneer dress
and distinctive hairstyles with waves, dips, braids, and buns. Their hai
clothing, and faces were all well groomed and "squeaky clean and shiny
Many men and boys wore suits or vests, long-sleeved shirts and ties, ar
cowboy boots. Everyone was "spiffed up" and neat. Seeing several hundre
people in clothing reminiscent of a bygone era added to our general feelin
of having been transported backward in time to rural America of mai
decades ago.

On entering the meetinghouse we were escorted to seats of honor on a
elevated platform at the center of one of the long axes of the hall. Or
seats were adjacent to the musicians and to the announcer's position. Seate
on the platform or arriving during the evening were religious and civ
leaders of the community, including elders of the council and the prophe
Throughout the evening people of all ages came up to the platform, shoc
hands with the prophet, introduced themselves to us, and offered words c
welcome and greeting. People were very polite and showed respect for th
prophet, and he reciprocated with friendliness. The presence of religiou
notables and the prophet at the physical center of the place indicated th;
the dance was both a religious and social event.

Our feeling of being transported to an earlier era increased as the evenir
progressed. The "band" consisted of three pieces, a piano and two violin
All the dances exemplified rural life or the pioneer era in American histor
square dances, waltzes, reels, and quadrilles. Sometimes a male and fema
danced together; sometimes a male danced with two females in a stylize
format; sometimes couples formed squares. Many of the dances began i
one end of the hall and proceeded linearly toward the other end of th
building. Other dances moved around the room in a long oval. The danc
tended to be formal and structured, with little spontaneity and free bod
movements characteristic of contemporary dancing. And no one dance
body to body or cheek to cheek, nor were there any "slow" dances.

Dancing partners were of all ages. Young men and women or boys an
girls danced together, as did older men and women; women and gir
danced together; youngsters and older people were partners in all comb
nations of age and gender, across and within family and friends. Thus mar

ommunity members participated in the event, a pattern common in American community dances in rural settings and earlier eras. Everyone seemed o be having fun, and people smiled, laughed, and joked with one another n an easy and lighthearted way.

Each dance began and ended according to a strict routine, under the nstructions of an elder of the community who was an adviser to the rophet. He announced each dance by title, for example, "The next dance vill be a quadrille." He then said "gentlemen's choice" or "ladies' choice," ndicating which gender should seek out a partner. (Our recollection is that nost dances were "gentlemen's choice," although there were many opporunities for "ladies," women and girls, to choose a dance partner.)

At the end of each dance, men and boys formally escorted their partner o a seat or area off the dance floor. Girls, women, and elderly people sat n chairs around the dance floor, with most at one end of the room. Men nd boys stood behind and apart from the girls and women. As a dance vas announced – for example, "gentlemen's choice" – men and boys approached a woman or girl, formally invited her to dance, and escorted her o the dance floor. This pattern of invitation, dancing, escorting females to eats, and the separation of genders while awaiting the next dance, was epeated throughout the evening. People also freely wandered about the oom informally, chatting with friends and family.

The whole scene and flow of events was a vivid, rich, and unique cultural vent. Decorum between dancers and genders was stylized and polite, with a sense of order and organization. Some dancers were highly skilled and graceful; others were stilted and strained (as we were in the few dances in vhich we participated – to the good-natured amusement of many who vatched us). Some dancers were outgoing and joyful, others were shy and eserved. Many young teenagers were stiff in their movements and interpersonal interaction; parents and grandparents dancing with their youngters were joyful and smiling broadly; those not dancing, especially the lderly, took in the scene with great pleasure.

As already mentioned, the religious underpinning of the dance was alvays evident – in the prophet's presence, the site of the dance, and the fact hat the announcer was a religious leader. Furthermore, in the middle of he evening the announcer gave a short speech about social and religious values. On one occasion he noted that people wanting to be liked by others 1ad to like themselves, be willing to be alone, and to be polite, decent, and 1onorable even when no one was watching. He also emphasized patriarchal values, noting that men are leaders of the family and as such should be polite and dignified, treat women and girls with respect, and protect and be responsible for them. At the second dance we attended, he stated that 'those who have not achieved the spirit of God are not welcome at the dance and should not come again." As examples, he cited boys and girl who quarrel with their mothers, girls who wear tight skirts or shoes wit high heels, and boys who wear jeans to the dances and no ties. He als stated that chewing gum was an undesirable form of behavior to be avoide by all young people. He went on the say that the community dress cod ensured proper dignity and representation to the world and that dress ir dicated the degree to which people were willing to uphold the standard of the community. To emphasize his point, he reminded the assemble group that the dance was under the strict control of the prophet and tha several years ago the prophet canceled dances because of problems in th community. Finally, he urged young people to go to their homes immedi ately after the dance and not delay or go anywhere else.

Another event toward the end of one dance also highlighted the impor tance of loyalty to the community. As he had done at Sunday evening' social event, Uncle James asked for volunteers to help pitch hay that ha been blown astray by wind and needed to be gathered in piles so that th community bailing equipment would work properly. The work had to be gin at 4 a.m. the next morning. Without a moment's delay, about a doze young men walked toward the center of the floor from all parts of th room. There was a burst of applause by the assemblage, Uncle Jame praised them, and the faces of the volunteers shone with pride. Once again people displayed loyalty to the community, achieving recognition througl contributions to the group.

At the end of the evening, everyone assembled around the platform on which the prophet and elders sat, and the prophet gave a final prayer Thereafter, a long line of people formed and shook hands with the prophet one by one. He and they greeted each other warmly.

We learned about other aspects of the dance in subsequent conversa tions. The next morning a daughter in one of our participating families tol us how much she liked the dance. She had not yet been asked to dance by boys outside her family – she said that they were too shy – so she had to depend on her brothers and cousins. She also said that girls try to sit in the front row so that it is easier for boys to ask them to dance. And girl and boys use the dance as one of the few opportunities they have in th community to be with someone they like. A young married woman witl whom we spoke on another occasion confirmed that young people use the social dance as a means for social interaction. For her and others it was the highlight of their week, and everyone tried to go as often as possible She also mentioned how nervous she was at first. Only gradually did she become comfortable dancing and relating to boys. She also described the event as one of the few settings in which boys and girls can freely and informally socialize.

One final anecdote reveals how the dance is linked to the religious structure of the community. On our drive to visit the town we stopped for lunch in a nearby larger community and accidentally met Uncle James. We asked him if there was to be a dance that evening, since our wives had not attended one and hoped to do so. To our disappointment, he said that no dance had been scheduled for that evening. By the time we reached the community some two to three hours later, however, we learned that a dance had suddenly been announced for that very evening and that all the young girls and women in the family we visited were busily getting their dresses ready and combing their hair. Although the number of participants at the dance that evening was smaller than usual, there were still several hundred people in attendance. Community organization and the influential role of key religious leaders were clearly evident!

In summary, the dress, stylized dances, gender roles, involvement of religious figures, sermons and prayers, and emphasis on community loyalty illustrate the powerful role of religious and social norms in the Redrock community.

Community service. Community loyalty and responsibility are also reflected in other activities. For example, we visited a park that church members had built as volunteers – clearing the land and constructing picnic tables and facilities. And we were told of a widow who moved into town without a home but who had a house built for her by members of the community within a short time.

We also learned about a summer volunteer service program for boys and girls. About 100 boys between 5 and 15 years of age meet each morning at the local school and receive assignments such as weeding, minor construction, and clearing drainage ditches under the supervision of men. They participate in work groups between 8 a.m. and noon, although they are not expected to do so every day. If they have no other responsibilities at home on a given day, boys usually join the community work crew. At noon they are served lunch at the church meetinghouse and then return home to do family chores. Girls help prepare and serve the lunches, the food for which comes out of the religious community's storehouse. The lunch is supervised by a senior member of the community, who sits at the front of the room with a microphone and ensures that the boys behave themselves.

Some boys we talked with said that everyone they know joins the work groups, although some attend more than others. The boys also reported playing sports only infrequently and instead spent a great deal of time helping their older brothers and relatives build homes, do chores around their house, or assist in whatever way they can.

Headquartered in the town of Redrock, the United Fundamentalist

Church is a powerful presence in many facets of the life of its members and their families. The influential role of the Cooperative Alliance Agency in controlling land use and home ownership, the involvement of the church in the town's school system and civil governance, church services, social dances, expectations of volunteerism, and service all speak to the pervasive role of religion in everyday life. And these religious-community controls are congruent with a conservative and traditional lifestyle, in which individual differences and values are manifested through loyalty to the community and adherence to explicit behaviors, roles, and norms.

The conservative Church of Latter-day Apostles

In contrast, the church services, social activities, and the everyday life of members of the Church of Latter-day Apostles tend to be more freewheeling, and less rigidly structured than in rural Redrock.

Dress and clothing. As in Redrock, modest dress is the norm in the Metropolitan City urban community. Tight-fitting dresses, short skirts, shorts, sandals, short-sleeved shirts, and other clothing styles that reveal too much of the body are discouraged for both men and women. At the same time, the clothing of women and girls is diverse and similar to that of the culture at large. Whereas women in the rural community are easily identified by their distinctive dress style, those in the urban community "look like everyone else." Even pants and jeans are acceptable everyday wear, as long as the principle of modesty is observed. Some women do wear pioneer-style clothing, usually in church or at formal occasions; some even follow the rural female hairstyles. But this is not always the custom. And although well groomed, many women have loose and flowing hair or adopt hairstyles fashionable in the general culture.

Similarly, the clothing of the urban men and boys is varied. Although the principle of modesty applies, men and boys are indistinguishable from most of their counterparts in the larger urban community. Shirts and ties, sport shirts, casual and formal pants, and slacks and jeans are all acceptable. Most men and boys have short and neatly combed hair, although we recall seeing a number of teenage boys with longer or more contemporary hair styles. Thus both communities emphasize modesty and cleanliness in dress, but members of the rural group follow a stricter dress code.

Church services. The main church building, a large plain cement structure, is in a semirural area near Metropolitan City, on land owned by the Church of Latter-day Apostles. In the 1950s, when the group was small, church services were held in members' homes. Some years later they bought and remodeled a home for Sunday services and meetings and then built the present meetinghouse about 15 years ago. It is a plain building with few decorations or embellishments and has modest furnishings. The building has a large all-purpose hall for church services, social events, and athletic activities, and small meeting rooms, and offices. The plainness of the building contrasts with the elegant meetinghouse in the rural community in Redrock.

The church services we attended began at 3:30 on Sunday afternoons, with about 600 to 800 people present. Congregants were dressed in a variety of clothing but most of the men wore long-sleeve shirts with or without jackets, and a goodly number wore ties. Some men and boys were dressed informally in jeans or work clothes. Women wore many different kinds of dresses – from pioneer to contemporary styles. Their hair was combed in a variety of ways, mostly contemporary, but a few in the unique hairstyles characteristic of the rural community.

Services were led by the religious leader and church elders, several of whom sat on the stage and assumed various responsibilities during the meeting. A choir of young and older men and women sat on a raised platform on the main floor to the left of the stage. At one service we attended, the members of the choir, a woman piano accompanist, and the church elders and prophet all wore a flower to commemorate Father's Day.

The church services included announcements of various activities, songs and readings, and religious speeches. A range of congregants – young and old, males and females – participated. Whereas the church service in the rural community was solemn and strictly devoted to religious activities, and the entertainment took place at night during a different event, the Church of Latter Day Apostles schedules all these activities in a two-hour service. Because people live all over the region, it is probably not feasible to hold two events on Sundays. Whatever the reason, the service tended to be reasonably informal and relaxed. The leader joked or addressed individual members of the congregation, some participants acted informally, and the congregation occasionally laughed at someone's comment or action.

One of the church services we attended began with the religious leader welcoming everyone. (He was absent from the other service because of illness.) Members of the community then made a series of announcements. Several young girls came up on the platform and gave information about various camps, workshops, and other social events. Then a young man, deliberately dressed casually in a denim jacket with the collar turned up, swaggered in an exaggerated way onto the stage and announced a forthcoming "1950s dance." His manner and dress elicited good-natured laughter from the congregation and elders.

There were other announcements at one or the other service we attended: a woman called for donations of white shirts for a boys' religious class; a man asked for blood bank donations to serve the congregation; another man described plans for renewing publication of *Truth* magazine, the fundamentalist journal that had ceased publication in the 1950s; a young man announced a forthcoming dance at which attendees would be invited to dress up in pioneer clothing; another young man described a forthcoming weekend trip for young people.

Following these announcements an older woman led the congregation in a religious song. Then the leader called up a young man to present a prayer, after which a young girl read a poem, "Trusting in the Lord." This was followed by a lengthy sacrament service in which 15 young men and adolescents, led by an adult, came to the front of the room, gathered around a table, offered a prayer, broke several loaves of bread into small pieces, and then passed among the congregation giving out sacramental bread. They then made another blessing and offered water to each member of the congregation, completing the sacrament service.

Other announcements followed. One woman outlined plans to start a religious newsletter for children containing scriptural material and stories to be written by members of the congregation. As part of her presentation she spoke against pornography in the media and literature and stated that the proposed newsletter would be a healthy substitute for children. Two young sisters then sang a religious song, after which one of us addressed the congregation (at one service the prophet invited both of us to sit with him and the elders on the stage; both of us spoke on that occasion). Our talks were followed by a violin and piano selection played by two women.

Next, the religious leader and some members of the religious council made a series of speeches. In his sermon the leader highlighted problems in the contemporary world – the lack of attention to religious roots, passiveness in the face of evil, the likelihood of a world crisis because the prophets have not been respected, and the blasphemy, immorality, and evil in the world. It was a "fire and brimstone" sermon that alerted congregants to the challenges they faced and the need for proper religious behavior. Members of the religious council then offered their thoughts. On Father's Day two speakers discussed the importance of patriarchs and fathers and the need to obey and respect holders of the priesthood. Another speaker focused on women, describing mothers as "jewels of the world" and "jewels in their husband's crowns," and the importance of men appreciating and helping their wives. Still another elder called on members of the congregation to repent their misdeeds, love one another, study and practice the gospel, and try to emulate Jesus Christ.

The church service ended with the congregation singing a song and a member offering a benediction. Afterward people mingled in the meeting hall and outside the building, greeting and interacting with one another. The religious leader and church elders circulated and talked informally with congregants (in contrast, people in the rural community lined up to greet the elders following the service).

In general, the atmosphere and flow of events in the urban church service were more informal and relaxed than what we observed in the rural community – even though the religious themes of speeches were similar in the two communities. Several factors undoubtedly contributed to the more informal tone of the service: the varied clothing styles of congregants, the congregation's participation in the service, the meeting's blend of religious and social content, and the easygoing relationship between congregants and the prophet and church leaders.

The social dance. One of us also attended a social dance at the church meetinghouse. It was informal and did not focus on religious and community affairs. Some of the dances were traditional (e.g., quadrilles and reels), but others were more contemporary. Sometimes men and women and younger boys and girls danced together, but it was at arm's length and not cheek to cheek or body to body. Women and girls freely asked boys and men to dance, and the atmosphere was similar to that of a typical church-sponsored dance. The contrast with the formal, stylized, and religious-community tone of the dance in the rural community was striking.

Schooling. Although the Church of Latter-day Apostles operates its own elementary school, most children attend public schools in the neighborhoods in which they live. (All high school students attend public schools.) Because they live throughout the metropolitan region, children in fundamentalist families are usually in the minority in public schools. As a result, they are in daily contact with children from monogamous Mormon and non-Mormon families and are exposed to the values, attitudes, dress, and customs of the larger culture. (The situation is different in the small United Order satellite community of the Church of Latter-day Apostles, where the elementary school is controlled by the group.) In contrast, students, teachers, and administrators in the rural Redrock community are group members, so public schools are homogeneous and essentially controlled by the fundamentalist community.

In summary, the two fundamentalist Mormon communities are similar in many ways. They are both patriarchal societies with long-standing Mormon religious values and with men serving as community and family religious and social leaders. The communities are also tightly knit, in part because they are physically and socially isolated from mainstream American

Mormon cultures. As a result, group members are dependent on one another and on their churches for social and economic support, friendships and many aspects of day-to-day life. Indeed, the long-standing ideal in fundamentalist beliefs (and to some extent in Mormon beliefs in general) is of a "united order" in which people share work, production, resources, social life, and religious values. Conformity, loyalty, service, and bonding of individuals and families to the community are advocated as an ideal state of affairs.

Although the Church of Latter-day Apostles and the United Fundamentalist Church share these broad values, they vary along conservative and ultraconservative lines. The rural United Fundamentalist Church is very conservative. With most of its members residing in the town of Redrock in an isolated geographical region, the church directly or indirectly controls many aspects of day-to-day life: land, homesites, agriculture, businesses, schools, public agencies, services, and community social activities. Although the church and community provide a great deal of security, they expect conformity and allegiance to fundamentalist religious and social values. On the other hand, the economic and social life of the members of the urban Church of Latter-day Apostles is quite diverse because people live and work throughout the region. Furthermore, many members are converts and probably bring in new and varied ideas. Consistent with its diverse character, church services, social events, and other activities tend to be more informal, and less highly structured than those of the rural group.

Although the focus of our work is on husband–wife and wife–wife relationships in contemporary plural families, those relationships are inseparable from the broader communities in which they occur. With this background in mind, we now present a brief description of the individuals and families with whom we worked. Following that we turn to the dynamics of day-to-day life in contemporary plural families.

The people and families

Members of 26 families participated in our project, although we worked most closely with about a dozen families. As described in appendixes A and B, our contacts with families varied widely. In some cases we met with participants on numerous occasions at their homes, in our homes, in restaurants, on trips, and elsewhere. In one case we lived in a family's home for several days (actually, Joseph Ginat has done so on many occasions over the years). In other cases our contacts with a family or family member were limited to only one or a few meetings.

The families with whom we worked for several years were not selected randomly. Some satisfied criteria we had in mind in advance; others joined our project more fortuitously – we met them by chance, were introduced by someone, or happened to be with them at a gathering or event. In conducting the research we decided at the outset to adopt a "depth-over-breadth" strategy. That is, instead of surveying a large sample of people and families on a few topics, thereby ensuring representation of the whole population, we did intensive case studies of a smaller number of families regarding many aspects of their lives. We realize that this strategy limits our ability to draw conclusions about plural families "in general." However, we decided to try to "learn a *lot* about a *few* families" rather than "learn a *little* bit about *many* families."

In selecting families we kept several criteria in mind. First, we sought plural families with two or more wives, even though many families in the fundamentalist movement are monogamous. (We did interview a few monogamous husbands or wives, some of whom were children of other participants; they provided a good perspective on specific issues.) Second, we included families with varying numbers of wives – from two to eight wives. Third, we worked with families at different life stages. Some are well established, with members at middle or later ages; others are younger families and still growing. Fourth, we selected some multigeneration plural families and some who are converts and new to the fundamentalist movement. Fifth, some families belong to the conservative urban group, whereas others are affiliated with the ultraconservative rural group (although most families are from the urban group). Sixth, we included relatively stable and viable families, as well as those experiencing serious conflict and upheavals (we interviewed four women who divorced their husbands or left a plural family). Seventh, our participants vary in status in the fundamentalist movement – some husbands are in central leadership positions in the church, others are rising in status, and others are not in influential positions. To satisfy systematically this array of criteria would have required sampling a very large number of families. Since that was not possible because of time and resource limitations, we did our best to satisfy some of these selection criteria.

Before approaching and meeting families, we consulted with and received permission from a church leader and from a family elder. Perhaps because Joseph Ginat has long-standing relationships with church leaders and many families in the rural and urban groups, everyone we invited to participate in the project agreed to do so.

We described the project to each family, our plans to publish the results, the voluntary nature of their participation, and our intention to honor their anonymity and confidentiality. As our work with a family progressed, we included them as primary or selective participants on the basis of their circumstances and interest in the project and how they fit with the goal of sampling different types of families. We eventually worked closely and over a long period with 12 families, and others provided valuable but more selective information.

We learned about plural family life through interviews, observations, and participation in family and public events. We also used a variety of archival sources, including scholarly books and treatises, newspaper and investigative accounts, personal autobiographies, and historical and ethnographic material. Observations and interviews were our primary source of information, however.

We met with many individuals and groups: husbands, husbands and all or some of their wives, parents, and children (most interviews were arranged through husbands, and we only occasionally met alone with a wife or wives). We observed public community events such as dances and church services. During our many visits to family homes we noted decorations, furnishings, and sleeping, eating, and living arrangements. And we talked with participants in an informal, open-ended style. Altogether we conducted almost 200 interviews and observations. (The number of interviews and observations per family varied from 1 to 49; the largest number were with a family in the rural community whom we visited for several days.) More than 100 husbands and wives and others participated in the project.

Because our sample is small and there is a great deal of variation across families, the averages and general statements that follow should be viewed with caution. Appendix B presents demographic information in more detail.

Number of wives

The fact that records and census information are either not kept or were not available made it difficult to obtain direct information about the number of polygynous families in the rural and urban groups. A senior member of the rural group estimated that about 30% of the families include plural marriages. The leader of the urban group provided us with some older data indicating that about 40% of the families in his community are plural families (on another occasion he and a senior member of the community independently estimated the figure to be 20%). In contrast, about 20% of marriages in the pioneer era involved more than one wife.

As for the number of wives per plural family, about 30% of the families in our sample have two wives, 43% have three or four wives, and 26% have five or more wives. A senior elder of the urban group described a survey they did in the 1980s showing that 78% of men in the group practicing plural marriage had only two wives; in a separate discussion another elder estimated that about half the men practicing plural marriage had two wives. These surveys/estimates are similar to those arrived at in studies of 19th-century Mormon pioneers (see chapter 2 and appendix B), which report that 60–70% of plural families had only two wives, with the number having more wives tapering off rapidly. Therefore, our sample probably underrepresents the proportion of two-wife families in the rural and urban communities.

Age of marriage

The typical first marriage in our families took place when husbands were about 21 years old and wives were in their later teens – averaging 17. Second and third wives married into families about 10 or so years later, when husbands were in the early 30s and the new wives were in their early 20s or late teens. Thus there was an age gap of about 10 to 14 years between husbands and their second and third wives. And these later wives were a few years older than the first wife when she and the husband married. A similar pattern occurred in later marriages; that is, new wives were in their 20s, and the husband was in his 40s and beyond, with an increasing age gap between them.

Although our sample is small, the pattern is similar to 19th-century Mormon plural marriages, in which

> the composite [Mormon pioneer] polygamist was first married at the age of twenty-three to a girl of twenty. Thirteen years later he took a plural wife, choosing a twenty-two-year-old girl [when he was about thirty-six]. The chances were two to one that, having demonstrated his acceptance of the principle of plurality, he was finished with marrying. If, however, he took a third wife, he waited four years, then selected another girl of 22 [when he was 40]. [If he married a fourth wife] he waited another four years, and once more chose a twenty-two-year-old girl, although he had reached the ripe age of forty-four. (Ivins, 1956, p. 234)

Although our data are generally consistent with 19th-century cases, averages do not tell the whole story. There is considerable variability from case to case, meaning that the ages of husbands and wives in first and later marriages vary greatly (see appendix B).

Number of children

Although we did not have complete information on the number of children in every family in our sample, it appears that families average about two dozen children and that some are likely to continue growing into the fore-seeable future. But these figures need to be adjusted according to the num-bers of wives. Plural wives in our families have, on average, about 5 to 6 children. Some women have many more children; almost 18% have 11 to 19 children. At the other extreme, several wives have either no children (3%), or 1 to 3 children (18%).

These figures are comparable to those for pioneer families. About a quar-ter of 19th-century plural families had 20 or more children (Ivins, 1956) and three-fourths had 11 to 25 children (Embry; 1987). (Our figures for overall family size are probably higher because we had a greater proportion of families with more than two wives than was typical for the pioneer period.)

The average number of children per wife in our sample, 5 to 6, is also roughly comparable to pioneer numbers, which reportedly ranged from 6 children per wife (Ivins, 1956) to 6 to 10 children in 50% of wives (Embry, 1987), and 7.5 children per wife (Smith and Kunz, 1976). Our somewhat lower figure may eventually prove to be an underestimate since several wives in our families are likely to continue having children.

Work and occupations

Most contemporary plural families struggle financially and are hard put to make ends meet. We neither met nor heard of very well-to-do families. In most cases some wives – often many wives – and all husbands worked to earn money. Families in our sample are from middle to lower socioeco-nomic levels; our impression is that most families in the two large funda-mentalist groups are in the same socioeconomic strata.

Some men run small businesses by themselves or with partners. These include an automobile body repair shop, a lumber business, a long-distance trucking operation, a small assembly factory. Others have had managerial or professional positions at one time or another: for example, school teacher and school principal, security manager, supervisor in a small con-struction company. Other men are cabinetmakers, sawmill and steelmill technicians, engineering technicians, and carpenters. Several others work in construction and other industries in a variety of capacities, including man-ual and unskilled labor positions.

Our impression is that some men do not have permanent jobs but work intermittently, often change occupations as opportunities arise or because they cannot find work in their own field, and often hold more than one job at a time. Except for those who run their own successful businesses or who are in stable fields, men shift occupations and jobs with the vagaries of the local and national scene. In other words, men struggle to earn an adequate living, and no matter how well they do it is usually not sufficient to meet the needs of large and growing plural families. As a result, wives in plural families, like many of those in present-day monogamous families, often work for pay outside the home to supplement family income.

We found that at least one wife in most families works outside the home at any given time; indeed, more than half of all wives about whom we have information regularly work in more or less full-time jobs. Several wives work in offices as receptionists, secretaries, clerks, and telephone operators. A few hold managerial or professional positions such as teacher, nurse, and realtor. Two wives run their own small business – a health food and sandwich shop, and a small seasonal fireworks company. A number of wives clean houses, baby sit, or have other low-paying jobs. And wives who do not work often take care of their working co-wives' children and manage the family home. Like their husbands, many wives work intermittently, dropping in and out of jobs as circumstances warrant, although a number also work on a regular and sustained basis.

The communities and churches of contemporary Mormon polygynous families play an important role in relationships between husbands and wives, and between wives. Indeed, dyadic and communal relationships within families are inseparable from the social and environmental contexts of which they are part – an essential thesis of our transactional perspective.

Early stages of relationships

The five chapters in this section examine the earliest stages of plural family relationships. Chapter 5 deals with the question of adding a new wife to a fundamentalist family. This important decision involves a complex set issues between a man and his established wife or wives and a prospective wife.

Chapter 6 is about the courtship stage of relationship formation. Here we describe the nature and length of courtship, dyadic relations between a husband and a prospective wife, and the communal involvement of established wives in the courtship.

Chapter 7 describes wedding and marriage ceremonies among contemporary Mormon fundamentalists – their location, participants, and associated events. Of particular importance are the dyadic roles of the bride and groom, and the communal participation of established wives.

Chapters 8 and 9 deal with the earliest stages of new plural marriages. Chapter 8 summarizes honeymoon customs: their form, length, and location; participation by established wives; and the ways in which husbands conduct themselves with the new bride and other wives.

Chapter 9 explores dyadic and communal aspects of adjustment to new marriages in plural families. How do the bride and established wives relate to one another early in the new marriage? What challenges face each of them during this difficult period? How does the husband manage this transitional phase?

In addition to focusing on the dynamics of dyadic husband–wife and communal wife–wife relationships, we highlight the tensions, stresses, and complexities of these early stages of plural family life.

5

Deciding to add a new wife to a family

Adding a new wife to a fundamentalist family is usually approached with considerable thought and deliberation and ideally requires approval by a fundamentalist group's prophet, the prospective wife's parents, and an established wife or wives. Although a possible new marriage is a significant religious matter, it is also an important interpersonal or *dyadic* event involving a prospective husband and wife and an important *communal* issue of relationships between potential co-wives.

The decision-making process by which a woman joins a family as a co-wife varies across fundamentalist groups. In the urban community, the participants themselves – a husband, his wife or wives, and a prospective wife – play an active role in initial explorations of marriage possibilities. Although the group's leader must approve, individuals have considerable latitude to pursue possible relationships. In the rural community, the prophet plays a strong role in arranging marriages, sometimes without consulting prospective partners or families in advance, and sometimes with input by parents and participants themselves. Furthermore, the process in both fundamentalist groups varies from family to family and marriage to marriage, depending on relationships between husbands and wives and other factors.

The decision to add a wife to a fundamentalist family is rooted in religious values promoting the idea that a righteous patriarch should participate with good women in creating a proper and upstanding family. By meeting a variety of religious obligations, including marrying for time and eternity and having many children, members of a modern plural family are ensured of living together as a unified family in a celestial kingdom in the hereafter.[1]

By way of background, the discussion opens with the rationale for and process of adding wives to a family in non-Western traditional polygynous cultures. It then turns to the dyadic and communal issues associated with the decision to add a wife to a fundamentalist family. Dyadic factors include the mutual interest and attraction of prospective partners to a marriage; communal aspects of the process involve the role of other wives and the family as a whole. We also examine the tensions, complexities, and stresses facing husbands and wives as they ponder the possibility of a new wife in their family, as well as the part played by parents and kin, the prophet, and the religious leadership of the community in the decision to add a wife to a fundamentalist family.

Deciding about new wives in other polygynous cultures

The right to have more than one wife in non-Western polygynous cultures is often reserved for men with high economic, political, or social status. Because it is customary in many cultures for prospective grooms and their families to give bridewealth gifts to a potential wife or her family in the form of money, animals, crops, or land, it is often only the wealthy and powerful men who can afford to have more than one wife. Having many wives can also be an economic and political stepping stone upward in society. And because families are often holistic economic units, with men, women, and children engaged in fishing, agriculture, animal husbandry, or trade, the more hands the better. Wives are central to the economic viability of families in traditional cultures because they often do a great deal of the work, and they bear children, who also contribute to a family's labor pool. Thus many anthropologists believe that economic factors strongly motivate people to add wives to a family in traditional cultures (Brabin, 1984; Clignet, 1970; Kenyatta, 1973; Lamphere, 1974; Little, 1951). Along with economic advantages, polygyny may help to establish or strengthen political and social bonds between families (Mair, 1977; Murdock, 1967; Stephens, 1963).

Although economics, politics, social status, and family alliances are important, the personal attraction of potential partners often enters into the decision. In the !Kung Bush culture of Africa, for example, most first marriages are arranged by parents when a boy and girl are quite young (Marshall, 1976), but subsequent polygynous marriages are voluntary, often based in part on mutual dyadic attraction of a man and woman. A similar situation occurs among the Swazi of Africa (Kuper, 1963). In the Bedouin society of Israel, a male's parents send a delegation to the family of a prospective bride to discuss a possible match (Ginat, 1982). In later plural marriages a man has more freedom to select a wife; but women do not directly initiate a possible marriage.

Sometimes established wives encourage or even pressure a husband to add a wife to the family. This behavior reflects a communal basis for polygyny. In traditional Sioux Indian societies, for example, older wives sometimes encouraged a husband to marry a younger woman, who could assist with economic and household tasks and add to a senior wife's social status (Hassrick, 1964). Similarly, an expectant wife among the Kikuyu of Africa sometimes encouraged a husband to add a new wife so that she would have both a companion and someone to assist in managing domestic responsibilities (Kenyatta, 1973). Similar motivations, including the desire of some women to have the support of co-wives when dealing with the husband, have been observed in other cultures (Stephens, 1963).

At the same time, wives in some cultures actively resist the addition of new wives to a family. In the Gusii culture of Africa wives often openly oppose a new marriage on the grounds that their power and status may be diminished by a new wife or that the husband may favor a younger wife (LeVine and LeVine, 1963). !Kung wives of Africa also often resist plural marriages (Marshall, 1976), as do some wives in the Bedouin culture of Israel (Ginat, personal observation).

Among pioneer and contemporary Mormon fundamentalists, religious doctrine has been a main reason for plural marriages, but mutual interpersonal attraction, compatibility, and a desire for social support also play a part in many cases. Although we informally observed that political and social factors entered into some Mormon plural marriages, this was not a primary focus of our analysis.

An important communal issue in plural marriages is whether an established wife or wives are asked for their opinion or have veto power over a prospective marriage. The practice here, too, varies from culture to culture. In Dakar, Africa, a man is "required" to discuss his marriage plans with his wife; if he fails to do so, she has legitimate grounds for a divorce (Falade, 1963). Because wives live and work together and mutual trust and cooperation are important, a wife's opinions are likely to play a significant role in the decision. Similarly, a senior wife in the Aboure culture of Africa supervises the work of younger wives and as a result is usually consulted about a prospective marriage (Clignet, 1970). Yet in some societies, husbands act unilaterally. Among some Bedouins in Israel, a husband does not consult with his wife or wives; he simply announces his decision, either before or after the marriage (Ginat, personal observation). Similar practices occur among the Javanese of Indonesia (Geertz, 1961) and the Winneba of Africa (Hagan, 1983).

Conflict, competition, jealousy, and a variety of stresses are common in polygynous families in many cultures, as noted throughout this volume. To alleviate such problems and help family members accept the decision, some cultures practice sororal polygyny, or the marriage of sisters to the same man, on the assumption that sisters may be interpersonally compatible and can live and work together in a harmonious way. This was the case among the traditional Sioux Indians of North America (Hassrick, 1964). The Zulus of Africa even have a saying to this effect: "The love of sisters overcomes the jealousy of polygyny" (Gluckman, 1950). But some cultures are sensitive to the fact that not all sisters are compatible. The Lozi of Africa for one, believe that "the jealousy of polygyny spoils the love of sisters. It will break up their family" (Gluckman, 1950). Interestingly, the Old Testament and the Koran prohibit men from marrying living sisters, presumably to avoid conflict between them.

Another practice is for a man to marry his brother's widow, support her economically, and provide her and her children a legitimate status in the culture. By one estimate (Murdock, 1967), 69% (127/185) of societies for which information was available followed this practice.

In general, therefore, the decision to add a wife to a family varies widely across cultures in rationale (e.g., economic, political, social, religious, personal), the role of other wives in decision making, sororal polygyny, and the like. As discussed next, the decision to add a new wife to a contemporary Mormon fundamentalist family is based in part on religious values. At the same time, there is a strong interplay of *dyadic* and *communal* processes as husbands, wives, and a prospective wife deliberate about whether to pursue a new marital bond.

Religious beliefs and Mormon polygyny

As noted earlier, contemporary Mormon polygyny is deeply rooted in 19th-century religious doctrine and practices. Although plural marriage was alien to personal experiences and cultural heritage, many pioneer Mormons eventually accepted the practice. But it was not easy for them to do so. Ann Eliza Young (1908), a wife of Brigham Young, described the pressure put on her father and mother, first by Joseph Smith and then by Brigham Young, to enter into plural marriage on religious grounds. They resisted vigorously but finally succumbed because of their religious beliefs. And according to Dorothy Solomon (1984), her grandmother vacillated and resisted her grandfather's desire to enter into plural marriage but eventually agreed because of her deep religious feelings.

The early Mormon Church clearly pressured its leaders and potential leaders to engage in plural marriage as a demonstration of their loyalty to religious values. Church leaders "counseled" particular men (and sometimes their wives) to add new wives to their families (Young, 1954), and in some cases church presidents publicly stated that those who refused to practice plural marriage would be removed from their church positions (Embry, 1987). In one study of 200 cases, "78 of the men or their descendants identified a Church official who asked them to marry in polygamy or who approved the marriage. Over 80 percent of these 78 reportedly received a direct request to marry a plural wife" (Embry, 1987, p. 62). Wives, too, were pressured to accept another wife and encourage their husbands to enter into plural marriages on religious grounds. Joseph Smith's 1843 revelation was invoked many times to demonstrate to pioneer wives that resisting plural marriage violated God's law and would lead them to forsake eternal life in a celestial kingdom in the hereafter.

The religious rationale for polygyny almost always came to the forefront in many of our discussions with men and women in the modern fundamentalist movement. Some people expounded articulately and at length on the religious doctrine that guides their behavior, especially on the patriarchal nature of families; life in the hereafter in which a husband, his wives, and their children would live together in an exalted state; and the links to biblical patriarchs who practiced polygyny. Others were less specific in their reasons for living a plural family life but referred fervently to their "religious beliefs and faith," "reaching salvation," "following the teachings of Joseph Smith," achieving "the fullness of the gospel," and following "the Principle." In addition, men and women often appealed to prayer, heavenly guidance, and religious doctrine to help them cope with the inevitable complexities and stresses of plural family life.

Each of the fundamentalist groups with whom we worked has a strong religious hierarchical structure that regulates the practice of polygyny, avowedly in accordance with the principle that it is only "righteous men" who are to have the privilege of being patriarchs of plural families. The religious leader of one community told us that he screens men and women carefully before approving a plural marriage, because he wants to be sure that their motives and past behavior qualify them for such an important step. Whether this ideal is acted upon in every case is not known, but the religious principle at least serves as a theoretical standard. Most men in our sample of plural families had some combination of the following characteristics: they were elders in the church hierarchy, they were younger men who appeared to be targeted for leadership positions, they were above average in education, they were from multigeneration polygynous families or had plural wives from multigeneration families, and they were linked to the religious power structure through marriage.

Dyadic and communal factors in adding a wife to a family

The decision to bring a new wife into a family can be examined from several perspectives: how and when the issue is raised, who broaches the matter, who initiates contacts with possible wives, and the extent of participation in decisionmaking by wives.[2] We learned that there is no universal answer to these questions. Rather, contemporary plural families experiment and adopt trial-and-error approaches that are tailored to specific circumstances. In so doing, they struggle to attain a viable balance of dyadic relationships (husband–wife and husband–prospective wife), and communal relationships (in the family as a whole, between established wives and between wives and a prospective wife).

Dyadic processes

Dyadic factors play an important role in deciding about a new wife joining a family. As in the larger monogamous American culture, a fundamentalist man or woman may hear about, meet, or see someone they find personally attractive. Other dyadic factors might include prior friendship and individual or joint economic, political, or social status. It is also possible that a religious revelation may guide a man or a woman toward a potential marriage partner.

The following case examples illustrate the way in which dyadic relationships between a man and woman facilitate the possibility of a plural marriage. Some of these examples also show how communal processes come into play along with dyadic considerations. For example, although a man or woman may be personally attracted to one another and initiate contacts, other wives may be consulted or participate in subsequent judgments about a potential wife.

Family 5
Howard and Constance, the first wife, knew one another in elementary school, and their families were also acquainted. Over time they met at church dances, dated, and gradually became attracted to one another, eventually marrying.

Howard and Valerie, the second wife, met at a dance in seventh grade, although they had casually known one another previously. Much later, after his marriage to Constance, Howard began noticing Valerie at community events and was attracted to her. At first she resisted his advances, but they eventually were mutually attracted and married.

Barbara, the third wife, was attracted to Howard as a teenager and "knew" that she was going to marry him someday. They gradually came to know and like one another and were married.

Howard had known Rose, his fourth wife, since she was a child.

When she was a teenager he was personally attracted to her and began to have a premonition of the possibility of their marriage. Their relationship evolved and they were eventually married.

Dyadic factors involving Howard's or a particular wife's feelings of personal attraction tripped off most relationships in this family. In each case, however, wives participated in the decision to pursue a particular relationship, to yield combined dyadic and communal processes. Other examples illustrate variations on the interplay of dyadic and communal aspects of the decision to add a wife to a family.

Family 2

David and Judith, the first wife, had known and liked one another during childhood. They lost contact for a while, met again as adults, and were immediately mutually attracted. David pursued her at dances, church meetings, and other events, and they were eventually married.

Several years after he and Judith were married, David noticed Rebecca in church and was attracted to her. Before meeting her, however, he asked Judith whether she knew Rebecca and what she thought of her. Judith was quite positive about Rebecca, and they agreed that David should pursue a possible relationship. He did, they got along, and were eventually married. This relationship consisted of a blend of dyadic features involving David and Rebecca and communal qualities involving Judith, David, and Rebecca.

Emily, the third wife, introduced herself to David and Rebecca when they were visiting the town in which she lived. The three of them immediately liked one another. The relationship was pursued, and David and Emily were eventually married. In this case, a prospective wife initiated the relationship in both a dyadic way with a husband and in a communal fashion with an established wife.

In a somewhat different pattern, Phyllis, the fourth wife, was especially assertive in launching her relationship with David, Judith, Rebecca, and Emily. She not only found David to be appealing, but she liked the wives and wanted to join the family. The women all got along and wanted to pursue the relationship, but David was resistant at the outset. He was not personally attracted to Phyllis and was also concerned that she hadn't been raised in a plural family. But he agreed to a later courtship because the wives liked her and felt that she would be a good family member. Over the course of a year, the relationship progressed, the women favored the match, and David and Phyllis eventually married. This case is interesting in that the relationship had strong dyadic and communal components by Phyllis at the outset, strong communal interests by the wives throughout, but only weak initial dyadic features on David's part. Eventually, dyadic and communal aspects of the relationship were all favorable, and the relationship worked out.

Following is another variation, involving two cases in which dyadic processes were set in motion by a prospective wife.

Family 1

Charlotte, Hal's third wife, was the prime instigator of their relationship. She had been a plural wife in another family, but the husband left the community and abandoned his wives. Charlotte had known Hal, liked him, and decided that she wanted to join his family as a third wife. Unbeknownst to him, she sought and received approval from a church elder to initiate their relationship. She then approached him at a church meeting and asked him to escort her to an office party. Approaching the same church elder for permission, Hal was surprised to learn of Charlotte's having done so earlier. He then realized what Charlotte had in mind. They were eventually married.

Family 6

Holly, the fifth wife, described how she approached Seymour with a proposal to join his family. She had had a very unstable early home life and an unsuccessful earlier marriage and was desperately seeking a decent family. Seymour's status as a religious leader and the stability of his family were appealing to her. She eventually overcame his initial resistance to the idea, and they were married.

Thus the possibility of a new wife joining a family often involves a direct dyadic process: a man or woman may be personally attracted to one another and initiate contact. But there may also be communal processes at work: wives may stimulate a relationship between their husband and another woman or participate in a decision to add a wife to their family. The flow of events varies from case to case, with dyadic and communal processes played out in a variety of configurations.

Dyadic and communal issues also entered into decisions about new wives for 19th-century Mormons. Diaries, historical records, and scholarly analyses point to personal attraction between men and women as a basis for many relationships (Embry, 1987; Young, 1954). In some cases, married men and single women fell in love, engaged in secret or public courtship, and eventually married. Other dyadic factors have been a woman's desire for the economic security that a particular man could provide, widow or widower status, and social status that a particular match might offer a man woman (for a discussion of these and other factors, see Dunfey, 1984; nbry, 1987).[3]

Who raised the issue of a new wife in the 19th century – the husband the wife? Account after account suggests that men were usually the prime stigators (Dunfey, 1984). At the same time, some 19th-century wives irted the ball rolling, often coaxing reluctant husbands into pursuing plu-l marriages (Mehr, 1985) or helping them select potential candidates oodson, 1976; Embry, 1984). In other instances, a husband and a wife ntly agreed to enter plural marriage. After one such couple recognized e virtues of polygyny, the wife played a major role in adding five wives the family within a year (Watt, 1978). How often a husband, wife, or th of them, actually initiated the process among 19th-century Mormons impossible to discern. As in the case of contemporary fundamentalists, wever, it appears that the decision to add a wife to a family may be tiated by any party to a possible marriage.

To what extent were 19th-century wives consulted about adding a new fe to a family? Ideally, a man was expected to seek the consent of his fe or wives before entering into a new plural marriage (Young, 1954). d consultation occurred in many cases. Ann Eliza Young (1908) said at when her mother and father sought a wife, they tried to make sure e would be compatible with both of them: he would "propose" possible w wives and she would "second" them. In several dramatic cases, wives toed the idea, in general, or the specific candidates, in particular:

One elder . . . wanted a second wife, but he feared to ask the consent of his first. Finally, he told her he had a revelation to marry a certain girl and that in the face of such divine instructions, she must give her consent. The next morning she announced that in the night she, too, had received a revelation "to shoot any woman who became his plural wife." Being the more drastic her revelation ended the matter once and for all. (Young, 1954, p. 123)

Another man explained his first wife's reaction to a possible match and iy he finally decided not to proceed with it as follows: "She wouldn't let e." She told him that "if he ever took another wife, when he brought her the front door [she] would go out the back" (Young, 1954 p. 123). Even ough the principle was for wives to be consulted "in a number of cases, iefly in the families of the elite, it was the norm to consult all the wives out any further ventures in matrimony . . . but in such prominent families is doubtful if a wife would dare not follow the wishes of her Lord and aster. Social position demanded conformity in such matters" (Young, 54, p. 122).

In fact, many 19th-century church leaders interpreted Joseph Smith's

1843 revelation on plural marriage to mean that a man could marry
plural wife even if his wife or wives objected. According to Orson Pra
the church authority who officially and publicly announced the practice
polygyny, when a wife

> refuses to give her consent for him to marry another according to that l
> [God's law], then, it becomes necessary, for her to state before the Presid
> the reasons why she withholds her consent; if her reasons are sufficient a
> justifiable and the husband is found in the fault, or in transgression, th
> he is not permitted to take any step in regard to obtaining another. Bu
> the wife can show no good reason why she refuses to comply with the l
> which was given unto Sarah of old, then it is lawful for her husband
> permitted by revelation through the prophet, to be married to others with
> her consent, and he will be justified, and she will be condemned. (Van W
> oner, 1989, p. 103)

Brigham Young was also quite forceful on the point: "If it is the duty o
husband to take a wife, take her. But it is not the privilege of a woman
dictate to the husband, and tell who or how many he shall take, or wl
he shall do with them when he gets them, but it is the duty of the wom
to submit cheerfully" (Warenski, 1978, p. 150).

As in pioneer times, dyadic factors clearly play an important role in
decision of modern Mormon fundamentalists to add a wife to their fam
In both periods the matter could be initiated by a husband or wife.
though consent by wives was historically stated as an ideal, it did not occ
in all cases. Among our participants, the consent and approval of esta
lished wives in the decision to bring a new wife into a family was affirm
as a principle and practice. (Indeed, no one ever mentioned the stateme
to the contrary by Brigham Young and Orson Pratt.) In general, therefo
some dyadic aspects of the decision to engage in polygyny were simi
among 19th-century and contemporary Mormon polygynists.

Communal processes

The idea of having a new wife in a contemporary fundamentalist family
often initiated as a communal activity, either by wives or jointly by
husband and wives. Sometimes the idea is discussed without any candida
in mind; at other times a particular woman is mentioned. Although re
gious reasons are central, other factors also enter in. These include
economic status of the family, stability of relationships among family me
bers, stimulation, friendship, and social support that a new wife may p
vide.

Family 1

The first three wives – Joan, Norma, and Charlotte – had been trying to persuade Hal to marry a new wife for some time. They didn't have anyone in particular in mind but believed that a new wife would further satisfy their religious principles. There were other reasons as well. They were very busy with work and children, lived in suburban neighborhoods with no other plural families nearby, and pretty much depended on one another for their social life. They felt that a new wife would be a new friend and someone else to socialize with.

Another communal process occurred soon after Hal met Cynthia, when the other wives spent time with her and collectively agreed that she would fit in nicely in the family. They then all went with Hal to formally express their interest in her.

Family 2

David, Judith, Rebecca, Emily, and Phyllis agreed that they needed to be on the alert for a new wife in the family. Even though they didn't have anyone in mind, the wives all felt that the time was ripe since the family was stabilized, everyone got along, and they desired to continue meeting "the fullness of the gospel."

There were other communal reasons as well. The four wives said that a new wife would be stimulating and a challenge for all of them, including David. They would have to learn to live together, and their relationships with David and with one another would be tested and would grow by virtue of a new wife in the family. An odd number of wives would also ensure that no wife would ever be alone (when David was spending time with one of them).

The wives also observed that although David is ready and capable of having a fifth wife, he doesn't quite know it yet. (He didn't disagree or respond to their analysis!)

Family 3

William, Carlyn, Danielle, and Alayna have been discussing the possibility of bringing a new wife into their family for some time. They even explored possibilities with two other women but decided communally that neither would fit in their family (one woman was also not interested in them).

William stated that a new wife would help the family better meet their religious values; everyone concurred. He also said that a new wife would force him to provide more organized family leadership since their life would be more complex. Danielle, the second wife, agreed and pointed out other qualities a new wife would bring to the family. Because they live in an isolated area and have few friends, a new wife would be a source of social support and companionship to the other wives. Sl added that a new wife might also have innovative ideas about fami life and would be another helper in managing the home. At the sam time, Danielle was a bit ambivalent, because a new wife might crea complexity, tension, and conflict, as everyone adjusted to one anothe All in all, however, she concluded that a new wife would be a plus f the family. Indeed, she had even taken the lead from time to time, searcl ing out and making initial contacts with potential new wives.

The others generally agreed about the positive aspects of a new wi but also reflected some ambivalence about when to proceed. Willia said that he is not quite ready for another marriage, but will intuitive know when it should happen. Carlyn, the first wife, agreed, reiteratii what William said. When we probed about what it means to "be ready, William explained that he would be prepared to have a new wife whe he becomes more worthy, more polite to his family, and better able lead the family properly.

In spite of their reservations, they all agreed that they needed to I open to the possibility of a new wife joining the family. They also co curred that any of them could identify potential wives, but that they a would communally decide on the appropriateness of a particular woma for the family.

Communal initiatives were also important among 19th-century Mo mons, albeit for many reasons (Young, 1954). For example, one wife e couraged her husband to enter plural marriage as soon as possible so tha she would not be too old and lose her influence over a younger woma Because of religious beliefs, some childless women urged their husbands t marry again or encouraged other women to join their family so that th husband could have offspring. In this way, they could follow in the foo steps of Sarah of the Old Testament. (In keeping with this principle, newer wife once "gave" one of her children to a childless sister wife t raise as her own; see Young, 1954.) Other wives encouraged their husban to marry a family domestic servant so that the senior wife could maintai control over the junior wife and have a permanent source of labor in th home. And sisters sometimes married the same man, partly for social su port (Embry, 1984). Finally, personal compatibility of women played a important role in bringing a particular woman into a pioneer fami (Eaton-Gadsby and Dushku, 1978).

These cases illustrate a communal basis for deciding to add a wife to fundamentalist family. Wives, or a husband and wives, may deliberate to gether about a new marriage even when they do not have a particula candidate in mind. And a wife or wives, alone or with the husband, ma

proach a woman who they think might be a good addition to their fam-
. The decision to have a new wife in a fundamentalist family may unfold
many ways. It can begin on a dyadic basis, with a man or a prospective
ife seeking one another out. Or it can begin communally, with wives or
husband and wives collectively pursuing various possibilities. At the same
ne, there is often an interplay of dyadic and communal processes, re-
rdless of the initial impetus. That is, the process may start in a dyadic
ay (e.g., a husband may be attracted to a woman), and then his wife or
ives may enter into the deliberations, in a communal process. If the matter
first approached communally – for example by a wife or wives – the
usband's dyadic relationship with a potential wife will eventually affect
e decision. Thus the pattern of events may unfold in many ways across
d within families as participants struggle to achieve an acceptable inter-
ay of dyadic and communal processes.

he role of elders and parents

s already indicated, deliberating about the possibility of a new wife is
ore than the business of a husband and wives alone. Even the earliest
ploration of a new marriage is subject to the approval of the religious
adership. In the rural community, marriages are arranged by the prophet;
the urban community, the religious leader or an elder must theoretically
prove any formal contact between a man and a woman. In addition, a
oman's parents must ideally approve of a potential match. Decisions
out potential marriage relationships therefore involve a network of social
ntexts in which fundamentalist couples and families are embedded. The
rticular confluence of participants may vary from case to case.

Family 2
In all cases, David had been careful to ask permission of the religious
leader and each of his prospective wife's fathers before exploring a relationship. He said that if he hadn't received their approval he probably
would not have pursued the matter further.

Family 5
When Howard became interested in Valerie, his second wife, the religious leader instructed him to seek her father's permission to date her.
Her father then approached her about the matter, and she agreed, even
though she was initially reluctant to do so.

Following the same procedure in the case of Barbara, the third wife,
Howard found her father resistant to a possible match. However, because she was interested in Howard, her father relented, although he

insisted that they not have any contact for six months so that they cou
test their true feelings.

In discussing the matter, the leader of the urban group was forceful an
articulate. Before approving formal dating or courtship, he careful
probed the motives of potential partners, wanting to be sure of their rel
gious commitment, family status, economic situation, and general attitud
about a possible marriage. He disapproved of potential matches in whic
a man could not support a new wife, was too old for a particular woma
was more interested in having a new wife primarily for personal versus r
ligious reasons, or in which a woman wished to explore a potential ma
riage for other than appropriate theological values. He acknowledged th
challenges faced by members of plural families and stated that he tried h
best to assess the probability that a potential plural marriage would b
successful.

In addition, the religious leader or parents sometimes act as matc
makers.

Family 13
After her first husband's death, the leader introduced Gloria to his ow
son. Gloria felt that the leader was encouraging and even pressuring h
son to consider establishing a relationship because of her unfortuna
family circumstances.

Family 15
After her divorce, the religious leader gave Henrietta a list of men wh
he knew were interested in adding a wife to their family. She contacte
some of them and was attracted to Michael and his wives. They even
tually married.

Nineteenth-century Mormon parents also played matchmaking roles i
plural marriages, presumably with the support of church leaders. Som
parents encouraged their daughters to become plural wives of particula
men in order to have economic security or social status. At times, a ma
would first approach the parents about marrying their daughter, withou
her even being aware of his action. It was also said (by anti-Mormons) tha
older men "traded" their daughters with one another.

Tensions and stresses

In view of the number of participants in the decision and the comple
process by which a new wife is added to a fundamentalist family, it shoul
not be surprising that disagreements, uncertainties, anxieties, and stresse

metimes arise. Potential threats to existing husband–wife and wife–wife
ationships, anticipation of disruptions in home life and family routines,
ncerns about a variety of adjustments to and by a new family member,
d other issues – whether explicitly stated or not – surely make stressful
e very idea of a new wife in a fundamentalist family. To begin with, a
sband may not be attracted to a particular woman but may be pressed
to a relationship by his wives; a wife or wives may object to a husband's
erest in a particular woman. Or a husband or his wives may not feel
at the timing is right, regardless of particular opportunities; family prob-
ns may be such that some members object to additional complexities in
eir life, and so on. And a woman in whom a family is interested may not
sure of her interest in them. Thus a variety of dyadic and communal
ues – not to mention the fact that parents, elders, or the religious leader
ay delay, question, disapprove, or encourage a new wife – may make the
cision process extremely stressful.

Family 1

When Hal, Joan, Norma, and Charlotte agreed that they wanted Cynthia to consider joining the family as a fourth wife, they approached her
together. She was overwhelmed by their proposal, felt surrounded by
their collective presence, and rejected their overture. This upset everyone.
Later, she became friendly with Norma and explained her feelings and
her interest in another man's family. Over a period of several months,
however, their friendship grew, and she also consulted with Norma's
father, a religious elder in the community. In some respects he acted as
a matchmaker and mediator, and Cynthia eventually accepted the family's proposal to further explore joining their family. But it was a long
and stressful experience for everyone.

Family 2

As noted earlier, Phyllis, the fourth wife, actively wanted to marry David
and join the family. Judith, Rebecca, and Emily, his three wives, liked
Phyllis and encouraged David in the matter. He resisted, but they persuaded him to proceed. There was considerable tension and stress between David and his wives about the matter that continued on into the
courtship phase of the relationship. (David and Phyllis were eventually
married, and happily so.)

On another occasion David became interested in a woman and discussed the matter with his wives, her parents, and the prophet. Judith
and Rebecca had reservations about the prospective wife, and tension
arose between them and David. But he went ahead in spite of their
concerns. Eventually the relationship was terminated when it became
clear that a marriage would not work.

Family 5

Howard was very much attracted to Valerie, and Constance, his fi
wife, also liked her. But Valerie was resistant at first. She had just t
minated a three-year engagement, was despondent, and not in the mo
to explore a new relationship. Nevertheless, Howard was persistent, a
they eventually dated and married. But it was hard on all of them
they struggled with the decision to explore their dyadic and commu
relationships.

Family 13

When Paul wanted to court Sherry as a third wife, the religious lea
prohibited any contact between them for four months, in order to ens
that they had a strong and valid interest in one another. Muriel, the f
wife, was not pleased at the prospective match but eventually approv
albeit only in a grudging way. The whole experience was very upsett
for Muriel.

Family 16

When Ralph expressed a possible interest in Beverly, several of his wi
discouraged him because she was a divorcee who had only recen
joined the community, and they were uncertain of her religious co
mitment. Ralph nevertheless proceeded, amid a fair degree of fam
conflict. He eventually married Beverly, with the other wives still o
posed, but reluctantly acquiescing.

Tension can also arise when other wives are not asked to participate
the decision to consider a new wife joining a family. In her autobiograph
Melissa Merrill (1975), the first wife in a dysfunctional contemporary fa
ily, described how she supported her husband in his first plural marria
When internal family conflicts developed, however, her husband married
third and fourth wife without consulting her at all. His actions accentuat
general tensions and upheaval in the family, all of which eventually led
their divorce. One of our participants had a similar experience:

Family 13

Contrary to custom, Paul secretly married his second wife, Gloria, wit
out telling Muriel, his first wife, or asking her opinion. It was only se
eral years later that Muriel found out what Paul had done. Needless
say, this created considerable turmoil in the family.

The prospect of a new wife also often created stress, anxiety, and em
tional turmoil in pioneer Mormon families. As discussed in an earlier cha
ter, Emma Smith, Joseph Smith's first wife, greatly resisted his plur
marriages. Of the numerous cases of conflict or personal turmoil at t

prospect of plural marriage, one pregnant wife was so upset by her husband's marriage to a younger woman that she remained resentful for years after (Young, 1954). In other cases, as already mentioned, some wives were so upset that the prospective matches were quickly aborted. Another wife attempted to thwart her husband's initial interest in a prospective wife by encouraging her children to be noisy and disobedient whenever the other woman was around. And a wife who finally agreed to the plural marriage of her husband stated that doing so "nearly broke her heart." A number of daughters have left a record of the unhappiness their 19th-century Mormon mothers endured at the prospect and consummation of a plural marriage.

"She knew who it was that Papa was courting, and of course, that broke her heart. Papa knew she didn't want it, but Papa was between the devil and the great deep blue sea" because he felt that he had been commanded by revelation to marry another wife. . . .

"Mother just cried her heart out when she found out about it. No, he probably never did consult mother about the marriage to Isabel, and the marriage just finished her." . . .

"My mother . . . accepted it; she lived it graciously, but it was always a heartbreak." (Embry, 1987, p. 59)

Some pioneer husbands also struggled with the prospect of a plural marriage. One man who was told by his bishop that a young woman wanted to marry him was upset because he did not want to marry again and was not personally attracted to the woman. But he finally acquiesced, persuaded by his wife that it was the proper thing to do (Embry, 1987).

Although firm in their religious beliefs, many people in the pioneer era had mixed emotions about plural marriage. In one case a first wife said to a prospective second wife: "It's hard, the hardest trial that ever came into my life. I can't help but feel bad, but I still want you to marry him . . . you are the one we both felt we could love and respect enough to come into the family, and we made the decision after much prayer and serious thought" (Embry, 1984, p. 58).

The special case of the United Fundamentalist Church in the Redrock community

As discussed earlier, the two groups with whom we worked subscribe to fundamentalist religious doctrine, including plural marriage, but the rural community is more conservative in its practices, including marriage. Marriages are arranged by the prophet, who theoretically chooses partners, with varying degrees of involvement by couple members or their parents. Thus dyadic and communal factors play a smaller role in the rural community of Redrock than in the Metropolitan City group, as is evident from the following examples.

Family 19

Abigail said that she knew of many cases in which a man and woman were informed of their marriage by the prophet without having known or having had any prior contact with one another. In some cases they had never even seen each other previously.

In her own case, Abigail's father told her that the prophet had selected Horace as her husband and that they were to be married in ten days. Horace only learned of the prophet's decision two days before the wedding because he was away at school. Abigail was pleased and not at all surprised, because they had spent a great deal of time together, and their families were friendly.

Family 4

Phillip (a son of Harry and his second wife Ruth) told us that he was informed by the prophet that he was to marry Sarah two weeks hence. Sarah learned of the prophet's decision a week before they were married. Phillip and Sarah had known each other over the years because the families were friendly, but they had never had a close relationship. Phillip said that he and Sarah were surprised but pleased about their marriage.

Belle, Harry's third wife, said that her own and her children's marriages were arranged by the prophet and that it is properly his decision about who marries whom. She also said how lucky she and her family were to have had such successful marriages.

Family 11

Benjamin and Katherine had been married for several years and had five children. One day the prophet informed Benjamin that he was to marry three sisters, each of whom had several children. The prophet decided on this unusual arrangement because the sisters' husband had been killed in an automobile accident.

At the same time, the prophet does not always act without the input of families or prospective partners.

Family 4

Harry, a senior member of the community, explained that although the prophet plays a central role, there is often considerable negotiation and consultation with parents and prospective partners before a decision about a marriage is made and announced. He also said that if either potential partner resists, a marriage is not likely to be forced on them.

At the same time, Harry emphasized that the prophet is the final decision maker, and while someone may have questions or feelings about a particular decision, they accept the prophet's judgment.

There are also cases in which the participants initiate a possible match themselves, with the prophet being an intermediary.

Family 4

Harry and Eve, the fourth wife, were married only one day after their match was announced by the prophet. Months before, however, Eve asked the prophet to arrange a marriage for her. When he asked her who she might like to marry, she named Harry. When the prophet later asked Harry how he felt about Eve, Harry said that he had been attracted to her but had been reluctant to raise the matter. Three months later, after she had not heard from the prophet, Eve pressed the issue with her father, who later told her to approach Harry directly. Around that time, the prophet informed Harry of her strong interest in him, whereupon Harry agreed to the match. When Eve approached him face to face – essentially proposing to Harry – they agreed to be married. Their wedding took place the following day.

We can assume that a variety of informal negotiations between families and the prophet occurred over a period of time before the marriage – a possibility that is reasonable in view of the fact that Eve and Harry came from prominent families in the community.

Here is another case from the same family:

A year after Shirley's husband was killed in an accident she asked the prophet to "place her" with another husband. The prophet mentioned Harry as a possibility, and she expressed interest in becoming his fifth wife. The prophet then raised the matter with Harry, and he was positive about Shirley. It is not clear how much discussion occurred back and forth between the prophet and the prospective partners, or between the partners themselves. But when both formally agreed to the match, they were married the next day. Although the prophet formally decided on the marriage, he also served as a "go-between" and matchmaker who seriously considered Harry's and Shirley's views in the matter.

Thus although the decision to marry is ultimately made by the prophet in the rural community, the system is not entirely monolithic. Sometimes informal dyadic processes come into play for some couples; sometimes parents foster relationships and negotiate with the prophet; sometimes partners initiate or veto a match. On the other hand, we did not hear of any instances of communal participation in decision making by wives in the rural group.

Summary

The motivation to have a new wife in a fundamentalist Mormon family is based on religious doctrine that views polygyny as an ideal family structure in earthly and eternal life. However, the pragmatic decision to add a wife to a fundamentalist family can be complex and multifaceted.

In the reality of everyday life, decision making about having a new wife by fundamentalist Mormons involves interpersonal dyadic and communal processes, as well as religious values. Thus one aspect of the decision centers on the dyadic relationship between a man and a woman. Are they attracted to one another? Do they share common values? Does a marriage serve some unique need for either or both partners? At the same time, fundamentalist families must deliberate at a communal level. Is a prospective wife compatible with other wives? Is the family economically, interpersonally, and in other ways ready to absorb a new wife? Deciding about whether to add a new wife to a fundamentalist family therefore involves both couple-oriented and family-oriented considerations or, in our terms, a balancing and interplay of dyadic and communal processes.

The decision to take a new wife may be initiated in several ways: a husband or prospective wife may start the process; or established wives may encourage or press the husband to think about a new marriage, in general, or in regard to a particular woman that they have in mind. It is customary for wives to participate in the decision at some point, at least in the urban community. This behavior also reflects a communal process. Ideally, it is expected that a man and a prospective wife will be attracted to one another. This expectation reflects a dyadic process.

Couple members and plural families are not the only ones to have a say in the decision about a new wife joining a fundamentalist family. Parents and the religious leader are also central players. Even the earliest contact between prospective partners requires approval by the religious leadership and by the woman's parents (who may also initiate and encourage some potential matches). In the rural community the prophet arranges many marriages, although parents and prospective partners often are involved informally.

Finally, deliberations about adding a wife to a family vary from case to case, within and across families. Each circumstance is unique and requires husbands, wives, and prospective wives to approach the matter anew each time. Because the issue is complex, so many participants are involved, and many men and women have had little prior experience with plural family relationships, they must discover for themselves how to achieve an acceptable interplay of dyadic and communal processes within the broader context of their family, community, and religious bonds.

6

Courtship

Courtship is widespread among world cultures and encompasses how, when, and where prospective partners meet, explore their potential match, become committed to eventual marriage, and participate in various activities prior to marriage. It is also customary in many cultures for family and kin, friends and peers, and others to participate in courtships. We focus on dyadic and communal aspects of courtship in contemporary Mormon plural families, with a view to determining how prospective partners and other wives participate in courting activities. We also describe the roles of families and the religious hierarchy, and compare pioneer and present-day Mormon polygynous courtships.

Courtship and culture

Courtship varies across cultures in several ways. First, in some cultures courtship is primarily a function of the families, not the prospective partners (Stephens, 1963). In other cases, especially Western cultures, courtship is largely the business of couple members, with families playing a secondary, albeit sometimes significant role. Likewise, the two Mormon fundamentalist groups with whom we worked vary in this regard. In the urban and somewhat less conservative Church of Latter-day Apostles, courting activities are couple-oriented once families and religious authorities sanction the process. In the ultraconservative United Fundamentalist Church many marriages are arranged by the prophet (sometimes in collaboration with families or potential partners).

Second, some cultures have short courtships, whereas others stretch them out over months or even years, and marriage does not occur until the betrothed pair has achieved maturity (or even borne a child). In the Mormon fundamentalist groups we studied, courtships are usually either fairly brief or do not take place.

Third, although wives in polygynous families in other cultures sometimes participate in the decision to add a wife to a family, most ethnog raphies are silent on the role of established wives in courtships. In ou conservative fundamentalist group, wives play a very active role i new courtships; in the rural ultraconservative group, wives are less in volved in courtship, largely because courtships do not occur or are ver brief.

The formality and duration of courtship varies widely across societies In some cultures there is essentially no courtship. Among Trobriand Is landers in the South Pacific, for example, marriage occurs when coupl members publicly eat together and exchange gifts (Mair, 1977). There i little formal courting or extensive negotiation between couple member or their families. At the other extreme, some courtships (or premarita phases) transpire over several years. In the Fulani culture of Africa, a boy who passes an initiation ritual is given a herd of animals and is betrothe to an infant girl (Stenning, 1971). At puberty she moves to the home stead of the boy's parents and works under his mother's supervision. O becoming pregnant, the girl returns to her family for about two and a half years and only then is the couple recognized as being married. Thu the Fulani premarital relationship lasts for years. Similar practices occu among the Bemba of Africa (Mair, 1977), Comoro Islanders of Mozam bique (Ottenheimer and Ottenheimer, 1979), and Yako of Africa (Forde 1950).

Cultures also differ in the courtship roles of couple members and fam ilies. In many cases families do the primary courting, often in lengthy anc elaborate negotiations involving bridewealth or bride service by the pro spective groom or his family, or dowries provided by the potential brid and her family. Couple members may also participate, but marriages i some such cultures primarily involve the bonding of families, with the cou ple serving as a vehicle for family ties.

In other cultures, couple members are free to initially choose a part ner, often first meeting in public places and according to some standarc ritual. Formal courtship may then involve families engaging in extensive negotiations for bridewealth and dowries, gift exchanges, and the like. I the Nuer culture of Africa, girls in their early teens are first courted a public dances, where boys display their skills in spear throwing and du eling activities (Evans-Pritchard, 1951). Although boys normally pursue girls, a girl sometimes goes with her companions to a boy's homestead even taking some of his father's cows to her home as a signal of her in terest. Her father returns the cows if he disapproves of the young man, but otherwise waits to see if the boy's parents are willing to enter nego tiations. Or a girl may remove the tether from a boy's oxen, and if the boy is interested in the girl, he will send a small brother to retrieve it. Assuming progress to this point, the boy and his friends and relatives make a series of visits to the girl's family and engage in brideprice and bridewealth negotiations. If all goes well, a betrothal ceremony occurs, in which cattle are transferred, and the boy's family and friends dance, sing war songs, and make speeches. Although the bridegroom's family does not participate in the betrothal ceremony and celebration, they are given food for their enjoyment.

Among the Kikuyu people of Africa, a boy who is attracted to a girl visits her home with his friends. If she signals acceptance of his advances and they receive parental approval, his parents bring gifts of honey or beer, her parents provide food, and family negotiations proceed (Kenyatta, 1973). At a later time the boy's parents present her family with sheep, goats, or cattle, as a first installment of bridewealth. Bridewealth payments continue until an appropriate number of animals have been given to the prospective bride's family, whereupon a feast is held at the girl's homestead and a public announcement is made of the betrothal. Still later, the marriage contract is signed by representatives of the families. This event is followed by another feast, gift exchanges, and ritual dancing. Thus courting involves couple members and families, the latter engaging in complex and lengthy negotiations.

The interplay of partner and parental roles in courtship can be seen in the Hagen culture of New Guinea (Strathern, 1972). Courtship begins in public parties where males and females "turn heads," that is, a pair kneels with their foreheads pressed together, and they sway backward and forward and side to side while others sing. A woman who has turned heads with a particular man on several occasions then visits his family settlement for a short time and receives gifts for her father and brothers. Over time there are gift exchanges between couple members and between families, as well as bridewealth negotiations for highly valued pigs and shells. Following a public display of the bridewealth as a signal of an agreement between families, a final transaction symbolizing the marriage itself occurs weeks later, when the groom's parents give a gift of pork to the bride's parents. Here again, courtship is a multistage process involving couple members at the outset and families later on.

As another example, young men and women of the Sioux Indians of North America historically participated in a stylized courting dance held in a large tipi (Hassrick, 1964). A young woman would invite a man to dance by kicking the sole of one of his moccasins; then several couples sang and danced around the fire. Next, young men danced before the women, chose a partner, and they danced together. This pattern was repeated until mutual choices emerged. At a later time, the couple might meet privately and develop their relationship further. Eventually, a formal proposal was delivered by a close friend or a brother of the man to the woman's brother or other male relative, whereupon a brideprice was negotiated. If everything proceeded satisfactorily, the marriage was considered consummated; there was no particular marriage ceremony.[1]

Thus courtships vary cross-culturally in their duration, role of couple members, and families, and the flow of events.[2] Courtship practices also change over time within cultures. Courtship in America has increasingly involved couples alone and apart from their families and chaperones, "dating" widely with others as a precursor to eventual formal "engagement" and courtship with one partner, and, in recent years, cohabitation and living together by couples prior to or at the same time as a commitment to eventual marriage (Rothman, 1984; Bailey, 1988).

Courtship among contemporary Mormon fundamentalists

Mormon fundamentalists who practice courtship, primarily those in the urban Church of Latter-day Apostles, view it in much the same way as American society at large. It is a time when a man and woman seriously explore their mutual compatibility and desire to marry. The earliest stage of courtship may be informal, as described in chapter 5. A later stage occurs when the prophet, parents of the woman, and other wives in a family sanction the beginning of courting – in essence defining a formal "engagement" period. Serious exploration of a dyadic relationship theoretically begins when couple members and other parties agree to the possibility of their eventual marriage. Any of these people theoretically have "veto power" over the initiation or continuation of a courtship.

In the rural United Fundamentalist Church, courtship either does not occur or is informal. Marriages are arranged by the prophet, often with families or participants informally involved, and formal courtships are not practiced.

Our discussion of courtship among contemporary Mormon fundamentalists focuses on *dyadic* and *communal* family processes. Specifically, we are interested in learning how a prospective husband and wife, and other plural wives, function during courtship to achieve the ideal goals of a new unique dyad in the family, ensure the well-being of other husband–wife dyadic bonds, and foster positive communal relationships between established wives and a prospective new wife. We are also interested in the tensions and complexities arising in courtship that threaten either the dyad-in-formation or the workings of the plural family.

Dyadic and communal features of courtship

On the one hand, courtship among Mormon fundamentalists is a distinctively dyadic process, with couple members acting in much the same way as their counterparts in the larger monogamous American culture. They explore one another's personalities, beliefs, and values; they test their interpersonal compatibility; they engage in intimacies (albeit in a restricted way); and they date and spend time together alone. At one level, an outsider would see no difference between the courting behavior of Mormon fundamentalists and that of many other American couples. And dyadic courting activities frequently occur with any wife – first, second, or later.

What is distinctive about fundamentalists is that other wives also court a prospective wife. In keeping with religious and cultural values, a marriage not only involves the union of a man and a woman in a unique dyadic relationship; it also involves a potential wife "marrying a family" whose members will live together in this world and throughout eternity. Because co-wives are ideally expected to be mutually loving, harmonious, compatible, and supportive, courtship is as much a test of the viability of family communal relationships as it is a test of the viability of a dyadic bond between a man and a woman.

What dyadic activities occur during courtship? As the following cases show, courting couples spend a fair amount of time alone, as they do in general American society. They go on "dates" to movies, restaurants, and other special places. What about communal activities? An established wife or wives may spend time with the couple in public or private settings. For example, they may all go to a movie, attend church together, or invite the fiancée to a family home. Or a man and his wives may visit a fiancée at her parents' home. Wives and the prospective co-wife may spend time alone themselves – at restaurants, movies, or in one of their homes. In some cases, a fiancée may live with one of the wives and her children for a period of time.

Family 2

In their courtship, David and Judith, the first wife, went on dates to movies, restaurants, dances, and elsewhere. They discussed their personal and religious values, the way in which David would lead the family as patriarch, and their mutual expectations of one another. On one occasion Judith tested his religious testimony by falsely telling him that she was opposed to plural marriage. He replied that he could not marry her if she held such a view, whereupon Judith expressed relief, told him of her true feelings, and the courtship progressed.

During Rebecca's courtship with David, the couple also dated alone, although Judith sometimes joined them, and Rebecca frequently visited the family home. And when David visited Rebecca's family, Judith went along. Rebecca and Judith also spent a fair amount of time together when David was not around. So courtship was a blend of dyadic and communal activity.

A similar pattern occurred when David courted Emily, the third wife and Phyllis, the fourth wife.

Family 5
Howard, Constance, the first wife, and Valerie, the prospective second wife, all went out together on many courting dates. This happened so often that Constance finally encouraged them to go out alone once in a while, so that they could build a relationship of their own that was independent of her. Constance was therefore sensitive to the need to achieve an acceptable balance of dyadic and communal processes during Howard's and Valerie's courtship. (She had also begun to find it burdensome to always be out courting, since she was working and also had children to care for.)

Family 9
This family developed a unique approach to achieving a balance of dyadic and communal activities in one of their courtships. While courting Marjorie, the third wife, John found it increasingly difficult to simultaneously meet the day-to-day needs of Joyce and Clara, the first and second wives and their children, and also spend time alone with his fiancée. Collectively, they eventually worked out a plan whereby he spent one evening a week alone with Marjorie, had some private time alone with Joyce and Clara, and Marjorie regularly visited the family home. In this way they attempted to achieve an acceptable interplay of their three dyadic relationships and their family communal needs.

Some combination of couple and family courting is quite common in the urban group of fundamentalist Mormons. Although each family works out its own courting pattern for prospective marriages, which may thus vary from case to case, participants generally strive to build unique dyadic bonds between couple members while simultaneously seeking communal ties between wives and a fiancée.

Although many participants emphasized the importance of couple members developing an intimate and unique dyadic relationship during courtship, they pointed out that there are strong norms against extreme physical intimacy prior to marriage. Even being alone in too private a setting is disapproved of, because it may imply inappropriate sexual activity. So although the development of a dyadic bond is important, couples are expected to observe strict norms regarding physical intimacy.

Family 2

Although David, Rebecca, Emily, and Phyllis agreed that hand holding, kissing, and hugging are acceptable, more intimate expressions may occur only in later stages of courtship or after a couple is married. They noted that some people in their group feel strongly that there shouldn't be *any* close physical contact until a couple is married. On the basis of his own experiences in successful and unsuccessful courtships, David said that he would never again become too intimate with a woman – including kissing her – until he was absolutely certain that they would marry.

Family 1

Norma, Hal's second wife, openly criticized him for not behaving properly when he was courting Cynthia, the fourth wife. He was wrong, she said, to have visited Cynthia on several occasions, until late at night, when she was alone in her apartment. Norma felt that someone else should have been present – her parents, one of the wives, or a church elder. She said that a man should only be alone with a prospective wife in a public place.

Hal, Joan, Norma, Charlotte, and Cynthia agreed that some level of interpersonal intimacy in courting couple members is all right, although very intimate physical contact is not acceptable. They pointed out that some people in their group even object to kissing before marriage.

Although wives often play a communal role in courtship, there are some unusual ways in which this occurs.

Family 2

During David and Rebecca's courtship, her father called for a temporary cessation of their contact with one another, because he wanted her to be sure of the match. During the moratorium, Judith, the first wife, maintained contact with Rebecca and essentially continued the courtship herself. The two women became close friends, the marriage eventually took place, and Judith and Rebecca continue to be good friends and companions.

In another case, Emily's father (she is the third wife), also stopped her courtship with David. He did so because a male neighbor stated that he had received a revelation from God that Emily should marry him, not David. Emily's father wanted her to ponder and pray on the matter, so that she would eventually marry the "right" man. During the several-month moratorium, Judith and Rebecca communicated regularly with Emily by mail. They and David would discuss the correspondence and decide how to reply to Emily's letters. In effect, the courtship continued, with Judith and Rebecca acting as surrogates for David and fostering both his dyadic and their communal relationships with Emily. The formal courtship eventually began again, and David and Emily were married shortly thereafter. It is possible that the outcome might have been quite different if Judith and Rebecca hadn't played such an active role.

Family 10
At one point in their courtship, Naomi, Barry's second wife, broke off the relationship. She just wasn't sure that marrying him was the right thing to do and wanted some distance between them. They had no contact for several months, during which time Anita, the first wife, tried repeatedly, but unsuccessfully, to convince Naomi to renew the relationship.

Eventually, Barry and Anita approached Naomi together. Naomi told them that she had been praying and fasting about the matter and had come to believe that she did want to marry Barry. Their wedding took place three weeks later. Here again, a wife stood in for her husband during a courtship and also probably built her own relationship with the prospective co-wife. It is possible that Barry's marriage to Naomi might not have occurred without Anita's persistence.

Thus courtship among present-day Mormon polygynists is strongly dyadic, with couple members attempting to develop an intimate and unique relationship. They do this by courting alone and in ways that are similar to those in the larger monogamous culture. At the same time, the Mormon fundamentalist culture values harmony, love, and unity among all family members, including wives. To cope with this communal value, wives actively participate in courtship with a prospective fiancée in any of several patterns – with the husband, with the fiancée themselves, and even as surrogates for the husband. Although variations occur within and across families, some blend of dyadic and communal activities is customary in most courtships.

Length of courtship

The period of courtship among fundamentalists is generally short, but not universally so. Its length depends on many factors – parents, the judgment of the prophet, the flow of events between couple members, other wives, and the demands of family life.

Although the religious leader must theoretically approve the initiation of courtship, in reality there are many cases in which couples informally court beforehand. So it is not always possible to specify the precise length of a given courtship. In general, the typical courtship among the urban group of fundamentalists rarely lasts longer than several months: in Family 1 Hal and Cynthia, the fourth wife, courted for about five months; in Family 9 John and Marjorie, the third wife, courted for three months; and in Family 14 Harvey and Molly, the second wife, courted for a couple of months (including a period when she and her child moved into the family home). In some cases, however, the courtships were either longer or shorter. In Family 9, John and Clara, the second wife, courted for just a few weeks. In Family 5, Howard courted Valerie, the second wife for about a year. And in Family 8, Ira and Ethel, the second wife, courted for about eight months. There were also a few cases in which a courtship was either shorter or longer than usual because of special circumstances:

Family 1
The religious leader wanted Hal and Cynthia, the fourth wife, to court for a full year because she had not been fully released (divorced) from her former husband.

Family 3
William and Danielle, the second wife, formally courted for only a week. However, they had participated in group religious teaching sessions with his Mormon fundamentalist colleagues for several weeks beforehand and agreed during that time that they wanted to marry. And, unbeknownst to Danielle, William had received approval from the church's leader to pursue the relationship. So, in effect, he had been courting her for several weeks.

William's courtship with Alayna, the third wife, who was Danielle's sister, followed a somewhat similar pattern. Soon after Danielle introduced them, and perhaps even encouraged the match, William knew that he wanted to marry her. They also participated in a religious teaching group and agreed to marry within a few weeks. Together with Carlyn and Danielle, they asked for and received the prophet's approval and were married shortly thereafter.

Family 13
The religious leader delayed giving Paul and Gloria permission to court and prohibited contact between them for four months because he wanted to be sure that they were serious about one another. Once the courtship was renewed, they married a month later.

Family 18

Charles was encouraged by a religious leader to marry Angela, a woman in the group who lived in another country. He did so with essentially no courtship, and they lived apart for six months until she was able to join him and his three other wives. Thus there was no true courtship before the marriage, although they corresponded after they were married.

A unique factor affecting the length of courtships is the communal involvement of other wives. As discussed later, courtship may produce a variety of tensions and disruptions in a plural family. Not only must a husband attend to his wives and families during courtship, but he must also direct time and energy toward building a relationship with his fiancée. Depending upon the number of wives and children in a family, as well as their living locations, a husband can be spread thin in his day-to-day life. Wives are also under enormous pressure, as they care for their children, often work outside the home, and manage domestic affairs without the husband being present every day because they share him with other wives. Courting a new wife adds to their burdens, as they go on dates with the new couple, entertain the prospective wife in their home, and play an active role in courtship. In many respects, shortening a courtship enables a family to address the new task of weaving the new wife into the family system. Extending a courtship over a long period of time simply adds to the daily challenges they already face.

Family 5

During Howard's courtship of Valerie, the second wife, Constance, began to feel that it was dragging on for too long. She found that it was hard to go on dates with them because she was working, had small children at home, and had to manage her household. She also felt that her relationship with Howard was suffering because he was spending so much time with Valerie. As a result, she encouraged (almost demanded) that Howard marry Valerie quickly so that, as she put it, "We can have a normal family life."

Howard also felt that courtships were hard on him, as he tried to meet his obligations to his wives, children, and fiancée. There was never enough time to be with his families or to develop a relationship with his future wife. He, too, was glad when courtships were over and they could all work through the new family situation.

Courtship among 19th-century Mormons

The typical courtship of many prospective partners in 19th-century Mormon society was mechanical, businesslike, hurried, and brief. (For comprehensive accounts of life in pioneer plural families, see Embry, 1987; Young, 1954.)[3] As one wife remarked, it was simply inappropriate for a married man to engage in a lengthy or romantic courtship: "Married men didn't do any courting of their plural wives. Why, we would have thought it dishonorable for a mature married man to go sparking [courting] around like a young man. They just came and asked us, and if we wanted them, we agreed [to marriage]" (Young, 1954, p. 129).

A brief or hurried courtship among pioneers may also have been due to the lack of personal experience or cultural norms about how to court in plural families, pressure to enter into plural marriages primarily for religious reasons, and the lack of leisure time in a frontier society. Mounting threats from the federal authorities drove many polygynists into hiding and probably hastened or even prevented courtship. These factors, coupled with the distance between wives and fiancées in different communities, made long courtships among Mormon pioneers difficult, if not impossible in some cases.

Some men and women gradually fell in love, courted over long periods, sometimes engaged in sexual intimacies, and eventually married (Young, 1954). And Embry (1987) pointed to instances of men and women "falling in love," a woman being attracted to a man's smile, personality or friendliness, of men and women falling in love "at first sight," and courting in ways that reflect other than a mechanical or always brief set of encounters. This pattern of romantic love and courtship is consistent with practices among monogamous middle-class Americans of the era (Rothman, 1984). Thus dyadic aspects of courtship varied widely among 19th-century Mormons, from being absent to being a central feature of relationships.

The communal role of established wives in pioneer courtship also seems to have been variable. On occasion, wives participated in courtship (Embry, 1987; Young, 1954). In some cases, courtship was secret, with wives explicitly not involved (Brooks, 1934; Embry, 1987; Goodson, 1976; Young, 1954). In other instances, wives knew and supported (or accepted) the match but did not actively participate in courtship. On the other hand, some wives initiated and were deeply involved. For example, a first wife in one pioneer family not only participated in courtship, but was the "spokesperson" for her husband in the early stages of the relationship (Embry, 1987). In general, however, wives in 19th-century Mormon families seem to have participated only infrequently in courtship, or not consistently from case to case.

Taken together, courtship in our sample of contemporary Mormon fundamentalists, although variable, seems to have focused more consciously on dyadic and communal issues than did courtship in Mormon pioneer plural families. We attribute these differences to a variety of factors, including the social, religious, and political milieu of the era.

Tensions and complexities in courtship

Although many courtships in our sample of contemporary plural families worked out reasonably well, sometimes they were challenging and stressful. During a new courtship, wives are often troubled by feelings of jealousy, loneliness, personal neglect, and a desire for attention and support. And husbands sometimes feel pressure and stress as they struggle to spend time with their wives and families, court a prospective wife, work at their job, and participate in a variety of church activities. Many tensions in courtship derive from the unique demand in plural families to simultaneously satisfy dyadic and communal relationships, a task with which many participants have had little prior experience.

From an established wife's perspective, the situation can be very stressful. She sees her husband in a close, intimate, and often romantic relationship with another woman – who is often younger, seemingly more attractive, and relatively freer of household and child responsibilities than she is. A wife may also see her husband romantically courting the fiancée, treating her in a special way, and taking her on dates and to special places, while she is burdened with an endless array of responsibilities. Feelings of jealousy, loneliness, and the perceived vulnerability of her own dyadic relationship with her husband may mount in her mind, contributing to feelings of stress and worry.

The husband also faces dyadic stresses. On the one hand, he may enjoy the stimulation of a new relationship with a young and perhaps attractive woman. Yet he too may feel that his dyadic relationship with his wife (or wives) is suffering, it is difficult to adjust to the unique personality of another woman, the time and attention he is able to give to his wives and children is insufficient, and the physical and psychic costs of fostering still another close dyadic relationship are draining. The following examples illustrate dyadic and communal stresses experienced by some husbands and wives in plural families.

Family 1
Joan, the first wife, was very jealous during Hal's courtship of Norma, the second wife. For a variety of reasons she and Hal hardly courted before being married, and she felt that they hadn't had a chance to develop a close and intimate relationship. Then shortly after their marriage, he began courting Norma, and for a much longer period than her

own courtship. Once again she felt that their relationship had never had a chance to grow. She was envious of Norma and angry with Hal, believing that he loved Norma more than he loved her and that her marriage was in jeopardy. She withdrew from him, felt alienated and very much alone, and only regained confidence in their relationship after a long personal struggle.

Norma also had a difficult time when Hal courted Cynthia, the fourth wife. She was upset that Hal visited Cynthia without anyone else present. Communal stresses also arose, in that Norma felt that Cynthia was insensitive to the other wives during the whole courtship. For example, when guests were staying with Norma during Christmas, Cynthia insisted that Hal spend time with her and not with them, and in other ways made herself the center of his attention. To make matters worse, Hal didn't correct the situation, and went along with Cynthia's demands.

Family 2

Judith, the first wife, was lonely and jealous when David was courting Rebecca, the second wife, and wondered about his love for her. She was especially upset and felt left out when the courting couple went alone to restaurants and movies. On the other hand, she was very comfortable when the three of them were together.

Rebecca went through the same stresses when David was courting Emily. But her feelings were eased by the fact that she and Judith were good friends and spent a lot of time together – including "having parties" themselves when David and Emily were out alone. And Judith was very understanding of Rebecca's feelings, and helped her through this difficult period.

Family 5

The wives agreed that during courtship they had sometimes been angry with Howard for spending so much time with his latest fiancée, and even felt that he had betrayed and abandoned them, didn't love them as much as he loved the fiancée, and was neglecting them. Constance, the first wife, pointed out that courtships, especially long ones, are especially difficult because a husband is away for too long, the woman being courted is not part of the family, and the wives are not part of the new relationship. It can be quite unsettling as each established wife feels she is competing with a fiancée for the husband's attention and love. For these reasons, Constance, Valerie, Barbara, and Rose agreed that short courtships are best, because they ease the distress experienced by some established wives.

Family 9

As noted earlier, John, Joyce, Clara, and Marjorie agreed that courting Marjorie created some stress in the family. John described his problem as one of maintaining an "emotional balance," meaning that he was torn between wanting to spend time alone with his fiancée Marjorie and also wanting to be home with Joyce and Clara. On their side, they felt that he was spending too much time with Marjorie and neglecting them. We described earlier the plan they finally worked out – John and Marjorie courted alone one evening a week; all of them were together on some nights; and John and each wife had special time alone on a rotating basis.

The time and energy required of all members of a plural family to court a new wife can be extensive. With pressures on wives to work, care for children, manage a home, participate in church affairs, and deal with one another on a regular basis, it is not easy to add another activity to their daily lives, especially one that can be emotionally powerful. Similarly, husbands have heavy ongoing responsibilities while they are involved in a courtship – spending time with each wife and their children, solving family problems, working at one or more jobs, participating in numerous church activities, keeping their personal relationships with wives on an even keel – in essence, maintaining a viable balance of dyadic and communal family processes.

Courtship among 19th-century Mormon polygynists also often involved stresses and strains. For example:

> In the Roger Knight family the first wife was none too pleased when her husband, under the impress of preaching, began paying attention to the hired girl in the home. Moreover, the manner in which he carried on did not improve the first wife's readiness to accept another into the family. Wife number one was pregnant at the time and he would bring the girl into their home nights and make love to her while his wife looked on. "I felt so ungainly and awkward at the time that it was more than I could endure to see the attractive young girl sitting on my husband's lap, being kissed and fondled by him." (Young, 1954, p. 133)

One disappointed wife actively interfered with the courtship; in other cases wives suffered emotionally or were unhappy but were resigned to the process (Young, 1954). Another wife who was angry about her husband's courtship of a woman locked him out of the family home – but to no avail, since the husband eventually married the woman (Embry, 1987).

How do members of contemporary plural families cope with the stresses of courtship? As noted earlier, relatively short courtships are the norm, perhaps to absorb a fiancée into a plural family as quickly as possible so that they can establish stable everyday routines and relationships with one another. Another coping mechanism used by a wife or wives is to facilitate a courtship, speed it up when necessary, or console or counsel wives experiencing stress about aspects of a courtship. In some cases, a husband, wives, and fiancée talk through their stresses and work out acceptable family and courting schedules. Another mode of coping with dyadic and communal strains during courtship is to focus on religious values, the theological basis of polygyny, and to engage in prayer and self-study. Nineteenth-century Mormons seemed to cope with the stresses of courtship in similar ways (Embry, 1987; Young, 1954).

In some cases, successfully coping with the stresses of courtship results in positive outcomes – friendships and strong bonds between wives, reaffirmation of religious beliefs, greater commitment to the idea of plural marriage, and greater self-insight by wives and a husband. In one family wives felt that the challenges of courtship made the husband a "better person":

Family 5

Constance and Valerie said that each courtship brought out the best and worst in Howard, as he struggled anew each time to develop a distinctive relationship with each fiancée and maintain healthy bonds with established wives. They believed that every new courtship helped him become even more sensitive to his relationships with each of them. As such, courtships were a microcosm of their future ideal family, where Howard and each wife would have a unique dyadic relationship, but when there would also be strong communal bonds between all of them.

Many case examples implied, but did not highlight, the fact that courtships vary *across* and *within* families. Not only may different families have unique courtship practices, but courtship may also vary from marriage to marriage within a family. In many respects, each new courtship in a family calls for a unique process, since family circumstances often change on a variety of fronts. Furthermore, life in contemporary plural families is complex for a variety of reasons, not the least of which is that many participants are from monogamous families and monogamous society and have had little experience with plural family life. Because the Mormon polygynous culture as a whole is relatively new, strong societal norms about a variety of life activities, including courtship, have not been firmly established. Thus participants in plural families lack both personal experience and cultural guidance as to how to live in a polygynous lifestyle. As a result, they must experiment and find their own unique individual and family solutions to a variety of everyday issues, including courtship.

The special case of the rural United Fundamentalist Church

As noted earlier, the rural fundamentalist group does not have a formal courtship period. Instead, the prophet of the group arranges and announces many marriages, and weddings take place shortly thereafter, often within a matter of days. Although we heard of cases in which the bride and groom first met at or around the time of their marriage, we also learned that some prospective partners had an informal courtship.

Family 19
As described in chapter 5, Abigail, the first wife, was not at all surprised when the prophet told her that she would marry Horace. She had known him for many years because their families were close, and they had spent a lot of time together as children. She also described an incident about a year and a half before their marriage wherein Horace, a long-distance truck driver, came home for an overnight stay. Her father spontaneously asked if anyone wanted to go on a trucking trip with Horace. Because she liked him, Abigail eagerly volunteered. With parental approval, the young man and Abigail and a friend went on a several-day trip together. She now realizes that her father had probably anticipated the possibility of their eventual marriage and gave them an opportunity to have an informal courtship. It is also possible that Abigail's father – an influential member of the community – had informal discussions with the prophet about the match.

We also heard of other cases in which there had been no formal courtship, but the couple members had known one another for a long time, were compatible, and were not at all surprised when the prophet announced that they would marry. Thus, there are cases in which potential partners informally court or the wishes of individuals or their families play a role in the prophet's decision about a match.

Summary

Courtship among many present-day Mormon fundamentalists consists of both dyadic and communal activities. A man and a woman date, spend time alone, explore their mutual compatibility, and attempt to build a unique dyadic relationship. In so doing, they are similar to monogamous couples in American society. At the same time, courtship among fundamentalists is often communal, with other wives playing an active role. Wives may join the couple on dates or spend time alone with a prospective wife, and the fiancée may visit the family home(s). Thus, as is consistent with fundamentalist values, a marriage is both the dyadic union of a man and a woman and the communal bonding of all members of a plural family. Although there is variation across and within families, many Mormon fundamentalist courtships are fairly brief. And in the rural community, where marriages are arranged, formal courtships are essentially nonexistent, although in some cases individuals and families play an informal role in selecting and facilitating contacts between prospective couple members.

Given the complexity of the process and the relative absence of personal experience and well-grounded cultural precedents, fundamentalist courtships often experience tensions and complexities – jealousy, loneliness, uncertainty by wives about their relationship with the husband, and pressures on husbands to attend to their wives and families while building a new close relationship.

The challenges faced by members of contemporary polygynous families to maintain dyadic and communal family relationships during courtship are similar to the challenges they face in all aspects of life. These challenges derive from the fact that contemporary Mormon fundamentalist families are part of "a culture in search of itself" and must experiment and struggle with a lifestyle with which many participants have relatively little individual, familial, or societal experience. As a result, members of plural families must find their own way, develop their own norms, and cope daily with a complex and often unpredictable set of demands that impinge on their dyadic and communal relationships.

7

Wedding and marriage ceremonies

Wedding ceremonies signify the end of courtship or other premarital events and the formal beginning of a husband–wife relationship. Weddings may consist of a series of activities, including the bride and groom's arrival at a ceremonial site, vows and rituals, gift exchanges, feasts and celebrations, and immediate postnuptial events. Couple members, families, friends, and community members often participate in weddings, playing roles in accordance with cultural practices.

Weddings of present-day Mormon fundamentalists vary with regard to where ceremonies are held, who officiates, who attends, what participants wear, and what role established wives play. At the same time, fundamentalists weddings follow the general format of Western Christian marriage ceremonies. The bride and groom appear before an official of the church, prayers and pronouncements are made regarding the religious basis and importance of marriage, the bride and groom are told of their responsibilities to one another and to their religious values, and the couple exchange vows of love and loyalty. Although a fundamentalist wedding formalizes the dyadic bond between a man and a woman, established wives often participate in the marriage ceremony, thereby also symbolizing the communal nature of weddings and plural family life.

We first describe wedding and marriage ceremonies in a sample of world cultures, to illustrate the variety of ways in which the event is observed. We then turn to the dyadic and communal aspects of marriage ceremonies and the location, management, participants, and tensions and stresses of fundamentalist weddings.

Weddings in other cultures

Marriage and wedding activities in other cultures usually involve some of the following activities.

1. There may be an exchange of bridewealth gifts or dowries, often reflecting the consummation of a "contract" between families that began during courtship. In contrast, in modern Western cultures gifts are usually given to the couple, not to their families, thereby highlighting the central and independent role of the dyad.
2. Elaborate wedding events may occur over an extended period of time, or they may be brief and relatively simple.
3. The mode of arrival of the bride and groom at the wedding place varies across cultures. In some cases, both in Western and other societies, parents escort the bride, and perhaps the groom, to the site. In some cultures, the bride (or groom) is symbolically "captured or abducted" and taken to the wedding place.
4. The couple or some participant often performs an act of commitment to the match: for example, a "vow," gift exchanges between families, or a ritual act finalizing the marriage. In Western cultures, the bride and groom make public vows to one another, following which the wedding official pronounces them to be married.
5. Rituals that immediately follow the wedding may include a feast, party, or reception and, in some cases, participation by guests in a sexual or symbolic consummation of the marriage.
6. After the wedding, there may be a period of isolation or special treatment of the groom and bride, visits to one or both parents' residence, or the traditional western "honeymoon."

Most ethnographic reports of polygynous societies we consulted made hardly any mention of the involvement of established wives in second or later marriages in a family. In contrast, in the urban Church of Latter-day Apostles, whose headquarters are in Metropolitan City, it is customary for wives to actively participate in the wedding ceremony of their husband to a new wife. This is not the always the case for the United Fundamentalist Church in Redrock.

Bridewealth, dowries, and gift exchanges

Gift exchanges are aspects of courtship in many cultures and may also occur during wedding and marriage events. In some cultures, bridewealth gifts or dowries consummate the marriage "contract" between families, and may reflect symbolically the "purchase" of the bride by the groom and his family. In fact, the term "wedding" derives from an earlier historical era in Western society where the bride and groom were pledged to one another by a familial contractual arrangement (Radcliffe-Brown, 1950). During the marriage ceremony, the bridegroom made a symbolic payment – the "wed" – to the bride's family, thereby fulfilling the terms of the contract. The contemporary Western practice of the bride's father "giving away" the bride is a symbolic vestige of marriage as a contract between families.

The payment of bridewealth at weddings is a widespread practice. For example, when a bride of the Masai in Africa arrives at the homestead of the groom's family, she is given a gift of livestock (Talle, 1987). Her acceptance of the animals is a crucial precursor to being married. At North American Tenino Indian weddings, the groom's family makes a gift of horses to the bride's mother and kin, whereupon the families exchange gifts (Murdock, 1980). When a Bedouin of Israel marries a second wife, he "compensates" his first wife with a gift of jewelry equal in value to the jewels he gives to the new wife. This pattern is repeated for the second wife when he marries a third wife (Ginat, personal observation).

In contemporary American society, bridewealth payments to a bride's family are uncommon. However, gift giving to the bride and groom is customary, to help them start their life together. Gifts from parents, family, and friends may include money, household items, or property. Contemporary Mormon fundamentalists also give gifts to newlyweds, albeit modest ones because many families have only limited resources.

Arrival of participants

In many Western cultures the bride and groom proceed separately to the marriage place, usually escorted by their parents or family. Other cultures also have wedding-arrival rituals, some of which symbolize the "purchase" of the bride by the groom and his family, the joyous nature of the event, and the ritual "abduction" or "protection" of the bride.

Bridal processions in medieval Europe during the Protestant Reformation departed from the home of the bride's family accompanied by musicians and young women dressed like the bride (in order to hide her from demons who might steal her away) (Stephens, 1963). The bride's escorts sometimes carried wheat sheaves, later throwing wheat grains on the couple as symbols of their future fertility.

In Bena Bena, New Guinea, the bride's family and clan bring her – hidden among their assemblage – to the homestead of the groom (Langness, 1969). They traverse a path of flowers in the groom's village, make speeches, and open ranks to reveal her. She is dressed in a new skirt and special headdress, and her body is covered with pig fat and has pieces of

ork suspended from her shoulders and waist (pigs are a prime resource in
Bena Bena). She is greeted by the groom's spokesperson, given pork cooked
especially for her, and is then escorted among the men and women of the
groom's clan, to whom she gives gifts of pork.

Some cultures practice symbolic "capture" or "abduction" of the bride
by the groom or his clan, with the bride "forcibly" brought to the wedding
site. The Bedouin of Israel perform ritual abduction after all bridewealth
payments have been made, as a symbol of the bride's transfer to the bridegroom's family (Marx, 1967). At the same time, the fact that the bride is
"abducted" means that she still has ties to her own family because abduction is an "illegal act." These ties are further symbolized by the absence of
the bride's parents at the wedding celebration.[1] Among the Gusii of Africa,
members of the groom's clan seek out the bride from a hiding place and
symbolically capture her (LeVine and LeVine, 1963). In a mock display,
she cries and resists her captors as they bring her to the wedding site.
Similarly, among the Kikuyu of Africa the groom's female relatives capture
the bride. She feigns resistance, and everyone begins laughing, singing, and
dancing (Kenyatta, 1973). In contrast, the !Kung of Africa practice a form
of "groom capture" (Marshall, 1976). In this case, the bride is escorted
voluntarily to the wedding site by her friends, and it is the groom who is
"captured" by his friends and brought to the place of marriage. To our
knowledge, Mormon fundamentalists do not have a specific protocol for
the manner in which brides and grooms arrive at wedding sites; much depends on family circumstances at the time.

Marriage vows and rituals

Many cultures have wedding rituals that formally bond couple members to
one another. In Western cultures, the bride and groom publicly make a
vow before a religious or civil wedding administrator and assembled guests
or witnesses. The vow often includes a commitment "to love, honor, and
cherish [the partner by name] . . . in sickness and health." In medieval Europe, the bride and groom made somewhat similar vows (often involving
commitment by the bride to "obey" the husband). The clergyman conducting the wedding then kissed the groom as a benediction from God, and
the groom "transferred" the benediction to the bride by kissing her. These
rituals clearly symbolized the hierarchical gender relationship of couple
members during the Middle Ages (Stephens, 1963).

Marriage rituals vary widely across cultures. For example, Hindu couples in India join hands and walk around a ritual fire to demonstrate
their marital commitment. In another Indian culture, the groom ties an

ornament around the bride's neck to symbolize their union (Mair, 1977).
A Mendi, New Guinea, bride cuts a gourd with a special knife, and each
member eats half, thereby symbolizing their unity as a couple (Ryan,
1969). (This practice is not unlike the bride and groom cutting their wedding cake in present-day American culture. And it is the bride who either
cuts the gourd or "feeds" the cake to the groom, perhaps in recognition
of future gender roles.) To symbolize the fusing of their lives, the Tai-
wanese bride and groom sit on adjoining stools, over which a single pair
of trousers is draped, with one pant leg on each stool (Fried and Fried,
1980). And Javanese newlyweds exchange potted plants, stand together
on an oxen's yoke, eat from the same bowl, sip water from a common
vessel, and are enclosed in a single shawl by the bride's mother. The
bride also washes the groom's feet as a sign of her deference to him
(Geertz, 1961). A bride of Druze, Israel, places dough on the front door
of the couple's home to indicate that the newlyweds will "stick together"
in the future (Ginat, personal observation). Modern fundamentalist couples make relatively standard marriage Christian vows of love, loyalty
and responsibility to one another. But other wives also make public vows
accepting a new wife, as an expression of the fundamentalist concept of
a unified communal family.

Feasts, celebrations, and postnuptial events

Many cultures celebrate a marriage with feasts, dances, speeches, and other
activities. For example, the groom in the Hottentot culture of Africa provides a cow and hunting game for the marriage celebration (Freeman,
1968). In one Indian culture of Asia, the groom's family provides music at
the wedding feast and the bride's family provides food. The two families
also sponsor separate celebrations in their own villages (Mair, 1977). In
New Guinea Highland cultures, weddings last for two or three days and
include bridewealth payments, eating, singing, gift exchanges, and speeches
of advice to the couple by elders (O'Brien, 1969).

Among Bedouins of Israel, first marriages involve lavish celebrations
whereas wedding events for later wives are much more modest – to some
extent because the state of Israel prohibits polygyny (although cohabitation
is accepted) (Ginat, personal observation). A large tent for guests is decorated with white flags symbolizing purity and peace, and a scarecrow
shaped like a woman wearing a red dress, to denote virginity, is mounted
on the tent. A smaller tent is pitched nearby, and the newlyweds remain in
it for several days. Women guests and relatives spend their time in a third
tent, where they sing and dance hidden from public view. Guests from the
groom's family and community bring a sheep or goat as a gift, and the

occasion is festive. In subsequent marriages, only family and close friends usually attend, and the event is much more modest.

In contemporary American society, a wedding celebration is common – often sponsored by the bride's family, with selective contributions by the groom's family. Depending on wealth and custom, celebrations may be relatively modest or quite opulent. Wedding parties and receptions among contemporary Mormon fundamentalists are often simple, sometimes include only a few people, or may not even occur. A great deal depends on a family's financial and other circumstances.

Some cultures also have sexually oriented rituals following marriage ceremonies. In Western societies of the 16th and 17th centuries, for example, relatives and friends brought the bride and groom to the bedroom after their wedding, often amid joking and teasing (Stone, 1977). It was customary for the bride to remove her gloves before going to bed, to indicate the loss of her virginity. Medieval celebrants then engaged in the "throwing of the stocking" (Stephens, 1963). Two of the groom's friends and two of the bridesmaids threw the couple's stockings over their shoulder, attempting to hit an opposite gender celebrant. If they succeeded, tradition held that the thrower was likely to be married within a year. In contemporary Western cultures, the practice has changed; now the bride throws her bouquet to a group of female friends and relatives, and the person catching the bouquet is said to be the one who will be married next.

Postmarriage activities occur in many cultures. On the wedding night of a Gusii in Africa, for example, the groom prepares for sexual activities by eating bitter herbs and large quantities of coffee beans (which are believed to be an aphrodisiac) (LeVine and LeVine, 1963). The bride seeks to resist his sexual advances by chewing on a piece of charcoal and by putting a piece of knotted grass under the marriage bed. When the couple is escorted to their room after the wedding, the groom's male friends may forcibly disrobe the bride and assist him in achieving sexual intercourse. A Bedouin groom in Libya, Africa, fires a rifle shot in the air to proclaim the symbolic loss of the bride's virginity (Peters, 1965).

Although wedding and marriage events vary from culture to culture, they mark the culmination of the bonding of couple members to one another and symbolize their expected or ideal future role relationships. Family, kin, and friends usually participate in weddings, thereby linking the couple to the broader social contexts of their lives.

Marriages and weddings of Mormon fundamentalists

Many first marriages of Mormon polyginists are legal civil marriages, whereas subsequent plural marriages take place within the fundamentalist church but are not performed by publicly authorized officials or documented in civil records.

Fundamentalist wedding ceremonies vary in several respects. First, marriage ceremonies may be held in any of several places: in church, at home, in the religious leader's home, at a sacred altar, or elsewhere. During the time that the authorities were arresting and prosecuting polygynists, one wedding among our participants was even held at night in the middle of a wheat field. Second, people may wear a variety of wedding clothing, from formal wedding attire to "nice" dresses and suits, to even casual clothing. If a wedding takes place at the sacred altar, however, everyone who participates, including other wives, wears white clothing. Third, although the administrator of a wedding must in some way represent the religious hierarchy in the community, any of several men may officiate. Many weddings are conducted by the prophet or leader of the community, but a religious elder may also conduct weddings. And it is permissible for the groom's father or the bride's father to conduct a wedding, as long as they are religiously observant and are delegated to officiate. When someone other than the group's leader conducts the ceremony, it is presumed that the religious hierarchy has authorized him to do so.

Family 1
Hal and Joan, Hal and Charlotte, and Hal and Cynthia were all married by the religious leader. When Hal and Norma, the second wife, were married, her father officiated at their wedding.

Family 4
Harry's father, a religious leader in the group, officiated at his marriage to Anna. When he and Ruth were married, his father explained to Ruth's father how to conduct the ceremony, and her father then married them. At Harry and Belle's wedding, an elder of the group who subsequently rose to a position of high leadership administered the wedding rites. When Harry married Eve, the fourth wife, her father officiated. In the last marriage, Harry and Shirley were married by a senior religious leader in the community.

Although most husbands and wives readily told us who officiated at their wedding(s) and where they were held, a few were reluctant to do so. Apparently some fundamentalists do not wish to disclose who married them in order to protect the wedding official from prosecution. We were told that this practice was adopted years ago, at a time when the civil authorities were arresting and prosecuting those who were conducting plural marriages. At present, this custom is followed only sporadically.

Family 3

William, Carlyn, Danielle, and Alayna, all rather fervent converts to fundamentalism, would not tell us who conducted their marriages. William was especially adamant on the point, saying that he had made a covenant to maintain secrecy about the matter, in accordance with traditions.

Family 6

When asked who officiated at her marriage to Seymour, Nina replied, "It is not for me to say." Seymour, a religious elder in the group, explained the historical rationale for the custom, adding that the person's name could be disclosed after he died. At the same time, Seymour said that he no longer feels strongly about maintaining secrecy, whereas Nina believes firmly in keeping the covenant. In the same family, Andrea, the fifth wife, didn't hesitate to tell us who married her and Seymour.

Fourth, most fundamentalist weddings are relatively simple, unpretentious, and pragmatic. The wedding ceremony is straightforward and follows Christian and Mormon religious practices, including plural marriage (although this may vary from one fundamentalist group to another).[2]

Fifth, as in most American weddings, family and relatives, friends, and members of the community may attend the ceremonies. The number and configuration of guests depend on the wedding site, desires of the couple and their families, and other factors. In some cases, many guests are present; in other instances, only a few people or the immediate families attend.

Finally, a reception or party, usually modest, sometimes follows a wedding ceremony.

Family 4

There were small receptions for their families following Harry and Anna's wedding and Harry and Eve's wedding (the first and fourth wives). However, there were no receptions when Harry married Ruth, Eve, and Shirley.

Family 5

Wedding receptions were customary in this family, but they usually included only close family members. Several of the wives pointed out that it is up to the bride and groom to decide on a reception. Constance, Barbara, and Rose, the first, third and fourth wives, all had small wedding receptions when they married Howard; Valerie, the second wife, decided not to have a reception.

They also agreed that wedding receptions are usually larger and more elaborate for the first wife than for later wives.

Family 9

When John married Joyce, they were members of the main LDS Church and had a large reception following their wedding. After they joined the fundamentalist group, however, there was no reception following John's marriage to Clara, the second wife.

In contrast, when John and Florence were married, a large reception of more than 100 people was held a week prior to the wedding. This probably was the case because Florence is the daughter of a prominent religious leader in the community and also belongs to a multigeneration fundamentalist family.

Family 3

Danielle, William's second wife, said that they had a small wedding reception, with only a few of his friends attending. They did this because their marriage was kept secret. When William married Alayna, the third wife, she didn't want a reception, but preferred to spend their limited funds on a honeymoon.

The variability and simplicity of wedding and marriage events can be attributed to a combination of factors: the newness of the culture, the pioneer heritage of simplicity, pragmatism, the need to get on with everyday life in a challenging environment and fledgling society, and the modest financial resources of many contemporary fundamentalists.

Dyadic and communal aspects of marriage ceremonies

As in American and Western society, Mormon fundamentalist wedding ceremonies focus on the dyadic union of a bride and groom. Much of the ceremony is directed at the couple, as they stand side by side facing the wedding administrator, or as they kneel facing one another at a sacred religious altar. The marriage rites address the couple members' love, loyalties, rights, and responsibilities to one another, as well as their religious obligations.

What is unique about contemporary fundamentalist practices is that other wives also participate in marriage rites, adding a communal aspect to weddings (this occurs primarily in the urban community). Beyond attending a new wedding, wives often stand with the bride and groom facing the wedding official. Or if the wedding takes place at the sacred altar, they kneel alongside the bride, facing the groom on the other side of the altar.[3] Furthermore, during one part of the ceremony wives are each asked if they give their blessing and consent to the marriage. They are, in effect, asked "if you are willing to stand as Sarah and give this woman to be this man's wife." This reference to the biblical patriarch Abraham and his wife Sarah sanctions the idea of plural marriage. The practice of asking an established wife's support of a plural marriage began in the early days of Mormonism. Dorothy Solomon recalled that at the wedding of her grandfather to a second wife, "when President Ivins [the wedding officiator] asked [the first wife], 'Do you, Charlotte, willingly give this sister in eternal marriage to our husband?' Charlotte had murmured perhaps her only words of the day: 'I do' " (Solomon, 1984, p. 3).

Another way in which established wives communally participate in the marriage of their husband to a new wife follows early church doctrine enunciated by Orson Pratt in 1852. The established wife is told: "If you [approve of the marriage], you will manifest it by placing her right hand within the right hand of your husband" (Young, 1954, p. 45).

Similarly, a 19th-century plural marriage ceremony has been described as follows: "The first wife stood in between her husband and the bride during the ceremony and, after agreeing to give the woman to her husband, she was instructed to place the bride's right hand in her husband's" (Goodson, 1976, p. 99).

In her autobiography, a contemporary plural wife commented on her feelings as she placed the bride's hand in her husband's hand, and then placed her own hand on theirs:

> This would symbolize my support of the union. I would be agreeing to share him with her – not till death parted them as are the ways of the world – but for time and eternity. This was to establish our way of life forever. He would no longer be "my" husband but "ours," and as time passed, perhaps we would be called upon to share his love with other wives. (Merrill, 1975, p. 8)

It is also customary for the *most recent* wife to place the bride's hand in the husband's hand, thereby symbolizing the newest wife's overt communal commitment to share her husband with the bride, just as another wife did when she entered the family. It is also customary for the most recent wife to then place her own hand on top of the clasped hands of the bride and groom. The other wives follow suit, placing their hands on top of the other hands. This reflect the communal unity of the husband and wives. Thus the fundamentalist Mormon marriage ceremony symbolizes *both* the dyadic bonding of a man and a woman and the communal bonding of the bride and other wives. The wedding is, in effect, a marriage both of a man and a woman and of a bride and wives to one another.

The following examples illustrate the dyadic and communal aspects of wedding ceremonies and the variation in those of contemporary fundamentalists.

Family 6

Seymour, who has seven wives, is a long-standing leader in the funda
mentalist movement and is very knowledgeable about church doctrine
and traditions. He described the ideal flow of events, although he said
that it wasn't always followed and that it wasn't a serious matter if there
were deviations.

Ideally, all wives should attend the wedding ceremony of a new wife
The correct arrangement is for the wives to stand on the left side of the
husband, with the bride closest to the husband and the other wives to
her left. Following the wives' approval of the marriage, the most recent
wife places the bride's and groom's hands together in a "patriarchal
grip" – essentially a handshake. Then each wife places her hand over
the hands of the bride and groom to symbolize the unity of the family.

In performing this act, the wives position themselves behind and be
tween the couple. When the marriage is performed at a sacred altar,
however, the wives reach across the altar to place their hands on those
of the bride and groom.

Family 1

In Hal's first plural marriage to Norma, they stood side by side; Joan,
the first wife, stood behind and between them. When he and Charlotte,
the third wife, were married, she stood on his left and the two other
wives were to his right. Hal and Cynthia, the fourth wife, were married
at the sacred altar. They knelt on one side of the sacred altar, and Joan,
Norma, and Charlotte knelt on the other side of the altar. In each mar
riage the most recent wife gave the hand of the bride to the husband in
the patriarchal grip.

Seymour, an elder from another family who joined in the discussion,
jokingly commented: "You did it all wrong. They should have *all* stood
on your left side. And the bride has to be the closest to you and then
the others are to the left. And they are to stand in a row. So you did it
all wrong!" After some good-natured banter, they all agreed that it really
didn't matter where people stood, even though Seymour was technically
correct, according to tradition.

Family 2

David's wives – Judith, Rebecca, and Emily – attended all weddings and
gave their consent in each case, including the most recent marriage to
Phyllis. David, an up and coming young church leader, said that it really
doesn't matter where wives stand at a marriage ceremony, and it isn't
even absolutely necessary for the newest wife to give the hand of the
bride to the husband. It is custom, he said, but is not required.

Family 4

When Harry, a senior leader in the rural Redrock community, married his first wife, Anna, and his second wife, Ruth, the only people present were the fathers of the bride and the groom. And Anna was not present at Harry and Ruth's wedding. Nor did Anna or Ruth attend the wedding of Harry and Belle, the third wife. When Harry and Eve were married, however, all the wives were present, although they didn't participate in the ceremony or give the bride's hand to him. None of the wives attended Harry and Shirley's wedding. When queried about not following customs, he said, "We don't follow all that 'goop' about patriarchal grips, placing a bride's hand in the groom's, and so on. We just get married in a straight and simple way."

Although not all fundamentalist marriages follow the full set of ideal practices, many other people said that wives often attend weddings in their family, are asked to give their consent to a new marriage, place the bride's hand in the husband's hand, and then put their own hand on the couple's joined hands. Although other features of weddings vary somewhat from case to case, these basic elements seem consistent. As such, they indicate that wedding ceremonies and cultural customs address both dyadic and communal aspects of husband–wife relationships among Mormon fundamentalists.

Wedding clothing. The dyadic bonding of the couple members is also symbolized in their clothing, as it is in the larger monogamous culture. In most cases, the fundamentalist bride and groom dress up for their marriage, although clothing may vary from family to family and marriage to marriage within families. Some brides wear a white wedding gown, a white religious garment, or a white dress. However, many brides wear dresses of another color. It is also customary for a groom to dress up, usually in a suit and tie; in some cases, grooms even wear a tuxedo. If the marriage takes place at a sacred altar, the bride and groom (and other wives) wear white clothing or religious garments.[4] Thus although a bride and groom have considerable latitude about what they wear at their wedding, dressing up is customary and reflects the importance of the dyadic event.

The clothing worn by other wives at weddings illustrates communal aspects of plural family life. They, too, dress up in their best clothing in acknowledgment of the importance of the event. And like the bride and groom, they may wear a variety of colors and styles. We were even told of a wife who wore her own wedding dress to the marriage of her husband and a new wife. Although only an anecdote, it may symbolize the established wife's "marriage" to the bride as a future sister–wife and member of the communal family or may signify a reaffirmation of her marriage to the husband. In another instance, we were told of a wife who wore especially plain clothing to her husband's wedding to a new wife in order to express her dissatisfaction with the event.

Family 1
At their wedding, Joan, the first wife, wore a white dress, and Hal wore a tuxedo. When Hal and Norma and Hal and Charlotte, were married, he wore a blue suit and they wore white dresses. When Cynthia, the fourth wife, and Hal were married at the sacred altar, he wore a white suit and the bride and three wives wore white temple garments.

Family 2
None of the four marriages in this family took place at the sacred altar. At each wedding David wore a suit and tie, and each bride wore a white dress. Wives also dressed up at each other's weddings, but they usually didn't wear white dresses. Rebecca, the second wife, did recall, however, that she once wore a white dress at one of the weddings of another wife. The others agreed that it was perfectly acceptable to do so. In fact, they told of cases in which everyone wore white, even when the marriage didn't take place at the sacred altar. To emphasize the significance of the event, Rebecca said that she made a new dress for herself for each wedding in the family.

Family 3
The family has always struggled financially, so that weddings have been quite simple. William always dressed up in his best clothing at his three marriages, and each bride did her best to do so as well. When he married Carlyn, the first wife, she wore a friend's wedding dress. Danielle, the second wife, also borrowed a friend's dress, although it was not formal wedding attire. And Alayna, the third wife, married William in her high school graduation dress.

Family 5
Howard wore a suit at each of the four weddings in the family. Everyone laughed when Valerie, the second wife, reminded them that Howard wore the very same tie to three of their weddings. Connie, Valerie, Barbara, and Rose didn't remember the specific dresses they wore at their weddings, although they remembered them to be white. They did say that their dresses were not especially elaborate since they couldn't afford expensive clothing.

They also did not remember what dresses they wore at each other's weddings, although they agreed that they always dressed up. They also pointed out, however, that it was the sacred events at marriage cere-monies that were important, not the clothing they wore.

Dressing formally at their own and their co-wives' weddings was cus-tomary in most families in our sample, although styles varied from family to family and marriage to marriage within families.

Family 6
As a special custom, Seymour's fourth wife, Tamara, said that he always bought a new pair of shoes at each of his weddings. Now, she said, whenever he comes home wearing new shoes she worries that he is think-ing about marrying another wife. The other wives laughed when she told this story; Seymour merely smiled coyly.

Family 12
At their wedding, Fred and Lauren, the second wife, dressed informally. She wore blue jeans and a simple blouse; he wore everyday pants and a shirt. They were married during a period when the authorities were clamping down on plural marriages, and since she was a minor at the time, their situation was precarious. As a result, they were married hast-ily and secretly, with little fanfare, celebration, or publicity.

Tensions and stresses in wedding ceremonies

Plural marriage weddings do not always proceed smoothly. Our partici-pants did not say much about their feelings at the time of weddings, and there is not a great deal in the pioneer literature or in contemporary bi-ographies about this subject. Nevertheless, some of the information we gleaned suggested that weddings can be stressful.

Our sense is that both dyadic and communal factors make plural family weddings stressful. Some wives even described the event as a threat to their own dyadic relationship with the husband. And wives who were not per-sonally compatible with the bride could see communal difficulties ahead. In spite of their feelings, some wives participated in, or at least attended, wedding ceremonies. In other instances, a disgruntled wife did not attend a wedding.

Family 13
Muriel was very unhappy about Paul's marriage to Gloria, the first plu-ral wife-to-be. Paul and Muriel had been married for several years, and although she agreed to live in a plural family, she was very upset when it came down to an actual wedding. After she gave her consent during the ceremony, she found herself unable to place Gloria's hand in Paul's

hand. She was so upset that she collapsed and had to be supported during the rest of the ceremony.

Family 14

Sally, Harvey's second wife, told an interesting story about her own mother and father. Although they believed in the principle of plural family life, they had been married monogamously for almost 50 years. In their 70s, the father wanted to marry another woman in order to satisfy religious doctrine. Sally's mother resisted strenuously but eventually consented on religious grounds, participated in the wedding ceremony, and even placed the bride's hand in her husband's. But she still resented the marriage and at the time the story was told to us was considering divorcing the husband, feeling that he had betrayed her after all their years together.

Family 9

Joyce and John had been married for 20 years when they decided to add Clara to their family. Although she strongly favored the marriage, Joyce said it "was a hell of a time" during the few days before the wedding. The idea of a new wife in the family and fears about her relationship with John and Clara resulted in considerable anxiety. But after thinking it through and recognizing that she was committed to plural family life, Joyce felt fine at the marriage ceremony.

In the following case, a wife was angry with her husband because of the way he handled their wedding in comparison with those of the other wives in the family.

Family 3

William's marriage to Danielle, the second wife, was kept secret, because he was afraid it would become known to the authorities and to their supervisors and colleagues at work. As a result, she didn't tell anyone about the marriage, wore no wedding ring, had a small wedding reception that he organized and to which her family was not invited. She described the event as a "humbling experience bordering on humiliation." What added to her bitter feelings was that the other wives had had open and festive weddings. For years afterward, she had a hard time "choking" out of her mind anger about what she termed her "nonwedding." And Danielle expects her negative feelings to arise again when William marries a new wife. William admitted that he had blundered when it came to his and Danielle's marriage, was apologetic, and said that he would be sensitive about such matters in the future.

Summary

Wedding ceremonies among contemporary Mormon fundamentalists illustrate a blend of dyadic and communal processes. On the one hand, marriage ceremonies focus on the dyadic union of a man and a woman. On the other hand, they embed the couple in the social context of the plural family. Unique to fundamentalists, other wives often play a central role in marriage ceremonies. They publicly consent to the marriage, symbolically "give" the bride to their husband, and then join hands with the bride and groom. These rituals reflect acknowledgment of the unique dyadic relationship between the bride and groom and the communal unity of wives with one another and with the husband.

Although wedding vows are prescribed by Mormon religious doctrine, they also reflect a blend of customary practices and permissible variations. For example, weddings are usually administered by qualified religious leaders, including the religious leader or certain religious elders. If granted permission by the religious hierarchy, others may also perform wedding ceremonies, including the father of the groom or bride. Although a marriage ceremony must be presided over by a "qualified" religious person, there is some flexibility as to who can do the job.

Wedding ceremonies also vary in the position of the participants. Custom calls for the bride to stand to the left of the groom, with other wives on her left and with everyone facing the wedding administrator (except for marriages at the sacred altar). However, this arrangement is not always followed. Some weddings do not rigidly adhere to the custom, some people and administrators are not aware of proper positioning, and it does not seem to be a matter of great importance.

It is also customary for all participants – bride, groom, and attending wives – to dress up. Although participants must wear white clothing or ceremonial garb when a marriage takes place at the group's sacred religious altar, there is no prescribed dress elsewhere. The bride and other wives may wear any color dress, although white dresses are worn by many brides. The groom usually wears a suit. Again, although custom calls for "dress-up" clothing, it is not absolutely required, and the couple may follow personal preferences for color and style.

In addition, weddings can take place almost anywhere – the sacred religious altar, the prophet's home, the bride's or groom's parents' home, or elsewhere. Any wedding location seems to be perfectly acceptable. And there are variations in post-wedding events. Sometimes there is a celebratory reception, sometimes not. And when a reception is held, it varies in its participants and scale. Indeed, weddings also vary in their marriage officiators, location, the involvement of other wives, the position of participants, wedding receptions, and other events and roles.

In contrast to many other cultures, contemporary fundamentalists have simple, short, and pragmatic wedding activities. They do not engage in elaborate brideprice or dowry negotiations and gift exchanges; there are no formal practices about brides and grooms arriving at wedding sites; the vows taken by participants are relatively straightforward and simple; weddings are not elaborate in terms of dress, receptions, and feasts; there are no prescribed postnuptial rituals. There is, therefore, considerable freedom to shape events from wedding to wedding, depending on the desires of the participants.

There are probably many reasons for the flexibility of fundamentalist weddings. Their heritage is one of simplicity and pragmatism; its roots lie in a pioneer culture that struggled to survive amid difficult environmental and social challenges. They also have a history of arrests and prosecution, which often led to hurried, secret, and simple weddings. In addition, immediate and extended families can be quite large, so that elaborate weddings are likely to be very expensive – and to occur often. Because many present-day fundamentalists are working people with limited resources, elaborate weddings are just not possible.

Variations in wedding practices are also consistent with other aspects of life in contemporary Mormon polygynous families. Plural family living is a new experience for many participants, and they continually struggle to succeed in their complex dyadic and communal relationships. Furthermore, their relatively new culture itself provides only minimal guidance as to how to balance dyadic and communal processes. As a result, flexibility, trial and error, and experimentation are commonplace in the day-to-day life of contemporary plural families, including their wedding ceremonies. This variability reflects our theme of an emerging "culture in search of itself."

8

Honeymoons

In Western cultures the honeymoon is a transition between a couple's wedding and the time they settle into everyday married life. The modern honeymoon is usually a dyadic event that enables the bride and groom to be alone with one another, away from family and friends and often in a special place. In many cases the honeymoon site is kept secret by the couple, and they often steal away after the wedding ceremony to embark on their private trip. In the contemporary Western stereotype, the husband and wife engage in seemingly endless sexual and interpersonal intimacies and are free from everyday responsibilities. It is a phase of marriage, albeit brief, during which the two direct all of their energies to one another and to the uniqueness of their relationship. The modern honeymoon is the ultimate dyadic experience, to use the term of our analysis.

Although contemporary Mormon fundamentalists generally follow Western cultural traditions, honeymoons vary across and within families. However, the special challenge for the fundamentalist couple is how to achieve a unique dyadic relationship on the honeymoon, and simultaneously maintain dyadic and family communal relationships with other wives. In other words, is the honeymoon a strictly dyadic event, with the couple completely cut off from other members of a plural family?

The chapter first describes honeymoon or post-wedding activities in a few other cultures and in earlier periods in Western societies. It then turns to honeymoons of present-day Mormon fundamentalists and the stresses and challenges faced by family members.

Historical and cultural differences in honeymoons

Before the 18th century, newly married couples in some Western societies traveled and visited family and friends for weeks or longer, often with no opportunity to be alone (Stone, 1977). By the late 18th and early 19th centuries, however, newlyweds began to go away alone on a post-wedding trip, in accordance with the changing view of marriage (Rothman, 1984). That is, the concept of the couple simply as an agent of the extended family was giving way to that of the independent dyad and nuclear family as the primary societal unit.

Many cultures have a transitional period between weddings and the beginning of married life, although they differ widely in its purpose, participants, activities, and duration. At one extreme, the !Kung of Africa, a nomadic group, have simple weddings, and no post-wedding period for newlyweds (Marshall, 1976). The wedding consists of the mothers of the bride and groom cooperatively building a wedding fire and a wedding hut midway between their two encampments, the "capture" of the groom by his friends, and a celebration at the site by friends of the couple. The only post-wedding activity occurs the next morning, when the bride's mother rubs her body with fat and draws special designs on her face with red powder. There is no "honeymoon" or other activity; the couple immediately lives an everyday !Kung life. The Iban of Borneo have a slightly longer transitional period (Stephens, 1963). After the wedding the couple spends a few days in the home of the groom's parents and then briefly visit the bride's family before settling in their own dwelling.

Many other cultures have extended post-wedding activities that may last for weeks or months. Javanese newlyweds, for example, live with the bride's parents for about a month. During this time they are isolated from the community and rarely leave the dwelling (Geertz, 1961). They subsequently visit the groom's parents, who give a party in their honor. It is not uncommon for the couple to live with either of the parents for up to a few years, until they are able to establish their own residence. This pattern of post-wedding events and living arrangements reflects both dyadic, couple-oriented practices during early stages of married life and the couple's communal involvement with both sets of parents.

Other examples come from the Gusii of Africa (Le Vine and Le Vine, 1963) and the Bedouin of Israel (Marx, 1967). Following their wedding, a Gusii couple lives in the groom's family's homestead for two to three months. The bride then lives with her parents for a couple of months, after which she returns to live permanently with her husband. Among Bedouins of Israel, the newly married couple is not fully independent of the groom's family until a few months after their marriage, sometimes only after the birth of their first child.

In some instances, weddings and post-wedding activities are continuous and almost inseparable. Among the Kikuyu of Africa, wedding events occur for several days, beginning with the "capture" of the bride and her "abduction" to the homestead of the groom's parents, where she lives for eight days in a hut built specially for her (Kenyatta, 1973). A variety of festivities occur during that period, and the bride is visited by boys and girls of her age group. She receives gifts and entertains them with songs about her loss of the companionship of friends. The bride does not do any work during this period, and she only leaves the hut when accompanied by her female friends. Each evening the bride and groom are left alone in the hut until the next morning, when the activities are repeated. On the eighth day, she is anointed with sheep oil to indicate her adoption into the groom's family. For a while thereafter she visits her parents periodically, always returning in the evening. As in other cases, Kikuyu marriage and post-wedding customs focus on the dyadic relationship between the bride and groom and on a variety of communal relationships between the bride and her friends, family, and the groom's family.

One unique example showing a difference between first and later marriages is found in Bedouin society in Israel (Ginat, personal observation). As mentioned in chapter 7, first marriages involve an elaborate wedding celebration over a period of several days, whereas later marriages are quite modest. There is no counterpart to honeymoons for first marriages, although in recent years the husband and each subsequent wife have been known to take a private trip with one another for a few days.

Honeymoons in contemporary plural families

Several questions arise regarding honeymoons of contemporary polygynous couples. What kind of honeymoon do they have and how long does it last? More important, are honeymoons in plural families primarily dyadic, involving only a groom and bride, as is the case in American culture at large? Or do honeymoons have communal aspects that involve other wives, as in courtships and weddings? And do family tensions and stresses develop when newlyweds are away from other wives in a plural family?

General characteristics of honeymoons

First, it is customary for a fundamentalist bride and groom to have a honeymoon following their wedding. Honeymoon trips occur in many marriages, whether a first marriage or a subsequent plural marriage. However, honeymoons are not universal or required, for various reasons: the need to keep a plural marriage secret, work obligations, family circumstances, finances, and other factors.

Second, as in American culture at large, honeymoons offer newlyweds the opportunity to be alone for a period of time in order to "get to know one another," exchange intimacies, and celebrate and initiate their marriage. Thus honeymoons have a strong dyadic aspect, as they do in other cultures.

Third, most polygynous honeymoons are celebrated away from the community, family, and friends. Although some couples visit relatives for part of their honeymoon trip, this is rare. Most seek out places where they can be alone, as is typical of a dyadic honeymoon. At times, however, honeymoons may involve communal actions by husbands and established wives.

Fourth, honeymoon trips are usually not extravagant, and no couples in our study reported flying to distant places, staying at fancy hotels, or going on luxury cruises. Honeymoons are simple, because few contemporary Mormon fundamentalists are wealthy and opulent celebrations are not part of their pioneer heritage. Honeymoons are celebrated in nearby cities or at modest resorts, in national and state parks, in camping settings, and the like.

Fifth, most honeymoons are brief; they usually last only a few days and rarely longer than a week owing to the expense, lost work time, and the difficulty of being away from other wives and children.[1]

Dyadic and communal aspects of honeymoons

The honeymoon is a powerful dyadic experience for contemporary polygynous couples. They go away alone as a couple, often to special places, and other wives do not join them. Sometimes they collect mementos of their honeymoon. Not only do many newlyweds go away alone, but each couple in a family usually visits a different place, thereby enhancing the idea that each husband–wife couple has a unique dyadic relationship.

Family 1
Hal and a wife whom he subsequently divorced spent a week on their honeymoon trip at the Grand Canyon. He and Joan celebrated their honeymoon on a three-day trip to a city in the region. Following their marriage, Hal and Norma, the current second wife, spent three days camping in the southern part of their home state. Hal and Charlotte, the third wife, celebrated their honeymoon on a three-day trip to a neighboring state to the north. Finally, Hal and Cynthia visited a nearby resort for three days following their wedding.

Cynthia remembered her honeymoon with great pleasure. When we toured her home, she eagerly showed us her honeymoon album, which was artistically prepared. The album contains photographs of her and Hal, prose and poetry she wrote celebrating the event, calligraphy, and souvenirs, such as tickets of admission to shows and museums. Hal also expressed pride in her artistic talents and told of the fun they had on their honeymoon.

Family 5

On their honeymoon, Howard and Constance visited a national park for three days. When he and Valerie were married, they spent a one-day honeymoon in a different national park. And Howard and Barbara, the third wife, visited a resort for three days after they were married. Finally, Howard and Rose celebrated their marriage on a three-day honeymoon in the southern part of their state. All of these honeymoons were camping trips.

Family 9

John and Joyce, the first wife, went on a honeymoon trip in their home region. He and Clara, the second wife, spent their honeymoon in the region where she grew up, also visiting with her family. When John and Florence married, they observed their honeymoon in the state where he was born and grew up. Each honeymoon lasted four or five days.

Family 3

William and Carlyn, the first wife, spent several days on their honeymoon visiting his family in one state and her family in another state. He and Danielle, the second wife, did not have a honeymoon because they kept their marriage secret. When he and Alayna were married, they went away alone for a few days.

Not all families celebrate honeymoons, nor are they of similar duration.

Family 4

Harry and Anna, Ruth, and Shirley, the first, second, and fifth wives, respectively, did not have a honeymoon. Harry and the third wife, Belle, had a one-day honeymoon; Harry and Eva, the fourth wife, celebrated their marriage on a four-day honeymoon. Whether they had a honeymoon and how long it lasted varied with the demands of everyday life.

Although honeymoons testify to the importance of the marital dyad, communal actions also sometimes occur. For example, successive honeymoons within plural families are often similar in length, cost, and type of activity so as to ensure that each relationship is treated fairly and to reinforce the ideal of a unified communal family. Furthermore, although economic factors probably play a role, the brevity of honeymoons may also minimize a husband's (and a new wife's) time away from others in the family, not only to allow him to attend to family needs and his relationships with other wives but also to hasten the new wife's entry into the family's day-to-day life.

In some cases, a husband may be sensitive to established wives' feelings about him going off on a honeymoon with a new, often younger wife, and he will try to reaffirm the importance of his and their dyadic bonds. In so doing, a husband also acknowledges the communal unity of the family and of all husband–wife and wife–wife relationships.

Family 2

As described later, Judith, Rebecca, and Emily, David's first three wives, each experienced stress when David went on a honeymoon with his newest bride. In discussing this, David said that he should have been sensitive to their feelings earlier, but realized how they felt when he married Phyllis, the fourth wife. While on that honeymoon he made a point of regularly telephoning each of the other wives to see how they were doing. The wives agreed that this greatly helped to ease their feelings of stress and also made it easier for them to feel good about Phyllis and her future role in the family.

Sometimes wives help one another deal with the stresses of honeymoons.

Family 2

Judith, Rebecca, and Emily readily told of their feelings of jealousy, abandonment, and worry about David's love for them during each honeymoon with a new wife (strongest when each was the most recent wife and hadn't previously experienced his marriage to a new woman).

However, they also supported one another emotionally during honeymoons and fostered a communal feeling among themselves. For example, Judith and Rebecca said that they "partied" every night when David and Emily were away on a honeymoon. The two wives at home went to the movies, had meals together, and spent a great deal of time with one another. They agreed that they had a lot of fun during David's and Emily's honeymoon.

Emily reported that she, Judith, and Rebecca also spent time with one another when David was on honeymoon with Phyllis, the fourth wife. She also said that she was able to discuss her feelings of loneliness, jealousy, and anxiety with the other wives and that they helped her a great deal. They in turn described how they kept her busy, encouraged her to express her feelings to them, and tried to be with her as much as possible during this stressful and uncertain time.

The husband and wives in another family also acted to preserve the dyadic and communal underpinnings of their family, although they did so in a different way.

Family 9

Joyce, John's first wife for 20 years, had a difficult time during his honeymoon with Clara. She said, "Those were five long days." And even though she wanted to be alone with John when the newlyweds returned from their honeymoon, she insisted that he spend the first night home with Clara, because she felt that Clara would feel isolated after having been alone with him during their honeymoon. She went on to emphasize that wives in plural families must be sensitive to one another and think more about others than about themselves. Thus she said that she was only trying to help Clara adjust when the honeymoon was over.

When John and Florence, the third wife, married and went on their honeymoon, Joyce and Clara spent a great deal of time together, talking about their feelings about the newest marriage and their relationships with John and Florence. They admitted experiencing some anxiety about this new marriage, even though they supported it. After all, Florence was young and attractive, and they worried about how John would feel about them after the new couple returned home.

But their fears were allayed when John and Florence came home. He greeted each of them warmly, hugged and kissed them, and expressed his love for them. Joyce described how relieved she was; her feelings of loneliness and neglect had vanished, and she felt wanted and needed by John. What also made it easier was that she had bonded with Florence and tried to support all of their relationships with John and with one another. Clara confirmed everything Joyce said and also mentioned that John had swept away her feelings of nervousness by being warm and supportive when he and Florence returned from their honeymoon.

Tensions and stresses during honeymoons

As the preceding examples illustrate, new marriages and honeymoons are not without their stresses and strains. The honeymoon can be a time of emotional upheaval, especially for established wives who are "left behind" as the new couple goes off on a romantic pleasure trip to celebrate their marriage. Some wives feel abandoned, some are jealous about the husband being with a younger and seemingly more attractive woman, some worry that the husband will not love them anymore, and some feel neglected and lonely. A wife who did not have a honeymoon herself may be especially upset and jealous.

Such negative feelings among established wives are understandable. After all, the very purpose of the honeymoon is to foster a close and intimate relationship between newlyweds, which might be seen by other wives as a threat to their own dyadic relationship with the husband. And being "left behind" and out of touch with their husband, even for a short period of time, may accentuate their feelings of anxiety. Furthermore, many wives were not raised in plural families, so that the honeymoon of their husband with a new wife contradicts the American monogamous concept of marriage as a unique and intimate bond between one man and one woman.

Family 18

When Charles and Nancy, the second wife, went on a honeymoon, the first wife, Susan, told us, "I was not very happy. Even though we wanted to abide by the principle of plural marriage, it was not easy seeing him go off on a honeymoon with someone else. After all, we had been married for more than 20 years when he married her. I wanted to see and be with him, and I felt peculiar about the whole thing."

She explained how natural it was for her to be insecure when her husband was with another woman, and she told us that she slept very little during the time of the honeymoon. But she coped through prayer: "What really helped me was my testimony. I prayed and asked the help of the Lord."

Family 2

The three wives in this family who experienced a new marriage and honeymoon of their husband David all remembered worrying about their relationship with him. After a couple of days into David's and Rebecca's honeymoon, for example, Judith, the first wife, began to wonder whether he remembered her or still loved her. And Rebecca had the same feelings when David was away with Emily on their honeymoon. Had he forgotten all about her? Was she going to be neglected and abandoned in favor of Emily? And the cycle repeated itself when David married Phyllis. Emily wondered if David missed her or if he even loved her anymore.

They did admit, however, that it became easier with successive marriages and that they did support one another during the honeymoons. As noted earlier, they even had fun "partying" together when David and his newest bride were off on a honeymoon.

Family 9

Joyce, John's wife of 20 years, described her experience during John's and Clara's honeymoon. She recalled leaving the wedding ceremony alone to go home, after watching the newlyweds depart on their honeymoon. The first few days that they were gone were all right, as she kept busy with various chores and activities. But by the fifth day she began to worry and feel anxious. She claimed not to be jealous but felt lonely, needed to talk with him about various matters, and wanted him to tell her that he loved her.

Loneliness, fear of the loss of love, and the threat to a wife's relationship with her husband are not the only sources of stress during honeymoons. Sometimes a wife's negative feelings are directed at the new wife or husband because of their actions.

Family 1

As described in an earlier chapter, Norma, the second wife, was upset about Hal's courtship with Cynthia, the fourth wife. She also resented the fact that immediately after their honeymoon, Cynthia insisted that Hal spend more time with her than with the other wives. Norma felt that Cynthia was insensitive to the fact that the other wives also needed to be with him, especially since they had been alone during the honeymoon. She was also angry that Hal was passive about the whole matter and didn't seem to appreciate how she and the other wives felt.

There are other reasons for wives being upset about new honeymoons in their family, including the fact they did not have a honeymoon whereas other wives did or feelings of inequity about the length or other features of their honeymoon.

Family 3

As already mentioned, Danielle, the second wife, resents to this day William's insistence at the time that their wedding be kept secret. As a result, she felt that it was not properly celebrated and that they did not have a honeymoon. What made matters worse was that William and Carlyn, the first wife, had a nice honeymoon visiting their families and attending receptions in their honor. And Alayna, the third wife, and William also had a honeymoon.

Family 1

Not only did Joan feel mistreated by a first wife (who later divorced Hal), but she resented the fact that her honeymoon with Hal was too short. She was envious that Hal and that wife had a week-long honeymoon, whereas hers was half as long. Then Hal married Norma shortly thereafter. The combination of being treated badly by the first wife, not having an adequate honeymoon, and Norma entering the family so soon made Joan feel that she had not been able to develop an adequate emotional relationship with Hal. Although she and Hal are now secure in their marriage, she expressed her feelings about this earlier period with considerable emotion.

Sometimes new wives also experience some anxiety about honeymoons, especially in relation to established wives.

Family 9
Florence, the third wife, told how difficult it was for her to return home from her honeymoon and face the other two wives. She was young, felt inexperienced compared with the other wives, and said that she felt like a stranger. She wondered how she was supposed to behave with them and with John. As she and John drove up to the house, she remembers saying to herself: "I wish I could be with my momma."

And it is not always easy for husbands.

Family 9
John described how strange he felt as he and Clara, the second wife, began their honeymoon. After all, he said, he had been happily married to Joyce for 20 years, had never been with another woman during that time, and here he was, in a car and on a honeymoon with a new wife. He felt nervous, naive, and uncomfortable knowing that he would be spending the night with a new wife, a young woman. He wasn't sure how to behave. It was fairly stressful.

Summary

As in American society at large, honeymoons of contemporary fundamentalists are strongly dyadic. The newly married couple, whether it be a first marriage or a plural marriage, usually goes on a short trip alone – away from home, other wives and children, work, and the community. The honeymoon symbolizes the unique and intimate relationship of the new husband and wife. The distinctive dyadic quality of this relationship is also clear from the fact that couples within families usually celebrate their honeymoons in different places.

At the same time, contemporary Mormon polygynous honeymoons often have a communal quality. Some husbands telephone or maintain contact with other wives during their honeymoons. And honeymoons tend to be relatively brief, thereby reducing the time newlyweds spend away from the family. Furthermore, honeymoons in plural families tend to be similar in length and cost, in "fairness" to the other wives. Finally, established wives sometimes provide social and emotional communal support to one another during a new honeymoon in the family.

Nevertheless, honeymoons can be stressful to members of contemporary plural families. Established wives are sometimes jealous and envious, feel lonely and abandoned by their husband, wonder whether he still loves them, and worry about their dyadic relationship with their husband. New wives and husbands, too, may experience stress during honeymoons – wondering and worrying about how they will relate to established wives as a result of the new marriage. Thus the honeymoon may create an upheaval and tension in both the dyadic and communal aspects of plural family life.

Modern plural families develop their own customs and practices for honeymoons and for dealing with the inevitable stresses and complexities of this earliest phase of new marriages. The honeymoon period is another example of the emerging and experimental nature of contemporary plural family life, as participants struggle to achieve a satisfactory balance of dyadic and communal family processes in their distinctive way of life.

Adjusting to a new plural marriage

With their honeymoon and wedding behind them, newlyweds begin everyday life together. A period of adjustment ensues, spanning weeks or months, in which couple members learn how to live with one another, accept each other's idiosyncrasies, and work to forge a viable dyadic relationship. The high incidence of marital divorce or separation, reports of marital stress and discord, and the use of professional counseling services suggest that monogamous couples in contemporary society often fail to cope successfully with both long-run and early problems in their relationships. Even in marriages that eventually succeed, initial adjustments can be challenging, complex, and stressful.

Hard as it may be for monogamous relationships to gain a firm footing, the earliest stage of marriage in a polygynous marriage is fraught with even greater challenges. Not only must newlyweds learn to relate to one another, but other wives are also in the picture. New and complex relationships emerge from the new configuration of wives, or between the husband and his established wives and new wife. One husband used the atom to describe the early days and months of a new marriage. Before a new wife joins a plural family, the family is like a stable atom, with the husband at the nucleus, and the wives revolving around him like electrons. But when a new wife joins a family, the stability of the family is disrupted and thrown into turmoil. Equilibrium is only reached, he said, when the new wife achieves a regular place in the family system.

The adjustment to a new marriage can be difficult for all family members. It is hard on a new wife in several ways. She often moves into another wife's home for a period of time, sometimes even permanently. Here she finds herself in a dwelling in which the furnishings, style of home management, and general routines are those of another woman. Yet her cultural and religious role is to be the creator of a proper home for her husband and family. How is she to do this in someone else's home? Moreover, the newlywed wife may see her husband in an established and often comfortable relationship with his other wife or wives. They may have worked out smooth communication patterns and unique modes of relating to one another, may be at ease in each other's company, and may depict a mature and generally stable relationship. Thus the new, often younger, and inexperienced wife may feel like an outsider or visitor, be ill at ease living in someone else's home, and feel insecure about her relationship with her new husband.

Conversely, an established wife also faces some adjustments. She now has a "stranger" living in her home, may feel obligated to give the new wife some say in how the home is managed, but be reluctant to do so since her home symbolizes her role and unique personality. In addition, the new wife may be younger (and may appear to be more attractive than she is), and the older wife may see her husband paying special attention to the new wife (even acting foolishly romantic). As a result, she may feel that her own relationship with the husband is threatened. An established wife may well think that the new wife has disrupted the previously stable family "atom."

The early period of marriage may not be easy for the plural family's husband, either. Although a new and younger wife may be stimulating and exciting, a husband must be sensitive to his relationships with other wives. He may have to pay special attention to wives who are worried about his feelings toward them. At the same time, he has to build a relationship with the new wife, help her become integrated into the family, work out a new system for sharing time with his wives and families, and cope with additional financial pressures resulting from another wife in the family.

A new plural marriage clearly involves a complex array of dyadic and communal processes. That is, each new couple in the family must ideally develop a unique, intimate, and special dyadic relationship. But doing so is difficult, because at the same time that the new marital bond is being solidified each of the other dyadic relationships in the family must be kept viable. The fundamentalist religious and cultural value system calls on couples to maintain positive communal relationships in families, with co-wives living and working together in harmony and love and supporting one another as individuals and as wives of the same husband. In this chapter we examine the ways in which plural families make their dyadic and communal adjustments to new marriages.

Communal and dyadic aspects of adjustment

Communal adjustments to a new marriage

Some adjustment obviously has to be made to day-to-day living, home management, and domestic routines. In addition, considerable change takes place in the interpersonal relationships between wives, where tensions may revolve around friendliness, dominance, control, and mutual sensitivity.

Day-to-day communal adjustments. Everyday matters of home management, meal preparation, cleaning, cooking, and decorating are common sources of tension between new and established wives. Because a new wife often lives with another wife or wives for some period of time, she necessarily becomes involved in day-to-day home management. In general, this is not an easy time for a new wife. An established wife usually has lived in her dwelling for some time and decorated according to her tastes, and she manages cleaning, cooking, and use of the home according to her preferences. If two established wives have lived in the same dwelling, they have probably accommodated one another and worked out an acceptable living routine. A new, often younger wife will almost inevitably find it difficult to come into such a situation.

Family 1
Joan was originally Hal's second wife. After their marriage, she lived with Mary, the first wife (who eventually left the family). Mary mistreated her and told Joan that she was to "live in a little downstairs corner of the home," almost as a boarder. Although Joan had free rein of the house, Mary maintained full control of all aspects of home management. Joan was miserable and very upset until she was able to have her own home.

Family 5
Valerie, the second wife, found it very hard to live with Constance after she was married to Howard. She felt as if she was living in someone else's home, was hesitant to add or change the decor of the home, and said, "I didn't know how to be a wife to Howard."

Rose, the fourth wife, lived with Valerie, the second wife, right after she was married. She found this hard to do for several reasons. For one thing, she wanted to have her own home immediately, and didn't want to live with another wife. For another, Valerie's daughters were almost as old as she was, and they resented her status as a wife.

Family 6
Tamara, the fourth wife, emphasized that not being able to decorate or arrange the home according to her own personal tastes, or to make decisions about home management, made living with another wife difficult when she was a newlywed. And doing her best to adjust to the other wife's daily routine added to the stress she experienced. She felt a wife should have her own home, be free to express herself in her home,

and raise her family in a setting suitable for her. The other wives agreed with her.

Nina, the second wife, described how hard it had been to become her own person when she lived with Hilda, the first wife, soon after marrying Seymour. She tried desperately to meet the very high standards set by Hilda in regard to home management. But it didn't work out because Hilda's standards were always too demanding and too rigid. As a result, Nina always felt inferior and inadequate (another wife said she had the same feelings when she lived with Hilda). After great stress, Nina eventually decided that she had to be her own person, live her own lifestyle, and not model herself after anyone. This was not easy to do, and it was a long time before she began to feel good about herself.

Hilda admitted that it is hard for new wives to feel comfortable when they enter established families and that sometimes older wives – herself included – aren't always as understanding as they might be in helping new wives adjust to the situation.

Family 8
Ethel, Ira's second wife, had somewhat unusual problems when she lived with Gloria, the first wife. Gloria had been raised in a small town and didn't know how to cook or manage a home. Being quite assertive, Ethel took over the home right away, but in so doing caused some conflict and upheaval in the family. She laughs about those early days now but admits that it wasn't so easy then.

Family 9
Clara experienced some troubling aspects of being a new second wife and living with Joyce, John's first wife of 20 years. Clara had lived on her own for 10 years, managed her home according to her tastes, had her own furniture, and was quite independent. As she put it, she had to "swallow hard" when she moved in with the family and had to adapt to their lifestyle. It was quite an adjustment, even though Joyce did her best to welcome and make it easy for her.

Marjorie, the third wife, felt very intimidated when she moved into Joyce's and Clara's home. She was much younger than them and had very limited home management skills but was expected to assume equal responsibilities with the two other wives. Although they were supportive, Marjorie still felt very inadequate.

Marjorie also described how difficult it was to relate to the other wives after her honeymoon. She didn't feel as if she was really "coming home"; she felt more like a visitor or stranger and wasn't sure how to behave. Still a relatively new wife, she hasn't completely worked through all these feelings.

Family 10

Naomi, the second wife, had a very difficult early adjustment to living with Anita, the first wife. She worked full time, was only home in the evenings and on weekends, and didn't have a sense of "fitting" into the scheme of things. Anita had been Barry's wife for several years, had children, and managed the home in her own way. Even though Anita was very supportive, Naomi struggled to find a distinctive role and tangible responsibilities – but found this difficult to do.

Family 11

Benjamin and Katherine had been married for several years when the prophet of the rural group informed Benjamin that he was to marry Melba, Kelly, and Mary – three sisters who were recently widowed. The three marriages occurred on the same day, and the new wives and their many children moved in with Benjamin and Katherine. Kelly, one of the new wives, described how hard it was for them. She and her sisters felt like visitors or guests, were uncomfortable using Katherine's dishes and utensils, hadn't done any decorating of the home, tried to follow Katherine's daily routine, and generally felt like intruders. It was especially difficult because they had previously managed their own home and daily life.

Adjustment stresses may be especially serious for new wives who are converts to the fundamentalist movement and who have had no prior experience with plural family life. Not having the freedom to create and manage a home according to one's personal tastes is also likely to be stressful to many new wives.

It is important to remember, however, that when the husband brings home a new bride, an established wife experiences a radical change in her everyday life as well.

Family 1

Joan and Norma, the first two wives, had some problems with Charlotte when she joined the family. Charlotte was older, came from another plural family, and wasn't reluctant to criticize them about aspects of their home management. Although they resented her intrusions at first, she provided them with some sound advice on other family matters, and they eventually got along quite well.

Family 6

Recall that several new wives in this family had problems with Hilda, the first wife, because she was so demanding about managing household activities. She found it very difficult to have someone else in her home, because she was a very particular housekeeper – a perfectionist, she said – and was not able to accept the looser and more lax lifestyle of other women. She admitted being extreme in this regard and described her struggles over the years to become more flexible and to accommodate to wives with different personalities and attitudes about household management.

Tamara, the fourth wife, also found it difficult to adjust to new wives who lived with her. In one case, she decided that she wouldn't accommodate at all but would maintain exactly her routines and lifestyles. Although this worked for her, it probably made things harder for the new wife.

Family 11
Not only was it difficult for Melba, Kelly, and Mary, the widows who married Benjamin on the same day, but Katherine, the first wife, was suddenly faced with a dramatic change in her life. Accommodating three new wives (who were sisters) and their approximately two dozen children in a home that had been hers alone was an overwhelming experience. Running the home, cooking, cleaning, and deciding who would be responsible for various chores created a great deal of stress and tension for her when they all first lived together. Thus the adjustment was no easier for Katherine than it was for the new wives.

Family 18
Susan had been married to Charles for many years when Nancy joined them as the second wife. Susan not only felt that Nancy seemed like a permanent guest, but there were other problems. Nancy had grown up in a poor community and family and had very few homemaking skills appropriate to a middle-class family. Susan found herself under great duress as she tried to teach Nancy how to live in her home and meet her standards of home management.

It seems that 19th-century pioneer Mormons ran into much the same problems of adjustment: "It's not an easy way to live. We never fully conquer ourselves. . . . It's not jealousy so much, for I had made up my mind to that, but the constant pressure of adjusting yourself to another woman. Each woman should be a queen in her own home, my mother always said, and it is the natural way" (Young, 1954, p. 215).

These adjustment problems sometimes revolve around the personalities and social relationships of new and established wives.

Family 1
Recall that Joan, the present first wife, felt that a former wife (who eventually left the family) mistreated her personally, treated Joan as an inferior, and was domineering and coercive about what Joan could do in the home they shared. Joan was very young at the time and felt intimidated by the first wife. To make matters worse, it took a long time

for Hal to intervene and solve the problem, so that Joan's feelings of mistreatment eventually affected her relationship with Hal. She portrayed him as a "jerk" during that time and was quite angry with him. Joan felt as if she wasn't important to him during the early days of their marriage. Thus, a communal issue between wives can spill over into or arise from dyadic relationships between a husband and wife.

Family 2
Emily, the third wife, described herself as being somewhat shy and reserved. Because Judith and Rebecca, the first two wives, were outgoing and friendly with one another, Emily felt like an outsider. In the early days of her time in the family, she was quite envious of their relationship and felt that she would never be able to be as friendly with them as they were with each other.

Family 3
Danielle, the second wife, had an unusual adjustment problem when she first married William. Carlyn, the first wife, was intrusive, wanted to do everything together with Danielle, share all of their clothing, and be a close co-wife. Such a loss of independence was not to Danielle's liking, and it took a while for them to assuage their different feelings.

Family 12
Lauren, the second wife, never really adjusted to living with Elaine, the first wife. She always felt that Elaine was controlling and domineering and made Lauren feel subordinate and unwelcome in her home.

Family 1
Norma, the second wife, had serious adjustment problems when Cynthia, the fourth wife, joined the family (recall that there also were problems during courtship). She felt that Cynthia did not understand plural marriage and was insensitive to others. Norma was particularly irritated by the fact that Cynthia expected special attention from Hal. For example, she expected him to close car doors for her when he didn't do it for the other wives.

Norma was also jealous of the friendship between Joan, the first wife, and Cynthia, that had sprung up when Cynthia joined the family. Joan and Norma had been close friends up to them, and Norma was afraid that their relationship would suffer if Joan and Cynthia became very friendly.

Although adjusting to a new plural marriage can be difficult, there are cases in which it proceeds smoothly.

Family 1

Although there were some tensions when Charlotte, the third wife, joined the family, she immediately helped them resolve a major issue – how Hal should rotate and spend time with each of the three wives. Charlotte was older, had been a member of another plural family, and had wisdom and experience in this regard. Hal, Joan, and Norma voiced their appreciation of her assistance with this problem; her joining the family was an immediate plus.

Although Norma, the second wife, had serious adjustment problems when Cynthia, the fourth wife, joined the family, neither Joan nor Charlotte shared her views. Joan, the first wife, admitted to some initial jealousy because of Cynthia's youth and attractiveness, but it was only momentary. She described Cynthia as an easygoing person with a pleasant personality who fit nicely into the family. In addition, she felt that having a new wife in a family helps everyone get out of their everyday ruts, shakes things up, and creates new challenges for family members. Joan felt that Cynthia filled that role well. Charlotte agreed wholeheartedly.

Hal pointed out how easy it had been for him and the wives to adjust when Cynthia joined the family. He felt that this was the case because all of them, including Cynthia, were older and more mature and dealt with the situation better than when they were all much younger.

Family 2

There were some minor adjustment problems when Rebecca, the second wife, joined the family. However, she and Judith quickly worked things out. They had similar and compatible personalities, were open and communicative with one another, and had known each other before. Rebecca described how they worked on home projects together, learned about one another, and developed a close friendship right from the outset. If there ever were any problems, they were quick to discuss and resolve them.

When Emily, the third wife, joined the family, she was very shy and envious of Judith's and Rebecca's relationship. But they understood her personality and feelings and tried to make her feel comfortable. They all agreed that things worked out quite well shortly after Emily joined the family.

Phyllis, the fourth wife, was also very shy and reticent, had difficulty talking about issues, and withdrew into herself. Despite some adjustment problems, the three other wives drew her out, established friendships, and wove her into the family. It worked.

Family 3

Carlyn, the first wife, was delighted when William married Danielle. She had been waiting several years for them to satisfy their religious beliefs and also longed for female companionship. (Recall, however, that Danielle felt that Carlyn was unusually intrusive in the early months after she joined the family. So although one wife had no adjustment problems, the other one did.)

Family 6

Hilda, the first wife, and Holly, the fifth wife, felt very positive about one another when Holly joined the family. Hilda felt a "burning of her bosom" – a wonderfully vibrant feeling – that told her Holly's marriage to Seymour was a good thing. This proved to be the case because Holly, a young and inexperienced new wife, was a hard worker in the home and willingly learned from Hilda. For her part, Hilda was protective of Holly and ensured that Seymour treated her fairly. In some ways, she felt that Holly was almost like a daughter.

Holly also felt good living with Hilda at the outset of her marriage. She was happy to join the family. Hilda was like a mother to her, taught her how to cook, do housework, and take care of the home. Holly described Hilda as patient and caring and as having helped her develop positive self-esteem, which she had lacked for many years.

Family 10

The eight wives in this family admitted to difficulties adjusting to a new wife, but the problems were often ameliorated by mutual support. For example, Anita and Naomi, the first and second wives, had few adjustment problems with one another. Anita had tried to make Naomi feel at home and emphasized that she was not a guest, but a true member of the family. Naomi concurred wholeheartedly, and recounted what Anita had said to her: "Do what you will in this home; let's rearrange the furniture if you want to." Naomi said Anita has always been giving, understanding, and helpful to her and all the other wives from the moment each of them joined the family. The others agreed.

Family 14

Molly, the second wife, had no serious adjustment problems when she married Harry and lived with Sally, the first wife. The two wives shared everything, restyling their eating habits to match one another, disciplining and treating children in the same way, cleaning and changing each other's beds, and cooking and eating together.

Family 7

Many years after Norman and Sarah had been married, Patricia, recently widowed, joined them as a second wife. Several years later, Norman married Audrey, Patricia's teenage daughter. Did this unusual situation, of a mother and daughter being co-wives to Norman, create special adjustment problems?

At first, Audrey, the new third wife, had some problems with other children in the family, by virtue of her changed status, but felt that things worked out reasonably well within a short time. She claimed not having any problems with Patricia, who was now both her mother and sister wife. She felt that Patricia did not treat her like a child and gave her considerable independence. And she feels free to call on her mother for advice and assistance in a variety of matters. Patricia, an easygoing person, claims to have easily adjusted to their new multifaceted relationship.

There are also examples of positive communal relationships between wives in 19th-century plural families. One first wife helped her husband select five wives within a year, shared her home with them, was compassionate and understanding, and served as a mediator when conflicts arose (Watt, 1978). Similarly one second wife is reported to have said: "I married with an intense desire to make a go of it. I felt that going in as I did, I should not assert myself over the other wives, and that I should do the best I could to make a place for myself in the household" (Young, 1954, p. 215).

Dyadic adjustments to a new marriage

The evidence clearly indicates that dyadic adjustment creates serious stresses in new plural marriages. Established wives often feel that their personal relationship with their husband is threatened by a new wife, they express a sense of loneliness, sometimes to the point of feeling abandoned, complain that they spend less time with the husband than before, and so on. Many wives are jealous and envious of a new wife and her relationship with the husband – perhaps because she may be younger and seems more attractive, or because the husband spends more time with the new wife or seems romantically attached to her. Even more powerful and disturbing is the feeling that the husband no longer loves the established wives, who may therefore harbor feelings of inadequacy and low self-esteem.

New wives also experience dyadic stress during the adjustment phase of their marriages. They want to build a close relationship with the husband but must share him with other wives and interact with him in their presence. They see their husband in what appears to be a smooth and easy relationship with other wives, feel inadequate and inexperienced, and sometimes are jealous of other wives' relationship with the husband.

Husbands, too, feel the strain of adjustment in a new marriage, as they seek to build a dyadic relationship with the new wife, while trying to maintain relationships with each of the other wives and reduce the stress on everyone else.

The established wives we interviewed reported a variety of problems.

Family 1

Not only was Joan upset with a former wife who mistreated her, as described earlier, but subsequent events involving Hal and a new wife, Norma, added to her misery. Shortly after Hal's divorce, which wasn't that long after he had married Joan, Norma joined the family. Joan was very upset with this turn of events. She had never had a chance to develop an intimate relationship with Hal, and here he was with a new wife. The fact that she never had a real courtship or honeymoon with Hal, whereas Norma did, added to her personal turmoil. She came to believe that Hal loved Norma more than he loved her and that her relationship with him was not maturing as it should. Things were so bad in those early days that Joan thought seriously about leaving the marriage but stayed only because of her strong religious testimony. A very mild-mannered and easygoing person, Joan described these events in an aroused and emotional manner and noted that it took nine years to fully resolve her anger and personal turmoil. She and Hal observed that they both were very young and inexperienced at the time and feel lucky that they were able to persevere during that difficult adjustment phase of their life. They both said they now find great pleasure in their marriage and feel it would have been tragic if they had separated.

Recall that Norma, the second wife, also had serious communal adjustment problems when Cynthia, the fourth wife recently joined the family. Norma feels that Cynthia is insensitive to the other wives and to her present status as a new wife. But Norma is also upset with Hal. She thinks that he spends too much time with Cynthia and thus feels abandoned. Hal acknowledges Norma's feelings, claims that he is trying to be especially supportive and attentive to Norma, and assured her in our presence that things would be all right. She agreed that they were making progress but needed to continue working at it.

Family 3

Danielle, the second wife, had a very hard time when William married Alayna. Although she supported the marriage, especially since Alayna was her sister and they were good friends, the situation put great strain on her relationship with William. They had only been married a short time, and Danielle felt that she and William had never had a real chance to develop their own relationship. Furthermore, William and Alayna had a public wedding and went on a honeymoon, whereas Danielle's marriage had been secret, which added to her feelings of having been mistreated and humiliated by William. All of this made for a very difficult adjustment for Danielle.

Family 6

Hilda, the first wife, was very upset during the first months after Seymour married Nina, the second wife. She was jealous of Nina and Seymour's relationship and felt that he was more attracted to Nina than to her, in part because he was spending more time with his new wife. At the same time, she felt very guilty about her negative reaction because she believed in the principle of plural marriage and was not handling matters very well.

She became so overwrought that she finally told Seymour about her emotional turmoil. His response was supportive and along the lines of "I love you more than I can say; but I love her as well." His perspective helped somewhat, but not completely, because she admitted that she always wanted to be the "queen" of the wives in his eyes.

The same feelings of jealously and abandonment arose when Seymour married Andrea, the third wife, even though Hilda supported the match. This made her realize that she was still unable to cope with a new wife joining the family. Once again, she felt guilty and inadequate about not being able to handle the situation. She did say, however, that the problem eased as subsequent wives joined the family.

Family 10

Several wives agreed that jealousy and having less time with the husband were sources of stress when a new wife joined the family. Joanne, the third wife, said that she had always wanted to be the "perfect wife" to Barry, but felt threatened when Dorothy joined the family as the fourth wife. Joanne felt that Dorothy was more attractive and that Barry loved Dorothy more than he loved her. She even said to him, "Please don't forget that I am here."

Dorothy, the fourth wife, pointed out that jealousy takes many forms during the adjustment period. For example, every time she saw Barry hug or express affection to a new wife, feelings of jealousy overcame her. And it happened with every single new wife. All the wives laughed, admitting that they, too, had experienced the same feelings over and over.

Family 11

As described earlier, Benjamin married three widowed sisters on the same day. In addition to communal problems, Katherine, the first wife, experienced severe dyadic stress. She now had to share Benjamin's time with three other wives and their children and had exceptional feelings of jealousy toward the fourth wife, Mary, who was much younger and who Katherine thought was more attractive and appealing to Benjamin. She was very worried that he would soon love Mary more than her.

Family 18

Susan, who had been married to Charles for 20 years when they decided to have a plural family, described her feelings when Nancy joined them as the second wife. She liked Nancy but was envious of her youth, became upset and jealous when Charles and Nancy spent the night together, and was very insecure about losing his love. When we asked if she had overcome these feelings – after many years of life in a plural family – she laughed, saying, "Yes, about 90% of the time."

In her autobiography, Melissa Merrill (1975), a modern plural wife who left her husband, told how emotionally distressful it was to hear sounds and voices of her husband and his new bride at night in their adjoining bedroom. Dyadic adjustment stresses were also common in 19th-century Mormon plural families and were not unlike those that present-day family members experience. One first wife vividly described her inability to adjust to the relationship between her husband and newer wives: "Three of us lived in the same house for a year. I said I couldn't stand it, I was going to lose my mind. I couldn't stand to see him fondle over the others. Oh, he had to show them a little affection. . . . No, he never slighted me, but I just couldn't stand it. I'm not the jealous kind, though" (Young, 1954, p. 201).

Another 19th-century Mormon first wife who opposed her husband marrying a second wife continued to balk during the early days of the new marriage. The wives lived together for a while, during which time "the first wife kept close watch on her husband and his new wife. For example, [the first wife] was in the habit of getting up early and doing her household chores promptly. If she found that [the husband] and the second wife were still lying abed, she would go over and throw rocks on the roof to awaken them and get them up" (Young, 1954, p. 195). Once, when the husband and second wife in the preceding case were away, the first wife unilaterally moved the younger wife's belongings out of the home to a new place, because of her continuing disapproval of the marriage and rejection of the newer wife. Neither the husband nor the newer wife ever said a word about this drastic action!

The initial period of adjustment is also stressful for new wives. Developing an intimate, unique and close relationship with their new husband is not easy for them. They are often younger than the established wives, see the husband and other wives engaged in a seemingly smooth relationship, communicating easily, and acting in confident and mature ways. They wonder if they can ever achieve a comparable bond with the husband. Their uncertainty, insecurity, inexperience, and feelings of inadequacy about how to relate to their new husband in the context of his relationships with other wives often upsets new wives.

Family 5

In addition to having problems about home management with Constance, the first wife, Valerie, the new second wife, was disturbed about her dyadic relationship with Howard. She reflected her feelings of inexperience by saying, "I didn't know how to be a wife." And she was confused about how to develop a relationship with him when they couldn't be alone very much and didn't communicate on a personal or intimate level. She felt shunted aside by him and unable to make progress in their marriage. What made things worse was seeing how well Howard and Constance seemed to get along. She even tried to imitate Constance's behavior for a while, but that didn't work. Those early days were very trying, she said.

Family 10

We discussed dyadic adjustment problems with all eight wives in this family as a group. Because the conversation was so lively, we were not always able to identify which wife said what. The general consensus was that as new wives they all worried about whether they would ever achieve the kind of marital relationship that Barry had with other wives. They had serious doubts that they "could ever catch up" in this regard. One wife told herself early in her marriage that "the relationship between Barry and the other wives is much more beautiful than I can ever hope to achieve" and wondered how she could match the quality of their relationship. Another wife said at the time that she would rather have been an "old wife" than a "new wife." As an older wife, she would have had an established relationship and a sense of understanding and trust with Barry. As it was, she was intimidated by the strangeness of his and her relationship in the context of other marriages in the family, had too little time with him, and didn't know what to do about it.

Naomi, the second wife, stated: "When I entered the principle I was in shock." Even though she grew up in a plural family she said that she never anticipated several things – being so jealous of other wives' relationships with Barry, finding it difficult to be a wife to a man who was married to other women, being upset when Barry was affectionate with other wives, and feeling guilty about her emotional distress at the time. The other wives confirmed that they, too, had experienced similar feelings of jealousy, stress, and difficulty when they first joined the family.

In some cases, however, the adjustment to new marriages is easy.

Family 1

As noted earlier, Norma, the second wife, experienced serious dyadic and communal stress when Cynthia, the fourth wife, married Hal. But Joan and Charlotte didn't. Except for some initial feelings of jealousy, their adjustment was easy. In fact, they both said that Cynthia's entry into the family gave them a lift and new challenge in respect to their own dyadic relationship with Hal. They said that it had stimulated personal growth, added new and unique dimensions to their marriages, and enabled them to break out of "old ruts."

Charlotte went on to say that she didn't feel at all threatened in her relationship with Hal because she felt quite secure in their marriage. Indeed, having another wife in the family gave her more freedom to pursue her own interests since Hal's time now would be divided among four wives. Unlike many wives in plural families, Charlotte did not feel that less time with Hal was a problem; it almost seemed to be an advantage! (Hal didn't seem at all insulted or chagrined when she said this.)

Our information about the adjustment problems of husbands when a new wife joins the family is somewhat more fragmentary, because wives were much more vocal and dominated the discussions on this topic. Some husbands did speak about the importance and challenge of attending to their new marriage relationship while also dealing with other wives. (To judge by the wives' feelings discussed earlier, some husbands were not always successful or even sensitive to this principle.) Several husbands said that they tried to be understanding of their wives' feelings during adjustment phases and that they felt the responsibility – as a husband to all wives and as family patriarch – to achieve appropriate relationships with all wives during this time of upheaval. Many of their comments were at an abstract level; they rarely referred to specific wives or marriages, perhaps because the wives had already done so when we discussed the matter or because they didn't want to put too much emphasis on specific relationships.

Family 1

Hal was philosophical about the stresses and strains he and his wives faced during marital adjustments. Although he acknowledged that wives often had problems during adjustment phases, he never described any emotional turmoil that he personally experienced. However, it was also evident that he had spent a great deal of time helping his wives adjust to new marriages, explaining his behavior toward them and toward a new wife, and trying to keep family life stable and secure. To use his metaphor, he struggled to restore the family-as-atom to a new and stable equilibrium.

Family 6

Although Seymour was not specific about his feelings when new wives joined the family, he did say that husbands face challenges with every new marriage. A husband's special burden is to attend to each wife's needs and personality and to ensure their well-being during this difficult time. In some ways, it is easier for wives to work through the problems of a new marriage, he said, because they can lean on one another for support. On the other hand, he felt pretty much alone in struggling to relate to the new wife and other wives.

In general, husbands were fairly quiet when we talked about adjustment problems. The wives did most of the talking, often in an animated way. When husbands participated, they usually commented on wives' feelings, not their own. They said they understood how and why wives felt as they did and then focused on their responsibility to ameliorate and resolve the problems wives were having with new marriages. On the face of it, if husbands experienced any stress when a new wife entered a family, it had to do with figuring out how to deal with wives' anxieties and difficulties, not *their* personal feelings of, say, jealousy or loss of love. Of course, it is possible that they did have other adjustment problems but chose not to express them in the presence of their wives or to expose a weakness in their patriarchal leadership role.

Coping with a new marriage

Although a new marriage can be stressful, husbands and wives told us they tried to work things out, because they believed in and wanted to succeed in their plural marriage. Their methods of coping involved *individual, dyadic,* and *communal* actions.

Individual coping responses

Over and over, participants expressed their commitment to fulfilling the religious commandment to live in a polygynous patriarchal family in earthly life, as a prelude to a celestial existence in the hereafter. They repeatedly spoke about praying for solace, guidance, and the strength to help them adjust to the new family situation and abide by their religious beliefs.

Family 1
In recounting her severe stress when she was a new plural wife, Joan said that it was only her strong religious testimony that carried her through those trying days. Things were so bad that she thought about leaving Hal. However, prayer, pleas for guidance from God, and reliance on her religious faith helped her work things out. To this day she is grateful that she succeeded, because they have a good marriage, and she was able to hold to her religious beliefs.

Families 5, 6, 10, 18
Nina and Cynthia, the second and third wives in Family 6, said that prayer and examination of their own religious testimony not only helped them adjust to new marriages but also allowed them to take charge of their lives during that difficult time.

Joanne, the third wife in Family 10, said that meeting the challenge of adjustment to a new wife helped her "grow toward God," better understand her own religious feelings, and gain a better sense of what God is.

Angela, the third wife in Family 18, said she centered her energies around Jesus Christ as a way of adjusting to the stresses of adjustment to a new marriage.

The daughter of Susan, the first wife in Family 18, agreed that one has to pray in stressful situations, such as a new plural marriage. "God comes first," she said, "even before one's husband, and the resolution of bad feelings will come by praying to Him." Susan agreed, saying that she was better able to adjust to a new marriage when "I prayed and asked the help of the Lord."

Along with turning to religious values, some wives were introspective and attempted to grow and become "their own person."

Family 5
During the early days of her marriage, Valerie, the second wife, was very envious of the smooth and mature relationship between Howard and Constance, the first wife. She was so upset that, in desperation, she tried

to imitate Constance's behavior, but it didn't work. After much personal reflection, she decided that she had to be her own person and once even blurted out to Constance: "I don't want to be like you."

Family 10

Joanne, the third wife, found it difficult to adjust when Jane and Leslie, the seventh and eighth wives, joined the family following their divorce from other husbands. Each had several children, and Barry was very busy helping them adjust to the family. After thinking about it, Joanne realized that she needed to become more independent and less reliant on Barry. She described this as a growth-promoting experience that enhanced her sense of self-esteem and self-worth. She went on to say that one of the important qualities of plural family life is the growth that can occur when one is faced with such challenges.

Other wives agreed, adding that each of them must be sensitive to one another's personalities while looking into their own. And, they said, living a plural family life is not only important for religious reasons, but it can also enhance one's self-concept and sense of self-worth.

Family 18

The daughter of Susan, the first wife in the family, herself a plural wife, stated that being a plural wife required a certain personal maturity. She said: "If one looks for faults in others, one will find them. One must accept others, love them, take other wives on their own terms, and do the best you can."

Thus participants often describe the challenges of adjustment to a new plural marriage as a vehicle for reaffirming and strengthening their religious testimony and as an opportunity for self-improvement.

Dyadic coping responses

Husbands and wives also worked through the problems of new marriages in a dyadic fashion – explaining and discussing their feelings and talking about their relationship. Wives aired their adjustment stresses with husbands, sometimes only after suffering frustration and emotional turmoil alone. Husbands were sometimes sensitive to wives' stresses and attempted to alleviate their concerns or intervene directly when a situation seemed serious.

Family 6

Seymour, an elder in the community, acknowledged that it is common for wives to feel betrayed, neglected, and not loved when a new wife joins a family. He said that it is important for a man to recognize and resolve these stresses as quickly as possible. For example, as described earlier, Hilda, the first wife, was very upset when Nina joined the family. To work things out, Hilda and Seymour together addressed the issue, with him affirming his love and commitment to her.

Family 9
Joyce and Clara, the first and second wives, had similar feelings of anxiety about their and his relationships when John returned from each of his honeymoons with a new wife. But in each case, he immediately expressed afection and love toward them after arriving home, thereby easing their minds. They both stated that John has always been sensitive to their feelings, especially during the early phases of a new marriage.

Family 18
Charles and Susan had been married for many years when Nancy joined them. The new marriage put enormous stress on Susan. Charles realized her plight, and paid a great deal of attention to her, going over their relationship, reaffirming his love for her, and being conscious of her feelings and stresses.

Communal coping responses

Another coping strategy during periods of adjustment shows wives supporting one another – new wives reaching out for assistance, or established wives being sensitive to one another or to a new wife.

Family 2
Judith and Rebecca, the first and second wives, are good friends who are especially sensitive to one another (and to other wives) during adjustments to new marriages. Whenever a problem arose, they talked it over and showed their love for one another. For example, when Emily, the third wife, joined the family, they were sensitive to her feelings of being a newcomer and worked hard to make her feel comfortable. Similarly, when Phyllis, the fourth wife, married David, they encouraged her to express her feelings and become an integral part of the family.

Family 5
Barbara, the third wife, was very jealous when Howard married Rose, the fourth wife. Although it was difficult for her to talk to the other wives, she eventually confided in Valerie, the second wife. So doing was very helpful to Barbara.

Family 9

Clara, the second wife, told us that Joyce, the first wife, helped her adjust to plural family life. Joyce was warm and supportive, and always ready to talk with Clara about her problems. Joyce also suggested that they combine their furniture to decorate an area in the home.

Marjorie, the third wife and a young woman, was very intimidated about living with Joyce and Clara. But they were sensitive to her fears, encouraged her to discuss them openly, and did their best to be supportive and warm toward Marjorie. It helped her a great deal.

Family 10

One wife said that other wives helped her build a relationship with her new husband: "I learned everything I needed to know about Barry from living with Anita."

A daughter of one of the wives, herself a plural wife, not only acted positively toward a new wife, but tried to consciously share space in the home with her. Among other things, she gave the new wife separate drawer space in the bathroom that they shared.

Family 11

When three widowed women married Benjamin all at once, Mary, the new young fourth wife, gave support and advice to Katherine, the first wife, who was also Mary's cousin. Katherine was not only jealous of Mary, but she was overwhelmed by the whole situation. Mary encouraged her to talk about her fears and stresses. Mary also assured her that she would not attempt to subvert Katherine's relationship with Benjamin and that she would assume a proper role in the family. Their talks resulted in a strong bond between the two women.

Some wives sought assistance from friends or relatives in other plural families.

Family 10

Naomi talked with her mother when she was upset during the early months of her marriage to Barry. She discovered that her mother, also a plural wife, understood her feelings of jealousy and loneliness, having experienced them herself. Being able to vent her frustrations and knowing that her mother understood were very helpful to Naomi.

Family 18

Susan, the first wife, said that part of her solution to adjusting to new marriages was to talk with other women in the community. Doing so made her realize that she wasn't alone; other women shared her feelings and also helped her cope with her stresses and anxieties. It relieved her greatly to know that other women went through the same thing.

One husband attended to both dyadic and communal issues in the adjustment phases of his new marriages.

Family 4

Harry traveled a great deal on business and family matters. During the early weeks and months of a new marriage, he always brought his new wife and an established wife on these trips. His goal, he said, was to spend extra time with the new wife, in order to further develop their marital relationship, and to give the new wife and established wives a chance to be with one another, both in his presence and when they were alone waiting for him to finish his business.

It is impossible to say which combination of individual, dyadic, and communal coping mechanisms are most effective or which are used most frequently during adjustments to new plural marriages. So much depends on the mix of personalities, the ethos of a particular family, the number of wives and their relationships, and one's position in the sequence of wives. Because the plural family lifestyle is so unique, the mix of personalities and intensity of relationships so complex, and their life circumstances so changeable, modern plural families must experiment and engage in trial and error to adjust to new marriages. Maintaining viable and healthy dyadic and communal relationships during this crucial phase of plural family life is surely a challenging task!

Sometimes the challenge is not met, and marital crises erupt. Melissa Merrill (1975), a former first wife in a contemporary plural marriage, has indicated that unresolved communal and dyadic stresses early in her husband's marriage to a second wife eventually destroyed her marriage to him. In the early months of the new marriage, she felt an increasing sense of despair and personal inadequacy: "A terrible fear engulfed me. He will love her more. I'll be forgotten. His love for me will die. This fear was to haunt me for years to come. . . . [F]or now and for most of the next five years, I was heavy hearted and shed bitter tears" (Merrill, 1975, p. 43).

As the months progressed, the situation grew worse. The husband was more attracted to the new wife, spent more time with her, and even began to make disparaging comparisons between Melissa and the new wife. Clearly, the dyadic stresses were serious, and dyadic coping mechanisms were not even being tried. The situation was exacerbated by communal stresses. The two women argued about managing the home and children, and the second wife was verbally abusive. Melissa, who cared for the children and ran the home while the second wife worked, even became jealous of the other wife's clothing that she laundered. Things simply never worked out between the women from the beginning, and eventually Melissa left the family.

Does experience help? Some further questions

Two other questions regarding adjustment arose in a few cases. First, "Is adjustment to a new marriage easier if a wife has grown up in a plural family?" Having seen firsthand the entry of new wives into one's childhood family, a wife might be better prepared to adjust when she faces the same situation – if, of course, those childhood experiences were positive. Negative experiences or a lack of awareness about the crises one's parents faced might also contribute to a rocky adjustment.

Second, "Does adjustment become easier as successive wives enter a family?" One might expect established wives to gradually become accustomed to the idea of new plural marriages and over time to grow more secure in their dyadic and communal relationships in the family. A great deal may still depend on the experience of an established wife, her relationship with the husband, the husband's behavior, the extent of wives' support of one another, and the effectiveness of the communal and dyadic coping mechanisms.

"Is adjustment easier if a wife has grown up in a plural family?" Several husbands and wives in our study grew up in plural families, some in multigeneration polygynous families. The issue was vigorously discussed by wives in one family, and only occasionally elsewhere.

Family 10

Several wives who had grown up in plural families argued that it had indeed been easier for them to adjust when new wives joined their family. The fact that they had childhood role models helped them anticipate and cope with the adjustment problems they faced.

Other wives disagreed. Naomi, the second wife, said that she had grown up in a compatible plural family home, but it hadn't helped her as an adult. She felt that a child does not always see below the surface of family relationships or is shielded from stress and conflict by parents. This conclusion was confirmed when, to her surprise, she learned as an adult that her own mother had suffered adjustment problems.

In general, wives and husbands raised in monogamous families do not seem to have experienced more dyadic or communal adjustment problems to new marriages than participants reared in plural families. There are so many factors at work in the adjustment phase of marriages that no single one, including childhood experiences, can make a difference across the board. Thus husband–wife and wife–wife relationships, intervals between marriages, age differences between wives and between husbands and wives, living arrangements, and other dyadic and communal factors all contribute to the adjustment process. Thus a plural family heritage in itself is probably not sufficient to ease the adjustment by and to new wives in a contemporary fundamentalist family.

"Is adjustment easier as successive wives enter a family?" Here, too, the answer is not simple. Some wives found it easier to adjust to successive new marriages in the family because they became increasingly secure in their marriage and their relationships with other wives. But it sometimes took several marriages before they felt that way. On the other hand, some wives said that they were never completely free of adjustment problems, no matter how many marriages occurred. And sometimes adjustment problems were as serious later on as in earlier marriages. So there is no universal pattern, although there appears to be some general easing of adjustment stresses with successive marriages, especially in families with many wives.

Family 5
Constance, the first wife, said it was easier for her to adjust to each of Howard's new marriages. It was extremely difficult when he married Valerie, the second wife, but much easier when Barbara and Rose joined the family – easier, she said, but still not without problems.

Family 6
Hilda, the first wife, had an extremely difficult time when Seymour married Nina, and she was almost as upset when Cynthia joined the family. But thereafter, with each of the next five wives, adjustment problems eased. She was not only more secure about her status in the family, but she and the other wives helped one another adapt to each new marriage. In fact, Hilda said, it is always the most recent established wife who suffers the most, because it is her first experience facing a new marriage. Conversely, new wives who enter a family with many wives may have an easier adjustment than earlier new wives, because they often have the understanding and support of older wives.

Family 9
Joyce, the first wife, found her adjustment to be much easier when John married Marjorie, the third wife, compared with the difficulties she faced when Clara, the second wife, joined the family. At the same time, the

adjustment goes on even after several years. It is, she said, a "day-to-day struggle," and she still has "certain feelings" when she sees John kiss or hug Joyce or Marjorie. While subscribing firmly to the principle of plural family life, she said, "I am still a human being and we all have our weaknesses."

As evidence that it is never easy to adjust, when John mentioned the possibility in one of our discussions of adding a new wife to the family, Joyce responded in a very low but authoritative voice: "John, let us breathe for a while. Let us breathe for a period of time." He immediately dropped the matter. So in spite of successively better adaptation to new plural marriages, Joyce has not completely overcome all the problems of adjustment.

Family 10
The eight wives had a spirited and articulate discussion about the issue. The consensus was that it did become somewhat easier to adjust as successive wives joined the family, but that it varied widely from case to case, depending on many factors. Having the support of other wives certainly helped, as did a sense of greater security about one's place in the family. But they agreed that it isn't all that simple. Personalities play a major role in adjustment, sometimes making it easier or harder. And sometimes unique circumstances enter in. For example, it was quite difficult when the last two wives joined the family, each coming out of a divorce and bringing several children into the family. Adjusting to them, and their adjustment to others, was very challenging since no one had experienced such a situation before. Although it does become easier from marriage to marriage, each case is also unique, and this makes it difficult to predict in advance how adjustment to a new marriage will work.

Thus it is probably somewhat easier for wives to adjust to successive wives joining a plural family. But it may take several marriages before it becomes very much easier. Even then, the adjustment is not without its problems and stresses. At the same time, each marriage is a unique event, with different personalities and family circumstances entering into the picture.

Summary

Marital adjustment by wives and husbands when a new wife joins a contemporary polygynous family is clearly a difficult period. Adjusting to a monogamous marriage in American society is challenging enough, but it is many times harder in a plural family. Not only must a bride and groom learn about one another and develop a unique and close dyadic relationship, but they must do so in the context of other husband–wife relationships in the plural family. In accordance with religious and cultural values, fundamentalist Mormon husbands and wives must also strive to establish a harmonious, loving, and supportive communal relationship among family members.

Achieving a viable balance of dyadic and communal relationships in contemporary polygynous families is especially difficult when a new wife joins a family. On the one hand, communal pressures may arise when a new wife lives in the home of one or more of the established wives. New wives are often unhappy about this arrangement, because they feel like visitors and have little control over home management and decorating. At the same time, established wives often feel as if they have a permanent visitor and intruder who interferes with their lifestyle. Interpersonal incompatibilities between wives sometimes add to the stresses of adjustment. Taken together, communal adjustment stresses can be serious, although in several of our families wives reported immediately adjusting well to one another.

On the other hand, a new marriage in a plural family can also generate dyadic stress. Some established wives are jealous of younger new wives, feel abandoned, betrayed, and lonely if they perceive the new wife as a threat to their relationship with their husband. New wives, too, often feel inadequate and uncertain about how to develop a close, unique and intimate relationship with their new husband, especially as they observe a seemingly smooth and mature relationship between the husband and his other wives. Some husbands make an effort to deal with dyadic and communal problems during adjustment phases of new marriages, but this becomes a challenge for them as well.

To deal with this multiplicity of adjustment pressures, participants use a variety of individual, dyadic, and communal strategies. Wives often rely on individual prayer and their religious beliefs to help them cope. Among the dyadic mechanisms, husbands may discuss their problems, reaffirming their love for one another, try to be supportive of one another, and respect each other's feelings. Many wives also rely on communal coping strategies, airing their feelings with other wives, comforting one another, and offering support to new and established wives during the adjustment phases of plural family life.

All in all, adjusting to a new marriage is a challenging and complex task for husbands and wives in present-day plural Mormon families. There are many sources of dyadic and communal stress, a variety of coping mechanisms, and a range of outcomes. Personality factors, interpersonal factors, husband–wife and wife–wife relationships, ages and background of wives and husbands, living circumstances, and economic factors all play a role in the process. As a result, it seems that individuals and families must develop their own coping mechanisms to deal with the unique dyadic and communal stresses of each marriage. These challenges may well be intensified by the fact that many participants have had little or no experience in plural family life and can find few broadly based cultural norms and mechanisms on which to rely.

Home environments of plural families

The three chapters in this section examine environmental aspects of the lives of present-day Mormon fundamentalists, especially their homes and dwellings. Chapter 10 concentrates on the living arrangements of plural families: wives living separately from one another, sharing dwellings, or residing in combinations of separate and shared dwellings. Attention is also given to changes in living arrangements over a family's history, the factors responsible, and the ideal residential arrangements to which modern plural families aspire.

Chapters 11 and 12 explore the psychological attachments of wives and husbands to their homes. As chapter 11 illustrates, homes are very important to plural wives, and they have control over decorating and access by others, achieve solitude and privacy, and display their personal identity, relationships with their husband, and links to their religious and cultural community.

By contrast, husbands in contemporary plural families have little psychological attachment to their family's homes, as explained in chapter 12. They play little part in managing, furnishing, or decorating homes; often do not have places of their own in these dwellings; and generally display weak bonding with family residences. Even the management of their clothing and personal possessions reflects a lack of attachment to dwellings and attests to their somewhat "nomadic" status in plural families.

10

Living arrangements

Living arrangements in 20th-century America have been geared to the idealized monogamous nuclear family: a mother, father, and a few children. However, this residential pattern is changing. With the rise in the divorce rate, there are now many single-parent households, usually consisting of women and their children. There are also a large number of blended families, in which divorced adults who have remarried have brought together children from earlier marriages; singles living together; group and shared homes for the elderly; single or divorced older children returning to live with one or both parents; poor and elderly occupants of single rooms in public facilities; and homeless people and families living in shelters. Although the housing stock continues to be designed for the traditional monogamous nuclear family, changes are afoot, with proposed new residential designs for different family configurations, such as suite arrangements for single-parent families that provide separate and common spaces (for a variety of design alternatives see Franck and Ahrentzen, 1989).

What about contemporary Mormon plural families? Do they live in communal arrangements, with wives sharing dwellings? If so, how do they arrange space and share various parts of homes. If they live apart, in a dyadic arrangement, how do they manage to function as a unified family? And do plural families maintain the same living arrangements permanently, or do they shift from dyadic to communal to dyadic configurations from one time to another? These are the questions we address in the present chapter. To begin, it may be helpful to examine housing patterns in other polygynous cultures.

Living arrangements in traditional cultures

People in traditional polygynous cultures live in a variety of residential patterns. Some are nomadic and have either temporary dwellings or portable ones that they carry from place to place; others live in permanent homes on stable sites. In some polygynous cultures, people reside in homesteads or compounds with several wives and their children. In other cultures, co-wives live separately on adjacent or distant sites. In still other cases, wives share a single dwelling. To facilitate the comparison of traditional polygynous societies and modern Mormon plural families we examine (1) the extent to which polygynous wives in other cultures live together in communal arrangements versus dyadic, independent dwellings; (2) the place in which husbands reside in polygynous families; and (3) changes in living arrangements.

Living configurations of wives

Plural wives in some cultures live in primarily dyadic arrangements, each having their own separate dwelling or part of a dwelling and managing their household lives independently of one another. These arrangements may also be communal in some respects: for example, the wives in a polygynous family may all use certain parts of a home, yard, or compound area. In primarily communal arrangements, plural wives share areas in and around a residence. Even in extreme communal situations, however, it is customary for each wife to have some control over parts of a dwelling, such as a bedroom or sleeping area. Mixed dyadic and communal formats occur when some wives in a family live communally and others live in separate dwellings.

Ethnographic information in the Human Relations Area File indicates that wives in many traditional polygynous cultures have separate living quarters, in part because of the desire to minimize conflict, and in part because wives often function independently in agriculture, animal care, and other economic activities (Murdock, 1967).[1] Dyadic living configurations among wives living far apart and rarely having contact differ from those among wives having separate dwellings in a community or compound or wives living in separate parts of a dwelling and sharing some joint spaces. Wives in the Comoro Islands, Mozambique, for example, often live in their mothers' communities, far from one another, and the husband travels from place to place to visit them (Ottenheimer and Ottenheimer, 1979) in what has been termed "bicycle polygyny" (Mair, 1977). In another dyadic pattern, plural wives among the Hagen of New Guinea sometimes live apart from one another, amid other families and their own kin, in order to have a broader base of interaction (Strathern, 1972).

In many cases, wives live in separate dwellings near one another in compounds or homesteads, share some communal space, and have daily contact with one another. The Swazi of Africa arrange their homesteads in a semicircle, facing a central cattle corral (Kuper, 1950, 1980). Each wife has a dwelling, storage hut, and kitchen enclosed by a fence. The husband's mother often lives in a large hut in the middle of the semicircle, with the first wife on the right of the mother's hut, the second on her left, the third on her right, and so on. Among the Gusii of Africa, polygynous wives have adjacent dwellings, separated by a field or pasture (LeVine and LeVine, 1963). And in the Lango district of Uganda, Africa, each wife has her own dwelling, kitchen, small structure for children, and a corral for animals on a 30-square-yard clearing; these homes are separated by high grass (Curley, 1973). In another configuration, among the Ijaw of Africa, wives have separate apartments in the same dwelling (Leis, 1974).[2]

In some cultures, co-wives reside in primarily communal arrangements. In Dakar, Africa, wives often live together, share space, and work in the home (Falade, 1963). In other cultures, wives reside in mixed dyadic and communal configurations. The Mende of Africa for example, live communally during busy periods of farming, with the main wife organizing household meals and other activities (Little, 1951). At other times, each wife has her own hut and work responsibilities.

Cross-cultural data suggest that dyadic living arrangements are quite common, although many such configurations include communal sharing of some public spaces. The wide variations in dwelling arrangements across polygynous societies mirror the situation in contemporary plural families, where co-wives live in a variety of residences, from dyadic to communal to mixed dyadic and communal.

Living arrangements of husbands

Do husbands have their own dwelling? Do they live with particular wives? Or do they rotate from dwelling to dwelling? In many cases men do not have their own dwelling but rotate from wife to wife. This occurs among the Bedouin of Israel (Marx, 1987), Comoro Islanders in Mozambique (Ottenheimer and Ottenheimer, 1979), and the Nuer of Africa (Evans-Pritchard, 1951). In other instances, husbands have separate dwellings, usually in compounds or homesteads, and in proximity to their wives as do the Kikuyu of Africa (Kenyatta, 1973), the Hagen of New Guinea (Strathern, 1972), the Mende of Africa (Little, 1951), and the Kiganda of East Africa (Kilbride and Kilbride, 1990). In a variant of this arrangement, the Mundurucu of Brazil locate husbands in a communal men's house. Husbands then visit their wives from that home base (Murphy and Murphy, 1974). In most cases where men have separate dwellings, women also have their own home.

In some cultures, men live in wives' homes but also have their own place in those dwellings. Among the Bedouin of Israel, wives and their children often live in their own tent (Marx, 1987). One tent of a tribal or family leader may be divided into a guest area and a family area, and the guest area may be reserved for meetings and receptions held by the husband, or for overnight male guests (Ginat, personal observation). Similarly, wives of the Gusii of Africa live separately, and each of their dwellings has two rooms (LeVine and LeVine, 1963). One room is the wife's area; it has a fireplace for cooking and a bed on which she and the husband and small children sleep. It also has a separate entrance and a partitioned alcove where adult sons eat without being able to see into the wife's private area. The second room is the husband's place, and it contains some of his personal possessions. It has a separate entrance and is used by men to entertain guests.

A somewhat similar arrangement can be found among the Masai of Africa, who give each woman in the compound her own hut (Talle, 1987). The interior is divided into different sections: a "little bed," a "big bed," a sleeping place for animals, and a hearth area. The little bed is a wife's special area where she maintains utensils and personal property and where she and the youngest children sleep. No one enters the area without permission, including the husband. The big bed is a reception area used by the husband and family for visitors. It is also a place to eat, drink, gather, and even sleep. Interestingly, sexual relationships between the husband and wife occur on the big bed, not in her private area.

Changes in living arrangements

Living arrangements in many traditional societies change over the course of courtship and betrothal, weddings, and in early and later years of marriage. These shifts often mirror changes in family status, partner and parent–child relationships, economic status, and other factors. For example, a betrothed young girl in the Fulani culture of Africa moves into the boy's family homestead and works under his mother's supervision and without any of her own domestic utensils and possessions (Dupire, 1963; Stenning, 1958, 1971). On becoming pregnant, she moves to her parents' homestead for two to three years and then returns to live with her husband. At that time, the women of the husband's camp build her a hut, and the men organize the area around the dwelling so that she can assume full wifely responsibilities. She then settles into managing her own property, working with the husband to raise and milk cattle, and independently manages her dwelling. Thus it is several years after betrothal and marriage that a Fulani woman obtains her own residence.

A slightly different arrangement occurs in the Gusii culture of Africa (LeVine, 1964; Levine and LeVine, 1963). A new bride first lives in her father's homestead for the first few months after her marriage. She then moves to the homestead of the husband's family, sleeps with her husband in his bachelor's hut, but is otherwise supervised by her mother-in-law. She does not obtain her own home in her in-laws' homestead until after the birth of her first child.[3]

Although living arrangements in many cultures shift during the early stages of family life, they may also evolve over longer spans of time. Among the Bedouin of Israel, a new couple lives in the tent of the husband's father until they are financially independent (animals and land are given to them by the groom's father after the birth of their first child) (Marx 1967, 1987). Later in life, elderly Bedouin couples spend more time apart, husband and wives each living with different sons. As the older couple shifts their property and assets to their sons, their links to their children become stronger, their own grow weaker, and their living pattern reflects this change in status.

Living arrangements of contemporary Mormon fundamentalists

Two observations can be made about the dwelling patterns of the Mormon plural families with whom we worked. First, their homes are of three general types: dyadic, communal, and mixed dyadic and communal. Since many variations occur in each category, contemporary plural families clearly do not have homogeneous living arrangements. Second, living configurations in modern fundamentalist families change as a result of pragmatic, psychological, and social factors.

Primarily dyadic living arrangements

In dyadic dwellings, plural wives and their children live in separate homes or apartments and exclusively use and control all or most living spaces. Dyadic arrangements take several forms: homes or apartments in different regions or in the same community, homes near one another in a compound area, separate apartments in a home, or combinations of these patterns. The important feature of dyadic arrangements is that a plural wife lives by and large independently of other wives. Some dyadic living arrangements also have communal features. Wives and their families may share an entranceway to a home, a yard, garden, driveway and garage, basement, laundry room, or other areas. Relatively "pure" dyadic residential configurations occur in several families.

Family 1

At one time Joan, Norma, Charlotte, and Cynthia each had their own home. Joan and Norma lived in rambler homes and Charlotte lived in a mobile home, all in different neighborhoods in the urban area. Cynthia lived in her own apartment a few blocks from Norma's home. In other words, they lived completely independently of one another.

Family 5

At present, Constance and Barbara, the first and third wives, live in separate homes within a few hundred yards of one another. Valerie and Rose, the second and fourth wives, each have their own apartment in the same multifamily apartment building; they live several miles away from the other wives.

Wives in other families live apart but share some aspects of their home areas.

Family 4

Ruth, Belle, Eve, and Shirley, Harry's second, third, fourth, and fifth wives in the rural community, each have their own home in a compound area. The dwellings are within easy sight and walking distance of one another. They and their children share communally the area between their homes, use it for gatherings, gardening, children's play, and other family activities. Anna, the first wife, lives in a home about a mile away from the compound.

Family 6

Seymour's seven wives have separate apartments, with some sharing common spaces. Five wives live in three dwellings in a large compound. Two dwellings have independent upstairs and downstairs apartments, with private entrances for each family. The other home is occupied by one wife. But the wives – Hilda, Nina, Sarah, Holly, Marlene, and Jane – share lawn, walkway, play, and other areas, as well as a garden and fields around the compound. Tamara, the fourth wife, and Mary, the seventh wife, live several miles away, each in their own home and distant from one another. All wives in this family live in dyadic arrangements, albeit in several forms.

Family 8

Ira's eight wives all live in dyadic arrangements, with some wives sharing parts of homes and outside spaces. Four wives – Gloria, Augusta, Betty, and Helene – have separate apartments in the main house of a compound area. Pairs of wives share a common entranceway at each end of the dwelling, with full apartments upstairs and downstairs on each side.

(The center of the structure has a large meeting room for family gatherings; Ira also uses part of this room as an office.) Two other wives live in separate apartments in another dwelling in the compound. The six wives and their children residing in the compound also share outside spaces.

Ethel, the second wife, and Marilyn, the eighth wife, live in other parts of the region, apart from one another and from the wives living in the compound area.

There are many social, psychological, and interpersonal reasons for the diversity of dyadic living arrangements in modern plural families. But some pragmatic factors are also at play. For example, many families in the urban group live in towns, suburban neighborhoods, or in Metropolitan City. As a result, they are more or less restricted to the existing housing stock, which is targeted for monogamous families. Therefore, many Mormon plural families in the urban group live in duplex homes, existing single-family homes that have been modified to accommodate them, or available apartments. In the Redrock community, and in more rural areas surrounding the urban and suburban metropolitan region, it is possible to build dwellings with multiple living areas, or to have compounds with several homes on a large plot of land. Part of the reason for diverse dyadic arrangements is thus wholly pragmatic.

Many plural Mormon families of the 19th century had similar arrangements (Embry, 1987; Young, 1954). Pioneer polygynous families lived in a variety of configurations, depending on practical and social factors, and living arrangements shifted from time to time. The most typical and preferred residential pattern among pioneer families was dyadic: oral history records show that 55% of plural wives lived in separate dwellings in the same community in later stages of marriages; and an additional 16% lived in their own home in different communities (Embry, 1987). Thus almost three-fourths of pioneer wives lived in separate dwellings in the later years of their marriages (dyadic living was less prevalent in early stages of marriage). Although our sample of families is small and selective, we, too, find that many contemporary plural families eventually live in dyadic arrangements.

Although one-third to one-fourth of pioneer co-wives appear to have shared the same dwelling in some areas, it is not clear what proportion lived in dyadic versus communal arrangements in the same home. Reports of wives in separate apartments in the same dwelling suggest a dyadic pattern:

> This home was divided into at least three apartments, each with its own kitchen, parlor and bedroom opening along common hallways. Each of the

wives . . . occupied one of these apartments. . . . [The husband] was said to be in the habit of dividing his time roughly into thirds, eating meals at the table of his individual wives and those children who were still living with their mothers. (Driggs, 1988, p. 116)

Two wives lived in the same house and the third in another a few yards in the rear. The single dwelling was really a duplex because each family had its own apartment, kitchen and all. The three kitchens, however, opened on a small yard about ten yards square. This provided an opportunity for the wives to see each other many times during the day. There was one cellar for the three families but the food was stored separately. Each wife had her own barrels and bins for supplies. (Young, 1954, p. 156)

According to numerous reports, the dyadic arrangement, in one form or another, was preferred by 19th-century plural families (Campbell and Campbell, 1978; Embry, 1984, 1987; Foster, 1981, 1982; Goodson, 1976; Young, 1954). In some cases, this was so apparently because at that time Mormon polygyny did not override the traditional American value of a wife having her own home. Furthermore, there was so little experience with plural family life at the time that communal living may have produced enough tension and conflict to make it a less desirable arrangement.

Primarily communal living arrangements

In communal residences, all or some wives and their children live in one home, sharing a kitchen, dining room, living room, bathrooms, and other areas within and outside the home. Wives living in communal settings usually coordinate and share responsibilities for cooking, cleaning, and using public areas, although cooperative arrangements vary, depending on work schedules, interpersonal relationships, and other factors.

There are several variations in communal living styles, the "purest" occurring when all wives live in a single dwelling and share all spaces, even sleeping areas. The hypothetical pure communal living arrangement is rare. More common are communal arrangements with some dyadic features: that is, a wife has at least her own bedroom and possibly her own bathroom and sleeping areas for her children. Another communal plan involves subsets of wives in a plural family sharing dwellings. Although living with one or two other wives is communal, it nevertheless offers somewhat more independence than all or most wives living together.

Family 7

In a relatively pure communal arrangement, Norman, Sarah, Patricia, and Audrey and their 13 children live in one home. In addition to communal use of all areas in the home, the four adults share a sleeping area. All of the infants sleep in an adjoining communal nursery room, the older girls share a bedroom, and the older boys sleep in a trailer adjacent to the home. Thus the children are housed according to age and gender. The home is being remodeled to have a large living room and a combined kitchen and eating area that will be used by the whole family.

Family 3

William, Carlyn, Danielle, Alayna, and their 12 children at present live in one home in a communal arrangement. The home has a single large kitchen and eating area, and several public rooms. The older children sleep in bunk beds in a large dormitory area subdivided for boys and girls. The infants and babies sleep in a small adjacent nursery. Thus children do not sleep near their mothers but in a highly communal arrangement.

Although each wife has her own bedroom, at one time they didn't have regular sleeping places. Instead, they shifted around nightly or every few days, sleeping here and there on no particular schedule.

Although several other families live in primarily communal patterns, most include dyadic features, usually with wives at least having their own bedrooms.

Family 9

John, Joyce, Clara, and Marjorie and four of their children live in a one-family dwelling in a suburban neighborhood. The first floor of the home has a living room, family room, and kitchen that everyone shares, a small room that John uses as an office, Joyce's bedroom, and her 18-year-old daughter's bedroom. Clara and Marjorie each have their own bedroom in the basement of the home.

Family 11

When Benjamin, married to Katherine, also married Melba, Kelly, and Mary after they were widowed, this rural Redrock family suddenly expanded to four wives and 30 children. They all live in Benjamin's and Katherine's home and are in the midst of a major remodeling to better accommodate everyone. The plan is for the wives to share one large kitchen, as well as cooking, cleaning, and shopping. The home is being converted into a three-story structure, with one floor for each wife and her children. Wives will have their own bedroom, with rooms for their children and a separate bathroom nearby, in a combined communal and dyadic configuration. The main floor will have a large living room and meeting room, an office for Benjamin, kitchen, and auxiliary space.

Communal living is not uncommon in Redrock, where land is owned by the United Fundamentalist Church and zoning permits large homes and multiple families. But communal living is not always possible in the urban area around Metropolitan City. For example, it is not feasible for a husband, four wives, and 18 to 20 children to live in a typical suburban home, even if it is partly remodeled. As a result, the limited housing stock (and zoning restrictions regarding the number of families and occupants in dwellings) force large urban plural families to live in primarily dyadic arrangements, or in communal arrangements involving subsets of wives and children.

Communal living also occurred among 19th-century Mormon families, although it was less common than dyadic housing (Embry, 1987; Young 1954). In one group of families, 47% of the wives shared homes early in their marriage, but only 10 to 15% did so in later years (Embry, 1987). We found much the same pattern in a smaller sample of contemporary plural families.[4]

Nineteenth-century communal living arrangements took several forms. In one reported case, a first and second wife lived in the lower and upper half of a home, respectively, but shared cooking, washing, and other household chores (Foster, 1982). (It is not known whether they had separate living rooms.) In another case, two wives shared a common living area and other facilities, although each wife had her own bedroom (Embry, 1987). Communal living arrangements were also adopted by some of the wives of Brigham Young (others lived independently and in dyadic configurations). According to one of Young's daughters,

> There were usually about 12 families living in the Lion House. When the families grew too large . . . they were moved to individual homes. (Spencer, 1961, p. 24)

> There were three floors in the house, with a long hallway running straight through the center of each. On the upper floor were twenty bedrooms where the childless wives and the older boys and girls slept. Each bedroom had its own . . . window, many of them had fireplaces, some had stoves and all were very comfortable. (Spencer, 1961, p. 26)

> The middle floor held the apartments of the wives with small children and the parlor or prayer room as it was generally known. (Spencer, 1961, p. 26)

The basement contained a large dining room in which some 50 members of the family had meals together. There was also a laundry room on that floor, and each wife had her assigned wash day.

The wives also used to take their turns at ironing at night by two or three of them so that they could go through the house occasionally and keep a lookout for fire at the same time. During the following day when these women slept their children would be cared for by some of the other wives. ... One wife had entire charge of the kitchen with as many girls as she needed to help her. (Spencer, 1961, p. 27)

All the wives had equal rights and privileges and each was, in turn, expected to do her share in keeping the establishment running smoothly. Each wife took care of her own apartment and her own children and assisted in doing other necessary work around the place. (Spencer, 1961, p. 65)[5]

Each wife in this latter case also assumed duties consistent with her skills; some were responsible for the kitchen and some for other duties.

Mixed dyadic and communal arrangements

Mixed dyadic and communal living patterns occur when some wives in a family live in dyadic arrangements and other wives live communally.

Family 10
Barry and his eight wives live in three separate dwellings in different parts of the community. Four wives live in one large home, the family headquarters, which also has a very large meeting room. Naomi and JoAnne and their children live in separate upstairs and downstairs areas on one side of the home, and Dorothy and Kay live in a similar configuration on the other side of the home. Wives have separate sleeping areas and bathrooms, but each pair shares a kitchen and living room. Subsets of wives shop, cook, and plan meals cooperatively and alternate in household responsibilities Thus these wives live in a communal arrangement with strong dyadic features.

Jane, Tricia, and Darla live in a different dwelling, with Jane and Tricia sharing cooking and public facilities, but having their own sleeping areas. Darla has a completely independent apartment in the home, which includes bedrooms, a living room, and kitchen. Thus two wives in this dwelling live in a communal pattern and the other wife follows a dyadic plan.

Anita, Barry's first wife, lives in a separate dwelling with her children in a strictly dyadic arrangement.

The wives said that they have lived with one another in different combinations and configurations over the years, as dictated by job requirements, number of children, child care needs, and other circumstances. In all cases, however, children always slept in their mother's area of the dwellings.

Family 4

Eve, Harry's fourth wife, said that her childhood family lived in one dwelling, as did many others in Redrock. Without using our terminology, she indicated that her mother and other wives in the family lived in a mixed dyadic and communal pattern. For example, there were three kitchens in the home, with sets of wives sharing two kitchens, and an older wife using one kitchen by herself. And young children slept near their mothers, but older children had bedrooms according to gender and age.

Family 18

Charles, Susan, Nancy, Angela, and Linda and their unmarried children live in two homes on the same street in a suburban neighborhood. Nancy, the second wife, lives alone in one home (it is hers from a previous marriage), and the three other wives share the other home, in a mixed dyadic and communal living configuration.

The three wives who live communally share the upstairs kitchen, dining room, living room, entranceway, yard, and other facilities, but each wife has her own bedroom. Susan, the first wife, sleeps upstairs, and Angela's and Linda's bedrooms are downstairs.

(It is interesting to note that one of Susan's daughters, herself a plural wife, and her baby also live temporarily in the communal home. Her own plural family does not yet have a large enough home or money for another home to house her, so she has had to live with her mother and the other wives.)

Transitions and stabilities in living arrangements

Transition, change, and experimentation with living arrangements are a hallmark of contemporary Mormon polygynous families. The factors that account for variability in dwelling practices are finances, family size, work requirements, child care, personal desires, interpersonal relationships between wives, and other issues faced regularly by modern plural families.

Family 1

Hal, Joan, Norma, Charlotte, Cynthia, and their 24 children have lived in several configurations over the years.

Their first home, still used by them, is a bi-level rambler in a suburban neighborhood. It has a single entrance leading to upstairs and downstairs areas. The upstairs has a kitchen, living room, dining area, and bedrooms. At first, Joan lived in the home alone but was joined by Norma when she and Hal married. Joan lived upstairs, Norma slept downstairs, and they shared the kitchen, living room, dining area, and the rest of the home. They lived in this primarily communal way for about two years. Then they built a separate kitchen, living room, and additional bedrooms downstairs, thereby allowing Joan and Norma to each live in a more dyadic configuration with their children – the numbers of which were steadily increasing. But they still shared some parts of the home. Thus they shifted from a primarily communal to a primarily dyadic arrangement.

When Charlotte joined the family, Joan moved into her own home in another part of the community. Norma moved to the upstairs part of the original home, and Charlotte resided downstairs. They lived this way for about two years in a dyadic and primarily dyadic arrangement. But Charlotte began to feel a loss of privacy and eventually persuaded Hal to allow her to move. When she was in her own home, all wives lived in a purely dyadic pattern, in separate dwellings in different parts of the community.

They continued in a dyadic mode when Cynthia joined the family; she simply remained in the apartment in which she had been living.

In part for financial reasons, they recently changed from purely dyadic to subsets of communal living arrangements. It was also becoming very difficult for Hal to see his four families, who lived in different parts of the community. Joan and Norma now live together in the original home – as they did in earlier years. Joan continues to live upstairs, and Norma lives downstairs. Even though they have separate kitchens and living areas upstairs and downstairs, however, Joan and Norma share one kitchen; shop, plan, and eat meals in combined families; and generally live in a communal pattern. In addition, their children do not necessarily sleep near each of them but are grouped according to age and gender. Clearly, Joan and Norma have shifted from a highly dyadic to a predominantly communal lifestyle.

So have Charlotte and Cynthia. They now live together in a one-level trailer home. They each have their own bedroom on different sides of the dwelling but share the living room, kitchen, dining area, and most other places in the home. And the children also sleep in areas selected according to age and gender, not according to their birth family. Thus, they also moved from a dyadic to a communal living arrangement.

Recently they moved again, after a relatively short period in the preceding arrangements. Because Charlotte's father became ill, he moved in with her and Cynthia moved into a newly purchased home with Norma. Joan stayed in the original family home with her children. Joan and Charlotte now live independently, and Norma and Cynthia live communally.

This is still a relatively young family, and they will no doubt continue to experiment with different living patterns as family size, finances, and other circumstances require. And it will come as no surprise if they cycle between a variety of dyadic and communal living configurations for years to come.

Family 2

A young and growing family, David, Judith, Rebecca, Emily, Phyllis, and their 21 children have lived in a variety of dyadic and communal patterns over the years.

The first home, in which Judith has lived for more than 15 years, is in a suburban neighborhood. When Rebecca joined the family, she and Judith lived communally in the home – sharing the kitchen and most other areas, cooperating in household chores, they and their children eating meals together, and so on. At the same time, they had separate bedrooms and sleeping areas for their children. As the family grew, they built a completely separate apartment in the downstairs area, and the two wives and their children lived in a predominantly dyadic arrangement. However, they continued to share a common entrance to the home, yard, and other facilities.

When Emily joined the family, she also lived in the home for a while, sharing living space with Rebecca downstairs in what was a mixed communal and dyadic living arrangement. But she eventually moved to a separate dwelling and thereafter was joined by Phyllis when she married David. As in the first home, Emily and Phyllis had separate upstairs and downstairs apartments. Thus all four wives lived in primarily dyadic configurations. These arrangements lasted for a few years.

But there have been major changes recently. Because of the wives' work schedules and the need for child care, different pairs of wives live in the first home and in a new second home (they sold the other home). For a while, Judith and Emily lived in the first home, and Rebecca and Phyllis lived in the new home. The new home had separate upstairs and downstairs apartments, but only one kitchen, which Rebecca and Phyllis shared, adding a significant communal component to an otherwise dyadic floor plan. Thus they resided in another type of mixed dyadic and communal arrangement, with wives in the first home in a strongly dyadic situation and those in the new home in a more balanced dyadic and communal plan.

The most recent configuration is even more complex and fluid, with shifts in living patterns occurring more rapidly than before. David now buys, remodels, and sells homes, and Emily and her children live in the homes he is redoing as repairs and sales progress. As a result, Judith continues to live in the original home in a strictly dyadic format. Emily is also living in a dyadic arrangement, albeit a transient one since she moves as soon as a home is renovated and sold (she has lived in three homes in the past year). And Rebecca and Phyllis continue to live together in a balanced dyadic and communal mode.

But there are more recent changes! Emily is due to have another child, and she and her young children need assistance and care before and after the birth of the new baby. So Emily now lives in the second home with Rebecca and Phyllis in a highly communal arrangement. The three wives and their children not only share most of the space in the home (although each wife has her own bedroom), but the children now sleep according to age and gender, not with their mothers. They expect this strongly communal pattern to prevail for at least several months. Thus the family now lives in a mix of a pure dyadic configuration for the first wife and a highly communal arrangement for the other wives.

Family 3
Another young family, William, Carlyn, Danielle, Alayna, and their 12 children, have also lived in several configurations.

When William and Carlyn first joined the fundamentalist group, they moved about half a dozen times in as many years – living in rental apartments and a trailer. When Danielle joined the family, all three shared a trailer. When Alayna married William, Carlyn moved into a tent they purchased (and lived in it during a winter), while Danielle and Alayna lived in the trailer (they were both pregnant at the time). Somewhat later, they rented a basement in a private home until their present home was habitable. In this array of settings much of their day-to-day life was communal.

A predominantly communal arrangement continued once the home was built, although not always. During one extended period, for example, William and Carlyn lived and worked in a distant place, only returning to the main home on weekends. They lived dyadically during the week, whereas Danielle and Alayna lived in a communal format, and the whole family lived communally on weekends.

Danielle and Alayna each had their own bedroom but managed the home in a communal fashion, sharing work and all other facilities. Since Carlyn did not have a regular place of her own, when she and William came home on weekends, family sleeping arrangements became somewhat arbitrary. Altogether, this led to a highly communal arrangement, since all spaces were shared, albeit temporarily.

A highly communal pattern also prevailed when William and Carlyn obtained jobs closer to home and rejoined the others. They continued to be quite casual about fixed sleeping spaces for the adults, shared most parts of the home, and housed the younger children in a nursery and the older children in a gender-separated dormitory arrangement. But later on they shifted the living configuration in a dyadic direction. Although they still shared kitchen and other public areas, Danielle and her children lived on one floor and Alayna and her children lived on another floor. And Carlyn, who didn't have children, had her own bedroom. They deliberately redesigned their living arrangements to have more privacy and to increase contact between a mother and her children. Indeed, they even had separate laundry facilities for each wife and her children. So, although still sharing communally many places and aspects of day-to-day life, they incorporated major dyadic features into their living arrangement.

But their story isn't over. William, Danielle, Alayna, and their children recently moved to another state to seek better employment. Carlyn remains in the original home, living there with two families, who are renters. William and Alayna live alone in a community different from Danielle's, and Danielle is caring for all their 12 children while the others work. They come together on weekends. So all the adults are living in one or another dyadic or independent arrangement, except on weekends, when William, Danielle, and Alayna live communally.

Taken together, these cases illustrate the transient living arrangements among present-day plural families, especially among younger families, as they seek and experiment with different lifestyles amid a variety of internal and external circumstances.[6] It is also useful to consider older families, many of whom eventually established stable living configurations.

Family 4
Harry, Anna, Ruth, Belle, Eve, Shirley, and their 65 children, members of the United Fundamentalist Church in Redrock, have lived in many configurations over the years. When they were first married, Harry and Anna, the first wife, lived with his parents. They continued to do so when Harry married Ruth, at one time in a tent on his father's property. For several years thereafter, they and later wives often lived communally

in the same dwelling. And different pairs of wives lived together at various times. At other times during their earlier years, the wives lived in other communities, because of fear of prosecution. Sometimes they lived apart from one another; sometimes they lived together as a whole family or in subsets of wives.

Now each wife has her own dwelling in the rural community, four of them in a compound adjacent to one another, with Anna, the first wife, living in a separate home about a mile away. Thus, after years of primarily communal living interspersed with various combinations of communal and dyadic residential arrangements, the family has adopted a permanent dyadic pattern (it is likely to be permanent because only one wife is still having children, most children are older and on their own, and the family is relatively secure economically and otherwise).

Factors affecting living arrangements

Several major factors seem to play a role in plural family choices of dyadic or communal living arrangements: (1) societal pressures, (2) the demands of everyday life, and (3) the social and psychological aspects of family life. All of these factors do not necessarily enter into every decision about living arrangements, nor are they necessarily equally influential in every family.

Societal pressures

Nineteenth-century Mormon families were repeatedly threatened with legal action for practicing plural marriage. As a result, many families split up – with wives and children living in separate dwellings in a community or fleeing to other regions in order to escape federal authorities, and the many so-called spotters, skunks, and Mormon eaters who engaged in "cohab hunting" in order to gain rewards for informing on plural family members (Dredge, 1976; Embry, 1987; Young, 1954). Some families in the modern era also followed a dyadic lifestyle when raids, arrests, and the prosecution of Mormon fundamentalists flared up again. Dorothy Solomon (1984), daughter of a former prophet of a fundamentalist group, recounted that wives in her family sometimes moved to distant communities during those years, living apart from one another in order to avoid prosecution. Although most members of our sample gave other reasons for selecting a particular housing arrangement, many are still wary about openly admitting that they are members of plural families, avoid public appearances as a plural family, and have little contact with neighbors when they live in monogamous communities. In earlier years (but less often nowadays), they also registered school children under a wife's maiden name. Although the fear of prosecution or discrimination is not at present considered a basis for selecting a living arrangement, this factor no doubt enters in occasionally, even if only indirectly.

Demands of everyday life

Over and over again, members of families gave practical reasons for changing their living arrangements toward either a more communal or a more dyadic situation. In young families that live communally, the simple facts of a "mini-population explosion" often lead to a more dyadic housing arrangement. Since it is customary for plural families to have children soon after marriage and frequently thereafter, families grow rapidly and consist of children of all ages. In younger families, there can be many infants, toddlers, and preschoolers at home; in more established families, there are also many school-age children at all levels. It is easy to imagine how tumultuous day-to-day life can be if two wives and 10 to 15 children live in a typical suburban tract dwelling with a few bedrooms, a kitchen, living room, and a couple of bathrooms. No matter what system is used to handle the everyday business of meal preparation, eating, bathing, and sleeping, the complexity of life must be extraordinary.

As noted in earlier case descriptions, at some point younger plural families shift from a communal to a more dyadic living plan as families grow. In urban areas, solutions include creating separate apartments in a home, moving one family to another dwelling in the community, and so on. Those in more rural areas sometimes build large homes with separate areas for several wives in the same structure, or they build homes in a compound where wives live separately but in nearby dwellings. And in other cases, families adopt a mixed strategy, with some wives living communally and others in dyadic arrangements.

The practical problems of day-to-day density in communal dwellings may also interact with wives' personal backgrounds and experiences. Although many fundamentalists are converts from the main Mormon church and grew up in large families, living communally with other wives and many children is bound to be stressful. In visits to family homes, we were always amazed at the levels of energy, noise, and hubbub as "hordes" of young children circulated through the home, even though they were polite and subdued in our presence. We can only imagine the adaptability and flexibility required of young mothers as they manage day-to-day affairs in a densely populated communal dwelling. Therefore it is easy to see, why pressures toward a dyadic living configuration often arise in growing plural families. The complexity of the situation is all too clear from statements such as "It just became too crowded, so we moved."

Nineteenth-century plural families faced similar problems: "Sometimes there were two homes because the families needed more room. John Brown's first two wives shared a common living area as well as the loom house and outbuildings, each wife having her own bedroom. Eventually the wives had so many children that John built two homes a few rods apart" (Embry, 1987, p. 77). At the same time, practical considerations forced families to move toward communal or shared living configurations. One important factor for many fundamentalist families in modest circumstances is finances. Many men work in seasonal occupations such as the construction industry, and their incomes are not always steady. And many women work in clerical and secretarial office positions, or in low-paying jobs such as housecleaning. As a result, people lead a prudent lifestyle – they have modest furnishings in their homes, grow some of their own food and make their own clothing. Many wives work, as do older children, in order to make family ends meet.

In addition, the fact that families have many children, all of whom need daily attention, may persuade wives to live in a communal configuration, or at least in communal subsets. In this way, wives can share child care while some are at work. (For example, Phyllis, the fourth wife in Family 2, cared for up to 18 young children every day – her own children; the children of her working co-wife Rebecca, with whom she shared the home; and a few children from another family who paid her to baby sit.) Wives who live communally can also share management of the home, save on joint purchases of food, cut down on utility costs, and share an automobile. It is also more economical to rent or own one or a few homes than it is to maintain separate dwellings for each wife. In spite of the practical problems associated with high density, financial issues can be a powerful impetus for families to live in a communal arrangement.

Another practical motivation (with some psychological and social aspects) that sometimes draws a family toward a communal configuration is the desire by husbands, wives, and children to spend more time together.

Family 1
As noted earlier, Joan, Norma, Charlotte, and Cynthia moved into two homes after having lived in separate homes for several years. Finances were one reason for doing so, but time constraints were also an important consideration. Hal found it increasingly difficult to travel around

the community, spending one evening at a time with each wife and family. This became all the more difficult when he began assuming more and more responsibilities in the church and had many meetings and appointments in the evening. With everyone now in two homes, Hal sees his wives and children more often and commutes less, and their new arrangement better accommodates their busy life.

A somewhat similar situation arose in one 19th-century family with three wives (Embry, 1987). The wives lived in separate communities to avoid federal authorities but also because they each ran one of the husband's businesses in their community. Feeling too distant from one another, they eventually moved into the same town, with two wives sharing a dwelling and the third wife living nearby.

Psychological and social factors

A network of social and psychological factors may also enter into a family's decision to change its living arrangements in either a dyadic or communal direction.

On the one hand, shifts in a dyadic direction may take place because wives wish to have their own home, manage it in their own way, have more privacy, and fulfill the American ideal of a family in its own dwelling. Incompatibility between wives may be another significant factor in this regard. Moreover, some wives and husbands find it difficult to develop a unique and intimate relationship in a communal living situation, and they want their own home in order to better foster their dyadic bond.

On the other hand, social and psychological factors may draw families toward more communal living arrangements. The concept of a harmonious, unified, and integrated plural family, led by a husband or father patriarch, is a deeply rooted value of contemporary Mormon fundamentalists. What better way to live this principle than to have a whole family under one roof – eating, sleeping, praying, and engaging in everyday activities as one family. Thus on occasion some participants feel that their plural family is too fragmented, that the husband and each wife and their children operate almost like independent monogamous families. And in strictly dyadic situations, the husband or father patriarch does not preside over a unified family but often scrambles about, visiting his separate families who are spread out across the community. In such living configurations, he is almost a transient, an occasional visitor whose leadership and parental role is fragmented and not present on a daily basis. Like practical factors that sometimes work at cross-purposes, social and psychological issues may predispose plural families toward either dyadic or communal living arrangements.

Members of some families were sensitive to the complex interplay of social and psychological factors and recognized that it was appropriate for them to live more dyadically at some life stages and communally at other times. And they articulated well the point that they probably would have to shift their living arrangements for many years to come, as their family, work, and other circumstances changed.

Family 1

In one discussion, Joan, Norma, and Charlotte, Hal's first three wives, strongly agreed that each wife should ideally have her own home. It is intrinsically difficult for women – especially new and young wives – to live with other women, they said. A woman needs to develop her own home management system, feel that a home is hers alone, and build a sense of competence and identity as a homemaker. And they also agreed that it is easier to develop an intimate relationship with the husband in separate homes.

They recounted their own experiences, noting, for example, how difficult it was for both Joan and Norma when Norma joined the family as Hal's second wife. Aside from practical issues, tension mounted as they each sought to develop a strong marital bond with Hal in one another's presence. For many reasons, they eventually decided to live dyadically, upstairs and downstairs in separate apartments. Doing so helped immeasurably in their relationships with him and with one another, and in developing their own sense of identity as homemakers. The same feelings occurred when Charlotte joined the family and lived with Norma, and the same solution eventually emerged – dyadic living in separate dwellings.

But recently they moved from completely separate dwellings for each wife to two homes for pairs of wives – a more communal arrangement than they had had for many years. This was done not only for practical reasons, that is, finances, but also family reasons: Hal can now see the four families more often. He had begun to feel that he was losing close contact with his wives and children and that he was being treated as a guest. In addition, it was becoming difficult to relax and enjoy his wives and children because the minute he walked in the door he was faced with all the serious problems that they had been saving for him on his twice-weekly visits to each of the four separate homes. Each wife felt the same way. They said "it was hard to get it all in" when he visited each of them so infrequently, and they too felt under great pressure.

They also said that living apart made it difficult for them to meet their religious obligations and goals of being a unified and cohesive family. Although they only partly achieve this in the present arrangement, with pairs of wives living together, it is at least a step in the right direction. They hope someday to achieve a more unified living plan in which all wives and children will live in proximity.

Norma emphasized that things work differently at different phases of life in plural families. Right now, she said, it is a good idea for them to share responsibilities and live in a more communal fashion. It wasn't right for them earlier, and it might even change again. Hal summed up the situation: "In plural family life, nothing is forever; change is inevitable."

Hal went on to say that his family has matured over the years, everyone has a greater sense of self-confidence, and they are now better able to live communally. Furthermore, he said that it is now important for the children, while they are growing up, to identify with the family as a whole – to build bonds with one another, and to see him as family patriarch and the wives as mothers in the same family. He also said that family members who live near or with one another provide important social support. "No one is ever alone"; "everyone's needs are met"; "no elderly people are put in rest homes." (Norma, who grew up in a plural family in which many family members lived together or close by, reinforced Hal's theme, describing how secure she felt as a child because of the support and help she received from other mothers and children in her family.)

Hal, Norma, and the other wives are articulating the principle that now is a time in their family history when communal living is essential, whereas earlier it was crucial to emphasize dyadic relationships in the family. In their view, living arrangements should mirror and be compatible with family circumstances.

Some of these views were expressed by other families, although in a less comprehensive way. Many wives and husbands mentioned that dyadic living was a means of enhancing the self-identity of individual wives, and a vehicle for facilitating an intimate and unique relationship between each wife and the husband in a plural family. Thus dyadic issues are often salient.

Family 5
When Rose, the fourth wife, joined the family, she lived with Valerie, the second wife, for three and a half years. But from the first day of her marriage she longed for her own home, even though she and Valerie got along well. The other wives chimed in, saying that it was important for

them to have separate homes in order to build more intimate and distinctive relationships with Howard at early stages of their married life.

Family 6
Seymour and five of his seven wives with whom we spoke feel strongly about having individual homes. He emphasized that separate living allows him and each wife to have time alone to develop their relationship, and leaves wives free to run their homes as they see fit.

The wives agreed, saying that living separately enables each of them to be her own person, live her own lifestyle, and not be subordinate or dominant over one another in home affairs. Nina stated that managing a home is a form of religious obligation or "stewardship" to raise children and create a place for her and Seymour. When wives lived together, she said, "Our stewardships were overlapping and sometimes in conflict," the implication being that living communally prevented them from meeting their domestic religious responsibilities.

The wives also pointed out that the five of their number who live in the same compound in separate dwellings or apartments in three homes have privacy and freedom but also visit, enjoy, and rely on one another. For them, this is an acceptable blend of communal and dyadic living arrangements.

Family 8
Ira, an elder in the community, feels that it is best for wives to have their own separate dwellings, to avoid inevitable tensions and conflicts. At the same time, he believes that wives should ideally live near one another so that they can be part of a single family. Ethel, the second wife, agreed, saying that living close to one another allows wives to develop a group spirit and camaraderie that encourages their mutual support and sense of unity. She went on to say that when wives and their children live apart, they are actually engaging in "plural monogamy," not a unified plural family life, and this is not what they are supposed to do.

Because five of seven wives live in a compound, in separate homes or apartments, they feel that they have achieved a workable living arrangement that meets their individual and collective family needs and ideals – a balance of dyadic and communal relationships.

Social and psychological factors also entered into decisions about living arrangements in 19th-century plural families – often leading to moves toward dyadic configurations. For example, in one family in which the wives did not get along the husband divided the house into two apartments. But the two wives still argued about the time the husband spent with each family. Wives would even listen through the keyhole of each other's apartments. Eventually the husband built a second house close by, but the women continued to argue and even came to blows (Young, 1908).

Another large issue in the 19th century had to do with the Victorian ideal of a wife having and managing her own home – a common view among wives in our modern families as well. A second wife who had lived with the first wife for a period of time finally obtained her own home, according to her daughter, when she "got backbone enough to demand a place for herself. She told Father that when a woman's hearthstone was taken away, everything was gone" (Embry, 1987, p. 76).

Another wife who had shared a home with the first wife "prayed for a separate home. After her husband returned from a seven-month mission, her father gave her some land, and her husband built her a small adobe house. She later wrote, 'I shall never forget how happy I was, and as soon as we were moved in and I was alone, I bowed down before the Lord and poured out my soul in prayer and gratitude for having a house of my own' " (Embry, 1987, p. 77).

And Annie Tanner, a turn-of-the-century plural wife, said that not having her own home, and having to live with strangers or in hiding for several years, left her unfulfilled as a wife and mother. It made her feel like a "wanderer without a home" (Tanner, 1983 p. xxiii).

The complex array of practical, psychological, and social factors that contribute to mobility among present-day plural families do not operate in a mechanical and uniform fashion. An issue that may be important for some families may be of little concern to others; some factors may play crucial roles during certain phases of a family's life and be less important at other times; some factors press toward dyadic living arrangements, whereas others move a family in a communal direction. As in many other aspects of their lives, what they often do is try to experiment with different configurations as they go along. If a particular arrangement works for a while, they are likely to stay with it. If it doesn't work or if family circumstances change, they will shift into another living mode. Because there are so many factors at play, sometimes working at cross-purposes, because participants have usually had so little personal experience with plural family life, and because the polygynous culture at large has few norms about living configurations, each family is more or less on its own when figuring out its housing needs.

The shift to a new living configuration may solve some problems, but it can sometimes create new ones. Thus the move from a dyadic to a communal arrangement can reduce privacy, to which a wife may have become accustomed; a move from a communal to a dyadic situation may result in the loss of previous companionship with other wives; and there may be disruptions in family routines.

Family 1

When Joan and Charlotte, and Norma and Cynthia, moved from separate homes into two homes, where each pair of wives shared a dwelling, the children had some problems adjusting. Some of the very young children were sometimes confused about who their mother was and were territorial about their rooms and possessions. Some even asked when they were "going home."

Family 2

As already mentioned, the family has been moving quite a bit recently, with three wives now living temporarily in one home. Phyllis, the fourth wife, who is responsible for caring for many of the children while the other wives work, said that she has been having an especially difficult time with all the moves. Because she cares for different children in the family at different times (and in large numbers – a dozen and a half children or more on some occasions) she must constantly reinvoke rules that she had previously established with them. She described this need for repetition and "resocialization" as very frustrating, and recounted how she blew up at David and the other wives for not understanding or appreciating her situation.

Phyllis also disliked several features of the new home that contrasted with her previous residence – she did not have a separate entrance to her downstairs apartment, but had to enter through the front door into Norma's apartment.

Family 9

John, Joyce, Clara, and Marjorie, and several children, including new babies, live in a typical suburban dwelling. Because it has become so crowded, one of the older sons in high school now lives in an apartment with several boys from other plural families; another son lives in the garage of the home. No one is happy with these arrangements, but there is no alternative at the moment.

Family 12

Even though they moved around quite a bit, Lauren, the second wife, has never had an arrangement with which she was completely satisfied. At one time, she had her own bedroom but shared a bathroom in Elaine's bedroom – which was quite inconvenient and not very private for either of them. At another time, they moved into a duplex where she had her own apartment. However, there was no private entrance to her home, so her visitors had to enter through Elaine's home – again an invasion of privacy.

At still another point in their marriage, the three of them shared a room in his mother's home. It was very crowded, and the wives had to take turns sleeping with Fred – yet another invasion of privacy.

In summary, although moving from one living configuration to another may solve some problems, it can also create other ones.

Life cycle of living arrangements

In spite of tremendous variability in dyadic and communal living arrangements among contemporary fundamentalists, and at the risk of over-simplification, we now describe a prototypic pattern of living arrangements over the life cycle of an "average" plural family in the Metropolitan City group.[7]

The story begins in the traditional American way. A newly married couple establishes an independent residence in an apartment or home, which they rent or purchase, depending upon their finances. When another wife joins the family, she often lives in the home with the first wife. Each wife usually has her own bedroom, but they share the kitchen, living room, and other public places. The end result is a communal arrangement with some dyadic features. This arrangement lasts for a while, but pressures slowly build for the wives to have greater independence. These pressures mount for several reasons: practical reasons associated with increasing numbers of children, and the complexities of managing two young families in a small suburban home; and social and psychological factors associated with wives' needs for privacy, differences in home management styles, the desire of wives to put their personal stamp on their homes, and their need to develop a unique relationship with the husband in their own physical setting. Now the family is drawn to a more dyadic arrangement – separate upstairs and downstairs apartments or different homes.

This same pattern often recurs as successive wives enter a family. Each new wife will live with an established wife for a while but eventually will set up her own residence as practical, psychological, and social factors come into play. Thus a pattern of dyadic–communal–dyadic living arrangements is not uncommon in the early phases of present-day plural family life.

Thereafter, in the growing and middle years of a plural family, they may live in a variety of dwelling configurations – from dyadic to communal or subsets of wives living communally, to mixed dyadic and communal, to dyadic, and so on. This is a period of great flux and variation in living arrangements, again as a result of the interplay of practical, psychological, and social factors in their lives. Some families maintain more or less dyadic configurations. But many move from dyadic to communal arrangements when there are too many dispersed dwellings, financial pressures mount, children of working wives need to be cared for by other wives, and so on. The opposite pattern, toward more dyadic living, also occurs, as the factors mentioned previously continue to be relevant. So there are frequent shifts in living arrangements during these "growing years," as modern plural families attempt to cope with the network of practical, social, and psychological factors in their lives.

The swings between communal and dyadic living arrangements during a family's growing years are likely to depend on the differential importance of pressures at various life stages. Thus overcrowding and loss of privacy during one stage of a family's life may lead them to a dyadic solution. At other times, financial and practical problems regarding child care, work schedules, and other factors may become salient and encourage the family to make more communal arrangements. In any case, growing families seem to oscillate between many forms of dyadic and communal living arrangements during the early and middle years of their lives.

In a family's later years wives tend to live in predominantly dyadic arrangements – in completely separate dwellings, apartments or areas within a common dwelling, or in a compound arrangement. In many cases, there is some communal sharing of public spaces, such as yards, gardens, and garages. The blend of dyadic and communal living arrangements is an ideal toward which many plural families aspire. On the one hand, communal living is congruent with their religious beliefs in a patriarchal family living in harmonious unity. On the other hand, they hold that each wife should have independent "stewardship" over her home. The tendency for many established and older families to live in dyadic arrangements, often with communal aspects, is consistent with these ideals.

Although there are many variants, the pattern of living arrangements in plural families usually begins with a dyadic format, becomes communal, shifts to dyadic patterns, and then through the years evolves in a variety of communal and dyadic configurations. Eventually, many families gravitate toward dyadic living forms – often with some communal features. Central to our analysis is the idea that experimentation and transition with living arrangements are customary among contemporary polygynous families; as they cope with a variety of pragmatic, psychological, and social factors in their lives.

The ideal: A blend of dyadic and communal living

Several families described an ideal living configuration that they hoped to have someday. They did not use our terminology, but essentially they looked forward to the time when they might have a dwelling arrangement that *combined* communal and dyadic qualities. On the one hand, they seek communal dwellings or homes in close proximity in order to meet their religious beliefs in a unified, harmonious, and integrated family. This is consistent with the ideal of a plural family eventually living throughout eternity in its own heavenly universe in the hereafter. (To be sure, they also acknowledged other reasons for living communally in "this world": child care, economic considerations, social support and companionship among wives, husbands having easier frequent access to families, and so on.) At the same time, many families want their ideal family home to possess dyadic qualities. They consistently emphasized the importance of privacy and independence for each wife and her family – for example, with the aid of separate entranceways into a communal dwelling, individual kitchens, living rooms, and sleeping areas for wives and their children. Over and over, husbands and wives explicitly stated that their ideal living arrangement was a combination of being together and apart – in our terms, a blend of dyadic and communal. And when they emphasized the communal aspects of a design, they were quick to incorporate dyadic features, and vice versa.

Family 1
Hal, Joan, Norma, Charlotte, and Cynthia – but mostly Hal – envision several ideal living arrangements, all of which have separate homes or apartments for each wife, with common areas for all four families to come together. One design is a quadrangular arrangement of four apartments, with a large room, courtyard, or atrium in the center for meetings, prayers, and joint family activities. We talked at length about alternative design arrangements, but each of them always involved the idea of families living independently but also having communal spaces for the whole family.

Family 3
William not only envisions living communally with Carlyn, Danielle, and Alayna, as they now do in one home, but he hopes to extend the concept to his children. He drew a sketch of what he has in mind – a small community in which his children, once they are grown and have their own families, live on plots of land around the main family home in which he and his wives now reside. For William, this symbolizes their eventual life in the hereafter, with him as patriarch surrounded by his wives and children.

Within this ideal family community, however, each family will have its own dwelling, so that they may live in an independent manner. Thus, although emphasizing the communality of the whole extended family, William acknowledges the importance of a design with dyadic features.

Family 6

Seymour's idea of an ideal home is entirely hypothetical. The perfect dwelling, he said, is a structure analogous to the state capitol, where each wife would have her own separate rooms for her and her children, but where there would be a common meeting place for everyone in the family to gather. Again, without saying so, Seymour sought a home that balances dyadic and communal processes.

Family 9

John, a recent convert to fundamentalism, offered a couple of ideas about the ideal home that are similar to those proposed by others. One concept involves a single dwelling in which all wives have separate living areas and kitchens. But the ideal home should also have a central family room where the whole family can gather. Another hypothetical plan is a multiplex dwelling with wives in separate apartments, each with its own entrance to assure complete autonomy. However, the apartments would all be clustered around and connected to a central family room where everyone could assemble for collective activities. Once again, the blend of dyadic and communal features is central to the ideal living configuration.

The idealized living configuration for several plural families is a blend of dyadic and communal processes. A communal arrangement is consistent with religious values that call for a plural family to live together in this world – as they will in the hereafter – in a harmonious unity and guided by a patriarchal husband/father. At the same time, families acknowledge that each wife must have responsibility for her own home and children, must have a place where she and her husband can develop and maintain a dyadic relationship. Thus, the interplay of dyadic and communal processes is salient in the minds of members of plural families when they imagine an ideal living arrangement.

Summary

In general, contemporary Mormon plural families live in three general dwelling arrangements. The first are dyadic arrangements, in which wives and their children live in separate homes, apartments, or areas of a home. In some cases, wives share spaces, such as entranceways, yards, and garages. The second category consists of communal living arrangements, in which wives live together and share kitchens, living rooms, and other areas. However, it is customary for wives to have their own bedrooms or sleeping areas, and this adds a dyadic dimension to primarily communal dwelling forms. The third kind are mixed dyadic and communal arrangements, in which some wives live communally and others live in dyadic configurations.

A variety of societal, practical, and psychological factors affect living arrangements of Mormon polygynous families. Earlier in their history, the fear of arrest and prosecution predisposed many plural families to live in separate or dyadic dwellings. The practical demands of large plural families living in restricted quarters and the psychological and social issues associated with individual identity of wives, fostering husband–wife relationships, and differences in lifestyles of wives sharing a home also contribute to moves toward separate dwellings. Because many members of plural families were raised in monogamous families, a preference for independent homes seems natural. At the same time, practical, psychological, and religious factors lead polygynous families to seek communal arrangements at some time in their lives. These include the lower costs of maintaining communal dwellings, ease of child care and home management for families with working wives, a husband's better accessibility to his families, and the religious ideal of members of a plural family living together in a communal fashion. Thus a variety of intertwined factors motivate contemporary plural families to live communally or dyadically, with combinations of factors entering in at various stages of a family's life. As a result, modern plural families change their living arrangements frequently, from more or less dyadic to more or less communal patterns, and vice versa, as they attempt to cope with the numerous pressures and complexities in their lives.

The prototypic pattern of dwelling arrangements over the life of a contemporary plural family (in the urban community) begins with new wives living in the homes of other wives. As families grow and other factors come into play, there is often a shift to dyadic dwelling arrangements. Thereafter, again as a result of a variety of factors, families oscillate between dyadic, communal, and mixed dyadic and communal arrangements. Eventually, when they are more established, have stable numbers of wives and children, and approach their later years, plural families often gravitate toward dyadic living arrangements, wherein each wife has a primarily independent apartment or residence.

When families described the ideal living arrangement that they would like in the future, they consistently mentioned housing arrangements that include a blend of dyadic and communal features. On the one hand, they want a home for each wife and her children, where they may live independently from day to day, much as in a traditional monogamous family. On the other hand, they also aspire to live near one another and to have a communal space where they can come together on a regular basis and be a unified, cohesive, and communal family. Thus, they seek a blend of dyadic and communal living arrangements in their hypothetical "dream" home of the future.

11

Wives and homes

A home is more than a place to eat, sleep, store personal things, and engage in the practical affairs of day-to-day life. A home is also where a marriage relationship is played out, children are cared for and taught, and people reveal, through their decorations and lifestyle, who they are and what they believe in. Thus a home is a place in which people display their values, idiosyncrasies, and personalities. In Western societies a home is also a person's or family's "castle" – a place over which they have dominion and control. The home is also ideally a place where people can have solitude, security, peace, and serenity or where they can interact with family, friends, and neighbors, as they desire.

The present chapter analyzes these psychological and social aspects of homes for wives in polygynous families. Specifically, it is concerned with wives' feelings about their homes, their home decor, and the extent to which homes reflect their individuality, dyadic relationships with their husband, and links to their co-wives and the communal plural family. Another topic of interest is the extent to which wives control and manage homes as personal "territories" and also use them to achieve solitude. The overall intent is to determine the degree and nature of "place attachment" to homes among wives in present-day plural families. Chapter 12 addresses the same issues for husbands in Mormon fundamentalist families.

Homes and culture

The social and psychological significance of homes has been the subject of numerous studies (see, e.g., Altman and Werner, 1985; Low and Chambers, 1989). Homes have been found to play a key psychological role in the spatial, temporal, and sociocultural orderings of our lives and to affect our conceptions of ourselves, others, and the social world in which we live (Dovey, 1985). Children first learn spatial orderings of up/down, near/far, right/left in their homes. People also view their homes as places of security and separation from the world, places to display personal and family identities, and a setting in which to engage in close relationships with partners, children, and others. Through decorations, symbols, and other means, homes connect people to their community and culture. The home also provides a temporal ordering to people's lives – it can be the repository of past events; it is an obvious indicator of the present; it can even signify future activities and events.

The psychological and social importance of homes is evident in many cultures around the world. For example, the word "marriage" in the Gabra culture of Africa is synonymous with the phrase "to build a home" (Prussin, 1989), and the words "home" and "getting married" are derived from the same root in the Javanese culture (Geertz, 1961). And in Jewish weddings the bride and groom are married under a canopy that among other things symbolizes the home in which the couple will live and raise a family.

Many ethnographies describe homes in other cultures in general or focus on "placemaking" in the early stages of marriage. The placemaking process is often rich in symbolic and practical details regarding role relationships between couple members and between new and established wives, and links of couple members to family, kin, and culture (Altman et al. 1992). In some cultures placemaking begins when young people or their families plan an eventual marriage; it can also occur following a marriage. The creation of a home may include financial savings, gift giving, bridewealth and dowry practices; the accumulation of household supplies and objects; and the construction of a dwelling. Placemaking often involves celebrations and rituals, such as engagement and house-warming parties, carrying the bride over the threshold, house blessings, and the decoration of the home on religious or social occasions.

The status of wives and homes

In some polygynous societies the placement of a new wife's dwelling reflects her status and relationship to other wives. Among the Masai of Africa,

> Every married woman has her own house . . . , and women married to the same man build their houses alternately according to seniority on the two sides of the family gate. The first wife begins by building her house on the right side [of the gatepost entrance to the family compound]. . . . The second wife builds her house on the left side, the third on the right again, etc. As a third and fourth wife is included in the polygamous unit, the first and second wife move away from their respective gate-posts. Thus the youngest wives will always live in the houses closest to the [gate]. (Talle, 1987, p. 64)

But more is involved than a wife's status. If a wife dies without sons to inherit her cattle, the livestock reverts to the sons of co-wives on the same side of the gate entrance. And children on each side of the gatepost tend to be socially closer to one another. For the Masai wife, the location of her home signals both her status and social bonds within the polygynous family.

Although new wives among the Pedi of Africa also place their homes alternately on the left and right of the first wife in a semicircle, in this case the more senior a wife the closer she is to the center (Kuper, 1980). The Swazi of Africa put the senior wife (or the husband's mother) in a "great hut" in a central position in a homestead (Kuper, 1950, 1980). Her hut contains a family shrine and skulls of cattle sacrificed to ancestors, and it is where the husband receives and entertains guests. The other wives' dwellings alternate right and left around the great hut according to their seniority. Thus the location of a Swazi home signifies both the status of wives and other important aspects of family history and social relationships with others. In contrast, we found no consistent evidence that the homes of Mormon polygynous wives are organized or differentiated according to their seniority.

Relationships with family and kin

In some cultures a new home may reflect relationships between a newly married couple and their family and kin. For example, the mothers of the bride and groom in the !Kung Bushmen culture of Africa cooperatively build a special wedding hut at the geographical midpoint between their two bands (Lee, 1984; Marshall, 1961, 1976). They also build a fire in front of the hut to symbolize home and family. The fire is started with a large and small stick, symbolizing male and female genders, respectively. A notch is carved in each stick and they are fitted together and placed in the fire. These placemaking rituals symbolize both the linkage of the newlyweds to their families and to one another.

Similar practices occur among the Gabra of Africa (Prussin, 1989). For these nomadic people, the transportable dwelling is symbolic of their marriage. During the wedding celebration the wooden frame and animal hides used to cover the dwelling are anointed, and the home is assembled at the home site of the groom's father. Women and girls from the bride's camp contribute some building materials and combine them with framing and animal hides from the home of the bride's mother's (a practice reminiscent of the "something old, something new" tradition in the dress of Western brides). And women from the groom's side provide a camel-skin bed mat and fat to polish the wooden frame. The home is then dismantled and reerected several times at the bride's family home. Then the groom anoints the home and builds a fire in it with fire sticks provided by his mother. Later the bride brings furnishings and arranges them in accordance with cultural customs. The Gabra placemaking process reflects important symbolic and physical links of the new dwelling and couple to their family and kin and also highlights their gender roles with respect to one another.

Similar practices occur among the nomadic Tuareg of Africa (Rasmussen, 1987). Women relatives of the bride prepare a dwelling tent for the newlyweds, and for three nights after the wedding the women dismantle and reassemble the tent, enlarging it and improving it at each construction. The families of the bride and groom contribute household equipment for the new dwelling. For six nights the bride enters the tent through a side flap, not the front entrance, and only on the seventh night, when the marriage is consummated, does she enter the front door. For the next year the couple only sleeps in the tent, returning to their parents' homes during the day; after that the tent becomes their permanent residence. Again, gender roles and links to family and kin are symbolically and tangibly reflected in new dwellings.

In summary, how homes are created by and for newlyweds – the placemaking process – often symbolizes personal identities, roles of couple members, and their ties to family, community, and the culture at large. To our knowledge, present-day Mormon fundamentalists do not engage in elaborate rituals when establishing a new home. They generally follow American traditions of gift giving, housewarmings, and the like.

Gender and family relationships in established marriages

One gender-related issue is who "owns" or is in control of the dwelling – the husband or the wife. As noted in chapter 10, in some cultures husbands and wives have separate dwellings that they each control. In others, husbands do not have their own home but may have an area of their own within a wife's home. In still others, wives completely control the home; husbands visit but do not have a defined place of their own in it.

In the Kikuyu culture of Africa, husband and wives each have their own hut in a family homestead (Kenyatta, 1973). Each wife's hut is under her strict control. It is a place where she keeps her personal belongings and where she cooks and cares for her children. The husband sleeps with wives in their hut, not in his. The husband uses his hut to entertain visitors and friends; wives are responsible for cleaning it, sweeping the yard, lighting his fire, and bringing food to him. In other words, each Kikuyu wife and husband identifies with their own separate dwellings, although they visit or have responsibilities in each other's homes.

Other polygynous cultures in which wives have their own dwellings designate certain areas in each home for the husband's use. Presumably he has some control over these areas and is psychologically identified with them. Among the Bedouins of Israel, each wife has her own tent, and the husband rotates among them (Marx, 1987; Ginat, personal observation). All or part of the tent is woven by the wife; she sets it up and takes it down when the family moves; and she manages day-to-day life in and around the dwelling. Bedouin homes mirror a woman's roles and identity symbolically and in practice. Bedouin tents of some men, including family or tribal leaders, are divided into a family area and a guest area. The family section is a "forbidden" place, and no man except the husband may enter it. The guest area is where the husband entertains visitors; it may be decorated with wall hangings, camel saddles, and the like.

Distinctive gender roles are also evident in the homes of the Fulani of Africa (DuPire, 1963; Stenning, 1958, 1971). The wife's family provides her with supplies and implements for the home, such as a bed, mats, and cooking implements. The groom's family gives him masculine-oriented resources, such as a pack ox and harness for transporting the home when the camp is moved. The home site is also divided along gender lines, with a calf rope separating the wife's and husband's areas. Her side of the homestead is reserved for domestic activities such as cooking and selling milk and butter, and it is the place where female members of the family eat. No male other than an infant typically crosses the calf rope into the wife's area, except when she and her husband have sex. By the same token, females do not enter the male area, except when a wife milks cows.

A final example illustrates how new and established homes involve gender roles and affective bonds with family, kin, and culture. In the Sakalava culture of Madagascar, a newly married couple's home is built near the groom's family home (Feely-Harnik, 1980). The home is oriented along sacred north–south and east–west axes, with the son's home to the south and west of his father's home. The father's home is closest to the graves of his ancestors. The interior of the home is similarly ordered, with the sacred northeast corner reflecting a connection between the worlds of the living and the dead. The north and east areas inside homes are also male places and are symbolic of patriarchal ancestors; the south and west areas in dwellings signify the world of women and visitors. Domestic supplies and equipment are arranged along the west wall, as is the fire, the latter reflecting women's importance to life. Also symbolizing gender differentiation, the placenta of a boy is buried in the sacred northeastern area of the home, and the placenta of a girl is buried in the southwestern part of the dwelling. Thus the Sakalava home not only mirrors gender roles, but it also links each home to a family/kin group, and to a husband's ancestral lineage.

Wives and homes in Mormon plural families

Although the living arrangements of contemporary plural families vary across and within families, most wives have a strong psychological attachment to their home or to places in the home. This is not always the case for fundamentalist husbands (see chapter 12). Contemporary plural wives also treat the dwelling as their "territory." That is, they determine the rules for family life and use of space, the home decor and furnishings, and the manner in which their values, beliefs, and preferences will be displayed. Territorial control enables a wife to regulate family routines, seek solitude from others, and determine who may enter or visit the home. Although wives are not able to fully exert their authority over a home when they share it with other wives, they each usually maintain territorial authority over their bedroom or some part of the home. In stable families, a woman's dominion over the home is usually acknowledged and respected by the husband and other wives and children.

The idea of a wife having her own home, being responsible for it, and using it to express her personality and beliefs is not only customary in traditional American culture (although in contemporary society many men also play an active role in the home) but is rooted in Mormon history and, indirectly, in Mormon theology. Like the main Mormon Church, fundamentalists have long linked women's roles to the home, leaving men to deal with the outside world and to serve as religious patriarchs of their families. A woman's responsibility is to create and run a home for her family, and make it a place of religious observance and teaching. The dwelling is a place over which she is given "stewardship" – a term reflecting responsibility in the socioreligious structure of the church and culture. Although many fundamentalist and mainstream Mormon wives work to help support their families, their responsibilities in the home continue.

These ideas about women and homes prevailed among 19th-century Mormons. Brigham Young once said:

> It is the calling of the wife and mother to know what to do with everything that is brought into the house, laboring to make her home desirable to her husband and children, making herself an Eve in the midst of a little paradise of her own creating, securing the husband's love and confidence, and tying

her offspring to her, with a love that is stronger than death, for an everlasting inheritance. (Young, 1954, p. 175)

Place attachment, territoriality, and privacy regulation in homes

Central to an understanding of close relationships is the concept of *privacy regulation*. Privacy regulation can be defined as a dialectic process involving the openness and closedness by a person or group to others. In other words, it is a process by which to control and regulate boundaries between the self and others (for a full discussion see Altman, 1975, 1977; Altman, Vinsel, and Brown, 1981; Altman and Chemers, 1989). Our thesis is that regulating privacy is a culturally universal process that is crucial to individual and group viability and well-being. Cultures differ widely in the behavioral mechanisms used by their members to regulate interaction. These can be verbal behavior; nonverbal behavior (or the so-called body language of gestures, facial and body expressions and movements); the use of the physical environment such as personal spacing; territorial behavior; and design, decoration, and other activities in the home and other places. Our main concern here is to determine how present-day plural families use the home to regulate their openness and closedness to others.

Since we view territorial behavior as an environmental privacy mechanism that people use to regulate their interactions with others, we focus on the use and control of areas and objects by individuals and groups (for a full technical discussion of the concept of territory see Altman, 1975; Brown, 1987). Territories can be classified as *primary, secondary,* or *public,* depending on their psychological importance to the occupants, the extent to which the occupants control a place, the duration or time of their control, the seriousness of intrusions or invasions of the space, and the extent to which people "mark" or decorate and personalize a place. Primary territories are those in which all these factors play a significant role. A home is a typical example. It is usually very important to its occupants, they control it almost absolutely and at all times, intrusion is a serious and potentially threatening matter, and a home is often extensively marked with decorations. In contrast, a seat on a bus is a public territory – it is far less important, duration of control is limited to the time a person occupies the seat, an intrusion is less threatening, and people rarely decorate or mark such places. Secondary territories are intermediate in these respects.

The third concept, *place attachment,* refers to the emotional and affective bonds that people have for places and things (for a discussion and examples of place attachment research and theory see Altman and Low, 1992).

We next examine the home as a primary territory and as a means by which plural wives regulate their privacy toward others. We do this by assessing the extent to which wives can control who has access to their homes, the manner in which they achieve openness and closedness, rules governing entry into different parts of the home, and the use of certain spaces for separation and solitude. We also studied wives' attachment to their homes as reflected in decorations and furnishings, as well as the other means they used to display their personalities and values in homes. Since these are complex issues, we begin with their clearest manifestation – in furnishings and decorations.

Who decides about furnishings and decorations?

Our information is unequivocal on the point that plural wives have the responsibility and authority for furnishing, decorating, and arranging their homes. Husbands usually play a minor role or have little part at all in how homes are furnished and decorated. Here is how wives and husbands view the matter:

Family 2
In discussing one of their planned moves – wherein wives would simply switch homes to help with child care – David casually suggested that they leave all the furniture where it was and that wives move only their clothing and personal effects. It would be so much easier, he said, than to move whole households. The wives vehemently opposed this suggestion, insisting that they would not move without their own furniture and decorations. Emily even said that her home was part of her and reflected her personality, and she was emphatic about moving her things with her. The others agreed and were so vocal that David quickly backed off.

They also discussed the fact that each of them decides how their homes are furnished and decorated, although David is involved in major purchases. He concurred, restating the theme that a home is each wife's domain and that they make decisions about decorations, furnishings, and use of the home.

It was evident that the wives are the key players, since each dwelling is distinctive. On our visits to their homes, some wives pointed out the special features of the decor – Emily, the third wife, decorated her home in a western motif; Phyllis, the fourth wife, decorated parts of her home to express her interest in horse showing and riding contests and in collections of angel figurines.

Family 4

On one of our visits to the family compound, Eve, Harry's fourth wife, described in detail the renovation being done to her home. The changes, she said, would solve many day-to-day living problems, and she was quite enthusiastic about the remodeling being done by family members. Harry made no comments and was clearly in the background. As we toured her home, Eve stated that Harry has no involvement at all in the renovation or in the furnishing and decoration of the home. He agreed, saying that it is completely up to Eve and the other wives to make all decisions about their homes.

Family 10

Over the years, the eight wives in the family have moved quite often. When they relocate, it is not uncommon to redistribute some of their furniture, depending on the configuration of the dwellings and the wives' needs (most of the wives live communally, sharing living rooms and kitchens). But they always keep their own bedroom furniture; everyone said those items are very important to them. Negotiations about what furniture to switch around are completely up to the wives. Barry has nothing to say about any redistribution, or the home decoration. In fact, he hardly said anything in this discussion, whereas the wives were quite outspoken about their feelings.

These few examples are typical of many other plural wives and their husbands. During our visits, a wife always led a tour of the home and described its features, or answered our queries about furnishings or decorations. Husbands usually went along, but rarely said anything and always seemed to be in the background. In addition, wives often expressed enthusiasm (or displeasure) about their home and its furnishings or arrangement, talked about what they would like to have, what was good and bad about the dwelling, and so on. Moreover, in case after case, each wife's home in a plural family was decorated and furnished in a unique way. Few had the same furniture, decorations were distinctive, and they reflected the specific interests, values, and preferences of wives.

How do things work when wives live communally? Even though many families live in some type of communal arrangement wives almost always have a place or area of their own – a bedroom, a suite of rooms for them and their children, or some other configuration. And in essentially every case that we encountered a wife at least determined how her bedroom and those of her children were furnished, arranged, and decorated. And communal spaces, such as kitchens and living rooms, were often jointly decorated by wives. In other cases, the first wife who previously lived in the dwelling determined by and large how the public spaces were furnished and decorated.

Family 3

William, Carlyn, Danielle, and Alayna lived in one home during most of our visits and discussions with them. On one of our visits, we observed that each wife has her own room, with everyone sharing public spaces. And the bedrooms are quite different. Alayna's bedroom is in considerable disarray – clothes are strewn about, the bed is unmade, there are no closets, and the room is disorganized. Carlyn's room is also unkempt, although she explained that she is only in that space temporarily and soon will move elsewhere in the home. In contrast, Danielle's room is well cared for, has wall hangings, photographs, displays of her jewelry, and a variety of objects neatly arranged on the dresser and tables.

The public areas of the home are not very well furnished or decorated, and there are no displays or items of furniture associated with any particular wife. However, on the main stairway to the second level we saw separate clusters of photographs linked to each wife. Groupings are not exactly the same, but they included photographs of a wife's parents, brothers, and sisters; each wife, the husband and their children; the husband's parents; and so on. This communal space in the home is clearly attached to each wife and to the family as a whole.

Family 9

Joyce, Clara, and Marjorie live in one dwelling, in which each wife has her own bedroom. The bedrooms are furnished and decorated quite differently. Joyce's room displays photographs of her children and John, her parents, small photos of Clara's children, a carved wooden figure of a kneeling camel, and other decorative items. Clara's bed has an attractive quilt made for her by Joyce and Marjorie, as well as photographs of her and John, their children, her parents, and a variety of objects. Both bedrooms are quite neat. Marjorie, who is relatively new to the family and a young woman, has a casual room, decorated with some posters and personal objects. Each room reflects the tastes of the individual wife and is decorated by her alone.

The main living room is furnished with a sofa and a few chairs. We assume that this was originally John's and Joyce's furniture – they were married for 20 years before entering plural family life. And a curio cabinet in the room is Joyce's; it contains her doll collection. Beyond this single item associated with a particular wife, the room has general decorations: a special Bible, the Book of Mormon, the book of Doctrines and Covenants, a print of Jesus and two women (suggesting his plural marriage), a decorative genealogy of the "history of mankind" drawn by John (beginning with the biblical tribes of Israel and going up through Joseph Smith). Interestingly, the living room has a photograph of John, the wives, and children. Except for Joyce's doll collection (and perhaps the furniture), the living room is not strongly linked to any particular wife but is a communal place.

Family 10

Barry's eight wives live in several configurations, a number of which involve pairs of wives sharing dwellings. They make decisions jointly about decorating the living rooms and common spaces but decorate their individual bedrooms according to their unique preferences and tastes.

One pair of wives said they display photographs of Barry and his parents in the living room but have pictures of their children, grandchildren, and of themselves and Barry in their bedroom. The public space is not used as dyadic space but primarily contains items associated with the family as a whole.

Interestingly, one pair of wives put their favorite chair in the living room. Although the chairs belong to each wife, they decided on the arrangement consensually.

Family 1

As described earlier, Joan, Norma, Charlotte, and Cynthia, Hal's four wives, each lived in separate dwellings until recently; they now live in pairs in two homes. We visited and toured Charlotte's and Cynthia's home a few months after they moved in together.

Each wife has her own bedroom (although their children's sleeping arrangements are decided on the basis of age or gender, not their mother's area of the home). They also share public spaces – kitchen, living room, and others. Their bedrooms are highly decorated with items meaningful to them, their relationship with Hal, and their children. For example, Charlotte has pictures of her and Hal and of her children on the wall behind her bed. Elsewhere in the room she displays a collage of photographs of her parents, sisters, and brothers.

In the same way, Cynthia's room contains many personal items, including pictures of her children and of her and Hal, her wedding flowers, and a lamp that Hal gave her as a birthday present. She also showed us her wedding and honeymoon album, which she meticulously prepared, and a framed poem she had written commemorating their marriage. Although they share a home, these two wives, like many others, have an area that they decorate according to their own tastes and that reflects their unique personalities.

As for the public areas, such as the living room, they discussed in advance how to furnish the room and selected furniture from each of their previous dwellings that would fit and be compatible (most of it came from Charlotte's home). So they were very sensitive to the joint nature of the spaces beyond their bedrooms. The living room is well furnished with a sofa, easy chairs, display case, and piano, among other items. They also have a variety of religious pictures on the wall and decorative objects around the room.

When we asked about some small objects in a display cabinet, they noted that each of them had put some of their own personal items on the shelves. And Charlotte said that she moved into the new home first but deliberately avoided putting photographs of her and Hal, her children, or other personal items in the living room, because doing so might have given Cynthia the impression that she was taking over the place and that it was not Cynthia's home to share. So, they were quite careful to negotiate and share in the design and use of the public spaces they shared in the home.

In general, wives in modern plural families are clearly in charge of furnishing, arranging, and decorating their homes. They and their husbands acknowledge their central roles in the home and the home's importance as a reflection of their personalities, beliefs, and values. Even when wives share dwellings, they almost always have significant control of their bedrooms and often make joint decisions about the furnishing and decoration of common spaces. This behavior reflects a combined dyadic and communal approach to shared dwellings. The home is therefore a primary territory for plural wives – a place that is important to them and over which they have long-term control. The fact that they extensively "mark" homes through decorations and furnishings also indicates the extent to which plural wives are closed and open about aspects of themselves. That is to say, they use their homes to manage the privacy regulation dialectic.

What level of territorial control do plural wives have about who can enter their homes or specific areas of homes?

Other members of a plural family – adults or children – do not usually enter another wife's home or area in a home without permission. This behavior confirms that homes are primary territories.

Family 1
At one time, Joan and Norma, the first and second wives, lived in separate upstairs and downstairs apartments in a suburban rambler dwelling. A stairway without doors connected their apartments. Although it was easy to move between apartments, they followed certain rules about access to one another's places. For example, Joan and Norma freely

entered each other's apartments if they needed to borrow a staple food such as sugar when the other was not at home, but they did so only when absolutely necessary. And they never borrowed or used special items or specially prepared food without permission.

They also had firm rules for children, who were taught that each home is separate, that they were not to go from one to the other unless they were invited or received permission. Indeed, we noticed on occasion that children who lived in the upstairs apartment sometimes peeked down the stairs to see or hear what was happening on the lower level but did not go down the stairs without permission.

Family 5

Constance, Valerie, Barbara, and Rose emphasize that children and adults should have respect for different homes in the family. They teach children not to enter another wife's home without knocking or asking permission to enter, even though all children are welcome in any of the family homes. And they noted that children tend to be a bit more reserved in another mother's home. They also agree that they themselves do not go into another wife's home without knocking or announcing their presence. In an emergency they do not hesitate to enter a home when the wife who lives there is away, and they sometimes do so to borrow something for cooking. But these are rare occurrences. Even within a family's home, children are expected to knock on closed doors, or to ask permission to enter.

Family 4

In contrast to the preceding cases, here children and wives seemed to enter the dwelling of the second wife, Ruth, without knocking or asking permission (although in the instances that we observed this behavior it was because they were preparing and bringing food for a family meeting that weekend). When we mentioned this to a gregarious young daughter of the fourth wife, Eve, she said "All the houses are Father's houses. I can go into any house whenever I please and so can everyone else." She emphasized the fact that her father "owned" everything, and that everyone's things, including the house, belonged to everyone in the family.

When we raised the issue with her mother, Eve, she agreed with what her daughter had told us, except to add that older children are expected to knock and ask permission to enter other mothers' homes. Everyone is more tolerant of younger children freely entering homes without formal permission.

In another discussion Harry stated that each wife's bedroom was her personal place. Children were very respectful of their mother's bedroom and did not enter without her permission. He said that he himself honored a wife's authority over her bedroom, implying that even he was "visitor" to her room. When we asked to tour Eve's home, and Harr encouraged her to do so, she refused, saying that this was not the righ time, but that we were welcome to return later. He quickly acceded t her wishes, out of respect for her control over the place.

The primary territorial characteristics of homes are particularly eviden in cases of family disruption or conflict. Although conflict between a hus band and wife, or between wives, is the result of many factors, it is reflecte in a malfunctioning of territorial control over homes. In several instances wives attributed family conflict in part to territorial violations by the hus band or another wife – for example, because they did not have a place o their own, were not able to control access to their dwelling, or had thei furniture or possessions taken away by their husband. Such intrusions ar quite serious in primary territories, because they attack the viability an well-being of a person (Altman, 1975).

How do plural wives use their homes to achieve solitude or separation from others?

Our analysis postulates that privacy regulation is a two-sided process o opening and closing oneself to others, which plural wives achieve in par through decorating and regulating access. But do plural wives have spe cial places in their homes or means for being alone? With a high level o contact between wives and their children, not to mention work and reli gious activities outside the home, plural wives rarely have any quiet tim and solitude. Many wives spoke about needing time to reflect, relax, at tend to personal matters, and simply restore their physical and psycho logical energy.

Family 10
One of the eight wives in this family said that it was not just the prob lems between them that created stress. The tremendous variety of re sponsibilities that each wife had to assume also made life difficult – working, managing the home, raising many children, tending gardens, canning and bottling food, teaching in Sunday School, and so on. An other wife said that they had so many activities and were so busy every day that "personal quiet time is a rare and valued commodity." The others agreed that it is very difficult to be alone in a plural family.[1]

The experience of these wives is not unique. If so, how and when do wives achieve solitude and separation from others, and how does the home play into the process? Some wives use a specific room or area to get away from others; sometimes they can only be alone at certain times of the day.

Family 1

Norma, the second wife, described her bedroom and a special chair in it as a "sanctuary" where she can be alone – to nurse a baby, read a book, think, relax, and escape the hurried pace of her day-to-day life. The room is a very special place for Norma, and everyone in the family respects her solitude when she closes the door. Another way she achieves separation from others is to get up at 4 o'clock in the morning, before her children arise, and work on personal projects, study, write, or just think. Charlotte and Cynthia also use their bedroom to be alone or to do some personal project, such as writing poetry, playing the piano, or reading.

At first, Joan, the first wife, said that she really has no place in her home to be alone. Her bedroom is a beehive of family activity, with children coming and going when she is in there. (Part of the reason may be that the family TV and VCR are in her bedroom!) She then mentioned a small room in the basement where she writes and has a sewing machine. Although it is not her favorite place, she does go there when she needs to be alone. And she went on to say that sometimes she stays up late at night or gets up very early in the morning to read, bake, do the laundry, attend to personal matters, or collect her thoughts.

Family 2

Judith, Rebecca, and Emily, the first, second, and third wives, respectively, all use their bedrooms as a place of solitude. Rebecca also treasures the early morning hours, when she reads, works at her desk, or simply wanders around the house by herself. In contrast, Emily described herself as a night person; she reads, watches TV, or just sits alone after everyone has gone to sleep. Emily said that on occasion she also goes for a walk to be alone.

Phyllis, the fourth wife, likes to go outside when she needs solitude. She sits on the patio, works in her yard, goes for a walk in the neighborhood, or takes a drive in the car.

Rebecca sometimes takes her children to her family's farm where she grew up. There her children run free, play with one another, and are not confined. She loves her childhood home, visits with her sister, wanders around the farm, and relaxes. It gives her a change of pace and a form of solitude when she needs to break away from everyday life.

Family 3

William, Carlyn, Danielle, and Alayna, who live communally, once built two small rooms/closets in a family room. The rooms are oriented toward the main LDS Temple and are used by family members to study be alone, think, or pray. Adults go into these rooms at unspecified times They also use another room – a "spiritual area" – in the home for the same purposes. It is a place where they go for personal conversation with one another, to be alone, or to pray. When anyone is in the room, no one else enters without knocking.

They also described the wives' bedrooms as places of solitude. And Danielle said that they have talked about putting locks on the mothers' bedroom doors in order to ensure separation.

They also recently shifted their living arrangements so that each wife and her children are on different floors in the dwelling. They made the move in order to give each mother and her children more independence and separation from one another.

Family 5
Constance, Valerie, Barbara, and Rose agree that each of their bedrooms is a place of respite and solitude and that children are expected to knock before entering.

Valerie went on to say that her favorite place is her living room, especially late at night or early in the morning. She especially likes to sit in a rocking chair carried down through the generations in her family. She herself had been rocked as a child, so it has special meaning for her. Valerie also sometimes walks in the nearby hills when she wants to be alone.

Along with her bedroom, Constance spends time in her garden; it is a place where she is able to tune out the world.

So, the home is an important vehicle for regulating privacy and is an important primary territory. This picture contrasts sharply with that of husbands, discussed in chapter 12. Husbands are much less involved with their homes, do not view them as a primary territory, and rarely use the dwelling to regulate their openness and closedness to others.

To what extent do wives have strong feelings of attachment to their homes?

Some wives are very proud of and positive about their homes, and they invest a great deal of time and energy in decorating and maintaining them.

Family 4
Each of the five wives has her own home: four wives live in a compound area, and one wife lives in another part of the community. They have lived in their homes for many years, and each is quite proud of and

satisfied with their dwelling. The homes vary in decorating style, and in every case almost every room is well decorated. As we toured each home, wives were enthusiastic, and eagerly described decorations, furnishings, photographs, and objects.

Anna, the first wife, has decorated her home extensively. Every room contains many photographs of Harry, her children, and grandchildren. Indeed, her home, like many others in our sample, is replete with family photographs. And religious items are displayed throughout the home – religious and inspirational sayings done in embroidery or prints, books, and photographs of church leaders.

Ruth's, Belle's and Shirley's homes, those of the second, third, and fifth wife, respectively, are also extensively decorated and furnished. Throughout their dwellings the same types of items are displayed, along with materials related to their special interests. For example, Shirley's interest in art is reflected in landscapes and other unique items. They all display a variety of religious items, along with many photographs of Harry, their children, grandchildren, and others. Each wife is satisfied and proud of her home and was pleased that we were interested in visiting their dwelling.

Eve, the fourth wife is also proud of her home, and it is very well cared for. When we had breakfast there, it was clear that she had gone out of her way to make this a memorable meal. She used her best dishes, prepared special food, and was extremely attentive to us. Her children's rooms were well decorated with photographs, religious sayings, posters, and the like. She also indicated with pride that each of her sons had his own bed, chest of drawers, and a desk. And she told that she does not permit her sons to decorate their rooms with pictures of horses, three-wheel cycles, or the like but insists on having them decorate with religious and spiritual items. Similarly, she does not allow her sons or daughters to decorate their rooms with movie stars but insists on them having religious sayings, photographs of the present and former prophet of the church, and photographs of Harry. She also encourages girls to hang pictures of domestic items from catalogs, such as furniture or bed-spreads (interestingly, girls' rooms were more extensively decorated than boys' rooms; for a discussion of gender differences in decorations see chapter 12). As we walked around the home, Eve described how she was redecorating the home, remodeling the kitchen, stairways, and painting rooms. She was very pleased with the process of redecoration. Eve's bedroom was also nicely decorated with a carefully prepared bed-spread, nice curtains on the windows, many religious books and sayings, and photographs of Harry, herself and Harry, her children, her parents, and the former prophet.

Family 5

Although they are furnished and decorated somewhat differently, Valerie's and Barbara's homes are well kept and a source of pride to them. All rooms have received considerable attention. Their living rooms are furnished with some combination of a sofa, chairs, tables, TVs, stereos, and a variety of decorations. Both homes contain photographs of family members; religious prints, objects, and embroidered sayings; and prints of various types. And their kitchens are also nicely decorated with similar items. The wives' bedrooms are similarly decorated with religious objects and wall hangings, and photographs of Howard, themselves and Howard, their children, and their parents. Children's rooms also have a variety of decorations and furnishings – some extensive, some simple, but generally including personal displays, photographs, and religious items.

Wives in several other families also expressed pride in their homes. Although furnishings were usually modest, homes were well cared for, and decorating incorporated a similar array of items from dwelling to dwelling. Thus many plural wives display their personalities, values, and beliefs in their dwellings, thereby using them as vehicles to be open and accessible to others.

Not all wives were enthusiastic, proud, or invested in all aspects of their homes. Some were neutral about their dwellings, acknowledging the fact that their present home was likely to be a temporary place – probably an adaptive stance in view of the fact that growing families move quite often. Others were more negative about the home in general – because of the neighborhood, the design of the home, its state of repair, and other factors. In many cases, however, wives felt strongly about their own furnishings and decorations and expressed attachment to them. And many wives were very much attached to their bedrooms and sometimes to other rooms in their home, for example, children's bedrooms or a family room.

Family 1

Joan, Charlotte, and Cynthia are satisfied with their homes, but Norma is not. She is frustrated and displeased with the design of the home, wishes she could live elsewhere, and has no feelings of attachment to it. There are several problems from her point of view – the kitchen is too small for her large and growing family, the kitchen is easily seen by people coming into the home, and it is also too close to the dining and living rooms. Furthermore, its equipment is poor. Several areas of the home, inside and outside, although clean, are in a general state of disrepair, which adds to her dissatisfaction.

On the other hand, her whole demeanor changed when she showed us her bedroom. She discussed each item in the room with enthusiasm and described the room as a sanctuary where she can be by herself, rest, and contemplate. Even though she talked about needing to do more to the room, it is clear that she treasures the room, invests a great deal in its decoration, and enjoys being there. There are many photographs of her children and of her and Hal all over the room. There are also objects in a curio cabinet, and an easy chair in the corner which she described with great pride. As noted earlier, this is the corner of the room where she nurses her babies, relaxes, and reads religious books. She also has plans to wallpaper and decorate the room with other photographs and objects – that is, when she has time. Norma is proud of her bedroom; she has not only invested in it but also wants to make it an even nicer place.

She then showed us a downstairs room that has been remodeled and of which she is proud. It is a place where she likes to entertain people with whom she wishes to spend time. Because it is away from the kitchen and living room, with all their noise and hubbub, she described it as "kind of a private public place" and is genuinely pleased about it. The room has a sofa, seating bench, and a large bookcase with religious and other books, some religious pictures on the wall, and photographs of her mother and her husband's mother. Norma has invested a great deal of time and energy in decorating this room, just as she did in her bedroom. She is also quite proud of her oldest daughter's bedroom, which she recently wallpapered, and which is decorated with a variety of objects, pictures, and hangings.

But she doesn't have the same feeling about some other rooms. The living room, for example, although clean and neat, is only modestly furnished with a sofa, a frayed chair, a piano, TV, and a few wall hangings and decorations. And a bedroom of two of her sons has basic furniture, but no other decorations on the wall or elsewhere.

Norma's feelings, like those of some other plural wives, demonstrate the idea of "levels of attachment" to home environments. That is, while homes in general may or may not be important to wives, specific items and personal possessions – photographs, furniture, objects, and others – are significant.

Family disruption and place attachment

The importance of homes to plural wives was particularly evident in several families in which disruptions were associated with, and perhaps exacer-

bated by, the violation of a wife's attachment and control of her possessions, furnishings, and objects by her husband or a co-wife.

Family 12

Lauren, the second wife, eventually left Fred and Elaine as a result of conflicts in many aspects of their lives. In general, Lauren feels that Fred favored Elaine and that he mistreated and was unfair to her and her
children. Some of her distress centered on living arrangements and his un-
willingness to allow her to have a home that she could view as her own.

They lived in very modest circumstances for years – renting apartments
in people's homes, basements, and elsewhere, with each wife having a
bedroom and sharing public spaces. Lauren claims that Fred often did not
allow her to decorate her bedroom as she desired. For example, when they
were once renting part of someone's home, she displayed trinkets from
high school on top of a chest of drawers. But he ordered her to put them
away, saying that her high school years were behind her. That upset her,
even though he didn't object to her displaying a quilt given to her by his
mother, a candle, doily, and a picture of him.

Later in the marriage she and Elaine had their own apartments on
two sides of a home. But Lauren always resented the fact that she had
old, hand-me-down furniture, whereas Elaine's home was nicely furnished. Her sofa was an old one that Elaine's mother had given her, she
slept on a mattress on the floor for years, and someone gave her an old
rocking chair. She and Fred rarely bought furniture together, and that
made her feel like a second-class person in the family (once they did buy
an item of furniture and she remarked how excited she was, because it
made her feel like a "real" wife to him).

Lauren also said they moved often, she never decorated very much,
and never was motivated to "make a house a home" – partly because
she had so little and Elaine had so much, partly because it was becoming
clear that her marriage was falling apart, and partly because Fred just
didn't seem to care about her or her home. She felt like a transient, never
hung things on walls, and didn't keep her homes very clean. As they
moved from place to place, she decided to "be mindless," "never think
about what I wanted in a home," and never become too attached to any
place.

To illustrate how bad things were for so many years, she recalled two
times where she truly loved a couple of homes. In one case she lived in
a separate dwelling, put up draperies and curtains, made quilts, kept a
neat house, and decorated it as best she could. She also planted a garden
and made friends with neighbors, all of which gave her a sense of being
rooted and helped her feel good about herself. In another case, even

though she had little furniture, she painted a life-size mural of Walt Disney's Snow White and the Seven Dwarfs on her child's bedroom wall. She also made a crib quilt with Bambi the deer sewn on it. She was very proud of the room, and when we asked why it pleased her, she said, "It was because it was me. I made it. I was being an individual." When she had to move, she cried for the first time when leaving a home, explaining to us, "I cried because I was leaving my mural."

Several issues of control and use of space added to stresses in this family. For example, Elaine was once angry with Lauren when Lauren lived in a bedroom that Elaine had previously used as a child's bedroom. She felt that Lauren had intruded into what she considered her space. At another time, Elaine and Lauren had separate apartments, with a connection between them in the basement. Lauren said that people came into her home freely, often without knocking or asking permission, making her feel as if she had no control over her own home.

They also had other problems of privacy. For example, in one of their homes, the bathroom entrance was in Elaine's bedroom, and it was very embarrassing when Lauren and Fred were in the bathroom together and Elaine was in her bedroom. In another home, Lauren had difficulty being alone in her room, because Elaine intruded or criticized her when Lauren tried to read, be by herself, or lock her door.

In summary, Lauren's complaints involved her pervasive feelings of being unable to establish a primary territory and govern access to her home, experiencing intrusions that she couldn't control, feeling that she couldn't always achieve separation and closeness to others, being unable to mark and personalize her homes as she desired, and not sensing that she could become bonded or attached to dwellings.

Family 13

Sherri, Paul's third wife, described many aspects of their stormy relationship over the years, which led her to eventually leave the family. In addition to interpersonal conflicts with Paul and her poor relationships with some of the other wives, she was especially unhappy about how he treated her with respect to her homes, furniture, and possessions.

For example, they moved quite often, and she was careful to always take her furniture and personal possessions from place to place. On a couple of occasions, however, Paul took some of her things and gave them to other wives. Once he gave a piece of her furniture to Gloria, his favorite wife, which added insult to the injury of his violating her property. That incident was very upsetting to Sherri. On another occasion Paul gave Sherri's television set to another wife when she was out of town. When she returned and wanted the TV, he told her that it wasn't hers anymore because she had been away for so long. She argued with him, successfully reclaimed it, but it was broken and she had to pay to repair it. Again, she was quite upset. But the really devastating event occurred when Paul asked Sherri to move out of the trailer she had lived in for four years. He then sold the trailer and used the money to buy a nice home for Gloria. Sherry was deeply humiliated. Although Sherri said that she divorced Paul for many reasons, his actions regarding her possessions and homes contributed to their breakup.

Family 14

Sally, Harvey's first wife, said that the way that she, Harvey, and Molly managed and decorated their homes mirrored the gradual deterioration of the marriage and their relationships. When Molly first joined the family she and Sally shared everything. They wore each other's clothes and cooperated in decorating the home. They discussed cooperatively how to furnish the living room, where to put furniture, what to hang on the walls, how to arrange objects. But over time things began to deteriorate, Sally claimed, because Molly became selfish and Harvey began to prefer Molly. In successive moves, Sally always kept her very personal things – books, desk, cedar chest, photographs, clothing, silverware. But she stopped caring about other things in the home, to some extent because Harvey began giving Sally's furniture to Molly without discussing it with her. Furthermore, soon after Sally bought a new car, Paul took Molly on a trip in it, crashed the car, and showed little remorse. In essence, Sally said, he showed little respect for her as a person, and demonstrated his feelings by the way he treated her possessions. Sally finally divorced Harvey for many reasons, but his violation of her attachment to places and things mirrored other problems in the family.

The importance of wives having control over their homes, achieving desired levels of interaction and solitude, and managing decorating and furnishing came to the forefront in cases of family upheaval and disruption. Although conflict between husbands and wives, and between wives, has many roots, disagreements about privacy, territory, and place attachment may play central roles.

Homes and personal identity, dyadic and communal relationships, and cultural ties

To repeat a central theme – the home is a reflection of peoples' personalities, beliefs, values, and associations with their family, community, and culture. In this section we look more closely at the ways in which a plural wife's *personal identity,* her *dyadic* relationships with her husband, her *communal* relationships with other wives, and her ties to the broader *cultural contexts* in which she lives are revealed in her home.[2]

Personal identity displays

Personal identity displays reflect the uniqueness and individuality of wives. They include a wife's preferences for particular kinds of furniture styles, decorations, arrangements of rooms, and the like. Even though many plural families are in tenuous economic circumstances and do not have elaborate furnishings, we illustrated previously how many wives tried to put a personal stamp on their home or bedroom. Personal identity displays include special objects, photographs, and other items that point to the person as a distinctive individual. Examples are items showing personal achievements, such as trophies, hobbies or collections, art objects, paintings, prints or posters, handiwork made by a wife or given to her, jewelry displays, plants, and framed poetry. The individual is the focus of personal identity displays. They make public and salient her tastes and preferences, interests and values, what she considers important aspects of herself that she is willing to disclose to others.

We also include items linking a wife to her parents, grandparents, and relatives in the personal identity rubric. Such items identify a wife as uniquely bonded to her birth family and her unique ancestry. Examples include photographs of grandparents, parents, siblings and relatives, and gifts and objects received from those family members.

Dyadic bonds with a husband

A major thesis of our analysis is that the dyadic bond between a husband and each wife is a crucial aspect of plural family life among contemporary Mormon fundamentalists. As a result, a wife's home may be expected to reflect their special relationship in a variety of ways – through photographs of the husband, the husband and wife, and their children; gifts given by the husband to a the wife; memorabilia of their wedding (marriage announcement, flowers, wedding photographs, honeymoon photos, etc.); gifts given to either of them as a couple; and displays of their genealogy and those of their parents. Other dyadic items might include photographs or objects connected with the husband's parents, which would thereby link a wife to the husband's ancestral line. These types of decorations and objects make visible the dyadic bond between a wife and husband and are an example of how the Mormon fundamentalist culture idealizes the special character of the individual marital pair.

Communal bonds within a plural family

Decorating practices provide considerable insight into the communal relationships between wives, as well as the intimate and unique dyadic relationships between each wife and the husband.

Communal relations may be reflected in displays of photographs of other wives or groupings of the husband and wives, photographs of other wives' children, gifts received from other wives or children of other wives, or similarities in decorating styles by different wives in a family. Other possible communal decorations are photographs of other wives' parents, grandparents or relatives, family genealogy charts or other items that include other wives and their children. Thus items that incorporate some aspect of involvement with other wives symbolize a communal bond in a plural family. Such bonds are also reflected in cooperative decisions about furnishings, decorations, and use of common spaces by wives who share a home.

Links to cultural contexts

Homes may also reflect cultural bonds. Broad cultural affiliations can be seen in religious photographs, drawings and objects, patriotic items linking residents to a nation, ethnic displays, styles of interior and exterior home furnishings that incorporate a cultural theme or that are similar to those of neighbors and community members, to name a few examples (Altman and Gauvain, 1981; Gauvain, Altman, and Fahim, 1983).

Since religion is a central cultural value for contemporary Mormon fundamentalists, the link between wives and the religious community should be evident in photographs of present and past church leaders, religious objects, memorabilia of significant religious events in the community, and so on. More general bonds to Mormonism and Christianity might also be displayed, in photographs, paintings, and sculptures or statues of the Mormon Temple, Joseph Smith, Jesus Christ, biblical patriarchs, the Book of Mormon and the Old and New Testaments, and in needlepoint and other artistic displays with religious themes, sayings and quotations.

Case examples of personal identity, dyadic, communal, and cultural displays in homes

We next present case studies to illustrate how the homes of plural wives reflect personal identity and dyadic, communal, and cultural values in different forms and combinations. The cases are representative of homes we visited, some of which have been described in part earlier in the chapter. However, we did not visit all homes in our sample, all parts of homes, or spend unlimited time in each room of a home. Doing so would have been inappropriately intrusive. As a result, our accounts are based on recollections and field notes, not on quantitative assessments.

Family 1

For several years Joan, Norma, Charlotte, and Cynthia, Hal's wives, each had their own home in different parts of the community. More recently, Joan and Norma, and Charlotte and Cynthia share two homes.

Joan's home, in which she lived for 12 years, is in some disrepair, inside and outside. Joan is a casual and easygoing person and housekeeper. There are many strong personal identity displays throughout the home. For example, the living room is furnished modestly with two sofas and an easy chair made from the same fabric. And Joan is very proud of the piano she purchased herself. She enjoys playing the piano, and it is a centerpiece of the room. Most of the other decorations in the living room reflect dyadic, communal, or cultural values, described later. Joan's bedroom is dominated by personal identity displays. She proudly pointed out her collection of panda objects and statues, and a large panda doll given to her last Christmas. And the quilt on her bed is decorated with figures of pandas. Joan also pointed out two pictures of butterflies that she enjoys and had purchased herself. Her bedroom also has a small curio cabinet containing several objects and statues, including pandas. Thus Joan's bedroom mirrors her personal identity in a strong way, as do other parts of the home. In addition to the piano in the living room, she also displays a collection of vases and other objects from Israel near the kitchen area.

Dyadic items reflecting her identity with her husband and her children appear in several places. The living room, for example, contains many photographs of her children, Hal's mother, and wooden figures of flying ducks given to her and Hal by his grandmother. There are also pictures of her children and of her and Hal in other rooms.

The only communal display we recall seeing was a picture of Norma's (the second wife's) grandmother in Joan's living room. This woman was a famous person in the religious community, so the photograph has both communal and cultural links.

Joan's home displays many cultural items associated with the fundamentalist group and the Mormon religion. The living room has a photograph of the current prophet of the fundamentalist church and a picture of the Salt Lake Temple. And when we visited her bedroom Joan proudly showed us her library of religious books. A picture of Jesus Christ also hangs on a bedroom wall.

Thus Joan's home contains personal identity, dyadic, and cultural or religious displays, but hardly any decorations symbolizing communal bonds with other wives in the family.

We already described aspects of Norma's home. As to *personal identity displays,* the upstairs living room is furnished modestly with a large sofa, chair, TV, and a small piano. The few decorations include a hanging lamp, planter, print of a landscape, some specimen butterflies, an embroidered wall decoration, and a clock. The adjacent kitchen is also modestly decorated. In showing us around Norma did not display much attachment to the living room or kitchen; in fact, she complained about them, as noted earlier. Norma expresses her personal identity in the extensive decorations of her oldest daughter's bedroom, which is wall papered and has a number of pictures and decorations of one kind or another. Norma is very proud of the room. Her own bedroom is even more revealing. As noted previously, she is very proud and strongly attached to this room and has invested enormous energy in making it a special place – "a sanctuary," to use her own words. Heavily decorated with all manner of items, it reflects vividly her personal identity and sense of self. Along with a bed and bureau, it has a small desk where she keeps personal items, and an easy chair that she described with great pride, because she uses it to nurse her children, read, and just "get away from it all." Norma also decorated the room with photographs of her parents, another form of personal identity display. She also had plans to put up some attractive wallpaper, furthering her personal stamp on the room.

Norma also redecorated a downstairs family room and is very pleased with it as a place to entertain guests. Aside from a new sofa, a seating bench, some other furnishings, and a photograph of her mother, the room is decorated with dyadic and cultural displays.

Norma's *dyadic* relationship with Hal is evident in her bedroom, in the numerous photographs of her children and of her and Hal on various occasions throughout their marriage. When we asked her to name most treasured things in the room, she immediately stated "the photographs of my family." The new downstairs family room also has photographs of Hal's mother (and her own mother), and a large genealogical chart. She and Hal are listed at the center, and each of their family histories is included in the remainder of the elaborate chart that she has worked on carefully and about which she and Hal expressed great pride.

We found no displays anywhere in Norma's home reflecting communal bonds. For example, there were no pictures of other wives or their children. Or if communal items are present, Norma made no mention of them.

Norma's home has many cultural displays reflecting her religious values and identification with the fundamentalist church. For example, a picture of the Mormon Temple hangs in the living room, religious statements are prominently displayed in the dining area, her bedroom has religious books near her favorite chair and is decorated with various objects and wall hangings with religious themes, and the remodeled family room contains religious books, pictures of Jesus delivering a sermon, Joseph Smith as a young man, and the genealogical chart noted earlier. Her small office off the family room contains church records and related material. And one of her children's rooms has a picture of Jesus.

Thus Norma's home has a variety of personal identity, dyadic and religious/cultural decorations, but no visible or salient communal decorations reflecting her links with other wives in the family.

Charlotte's home is decently furnished, well cared for, and she is very happy living there. The living room has sofas and chairs and is extensively decorated with a variety of items, as are her bedroom and the one child's bedroom we visited. Her personal identity is evident throughout the home in the furnishing style and decorations: plants, a clock with a painted design on it, sculptures, a sewing machine, her oil paintings in the bedroom and in the living room, and other items.

Charlotte's home also reflects her unique dyadic relationship with Hal. The living room has several photographs of her children, as does her bedroom. Her bedroom also prominently displays a *New York Times* front page of Hal's day of birth, photographs of their marriage and other occasions, photographs of Hal, and a dried rose under glass that he gave her on their first date.

Her bedroom also has a lamp that one of Norma's father's sons had made for her, perhaps reflecting a communal bond between Norma and Charlotte. Hal also mentioned that Joan, Norma, and Charlotte have the same bedroom furniture, because he was able to get a good price by buying them together. Although not a communal indicator in a social-emotional sense, having the same furniture may nevertheless symbolize family unity.

Religious/cultural displays are prominent everywhere. Photographs of church leaders are in her living room, along with a picture of Jesus and the apostles, religious books, a print of the Salt Lake Temple, and a sculpture of a book open to a page containing a picture of Joseph Smith and a picture of Jesus. And Charlotte's bedroom contains a collection of a fundamentalist magazine, *Truth,* published in the 1950s, and notebooks of her genealogical work (also a personal identity item). She also has a large pewter cup with the names of all the presidents of the United States.

Cynthia had recently married Hal when we visited the apartment in which she had been living for a while. It was very well decorated, with carefully arranged furniture and displays, and it was evident that Cynthia liked her home and had invested a great deal of time and energy into making it a well-designed place. As for personal identity items, her artistic talents and interests are strongly reflected everywhere. Although the living room is modestly furnished with a sofa and a few chairs, there are many pictures and displays. One item she takes pride in is an antique Wedgwood china piece that her mother gave her for her wedding (this is perhaps a symbol of both personal identity links to her family and dyadic ties to Hal). Her kitchen is also extensively decorated with water colors, needlepoint hangings, sewn butterflies done by her mother, and a poem that she wrote. In several places in the apartment she displays her own poetry and writings done in calligraphy script. Cynthia's bedroom is also very well furnished and decorated. She likes rainbows and has hung pictures of them around the room, along with her own poetic sayings.

Cynthia's apartment also reflects her dyadic bonds with Hal. For example, her bedroom has pictures of her children, her and Hal, her wedding flowers, and a special lamp Hal gave her as a birthday present that changes colors and plays music. She also showed us her wedding and honeymoon album, which had been meticulously prepared, and a book of her poetry, of which she and Hal were very proud. A framed poem on the wall commemorates their marriage.

We did not see, nor did Cynthia point out, any communal furnishings or decorations reflecting the unity of her and the other wives. (However, when we visited the newer home Cynthia and Charlotte shared, they described how they cooperatively arranged the living room and jointly use space in a cabinet for their own objects.)

There are many cultural or religious items on display in every room of Cynthia's apartment. The living room contains two religious pictures that she likes very much – one of Jesus being baptized by John, Mary, and Martha near Lazarus's tomb, and the other of Jesus and his disciples. There is a picture of Jesus on another wall. She also posted a number of religious sayings in the kitchen. The children's bedrooms also contain religious prints and a picture of Jesus. And her bedroom displays pictures of Jesus and Joseph Smith.

The four wives in this family have very distinctive decorating styles, each reflecting to one degree or another their personal identity, dyadic bonds with the husband and children, as well as links with their broader cultural and religious community. We saw few examples of communal bonds between wives.

Family 2
During one period, Judith, Rebecca, Emily, and Phyllis had separate apartments in two houses, and at another time Judith and Emily lived in separate dwellings and Rebecca and Phyllis shared a house. We describe those instances in which we visited most areas and rooms in homes.

Judith, David's first wife, has lived on the first level of the home for 13 years; she likes the place very much. Personal identity items are not abundant in the living room, which is modestly furnished with two sofas, some chairs, a TV, and a few pictures. Judith didn't express great interest in the room. She did point out a large painting in the hallway near the living room as being very special, since it was a gift from a now deceased friend. And she showed us some treasured objects displayed in the dining room and kitchen – especially candlesticks, copper ducks, and an old music machine and record player given to her by her grandparents.

There are no dyadic decorations in the living room or other rooms, but she has a collage of photographs of her and David in her bedroom. We do not recall seeing any cultural or religious items or decorations reflecting communal relationships with other wives.

Emily, David's third wife, lives in the same home as Judith, but in a downstairs apartment. She expressed strong attachment and pride in her home and was pleased to show us around the well-decorated apartment. *Personal identity* items are everywhere in the living room: a western style of decorating, her guitar, objects and figurines, and a photograph of her parental family to which she is strongly attached. Emily also decorated her bedroom with a variety of items, including small objects that she collected, gifts given to her on birthdays and other occasions, and a box of jewelry that she said was very important to her. She also decorated the walls and ceilings of the children's bedrooms with prints and objects showing various children's themes. As she showed us around, Emily repeatedly expressed her strong sense of attachment to her home.

There are also many dyadic displays throughout the apartment, including many pictures of David, her and David, and their children.

The only communal decoration that we saw, or that she pointed out, is an oil painting of a flower in her bedroom that the other wives gave her soon after she was married. Its colors match her sheets and bedspread and the painting is a centerpiece of the room.

Cultural and religious decorations are also displayed in several rooms, one of which is a large picture of some presidents of the Mormon Church.

At the time we visited the home of Rebecca, the second wife, she had recently moved in on the first floor; Phyllis lived downstairs. Rebecca's place is only modestly furnished. The living room has a sofa, a couple of new chairs, and a large chest. The other rooms are not extensively furnished or decorated.

Personal identity items in her bedroom include a small sculpture from her grandmother that she treasures and photographs of her parents; and the living room has a photograph of all of her sisters. Dyadic items include photographs of her and David, and of her children in her bedroom.

Rebecca's living room has a kind of communal display – all the objects and statuettes that Joseph Ginat had brought them from Israel over the years. Since they were gifts to the whole family, they represent, in a sense, a *communal* identity. Rebecca also said that she used to have candid photographs of the other wives on the mirror in her bedroom, but removed them when she cleaned it. They were not there when we visited her home. She also said that she hopes to arrange for a formal portrait of all of the wives at some time in the future.

We do not recall seeing any cultural or religious items in Rebecca's home.

Phyllis, David's fourth wife, now lives downstairs from Rebecca. She has decorated her home extensively and is very proud of the place. She has many personal identity displays – pictures of her parental family, personal objects, photographs, and trophies reflecting her hobby of horseback riding. One of her treasured objects in the living room is a figurine of a horse that her father painted to look like a horse that she once owned. There are also collections of bells, porcelain dolls, and figures in a cabinet on the wall. David commented that Phyllis loves her collections and cares deeply about treasured things. He joked that she wouldn't allow him to have the statue of an eagle given to both of them by her parents but displays it in her home. Her children's bedrooms are also extensively decorated with curtains, quilts, and a collection of dolls. And her bedroom contains a collection of figurines of angels and other items.

Dyadic decorations are in her bedroom, especially in a special curio cabinet containing items associated with her marriage to David. There is a glass crystal object with an engraving of their wedding date, her wedding flowers, and small china gifts given to her at the wedding. Phyllis takes great pride in this collection. And there are photographs of her, David, and their children in the kitchen and living room.

We saw no communal items in Phyllis's home. And our notes do not reflect any cultural or religious decorations, but the home is so extensively decorated that we could have easily missed seeing them.

In summary, wives in this family arrange and decorate their homes quite differently from one another. However, as in other families, they each consistently display some combination of personal identity, dyadic, and cultural or religious decorations. Only occasionally, and then in a very limited way, do their homes contain communal items.

Family 4

Harry, Anna, Ruth, Belle, Eve, and Shirley live in the rural community. Each wife has a separate home – four are in a compound area and one a short distance away.

Anna lives in the family's original home. It is well furnished and cared for and is extensively decorated. Personal identity displays are evident throughout the home: the style and quality of furnishings, a large landscape painting in the living room that Anna did herself, a piano in the living room, and several embroidered wall hangings that she made.

Dyadic decorations are everywhere in the home, and in great numbers. These include photographs of her children and her grandchildren. For example, one of her sons has 10 children, who are shown in a single framed collage. And pictures of Harry are in every room, many showing him at different ages.

We saw no communal decorations reflecting her bonding to the overall family, nor did she point out any such items..

Cultural and religious items are also everywhere in Anna's home – inspirational and religious sayings in prints and embroidery, religious books, a photograph of the prophet of the church, and so on.

As noted earlier, Eve, the fourth wife, is proud of her home. Her style of decorating and her great interest in the ongoing remodeling reflects her personal identity in every aspect of the home. Eve also displays photographs of her parents and family, another type of personal identity item.

Dyadic decorations abound in the home – her bedroom has two pictures of Harry and many pictures of her children; photographs of Harry are displayed in the children's rooms and in the dining room (to some extent his photographs also symbolize his patriarchal role, and might therefore be construed as both a cultural or religious and a dyadic symbol).

Cultural and religious symbols also appear in many rooms in Eve's home. As noted earlier, she doesn't allow her sons and daughters to display "secular" items in their rooms, such as three-wheel cycles or posters of movie stars, but insists that they decorate with religious and spiritual items. We saw many such items, with sayings such as "Do not pray for an easy life, pray to be a strong person," "Hold on to your dreams," "Love your neighbor as yourself," "Have a pure heart and clean hands," "Remember your prayers," and "The spirit of God and the spirit of peace." Her bedroom contains a photograph of the former prophet, religious books, and the like.

We saw no evidence of communal decorations reflecting her bond with other wives in the family.

The other wives' homes are similarly decorated, although each has a unique combination of personal identity, dyadic, cultural and religious items, and few, if any, communal displays reflecting bonding between wives. One exception occurred in Belle's home, where we saw a photograph in her living room of Harry and several of the other wives together; the picture had been taken many years ago when they were all much younger.

Family 5

Howard's four wives – Constance, Valerie, Barbara, and Rose – each have their own home, with pairs of wives living close to one another. We describe only Constance's and Valerie's homes because we had more of a chance to see them.

Constance's personal identity is reflected in the general style of furnishing and care of her home, and in some special items she displays. These include a piano, a wall clock made by one of her sons, and porcelain figurines made by her mother that she displays in the living room (some of these figurines are also displayed in her bedroom). The kitchen area has decorative plates given to her on various occasions by members of her family and a photograph of her grandfather that she described with pride, since he had been leader of an early polygynous group (this is therefore a cultural-religious and personal identity item). And in the hall she pointed to some paintings done by her brother. She described many of these gifts from her family with enthusiasm.

The living room and other rooms contain many photographs of her children; a cabinet near the kitchen displays china dishes that were wedding presents, and gifts from her children and family are in her bedroom – all of which reflect dyadic relationships.

Once again we saw no communal items linking Constance to other wives, nor did she point any out.

Constance's home is replete with cultural and religious items. There is a religious saying in the living room near the entrance to the home and a picture of Joseph Smith on another wall; her bedroom has several religious pictures, including two favorites of hers – of Jesus and his disciples, and Joseph Smith, the latter of which she described as a special item. There also are some embroidered items on the wall: "The Lord is my shepherd" and "A true friend is of God."

Valerie's living room is furnished and decorated with a matching sofa and chairs, a piano, stereo system, and needlepoint embroideries that she made, as well as other objects. The kitchen is also decorated with a variety of items. Additional aspects of her personal identity are reflected in her bedroom – which is extensively decorated with photographs of her parents, landscape prints, embroidered wall hangings, and other items.

Dyadic items are also everywhere in the home – photographs of Howard and her children, a photograph of Howard's parents, gifts from her children, a handmade pillow on her bed embroidered with the word "Mom."

Valerie also has a unique and interesting communal item in her bedroom, one we had not seen anywhere else. Hanging behind the bedroom door is a large embroidered tree. Hanging from the ends of its branches are 3 × 5 index cards. Each card represents a month of the year and lists the birthdays of all family members. Everyone joked about this chart, saying it is very useful to Howard, since he has difficulty keeping up with the birthdays of his 30 children and 4 wives.

Valerie's home also has a large number of cultural and religious items. A bookcase in the living room is filled with religious books, the kitchen and children's bedrooms have wall decorations and embroideries with religious sayings, and her bedroom displays religious objects and photographs.

Family 8

We visited four of Ira's eight wives' homes, but describe only that of Gloria, the first wife, because it has some unique features. The other homes, while interesting, are similar to many others in their furnishings and decorations. Gloria's home is one of four in a large structure that has four complete apartments, two on each side, upstairs and downstairs. Gloria's apartment, especially her bedroom, is the most extensively decorated place we saw. Almost every inch of the bedroom walls and furniture surfaces is covered with photographs, books, objects, and displays. And the furnishing and decoration have all been done carefully, as in the bedroom and in the other rooms. The place clearly is a display of her personal identity.

Dyadic decorations are everywhere, especially in her bedroom – dozens of photographs of her children and grandchildren, gifts and things made or given to her by them, weavings and embroideries, a special book of poems written in 1910 that she said was one of her favorite things, and other items. She was able to describe who gave her each item and the occasion that it symbolized. She said she greatly treasures the presents received from her sons, daughters, and relatives. And her home has many photographs of her and Ira or of Ira alone.

In addition to many decorations and photographs, her living room has a very large quilt on one wall. It was made by her daughters and depicts a tree. The main trunk of the tree shows her and Ira's name and the date of their marriage. Each branch has several apples, each of which lists the name and date of birth of her children and grandchildren. A quilted basket at the base of the tree also contains many apples, which are individually inscribed with the name and date of birth of each of Gloria's great grandchildren. And flying above the tree are embroidered birds, each of which carries a small basket in their beaks listing the names of children and grandchildren who have died. Gloria is very proud of this quilt, and we were impressed by it.

We saw no communal items in Gloria's home, nor did she point any out.

As in other cases, Gloria displays many cultural and religious items – religious objects, religious sayings, a large picture of a former prophet of the fundamentalist movement (which she described as a very important item to her), religious books, and other items.

Family 18

Charles's wives live in two homes on the same street. Susan, Angela, and Linda, the first, third, and fourth wives, live in Susan's original home, and Nancy has her own home. We visited only the main home and saw only its public areas.

The public areas are obviously Susan's domain, perhaps because she and Charles had been married for many years when they entered the fundamentalist movement, and because the other wives living there are much younger than she is. The living room and kitchen area are very well decorated and represent Susan's style preferences, thereby portraying her personal identity. Other items include photographs of her parents, a plaque and embroidered poem she received from the main Mormon Church women's organization for her service (before she joined the fundamentalist group and was excommunicated; these items also reflect cultural and religious values). The poem is especially interesting because it highlights expected gender roles in a patriarchal culture:

I love my kitchen
God bless my little kitchen
I love its every nook
Bless me as I do my work
Washing pots and pans and cook.

The public areas also contain the usual dyadic symbols – pictures of her and Charles, photographs of her children, photographs of Charles's parents, and comparable items. There are no communal decorations or other items linking her to the other wives; they apparently have not contributed anything to the furnishings or decorations in the public areas of the home.

Cultural and religious items are everywhere, including pictures of Jesus, Joseph Smith, and the Salt Lake Temple. There is also a large Bible on a table in the living room, and religious and inspirational embroideries and prints hang on the walls.

Comment on communal aspects of home decorations

As the preceding examples demonstrate, home decorations and furnishings mirror the personalities and values of plural wives – their personal identities, dyadic links to their husband and children, and their bonds to their religion and culture. We were surprised, however, to learn that wives' homes or areas in homes do not highlight the communal bonding of wives with one another or with their plural family as a whole, or do so only occasionally. We saw (or had pointed out to us) only a few objects or gifts from other wives or other wives' children, almost no photographs of other wives or their children, and only a few photographs of all or subgroups of wives, with or without the husband.

When we asked some wives whether they display photographs of other wives in their homes, almost none said that they showed photographs of co-wives in their homes. Some did have photographs of other wives in albums; others indicated that they planned to have pictures of other wives displayed but had not gotten around to doing so; and still others said it was too complicated to work out schedules for group pictures. A few didn't want to bring attention to their plural family status.

Family 1

Joan, Norma, Charlotte, and Cynthia stated that they don't display photographs of one another in their homes or areas in homes that they share – although they have candid photographs of one another and their children in albums. Why not? They said that the pictures in their homes are mostly formal photographs taken by professionals, and the expense and difficulty of getting wives together makes it prohibitive. However, they admitted that they had never even thought about this issue before, and one of them said "I guess that it just isn't a high priority."

Another reason for not taking group photographs is that it is too complicated to explain to a professional photographer who they are and why they are taking such pictures. They admitted, however, that such problems could be overcome if they took individual photographs and put them in a collage.

They also agreed that displaying group or individual photographs of other wives or their children is not a common practice in other families with whom they are acquainted, although they could recall a few instances in which it was done.

Family 2

Rebecca, David's second wife, said that she didn't display any photographs of Judith, Emily, or Phyllis in her home. She hoped that they could take a formal group portrait someday, but there was no immediate plan to do so. As noted earlier, Rebecca said that she had previously placed pictures of the other wives on the mirror in her bedroom but removed them to clean the mirror and hadn't had a chance to put them back. When we posed the question to Phyllis, the fourth wife, she stated that she doesn't display photographs of the other wives anywhere in her home but didn't elaborate.

Family 4

As described earlier, Eve, Harry's fourth wife, said that she has no pictures of the other wives shown anywhere in her home. She did say, however, that she planned to ask them for pictures but hadn't done so as yet. And she said that the five wives intended to give Harry a birthday gift of portraits of each of them clustered around his picture in a single frame.

Belle, Harry's third wife, showed us one photograph in her living room of her and some of the other wives and their children. It was a candid picture taken many years ago. Belle pointed out, however, that she has no other pictures of the other wives in her home. And she doesn't recall any of the other wives having pictures of one another in their homes.

Family 5
Constance, Valerie, Barbara, and Rose all said that they did not show photographs of one another anywhere in their homes, although they had candid photos in picture albums (and they once gave Howard an album with pictures of all of them and their children as a birthday gift). They said that it simply didn't occur to them, was too expensive, and they would rather spend their money on photographs of their children. Moreover, it would be awkward to explain to visitors or friends of their children who didn't know about their lifestyle.

Some wives simply reported not having photographs of one another shown in their homes, without providing much rationale.

Family 8
Betty, Ira's fourth wife, said that she did not display photographs of other wives anywhere in her home, although she had pictures of them in albums. She also did not remember seeing photographs of other wives in any of her co-wives' homes, nor were pictures of children of other mothers shown in various homes.

Family 10
When we raised the matter with the eight wives in a group discussion, they all said that they did not openly show pictures of the other wives in their areas of homes. Like other families, however, they kept pictures of one another in albums or in drawers.

In several cases we noted the absence of group photographs.

Family 3
William, Carlyn, Danielle, and Alayna live in a communal dwelling. As noted earlier, the main staircase wall has various groupings of photographs – each wife and her parents, brothers and sisters, along with photographs of William and a wife, sometimes alone and sometimes with their children. Groupings for each wife were on different parts of the wall. There were no photographs of all wives or subgroups of wives or of wives and their children, even though Danielle and Alayna were sisters.

Family 9
Here is a rare exception to the preceding examples. In the living room of the home shared by John's wives, we saw a photograph of John, Joyce, Clara, and Marjorie and their children.

Summary

This chapter explored the bonding of contemporary plural wives to their homes. Using the concepts of privacy regulation and territorial behavior, we illustrated that wives are strongly attached to their homes or areas in homes. They are responsible for and have control over furnishings, decorations, and general decor, whereas husbands have little to do with these matters. And wives express strong positive feelings about homes (and strong negative feelings when homes fail to meet their expectations, or when they are thwarted in decorating or controlling them). Wives also achieve solitude through rules they establish regarding entry into the home or its areas and rooms. Openness in homes is reflected in decorations and furnishings, which display aspects of wives' personalities, values, and beliefs.

In analyzing furnishings and decorations, we observed that homes often display personal identity decorations, such as a wife's hobby, art, poetry, or collections of objects. Personal identity displays include items associated with a wife's parents or relatives. Homes also contain many dyadic decorations, such as photographs of a wife's husband and children, gifts, and other items. And wives often display cultural and religious items – photographs of church leaders, religious scenes and figures, and embroideries with religious or spiritual themes and sayings.

Interestingly, wives rarely display communal decorations, that is, items symbolizing their bonds with other wives or with the plural family as a whole. They hardly ever show photographs of other wives or their children, or of the wives together or with the husband as a group. In general, a home is a personal, dyadic, and cultural place for plural wives, and it is not a setting where they portray their communal ties with one another.

On the whole, present-day plural wives are very much involved with their home, play a major role in its establishment and management, and use it to regulate their interaction with others. As a result, plural wives have strong emotional attachments to their homes. As discussed in chapter 12, the situation is quite different for husbands in plural families, who show relatively little emotional and psychological attachment to dwellings.

12

Husbands and homes

We now turn to husbands' feelings about their homes. In addition, we consider an aspect of attachment to homes that spontaneously arose in our discussions with husbands and wives, namely, the management of a husband's clothing. Where does he keep his clothing – in one home, or spread out among homes?

Place attachment, territoriality, and privacy regulation in homes

Do husbands in plural families have homes or areas in homes of their own?

It is quite rare for a husband in monogamous Western cultures to have a dwelling apart from that of his wife. In contrast, as explained in chapter 10, living arrangements in traditional polygynous cultures range from those in which a husband and his wives lived communally to those in which husbands and wives have their own separate dwellings. For example, husbands and wives among the Kikuyu (Kenyatta, 1973) and the Masai of Africa (Talle, 1987) have their own huts. In such cases the husband uses his dwelling to entertain guests, wives care for his dwelling, and the husband rotates among his wives' huts for sleeping and sexual relationships. Among the cultures in which husbands share homes with their wives are the Bedouin of Israel. Here, husbands entertain guests in part of a family's tent (Marx, 1987). And husbands in the Gusii culture of Africa use part of a wife's dwelling to spend time alone or with friends (LeVine and LeVine, 1963).

Husbands in 19th-century Mormon polygynous families did not have separate residences, except, of course, when they were away for long periods of time. They either lived with their wives in a communal dwelling, rotated among wives' homes, or lived more often with a particular wife or wives. We neither encountered nor heard of any cases in which a contemporary plural husband has his own permanent separate residence.

In some segments of contemporary American society it is not uncommon for men to have a room or area in a home that is theirs – a workshop, den, study, or office (Altman, Nelson, and Lett, 1972). The situation was not as clear for 19th-century Mormon pioneers. Some husbands had their own rooms or areas in homes. For example, Brigham Young had an office and bedroom in his main family residence that were adjacent to rooms used for formal parties and receptions and close to rooms in which some of his wives and children lived. Another man built a special room for himself in each of his homes so that he could have some time alone wherever he was staying (Young, 1954). In one 19th-century family in which the husband and his six wives lived in a single home, the husband used the living room as an office and also had his own bedroom. But these are isolated cases; the literature on family life in 19th-century Mormon plural families rarely gives examples of husbands having separate areas or rooms in homes. Given their frequent moves, the struggle to survive on the frontier, large families, and other factors, living space was difficult to find, and a husband having his own area would have been a luxury for the average pioneer plural family.

In our sample of present-day plural families, we found only a few husbands and fathers who had their own places in homes. When they did, it often was in a public part of the home (e.g., a desk in a living room). Furthermore, the husband usually had had the room for only a short time, may have had a place of his own at an earlier time or when he was ill. In general, therefore, it is uncommon for husbands in present-day fundamentalist families to have rooms or places of their own in homes. But there are a few exceptions.

Family 2

With the recent move to a new home, David has a room of his own for the first time in his many years of marriage. He is very excited about the new room, just finished decorating it, and showed it to us with great pride. The room is near the front entrance and adjacent to the living room; there is no door separating it from the living room (it seems to have been designed as a dining room in a rambler-style house). He also shares the room with Rebecca; since she has her own desk in the room and uses it as an office for her small business, the space is somewhat public in its design and use.

Although he is very pleased with the room, David said that he may have to give it up when the home becomes too crowded (as the family expands) or if they move again and do not find comparable space. As a result, his "personal" room is actually a semipublic and shared room, and probably his to use only temporarily.

Family 8
Four of Ira's wives live upstairs and downstairs on each side of a large dwelling. There is a large room, perhaps 30 to 40 feet long, in the center of the home, which is used as a meeting and reception area. Ira uses a corner of the room as an office; it is furnished with two desks, chairs, and file cabinets. Ira is quite busy with visitors and business matters, and he describes the room as a hectic place – not one where he can be alone or relax.

In other cases, special circumstances enter in, such as illness.

Family 6
When asked about whether he has a room of his own, Seymour laughed and said he never had one in his many years of marriage to his eight wives. Now in his middle 60s, he finally has a small workshop of his own in the compound where several of his homes are located. More recently, Seymour has been living in his own bedroom in Tamara's home, where he has a special hospital bed. He has been seriously ill, and it is more comfortable for him to live in this home.

Some husbands do not have a special room or area, but talked about future plans for a space of their own.

Family 11
Benjamin, Katherine, Melba, Kelly, and Mary are currently remodeling their communal home to better accommodate them and their many children. The plan is to have a large living and meeting room in the center of the home, part of which can serve as Benjamin's office. At present he has no such place. His area will be semipublic and in a section of a multi-purpose room.

Family 4
Harry's family is doing a fair amount of remodeling of some of the homes of the four wives who live in the compound area. His sons also built a new structure that can be used as a guest room, an office, or retreat for Harry, and a place where he can occasionally sleep overnight. Harry is now 70 years old, and this is the first time he has ever had a place of his own. How the space will actually be used remains to be seen.

In a few cases, a husband has a room that is his alone and that is clearly demarcated as such.

Family 9

John has his own room in the home in which he, Joyce, Clara, and Marjorie live. He uses the room as an office to make daily telephone calls and maintain records. He also uses the office to study, think, and be alone every Sunday after the Sabbath meal. John tries to spend part of a day every week alone in his room – reading religious material, thinking, exercising, and sometimes even sleeping alone overnight. At other times he occasionally goes to the room to be alone for a few minutes.

One contemporary plural wife stated that her husband tried to have his own room whenever possible, but they often didn't have enough space (Merrill, 1975). She also said that in one case he kept the room locked, used it for studying and personal projects, and occasionally invited a wife to sleep with him in the room.

It is easy to understand why a special place for a husband in modern plural families is given low priority. Polygynous families are large and grow rapidly as wives have many children, often in rapid succession. Moreover, many families face financial challenges and live in modest homes, where space is at a premium. In addition, many families in the urban group live in standard housing stock, which is not designed for very large families or for communal living. As a result, it is a luxury for a husband or father to have his own separate area amid the day-to-day pressures of family life (particularly since he usually rotates among families and would not use a place regularly).

Communal factors may also enter into the picture, especially when wives live in dyadic setting. That is, if a husband has a separate room in one home (it is highly unlikely that it would ever be possible for him to have his own room in all homes), that home and the wife and family who live there might become or be seen as being more important and special to him. And he would probably spend more time there on practical grounds. Since a husband is ideally expected to be fair and loving to all of his families, a special room in one wife's home might create tensions in the family and upset an acceptable balance of dyadic and communal family processes.

What roles do husbands have in decorating homes?

As noted in chapter 11, the modern plural wife is primarily responsible for, and has authority over, the furnishing and decorating of homes. Husbands do not play much of a role, except when significant expenditures are involved. For example, husbands had little to say about furnishings and decorations when we toured dwellings; wives always took charge and described the decor. Husbands were usually in the background, noncommittal, passive, and showed little affect or reaction to the decor and furnishings of homes. Husbands and wives also often agreed that it was the wife who was responsible for furnishing and decorating decisions and that husbands played little or no role.

Family 1

Hal remarked: "I am the head of the family, but the homes belong to my wives, and I do not interfere with how they decorate them." His avowed role is certainly confirmed by the wide variation in furnishing style in each home in the family, each wife's detailed description of aspects of her home, and his neutral and passive demeanor as we toured homes.

Family 2

David and each wife made it quite clear that he plays a small role in determining the layout of the furniture and in decorating any of the family homes (however, he does help move furniture around under his wives' direction!). His only input to furniture selection is trading or purchasing items when they are on sale or easily obtained.

Family 4

When Eve, Harry's fourth wife, took us around her home, she made it quite clear that Harry had little to say about the remodeling and decorating. She said in his presence, "He allows me to do anything I want to, and he doesn't say anything about how I decorate my home." He agreed, saying that it is completely up to her and the other wives to decorate and furnish their homes the way they want to.

Family 6

Seymour and his wives are unequivocal regarding his role in decorating homes. In their eyes, he is the patriarch of the family, with clear social and religious authority. The wives are given "stewardship" over the home and are responsible and accountable for caring for it properly. He emphasized repeatedly that he has no personal interest in furnishing and decorating homes and that it is completely up to the wives to act on their religious responsibility and authority in creating a home.

In general, husbands in modern plural families are somewhat "disconnected" from and "unattached" to their homes. They rarely have a place of their own in family dwellings, and when they do, the place is often temporary, in a public area, shared with others, and not permanently theirs. Without places of their own, and not having long-term, significant control over rooms or areas, husbands do not have primary territories in their homes. And they play little part in furnishing and decorating their homes. Thus husbands are almost visitors to the home territories of their wives.

How do husbands achieve solitude?

We know that plural wives use their homes to be alone – spending time in their bedroom behind a closed door, getting up early in the morning or staying up late at night, using a special room or going to the yard and garden. Almost every husband we asked said that he does not use his home to be alone, even though there are occasions when he wants to think and reflect, escape from everyday pressures, and just relax. So, what do husbands do? Some men use their offices at work.

Family 1
Hal doesn't have a place at home, so he goes to his office to be alone, read, relax, and think about things.

Family 10
Barry said that he has no real place of his own to be alone in any of his eight wives' homes. So he goes to his office at work. In fact, one of his children calls his office "Daddy's house." Or, if it isn't convenient to travel there, Barry said that he "borrows" one of his wives' bedrooms to be alone for a while.

Several husbands use other strategies.

Family 4
Harry often uses his car to be alone. He said that it is the *only* place where he can be alone and where he can do what he wants to do without having to answer to or deal with others. He also stores personal and work papers in his car.

Family 1
Although Hal sees himself as a "people person" and rarely needs to be alone, he recalls a short trip he took with a friend to another state. It was the first time in a long time that he had been away from everyone in his family – including his four wives – and it was quite enjoyable and restored his energy.

Family 2
David likes to be alone on occasion, especially when he is under stress. Recently, after leaving his long-time job, he felt a strong desire to be alone. He left the family for a week, camping in the outdoors. David was deliberately out of touch with the family most of the time because

he needed to ponder the future away from day-to-day problems. David said that he doesn't do this sort of thing regularly, but this was one of those times when he had to be by himself. At other times, when he is home and needs a short respite, he just goes for a walk by himself.

David emphasized that he struggles to find time to be alone and think. Being with a different wife and children each night is a time-consuming activity that never gives him a chance to be alone. On the other hand, he noted, each wife sees him only about twice a week, so they have some time to themselves without him, although they must deal with children all the time.

Family 5

Howard said that his solution to being alone – something that is very important to him because he is so busy with work and with his four wives and 31 children – is to go for a hike by himself into a nearby canyon.

Although several husbands gain solitude outside of and away from their home, a few use places in the home, the most obvious being a separate room if they have one.

Family 9

As noted earlier, John has his own room and office in the home where he lives with Joyce, Clara, and Marjorie. He spends time alone in the office, reading religious material, thinking, exercising, and periodically sleeping overnight.

John, a new convert to fundamentalism, feels under considerable pressure to lead his family. The financial problems are enormous, he feels that he must always be emotionally "up" and ready to deal with his three wives' daily problems and challenges, regardless of his own personal and business problems, and he is bombarded with family issues every day when he returns from work. There are times when he just needs to be alone and sort things out. Whether he can continue to have a separate room, if they stay in the home and the family grows, is a matter of conjecture, he said, but it works well for the present.

Family 2

Although he sometimes takes trips alone or goes for short walks, David also stays up late after the wife and children with whom he is staying have gone to bed. Thus he has various ways of finding solitude in and out of his homes.

Family 18

When Charles finds himself needing to be alone, he does several things: he works for a few hours in the garden of one of the two homes in which his four wives live; he sits alone in the living room late at night after everyone has gone to bed; he uses a wife's bedroom to read or be by himself; and sometimes he even spends the night alone.

Family 4

When he needs some serious respite and relaxation, because of physical and emotional fatigue or stress, Harry goes to Ruth's bedroom. She is always ready, he said, to help him relax and regain his energy. So her room is a special place for him to have some quiet and security from daily pressures.

Harry also told us the following story of an acquaintance's strategy for being alone. A man with two wives who lived in the same home allegedly married a third wife in order to find time to be alone. Instead of having the new wife live with the other wives, he arranged for her to live in a separate home and eventually did the same for the first two wives. Then, the story goes, it was difficult for the wives to keep track of him because he didn't follow a strict rotation schedule. This allowed him to check into a motel every couple of weeks and have some time alone.

How do husbands feel about their homes?

In general, husbands in modern plural families are much less psychologically involved in their homes than are their wives. There is strong evidence to support this conclusion. As noted earlier, husbands play a small role in decorating or furnishing homes, they were passive and deferred to their wives when we toured homes, and they rarely expressed any emotional attachments to homes. They also tended to respond in neutral or flat emotional tones when discussing moving, decorating, or home management; wives usually dominated discussions of these topics, with husbands entering in secondarily or simply listening. The fact that so few men have their own places in homes or have only semipublic or temporary places adds to the picture. Some husbands even expressed their weak feelings of attachment to their homes.

Family 2

Although David admits to some attachment to the original family home in which two of his wives have lived for many years, his feelings are not all that strong. Homes are simply not that important to him, he said.

Family 4

Harry expresses very strong attachment to the community and town in which he lives but claims to have no strong attachment to any particular home in which he and his four wives live. He said this might be because they have moved often over the years to escape the authorities and because of finances, family growth, and work.

In addition to accepting that wives have the right and responsibility to maintain "stewardship" over homes, husbands appear to view homes in a very pragmatic way, as places to house wives and children. As a result, they invest little of their feelings and emotions in homes, are ready to change homes and living configurations as the need arises, and leave wives to manage and control dwellings.

It is important to note, however, that some husbands do have strong attachments to some homes or to certain places in particular homes, for example, because of a special relationship with a particular wife, as discussed in the next section.

Homes and personal identity, dyadic and communal bonds, cultural ties

As explained in chapter 11, plural wives use their homes to display their personal, dyadic, and cultural and religious identities, but not their communal bonds with co-wives. How are rooms or areas over which husbands have control decorated with respect to these identities, if at all? And if husbands do not have their own places, where do they display or keep personal objects and items?

Family 2

David showed us his new room in one of the family's homes on two occasions, enthusiastically describing each item and decoration. The room is furnished with an easy chair that he relaxes in and two desks and chairs (Rebecca, the second wife, uses one desk for the business that she operates, and he uses the other desk for his work and projects).

The room is dominated by personal identity displays showing David's hobbies and interests. For example, he likes old sailing ships and has drawings and models of ships all over the room. He also enjoys collecting pictures of eagles, and they are prominently displayed. Other personal identity items include a sculpture of the head of an American Indian and another small statue given to him as gifts by people at his office. He also displays a small bank whose shape and design he likes. A bookcase contains a few books and objects, and his briefcase lies on the desk.

The only dyadic item is a formal portrait of Judith, his first wife, which hangs behind the desk. There are no photographs of other wives or of any children in the room. We also did not see, nor did David point

out, communal items such as photographs of himself and all or some of
the wives in single pictures, or cultural or religious items.

Clearly, David decorates his room with items reflecting his personal
interests, hobbies, and preferences. David's room does not mirror his
dyadic and communal bonds to his wives, individually or collectively,
or to his religious values. Perhaps because dyadic and cultural or religious values are prominent in the wives' homes, he focuses on *himself*
in the place over which he has control.

Family 9

John's room in the home he shares with Joyce, Clara, Marjorie, and
their children is furnished with a desk, chair, exercise equipment, and a
bookcase filled with books. Most of the things in the room reflect John's
personal identity and his cultural and religious values. Personal identity
items include a computer, a pair of old boots, and a hat that he keeps
as a memento of the time he served as a government security officer,
exercise equipment, a radio, a bottle of cranberry juice, and a box of fig
newtons. Cultural and religious items include an extensive collection of
religious books and religious archeological maps. The only dyadic item
is a small stuffed animal given to him by his newlywed wife, Marjorie.
We saw no communal decorations in the room.

John, like David in Family 2, uses his room to mirror aspects of his
personal identity that are not evident elsewhere in the home. However,
he also emphasizes his cultural and religious interests. Also like David,
he does not display many dyadic items in his room or any family communal objects.

Family 8

Ira's office area in a large reception room is furnished with two desks
(one of which is used by Augusta, his third wife, who helps him with
church business), a computer and typewriter, some file cabinets, and a
small curio cabinet on the wall near his desk. His office area is at one
end of the large meeting room, which is furnished with a piano and
several sofas and chairs (Ira uses the sofas and chairs to meet with business visitors, friends, and family). Pictures of church leaders, beginning
with Joseph Smith and extending up to the present time, are on one wall
in the main room.

Cultural and religious items are prominent around John's desk. There
are photographs of a former leader in the fundamentalist movement and
of members of the current governing council of elders, as well as gifts
with religious themes given to Ira by Joseph Ginat and others (the gifts
from Ginat might also be classified as personal identity items since they
reflect the friendship between the two men).

Ira also has a few photographs of some of his children and grand-children on the wall or shelves near his desk. These photographs symbolize his dyadic bonds with some wives and their children. Since Ira did not attach special significance to them, we assume that he displayed them because they symbolized a special event, for example, a school graduation, not because of some unique association he has with the children or grandchildren in the photographs (Ira has eight wives and 43 children, and many grandchildren). There are no other dyadic items, nor are there any communal decorations showing the unity of the whole plural family.

The few cases in which husbands have special rooms in a home are consistent in several respects. First, personal identity and cultural and religious displays, in different combinations and to different degrees, predominate in husbands' rooms or areas. Not present anywhere else in the home, a husband's personal identity displays are preeminent when he has a place of his own. In two of the cases noted above, religious items were also displayed – some of them, for example, religious and archeological maps and gifts from a special friend were also unique to the husband's personal interests. Second, dyadic items involving a husband and his wives are absent or only infrequently shown. Third, communal items involving the whole plural family are completely absent. So husbands' rooms are quite personal; perhaps they compensate for the fact that homes usually highlight the personal identity of wives, not that of the husband. And because wives use their homes to make salient their dyadic link with the husband, he doesn't "need" to do so when he has a place of his own. A husband's room therefore gives him an opportunity to express his own unique personality in the home environment.

What happens when a husband does not have a place or area of his own? If he has personally valued objects, photographs, or other items, where does he keep them? How are they displayed? And how does he feel about them? Some husbands are quite bland and casual about their possessions; they have some but don't express strong feelings about them or where they are located.

Family 5
For one of Howard's birthdays, Constance, Valerie, Barbara, and Rose gave him an album containing pictures of all the wives and their children – a kind of communal and dyadic gift. When we asked him where the album was, he didn't know. Constance finally entered into the conversation, saying that she has it. Howard was quite bland about the whole matter.

Family 10

Barry is casual about where he keeps his personal things. He said that he stores gifts and personal property in one or another wife's home, depending on where there is space. He doesn't have any special place for things and doesn't seem to mind. If a wife or her children gives him a gift, he might keep it in a drawer that he has in each home, or somehow display it. He was neutral and pragmatic about the matter, although it is interesting that gifts from each family stay in their home, thereby conveying a dyadic quality.

When we asked what he plans to do with a gift just given to him by Joseph Ginat, he said that he would put it in his office, just as he had done with an earlier gift from Ginat. An item such as this, from someone outside the family, is not kept in a home (perhaps to avoid showing any favoritism toward a particular wife). In general, Howard shows little affect or interest in his things and even said that he isn't at all concerned that his possessions are not consolidated in one place.

These few instances illustrate the rather casual attitude of some husbands to objects and possessions, perhaps resulting from the fact that so few have permanent places of their own. The men who did have rooms or areas in their homes seemed enthusiastic about them. But those who did not appeared to be quite neutral and not very attached to personal objects.

A few husbands do display preferences and feel attached to certain places or things in some of their wives' homes.

Family 4

When we visited the home of the second wife, Ruth, and were in her bedroom, Harry said that the room was a special place for him. He described with great feeling how one of their children died of cancer at the age of seven. They had a viewing in this room, he said, and he and Ruth slept that night in the room with the deceased child in the casket next to their bed. He described this tragic event as a touching and beautiful experience, and one that strengthened the bond between them.

He went on to say that Ruth's bedroom is a special place where he comes to seek respite and serenity and to work through life stresses. No matter how tired he is, or how serious the problem, he knows that Ruth is always ready for him to have a good rest. In a lighter vein, Harry said that Ruth's bedroom is the only one in which he has a separate closet and in which he keeps many of his clothes. We will return to this issue later but raise it here to emphasize the point that Harry – who never had a room of his own – has a unique identification with and attachment to Ruth's bedroom that is manifested in pragmatic and interpersonal ways.

Harry and his five wives have strong and stable relationships with one another. In families that eventually ended in divorce or separation, husbands sometimes had special attachments to the homes of particular wives. These preferences either added to or resulted from the conflict between a husband and wife.

Family 12
Lauren, the second wife, told us that Fred expressly told her that he preferred Elaine's home because it was furnished better and was more comfortable. He kept all his clothing in Elaine's home, always went there first when he came home from work, and referred to the bedroom as "our" bedroom (and referred to Lauren's bedroom as "your" or "her" room). Lauren often had the feeling that Fred was a "visitor" in her home and that his "real" home was with Elaine. After years of turmoil and conflict, Lauren left him and they were divorced.

At an even more particular level, we can examine seating patterns and the extent to which husbands are attached to or have "seating territories" at mealtimes or elsewhere in homes. Lower middle-class American nuclear families, for example, have generally fixed seating at mealtimes, with the husband/father often seated in a central position, at the end or "head" of a table (Altman, Nelson, and Lett, 1972).

Family 4
We had meals on several occasions in the homes of Harry's wives. Harry always sat in a prominent position – at the "head" of the table or in a central position in large groups. Harry once entertained us along with about a dozen other people in a restaurant. Again, he sat in a central position, where he was visible to everyone, and others were seated near him according to their status and seniority (he arranged the seating plan for this occasion).

Family 3
William, Carlyn, Danielle, Alayna, and their children have used various seating configurations at mealtimes. At present, they sit at one large table, with William at the end, in the "head" position. For a while, Carlyn, Danielle, and Alayna sat next to him, but that didn't work out because the children needed supervision. Now the wives sit among the children, especially near the young ones, but William still sits at the end of the table.

Family 5
Howard always sits in a particular place at mealtimes. The place varies in each of the four homes of his wives, but it is usually at the end or

corner of a table, depending on the configuration of the space. Everyone else also tends to have a regular seat.

Family 7
Norman, Sarah, Patricia, Audrey, and their children live in one home. Norman usually sits at the center of the table, with the wives sitting on either side of him. They recently rearranged the seating plan into a T-shaped arrangement, but Norman still sits at the center of the table with Sarah, Patricia, and Audrey nearby, and with the children spread out along the rest of the table.

Family 18
We had a meal with the family on two occasions. Each time Charles sat at the end of the table, at the head position.

There are also some exceptions to a husband having his own seat in a home, at mealtimes or otherwise.

Family 6
Seymour, a member of the religious council, is a senior elder in the community. He told us that he has no particular chair or seat reserved for him when he is with one of his seven wives. In fact, he said that if he is sitting in a wife's favorite chair, he leaves it when she comes into the room, and takes another seat. And at mealtimes he sits wherever a place has been set for him, although he acknowledges that most family members usually sit in particular places. Our impression is that he is rather casual and not attached to particular seating locations.

In general, husbands in plural families display weak attachment to their homes. Only a few men have rooms or areas of their own, and some of these are temporary places. When they do have such places and when they decorate them, they tend to emphasize their own personal identities and their personal cultural and religious commitments, neither of which are usually reflected in other parts of homes. In addition, a few men feel strongly about some parts of homes – a particular wife's bedroom, for example – or they have a particular seat at mealtimes (which may symbolize their patriarchal status in families more than an emotional attachment to the place).[1]

Dyadic and communal aspects of husbands, wives, and homes

The dyadic relationship between each wife and her husband is highlighted in the homes of plural family members. Wives, the primary interior designers of homes, display many symbols of their special dyadic relationship with their husband – photographs of him, her and him, and their children; gifts from the husband or their children; memorabilia of their wedding or honeymoon; and other items. Although husbands are not too involved in decorating homes and show little attachment to homes in general, the presence of many dyadic decorations in each dwelling makes tangible his unique marital relationship with each wife. As he rotates among his wives and families, a husband is exposed to strikingly different homes and lifestyles, which also make salient his unique relationship with each wife. Even though husbands show little attachment to homes and usually do not have a place of their own in them (and hardly show dyadic decorations when they do), wives do the job for both of them.

A husband's weak attachment to homes might be an indirect way of *supporting* family communality – or at least of not weakening it. By not becoming attached to homes in general, or to any specific home, he avoids showing favoritism for a particular wife. Such behavior reinforces, or at least doesn't threaten, the worthiness of all dyadic bonds and the cohesion of the communal family. Admittedly this suggestion is speculative, and there are many pragmatic reasons for low levels of attachment by husbands to homes – large families, economic pressures, the husband rotating among residences, and others. At the same time, the husband's low involvement in furnishing and decorating homes may enhance, or at least not detract from, the ideal of a cohesive communal family.

Another aspect of attachment: A husband's clothing

We accidentally stumbled onto a topic that also sheds light on the attachment of a husband to homes, namely, the storage and care of his clothing. If a man has several wives, where does he keep his clothing – in one home, in all homes, in a suitcase that he carries from home to home? How does he keep track of his clothing if it is stored in several places? Who cleans and cares for his clothing – the husband himself, a particular wife, or all wives? These questions relate to a husband's attachment to homes, and to dyadic and communal relationships in a plural family. If a husband always keeps his clothing in one home, for example, he may be highlighting his dyadic bond to a particular wife and to her home. If he stores some clothing in each home, he may be emphasizing a communal bond to all wives. In other words, the seemingly mundane matter of the location of a husband's clothing may reveal something about his potential dyadic and communal attachments to wives and their homes. (In discussing this issue we were regaled with stories and laughter about all sorts of mishaps regarding the management of husbands' clothing. Aside from the conceptual relevance of the topic, it was fun to talk about).

There are several strategies for managing a husband's clothing that relate to communal, mixed communal and dyadic, and dyadic aspects of plural family life.

Communal management of a husband's clothing

Most of the families with whom we worked distributed the husband's clothes among wives.

Family 1

Hal used to keep his casual, work, and dress clothing more or less equally in Joan's, Norma's, Charlotte's, and Cynthia's homes; no home was used more than any other, so as not to show favoritism. When they moved from four homes to two, shared by pairs of wives, he kept clothing in each of their four closets. In effect, Hal shows a communal attachment to all homes and wives and does not favor any one over the others.

But spreading his clothes out creates some problems. Hal recounted a day when he had an important early morning business meeting. He dressed up in a formal business suit, only to discover that he only had running shoes in the home in which he was staying. It took several phone calls to the other wives to locate his shoes and then a long trip to retrieve them.

He and the wives also joked about how confused he gets looking for his clothes in some of their homes. It so happens that Joan, Norma, and Charlotte all have the same bedroom furniture, which they bought together for a very good price. Hal's clothing is in different dresser drawers in each home, and he is forever getting mixed up about where his shirts, underwear, and socks are in each place. (Hal's wives said he often gets confused at night when he gets up to go to the bathroom. Not exactly sure which home he is in, Hal stumbles about, banging into furniture, heading in the wrong direction, and acting foolishly. They told these stories amid great laughter.)

Family 5

Howard distributes his clothing among the homes of his four wives, Constance, Valerie, Barbara, and Rose, all of whom live in separate dwellings. He keeps some of his clothing in his own drawer in a bureau in each wife's bedroom. They, too, have adopted a system that emphasizes his communal relationship to homes and wives.

They also told of the amusing confusion that arises in managing Howard's clothing. He sometimes ends up having to wear bizarre combinations of colors because he doesn't know where things are, sometimes all of his socks end up in one wife's home, or he is missing a key piece of clothing for a particular outfit, and so on. With great amusement, the wives said Howard bangs into walls and furniture in the middle of the night, not sure of where he is, and is always looking in the wrong drawers for his clothing.

Family 10
Barry and his eight wives live in separate apartments (some shared by pairs of wives) in three dwellings in different parts of the community. He keeps full outfits of dress and casual clothing in every wife's home or bedroom, even when they live communally. Several of Barry's wives said that he is very organized and keeps good track of his clothing.

Family 18
Charles, Susan, Nancy, Angela, and Linda live in two homes on the same street. Even though the homes are nearby, Charles keeps his clothing in every wife's bedroom, so as to avoid any semblance of favoritism. In fact, he always makes sure that his best suit, which he wears to church on Sunday, is in the wife's room where he is that day.

From the little information that is available about a husband's clothing among 19th-century Mormon pioneers, it appears that husbands often kept their clothes in several wives' homes (Young, 1954). There are also cases of husbands carrying their clothing from home to home. One son of a second wife said that polygamy

> was then so natural to me that I did not notice particularly his weekly packing of his leather valise to move over to "Aunt Caroline's" for the week, or his return the following Saturday with his things put away in the leather container. . . .
> Dad always shaved with a razor, and he had a little shaving kit. For years it was my responsibility for that shaving kit to be at the house where he was going to shave the next morning. (Embry, 1987, p. 81)

In summary, despite occasional inconvenience and confusion, plural husbands find it practical and convenient to have some of their things in different homes. Otherwise they would have to carry clothes with them or always go to a particular home for a change of clothing. At the same time, this arrangement fits the ideal of a husband being "fair" and not favoring any particular wife. Since a husband's clothing can be an important dyadic symbol to some wives, distributing his clothing across homes mitigates against perceptions that the husband is playing favorites.

Having his clothing in all homes is also consistent with the weak attachments that many husbands display toward their dwellings. It "doesn't matter" where he keeps his clothing, and keeping it everywhere symbolizes his lack of special feelings about any home.

Communal and dyadic management of a husband's clothing

In a few plural families the husband's clothing is kept with some wives but not with others; or some clothing is stored in all homes, but most of it is in one or two places. Although communal in some ways, these approaches also have dyadic features. It is done this way for any of several reasons: space availability, convenience – depending on where a husband works and where wives live – or simply because of habit.

Family 2
David's arrangement reflects a communal style: he keeps some clothing in the home of each of his four wives. However, most of his clothing is stored in Judith's and Rebecca's homes – which are upstairs and downstairs in the same dwelling. His suits, shirts, and pants are in a closet upstairs, and his underwear is downstairs. He uses this arrangement because these homes have more room for his things. He deliberately keeps some clothing in the other wives' homes as a symbol of his relationship with them.

When they shifted living arrangements, he moved a lot of his clothing to Rebecca's new home, only because it had more room. Storage space and practicality thus enter into why David keeps his clothing in a mixed communal and dyadic arrangement.

Family 8
Ira and his eight wives live in several dwellings – two are in a compound, of which houses several wives in separate apartments, and one is a home elsewhere in the community. Ira, now in his 80s, keeps most of his clothing in two places – in one of the wives' homes in the compound, and with Betty, the fourth wife, who lives elsewhere in the community. This is a mixed dyadic and communal arrangement.

In earlier years, Ira kept clothing in every wife's home but moved to the present arrangement because he is busy day and night with church affairs, his office is in one of the homes in the compound, and it is just too difficult to meet his responsibilities and suffer the inconvenience of having some of his clothing in every home. The demands of work and of everyday activities determine where he keeps his things.

Dyadic management of a husband's clothing

In a very few cases a husband keeps his clothing in one wife's home, thereby reflecting a dyadic orientation. The reasons for doing so may be practical, as noted earlier. Or a man may prefer a particular wife and may spend more time in her home. A dyadic approach to managing a husband's clothing is rare in the families we interviewed.

Family 6
Seymour, now in his late 60s, has been quite ill for the past several years. As a result, he lives mainly in Tamara's home, where he has his own bedroom, a special hospital bed, and a place to store most of his clothes (apparently he also has a few items of clothing in some other wives' places).

In earlier years, he kept clothing at each of his eight wives' homes, with the usual complications and funny stories. For example, one of his daughters remembers seeing Seymour all dressed up for a wedding in a nice suit, but wearing dirty work shoes because he didn't know which wife had his dress shoes.

Family 12
Lauren, the second wife, eventually left the family as a result of the long-lasting conflicts with Fred and Elaine, the first wife. The location of Fred's clothing also reflected their problems. Early in the marriage, he kept his things in Elaine's home because, Lauren claims, he preferred her and was more comfortable in her home. At another time, when they lived in adjoining apartments, he distributed his clothing more equally. But this changed from time to time, depending on where they lived and how their relationships progressed.

In general, contemporary polygynous Mormon husbands keep their clothing in most wives' homes, or at least in several wives' places. Storing a husband's clothing in only one place is relatively rare and occurs only in special circumstances, such as illness or family upheaval. Adopting a communal, distributed strategy for managing a husband's clothing symbolizes his concern for all wives and the plural family as a whole, avoids preferential treatment, and makes all homes (and the wives and children in each) symbolically equivalent. This practice is also consistent with the low level of attachment and involvement that husbands display with respect to decorating and furnishing homes, not having a room in homes, not using homes to regulate openness and closedness, and so on. Whether deliberate and conscious or not, the "placelessness" of husbands in modern plural families contributes to an aura of "fairness," nonpreferential treatment of particular wives and children, and family communality. And if he is less involved emotionally in homes, wives are also able to freely manage and control day-to-day life in their dwellings.

These case examples also reveal that change and experimentation apply to the handling of a husband's clothing, just as in many other aspects of modern plural family life. Families use different systems at different points in life, and in no particular order. Thus where a husband's clothing is kept depends on the living arrangements in which a family finds itself at different times, distances between homes, work schedules, the availability of storage space, how family members are getting along with one another, health, and so on. At the same time, plural family members seem to be sensitive to the fact that the location of a husband's clothing symbolizes aspects of interpersonal relationships in the family. This is clear from wives' feelings about their husband's clothing.

How do plural wives feel about their husband's clothing?

Unusual as it may seem, a husband's clothing sometimes has important symbolic value to contemporary Mormon plural wives. It is a symbol of their dyadic marital relationship with the husband, and some care deeply about where he keeps his things and their role in caring for his clothing.

Family 2
Judith, Rebecca, Emily, and Phyllis agree that having and caring for David's clothing in their home is an important symbol of each of their unique marriage relationships with him. Phyllis was emphatic about the matter. She said that she likes to have some of his clothes in her home, enjoys cleaning and taking care of them, and feels good about presenting him with fresh clothing when he stays with her.

Family 5
Constance, Valerie, Barbara, and Rose said that they "treasure" having Howard's clothes in their closets and that they take pleasure in washing and caring for them. They feel that his clothes in their home symbolizes his presence in their lives – whether he is there or not. Barbara said, "It is a privilege to do things for my husband," referring to taking care of his clothing. (They all laughed and agreed when one of them said that there certainly are times in their hectic lives when they would be quite happy to have other wives wash and iron Howard's clothing!)

Caring for a husband's clothing was also important to some 19th-century plural wives:

Such mundane matters as doing a husband's laundry, and mending, and keeping his Sunday clothes often became indicators of difference in status. ... A daughter of [a second wife] ... remarked on the high significance of doing the laundry: "I have seen my mother in tears because father didn't bring his laundry for mother to do. She was so afraid she hadn't done it right last time." (Young, 1954, p. 199)

Some contemporary plural wives showed how important a husband's clothing was to their dyadic relationship by establishing "proprietary rights" to certain items.

Family 18
Sometimes one of the four wives buys Charles a shirt or special item of clothing for Father's Day or his birthday and tries to keep it in her room and personally care for it.

Family 5
One of the four wives mentioned that they sometimes embroider *their* name or initials on a special piece of Howard's clothing that they bought or made for him, to ensure that it eventually comes back to them to keep and care for. (Wives in several other families either did a similar thing or knew of other such cases.)

A husband's clothing was a particularly telling symbol of a dyadic relationship in at least one case.

Family 2
Rebecca, the second wife, told us half in jest but half seriously that she sometimes sleeps holding one of David's shirts when he is not at her home. It comforts her by making her feel that he is with her in an indirect way.

Summary

Most husbands in contemporary Mormon plural families have rather weak attachments to their family homes, as revealed in the fact that they rarely have a room of their own, are seldom involved in decorating and furnishing homes and have little interest in doing so, often seek solitude outside the home, and do not display personal possessions in the homes of their wives. In a few cases in which husbands have their own area in a home, it often is a semipublic place and only temporarily theirs – there are pressing needs for space in many plural families. And husbands' rooms are largely decorated with personal identity and cultural and religious items; they do not reflect husband–wife dyadic relationships or communal relationships in the family as a whole. Furthermore, most husbands do not show preferences for particular homes and tend to keep their clothing in several homes, and not in a particular wife's dwelling.

The differences between husbands and plural wives is striking. For wives, the home is an important place to express themselves, their personality, and their values in the physical environment. For husbands, the home is a place to "visit," a site to house their family, and a place to which they make little emotional commitment and over which they exert little control.

A NOTE ON CHILDREN AND HOMES

Having examined how husbands and wives in plural families differ in psychological attachment to their homes, we were naturally curious about children. Are there comparable gender differences among boys and girls in present-day plural families, perhaps reflecting socialization into adult roles? As discussed throughout the book, traditional gender roles are strongly advocated among Mormon fundamentalists. As a result, we might expect to find the seeds of gender differences in the way in which boys and girls are socialized with respect to their homes. Although we did not collect systematic information, we learned a bit about children's sleeping arrangements and room decorations. The following observations provide preliminary information on a topic that merits additional study.[2]

Sleeping arrangements of boys and girls

Children's sleeping arrangements in present-day Mormon plural families vary widely as a function of living arrangements, age, and gender of children. When a family lives in dyadic arrangements, children live and sleep in their mother's dwelling. In communal arrangements, when wives share homes, our impression is that young children and infants usually sleep near their mother, in her bedroom or in rooms and areas close to her bedroom. However, older children of different mothers in a family sometimes share rooms or areas – boys with boys and girls with girls. But even these patterns vary as a function of family size, the particular configuration of children, and other factors. In some cases, children of all ages sleep together in separate gender groups because there is not enough space to do otherwise; one family created a "nursery" for *all* young children and a large single dormitory for older children, with boys and girls in different parts of a large room. Generally speaking, however, young children sleep near their mothers, and older children have a wide array of arrangements, depending on family circumstances.

Do girls have "better" and more regular places than boys – something one might expect if they are differentially socialized with respect to attachment to homes? In general, our impression is that older boys and girls have more or less equivalent sleeping places – they have rooms alone or share them with others, with no substantial gender differences in most cases. In a few cases, however, girls seem to have more stable or closer-to-home sleeping arrangements.

Family 4

Anna, Harry's first wife, lives in her own home. Two of her teenage sons sleep in a small one-room building immediately adjacent to the home. Some of her older daughters live inside the home.

Eve, Harry's fifth wife, also has her own home, and all of her children are teenagers or younger, so space is quite limited. Some of her older boys share a bedroom, as do the older girls. When visitors come, however, the boys are usually relocated to other rooms or the homes of other wives. Girls did not appear to be shifted around in the same way.

Eve and Belle, the fourth wife, are doing some remodeling of their homes. The plan is to build some rooms for older boys from Eve's and Belle's families to share together – across mothers – and for the older girls to have rooms in each of their mother's homes. It is also customary in the family for teenage girls to have their own rooms as soon as there is space in the home, with boys continuing to share bedrooms. Thus older boys seem to be less rooted to places in the family home and to sometimes have more casual and temporary sleeping arrangement than girls.

Family 7

Norman, Sarah, Patricia, Audrey, and their 13 children live in one home. The older children sleep in different areas of the home as determined by age and gender. The older girls have rooms inside the home; the older boys sleep in a trailer adjacent to the dwelling.

Family 9

John, Joyce, Clara, and Marjorie live in one home. Because there isn't enough room in their home, one of Joyce's older teenage sons lives in the garage adjacent to the home, and another older son who is still in school shares an apartment with several other young men from plural families. (The only older daughter in the family is married, so sleeping arrangements could not be compared by gender in this case.)

Family 2

In one home, some of Rebecca's young boys sleep in bunk beds in a curtained-off area adjacent to the kitchen. Her girls sleep in one or two bedrooms in the crowded home.

These certainly are not definitive data and represent only a handful of cases. However, they are consistent in suggesting that the sleeping arrangements of boys in a few contemporary plural families are somewhat casual, are not always in the home itself, and vary from time to time. In contrast, girls always sleep inside homes in bedrooms and in more stable arrangements. By inference, therefore, girls may be socialized to be more attached to homes than boys, perhaps in anticipation of their future adult roles.

Decorating practices of boys and girls

How boys' and girls' bedrooms in modern plural families are decorated may reflect gender socialization and eventual attachment to homes – as it does for husbands and wives. Thus we might expect girls' rooms to be more heavily decorated than those of boys and the decorations in children's rooms to be linked to gender.[3]

Volume of decorating in children's rooms

In the five families for whom comparisons were possible, we judged that girls' rooms were more extensively decorated than boys' rooms in 16 of 19 or 85% of the cases. In only three cases was the volume of decorations equivalent, and in *no* cases were boys' rooms more heavily decorated. The volume of decorating in boys and girls' rooms – whether the decorating was done by the children or their mother is unknown – is consistent with attachments to homes by husbands and wives.

Content of boys' and girls' decorations

We categorized decorations according to the same schema used for adults, namely, personal identity, dyadic, communal, and cultural or religious displays.

Personal identity items are the most frequent form of decoration for both boys and girls. Boys' personal identity items include posters or pictures from magazines of professional and college athletes, horses, trucks, and recreation vehicles. Boys' rooms also have rifles, sports equipment, cowboy hats, automobile models, athletic and scouting trophies, and a variety of other male-oriented things. Other items include TVs, stereo equipment, and coins or other collections. Personal identity items predominate in boys' rooms and mirror the traditional roles and interests of males in American culture. Some boys also have photographs of their parents and brothers and sisters – which can be classified as personal identity or dyadic items.

Girls' rooms are also heavily decorated with personal identity items that fit traditional gender roles. Posters and pictures of butterflies, cats and kittens, horses, and landscapes, are common. Other personal identity items include dolls, embroidered wall hangings, feminine curtains and bedspreads, delicate figurines, necklaces and jewelry, and plants. Girls' rooms also seemed to be nicely painted or wallpapered more often, decorated more carefully, and cleaner and better cared for than boys' rooms. Some girls also have photographs of family members – brothers and sisters, parents, and relatives.

As in other parts of homes, we did not observe or hear about decorations in boys' and girls' rooms depicting the communal plural family of other wives and mothers or their children.

Boys and girls also have cultural and religious items in their rooms that are similar to those in other parts of homes. These include photographs of present and past church leaders, pictures of Jesus, religious books, objects and figures, and so on. One boy has a poster of Jerusalem on his ceiling and a large thermometer on the wall that records his savings toward a trip to Israel; some girls – but never boys – have embroidered religious sayings on the walls of their room.

In general, girls' rooms are more extensively decorated than boys' rooms, although personal identity items – often gender-linked as they are in the larger culture – are predominant in both cases. Photographs of parents and siblings, which might be considered dyadic or personal identity displays, and a variety of cultural and religious items also appear in both boys' and girls' rooms but are much less prominent than personal identity items.

As is consistent with research by Csikszentmihalyi and Rochberg-Halton (1981), decorations in children's rooms tend to focus on the "here and now," as reflected in their contemporary interests and action-oriented items, such as sports equipment. Thus the rooms of boys and girls in contemporary polygynous families seem to be decorated in much the same way as those of children in the larger American culture.

We did not see striking differences between boys and girls in the distribution or proportion of decorations in personal identity, dyadic, communal and cultural categories. Girls do more decorating in general, but both genders emphasize personal identity items, and both have some dyadic and religious decorations.

Summary

Our limited information reveals some differences in sleeping arrangements and decorations in the rooms of boys and girls in present-day Mormon plural families. First, girls seem to have more stable sleeping arrangements – they usually have their own bedroom or share one with their sisters, and their sleeping places are more fixed and permanent. In contrast, boys seem to be treated more casually – older boys sometimes sleep outside the home in trailers or garages (or, in one case, with boys of other families) and are moved more often when space is limited.

Girls' rooms are also more extensively decorated than those of boys, although both genders rely heavily on personal identity items reflecting gender-linked interests. Boys and girls also decorate with cultural and religious items and with dyadic items linking them to their parents and brothers and sisters. Aside from volume, boys and girls do not otherwise differ in the decorations they display in their rooms.

In general, our information suggests that girls are probably socialized to have greater attachment to their home than are boys – a pattern consistent with what we observed for husbands and wives.

Managing everyday life

The three chapters in this section examine day-to-day life in present-day polygynous Mormon families.

Chapter 13 describes systems by which a husband's time is distributed among his wives and families. The so-called "rotation" process can vary from a *rigid* system in which a husband visits his wives on a strict schedule, to a *laissez-faire* arrangement wherein his visits do not follow a regular pattern, to a *flexible* system in which he rotates in a more or less regular routine.

Chapter 14 deals with a crucial day-to-day issue in polygynous Mormon families, namely, how they manage their financial resources. We examine the extent to which a husband and wives operate according to a strictly dyadic system in which each couple deals with finances and income separately, in contrast to a communal system in which family members pool resources and work out their finances collectively.

Chapter 15 examines the ways in which present-day plural families celebrate various events – the birthdays of children, wives, and the husband; wedding anniversaries; and holidays such as Christmas. Are all of these events celebrated communally by a whole family, or are some observed in a dyadic fashion, that is, by each wife and her husband separately from the other wives?

We also examine tensions and stresses in plural families that are associated with dyadic and communal aspects of rotation, budgets, and celebrations.

13

The rotation process: Husbands and wives alone together

Ideally, in a polygynous Mormon family a husband and each wife spend some time alone with one another and with their children, doing what any monogamous couple does – eating, talking, solving family problems, interacting with children, sleeping together, having sexual relationships, watching television, or engaging in some type of recreation. But how do they manage this essentially dyadic process in the context of a communal life involving several husband–wife–children units? Put another way, how does a husband "rotate" among wives and children so as to acknowledge the uniqueness of each dyad in a plural family and simultaneously preserve the family's communal unity?

Rotation patterns in polygynous cultures vary widely with regard to a number of dyadic and communal issues. To begin with, who visits whom – does the husband go to the wives, or do they go to him? Is "fairness" regarding the time a husband spends with different wives a consideration in rotation patterns? Who decides when and for how long a husband and wife spend time together – the husband, the wives, everyone? What type of "rotation systems" do plural families use – a rigid one in which a husband spends fixed times with each wife; a completely open system with no regular pattern of rotation; or a flexible system with some systematic rotation pattern but also with some flexibility and variation?

The question of particular interest here is the way in which rotation plans enhance or detract from dyadic and communal aspects of contemporary plural family life. On the one hand, achieving acceptable dyadic relations between a husband and each wife calls for some regular contact between members of each couple, in order to acknowledge the uniqueness and importance of their bond. On the other hand, a rotation system should acknowledge the communal importance of all relationships. Our analysis indicates that contemporary Mormon plural families struggle to meet these ideals, experimenting with various rotation schemes from time to time. As a result, different families develop unique arrangements to meet their circumstances. Achieving a viable interplay of dyadic and communal rotation practices is difficult because many participants have had little personal experience with plural family life and must often "invent from scratch" a system that will suit their needs.

Rotation systems in polygynous cultures

There are a variety of rotation systems in other cultures. In some cultures, husbands visit their wives' dwellings; in other cultures, wives come to the husband's place. In some cases, the husband rotates among wives on a daily basis or every few days; in other cases, the husband spends longer periods of time with each wife and her children. Some groups use a regular rotation system, others use a sporadic one in which husbands spend varying amounts of time with different wives. Some cultures expect a husband to be "fair" and to spend equal time with each wife; others do not explicitly follow this principle or do not consider it important. In some cultures, the husband decides when and how much time to spend with each wife and her children; in other cultures, wives may have some input into these decisions. In some societies, rotation is guided less by family issues and more by religious, political, or economic factors such as agricultural cycles, a husband's religious and political status and activities, his traveling patterns, and the like. Ethnographic evidence suggests that polygynous cultures have developed rotation systems that are uniquely appropriate to their social and cultural circumstances.

Who visits whom – a wife or the husband?

In many polygynous cultures the husband visits each of his wives in their dwellings. If the residences are matrilocal, that is, if the wives live near their natal family and kin as they do among the Comoro Islanders of Mozambique, a husband sometimes travels long distances to each of his wives' residences (Ottenheimer and Ottenheimer, 1979). A husband in this culture is truly a "visitor," living with a wife temporarily amid all of her relatives. The concept of a husband-as-visitor also occurs among the Masai of Africa (Talle, 1987), the Gusii of Africa (LeVine, 1964 LeVine and LeVine, 1963), the Lango, of Africa (Curley, 1973), the Bedouin of Israel (Marx, 1967, 1987), and the Tonga of Africa (Stephens, 1963). This rotation pattern is also customary in contemporary Mormon plural families, as it was among 19th-century Mormons.

In certain other cultures, wives periodically go to a husband's dwelling or place in a home. This is the practice among the Aboure of Africa (Clignet, 1970), the Kiganda of East Africa (Kilbride and Kilbride, 1990), and the Kikuyu of Africa (Kenyatta, 1973). In some of these cases, wives and husbands each have their own dwelling in a family compound or homestead; or a husband and his wives share a single dwelling in which the husband has his own area.

Some cultures have mixed rotation patterns; that is, wives sometimes go to a husband's place, and a husband sometimes rotates among his wives' homes. When a polygynous family in the Dakar culture of Africa lives in a single dwelling, each wife has a turn sleeping with the husband in his bed (Falade, 1963). If wives have separate dwellings, the husband rotates from home to home. Thus who visits whom may vary with living arrangements.

Fairness and equity in rotation systems

Husbands in many polygynous cultures are expected to be "fair" and to visit their wives and children regularly (Murdock, 1967). The principle by which a husband allocates his time and resources to his wives equitably is designed in part to minimize competition and conflict between wives and to enhance the economic viability of the family unit. Because marriages are often based on links between kin groups, fair treatment of wives maintains and solidifies those bonds. Several cultures explicitly call on husbands to demonstrate equity toward plural wives. This is the case among the Ijaw of Africa (Leis, 1974), Comoro Islanders of Mozambique (Ottenheimer and Ottenheimer, 1979), the Tonga of Africa (Stephens, 1963), and the Fulani of Africa (Stenning, 1971).

But the principle of rotational fairness is not always practiced. Husbands in the Lango culture of Africa sometimes have a favorite wife with whom they spend more time and whom they treat better; or a senior Lango wife who has more status may command more of a husband's attention (Curley, 1973). Although equality of a husband's time and resources is espoused by the Nyakyusa of Africa, here, too, a man often has a favorite wife, sometimes the newest one, toward whom he directs special attention (Wilson, 1950). Among the Gusii of Africa it is often the youngest wife who receives this kind of attention (LeVine & LeVine, 1963), whereas the Tonga of Africa expect a husband to spend time with the senior first wife before and after returning from a journey (Stephens, 1963). A similar practice occurs among Negev Bedouins of Israel (Ginat, personal observation). Some cultures ensure fairness by requiring a husband to compensate a wife when he fails to visit her regularly. If a husband in certain Bedouin groups of Israel does not visit a wife at her turn, he is obligated to give her a gift of a sheep or a goat (Ginat, personal observation).

Equal treatment of wives in time, attention, and resources is a long-standing principle among Mormons. It was espoused as an important ideal by 19th-century Mormons and continues to be articulated by contemporary fundamentalists. Although practiced by many, there are exceptions, as discussed in the next section.

Rotation systems: Regularity and length of visits

Some cultures expect a man to follow a rigid rotation schedule. Ideally, a Bedouin husband of Israel visits each wife on a regular schedule (Marx, 1967). And Fulani husbands of Africa spend one night with each wife (Clignet and Sween, 1981), Javanese husbands spend two nights with each wife (Geertz, 1961), and those in the Temni and Mende cultures of Africa visit each wife for three nights (Little, 1951).[1]

The Gusii, as noted earlier, follow a less regular system. Husbands spend whatever time they desire with wives, yet they are obligated to visit all wives on occasion, if for no other reason than to honor a wife's desire to have children (LeVine and LeVine, 1963). Likewise, Masai husbands of Africa visit and live with their wives when it suits them (Talle, 1987). Polygynous husbands in Mormon pioneer and present-day fundamentalist culture also use different rotation schedules, although in general husbands are expected to visit all their wives on a regular basis.

Who decides about rotation visits?

Although ethnographies do not always delve into these issues, the cross-cultural evidence suggests that husbands often determine which wife they visit and for how long. At the same time, wives are not always passive about rotation practices; they may be active players. A first wife in the Mende culture of Africa not only supervises a new wife in various day-to-day activities, but she can also decide when the subordinate wife is to see the husband (Little, 1951). Thus cultures vary widely in terms of husbands' and wives' roles in the rotation system.

Among present-day Mormon fundamentalists, the husband theoretically decides which wife he will visit and when the visits will occur – in accordance with his formal status as family patriarch and leader. At the same time, many fundamentalist wives play an active role in the process, albeit sometimes informally.

In general, therefore, there are cross-cultural consistencies and variations in rotational philosophies and practices. In most cultures husbands visit wives, although some cultures call for wives to visit husbands. Moreover, many cultures subscribe to the principle that a husband should be "fair" to plural wives – in visitations and provision of resources. But this does not always happen in practice; favoritism is not unusual. Systems of rotation also vary in length of visits – from a husband rotating daily among wives, spending several days with each wife, or visiting for longer periods. And although ethnographic accounts often state or imply that husbands decide on rotation visits, there is evidence that polygynous wives may be influential in rotation patterns, either informally or through culturally established roles. It is also important to note that ethnographic accounts usually describe only general cultural practices and norms; they rarely penetrate into variations within and across individual families. We suspect that there are wide variations in rotation practices in individual cases within cultures, as there are among Mormon plural families.

Rotation among fundamentalists

Modern plural families follow three general systems of rotation: *rigid* systems with a fixed schedule, in which a husband spends equal and regular times with his wives; *laissez-faire* systems, which have no predictable schedule of rotation; and *flexible* systems, which follow a loose and approximate schedule. Each type has dyadic and communal aspects in terms of scheduling, the roles husbands and wives play in developing and maintaining rotation systems, the principle and practice of "fairness" or equality with respect to a husband's time with his wives and children, changes in rotation systems, and problems and stresses associated with rotation.

Types of rotation schedules

Regardless of the specifics of scheduling, present-day fundamentalist husbands usually visit their wives and children in a wife's home or area of a home.[2]

Rigid rotation systems. In rigid rotation systems a husband visits each wife and her children according to a fixed routine, theoretically spending the same amount of time with each family, and in a known and predictable sequence of visits. This might involve a rotation every day, every several days, or some other pattern, depending on circumstances; but whatever the length of visitations, the cycle is prescribed, fixed, and unfolds on a regular basis.

Rigid rotation systems are used only rarely in the families we studied. Although several families had tried some form of rigid rotation pattern, they either modified it or eventually scrapped it completely. Many families feel that rigid visitation does not take into consideration the fact that issues might arise requiring the husband to alter the rotational pattern, for example, because of birthdays and anniversaries, travel and work schedules, or emergencies. For some participants, rigid rotation patterns can also become too mechanical and visits by a husband may lose their spontaneity. An unbending rotation schedule often ignores personal and interpersonal needs and feelings and is insensitive to day-to-day circumstances. Rigid rotation patterns sometimes become something everyone "has" to do as an obligation, not something that they look forward to and "want" to do. As a result, families often eventually reject a rigid system or incorporate some flexibility to meet their needs.

Family 1
In the earlier years of their family life, Hal, Joan, and Norma followed a rigid rotation system that had Hal spending exactly equal time with each wife. Eventually they all agreed that the system was not working well. It was simply too mechanical, did not always meet Hal's personal need to be with a particular wife or to attend to a particular family problem, ignored the desire of a wife to be with him, and made them all feel that they had to be with one another as an obligation, not as a time of pleasure, companionship, and satisfaction. One of them said that a rigid pattern of visits contributed to a feeling of not even being married. As a result, soon after Charlotte, the third wife, joined the family they shifted to a flexible system.

Family 9
John, Joyce, and Clara are recent converts to the fundamentalist group; Marjorie, the fourth wife, was raised in a plural family. The family lives together in a single dwelling, and they have adopted a rigid 24-hour rotation system. John spends a full day with each wife, beginning at noon and extending until noon the following day. When his time with a wife begins, John focuses his attention and energy on her and their relationship, sits near her, spends time alone with her, and so on. And when they are all out driving somewhere, the wife with whom he is spending the day sits next to him, and the other wives sit in the rear of the car. They carry the system to the point that if noon arrives when

they are shopping or out of the home, the wives shift their seats in the car in accordance with the rotation schedule. Because there are three wives, John spends alternating days and a night with each of them twice a week. On the seventh day and night of each week he spends time alone or with all the wives together, and sleeps in his office in the home. (They recently shifted this cycle, with John spending time alone only every 10 days or two weeks).

But even within this rigid system they acknowledge the need for some flexibility. Thus John does interact with Joyce, Clara, and Marjorie on a daily basis, and addresses major problems that arise, regardless of the rotation sequence. And they agree that John should spend extra time with a wife on her birthday and on their wedding anniversary.

They recently introduced a new feature into their rotation system that gives more attention to each dyadic relationship. During the summer John and each wife spend a couple of days on a "mini-vacation" away from the family home. Each couple visits a different place, thereby highlighting their dyadic uniqueness.

This family practices the most rigid rotation schedule we encountered. Yet they still maintain a degree of flexibility to handle special circumstances. It will be interesting to see if they continue their system over the years, as the family grows and as life circumstances change.

Rigid rotation systems are also followed by *Family 12,* which has Fred spending alternating nights with Elaine and Lauren, and *Family 13,* which has Paul rigidly alternating his time during the week with Muriel, Gloria, and Sherri. Then he spends a full weekend with each wife, also on a strict schedule.

Another family follows a fairly rigid rotation pattern but permits substantial flexibility to allow for special circumstances and occasions. In a sense, they use a combined rigid and flexible system of rotation.

Family 18

Charles alternates days as exactly and evenly as possible with Susan, Nancy, Angela, and Linda. Because three wives live in the same dwelling, he does his best to focus attention on the wife in the home where he is spending the day. For example, they may sit near one another at dinner or eat alone in the backyard or private area of the kitchen.

At the same time, they have incorporated flexibility into their system for special occasions. Thus the routine is changed to accommodate birthdays and anniversaries, at which time Charles and a wife may spend an extra day together. In addition, Susan, Nancy, Angela, and Linda may negotiate a change in the schedule with one another for children's birthdays, special problems that need to be addressed, and so on. Charles is quite open to the wives' desire for flexibility, and they all agree that the combined rigid and flexible system works well for them.

Some Mormon pioneer families in the 19th century also adopted fairly rigid rotation systems.

> [Father] . . . "used to be at our home every third day, regular as clock work. He stayed at one house one night, the next house another night, and our house the third night. He was in the temple full time, but he was home at one or the other of these three homes every night." . . .
>
> [A daughter] . . . said that her father['s] schedule was "just like clock work. . . . Father had a regular schedule to be over to mother's every night [on her turn] to have supper and breakfast the next morning. He would stay for dinner. Then he would go back to Aunt Clarinda." (Embry, 1987, p. 81)[3]

In some ways a totally rigid rotation system *theoretically* serves the communal unity of a family by ensuring that a husband spends equal time with each wife, taking the decision out of his or the wives' hands, and avoiding any visible favoring of particular wives. It also *hypothetically* reinforces the importance and worthiness of each dyadic relationship in a plural family. At the same time, totally rigid systems may not serve dyadic or communal aspects of plural family life very well. A mechanical rotation system dilutes the concept of each husband–wife pair as a distinctive, unique, and special relationship. It denies the diversity and special character of each marital bond, homogenizes those bonds, and ignores the special circumstances that may call for extra or out-of-sequence time in a marital and family relationship. If all couples are treated alike in a mechanical way, then none are distinctive, unique, or special. And if the time spent by a husband and wife together is rigidly prescribed, independent of their desire and need to be with one another, then the relationship can easily become obligatory and routine, as noted by some participants in our study. So a rigid system may violate the ideally unique nature of husband–wife dyadic relationships.

Moreover, rigid systems may not serve communal family goals very well, beyond ensuring that a husband spends equal time with his wives. With a predetermined rotational scheme, no one has control over special family needs, and participants may not feel part of an interpersonally cohesive family unit operating according to consensual and shared goals. Everyone is simply a cog in a machinelike system whose parts are linked in a superficial way. Perhaps that is why few plural families use rigid systems of rotation and eventually change to more flexible visitation patterns.

Laissez-faire rotation systems. Laissez-faire systems follow no particular order as to when and how much time a husband spends time with each wife. In the few cases we encountered, it is solely up to the husband to decide where he will spend an evening, day, or longer period of time. In some instances, he might inform a wife about when he plans to be with her; in other cases, he simply arrives at a wife's home unannounced and may stay for an indefinite time. Unlike a rigid rotation scheme, the laissez-faire system usually places full authority in the husband's hands, at least theoretically. He goes where he deems it appropriate or convenient, with or without advance notice, and for as long as he decides.

Family 8

Ira, a senior elder in the church, does not have any particular routine as to when and where he eats meals, sleeps, or spends time with his eight wives and their children. He often decides on the spur of the moment, depending on where he is and what he is doing at the time, and often appears in a home without advance notice. He believes that such a system is necessary because he is heavily burdened by church responsibilities, travels a lot, works late as circumstances demand, and simply cannot adopt a regular rotation schedule. In fact, he said, if he did so, his time with individual wives might be hurried, mechanical, and of poor quality, particularly since some wives live in different parts of the region. From his point of view, he and his wives of many years have adapted to the situation.

Family 4

Harry and his five wives do not follow a regular rotation pattern. He does not inform wives in advance about where he will be, often appears unpredictably in one or another home, and makes the decision himself. Viewing himself as the family patriarch, Harry explicitly rejects a fixed rotation schedule, stating that he spends time with different wives and children according to his desires and feelings, and his assessment of which wife and children require his time and attention. (Our observations and discussions with Harry indicate that in spite of his seemingly laissez-faire approach, he is careful to distribute his time among his five wives in a more or less equivalent or flexible fashion.)

Family 3

William, Carlyn, Danielle, and Alayna, all converts to the fundamentalist movement, have tried out several rotation systems over the years. At one time, William and Carlyn, the first wife, lived away from Danielle and Alayna, because they both worked in another community. On weekends they returned to the family home, and William shared his time with

Danielle and Alayna. On the way home he would call and tell the wife who answered the phone where he would sleep that night. Or he might ask the wife with whom he had decided to spend the night to drive half way and meet him, and they then drove back home together.

At another time, when William worked close to home and everyone lived together, they used a rather loose rotation arrangement. There was no particular schedule, and William's time with each wife was decided on the spur of the moment. Sometimes he came home in the evening with no particular plan about where he would sleep, and on occasion even broached the matter for open discussion.

Although neither of these approaches are "pure" laissez-faire systems, either because William consciously attempted to rotate among his wives on a regular basis or because they discussed the issue as a family, the unpredictability of decision making is somewhat characteristic of this rotational approach.

Some pioneer families also practiced laissez-faire systems of rotation, often because wives lived in distant locations (and, in some cases, because they might have been on the run from authorities):

"Brother Vernon had no set time for spending time with his wives. If he was needed, he was there. Whenever there was sickness, he stayed at that home. Sometimes he had to be on the farm and sometimes in town." . . .

"Father just stayed where night overtook him. We learned to expect him when he showed up." (Young, 1954, p. 178)

Charles was in the freighting business and his families were located in widely scattered communities. He had no regular time schedule for staying with them. Weeks might go by and then without any prior notice he would appear to spend anything from a day or two to some weeks with a particular family. (Young, 1954, p. 248)

Pure laissez-faire rotation systems, although rarely practiced, theoretically serve some aspects of dyadic and communal goals in plural families. On the communal side, vesting power in the family patriarch to decide on visitations to wives and assuming that he knows what is best for individuals and the family as a whole hypothetically preserves the well-being of the communal family. Doing so also theoretically minimizes conflict, negotiations, and competition between wives, since they have no role in deciding where the husband will be at any time. However, these potential communal advantages of a laissez-faire system may be outweighed by the realities of everyday life and the sensitivities and personalities of husbands and wives. A laissez-faire scheme does not foster relationships between wives since they have no say in a husband's rotation practices. Indeed, anxiety, jealousy, competition, mistrust, and uncertainties may arise and erode family cohesion and communality.

On the dyadic side, a husband who is perceptive and sensitive to his own and each of his wives' and children's needs and desires will be in the appropriate place at the right time. And if each relationship meets this ideal with a good "hit rate," then all dyadic relationships gain, as does the family as a whole. But families often fail to achieve this ideal in reality, owing to tensions and problems associated with loneliness, jealousy, insufficient time between husbands and wives, and other stresses in plural marriages. The fact that the few laissez-faire systems we encountered often incorporated some degree of predictability, regularity, and equality suggests that the theoretical advantages of this strategy may not work too well in practice.

Flexible rotation systems. Most families with whom we worked adopted some form of flexible rotation system. Although flexible approaches vary from family to family, they share some common features. First, as in laissez-faire systems, it is the husband who "officially" decides where he will spend his time. However, he and his wives operate under a cultural norm that calls on him to be fair to all his wives and children. Second, husbands and wives often discuss their rotation strategy and change it when they feel that an adjustment is warranted. Third, and most important, flexibility is built in to accommodate special family occasions, such as birthdays and anniversaries, or to address important family problems and emergencies. Fourth, flexible rotation systems vary from family to family and time to time within a family. As in other aspects of modern plural family life, Mormon fundamentalists experiment and try out different rotation approaches in their effort to achieve a viable family life.

Family 1

Hal pretty much decides himself, often on a day-to-day basis, which wife and children he will visit. In some cases, he lets a wife know in advance when he is coming; at other times, he decides on the spur of the moment. However, he tries to spend about the same amount of time with each wife and their children. Hal, Joan, Norma, Charlotte, and Cynthia agree that their system works quite well and is a far improvement over their formerly rigid approach. They like the flexibility, and it is a more natural way to deal with birthdays, special occasions, family parties, and family problems.

We observed their system in operation on several occasions when the wives lived in separate homes. When Joan and her children left Norma's home following one of our meetings, she and the children kissed Hal goodnight. When we asked Hal how Joan knew that he wasn't going home with her, he said that she probably realized that he would be staying with Norma that night because of where he had parked his car in the driveway, and the way he and Norma had acted toward one another.

On another occasion, when we were alone with Hal, we asked him where he was spending that night. He said that he hadn't decided but because he hadn't seen Norma for several days, that was a good possibility. Later, when he dropped us off at our car near Norma's home, he went in to see her. We assumed that he spent the night there. We don't know whether he had contacted her earlier or simply decided on the spur of the moment.

The family continues to use a flexible system even though pairs of wives now share two homes. Hal continues to rotate in a flexible way among individual wives. They all like the present arrangement very much because Hal has much more contact with all wives than before. He and the wives see and interact with one another and with the children more often, adjust their time together more easily, and find the new arrangement to be simpler and more responsive to their personal and marital needs and desires.

Family 5

Howard, Constance, Valerie, Barbara, and Rose are quite pleased with the rotation system they developed over the years. It is quite flexible, works in "a way that doesn't tie everyone down," and gives each of them considerable independence and freedom. And the wives all agree that their time spent with Howard is much more natural and personal than if they followed a fixed system. For the most part, Howard calls a wife to tell her that he will be visiting that evening. Sometimes he doesn't contact her in advance but just shows up. They agree that it generally isn't a problem if he fails to call ahead, because they more or less know when he is likely to be at their home. He is quite reliable in spending time fairly with each of them, and they assume that he comes or doesn't come at a particular time for good reasons.

Constance, Valerie, Barbara, and Rose are confident that if they ever need Howard for an emergency he will come without hesitation. Even if they simply need to talk to him, he is easily reached at another wife's home. And they support each other's right to talk with Howard wherever he is.

Although they express satisfaction with their rotation system, Howard's wives admit to some surprises and inconveniences. Sometimes Howard shows up quite unexpectedly, and they have to quickly rush to prepare an acceptable dinner. Or the opposite sometimes happens. A wife might expect Howard that evening, even though she hadn't heard from him, prepares a special dinner, and then he doesn't show up. Barbara said that there have been times she didn't expect him, made plans to be elsewhere, and then he arrived unannounced and she missed his visit. But all in all, the wives agree that these are not serious issues and that they are quite pleased with the way their system works.

Family 10

Barry and his eight wives follow a flexible rotation system in which he and each of them spend time together in an equitable but nonrigid way. They all expressed satisfaction with the way the system works, noting that they see him quite often because clusters of wives share the same dwellings. As a result, if anyone needs to see or talk to him about a personal or family matter, they simply do so if he is in the home or call him if he is elsewhere. The system is quite open, and everyone supports its flexibility.

Family 11

Benjamin, Katherine, Melba, Kelly, and Mary also use a flexible system, on the grounds that a strict rotation system would be difficult to maintain and would not meet each of their personal needs. In addition, Benjamin often invites a different wife to accompany him on weekly business trips, and he does so in an equitable fashion, adjusting to each of their work and personal commitments.

Flexible rotation systems were also common in 19th-century Mormon plural families. Because wives often lived in distant communities, however, rotation sometimes involved longer and more intermittent visits by husbands:

[In one case] when wives did not live in the same community, the husband would often visit one family only on the weekend, at harvest time, or at conference time. [In another case] he spent most of his time with her [his first wife] but visited his second wife . . . and their eight children . . . several times a year, almost always at general conference time in April and October. . . .

[Another informant] remembered that her father would come for conference twice a year and stay for a month. "Then he would go back to Canada because he had a large business there and he also had a large farm. . . . My memory of our father living with us is rather limited. He just wasn't around very much." . . .

[One informant said:] "Sometimes of a necessity he would be at one place and then the other. At least he would be staying nights at one place and then the other. I would imagine it was pretty well divided."

[Another informant stated:] "He wasn't stringent on it. But his wives didn't demand it that way either. They had an understanding; they knew that he was trying to make everything as nearly equal as he could. . . . It wasn't a hard and fast rule like some people like to make you think as long as it was fair." (Embry, 1987, p. 82)

Flexible rotation systems have the greatest potential for a viable interplay of dyadic and communal processes in modern plural families. Although they often place primary responsibility in a husband's hands, flexible systems enable wives to participate in changing particular visits because of personal or family needs. Thus a flexible system is "owned" by everyone and can function as an agreed-upon communal process. If the husband has primary responsibility, the onus is on him to make sure that the whole family is considered in visitation patterns and that the best interests of the whole family are served at any given time. If he is equitable and responsive and if the wives acknowledge another's unique circumstances, then a flexible system can enhance family unity as family members watch out for, care about, and are sensitive to each of the other situations. Naturally, whether communality is achieved depends on how fair and equitable a system is in practice.

A flexible system also has the best potential for strengthening dyadic bonds between a husband and each wife in a plural family. With flexibility, they can celebrate a wife's birthday or a husband's and wife's anniversary outside a regular rotation sequence and thereby make each dyadic relationship salient and special. Similarly, breaking a rotation to address a wife's personal problem, a husband–wife problem, or a family matter testifies to the importance of each dyadic relationship in a plural family.

In addition, flexible systems can enhance general family viability in light of innumerable practical issues faced by contemporary plural families. Husbands are busy with work and religious responsibilities; wives often work and have enormous responsibilities managing a household and caring for children – often many children. And when wives live in separate dwellings in different parts of the community, husbands have a commuting problem. In general, a flexible rotation system is the one most likely to adapt to a plural family's everyday life rhythms.

Variations and changes in rotation systems

The preceding examples testify to the diversity of rotation strategies *between* contemporary plural families. But there is also considerable variation *within* families, whether because of the desires of a husband or wives, family size, and ages of children, or illness, work schedules, and living arrangements. The result is an ongoing process of experimentation and shifting of the way in which a husband rotates among his wives and families.

Family 1

They followed a rigid and inflexible rotation system in their earlier years of marriage, with Hal spending alternating days with Joan and Norma, regardless of circumstances. They didn't like the arrangement, but didn't know what to do about it until Charlotte married into the family. She was older, had been a wife in another plural family, and helped them work out a flexible system that all are now happy with. The logic of the system is that Hal spends time with wives according to his and each of their individual needs, as well as family needs. Hal and each of them informally communicate their situation, although Hal makes the decision about where and with whom he will spend specific times. They all feel much less tension and stress about his visits, and a flexible situation suits them quite well.

Family 3

William, Carlyn, Danielle, and Alayna, all converts to fundamentalism, are continually experimenting with ways of living as a plural family – partly because of economic and living circumstances and partly because they admit not knowing how to live this lifestyle. They have tried out a variety of rotation systems and are still working at the problem.

At an early time in their marriage, when they lived in a trailer and tent, William rotated on a rigid schedule, spending one night with first Danielle and then Alayna in the trailer and one night with Carlyn in the tent. Later, when they all lived in one home and William worked nearby, they followed a somewhat haphazard laissez-faire pattern. William would come home from work and decide on the spur of the moment who he would spend time with and where he would sleep that night. Everyone agreed that this arrangement didn't work and generated considerable tension.

Then, as mentioned earlier, when William and Carlyn worked at a site far from home and only returned on weekends, he took turns staying with Danielle and Alayna. Sometimes he called in advance, telling the wife who answered the phone where he would sleep that night and asking that wife to inform the other wife about the sleeping plan. Needless to say, this created some awkwardness between wives. Sometimes he would call and ask the wife with whom he would spend time that night to drive and meet him and Carlyn halfway home. He and either Danielle or Alayna would then drive home together, leaving the other car, or Carlyn would drive the rest of the way home alone. Still later, when

William lived at home and worked nearby, they followed a flexible rotation schedule, with him spending roughly equal and generally predictable time with each wife during the course of a week.

Thus, the family has tried out a variety of systems, and its members are still not sure what works best for them. They expect to continue experimenting.

Managing rotation systems

Managing rotation schedules in modern plural families is a complex business. In keeping with religious doctrine regarding patriarchal family structure, it is the husband who theoretically decides when and how much time to spend with each wife and her children.[4] His decision is ideally based on family needs related to problem solving, interaction, and family events; religious needs; and his and each wife's personal needs and desires. In addition, a husband is also expected to maintain a "fair" rotation schedule among his wives and children. Our informants repeatedly stated that these principles are the essential components of a healthy rotation system and plural family.

Family 4
In deciding which of his five wives to spend time with, Harry considers which wife and family needs him – and where *he* wants to be. At the same time, he does his best to visit all wives regularly.

Family 5
Constance, Valerie, Barbara, and Rose agree that it is up to Howard to determine where he should be at any time. As noted earlier, Howard might inform a wife in advance of his visit, or he might appear unannounced. Everyone feels that Howard balances his time with them fairly and is available whenever they need him.

Family 10
Barry and his eight wives follow a flexible rotation system in which he decides who to visit. The wives agree that they have no right to control Barry's time, and it is their responsibility to be available when he decides to be with their family. He agrees: "This is my time, and it is up to me to decide where I need to be." But the wives all say that he is very sensitive to each of their individual and family needs and that they can always contact or see him if necessary, regardless of where he is.

Leaving the decision about rotation choices up to the husband serves both dyadic and communal aspects of plural family life. On the one hand, accepting his decision-making role acknowledges the communal legitimacy of his religious and social position as family patriarch. It reflects a common value shared by all family members, ideally binding them together around a set of core values and beliefs. At the same time, the husband is expected to care for the communal well-being of the family – to act fairly, weigh all family members' needs, and serve all wives and their children. If he acts judiciously, a husband engenders trust that everyone in the plural family will be treated fairly and that communal unity will be preserved. Furthermore, placing the decision in the husband's hands may simply be a more adaptive mechanism especially for flexible rotation systems. Consider how complex it would be if members of a plural family had to decide collectively each day where the husband would spend his time. It simply wouldn't be efficient to do so and might also upset an already fragile set of family relationships. In some respects, therefore, putting the everyday rotation decision in the hands of the husband may reduce the possibility of family upheaval.

The husband's central role in rotation may also serve dyadic aspects of plural family life, especially in flexible systems, by enabling him to address the individual and dyadic needs of each wife and her children. If he does the job well and is continually sensitive to and understanding of the circumstances of his dyadic relationship with each wife and family, then the system may work. In the ideal arrangement, he spends time with a wife and her children because he wants to be with them, because they need him, and because their unique and distinctive relationship calls for attention – not simply because it is their "turn." But this is all hypothetical and depends greatly on the personalities and circumstances of a plural family.

We learned of a few instances in which husbands consciously attempted to satisfy simultaneously dyadic and communal aspects of plural family life during everyday rotation processes. They did this not only by having special time with each wife but also by attending to all wives in some fashion.

Family 9

As noted earlier, John, Joyce, Clara, and Marjorie follow a more or less rigid rotation schedule – from noon to noon of each day. In spite of this rigid dyadic rotation, John also engages in communal actions every day. No matter which wife he is with on a given day, he says that he kisses all wives goodnight and greets each of them warmly every morning. And he always reads stories and puts Clara's two young children to bed at night, regardless of which wife he is with that day. These symbolic acts reflect an ongoing attempt to maintain both dyadic and communal relations in the family.

Family 18

Charles, Susan, Nancy, Angela, and Linda follow a daily rotation schedule. In addition to emphasizing special dyadic time between Charles and each wife, they engage in some communal practices. For example, Susan, Angela, and Linda share a dwelling, and Charles and the three of them usually eat dinner together, unless the wife with whom he is spending the day desires to eat alone with him – something they all respect and accept.

In addition, Charles tries to see each wife and family every day even though he is spending time with a particular wife. Thus every morning he greets each wife and even visits his other home down the street where Nancy lives, to wish her a good morning and to see if all is well with her. And every night he talks with each wife to see if they are all right and to wish them good night.[5]

Similar practices have been reported among 19th-century Mormon plural families:

> George Reynolds, one of the leading officials of the church, located his first two families in adjacent houses. Although he spent alternate weeks with each wife, he made it a daily practice to call on the other wife to "kiss her good morning as he was on his way to the office" and again, on his way home, in the evening, he would "stop in to kiss her good night."
>
> "Father spent one week with each wife. When he got up in the morning, he made the fire, called the family and fed the cattle. Then he would go over to the other house, make their fires, call the family, and feed the livestock there. After that he would go back to the place where he was staying and have his breakfast." (Young, 1954, p. 179)

In describing her father's practice, one child stated: "It also seemed perfectly natural that he should leave our house a little before bedtime to go over to say good night to 'Auntie' when it was our week, or for his coming just before bedtime to kiss us good night when it was his week over there" (Embry, 1987, p. 81).

Taken together, these simple communal acts embedded in daily dyadic relations acknowledge the importance of both processes by husbands and wives in some pioneer and contemporary Mormon plural families.

Although husbands usually manage rotation schedules, wives often influence what happens. As noted earlier, a decision to change a rotation system can result from deliberations of a husband and wives or may be guided by a particular wife. In some cases, wives agree among themselves to shift visits with a husband because of special family events, celebrations, or problems. Furthermore, wives sometimes act on behalf of other wives, ensuring that the husband pays special attention to another wife for some reason. And they may accept intrusions on their time by another wife because of some special need. In some cases wives negotiate changes in rotation with one another and then ask (inform?) the husband to do so.

Family 2
This family follows a flexible rotation system in which David decides where to spend his time. However, any of the four wives can discuss a shift in rotation to meet some special need. If he agrees, David informs the wife with whom he is supposed to spend the evening of a change in the rotation. Thus rotation changes are discussed in a dyadic mode with him, not communally between wives. The family also shifts schedules as a matter of course for wives' birthdays and anniversaries. Everyone actively supports this way of operating.

Family 18
Although Charles follows a relatively rigid schedule in spending time with Susan, Nancy, Angela, and Linda, they adjust the rotation for special occasions, such as birthdays and anniversaries. Whenever special circumstances arise, such as a family problem, the wives also often make arrangements among themselves – communally – to change his visiting time. Charles said, "I am willing to do whatever they want me to do," and we had the impression that he generally follows their requests. They also told of occasions on which wives encouraged Charles to spend time with another wife because that wife needed him.

In her autobiography of life in a contemporary Mormon plural family, Dorothy Solomon (1984) stated that her father's wives played a powerful role in the rotation process, even though he was the leader of a large fundamentalist group. On one occasion, a wife sent him away from her home even though he was scheduled to be with her. Unbeknownst to him, she and another wife had arranged for him to spend the night with her a few days later, on their wedding anniversary. Solomon said that upon being sent away, her father, the religious leader and patriarch, "sheepishly" left without comment to spend the night with another wife and her children.

Wives' involvement in the everyday operation of rotation schedules also contributes to dyadic and communal aspects of plural family life – especially in flexible rotation systems. On the dyadic side, a wife may influence the rotation process to meet her own personal needs or to have her husband deal with their special marital or family relationship. She may command the husband's attention and shift his time to her out of sequence, may communicate with him when he is with another wife if circumstances warrant, and has the right to do so on the basis of her own judgment. This freedom and influence attest to her unique dyadic relationship with the husband.

The fact that wives in many families accept or actively support changing a rotation schedule to meet individual circumstances also reflects their communal support of the special relationship each of them has with the husband. Their support of each other is, in effect, a communal agreement about a key aspect of plural family life. To the extent that there is consensus among wives, a rotation system will simultaneously preserve the dyadic uniqueness of each husband–wife bond and of the communal family system. Thus wives in modern plural families often have important and influential roles in regulating rotation systems.

Stresses and strains in rotation

The rotation of husbands among wives and families may also lead to friction and family upheaval. Such problems can be quite serious when wives begin to feel that their husband does not spend enough time with them in comparison with other wives (see also chapters 16 and 17). In most cases a wife's feelings about rotation are usually only one aspect of interpersonal problems between a husband and a wife or between wives. However, the visitation pattern of a husband is a visible indicator of interpersonal problems. Tensions and stresses associated with rotation thus need to be understood in the context of general husband–wife and wife–wife relations.

Feelings of not being treated fairly by the husband, jealousy about the amount of time a husband spends with other wives, and the quality of their interaction when he does visit are topics often raised by wives, especially in marriages that are not functioning well or that ended in separation or divorce.

Family 15
Henrietta, the first wife, eventually divorced Samuel for a number of reasons, including the fact that she didn't really like Jean, the second wife. At one point in the marriage, Samuel spent more time with Jean, which seriously upset Henrietta. Eventually, these and other problems convinced Henrietta that the marriage wouldn't work.

Family 16
Ralph, a leader in the church, is very busy. As a result, he relies on the wives to help him decide where and when he should spend his time. Beverly, the third wife, claims that one of the wives unfairly manipulates their rotation systems so as to have more time with Ralph. Although the

family is stable, there is considerable tension and anger toward the wife, who allegedly violates the principle of respect for other wives and their relationships with Ralph.

Family 12

Fred, Elaine, and Lauren had a stormy marriage, according to Lauren, and she eventually left. It was a dysfunctional family in many respects. For example, Fred spent much more time with Elaine. In addition, Fred and Elaine went on vacations together, but he rarely took Lauren on trips. Although their problems were not strictly related to rotation, Lauren also said that Fred didn't spend time with her children and would visit Elaine's parents but wouldn't do the same for her.

Family 14

Sally, the first wife, eventually divorced Harvey several years after Molly joined them as a plural wife. At first, everyone got along well, and Harvey split his time equally between them. But later they used a system in which the wives would ask him to be with them, and Sally felt that he didn't accede to her requests as often as he did with Molly. There were many other problems in the marriage, and the rotation issue was only one symptom of widespread family conflicts.

Tensions between wives and between husbands and wives about rotation also appear in accounts of 19th-century Mormon plural family life. For example, Ann Eliza Young (1908) describes an argument between two wives over the time their husband spent with each of them. And Emmeline Wells, a pioneer plural wife, said that her second husband married her only because she was a widow and spent little time with her, showed little affection, and was more interested in his other wives (Eaton-Gadsby and Dushku, 1978). She felt great sadness at his inattentiveness:

> This evening I fully expected my husband here but was again disappointed. If he only knew how much good it would do me and what pleasure and happiness it brings to my subsequent days, he would not be so chary of his attentions. I suppose it is rather an exertion for him to come, he is not in want of me for a companion or in any sense, he doesn't need me at all, there are plenty ready and willing to administer to every wish, caprice or whim of his, indeed they anticipate him, they are near him always, while I am shut out of his life, and out of sight or mind, it is impossible for me to make myself useful to him in any way while I am held at such a distance. (Eaton-Gadsby and Dushku, 1978, p. 468)

In general, therefore, tensions and stresses about rotation sometimes derive from family members feeling that a system is not responsive to their dyadic and communal needs. In other cases, rotation patterns are a symptom of deeper problems in a family – poor relationships between a husband and a wife, conflict between wives, and family upheaval.

Summary

Polygynous husbands usually follow some type of rotational system in visiting their wives and children. These types fall into three general categories: *rigid* rotation systems (a fixed and regular routine), *laissez-faire* systems (irregular visitation), and *flexible* systems (which more or less adhere to a schedule, but with variations depending on circumstances). Most contemporary Mormon polygynous families favor a flexible system, which allows for a husband to be with a particular wife and family on special occasions, such as birthdays and anniversaries, or to deal with problems that need immediate attention.

Two principles govern rotation processes in modern fundamentalist families. First, the husband, as religious and social patriarch, theoretically makes the decision about which family he spends time with. Second, the principle of fairness and equality in the time spent with each wife and children guides a husband's decision about rotation. But wives often play an important role in rotation. Thus a husband and wives often decide collectively about what type of rotation cycle best suits their family. And wives frequently negotiate with the husband or other wives when they want to change the pattern to meet a special family circumstance.

An effective rotation system can contribute to the dyadic and communal viability of a plural family. Flexible systems have the greatest potential in this regard – if they are handled well by a family. Dyadic issues are most easily addressed by flexible systems, since the particular needs of a husband and his wife and her children can be met as they arise. A cooperative rotation system, a willingness to be flexible so as to meet everyone's needs, and a husband who treats all wives fairly all contribute to the communality of a plural family. Rigid and laissez-faire systems do not seem to be as effective as flexible systems in satisfying dyadic and communal aspects of modern plural family life.

Modern plural families use quite diverse rotation systems that differ between and within families, depending on each of their circumstances. But they also change systems as new wives join families, children are born, living arrangements shift, and other factors intervene. Because plural family life is a wholly new experience for many participants, experimentation and trial and error with rotation systems is customary in many families – as it is in many other aspects of their lives.

The rotation process is central to plural family life, since it relates directly to the interaction of each husband and wife in a family. It is crucial, therefore, for plural families to work out rotation systems that optimize an appropriate interplay of dyadic and communal qualities in their lives.

14

Budget and resource management

All cultures – whether monogamous or polygamous, technological or agricultural, poor or wealthy or engaged in farming, animal husbandry, manufacturing, or information processing – generate, allocate, and distribute resources in the form of goods, products, and some type of currency. Ethnographies of world cultures illustrate that family life and family structure are inseparably linked to resource issues. The fundamental economic unit in many traditional societies is the family, with husbands, wives, and children generating resources. In polygynous cultures, plural wives and numbers of children serve as a crucial labor pool for the economic well-being of the family.

Budget and resource management is of utmost concern to contemporary Mormon plural families, for the challenges they face are numerous. Many fundamentalist families are in lower or middle-class socioeconomic groups (see appendix B). Although some participants in our sample are college educated and have their own businesses or are in professional fields, many have a high school education and work in skilled, semiskilled, or unskilled occupations such as carpentry, construction, truck driving, farming, office work, housecleaning, and sales. Thus few modern plural families are prosperous or wealthy. Many families struggle to stay afloat economically because they do not always have steady work or the financial resources to fall back on in difficult times. Moreover, plural families often have multiple households and numerous children. To make ends meet, many wives in present-day plural families work on a regular or intermittent basis (as do wives in monogamous families). Older children also contribute to a family's income. The typical plural family struggles economically, often living week to week or month to month on a modest income.

The question of interest here is: How do plural families cope with budgetary issues so as to address dyadic and communal aspects of their lives? More specifically, how is family income generated – by the husband alone, by the husband and wives, primarily by wives? And how are resources distributed – dyadically, by each husband–wife pair, or communally, with earnings put in a common pool and consensually allocated by the husband

and wives? And what control do husbands and wives have over family resources? As in other aspects of life, contemporary polygynous families manage their resources in a variety of ways, from almost purely dyadic systems, in which each husband–wife pair functions independently of other pairs in a family; to highly communal systems, in which everyone participates together in budgetary matters; to mixed dyadic and communal systems. Furthermore, modern plural families frequently change and experiment with budget and resource systems.

Resource management in other polygynous cultures

Economic resources are a central concern of many polygynous cultures. Courtship and wedding ceremonies often involve gifts or exchanges of land, animals, or goods between families, and married life is often organized around the management of crucial economic resources. Relationships between a husband and wives, and sometimes relationships between wives, often center on how they produce and distribute economic resources. In many polygynous cultures, wives are usually key players and major sources of labor in family economies. They may maintain animals, care for gardens, harvest and process animal and agricultural crops, and market and sell products.

Who controls these resources varies from culture to culture. At one extreme, husbands and wives are almost totally independent of one another, managing their resources separately. At the other extreme, a husband and each wife may be completely interdependent economically. Similar patterns obtain for plural wives. Although wives in many traditional polygynous societies appear to operate more or less independently of one another, some function as an integrated economic unit.

The economic systems used by families can be divided along dyadic or primarily communal lines. In dyadic systems, each husband–wife pair functions more or less as an independent economic unit. In some cases, wives have little to do with one another. In other instances, there may be some indirect communal relationship; for example, resources may be pooled and then distributed by the husband. Other cultures rely on communal systems, allowing family resources and incomes to be pooled and distributed through shared decision-making procedures.

Primarily dyadic systems

There are many versions of dyadic economic systems in polygynous cultures. In some cases, husbands and wives have a mixture of shared and independent economic responsibilities and authority, but wives have little to do with one another. In Hagen, New Guinea, each wife has her own garden and pigs. A husband builds and fences each wife's garden; she cultivates, cares for, and harvests crops in the garden, and they share in the outcome. (A man may also have his own garden, which he controls completely.) In addition, a husband and wife often have joint responsibilities for raising pigs (Strathern, 1972). Thus each husband–wife pair in a plural family operates independently of other couples, and it follows intricate rules regarding joint and separate links between a husband and each wife.

In another dyadic arrangement, each wife among the Shampla of Africa grows crops on land given to her by the husband (Winans, 1964). She decides what to grow and keeps some profits; husbands only have claim to certain crops. Husbands are expected to clear the land and assist each wife in heavy labor. At the same time, plural wives have little economic involvement with one another. This is also the case among the Tanla of Madagascar (Stephens, 1963). A husband's land is apportioned equally to his wives, each of whom is responsible for raising crops and supporting her children. When she has surplus crops or sales, the husband shares in the profits. A wife receives half of the game and fish he catches (or the money he receives from sales of his catch) on the day he spends with her. She has few economic ties to other wives. Husbands among the Winneba of Africa also catch fish, but here each wife is responsible for smoking, drying, and selling part of the catch (Hagan, 1983). Wives then share proportionately in the profits from sales. When the fishing season ends, each wife is expected to support herself in agricultural work (husbands often leave to fish in another region – sometimes with another woman or wife).

Some dyadic resource models have communal features. In many cases, a husband controls family resources, treats them as a communal pool, and distributes money and goods to each wife in a dyadic pattern. There is rarely any direct contact between wives in regard to resources; everything works through the husband, and he deals with each wife separately. The Bedouin of Israel let husbands control agricultural lands and animals, work the land, herd the animals, work in wage labor jobs, and buy and sell goods (Marx, 1987). Husbands distribute resources to each wife in a one-to-one dyadic arrangement.[1] Similarly, the Bete of Africa give husbands complete control over each wife's agricultural output, and let them regulate all family expenditures, presumably doling out resources to each wife (Clignet, 1970). Among the Gusii of Africa, the husband and each wife have their own agricultural fields and livestock (LeVine, 1964). However, the husband controls surplus profits from the wives' production. He sometimes uses extra resources and earnings from his own wage labor to give some wives luxury items, such as sugar, tea, and clothing. (He must do this cautiously in order to avoid showing favoritism and thus causing family dissension.) Although wives function independently of one another, the husband introduces some communal element into the system by pooling and redistributing some family assets.

There are a few other versions of dyadic systems with communal features. For example, wives may occasionally assist one another in gardening, animal care, and food or game production but still function separately most of the time.

Primarily communal systems

In relatively "pure" communal resource system, the family pools its resources and shares day-to-day responsibilities on an ongoing, often daily basis, with little consideration of each wife's unique needs. Such configurations often occur when wives live in a single residence, and they and the husband share a variety of economic responsibilities. In Dakar, Africa, wives live communally, take turns cooking, managing the home, and selling produce at a market or door to door (Falade, 1963). All resources appear to be used communally. A similar system can be found in Java. In one polygynous family there, a butcher and his three wives lived cooperatively, with one wife selling meat, one wife controlling its distribution, and one wife managing the home (Geertz, 1961).

Our impression is that family resource and economic systems in non-Western polygynous cultures are often primarily dyadic, with wives having separate economic responsibilities and authority. A husband is linked economically to each wife in any of several dyadic arrangements, with wives in different cultures having varying degrees of independence from their husband. Typically, however, wives have few economic links with one another, although wives do share responsibilities or resources in some communal cultures.

On the whole, budget and resource systems vary with cultural practices, economics, and social structure. The contemporary polygynous families with whom we worked tended to have budget and resource systems that involved both dyadic and communal features.

Economic systems in contemporary Mormon plural families

Primarily dyadic budget and resource systems

Mormon plural families practice several versions of the dyadic budget system. In "pure" dyadic cases, a husband and each wife negotiate resources separately, and no other wives participate. In other cases, family members pool resources communally, but the husband and each wife negotiate budgetary allocations separately from other couples. For the most part, budget systems in our families usually involve an interplay of dyadic and communal processes. In addition, husbands typically play a strong leadership role, often dealing with each wife separately and distributing and reallocating resources among wives as necessary. Although wives are not without influence in resource management, their role varies from family to family.

Purely dyadic budgetary systems have a strong monogamous quality, with essentially no ties between wives in a plural family.

Family 4

Harry is in his late 60s, no longer works regularly, and is assisted financially by his sons. Several of his five wives work and support themselves. If they need additional money, they ask him. He also checks with each wife every few weeks to make sure they are managing all right. Shirley, the fifth wife, has several young children and doesn't work; Harry fully supports her and the children. In essence, each wife is independent of the other wives, and all financial dealings occur between Harry and each wife. This is therefore a fairly "pure" dyadic budget system.

Family 1

Hal pays basic living expenses (including food, housing, car and utility bills) for Joan, Norma, Charlotte, and Cynthia from his income. Since the funds each wife receives are based on separate and private discussions with Hal, the system is highly dyadic. Wives are also free to work and keep all the money they earn for themselves and their children. Hal describes this system as a "surplus-order" philosophy rather than a "budget-order" philosophy, and it is an incentive to wives who wish to improve their situation. This system is therefore purely dyadic since there is no pooling of money or communal involvement of wives with one another.

Family 5

Howard, Constance, Valerie, Barbara, and Rose have used different budget systems over the years. A recent system is highly dyadic. Howard meets weekly with each wife, discusses her earnings and needs, and supplements her funds, if necessary, with money from his salary. Our impression is that there is little shifting of money from wife to wife and that the system is highly dyadic on the whole.

Some primarily dyadic systems also have communal features.

Family 8

Ira's eight wives do their best to be self-sufficient economically, and he helps out as needed. Gloria and Augusta are nurses. Ethel and the other wives work in a variety of jobs – some full-time, others part-time, some regularly and some intermittently. However, they have a communal element in their financial system. Ira discusses each wife's needs with them separately. Any surplus money from their earnings is given to him. He then redistributes funds to wives who earn less than they need or who aren't working at the time.

There are other instances of communal actions in this largely dyadic budgetary system. For example, Augusta, the third wife, has received a supplement to her salary from Ira for several years. When her son died in military service, she received insurance money from the government, which she gave it to Ira to help pay off mortgages on some of the family's homes. Similarly, when Betty came to the family after a divorce, she used some of her alimony and child support funds to help pay for some property.

Thus, Ira deals with each wife separately, and each wife tries to support herself, sometimes with his assistance, in what amounts to a highly dyadic system. At the same time, they incorporate communal elements, with surplus earnings and funds from other sources turned over to Ira to help other wives or to solve some of the whole family's financial needs.

Family 18

Charles coordinates the finances of the family to ensure that everyone's needs are met. The wives all work and give their earnings to Charles. After this communal pooling of funds, he meets separately with each wife, and allocates money to each of them on the basis of their dyadic negotiation.

Family 10

Barry and his eight wives follow a somewhat different dyadic system with communal features. Wives who work keep the money they earn according to an allocation system they privately negotiate with Barry (it is based on the size of their family, special needs, and other considerations). Any money they earn above and beyond their allocation is turned over to him. He distributes funds from his and his wives' surplus earnings to wives who did not earn enough to meet their needs. All negotiations and allocations are done by Barry and each wife separately, in a dyadic format, but with communality reflected in the pooling of surplus funds.

Primarily communal budget and resource systems

In communal systems, resource management shifts from husband–wife dyadic negotiations to collective family processes. Under a "pure" communal arrangement, wives and the husband pool all of their earnings, discuss family needs as a group, and then allocate the money to budget categories, such as shopping for food. Except for taking into account the personal needs of individual wives, a family deals with expenditures by budget category and do not allocate funds separately to wives.

Pure communal systems are rare and there often are dyadic components in many communal budget strategies. Thus money may be pooled and allocations collectively assigned, but wives then have control over their own funds. Or the special needs of a wife and her children may be taken into account (e.g., the number of children, medical costs, and clothing). Such practices reflect sensitivity to dyadic needs within the communal family.

Family 7
On the basis of family discussion, Norman draws money for food and other shopping trips from everyone's pooled income and gives it to Sarah, Patricia, and Audrey as a group. No wife has her "own" money; everything is in a common pool. They do not have sufficient reserves or steady income to develop a stable or predictable budget and seem to go from week to week, doing the best they can to keep afloat by operating in a completely communal fashion.

Family 5
Howard, Constance, Valerie, Barbara, and Rose have used different budgetary systems over the years. At one time, they met as a family once a week – pooling their earnings, and listing their bills and anticipated expenditures for the following week. Each wife was allocated a food and living budget that was based on the size of her family, as well as any special expenses. Utilities and rent were paid out of the central pool. Although all wives participated in the discussion, Howard made the final decisions.

This system is almost purely communal; it has a slight dyadic component in that each wife controls her allocation on a day-to-day basis. In all other respects, it is strongly communal.

Family 11
Benjamin, Katherine, Melba, Kelly, and Mary live in the same dwelling. The wives who work give Benjamin their salaries. Following family discussions, money is allocated to the wives as a group for food and other day-to-day purchases. Wives draw on the pool of money depending on

who is responsible for shopping, meal preparation, cleaning and other such activities. At the same time, wives who have special needs for themselves or their children, say, clothing, negotiate with Benjamin separately and thereby incorporate a dyadic component into a fundamentally communal budget system.

Family 9

John, Joyce, Clara, and Marjorie live in a single dwelling. Once a week the wives who work give John their earnings. At a family meeting the wives present their anticipated expenses for the coming week, and John allocates money to each of them. Although he makes the allocation to each wife, which adds a dyadic dimension to the process, the fact that they pool their money and collectively discuss their needs introduces strong communal features into their resource management system. They claim that publicly discussing and allocating money to each wife reduces the chances of conflict.

One family had a variant of a communal system in which subsets of wives assumed financial responsibility for one another as a supplement to the support provided by the husband.

Family 2

In his present job, David buys, remodels, and sells homes. Judith and Rebecca, the first and second wives, work in offices; Rebecca also runs a seasonal business of her own. Emily and Phyllis care for their own young children and those of other wives, while Phyllis sometimes earns money by caring for other people's children.

They have a complicated budget-sharing system: David pays the rents and mortgages for all wives, as well as utilities and related expenses. If he is unable to do so, he asks wives to help out. Judith pays for her own groceries and her children's clothing; Rebecca pays for her own groceries *and* for Phyllis's groceries; Phyllis buys clothing for her children from her baby-sitting activities; Emily pays for her own groceries by baby-sitting.

This complicated communal system with dyadic features is based on David's theory that all their money belongs to everyone. As a result, he doesn't want to control their resources completely and believes that all of them should help out one another as necessary. David and subsets of wives assist one another in different ways, although each wife tends to function more or less independently. The system and resource allocations are also communally known and agreed upon.

In an autobiography of her life in a contemporary plural family, Lorraine Bronson (n.d.) stated that each wife's earnings were given to her husband. He paid the bills and even purchased most food supplies on the basis of lists provided by the wives. If a wife needed money for personal use, however, she asked him. Although a communal system of sorts, this family's approach to resource management had some dyadic aspects.

In general, present-day Mormon plural families use a variety of systems for managing their finances. Some families use purely dyadic systems in which a husband and each wife function independently of other husband–wife couples in the family. And some use purely communal systems in which resources are pooled and money are assigned and spent collectively. But these are the exception. Most plural families adopt some combined dyadic and communal budget systems in which they simultaneously acknowledge their collective and separate lives. Furthermore, as is true of so many other aspects of their lives, present-day Mormon polygynous families develop systems that are unique to their own situation and that they change from time to time.

Budgeting and resource management by Mormon pioneers

Nineteenth-century Mormon plural families appear to have favored dyadic systems (Embry, 1987; Young, 1954). Perhaps this was because families functioned in a farming and ranching economy, often lived apart from one another, husbands were away on church business for long periods of time, and prosecutions led to secrecy and flights. As a result, wives and families were frequently independent of one another.

Extreme dyadic arrangements, in which wives received little or no financial support from their husbands, appear to have been rare. They turned up in only 12% of the cases in an oral history project of children of pioneer families (Embry, 1987). Similar figures were obtained in a sample of monogamous families of the same era. Interestingly, *no* pioneer monogamous or polygynous wives received *total* financial support from their husbands. Rather, in 19th-century families of both types husbands and wives usually contributed to family finances.

Some pioneer plural wives were financially independent, however: one woman owned and operated several farms with her sons, owned other properties, and engaged in various businesses; a wife in another family ran a chicken farm with her children and received very little support from her husband, who lived in a different region (Embry, 1987). In another case, in which the husband was on an overseas church mission, a wife operated a chicken farm and butter and egg business (and even sent her husband some money and helped support him!). Juanita Brooks (1934) reports that her grandfather gave her grandmother a farm and animals and thereafter provided little support (and rarely visited her since he favored his first wife and had married this second wife because she had been widowed). In situations of financial distress, some 19th-century plural wives supported themselves by working in traditional men's jobs on farms, for example, doing manual labor in the fields.

In one unique system, a husband gave full financial and managerial authority in different businesses to each of his wives:

> During his first decade there he married two other women [in addition to his first wife]. Almost from the outset he was a successful farmer, trader, and freighter. At first he had a common storehouse and doled out supplies to his families as they needed them. When he had accumulated considerable property, he hit on the novel plan of giving each wife certain capital – land, houses, or money – and then have them set up their own enterprises. His first wife was established in a hotel venture. . . . The second wife . . . was given a large farm. . . . The third wife he left in town in her own house and she depended on the earnings of her sons for her support. (Young, 1954, p. 168)

Many wives in pioneer plural families were self-sufficient and resourceful; ran businesses; were teachers, physicians, and writers; and were quite "liberated" in a contemporary sense. They had to be strong and independent for several reasons: wives in plural families were often geographically dispersed, they lived in a frontier subsistence economy, the men were occupied with church responsibilities and travel, and the fear of prosecution kept many husbands on the run (Foster, 1982).

In most pioneer families, both husbands and wives contributed to a family's resources (Embry, 1987). Only a small proportion of wives worked outside of the home; many women earned money from farming and animal husbandry, washing clothes, and taking in boarders.

Available evidence also suggests that resources were often managed in a dyadic fashion – between a husband and each wife. Once resources were allocated, wives typically managed the funds themselves. In one sample of 49 pioneer plural families, 65% of the husbands distributed resources to each wife, often using family size as the basis of his allocation (Embry, 1987). Once they received their share of resources, many wives apparently managed independently of one another, even when they shared a dwelling:

> There was one cellar for the three families [who lived in the same dwelling] but the food was stored separately. Each wife had her own barrels and bins for supplies. While there was occasional borrowing of such things as bread, these items were always paid back. Each wife had her own cows and made her own butter and cheese; likewise each had her own flock of chickens. There was a large orchard with apple, peach, and plum trees, and gooseberry bushes. When the orchard began to bear, the father counted off the trees

according to the number of children in the respective families. He was particular in dividing up the fruit and food and he thought this a method by which all would be fairly treated. (Young, 1954, p. 157)

There were several other types of primarily dyadic resource systems in 19th-century Mormon plural families. "A successful jeweler . . . gave each of his wives a definite allowance: $50 per month. In addition such staples as flour, sugar and coal were bought in bulk and given out as required" (Young, 1954, p. 170). In another family, "each spouse had an allowance and could buy what she wanted. The wives took care of the purchases [communally?] because 'Father was a very busy man, and he didn't have any time to attend to any of the buying. Of course he always had such staples as flour and potatoes sent out as they were needed' " (Embry, 1987, p. 127).[2]

One variant of a dyadic system with a different communal quality involved a husband "delegating" a wife, usually the first wife, to distribute resources to other wives. This arrangement was reported in about 20% of the cases in one sample of pioneer families: one informant remembered how her mother "split the raspberries, eggs, and milk based on the number of children. She placed the second family's share on the pantry window of her home, and [the other family's] children came to pick them up" (Embry, 1987, p. 124).

Another dyadic system with communal features involved a common family "storehouse" from which wives could individually draw supplies. Brigham Young organized such a family store in one of two adjacent homes to service wives and children who lived together. Wives could draw supplies as needed, "charging" them to their "account" (Spencer, 1961). Each wife also had an account at a local dry goods store where she could obtain other supplies. This system is dyadic in that wives operated separately from one another; it is communal in that they drew on pooled family resources.

Although 19th-century plural families tended to operate dyadically with respect to budget and resources, albeit often with communal features, a strong communal system turned up now and then. One man "tried to operate his households on the 'United Order' basis and any money earned by any members was supposed to go into the common fund. Purchases were made with money or script largely in terms of the particular need" (Young, 1954, p. 169). In another case, two sisters married to the same man and living in the same dwelling shared responsibilities: one wife did the outdoor work and cared for the animals, and the other one maintained the household (Embry, 1987). Similar patterns of cooperation and, presumably, communal use of resources, occurred in other families. For the most part, however, the available evidence suggests that wives in pioneer plural families operated primarily in a dyadic mode, or in a mixed dyadic and communal mode. Nineteenth-century plural families are quite similar to our sample of contemporary families in this respect.

Changes and experiments with resource management systems

Present-day plural families change the way they manage resources as circumstances evolve. Change and experimentation is a result of many factors: the tenuous and unpredictable economic situation of many families, the arrival of new wives and more children, the struggle to achieve an acceptable balance of dyadic and communal relationships between husbands and wives, the limited personal experience with plural family life in many cases, and absence of cultural norms regarding day-to-day life in polygynous families. Individual families seek to discover their own solution to problems with money and resources, and they do so in a more or less trial-and-error fashion.

Family 4
Harry, Anna, Ruth, Belle, Eve, and Shirley have used several budget systems over the years. At one time, the wives gave Harry their earnings, and he and each wife negotiated their allowance for food and other day-to-day expenses, using his and their earnings as a communal pool. Now that he is retired and receives financial assistance from his sons, most of the wives work and support themselves. Since Shirley doesn't work because she has small children, Harry supports her. If the other wives have needs beyond their income, he helps out. So they have moved from a somewhat balanced dyadic and communal system to a strongly dyadic one in which wives are quite independent of one another.

Family 5
Howard, Constance, Valerie, Barbara, and Rose have experimented with different budget systems over the years, largely because Howard's work in construction is often unpredictable and far from steady. As described earlier, at one time they had a communal system, meeting together weekly, pooling all their income, and allocating money to each wife according to her needs. They still pool their earnings but now give the money to Howard. He then meets separately with each wife and gives them money according to their needs. Thus they have moved from a relatively communal system to one with stronger dyadic features.

Family 3

William, Carlyn, Danielle, and Alayna have always been financially strapped. At one time, Carlyn was the only one working, and she supported the family; the money was used communally. At another time, when William and Carlyn worked away from home, he and she had one checking account, and Danielle and Alayna had another account – each pair more or less supported themselves, but shifted money back and forth as needed.

Most recently, Carlyn moved into the family home and now works and collects rent from the families occupying part of their residence. William, Danielle, and Alayna moved to another state to find work but barely earn enough to support themselves. Carlyn sends part of her salary and the rental income to them.

The family of a former prophet of a modern fundamentalist group, Rulon Allred, also used different budget systems from time to time (Solomon, 1984). During one period, wives and children turned their earnings over to him, and he gave each wife an allotment. This was by and large a dyadic arrangement, but with a communal pooling of resources. Interestingly, two wives who were sisters pooled their allowances and shared household management, child care, and grocery shopping, thereby organizing a minicommunal management system within the family. At another time, when several wives lived in a distant community because of Allred's flight from prosecution, the wives lived and managed their budgets communally – sharing income and resources. Thus this family used systems varying in dyadic and communal features at different times in their life, depending on the situation.

In some cases, family tensions cause changes in budgeting.

Family 2

We described earlier the complicated budget system used by David, Judith, Rebecca, Emily, and Phyllis: David pays many of the fundamental bills such as mortgage, automobile expenses, and utilities while the working wives sometimes share their income to cover food, medical bills, and clothing. In such cases, a working wife might be responsible for supporting a particular nonworking wife. They recently changed this system because some of the wives felt that they were inappropriately dependent on other wives. And the wives who were providing support did not like the responsibility of making decisions about other wives' financial resources and family management. Now David and each wife discuss their needs separately, and they pool some of the surplus funds from wives' income to balance things out.

At another time, they pooled *all* the money, and David apportioned it out to individual wives. One wife preferred this system because then she didn't have to make decisions for other wives about their income.

Tensions and stress regarding resources

Sometimes the management of money is a major source of tension in plural families and a symptom of other serious marital problems.

Family 12

Lauren, Fred's second wife, was very unhappy in her marriage for many reasons and eventually left the family. One cause of her distress was that she felt severely mistreated in matters of money and resources. At one point, she and Elaine were to have their own money for food and clothing. However, Elaine had the authority to give Lauren her allowance, which made Lauren feel inferior and subordinate to Elaine. Lauren eventually revolted and insisted that Fred provide her with money himself, not through Elaine. He agreed and did so.

But there were other aspects of resource management that indicated great stress in the family. Lauren claimed that Fred gave Elaine nicer furniture, a better and larger home, and gave more things to Elaine's children. In our terms, Lauren perceived herself to be the victim of poor dyadic and communal relationships regarding family resources, even when some attempts were made to change their allocation system.

Family 13

Gloria, the second wife, eventually divorced Paul because they were incompatible in many respects. For one thing, she felt mistreated when it came to money and resources. She said that other wives were free to overspend their budgets, whereas she was criticized for doing so. And he gave other wives more money than he gave her. At one point, he even took some furniture from her home and gave it to another wife. In her view, he violated their dyadic bond and her communal role in the family.

Conflicts about money and resources also appear in personal biographies of contemporary plural families. Melissa Merrill (1975), a former plural wife, said that her husband kept changing the family's budget allocation system. Sometimes, working wives covered their own expenses and turned surplus funds over to the husband in a primarily dyadic system. At other times, the wives gave the husband their earnings and he gave each of them an allowance, in what can be described as a dyadic system with communal features. At another point in the family's history, wives were totally self-supporting. The husband was rather capricious with respect to budgets and resources, and this created tension in the family. On one occasion, he took money sent by her mother for a baby crib and spent it on other baby furniture, much to her chagrin. On another occasion, he decorated a room in one of the homes for his own private use at a time the family was struggling economically.

Even in fundamentally stable plural families, resource issues sometimes produce tensions. In a biography of life in her father's family Dorothy Solomon (1984) notes that some wives and children resented turning over their earnings to him for redistribution among wives. Some sons wanted to save their earnings for their own education, rather than distribute them to wives and other family members. And one wife complained that she did not approve of her hard-earned funds being used to support other wives.

Budget and resources were also a source of tension in some 19th-century Mormon plural families (see, e.g., Brooks, 1934; Embry, 1984, 1987). Feelings of inequitable treatment were sometimes linked to jealousy because of another wife's furniture (Tanner, 1983), resentment about going to a senior wife to request supplies (Tanner, 1983), seeing other wives living in better quarters (Young, 1908), or observing other wives demanding and receiving more resources (Embry, 1987). In a dramatic case, Martha Cannon, a highly educated third wife, complained bitterly about her husband's unfairness. In letters to him she wrote:

> How do you think *I* feel when I meet you driving another plural wife about in a glittering carriage in broad daylight? [I] am entirely out of money – borrowing to pay some old standing debts. I want *our* affairs *speedily* and *absolutely* adjusted. . . . Will you send remittance – coal-flour etc. etc. . . . to say nothing of winter clothing essential to growing children. I find myself inadequate to *entirely* support them while they have a so called "handsome magn[i]fic" father living. . . . I should have appreciated the interest you should have felt more than the money – Tis the *little* things you could have done and not the larger things you could *not,* that have estranged us. (Van Wagoner, 1989, p. 96)

Summary

Budget and resource issues are important concerns in contemporary Mormon polygynous families. Resource management in modern polygynous families has dyadic and communal qualities. Many families adopt primarily dyadic resource systems, often with some communal features. In purely dyadic systems, a husband and each wife separately negotiate budget matters, without any involvement by other wives. In some cases, wives retain their own earnings; in other cases, a husband provides resources to wives.

Some dyadic systems also have a communal component. For example, a wife's surplus earnings may be given to the husband to distribute among wives experiencing a funding shortfall. Or all the money earned by family members may be pooled and then distributed by the husband on a dyadic basis to each wife.

Although dyadic systems are customary in modern plural families – as they were in Mormon pioneer days and are in other polygynous cultures – some families use communal resource management systems. Wives may use pooled money collectively in day-to-day management of the home, or, in a variation involving a dyadic component, family members may pool their earnings and then collectively decide how to allocate funds to individual wives. In other variants of a primarily communal system, subsets of wives share resources, with the husband involved as special needs arise.

Consistent with our general thesis is the fact that many contemporary Mormon polygynous families adopt resource systems of a dual nature: they acknowledge the importance of each husband–wife pair and simultaneously recognize the communal unity of the family. Although specific features vary from case to case, in general modern fundamentalist families attempt to achieve a viable interplay of dyadic and communal processes in their budget and resource systems.

As economic and family circumstances change, plural families often revise their resource systems, altering the balance of dyadic and communal features. In so doing, often amid internal family stress and tension, contemporary Mormon fundamentalists engage in a process of "experimentation" and "trial and error," much as they do in many other areas of their lives. With limited personal experience in plural life and with only the barest guidance from their culture at large, members of modern plural families must find their own solutions – and work through the inevitable stresses and tensions – to managing their finances and resources.

15

Celebrations and holidays

Celebrations and holidays are an integral part of family life. They punctuate and provide variation from daily routines of school, work, and home management; they mark important seasons, religious, and cultural events; they often include unique rituals and activities. Some celebrations single out individuals, families, or interpersonal relationships. Thus birthdays honor individuals; wedding anniversaries commemorate a couple, and families often display their unity through these same celebrations. In many cases, families develop their own traditions, such as vacation trips, reunions, picnics, and dinner gatherings, often symbolizing family unity and distinctiveness. Other celebrations and holidays are associated with religious, ethnic, and community occasions. Religious observances may occur daily, weekly, or less frequently and may be observed at home or in formal places of worship. Other events may involve ethnic or national heritages and national holidays such as the Fourth of July, Thanksgiving, Mother's Day, and Father's Day. Many of these events have community- or society-wide traditions and modes of observance. However, individuals and families often add their own unique celebratory twists, lending a sense of family unity to a community celebration.

Again, the key issue here concerns the interplay of dyadic and communal processes in holidays and celebrations observed by contemporary polygynous families. Are national and community events observed communally by a whole family, in separate dyadic family clusters, or in some mixed way? And what about birthdays or wedding anniversaries? Are these celebrated communally by the whole plural family, in subgroups, or separately within each dyadic family unit? Do the celebrations of plural families follow a pattern – some primarily dyadic, some largely communal, and some involving an interplay of dyadic and communal processes?

To these questions we add those posed elsewhere in this book, namely, How do celebrations vary across families, change within families as their lives evolve, and involve tensions and stresses? Celebrations provide further clues to husband–wife, wife–wife, and family relationships in present-day fundamentalist families.

Dyadic celebrations

Dyadic celebrations involve a husband and wife; a husband, wife, and children; or a wife and children. Typical dyadic celebrations include wives' birthdays, wedding anniversaries, and children's birthdays.

Wives' birthdays

In many families a wife's birthday is a distinctively dyadic event that finds her and the husband doing something special by themselves.

Family 2
David always tries to celebrate Judith's, Rebecca's, Emily's, and Phyllis's birthday in a special way – taking the celebrating wife out to dinner or to a movie and spending the night with her.

Family 5
The wife celebrating her birthday chooses what she wants to do on "her day." She and Howard might go to dinner or a movie, visit a temple, or see relatives or friends. It is a special time for a wife and for the two of them to be alone or out together.

Family 18
Charles and the wife whose birthday it is always spend an extra day together. They may go out for an evening or day and sometimes stay overnight at a hotel.

Lorraine Bronson (n.d.), a modern plural wife, has described the special celebration on her 40th birthday. Her children treated her and her husband to a movie. Bronson's two children joined them, making it a special occasion for that family in the larger plural family. Thus a wife's birthday celebration acknowledges both her individuality and her unique dyadic relationship with her husband and, sometimes, with their children. But other wives sometimes honor their co-wife, in a communal celebration of a birthday.

Family 1
Sometimes, Joan, Norma, Charlotte, and Cynthia have a birthday party for one another, depending on their work schedules and other commitments.

Family 2
The main way to celebrate a wife's birthday is for her and David to go out alone together. However, it is also customary for wives sharing a home to bake a cake for one another. And on occasion David, Judith, Rebecca, Emily, and Phyllis might celebrate a special birthday together.

There are also times when a wife reminds David about another wife's birthday, especially if she suspects he has forgotten about it.

Family 10
Being alone with Barry is the highlight of a wife's birthday celebration; however, it is also customary for another wife to bake a cake for the birthday celebrant.

Family 12
For Elaine and Lauren, the typical birthday celebration involves dinner and a movie alone with Fred. Either one contributes to the occasion by taking care of the celebrating wife's children. On one of Elaine's birthdays, Lauren honored her by cooking and serving a special dinner for her and Fred.

We learned of a unique communal aspect of children's and wives' birthdays in one family.

Family 5
Valerie, the second of four wives, has a large chart in her bedroom marking off each month of the year. On cards under each month she lists the names and dates of the birthdays and anniversaries of all members of the family. It helps her remember who to congratulate (and helps her remind Howard as well!). Valerie is, in effect, the communal source of information about important events in the family.

In general, then, a plural wife's birthday is an occasion to make salient her individuality and unique dyadic relationship with her husband. At the same time, communal elements sometimes come into play, with other wives often doing special things to honor a co-wife. Thus, while primarily dyadic, a wife's birthday may also be an occasion to reinforce the communal quality of a plural family.

Wedding anniversaries

Wedding anniversaries are handled in much the same way as wives' birthdays. As in a monogamous marriage, the wedding anniversary of a plural husband and each wife symbolizes their unique and distinctive relationship. To acknowledge the event, it is customary for a couple to spend special time alone, if only for an evening, going out to dinner at a restaurant, to a movie, or some other special place. In some cases, they may stay overnight at a hotel, go on a short trip, or spend extra time together at home. We encountered only one case in which another wife joined a couple for dinner on their anniversary – and it was not comfortable for anyone, especially for the "intruder." Thus wedding anniversary celebrations, are usually dyadic, highlighting the uniqueness of each marriage in a plural family.

Children's birthdays

Because our analysis focuses on husband–wife and wife–wife relationships in plural families, we know few details about children's birthdays. But what we learned is quite consistent. It is customary for a wife and her children to observe a child's birthday within their family unit. Children's birthdays are not usually celebrated communally with other wives and their children present. Thus children's birthdays are often treated as a dyadic family event.

On practical grounds alone, it is easy to see why a child's birthday is celebrated in a dyadic fashion. Suppose a family with a husband, four wives, and 20 children (not an unusual case in our sample) celebrated every child's birthday communally. The logistics would be awesome – there would be a birthday party almost every other week, people would be transporting many children to the birthday site and purchasing or making gifts all the time, and the day-to-day life of already very busy people would be constantly interrupted.

At the same time, as discussed in chapters 18 and 19, mothers and their children are strongly bonded to one another. Although children are encouraged to see *all* children in the family as "true" brothers and sisters and to respond to all wives as "mothers," the fact is that there are powerful bonds between a mother and her biological children. To some extent, therefore, children's birthday celebrations acknowledge and reinforce the special relationship between a mother and her children and distinguish her family from the larger communal plural family. Even so, communal elements are at times incorporated into children's birthday celebrations.

Family 1

It is customary for only siblings in a mother's family to participate in a child's birthday party. Yet there are occasions when the whole family participates. If the birthday is on a Sunday, for example, they might celebrate before or after church when everyone is together.

Joan and Norma, the first and second wives, also have some joint birthday parties for their children. They have several children who are close in age and are friends. Because they have separate apartments in the same dwelling, it makes sense and is easy to arrange.

What about the father's involvement in his children's birthday celebrations? Although our information is sketchy, it suggests that fathers usually attend birthday celebrations on an intermittent and "as-available" basis.

Family 5

With four wives and 31 children in the family, Howard attends only a few birthday parties. It is just too inconvenient, given his work and church responsibilities. Valerie, the second wife, said that they are always pleased when he comes to a party, but they don't generally plan on his being there. The three other wives agreed, saying that they do not expect Howard (or one another's children) to attend. Otherwise, they would be forever planning and celebrating birthdays and trying to work around his and their complicated schedules.

Family 10

Barry and his eight wives have more than 50 children. Groups of wives share dwellings, but typically celebrate their own children's birthdays separately. Barry attends some parties, but only if he happens to be at a home where a party is taking place.

Thus far, we have illustrated that some celebrations in modern Mormon plural families (children's birthdays and wedding anniversaries of a husband and each wife) are strongly dyadic and that other events (wives' birthdays) are dyadic but may also have communal features. Next we examine communal family celebrations, including a husband's birthday and community and cultural holidays.

Communal celebrations

Communal family celebrations take many forms, but generally involve a husband and all wives or subsets of wives and children participating jointly in some activity. Some communal celebrations, for example, a regular Sunday dinner or a family vacation, are unique to a family. Others may be community or cultural events, such as a church picnic, Thanksgiving, and Christmas. Some of these are almost "purely" communal; others have dyadic aspects.

Fathers' or husbands' birthdays

Very frequently a father's or husband's birthday is a communal event celebrated by wives or a whole family.

Family 1
Hal's birthday is celebrated differently from year to year, depending on family circumstances. On several occasions, Joan, Norma, Charlotte, and Cynthia have taken him out to dinner as a group. Sometimes a few children join them, but that is rare. This year they had a special celebration. The wives gave him a surprise party with the whole family in attendance. And they and Hal's mother also took him out to dinner.

Family 5
Howard's birthday is celebrated only intermittently, and then in different ways, sometimes with the whole family having dinner together. On his most recent birthday, Constance, Valerie, Barbara, and Rose gave him an album of the pictures of all the wives and their children.

Howard was born on his father's 50th birthday, and this is always acknowledged on his birthday. The celebration thereby embeds Howard and the whole family in an ancestral and cultural context of patriarchy.

Family 6
The family held a special celebration on Seymour's 65th birthday. About 100 people attended, including his 58 children and their spouses, as well as friends and other relatives. On his 67th birthday this year, they did the same thing, with between 150 and 200 people at the celebration.

Family 12
Fred's birthday is a special family occasion. Fred's mother and Elaine and Lauren and their children gather together for a family dinner and party, following which they give him presents. His mother and the older children present gifts to him, and Elaine and Lauren often make sweaters, socks, or other items of clothing for him.

Another example from the contemporary era can be found in Dorothy Solomon's (1984) account of life in her father's plural family. Rulon Allred, her father and former leader of a large fundamentalist group, and his wives and children often celebrated his birthday communally. On one occasion, each wife publicly described a personal memory of him, reflecting their common bond with one another and with their husband.

We also came across a few examples of how a father's or husband's birthday was celebrated communally by 19th-century Mormons – a notable case being the observance of Brigham Young's birthday. A former wife portrayed the typical celebration as a communal event in which all the wives gathered together at a dinner in Brigham's honor (Young, 1908). According to one of his daughters, the children of the family performed songs and dances in honor of his birthday (Spencer, 1961). Community and church leaders also visited and offered their congratulations. Although it was not customary to have presents, one year the family gave Brigham a "hair wreath," made up of strands of hair from every member of the family.

Not all present-day plural families observe a husband's or father's birthday in a strictly communal way. Some families do different things from year to year, varying from highly communal to highly dyadic modes of celebration.

Family 10

Barry's birthday is celebrated in different ways from year to year, with the eight wives respecting his desires about how to celebrate the event. On some occasions, the whole family, including children, celebrates together. At other times, his birthday is acknowledged separately by each wife and her children, and he has eight birthday parties! Sometimes, the subsets of wives and children who share a dwelling give him a birthday party.

In many of our discussions it was apparent that a husband's or father's birthday was an occasion to honor him personally and to acknowledge and reaffirm his status as family patriarch, in accordance with fundamentalist religious beliefs.

Family 4

Harry and his five wives and 65 children do not celebrate Christmas because he feels that it has become a commercial holiday and has lost its religious meaning. Instead they celebrate "Father's Birthday" every summer (see chapter 18).

Its key elements are a gathering of family members (there may have been 400–500 people at the last party we attended); food and drink prepared by wives and daughters; and a "show" put on by children and grandchildren that includes singing, the reading of poems and prose, the presentation of gifts to Harry, his giving of gifts to children (which each wife or mother arranges), and Harry making remarks and serving as master of ceremonies. His remarks emphasize the unity of the family, incorporate religious themes, and reflect his status as family patriarch.

In celebrating the husband's or father's birthday as a major communal event, some modern plural families symbolically bind family members together as a unified group. The fact that wives may cooperatively plan and conduct the birthday celebration may reinforce their communal relationships with one another.

Family events

Many families regularly spend time together on Sunday. They may go to church as a group, have a family meal before or after church, invite guests to their home on Sunday evening, or visit relatives and friends. Wives may take turns cooking Sunday dinner, or they may all share in the preparation of meals. Although practices vary from family to family, and even within families from time to time, Sunday is often an occasion to highlight the communal unity of the family in relation to church and religious activities.

Some families also come together on other occasions.

Family 1
Hal, Joan, Norma, Charlotte, Cynthia, and their children often spend the July 4th holiday at a family cabin in another part of the state. Other relatives sometimes join them.

Family 6
Tamara, the fourth wife, said that Seymour, the eight wives, and all the children have a large family party or picnic every couple of years. And her own parents' family has a large get-together every other year, usually on her father's or grandfather's birthday.

One of the most remarkable examples of an event symbolizing family communality is a monthly meeting held by family 4 (see chapter 18).

Family 4
More than twenty years ago, Harry organized a monthly meeting of his 37 sons and their families. No matter where they work – and many work far away – his sons and their wives and children return to the family home for a weekend of meetings and gatherings. Harry organized this communal event in order to foster and sustain family unity. The weekend includes formal and informal social activities, attendance at church services, group meetings of Harry with his sons, a large breakfast for all males in the family (including grandchildren and sons-in-law), and rec-

reational events. Harry presides over all these meetings as family patriarch, checks on each family member's personal status, gives advice, and in a variety of ways fosters a sense of loyalty and obligation to the communal well-being of the family.

Nineteenth-century Mormon families also engaged in a variety of communal observances. Nearly half of the children in one sample of pioneer polygynists stated that their fathers attended church with all wives and children (Embry, 1987). This reflects a communal orientation. One daughter remembers her father "going up the aisle of a church with one wife on either side. He took them both to all public places. He said where one went the other would go too" (Young, 1954, p. 221).

At the same time, about 15% of the husbands attended church with the wife with whom they were staying at the time, in a dyadic approach (Embry, 1987). One man who rotated weekly among his wives took the wife with whom he was staying to church and other public activities, and at church the other wives did not sit directly alongside the couple but were nearby (Young, 1954). Similarly, when they went for a drive in the family car, the wife the husband was visiting sat up front next to the husband, and the other wives sat in the back. (If that wife wasn't with them, the front seat remained vacant!)

Community and cultural events

Contemporary plural families also observe community and cultural holidays with dances, picnics, camping trips, adult activities, and celebrations of the birthday of the religious leader.

Family 12
When Fred, Elaine, and Lauren lived in one of the group's isolated rural settlements, they participated in monthly community activities coinciding with the visit of the group's prophet. On Saturday morning men and older boys worked on community projects, and women engaged in Relief Society (social service and mutual assistance) activities. There was also a dance on Saturday night. Sunday was devoted to religious meetings, church services, and discussions with the prophet. This was a special time, Lauren told us, because it was an opportunity to see everyone, have fun, change the regular routine of life, and have time together as a whole family and community.

The community also held a major summer celebration on July 4 and July 24 (a major holiday celebrating the arrival of the first Mormons in

Utah in 1847). Everyone gathered in the town park for a baseball game, greased pole contest, pet showing, costumes, barbecue, and a community meal. Community celebrations also coincided with the group's regular religious conference and with the birthday of a former prophet.

Nineteenth-century Mormon plural families also celebrated a variety of occasions. They held swimming parties, picnics, summer trips, impromptu gatherings, and family reunions that involved all or most wives and their children (Embry, 1987). Families also participated in extended family reunions, church plays and musicals, and community socials, dances, and concerts (Arrington and Bitton, 1979). It is important to recognize, however, that some pioneer families participated in public events in a communal way, whereas some adopted dyadic approaches. On the communal side, one man "remembered that his father took both of his wives to the Salt Lake Theater two or three times a year. . . . 'There was no reason to hide. They didn't talk about it, but they did things together' " (Embry, 1987, p. 85). A woman said that when her father and his two wives "were younger, they would go to dances and parties together" (Embry, 1987, p. 86).

On the dyadic side, one man "spent a week with each wife in turn and when he went out in public – to church, public dinners, dances, or other entertainment – he always took 'the wife of that week' with him" (Young, 1954, p. 179).

Many modern plural families also observe a variety of national cultural holidays in a communal fashion.

Family 1
Hal, Joan, Norma, Charlotte, and Cynthia and their children usually celebrate Thanksgiving and Halloween together. They explicitly say that their goal is to keep the family together on these and other holidays.

Family 5
On Thanksgiving the whole family – Howard, Constance, Valerie, Barbara, Rose, and their children – gather in the home of the wife or mother with the largest living room. The wives share responsibility for the meal and coordinate with one another who will cook what dishes. They also celebrate Memorial Day and Mother's Day as a whole family in different wives' homes. On the 4th and 24th of July they have a large family picnic.

Not all families celebrate all cultural holidays, nor do they do so in the same way. Some families do not celebrate Christmas because they view it as a pagan holiday. And in some cases wives and their children celebrate a holiday separately from one another. But such cases are rare; major holidays are often observed by whole families as a communal event.

A couple of families, most of whom are converts to the fundamentalist movement, rebel against celebrations that have a "pagan" or "commercial" tone; instead they are experimenting with more biblical and religious types of celebrations, including traditional Jewish holidays.

Family 3

William, Carlyn, Danielle, and Alayna have been trying to celebrate a number of Jewish holidays, to acknowledge the fundamentalist group's religious "roots." Thus at Passover they eat lamb and kosher food and watch the movie *The Ten Commandments*. (They acknowledge not knowing exactly how to act on these occasions and asked us many questions about various holidays that they hope to observe in the future.)

Family 9

John, Joyce, Clara, and Marjorie celebrate some Jewish holidays (one of John's parents was Jewish, and even though he had no religious background as a child, he is now interested in Judaism). The family observes the first day of the Jewish New Year, the Day of Atonement, Passover, and a few other holidays. (John even bought a Shofar – a ram's horn used on the New Year – which he occasionally blows, to the bewilderment, he says, of some of his suburban neighbors.)

These are unusual cases, but reflect attempts by some families to experiment with different forms of observance, partly to "discover" their own real or symbolic roots and partly to have meaningful occasions to enhance family communality.

Nineteenth-century Mormons also participated in major community and cultural events, such as Pioneer Day, which celebrated the arrival of the first wagon train of pioneers into the Salt Lake valley. They also celebrated the anniversary of Utah's statehood, the joining of the cross-country railroad in Utah, the Fourth of July, and other holidays. These events are still observed in Utah and the surrounding region.

Blending dyadic and communal processes: Celebrating Christmas

Although many polygynous Mormon families who celebrate Christmas emphasize communality in their activities, some also incorporate dyadic features in the *location* of Christmas celebrations, *gift-giving* practices, and other events during the holiday season.

Location of Christmas activities

In several families, everyone gathers in one home on Christmas Eve or on Christmas Day for a meal, opening gifts, and even sleeping overnight – all of which symbolizes their communality as a plural family.

Family 1
On Christmas Eve, Hal, Joan, Norma, Charlotte, and Cynthia and their 24 children all gather in one home. The adults sleep in the living room near the Christmas tree and gifts, and the children sleep elsewhere on beds, mattresses, sleeping bags, and in other makeshift places. They spend part of Christmas Day together opening gifts, eating, and doing things informally.

Family 10
Christmas day is celebrated by Barry, his eight wives, and their more than 50 children (plus spouses and children of married children) at the main family home. They eat a meal together, exchange gifts, and enjoy one another. Christmas is the only occasion during the year when all of the married sons and their families come to the family home, so it is a special occasion that reflects the communality of the immediate and extended plural family.

Family 12
Fred, Elaine, Lauren, and their children traditionally observe Christmas together – opening presents and having a special Christmas day dinner. Sometimes the whole family also entertains guests on Christmas night.

It is easy to imagine how the communal spirit of a plural family is theoretically enhanced when the husband, wives, and children sleep in the same home on Christmas Eve, open gifts together, and share meals. But think about the practical side of such situations – when there might be four wives, and more than two dozen children in a single dwelling – as is the case in a couple of families who follow this custom. The noise and activity level during waking hours must be extraordinary, meals must require extensive preparation, and one can visualize the challenge of managing some two dozen aroused and excited children of all ages. It must be an arousing celebration that becomes a memorable event – and that adds to everyone's sense of being part of a unified and communal family (and imagine the relief that some adults feel when the celebration is over!).

Some families also incorporate dyadic features into the location at which Christmas is observed.

Family 2

David, Judith, Rebecca, Emily, and Phyllis gather at one of their homes on Christmas Eve, sleep there overnight, open gifts the next morning, and spend Christmas Day together. However, each wife also has a Christmas tree in her home that she and her children decorate together (they also exchange gifts in their immediate family).

Gift giving

The exchange of gifts at Christmas time can be a real challenge in plural families. Do wives give gifts to their own and other wives' children, in a communal pattern? Or, do they give gifts only to their own biological children, in a dyadic orientation? We learned that families use a variety of gift-giving strategies, many emphasizing communal values, and others reflecting a blend of dyadic and communal processes.

Family 2

David, Judith, Rebecca, Emily, and Phyllis each give gifts to one another. The wives also purchase or make small gifts for *all* children in the family, not just for their own offspring – this behavior reflects a strong communal orientation to gift giving.

Family 3

Although William, Carlyn, Danielle, and Alayna do not celebrate Christmas, they exchange small gifts at the New Year. Each mother makes or buys gifts for *all* children in the family, in a communal approach. Gifts are modest; they consist of socks, toothbrushes, small items of clothing, and so on. The children also receive gifts sent by their grandparents. To add to the occasion, some of the children put on a play for the family.

Although other families also have a strong communal approach to gift giving at Christmas, several use a lottery system to keep the situation manageable.

Family 5

At Thanksgiving, family members draw names out of a hat, to determine Christmas gift-giving assignments. The names are drawn across the whole family, in a communal manner. In a family of a husband, four wives, and many children, this lottery system keeps gift exchange within reasonable bounds.

Other families combine the communal lottery system with a dyadic feature.

Family 1

Although family members draw lots to give Christmas gifts across the whole family, Joan, Norma, Charlotte, and Cynthia also give special gifts to their own children, thereby introducing both communal and dyadic aspects of gift giving.

Nineteenth-century Mormon pioneer families also varied in how they celebrated Christmas (and Thanksgiving). In one sample of informants, roughly equal numbers said that their pioneer families celebrated Thanksgiving and Christmas communally (40%) or dyadically (35%) (Embry, 1987). And some families alternated – celebrating Thanksgiving together and Christmas apart; in other cases the father/husband visited each wife and her children's families separately on holidays.

Clarissa Spencer (1961), a daughter of Brigham Young, recollected that wives and children celebrated Thanksgiving together and that all the children in the family hung up their stockings for Christmas, each receiving a toy and some clothing (see also Embry, 1987).

Some pioneer families celebrated Christmas and Thanksgiving in a more dyadic mode (Embry, 1987). The husbands/fathers simply celebrated the occasion in the home where they happened to be at the time; others decided on an ad hoc basis where to spend a particular holiday; still others traveled around on the holiday to visit their families.

Special observances

Now and then, a plural family would undertake an interesting blend of communal and dyadic activities.

Family 1

Joan's father was seriously ill during one Christmas holiday season, so Hal, Joan, Norma, Charlotte, Cynthia, and their children planned a special treat for him. Each wife and her children visited Joan's father's home on alternating nights during each of "the twelve days of Christmas," leaving an anonymous gift for him on the doorstep. On the twelfth night the whole family gathered in front of the home, sang Christmas carols, and presented Joan's father a single gift from everyone.

Here we see a strong blend of communal and dyadic activities – dyadic in that each wife and her children visited their ill relative separately, and communal in that the whole family planned the activities, sang carols, and gave a collective gift on the last night of Christmas. And they recounted this event with enthusiasm, describing how much fun it was, how good it made everyone feel, and how they continue to share in the memory of the event.

A similar blend of dyadic and communal activities is described by Samuel Taylor (1972). On Christmas Day his father dressed up as Santa Claus and visited the homes of each of his wives and children, in a dyadic approach. But later all his wives and children would gather in one of the homes, and he would arrive in a horse-drawn wagon, dressed in a Santa Claus outfit. The whole family then ate a Christmas dinner that had been cooperatively prepared by all the wives. These events highlight a communal aspect of the celebration. At the same time, each wife's home had its own tree, and each mother and her children exchanged presents among themselves, in a dyadic orientation.

Tensions and stresses in celebrations

Celebrations and observances are not always completely happy occasions. Sometimes they contribute to or reflect family upheaval and conflict. The tensions often center around dyadic issues – when a wife may feel that she and her children are not being treated fairly. Such feelings also detract from a sense of family communality, since the aggrieved parties are neither pleased with their dyadic relationship nor feel that the family is functioning as a unified whole.

Family 12

Lauren, Fred's second wife, eventually left him and Elaine for a variety of reasons – many arising from her feeling that he didn't treat her fairly and that he strongly favored Elaine. She recounted a number of conflicts and negative feelings related to the way they observed holidays.

Although they celebrated Thanksgiving fairly regularly, Lauren said that they never developed a tradition about how and where to do it. Sometimes they all gathered at Elaine's home; sometimes they joined Fred's family; and sometimes she and Elaine had separate dinners. Furthermore, Lauren claimed that she never participated in the decision about how to celebrate in a given year and was simply told what would be done after Fred and Elaine had talked about it. Lauren was angry about this issue, felt left out, and described herself as a second-class member of the family.

Problems also arose at Christmas. They followed the tradition of opening presents together on Christmas morning, having a family Christmas dinner, and entertaining guests. All well and good, according to Lauren. But then there were times when Fred, Elaine, and her children visited her parents or friends, leaving Lauren and her children behind.

Again, she resented both Fred's and Elaine's lack of concern for her feelings. As their relationships deteriorated, they even stopped having Sunday dinners together as a family. It was simply too stressful and difficult to plan and be together as a whole family.

Family 14

Sally, Harvey's first wife, eventually left him after several years of conflict and her feeling that he had come to favor Molly, the second wife. There was tension between the three of them about many issues, including aspects of holiday celebrations. For example, Sally claims that Molly saved money from the family budget to buy special Christmas gifts for her children and left Sally to pay for all the family's grocery expenses herself. As a result, Sally was unable to buy nice presents for her children, and she strongly resented Molly's selfishness. As time went on, Sally and her children celebrated Christmas with her parents, not with Harvey and Molly, to give her children a better holiday. What made matters worse was that Harvey refused to do anything about the situation.

Family 3

William, Carlyn, Danielle, and Alayna are all converts to the fundamentalist movement. William objects to celebrating Christmas because it is too commercialized and violates the true meaning of Jesus Christ's birth. He wants to have a Christmas observance in April, to coincide more closely with the birth of Jesus. Although Carlyn, Danielle, and Alayna accept his views, there is some tension over the matter – it is a difficult time for the children who only know that they aren't having Christmas like other families. Furthermore, the grandparents send gifts to the children and family and put pressure on them to celebrate Christmas. As noted earlier, they have compromised by having a small celebration and exchange of gifts around the New Year, but it still is a matter of some contention in the family.

They also expressed some family disagreements about celebrating birthdays. William apparently doesn't think they should observe the birthdays of family members, and it is evident that he and the wives view the matter in different ways. However, they did not wish to discuss the issue further with us until they themselves worked out their different opinions.

Patterns of observing celebrations

By and large, plural families seem to seek and often work out a pattern of observing holidays that incorporates both dyadic and communal processes.

In *Family 1,* Hal, Joan, Norma, Charlotte, and Cynthia celebrate holidays and other events in a range of ways – from purely dyadic, to mixed dyadic and communal, to purely communal. On one hand, children's birthdays, wives' birthdays, and wedding anniversaries are observed in a dyadic way: for example, children's birthdays are usually observed with families; and Hal and each wife celebrate her birthday and their wedding anniversary alone. On the other hand, his birthday is strictly a communal event involving all the wives, as are Thanksgiving, the Fourth of July, Sunday dinners, and other events. Christmas can involve a blend of dyadic and communal activities. Everyone gathers together and sleeps in one home on Christmas Eve, they open presents together, and draw lots across families to assign gift giving. But each wife also has a separate tree for her children and family, and mothers give their own children special gifts. And, on the occasion of the grandfather's illness, each wife and her children brought him gifts separately on subsequent days, but then the whole family gathered to sing carols.

Other plural families combine dyadic and communal activities as well, but the patterns of celebration vary from one family to another. It was also not uncommon for pioneer families to adopt a mixed dyadic and communal strategy. One husband reportedly took both of his wives to socials, "but took each in turn to General Conferences, leaving the other wife to manage the home and farm" (Embry, 1987, p. 86). After he married a third wife, the other wives concluded that "every wife ought to have good times after she is married and so they rather encouraged, or at least tolerated father showing [the third wife] a special good time by taking her to dances and other ward functions. Then after that, he gradually settled down to all of them going together" (Embry, 1987, p. 86). In another case, the husband seldom appeared in public with two wives, "except at church parties where he might take all three. He took his wives to concerts and plays by turns. These turns might not coincide with the time of his visits, but they worked out very well" (Young, 1954, p. 295).

Summary

Contemporary polygynous families celebrate holidays and special occasions – birthdays and anniversaries, religious holidays, and community and societal events such as Christmas, Thanksgiving, and the Fourth of July – in both dyadic and communal ways. Some events are observed mainly in a dyadic fashion, others are primarily communal, and still others have both dyadic and communal qualities. Wives' birthdays and wedding anniversaries are usually celebrated as dyadic events – with the husband and wife doing something special as a couple. On the other hand, husbands' birthdays are often observed communally, with the whole plural family or subsets of wives and their children participating in the event. Other occasions, such as churchgoing, Sunday dinners, Thanksgiving, and similar holidays, also tend to be communal occasions involving the whole plural family.

Other holidays involve mixed dyadic and communal features for some families. For example, all members of some plural families celebrate Christmas together, exchanging gifts across families, sleeping in the same home on Christmas Eve, and having meals together, in communal celebration. At the same time, mothers sometimes give gifts to their own children as well, have a Christmas tree in their home, and otherwise celebrate the holiday in their own way. In these cases, the celebrations are a blend of dyadic and communal activities. Some plural families develop their own unique customs.

In their holiday celebrations, as in other aspects of their life, present-day fundamentalists are seeking a viable lifestyle in the face of little or no personal past experience with plural family life. The fact that conflict and tension in some families reflects or results from various celebrations attests to the importance of holidays and other special occasions in polygynous family life.

Although plural families celebrate many events in essentially the same way as most Americans, the size and complexity of their families sometimes leads them to rather different forms of observance. For example, a husband's or a father's birthday, Christmas, and other occasions are usually celebrated communally. Thus the modern fundamentalist culture, while linked to the larger American value system, is also developing customs that are congruent with its distinctive beliefs and values and that are designed to foster viable and well-functioning plural families.

Social-emotional and family relationships

The four chapters in this section examine central aspects of plural family life. Chapters 16 and 17 address social-emotional relationships between a husband and each wife and between wives, respectively. Chapter 16 examines mechanisms by which each husband–wife pair in a plural family achieves a unique and distinctive relationship from other couples in the family and the implications of failing to do so. It also describes how wives communally facilitate or detract from each others' relationship with their common husband. Chapter 17 focuses on relationships between wives in regard to managing homes, childrearing, and general interpersonal relationships.

Chapter 18 turns to the question of plural family structure, including the patriarchal role of husbands/fathers, the role of wives/mothers, and the means by which they achieve family unity. These issues are explored in case studies of a stable and well-established family, an "experimenting" and growing family, and a composite of disrupted families. Chapter 19 considers family structure as reflected in relationships between husbands and wives and their children, names for newborn children, and the terms children use to refer to their birth mothers and other wives.

16

Social-emotional relationships of husbands and wives

In this chapter we turn to yet another domain of contemporary Mormon polygynous life: the feelings of intimacy and love between a husband and each wife as they seek to establish a unique dyadic bond with one another. We also discuss the ways in which a husband and each wife relate emotionally to one another as members of an idealized communal plural family.

It is, of course, impossible to separate emotional relationships between husbands and wives from other aspects of their lives. Emotions are intertwined with living arrangements, budget and resources, celebrations, and all of the topics discussed in this volume. At the same time, participants often talked generally about their feelings of jealousy, frustration, loneliness, anger, love, warmth, and affection for one another, above and beyond specific activities or life domains. Mindful of the complexities of their relationships, we pose the following questions: What principles guide each husband–wife couple in a plural family toward a viable and unique dyadic relationship? What communal principles do plural family members follow to ensure the well-being of each husband–wife couple? And what are the consequences of failing to follow these principles?

These issues are first examined in a few polygynous cultures around the world. The discussion then moves on to the complex and controversial matter of "love and romance" and social-emotional relationships in 19th-century and contemporary Mormon polygynous marriages.

Social-emotional relationships in other cultures

Anthropological reports generally focus on relationships between a husband and wives, or between wives, in regard to household management; resources of land, agriculture, and animals; the treatment of children; and other similar issues. Intimacy, affection, and social-emotional relations between husbands and wives are hardly ever discussed in and of themselves. (We do not know whether this is a result of an anthropological tradition that consciously or unknowingly ignores social-affective aspects of close relationships or the fact that they are not a key aspect of close relationships in other cultures.) Some clues to the nature of social-emotional relationships between husbands and plural wives in other cultures can be found in their general contacts with one another, feelings by wives about the "fairness" with which they are treated by the husband, and jealousy or compatibility between wives in respect to the husband.

Contacts between husbands and wives in some polygynous cultures appear to be limited. Husbands and wives in the Bedouin culture of Israel lead quite separate lives – men spend time with men and women spend time with women; a husband does not usually inform his wife about where he is going and when he will return; wives seldom participate in family decisions; and women and men do not shop or eat in restaurants together (Marx, 1987). And husbands in the Xesibe culture of Africa are aloof and domineering, rarely give wives any attention in public, are free to pursue young unmarried women, and spend little time with their wives (O'Connell, 1982). But in other cultures husbands and wives spend much more time together.

The ease with which marriages can be dissolved also provides some insight into the emotional side of polygynous relationships. In some cultures, marriages are easily ended, perhaps because social-emotional ties between partners tend to be weak. Among the Mundurucu of Brazil, a divorce occurs when either partner simply leaves the relationship (Murphy and Murphy, 1974). (The fact that there is no elaborate system of courtship, gift exchange, bride price, or formal marriage ceremony and that husbands and wives live apart early in their marriage suggests that marital ties are fragile in the Mundurucu culture.) Marriages can also be dissolve easily among the Akan of Africa, who allow husbands and wives to be quite independent (Asante-Derko and Van Der Geest, 1983). Their assets and incomes are kept separate, and marriage is primarily aimed at legitimizing the status of children. Although Bete husbands in Africa are dominant and couples live near the husband's family community, wives consider their marriage to be temporary, and they are free to dissolve it if they feel neglected or mistreated (Clignet, 1970). Marital bonds appear to be weak in these societies, which, on the face of it, do not emphasize intimate, social-emotional bonds between partners. In many other societies, however, marital ties are strong and not easily broken. Among the Kikuyu of Africa, divorce only occurs when there is serious marital conflict as a result of desertion, thievery, witchcraft, refusal to engage in sexual activity, inability to have children, and the like (Kenyatta, 1973).

Few ethnographies discuss "love," affective or emotional feelings, or the unique dyadic bond between a husband and wife. Rather, they tend to focus more on a husband's "fairness" to his wives, or the fairness of wives to one another, as an important ingredient of success in a polygynous family (Mair, 1977). When a husband in the Lobedu culture of Africa gives one wife certain supplies, he is expected to do the same for his other wives (Crige, 1964). Equal sharing or provision of resources is also the cultural norm among the Yako (Forde, 1950) and the Mende (Little, 1951) of Africa. Among the Nyakyusa (Wilson, 1950) and the Lango (Curley, 1973) of Africa and the Hagen of New Guinea (Strathern, 1972), a man is expected to divide his time equally among his families. Similarly, husbands among the Ashanti of Africa (Fortes, 1950), Comoro Islanders of Madagascar (Ottenheimer and Ottenheimer, 1979), and the Bedouin of Israel (Ginat, 1982; Marx, 1967, 1987) are expected to provide equal time, sexual attention, and material provisions to each of their wives. In a somewhat different vein, all wives in the Ijaw culture of Africa cook meals for the husband daily; he is expected to eat equal portions from each wife's meal in order to avoid showing favoritism (Leis, 1974). A similar practice occurs among the Gusii of Africa (LeVine and LeVine, 1963).

In practice, however, husbands do not always treat their wives fairly. Bedouin husbands of Israel, although expected to treat all wives equally, sometimes favor one wife over another – especially a new wife in the early stages of their marriage (Ginat, personal observation; Marx, 1987). Similar inequities occur among Africa's Lango (Curley, 1973), Nyakyusa (Wilson, 1950), Yoruba (Ware, 1979), and Gusii (LeVine, 1964) cultures, and among the Siwai of the South Pacific (Stephens, 1963). In a survey of Yoruba wives (Ware, 1979), the favoritism of husbands toward certain wives was a major source of dissatisfaction among plural wives. In this and many other cases, the perceived mistreatment revolves around economic and resource issues, as well as the treatment of children. It is not clear from ethnographic accounts whether the "loss of love" or emotional incompatibility are issues in other polygynous cultures. In contrast, unfair treatment of wives by contemporary Mormon fundamentalist husbands is often associated with both practical and social-emotional factors.

Another view of husband–wife relationships is gleaned from the manner in which plural wives relate to one another with respect to their shared husband.[1] The anthropological literature highlights jealousies, competitiveness, tensions, and strains between plural wives. Even though there are many examples of cooperative relationships, the majority of accounts emphasize negative feelings between wives in polygynous families. In some cultures, negative feelings are so prevalent that they have been incorporated into songs, stories, sayings, slogans, and practices. Co-wives are referred to as "the jealous ones" by the Ashanti (Fortes, 1950); the same words denote "co-wife" and "trouble" or "problem" in Bedouin and rural Arab society

(Ginat, 1982); there is a special word in Gusii meaning "hatred between co-wives" (LeVine and LeVine, 1963); the same word means "co-wife" and "rival" among the Yoruba (Ware, 1979); and the phrase "to be jealous" is synonymous with "co-wife" among the Kikuyu (Kenyatta, 1973).

Proverbs, sayings, and songs also speak to the widespread competition and jealousy of plural wives, as demonstrated by the Hindu proverb, "A thousand mustaches can live together, but not four breasts" (Stephens, 1963). The Lodagaba of Africa have a similar saying: "Men can always eat together; it is women [co-wives] who cannot" (Goody, 1958). A Hindu proverb directed at co-wives states, "Never let your husband rest with one wife" (Stephens, 1963). And Muslims refer to the stress connected with a new and often young wife in the saying, "The co-wife is bitter, even if she were honey in a jar" (Stephens, 1963).

Many of these examples pertain to competition and jealousy over property, resources, gifts, the treatment of a wife's children, and general relationships with the husband (Stephens, 1963). The Akon of Africa have songs describing the competition and jealousy of wives as they curry the husband's favor through lovemaking and cooking (Asante-Danko and Van der Geest, 1983). Other Akon songs caution wives to be alert to one another in order to protect their interests. Co-wives among the Gusii are rivals for what the husband can provide by way of wages, his unallocated fields and livestock, and surplus resources and luxuries such as sugar, tea, and clothing (LeVine, 1964). Anger and hostility between wives among the Bena Bena of New Guinea centers on a husband's economic allocations, the fact that he favors one wife's food over that of another, or sexual jealousies; these rivalries sometimes erupt in physical violence between co-wives (Langness, 1969).

About 85% of Yoruba women consider envy, jealousy, hate, and competition between co-wives to be negative aspects of polygyny: these issues are "first and foremost a rivalry to secure maximum access to scarce economic resources" (Ware, 1979, p. 190). At the same time, 60% of these women would apparently be pleased to have a co-wife with whom to gossip and socialize, share housework, and help care for children. Only a small percentage of women in this culture view marriage as ideally involving companionship, sexual satisfaction, and advice-giving between a husband and wife; when surveyed, none mentioned "love" as an important feature of marriages.

Thus jealousy and competitiveness with regard to children and resources seem to be at the root of much of the conflict between co-wives in polygynous societies; sexual and other forms of attention from the husband are often associated with these issues. At the same time, not all co-wife relationships are negative. Co-wives among the Masai of Africa sometimes form close and supportive relationships (Talle, 1987), and among the Mende of Africa (Little, 1951), a senior wife – "the big wife" – sometimes nurtures a young junior wife, almost as a mother would. Co-wives sometimes join forces cooperatively against the husband on certain issues, keep each other's secrets, and withhold information about one another from the husband.[2] Co-wives in many cultures also display a mix of cooperation and competition and of hostility and harmony in their behavior. Some !Kung, co-wives of Africa (Marshall, 1976) share a shelter and fire, cook together or take turns cooking, and even nurse one another's babies. Yet conflict can arise between them over other matters. The Nuer of Africa, too, can be both competitive and cooperative (Evans-Pritchard, 1951). They may cook for one another, feed one another's children, and require children to refer to other wives as "mother" or some other title of respect. Yet they can also be jealous and competitive regarding resources, access to their husband, and other aspects of day-to-day life. Similarly, wives of the Swazi of Africa tend to be suspicious of one another, even believing that their co-wives are practicing witchcraft against them (Kuper, 1950). Yet, they are also often cooperative – preparing and eating meals together and engaging in joint agricultural activities.

In general, there is considerable evidence of competition, jealousy, and conflict between co-wives in many polygynous societies. At the same time, some cultures have mechanisms for formalizing relationships and encouraging cooperation between wives. What is important for our purposes is that tensions and conflict between plural wives in many cultures seems related to practical concerns – over resources, the treatment of children, and a wife's general status in the family. Although some ethnographic reports point to sexual jealousies between wives or favored treatment by the husband of certain wives, scholars rarely focus on "love," attraction, or affection as sources of plural family divisiveness. If social-emotional feelings also contribute to conflict, they only seem to do so in regard to resources, status, and security.

In contrast, social-emotional factors – love, affection, and intimacy – are central to marriage and other close relationships in contemporary American culture. From an ideal perspective, they are the cornerstone of monogamous relationships. Although not always achieved in practice, as reflected in the high divorce rate and incidence of marital infidelity, affection and intimacy between couple members is a cultural ideal. This dyadic ideal is also important to Mormon fundamentalists (along with marriage as a religious obligation), as is their belief in the importance of positive and constructive communal relationships between plural wives. Thus present-day plural families abide by somewhat different marital principles than do traditional polygynous cultures. Some controversy has arisen over this issue, however, since it has also been argued that love, intimacy, and affection were not central features of 19th-century Mormon marriages and, by inference, are perhaps not especially important for present-day fundamentalists.

"Love," affection, and intimacy among fundamentalists

Scholars of 19th-century Mormon plural family life agree that religious values were salient reasons for men and women to enter into plural marriage (Embry, 1987; Young, 1954). Nineteenth-century records, diaries, autobiographies, and statements by church leaders repeatedly refer to men and women entering polygyny for the sake of their religious beliefs. Our interviews with present-day fundamentalists confirm the idea that plural marriage is, in part, a religious act.

Embry (1987), and to some extent Young (1954), leading scholars of 19th-century Mormon family life, claim that love and affection were not central bases for marriage at the time. Drawing on general Victorian and Mormon cultural values of the era, Embry (1987, p. 66) stated:

> The modern perception of men and women marrying for love [in the 19th century] was rarely mentioned in marriage manuals. According to them, love should not be a "guiding star" in marriage plans. "A married couple should feel love for each other, but the love should grow out of the relationship rather than being the cause of it." Instead, men and women were to consider religion, character, and physical traits rather than romantic love.

Brigham Young himself emphasized these values:

> I am almost daily sealing young girls to men of age and experience. Love your duties, sisters. Are you sealed to a good man? Yes; to a man of God. . . . Sisters, do you wish to make yourselves happy? Then what is your duty? It is for you to bear children, in the name of the Lord, that are full of faith and the power of God. . . . Do you look forward to that? Or are you tormenting yourselves by thinking that your husbands do not love you? I would not care whether they loved a particle or not; but I would cry out, like one of old, in the joy of my heart, "I have got a man of the Lord!" "Hallelujah! I am a mother – I have borne an image of God!" (Young, 1954, p. 174)

Many accounts have echoed these ideas, referring to marriage as a "business arrangement," a "chance for a good match," with "no special love" between them. In one case a man "married the second wife, . . . because he felt sorry for her," then married his third because "the principle was being preached," and he married his fourth because the third wife "recommended it" (Embry, 1987, p. 68). In the case of one husband, "there was nothing of romance like boys and girls have nowadays. His wives were selected with attention to heredity, education, and absence of defects. They later came to love and respect him, and were very glad to carry out their biological purpose" (Young, 1954, p. 63).

According to the daughter of a 19th-century polygamist, all six of his wives "profoundly respected" their husband, but he had no "particular" love for them, except for his first wife. "I don't think those polygamists knew what romantic love means," she concluded (Young, 1954, p. 185). One 19th-century wife retrospectively stated:

> Guess I had enough love to do for him as he ought to be done by. I didn't care for all that hugging and kissing stuff. I used to do everything for him. I knitted socks, made his shirts, and got his shoes for him. What more did a man need? . . . I never let any feeling enter into it. You just can't always be thinking about what they [husbands] are doing and watching for him all the time in polygamy. It wouldn't work. (Young, 1954, p. 185)

Indeed some records show that "where the wives did not seem to be particularly fond of their husbands in the romantic sense, they were able to make a better adjustment than were those who were romantically involved with their spouses" (Young, 1954, p. 209). As one plural wife remarked, "A successful polygamous wife must regard her husband with indifference, and with no other feeling than that of reverence, for love we regard as a false sentiment; a feeling which should have no existence in polygamy" (Van Wagoner, 1989, p. 101). In addition, there are numerous examples of men marrying widows or deserted women, women marrying for security or status, or men and women marrying for some reason other than love and affection. (Recall that Brigham Young and other church leaders married some of Joseph Smith's widows following his assassination.)

But that is not the entire story: there is also evidence that emotional attraction, love, and affection were important aspects of 19th-century marriages. One second wife said she was deeply in love with her husband "for years before we were married, and we courted each other for years. . . . He was the best man that ever lived, and good looking, too" (Young, 1954, p. 131). According to another wife, "In the beginning of the movement men took wives because it was a sacred duty, but in later years they were beginning to take them more because they fell in love with younger women" (Campbell and Campbell, 1978, p. 13).

Some scholars see Mormon plural marriages of the era as "essentially Victorian" and based on "the tacit assumption that romantic love was an ideal" (Iversen, 1984, p. 513). Although Americans had earlier associated romantic love with "immaturity, self indulgence, and impermanence," by the middle of the 19th century "romance was . . . emerging as the only acceptable basis for intimacy" (Rothman, 1984, p. 103). Their vision of romantic love, however, "stressed mutuality, communality, and sympathy between man and woman" built on a base of positive and strong emotional relationships (Rothman, 1984, p. 108).

Many cases of unrequited love speak to the importance of personal and affective bonds between a husband and wife as an ideal, even if it was not always the original basis for the match. In one case, a woman married a man to help him meet his social and spiritual obligation. She had hoped to have a deep and warm intimate relationship with him, but he did not seem interested in her: "O if my husband could only love me even a little and not seem to be perfectly indifferent to any sensation of that kind, he cannot know the craving of my nature, he is surrounded with love on every side, and I am cast out" (Eaton-Gadsby and Dushku, 1978, p. 467). In other cases, "there was intense love between husbands and wives; while the love had to be shared, plural husbands and wives did have romantic attachments" (Embry, 1987, p. 51).

Whether 19th-century Mormon marriages and, by inference, contemporary fundamentalist marriages, were based on "love and romance" or religious and other reasons can be debated endlessly. From a historical perspective, it is clear that these plural marriages were influenced to some extent by social trends of the times (Kern, 1981). With the dramatic liberalization of heterosexual relationships and life in general in Western society beginning in the mid to late 1700s, the idea of romantic love took hold. Families began to have less control over partner choices, sexual practices became more liberal, expectations for marital satisfaction mounted, divorce laws became more flexible, birth control and abortion were practiced more freely than before, and women's rights were expanded. Individual freedom of choice was the hallmark of the times (see also Rothman, 1984). But there was a conservative counterforce in the form of new religious movements, including the Mormons, who argued that the liberalizing trends were destroying the moral fabric of society, fostering the breakdown of the family, and resulting in unhealthy gender roles. These groups sought to combat the seeming immorality of society, restore community controls over individual behavior, reestablish proper gender roles, reshape the meaning of marital and heterosexual relationships, and provide a strong social order. Thus the early Mormons downplayed love and romance as the basis of marriage, minimized sexual pleasure and eroticism, emphasized the role of women as homemakers and as subordinate partners to males, and stated that their primary function was to bear and raise children.

Although marriage was expected to be based on religious values in the new Mormon culture, the ideas of individual love, attraction, and freedom of choice were also strong American cultural values. It was not easy to reconcile these opposing norms, and perhaps that is why 19th-century Mormon marriages occurred not only for religious reasons, but also because of feelings of attraction and love, or a mixture of both.

This line of reasoning seems to apply to present-day Mormon fundamentalists. The liberalizing values beginning in the 1960s have recently been rebutted by conservative religious and political movements. Today there is conflict and disagreement about standards of sexual and interpersonal behavior, with conservative factions emphasizing marriage and close relationships based on certain "family values," clearly defined gender roles, and adherence to certain theological and social doctrines. This is certainly the case for contemporary Mormon fundamentalists. At the same time, American culture is firmly anchored in the belief that individuals should have freedom of choice in many life domains and that marriages should be based on intimacy, love, and affection. Thus a variety of motives underlie the relationship between husbands and wives in present-day plural families. And this diversity of values presents extraordinary challenges to the members of those families. They must figure out how to satisfy their religious beliefs concerning the rationale for plural marriage and at the same time deal with cultural values about the unique, distinctive, intimate, and ideally "loving" relationships between the members of a dyad. In addition, they must cope with complex relationships between wives in a communal family that, on the face of it, conflicts with the special nature of each couple in a plural family.

What principles guide each husband–wife couple in a plural family toward a viable and unique dyadic relationship with one another?

We found that couples in modern plural families use several strategies to develop intimate and special dyadic relationships. In part, they try to make each relationship unique and different from others in the family, by highlighting the distinctive personal qualities of the husband and each wife and by "sealing off" each dyad from the others in a family, for example, by not revealing dyadic intimacies to others. Thus each couple works to make itself distinctive. But communal strategies are also used to strengthen each dyadic relationship. An effort is made to facilitate all dyads in a family, stay out of the affairs of other couples, and ensure that husbands are "fair" to all wives.

Making each couple unique. In our interviews, participants constantly emphasized the distinctiveness, uniqueness, intimacy, and special character of each husband–wife dyad in a plural family. Husbands and wives in many families almost seem to seek a kind of "plural monogamy," in which each dyad is similar to a monogamous couple in the larger culture. How do they do this?

There is no specific formula by which couples in plural families achieve a special character. They do many things: they spend time alone, discuss their dyadic relationship, behave in ways that demonstrate their distinctive relationship, ensure that the husband will be available to each wife when needed, pay special attention to or do special things for one another.

Family 1

When we visited Cynthia's home, some time after she became Hal's fourth wife, they acted like newlyweds – showing affection toward one another and telling us how happy and romantic they felt. As he told us previously, Hal believes it is important for each couple in a plural family to have a unique relationship. This principle was brought home when we visited Cynthia's bedroom. Hal pointed out a unique lamp that played music that he had bought for her as a birthday present – actually, it was an extra gift. It was a lavish and unique item that he had purchased on an impulse because he was so pleased with their relationship and wanted to do something special for her. They were both proud of the lamp as a symbol of their happy marriage.

In another discussion, Norma, the second wife, pointed out that it is easy for a wife to feel emotionally deserted if she and her husband don't have an intimate and distinctive bond. She said she felt that way when Hal first married Cynthia, in part because they didn't have enough quality time alone. Hal admitted that things had been difficult between them but that they had overcome that stressful period. Norma agreed but said that they had to continue working on their relationship.

Family 3

William claims that he works hard to learn about his wives and their unique needs. He also tries to spend special time alone with each of them, even though they all live in the same home. When each couple is alone, the others try not to disturb them.

Danielle, the second wife, said it wasn't always that way; at an earlier time, William failed to recognize that each of their dyadic relationships needed to be separate and unique. Sometimes they all met in one bedroom, for example, where he would lie on the bed (he had serious back problems) while the wives gathered around him. Danielle resented using a bedroom and bed in this way; it somehow violated the idea of each marriage being separate and special. William agreed, saying that he came to realize that he couldn't treat his wives as "a group" but had to have a distinctive relationship with each of them.

Family 4

When we arrived by car at the family compound, Harry greeted each of his five wives in a distinctive way, showing affection and saying some personal thing to each of them. During the course of the several days we stayed with Harry, Anna, Ruth, Belle, Eve, and Shirley, we observed that he was careful to say something special about himself and each wife in their presence. He showed pride in Eve's remodeling of her home, the special sanctuary Ruth's bedroom provided when he needed respite from his responsibilities, the fine children he and Belle had, and so on. In so doing Harry was representing each of his marriages as a unique and special relationship.

Family 9

Joyce, the first wife, said that she never feels neglected or abandoned by John, because he is very sensitive to their bond. He always calls her regularly, no matter where he is, and she is comfortable with the special nature of their relationship and knows that he will be there when he needs her. Clara expressed the same feeling.

Sometimes even simple actions contribute to the special quality of a particular dyad in a plural family.

Family 5

Valerie, the second wife, regularly cuts Howard's hair. She is skilled at it and is the only wife of the four who does so. Although a small act, it probably adds a measure of distinctiveness to their relationship.

Family 9

During one of our conversations, John was talking in an animated way and took off his glasses to clean them. Joyce got up from the sofa, went over to John, took the glasses from him, and cleaned them herself. He smiled and thanked her, and we sensed that they had followed this private routine many times before.

Family 10

Barry's eight wives, with whom we had a lengthy discussion, agree that they each work hard to have a special relationship with him and that they have generally succeeded in doing so. They all feel that he comes to them or attends to problems when they need him – day or night – and that they have "quality" and personal time with him, even though they sometimes wish that they could have more time together. They agree that it isn't easy to develop and maintain their unique marriage relationships but feel that they have done a pretty good job so far.

Nineteenth-century Mormon plural families were not too different in their emphasis on dyadic relationships. As one man said, "The same love burned in my heart for Maria as ever came in the love affairs with Ellen; that does not mean that I loved Ellen less nor Maria less. The heart of a man grows and expands with knowledge and understanding of the correctness of the plural wife system" (Embry, 1987, p. 128).

Highlighting the unique personal qualities of the husband and each wife. In addition to casting each marriage in a distinctive light, we also learned that some partners acknowledge each other's special talents or personal qualities. Most interesting is the conscious attempt frequently made to emphasize that a husband is (or should be) "a different person" with each wife. By construing each wife as a distinctive person and the husband as a kind of "multiple personality," every couple becomes unique.

Some husbands highlighted the special and different talents of their wives.

Family 1

As described earlier, Cynthia, the fourth wife, showed us her honeymoon album and a book of poetry she had written about their love for one another. Hal also showed us a framed poem that Cynthia had written commemorating their marriage. Hal was clearly proud of her artistic and literary accomplishments, and she was very pleased with his attention.

As Norma, the second wife, took us through her home, Hal expressed his pride in her writing talents, showing us some of her prose and poetry. He also said how proud he is of her work but added that she underestimates her abilities. She was pleased by his comments.

Family 2

Rebecca is extremely busy with two jobs – she has an office position and runs her own seasonal business. David not only praised Rebecca for her hard work but expressed sensitivity to the physical and emotional stress she faces in trying to do so much. They agree that as her business grows she will have to quit her other job and lead a more orderly life. In the discussion, he was not only sympathetic to and appreciative of her hard work but commended her business skills.

Wives also acknowledge their own talents and skills and their expectations that their husband will treat them as independent and competent.

Family 6

Hilda views herself as a very independent person – more so than many plural wives, she says. She undertakes a variety of projects on her own, visits anyone she wants and whenever she chooses, even though Seymour doesn't always approve. She recently attended a family reunion of her parents and relatives, even though he discouraged her from going and later criticized her. In front of him she said that part of the reason she went was to show him that he needed to respect her independence and that her children needed to learn that they too are individuals.

Family 10

Our sense is that the eight wives in this family are very independent on a day-to-day basis and express themselves as quite different people. They control their own funds, operate according to their own lifestyle, seem strong willed about various matters, and were not at all hesitant to question us about our work or lives. They also pointed out that, unlike monogamous wives whose husbands are around to help with or solve problems, plural wives must take care of their business alone – including home and automobile repairs, which are traditionally men's responsibilities. They noted that being alone much of the time increases their sense of self-confidence and self-worth, and they expressed these views with forcefulness and vigor. During the whole discussion Barry was either very quiet or simply concurred with what his wives were saying.

A fascinating mechanism for making salient the uniqueness of individuals is to treat the husband as a "different" person in each dyad in a plural family – it is almost as if he had a "multiple personality."

Family 1

To make their marriages work, the four wives agreed that Hal had to be a different person with each of them. To illustrate the point, Norma said, half jokingly, but also half seriously, "Sometimes I don't like *her* husband," referring to her co-wife Joan. (In another family, one wife said it a little differently to her co-wife: "Sometimes I like *your* husband better than I like *mine*.") The wives acknowledge that it isn't easy for Hal to be a different person with each of them. But, to the extent that he succeeds, each marriage benefits, and he grows personally.

Family 5

In discussing the challenges and complexities of being wives in a plural family, Constance, Valerie, Barbara, and Rose admit that it isn't easy for Howard. Valerie said to Rose "*You* had a better husband when you married Howard than *I* did," implying that he has changed for the better by virtue of his earlier three marriages, and is a "different" and "better" person than he had been previously.

Amplifying on the challenge she saw Howard facing, Barbara said, "I am glad that I am not a man; being a different person with each wife is more than I could do."

Family 9

John, Joyce, Clara, and Marjorie live in one home. John described how difficult it can be when he comes home from work and has to be three different people in three different marriages all at once – while still struggling with the pressures of work. It takes enormous emotional energy to deal with each wife in a unique way at the same time and to be sensitive to "who he is" in each relationship.

Protecting dyadic intimacies. An explicit norm in many contemporary plural families is that each husband–wife pair should not share personal intimacies about their relationship with other wives in the family. In personal matters, the ideal is for each couple to be "sealed off" from the others; that is, no details are disclosed about intimate marital issues, and no one probes into the affairs of other dyads in the family. In many respects, this norm is similar to that followed by monogamous couples. It may be that this principle is more openly defined in plural families because of the potential harm to dyadic and communal bonds if intimate matters between a husband and each wife are too widely known.

Family 1

Charlotte said that she never discusses with other wives the intimate details of her relationship with Hal, including their sexual relationship. Hal believes it is also important for a man not to disclose intimate things about his relationship with one wife to another wife. A husband needs to be trusted by each wife, he said, and each wife must be confident that her husband will keep their personal affairs and "secrets" private.

Family 5

Howard, Constance, Valerie, Barbara, and Rose agree that they should not tell one another about their personal relationships with Howard and that he has "to keep secrets" and treat each relationship as an independent and separate affair. Thus if a wife wants to become pregnant, she should discuss the matter with her husband so that he can make a decision about spending time with her; it is not a matter to be discussed with other wives. Or a husband should give money directly to a wife, rather than giving it to another wife to deliver to her. The principle they abide by, they said, is to avoid intruding on the personal and intimate affairs of each husband–wife relationship.

This was also an important principle in 19th-century Mormon plural families. Orson Pratt, an early church leader, advised that a husband should not "betray the confidence of one wife to another, nor speak of one wife's faults to another," and a wife should "never seek to prejudice the mind of her husband against any of his other wives, for the purpose of exulting herself in his estimation." She should also "speak no evil of her husband to any of the rest of the family" (Young, 1954, p. 51). Taking such advice to heart, one husband made "every effort not only to be fair and just about material things but also . . . to keep the confidences which he gets from one wife or the other" (Young, 1954, p. 202). Wives, too, were careful not to carry "tales from one wife to the other" (Young, 1954, p. 213). One wife said, "This, however, is as far as telling goes. Each wife knows that he respects her confidence." A daughter said of her father: "Father was very wise. He never carried the stories from one family to another and he never made a comparison" (Embry, 1987, p. 129).

Failing to meet principles of dyadic uniqueness

When these norms are violated, relationships may be marred by jealousy, loneliness, anger, conflict, separation, and even divorce, especially if conflicts and disagreements have crept into other life domains. A major source of stress and tension is a wife's feeling that she does not have enough time with her husband, is unable to build a unique and special relationship with him, or is not fully appreciated, understood, or loved by him. Very often these feelings are compounded by jealousy of the husband's relationship with other wives.

Family 1

Norma, the second wife, has been unhappy about her relationship with Hal since his recent marriage to Cynthia, the fourth wife. During the courtship, early in the marriage, and for a long time thereafter, Norma felt that Hal showed favoritism to Cynthia. Norma also felt that he didn't fully understand her as a person, their relationship became fragmentary, and they spent too little time developing their own marriage. She even said she felt abandoned by him. She explained that it is not jealousy between wives, but a feeling of being deserted by a husband – regardless of his relationships with other wives.

Hal admitted to Norma that he has only recently begun to understand the depth of her feelings, that he genuinely loves her, and that he is attempting to rectify the situation by spending more quality time with her. Part of the problem, he said, is that he is spread rather thinly and doesn't have the time to meet all of his obligations. They both agree that they still have a long way to go to work things out.

In a different discussion, Joan, the first wife, expressed strong feelings about the many years it took her and Hal to achieve the good relationship they have at present. She, too, had been unhappy for years, partly because Hal had failed to protect her from being mistreated by a former first wife. And when he finally acted and that wife left the family, he soon married Norma. As a result, she found it was very difficult for them to establish a distinctive marital relationship. It took her nine years to get over her anger and distress about her relationship with Hal. They are happy now, but she described those earlier events with intensity and considerable affect.

Family 6

Holly, the fifth wife, said that her relationship with Seymour is not as good as those of the other wives – she feels that they are not as close to one another as she would like, he is not patient with her, and he ignores her a great deal of the time.

Andrea, the third wife, is comfortable in her relationship with Seymour. Yet she still feels pangs of jealousy and becomes upset when she sees him expressing affection in her presence to another wife. She gets angry with herself for feeling that way but can't help it. (In another discussion, Seymour told us that he tries to avoid showing affection to any wife in the presence of others, to avoid feelings of jealousy and competition.) Hilda, the first wife, chimed in, saying that she has similar feelings of jealousy when Seymour opens the car door for Marlene, the seventh and youngest wife (he never does it for her!).

In emphasizing the need to keep each marriage separate, Seymour told a story about a man who slept with several wives in the same bed and had sexual relations with one in the presence of others. For this, and probably other reasons, there was a great deal of conflict and upheaval in this family. He told of another case in which wives could hear their husband having sex with other wives because of poor insulation and squeaking beds. Seymour claims that everyone was embarrassed by the situation, and the family suffered considerable stress. These stories illustrate what can happen when the basic principle regarding the privacy and uniqueness of each couple is violated.

Family 9

John and Joyce had been married for 20 years when they joined the fundamentalist group and entered into plural marriage. Even though they have a good relationship, Joyce continues to feel insecure about her relationship with John and is jealous of his relationships with Clara and Marjorie. She still gets upset when she sees him express affection to one of the other wives. And she struggles not to think about him in bed with another wife, saying, "If you think about it, you will 'lose it.' " Although she is adjusting to John's relationships with Clara and Marjorie, Joyce went on to say, "Plural family life is a mighty hard day-to-day struggle." Clara agreed, admitting that she, too, is sometimes jealous of John's relationships with the other wives, but that one has to cope. She said, "There are good days and there are bad days, and you either swim or drown."

Family 14

When Molly joined Harvey and Sally in a plural family, Harvey tried to be equally attentive to both wives. As a result, he often left the bed of one wife in the middle of the night to go to the bed of the other. After a while this practice began to be a problem for the wives, Sally said, because they were losing a sense of having separate relationships with Harvey. It was as if their identities as people and as wives were being blurred.

Many of these issues were confirmed by the leader of the Metropolitan City group, who does a great deal of marital and personal counseling. He told us that members of plural families, especially wives, often come to him because they are upset about not achieving satisfactory dyadic relationships. Many of these wives feel that their husband does not spend enough time with them, that he is not fully attentive to all his wives, that they feel abandoned emotionally, not loved, lonely, and so on. His experience and the case examples reported above indicate that certain couples in plural families fail to meet the principles enunciated earlier; that is, they fail to establish unique husband–wife relationships in each marriage, to highlight individual qualities of family members, or to maintain strong boundaries between dyads. These are among the important factors that lead to separation and divorce.

Family 12

Lauren, Fred's second wife, had many complaints about her relationship with Fred and with Elaine, the first wife. One major problem was her feeling that she and Fred never developed a close dyadic bond. She felt that it was hard to talk to him, he passed off her complaints and feelings as unimportant, and he wasn't there when she needed him. As examples, he showed no warmth or support when she had a miscarriage, he allowed her to do heavy yard work in the late stages of a pregnancy, and he did not act very concerned following a difficult birth. (As a counterexample, she described how elated she was when he once took her to a party at his company and once shopped with her for living room furniture. She said she felt like a "real wife" on those rare occasions.)

Lauren also claimed that Fred let it be known that their relationship was not as satisfactory as his marriage to Elaine. Late in their marriage Lauren said that he baldly stated that he cared for her less than he cared for Elaine, and that their sexual relationship was not very good. And he behaved in many ways to show those feelings – spending more time with Elaine, helping furnish her home more nicely than Lauren's, treating Elaine's children better, going on vacations with Elaine, making Lauren sit apart from him and Elaine when they went to the movies, spending more time with Elaine's parents and relatives than with hers, and so on.

Lauren also said that Fred violated the norm of maintaining each couple's intimacies. He discussed with Lauren his sexual relationship with Elaine, pretended that he was with Elaine when having sex with Lauren, and told Lauren on one occasion that he couldn't have sex with her because he had just made love with Elaine.

Lauren also said that Fred always demeaned her personal qualities – her cooking and house care, her artistic talents, her children and childrearing practices, her general demeanor – and he called any expression of her interest in sexual pleasure "evil." In such cases, he always compared her unfavorably with Elaine.

Here is a case in which every principle enunciated earlier appears to have been violated – through unsatisfactory development of each dyadic relationship in a plural family, denial of the special individuality of each participant, and insufficient "sealing off" of personal aspects of each marital relationship.

In some respects the challenges faced by a husband and each plural wife are similar to those of monogamous couples. They must develop a special and unique relationship, acknowledge the distinctive personal qualities of each participant, and keep the intimate and personal "business" of the relationship to themselves. But meeting these goals is especially challenging for members of contemporary plural families. After all, it is not easy for wives to see their husband in multiple intimate, personal, and affectionate relationships while proclaiming the special nature of their own individual relationship. Nor is it easy for a husband to make each relationship with his wives distinctive and unique and to be a "different person" with each wife. Managing multiple dyadic relationships is difficult for both husbands and wives, and feelings of jealousy, uncertainty, stress, and marital strain are common. So, it is challenging for everyone to work out healthy and satisfactory dyadic relationships in modern plural families.

What communal principles do participants in a plural family follow to ensure the well-being of each husband–wife couple?

It is challenging enough to develop a close husband–wife relationship in the context of other such relationships in a family. But it is also difficult for participants to foster close relationships with others in a plural family. Doing so is important, since a goal of contemporary fundamentalists is to have a healthy balance of both dyadic and communal relationships in a plural family.

Our analysis suggests that, in theory at least, they seek communality by actively facilitating the well-being of other husband–wife pairs (in addition to working on their own relationship), not intruding into the personal affairs of other relationships, emphasizing the notion that the husband should be "fair" to all wives, and acknowledging the uniqueness of other relationships and the special qualities of individuals in other relationships.

Enhancing and facilitating all dyadic relationships. Implicitly or explicitly, members of some plural families recognize and act in ways to foster, nurture, support, or facilitate each other's dyadic bonds. Given their common fate in a single family, if wives, for example, are able to support one another's relationship with their husband, and everyone does it, then each of their relationships, as well as the family as a whole, has a better chance of being viable and avoiding destructive conflict.

Family 4
When Harry was seriously ill and hospitalized, Anna, Ruth, Belle, Eve, and Shirley took turns visiting and staying with him for a day at a time. When he returned home to recuperate and was essentially bedridden, he still moved to each wife's home on successive nights. He could hardly walk but insisted that he rotate among homes every day. Here we see Harry and his wives acknowledging and respecting the worthiness of each of their marriage relationships during a time of family crisis.

In one of our discussions, Harry said that it is best to have a small number of wives in a plural family (he considered his five marriages to constitute a small number!). Doing so allows him to not only develop a good relationship with each wife but also helps him foster good relationships between wives, be aware of family events, and step in when conflicts or upheavals arise. So Harry is sensitive to maintaining both individual and collective relationships among family members.

Shirley, the fifth wife, told a story illustrating that every marriage in the family is respected by Harry and the other wives. She, Belle, and Harry met some people who didn't know that they were fundamentalists. Belle introduced Harry as her husband, and then Harry introduced Shirley as his wife. The people were flabbergasted and couldn't figure things out until they explained who they were. Shirley described the incident as having been great fun; it also indirectly reflects everyone's respect for each marriage.

Family 5

Barbara, Howard's third wife, emphasized that each marriage not only needs to be on its own but also requires support and help from all members of a family. She described an incident in which Valerie, the second wife, suddenly became ill, and the other wives encouraged Howard to take her home immediately. In reflecting on the event, she felt pleased that they all rose to the occasion and that each of their marriages is independent but still part of a whole.

In discussing this further, the wives agreed that they often encourage Howard to be with whichever of them needs him at the time and that by doing so they nurture each of their independent relationships with him. Indeed, they described incidents in which they sometimes actually "ordered" Howard to see another wife because they knew she needed him. As they put it, they have struggled to reach a level of maturity at which they respect the love between Howard and each of them, and doing so does not take away from their own love. In fact, they noted their feelings of regret and sorrow when Howard and one of them had conflict.

With respect to Howard's role, even though he isn't with them every night, they say that "day or night we have the security that he will come to any of us whenever we need him."

Although these ideals are not always easily put into practice, they are something to which the family members aspire. As such, they are a norm for achieving a viable interplay of emotional and affective dyadic and communal processes.

Family 6

Hilda, the first wife, said that she gets upset if Seymour does not behave properly toward the other wives and mentioned that she has taken on the role of making sure that he treats all eight wives in an appropriate way. As she has matured and become more successful in plural family life, she wants to see Seymour have good relationships with all his wives. "If he has a good marriage with them, then it is likely that he will have a healthy relationship with me," she said.

To illustrate her feelings of support for all the other marriages in the family, Hilda told two stories. First, when one of the sons in the family died suddenly, Seymour was spending the day with a different wife than the mother of the son. When she learned of the news, Hilda contacted Seymour and told him that his duty was to be with the wife whose son had died. He followed her advice. Second, Hilda told about the time that she and Seymour were present at the birth of another wife's child. After the baby was born, Hilda watched Seymour lean down close to the new mother and thank her for bringing a child into the world. Hilda was so touched that she broke down and cried because of her pleasure at this incident. Hilda told these stories to illustrate her active interest in supporting each of the marriages in her family.

To further illustrate their concern for each other, Seymour told the story of the death of a four-year-old son. He and the child's mother were crying and mourning, when one of the other wives heard them, came into their bedroom, and cried along with them.

Family 10
One wife indicated that she had gone through a difficult adjustment when Barry married two previously divorced wives with a total of 13 children. Barry was very busy with his new families, and she eventually learned that she had to "let go" so that he could spend time and absorb them into the family.

Joanne, the third wife, observed that now she has matured and better understands plural family life she actually feels joy when she sees Barry expressing affection toward another wife. Dorothy, the fifth wife, went on to say that she would be concerned if Barry was cool toward another wife; it might be that something was wrong between them.

Family 18
Charles spoke at length and with great feeling about loving each wife in a unique way and his special relationship with each of them. He highlighted the fact that each of his four wives has a distinctive personality, that he tries to support each of them, and that he wants each wife to support the other relationships with him. He put it this way: "I need to love each wife in her own individuality, but I must also try to make them feel as if they are not individuals, but are parts of a single and unified family."

Susan, the first wife, agreed and told a story illustrating the point. She was helping out at a girls' camp and was lonely for Charles and the other wives. One day she was surprised to see Charles and Nancy, the second wife, who made a trip on the spur of the moment to see her. She was so overjoyed and pleased to see them that she broke into tears. She was overwhelmed, she said, to see that Charles and Nancy cared so much for her, which added to her feelings of loyalty and pleasure at being part of the family.

Similar examples of wives supporting one another's marriages appear in accounts of 19th-century plural marriages. One wife would not allow her husband to favor her, and "did everything she could" to make another wife happy: "I think she told him ways in which he slighted me, for when she did he came to beg my pardon" (Young, 1954, p. 182). All the members of the family "wanted harmony and they were strong for loyalty and harmony in the home. They were all proud, proud of the fact that they could live together. Auntie [the first wife] believed that the family should be united and she did everything to make it possible" (Young, 1954, p. 213).

Avoiding intrusions on other husband–wife relationships. As discussed earlier, many families follow the principle that each husband–wife dyad should maintain strong boundaries around itself with respect to personal and intimate topics. Some wives also said that they tried to stay out of other couples' business and did not ask about or pry into their personal affairs. In this way, they ensured that each dyadic relationship would remain unique and independent, and that all would be communally respected and supported.

Family 5
Barbara, the third wife, spoke eloquently about keeping her relationship with Howard separate and distinct from those of the other wives but also emphasized that each of the wives should not intrude on Howard's other marriages. It is sometimes hard to do this, she said, but she eventually realized that it had to be done, or else her marriage and all the others would fall on hard times. "Letting go," staying out of the way, not becoming too involved, and allowing other relationships in the family to grow in their own way, she said, is crucial to the well-being of her marriage to Howard, and to his relationships with the other wives.

The husband being fair to all wives. Treating wives fairly in a variety of life domains is a normative ideal and an important communal principle in both pioneer and contemporary Mormon plural families. Difficult as it may be to follow this precept from day to day, the challenge is probably especially great in social-emotional, affective, and personal areas of marriage relationships. But failing to do so may jeopardize family viability, since the concept of close and unique relationships between a husband and wife often directly emphasizes emotions, love, and affective feelings. Husbands and wives in many plural families claim to be sensitive to the issue and address it in several ways. One strategy is to be careful about showing too much affection to one wife in the presence of others.

Family 18
Charles said that he is very conscious about not giving too much attention or showing too much affection to a particular wife when they are all together. Doing so can be upsetting and might give the impression that he is favoring one over the others.

Family 6
Tamara told us that Seymour was once sitting in one of their living rooms with several wives, and she came up behind him and put her arms around him. He removed her arms, whispering that she should not do that for fear of arousing the jealousy of the other wives.

Although they all acknowledge that Seymour should avoid expressing his feelings toward each of them in the presence of other wives, they accept the fact that there are occasions when he can treat a wife in a special way. And they accept this because they consider him to be generally fair and honorable toward them. In a lighter vein, they joked about Seymour occasionally getting in trouble by being unfair to one of them, and the way they all "gang up" on him to set things straight.

Family 8
Ira, an elder of the church who does a great deal of marital and family counseling, told of a wife who wanted to leave her husband because she felt that he was not treating her fairly. The other wives supported her, met with the husband as a group, and pressured him into changing his ways. It apparently worked.

Family 4
We mentioned earlier that Harry is careful to greet each wife in a special way when he returns to the family compound after a trip and thereby emphasizes his unique relationship with each wife. At the same time, by attending more or less equally to each wife, he is being fair and not favoring any of them. Therefore, his actions reflect attention to both dyadic and communal aspects of his relationship with each wife.

Fairness was an equally important principle in 19th-century Mormon plural families. One daughter recalled that her father was extremely fair "There was just too much love there. He would never play favorites at all. He was the kindest and gentlest of men" (Embry, 1987, p. 128). And a wife in the family said her husband was one "amongst a thousand," who was always "firm and decisive" yet kind and forbearing: "A good deal of good can be done in a family of many wives when the man takes a wise course. It is in a man's hands to make his family happy or unhappy to a very good extent; when they are striving to do right, if he is unwise in his course he will make them unhappy; and he can be to his family sunshine or shade" (Embry, 1987, p. 128).[3]

Thus, a sense of harmony in plural families can prevail if participants communally support one another's dyadic relationships, collectively protect the intimacy and special character of each husband–wife bond, and ensure fairness in the way wives are treated emotionally. Although many husbands and wives articulate these principles and some put them into practice, it doesn't always happen. And when they fail to understand or act in accordance with these ideals, conflict, upheaval, and family disruption may occur.

Failing to meet the principles of communal support

We described earlier a number of cases of martial disruption or stress associated with unsatisfactory dyadic relations between a husband and wife. Such problems are often exacerbated by or stem from communal issues involving other couples in a family.

Family 6
Three of the wives feel that Seymour is not always fair or sensitive to their emotional needs in comparison with those of the other wives. Holly, the fifth wife, often feels inferior to the other wives, sensing that she is not as skillful in relating to him. And he doesn't help – ignoring her expressions of insecurity, not being patient or listening to her, and seemingly treating her more casually than he does the other wives. Other wives also described instances of his insensitivity to them: his favoring a younger wife by opening car doors for her but not for the other wives, marrying a new wife and paying a great deal of attention to her shortly after having married another wife, and not working hard to develop their relationship before marrying again.

Family 13
Muriel has been in several plural marriages, a widow in one and a divorcée in a couple of others. In one case, her husband was much more openly affectionate to her than he was to her co-wife. The behavior caused a family upheaval. Muriel, the preferred one in this case, wasn't especially fond of her co-wife and didn't do anything to change her own

favored status – probably adding to the disruption in that family. So both Muriel and her husband violated some basic principles of communal support of all relationships in a plural family.

In another plural marriage that wasn't going very well, Muriel claimed that her husband gossiped about her to the other wives, saying that she was a demanding and bad person; he also gossiped to her about the other wives – all of which created a great deal of upheaval and poor relationships in the family. In this case, the husband apparently violated the principle of keeping personal aspects of relationships private and not supporting all relationships or individuals.

Family 14

Sally, the first wife, eventually left Harvey and Molly, the second wife, in part because of their social-emotional relationships. Sally claimed that whereas Harvey was equally attentive to them early in their plural family life, he began to ignore her later on. She asked him to spend more time with her, but he fended her off, devoting more and more time to Molly. And Molly became openly competitive with Sally in emotional issues, disclosing her own intimate activities with Harvey and probing Sally about hers, probably to show her advantage. Sally joined in this "emotional competition." As another intrusion, Molly once insisted on joining Sally and Harvey for dinner when they were celebrating a wedding anniversary; she then ruined their celebration by behaving badly toward Sally.

Here we see violations of all the communal principles described earlier – a husband treating wives unequally, wives disclosing and probing into one another's personal affairs with the husband, and wives not supporting each other's emotional relationships with their husband.

Family 12

As noted earlier, Lauren, the second wife, felt unfairly treated by Fred in comparison with the way he treated Elaine, especially on the social-emotional level. He was unusually affectionate and teased and tickled Elaine in front of Lauren – but never acted like that with her, did not show sympathy for her during stressful times, but did so with Elaine, and so on.

Lauren claims that Elaine didn't help either. She openly competed for Fred's attention, demeaned Lauren in many ways, and always tried to show that her relationship with Fred was better than Lauren's. And Elaine allegedly feigned illness on occasion in order to gain more of Fred's attention, even doing so on Lauren and Fred's second wedding anniversary and thus ruining the celebration. So both Fred and Elaine seemed to have violated some basic communal principles of plural family life.

Such preferential treatment by a husband has occurred in other contemporary plural families (Merrill, 1975), not to mention 19th-century Mormon families:[4]

> Whenever we went in the carriage, it waited for us at the first [wife's] home, and when we returned, it was unloaded there. It was assumed to be the proper thing for Aunt Harriet [the first wife] to always be in the front seat with father, and mother in the back. "See, there she goes," my mother would remark as father would drive off with Aunt Harriet. "She never lets him go without her." (Young, 1954, p. 198)

In one pioneer case, five wives complained of the husband's favoritism toward a new wife, who got to spend more time with him than the others: "she could have things" that they couldn't have, and could even make him "believe the moon was made of green cheese. She's caused me more trouble than a little bit. I don't mind saying it, because she knows" (Embry, 1987, p. 146). In her autobiography, Annie Tanner (1983) described her jealousy when her husband seemed to be giving greater attention to his other wife. She also recounted that in her father's family, one wife resented the fact that another wife was given a bureau that had a "better shine" than her own.

Mary Ann Young, Brigham Young's second wife, once commented on the displacement of still another wife as his favorite: "God will be very cruel if he does not give us poor women adequate compensation for the trials we have endured in polygamy." Another wife, once highly favored by Brigham Young but now replaced by a new wife, suffered "the torments of the damned" over being displaced by Brigham Young's younger wife, Amelia Folsom.

> When a friend asked one of Mary Ann's daughters if it did not grieve her mother to see Young's devotion to his new wife, she replied "Mother does not care. She is past being grieved by his conduct, but, on the other hand, it gives her most intense satisfaction to see Emmeline [the newly displaced wife] suffer as she does. She can understand now what mother had to undergo in past years. In fact, all the women are glad that Emmeline is getting her turn at last." (Van Wagoner, 1989, p. 100)

Summary

In this chapter we attempted to gain a glimpse into participants' emotions about one another and to understand how they manage those feelings in the complicated context of modern plural families. We discovered that plural husbands and wives follow several principles to help each couple achieve the cultural ideal of a loving, affectionate, and close dyadic relationship. They spend time alone, reinforce the special nature of their relationship, do special things for one another, and so on. They also try to acknowledge the distinctive personalities and talents of each family member, especially in regard to their marital bond. In some families the husband is even depicted as a "different person" in each of his marriage relationships, so as to underscore their unique and distinctive character. Another strategy is to avoid disclosing their private affairs to other wives and thereby to seal off close emotional aspects of each dyad from the others. We found several marriages in which some combination of these principles had been violated, and the result was conflict, upheaval, and even divorce.

Still another challenge for plural marriages is to build a communal and harmonious family composed of several close dyadic relationships. Members of some families try to actively support one another's dyadic relationships, for example, by acting on their behalf or helping out in times of stress. They also avoid intruding on the personal affairs of other couples, staying out of their way, and allowing others to develop their own approach to marriage. Participants emphasized that a husband must be fair and attentive to all wives, not favoring one over the others, not showing affection to wives in front of one another, and so on.

Members of contemporary Mormon plural families use these dyadic and communal principles and associated actions to ensure the social-emotional well-being of each couple and the plural family as a whole. But things don't always work out. These principles are not always put into practice or they are violated. Thus a husband might favor one wife over another and make his feelings known; wives may blatantly compete for a husband's affection or undercut one another; intimacies may be disclosed to others; or a husband may fail to be fair to wives in a variety of ways.

Although not wholly separable from aspects of plural family life discussed in other chapters, the emotional and personal relationships of a man and a woman, and of a man and several women, are central to the viability of modern plural family life. Equally important, however, are the feelings and personal relationships between wives, as discussed in chapter 17.

17

Relationships between wives

Plural family life is greatly affected by relationships between wives that are more or less independent of the husband. These relationships revolved around their general feelings about living with one another in plural families, their mutual responsibilities for managing homes, how they get along rearing their children, and their interpersonal compatibility.

Home management

Cooking, cleaning, meal preparation, and other aspects of managing a home are important social and religious responsibilities of contemporary plural wives. Needless to say, women in American and Western cultures have also have had the same responsibilities for generations – and still do today, notwithstanding the recent trends that have blurred rigid gender roles.

A fundamentalist Mormon woman's role in the home has both theological and cultural roots. According to Mormon doctrine, a man is the religious and social leader of the family, teaches his wives and children theological values, and may govern his family in their own heavenly "universe" in the afterlife. Women are expected to maintain "stewardship" of the home; raise and teach their children proper social, moral, and religious doctrine; and strive to build a healthy relationship with their husband. The home is also a place where a wife can display her own personality, creativity, and independence from other wives. Thus managing the home is a strong gender-linked responsibility of women in plural families. In this sense, caring for the home has strong dyadic meanings since it bears directly on husband–wife and wife–children relationships. This theme has been illustrated in other chapters dealing with wives' attachments to homes, living arrangements, and other aspects of plural family life.

Home management also bears on communal relationships between wives, especially when they share a dwelling. Although they are expected to be harmonious, mutually supportive, and part of a unified plural family

– and presumably to share in home management – one may wonder how this works out in practice. It is easy to envision conflicts and tensions since wives may have different styles, attitudes, and skills in meal preparation, cleaning, and other aspects of day-to-day life in homes. Problems in these areas often arise when new wives arrive to live with an established wife (see chapter 9).

Communal home management styles

There is no single formula for managing homes when wives live in the same dwelling. What they do depends on many factors – the configuration of the home, whether or not they work, family size, children's ages, and how well wives get along in general. Often, wives must experiment and work out a system that suits their individual and collective preferences and personalities. Sometimes they share tasks together; sometimes they have fixed responsibilities for different chores; sometimes they take turns doing things. Many wives seem to develop home management systems that have both dyadic and communal aspects. And when they do so to a reasonable extent, relationships between wives are often positive and constructive.

Family 1
Whereas they had all previously lived in separate dwellings for many years, Joan and Norma, the first and second wives, now share a home, and Charlotte and Cynthia live in another home. Each pair of wives uses a different system of home management. For example, Joan and Norma share a kitchen, shopping, and cooking, and they and their children eat meals together. They also have "teams" of children who do various chores that each wife supervises. Things have worked out quite well, they say, perhaps because they have been friends over the years, and even lived together once before.

Charlotte and Cynthia also share a home. However, they do things somewhat less communally. Although they shop for food and supplies cooperatively and do some joint planning, they and their children eat at different times because of work and school schedules. So they manage the home in a combined dyadic and communal fashion, whereas the other pair of wives tilt more in the communal direction.

Family 7
Sarah, the first wife, works outside the home, so she has few home-management responsibilities. Patricia and Audrey share many of the household duties; one of them regularly prepares breakfast and dinner, and the other takes care of lunch and tends to all the children. Although

primarily communal, this system has dyadic features in that the two wives at home can manage their separate assignments as they see fit.

Family 10

This family of eight wives lives in three homes; the wives have different systems for managing day-to-day life. Anita, the first wife, lives alone and takes care of her own place. Two pairs of wives live on separate sides of a large home; each pair shares a kitchen and living room. One set of wives alternate responsibilities for meal preparation every three days; the co-wife does other chores. The two wives on the other side of the home alternate the cooking every day. Another subset of wives living elsewhere also take turns daily in home management tasks.

Regardless of where and with whom they live, all the wives often participate together in bulk food purchases and give advice to one another on cooking, conserving money, and managing the home. So they engage in many communal home management activities, although their separate rotating responsibilities have a partly dyadic quality.

Family 18

Susan, Angela, and Linda the first, third, and fourth wives, share a home; Nancy lives in her own place. The three who live together share all household tasks on a rotating basis. In an interesting blend of dyadic and communal management, they link meal preparation to the days each wife spends with Charles. Thus on the day that a wife is with Charles she does the cooking, but they all eat together.

Family 11

Benjamin, Katherine, Melba, Kelly, and Mary live in one home. Mary is the only wife who is not working, and she is responsible for preparing breakfasts and lunches and also for caring for all the children in the family. The other wives assist with the evening meal, and they all clean the home together. Each wife has other independent responsibilities. For example, Melba does the shopping, Kelly manages the family budget, and so on. All in all, they have worked out a system that has a mixture of communal and dyadic responsibilities and independence.

Family 5

At one time, Constance and Valerie lived together and took turns cooking and doing other chores on a weekly basis. However, each of them was always responsible for cleaning and managing her own bedroom, doing her own laundry, and managing other aspects of her life separately from the other wife. (Caring for one's own room and personal things is quite common in most plural families.)

Similar patterns of sharing household responsibilities are reported in autobiographies and accounts of other contemporary plural families. Melissa Merrill (1975) managed the home and cared for her own and another wife's children when the second wife worked. In one family in a present-day rural group, five wives alternate weekly in managing the family's kitchen, gardens, and laundry (Bradley, 1990). Wives in another family divide responsibilities on a permanent basis, with one wife managing child care; another wife doing the family sewing, laundry, and ironing; and a third wife preparing meals (Bradley, 1990).[1]

It was also customary for 19th-century Mormon plural wives who lived together to share home management. In some families, wives divided the tasks: "Louisa enjoyed being outdoors and took charge of the cows, while Anna did most of the housework" (Embry, 1987, p. 98). A child stated, "I remember one mother was always sewing and mending. My mother was the cook; she was cooking for everyone. One of my aunts had a hoe. She was out in the garden hoeing weeds all the time" (Embry, 1987, p. 99). Some pioneer wives ran the family business, some did the weaving, and others did the housework (Young, 1954, p. 155). In another family, "Some [wives] were assigned to the laundry or to cleaning the house; others to the sewing room, or the kitchen. Each one's task was a duty performed for all the family. The fourth wife, for example, 'loved to cook' but didn't like sewing, so she used to trade jobs with one of the other wives who liked sewing" (Young, 1954, p. 218).

Even in communal arrangements, however, many pioneer wives often had independent, dyadic authority and responsibilities, such as being responsible for her own room or part of the home in which she and her children lived. Such was the case in Brigham Young's main family dwelling, where a dozen or more wives lived together: "On the upper floor were 20 bedrooms where childless wives and older boys and girls slept. The middle floor held the apartments of wives with small children and the parlor. . . . On the west side [of the basement floor] was the large dining room, where some fifty members of the family sat down to every meal" (Spencer, 1961, p. 26). One wife was in charge of the kitchen, another wife taught the children in a schoolroom in the home, and each wife did her own laundry and ironing. Furthermore, the family operated a "store" where wives could obtain individual items for themselves (Spencer, 1961).

When wives in present-day plural families live together, they often share household management responsibilities on a rotating or cooperative basis. They do so in many configurations, depending on personal and joint preferences, work responsibilities and schedules, and other factors. Many communal approaches to home management also have a dyadic component, in that individual wives usually exercise some autonomy in their tasks.

Dyadic home management styles

It should not be surprising that wives who live in separate dwellings function in a monogamous way – each wife having complete control over her day-to-day life. Yet, even wives who live apart may participate in some communal home management activities.

Family 1
Even when Joan, Norma, Charlotte, and Cynthia lived in separate homes they jointly planned Sunday dinners and Christmas and Thanksgiving meals. They discussed where to hold the event, who would cook what food, and how gift giving at Christmas would be done.

Family 2
When Judith and Rebecca, and Emily and Phyllis lived in two homes, with separate upstairs and downstairs apartments, each wife cared for her own apartment and cooked for and ate separately with her children. At the same time, there were communal aspects to their lives. Judith and Rebecca felt free to borrow food supplies from the other's apartment when the other wife wasn't home. And there were occasions when all four wives did joint shopping. It was also customary for them to do cooperative canning of food, store it in one place, and draw on it as needed throughout the year. So even though they generally managed their homes separately, the four wives worked communally on some household tasks.

Similarly, many pioneer plural wives did day-to-day activities in strictly dyadic ways or in a blend of dyadic and communal styles: "Aunt Phoebus . . . ran her place and my mother . . . ran her place. In our home, mother had supreme authority. . . . No one ever tried to interfere with Aunt Phoebus's living; she did not try to bother in our living. It was just like two different families. We did not try to live together as a family" (Embry, 1987, p. 98). In another family, two wives lived in one dwelling and a third wife lived in another house nearby:

> The single dwelling was really a duplex because each family had its own apartment, kitchen and all. . . . There was one cellar for the three families but the food was stored separately. Each wife had her own barrels and bins for supplies . . . each wife had her own cows and made her own butter and cheese; likewise each had her own flock of chickens. (Young, 1954, p. 156)

There also were dyadic relationships with communal overtones, as in the case of two sisters married to the same man who lived separately but did their laundry together in two wooden tubs on a bench: "One would scrub on the board, get the worst of the dirt off, and put them into the other tub. And then she would scrub" (Embry, 1987, p. 98).

Because families move often, wives work outside the home in different configurations, and new children and new wives come on the scene, home management may change from time to time. Wives must no doubt continually negotiate and deal with one another in this important aspect of plural family life. And home management matters don't always go smoothly, as wives sometimes disagree about how to do things, feel that others aren't sharing enough household responsibilities, or compete for control.

Family 3

Carlyn, Danielle, Alayna, and William live in a single dwelling. The wives share all household tasks, including cooking and cleaning, and the family members eat together. They have tried out many different systems for managing the home. At one time, they did things cooperatively, with adults and children having assigned tasks. At another time, when Carlyn and William lived away during the week because of work, Danielle and Alayna were casual about who did what. One of them would cook, for example, until she got tired of it, and then the other one would take over.

When all three wives were home, there was often confusion about who would do what, and tensions arose between them. Once things got so bad that William stepped in, developed a detailed schedule of responsibilities for managing the kitchen, cleaning, and caring for children. This system didn't work in the long run, so they had to change things again.

Now a particular job is done by anyone who happens to be available. But on Sundays one wife is responsible for cooking and cleaning, a second wife takes care of the children, and the third wife has the day off.

Although highly communal in many home-management activities, they recently introduced a dyadic component, with each mother living in a different part of the home with her children, caring for it by herself, and having separate laundry facilities for her and her children's clothing. As in other families, even their highly communal arrangements often involve some dyadic aspects.

Family 6

The eight wives in this family live in separate dwellings. They all feel strongly that this is the best arrangement because it allows each of them to lead their own lifestyle. And they cite examples of conflict about managing the home when they lived together in earlier years. Nina, the second wife, pointed out that each of them is responsible and accountable for creating an effective home but that "our stewardships were overlapping when we lived together" – the implication being that they could not effectively meet their social and religious responsibilities in running a home.

Family 7

Sarah, the first wife, works outside the home and sometimes is away for days at a time. Patricia and Audrey share household chores. On occasion, Sarah feels left out of certain decisions. She may come home and find that Patricia and Audrey have changed things around without consulting her. At such times she feels upset and even angry. The changes might be minor, such as rearranging furniture or hanging pictures in different places, and she claims that her feelings are not deeply rooted – but she is bothered.

Family 8

Ethel, the second of eight wives, is an energetic, outgoing, and exuberant person. She got into trouble in the past when she lived with another wife because of her strong ideas about how to manage, arrange, and rearrange furnishings and activities. Her boundless energy makes other wives insecure, and they don't want to live with her. Even now, when they all live separately, her visits are not always welcome because she jumps in and begins doing things in their homes. In fact, she no longer visits Betty, the fourth wife, because Betty told her flat out that she didn't appreciate Ethel's criticisms and suggestions about how to run her home. Ethel claims no malicious intent, only a desire to help.

Family 9

John said he once returned from a business trip and saw that Joyce and Clara, who shared a home, had each prepared a dinner for him. They were obviously competing for his attention, or perhaps challenging him to "choose" between them. His resolution to this dilemma? He ate half of each meal! Although this incident deals with the wives' dyadic relationships with John, it also illustrates tensions between them with respect to managing the home.

Tension also arose over shopping. Joyce felt that Clara, who was much younger, didn't know how to manage household money when shopping. They couldn't resolve things, so John finally intervened and asked them to shop together so that Joyce could teach Clara how to be more prudent.

Positive and negative relationships between plural wives in home management are also described in autobiographical accounts of contemporary plural family life. Melissa Merrill (1975), a former modern plural wife, recalls that a new wife refused to share in cleaning of the home, was verbally abusive, refused to prepare breakfast for Melissa's children, didn't allow her own children to help out with chores, and was generally disruptive. For these and many other reasons Melissa eventually left the family.

Dorothy Solomon, daughter of a former religious leader of a fundamentalist group, described the "pecking order" among wives in her family. It was partly based on personality and order of marriage (Solomon, 1984). The first wife was clearly the leader, at least for one period in the family's history. Some of the wives referred to her as "Boss 2" (the husband was "Boss 1"), and in the earlier days of the family's history, when all the wives lived communally, she ran the family like a military drill instructor. She controlled budgeting and entertaining and scheduled the wives in preparing meals, doing dishes, and cleaning the home. She also tended to go to public events with the husband more often and served as his "official wife."

Childrearing and discipline

Children are important in mainstream Mormon and Mormon fundamentalist cultures. They symbolize theological values involving "premortal spirits" who must enter human bodies and pass through earthly life before entering the hereafter. Children are also important status symbols for women, since wives are responsible for their upbringing and socialization.

Wives in modern plural families often are heavily involved with one another's children. This naturally occurs when families live communally in one home, and everyone is in daily contact. Although young children often sleep near their mother, older children may share spaces across mothers. Wives and children also have ongoing relationships even if families live in separate apartments or dwellings. Because many wives work, children are often cared for by other mothers in the family. As a result, wives help socialize, discipline, feed, and care for each other's infants, toddlers, young children, and even teenagers. To some extent, therefore, children reflect a communal aspect of family life.

Because fundamentalist families often have many children, one can imagine the complexity of day-to-day life when there are several wives and large numbers of children, or when one wife cares for the children of other wives (in one of our families, one wife cared for about a dozen and a half of the family's children while the other wives worked outside the home).

Because children are so important to wives for personal, status, and religious reasons, it is easy to see that children can be a source of competition, conflict, and tension between wives. For one thing, wives sometimes become upset about how other wives treat their children. And it is easy to see why this is so. Wives do not always have the option of child care but must depend on one another – even if they do not like one another or if they disagree with how their children are being treated. In some cases, the way children are disciplined and dealt with by other wives becomes a lightning rod for family stress.

Family 2

In general, Judith, Rebecca, Emily, and Phyllis are quite compatible. If they have any major problem nowadays, they say, it is not because of jealousy about their relationships with David; it has to do with disciplining one another's children. For example, Phyllis, the fourth wife, and Rebecca, the second wife, have periodic conflicts about their children. At present, Phyllis cares for many children in the family while the other wives work. She is a strict disciplinarian, because she believes that children must obey rules and because she cares for so many that some semblance of order is necessary. However, Rebecca is quite relaxed about discipline. As an example of their conflict, Phyllis sometimes refuses to allow children to do certain things. But on occasion Rebecca's children then call her at work, and wheedle permission to do the very thing that Phyllis prohibits – thereby circumventing her authority. When this happens, the two women end up in an argument. (Once it was so bad that they went to David for mediation. He supported the principle that Phyllis's rules should be enforced during the time that she is the caregiver.)

Judith, the first wife, gave an example of a similar conflict between her and Rebecca. Rebecca's babies tended to touch Judith's fragile things in the living room that they shared, and Rebecca did nothing to stop them and didn't seem to care. This created some tension between them, which took a while to work out.

Phyllis expressed general frustration about her role as caretaker for wives who work outside the home. Because they have moved so often recently, she has been caring for different wives' children. She finds herself repeatedly retraining children to observe her "rules," having conflicts with the other wives, and becoming exhausted at having to deal with large numbers of children. It is very frustrating, she said, and every once in a while she blows up because of the pressure she faces every day.

Family 3

Although the three wives espouse the principle that any of them can discipline children in the family, they sometimes argue about specific incidents. For example, Danielle feels that Carlyn, who has no children of her own, often inappropriately disciplines her children. As a result, Carlyn is now hesitant about criticizing Danielle's children, and this has created some tension between them. There is no such problem between Carlyn and Alayna or between Danielle and Alayna.

Family 10

Dorothy, the fourth of eighth wives in the family, observed that dealing with one another as mothers is very difficult – especially where disciplining the children is concerned. To be consistent, to establish ground rules with several different wives, to discipline in a way that is acceptable to oneself and another mother is very demanding. Dorothy said: "It's difficult enough to live the 'principle' with another wife; it's much more difficult to do so with another wife and her children."

Other child-related matters also contribute to poor relationships between wives. For example, a wife may feel that her children are not treated fairly by other wives or that other wives' children are favored in some way.

Family 14

Sally, the first wife who eventually left the family for a variety of reasons, also had complaints about how her children were treated by Molly, the second wife. Sally felt that her children were inappropriately disciplined and not cared for very well by Molly when Sally was at work. She also described an incident in which Molly obtained extra money from Harvey for counseling for her son but used the money to buy special Christmas presents for her children. Sally, who had been helping support the family financially, felt that her children had been treated unfairly by Molly (and by Harvey as well, since he did nothing to correct the situation).

Other contemporary plural families face similar problems. In her autobiography, Melissa Merrill (1975) states that another wife's children were disrespectful and disobedient to her but that wife did nothing to support Melissa when she tried to discipline them. And she claimed that her own children were mistreated by other children in the family, again with little sympathy or response from their mother. All of this made for great stress and difficulty, which, coupled with other problems in the family, eventually led her to leave the husband and two other wives.

On the other hand, many wives have good relationships regarding child care and discipline.

Family 1

Joan and Norma, the first and second wives, get along in general and feel good about how each of them deals with both sets of children. They are comfortable disciplining one another's children and have their children working in "teams" to do chores, now that they are living together after having been apart for several years. (On a couple of occasions we also observed that their children easily went from one of them to the other.)

Family 2

Earlier we pointed out some disagreements between Rebecca, the second wife, and Judith and Phyllis, the first and fourth wives. For the most part, however, they all agree that matters between them and their children are pretty smooth. They work on the principle that each mother is primarily responsible for disciplining her own children, but when she is not around any other mother can step in and correct a child.

Judith and Rebecca spoke positively about nursing each other's children from time to time. We also recall seeing two little girls from two mothers who were dressed identically and were jokingly referred to as "twin sisters." And on a couple of occasions we observed that children easily went from mother to mother and were warmly treated by all mothers.

Family 9

Joyce and John were married for 20 years when they joined the fundamentalist group and entered into plural marriage. Joyce admitted that her adjustment to a new wife had its difficult moments. At the same time, she is enjoying having small children around, now that Clara, the second wife, and John have had children together. She said that she never would have imagined the love and joy she feels for the two little ones.

Family 10

Dorothy, the fourth of eight wives, believes that all children in a plural family should feel that all mothers love them and care about their well-being and that wives must work hard to love one another's children in a genuine way. If that can be achieved, the family will be unified, to the point that anyone can legitimately discipline a child without the child or its mother feeling mistreated.

At the same time, Dorothy admitted to the complexities of living with another wife and her children and figuring out how to discipline, how to be consistent and fair, and how to establish ground rules acceptable to both mothers. They discussed this issue at length and appeared to agree with one another about principles. Barry entered into the discussion, saying that he, too, emphasizes the importance of the wives loving all the children in the family. For him it is a requirement for a unified family in this life, and a precursor for achieving a celestial kingdom in the hereafter.

As another example of their mutual concern, the wives share information about health care of the children and one another, try to learn some basic medical skills, and openly consult with one another about family medical matters.

Family 11

Melba, Kelly, and Mary, the second, third, and fourth wives, are sisters and are very close to one another. They take care of one another's children, speak of their love for all children, and say that they treat each other's youngsters as their own. They claim not to have any problems of discipline or unfair treatment of the children.

And there are cases of 19th-century plural wives who cared for one another's children in a positive and warm way. In one family, two sisters were co-wives, and they were so close that "one would nurse the other's baby if the other was busy" (Embry, 1987, p. 141). In the case of two other sisters, one did not have any children, but she was just as fond of the other's children "as if they had been her own" (Young, 1954, p. 216).

Interpersonal relationships among wives

The relationships between co-wives are also greatly affected by their personal compatibility and mutual liking, the social support and friendship they offer one another, and the values they hold in common. However, personality, personal background, and interpersonal relations are closely connected with other aspects of plural family life.

Not surprisingly, some wives in a plural family get along with one another better than others for reasons of personality and interpersonal compatibility.

Family 1

Joan, Norma, Charlotte, and Cynthia have very different personal relationships with one another. Although their compatibility is intertwined with their relationships with Hal and with other aspects of plural family life, they are also each very different personalities. Joan, for example, is an easygoing, open, and genial person who seems to have excellent relationships with each of the other three wives – and they feel positive toward her. Norma is very intense and serious, gets along with Joan and Charlotte, but not with Cynthia – who she feels is self-centered and not a "team player" in the family. Cynthia claims to be friendly with Joan and compatible with Norma because of their religious interests, but she doesn't see Charlotte very much. Charlotte, the third wife, who is older than the others, feels good about her co-wives, but tends to go her own way much of the time and seems to have cordial but not very close personal relationships with any of the other wives. Thus subsets of the four wives in this family have varied perceptions and interpersonal affiliations – some very positive, some distant and detached, and some negative.

In some respects their feelings about one another were acknowledged when they moved from separate homes into two dwellings. Joan and Norma, who got along well, shared one home, and Cynthia and Charlotte, who also were compatible, lived in the second home.

Family 2

Judith and Rebecca, the first and second wives, lived together for quite a while and are good friends. They describe their interests and personalities as being very similar, they grew up in the same kind of urban area, and hardly ever have conflicts. And the two younger wives, Emily and Phyllis, are also good friends. They were both raised in rural settings, have children of the same age, and provide companionship and social support to one another. Although we noted earlier some conflict between Phyllis and Rebecca about childrearing, the four wives seem to be compatible in general, albeit with special relationships between the two older and the two younger women.

The wives are attuned to one another in other ways. For example, Rebecca noted that they realized early on that Phyllis was reticent and didn't easily express her feelings and concerns. The three other wives worked hard to draw Phyllis out, make it comfortable and easier for her to be open about her feelings, and being supportive of her in general. She agreed that they had helped her a great deal. They also said that they spend a fair amount of time together, especially when David is away from home, and that they are good friends and rely on one another for companionship.

Family 3

The three wives in this family have rather different temperaments, personalities, and compatibilities. Alayna, the third wife, is easygoing, reserved, and an accommodating person who gets along very well with Carlyn, the first wife, and Danielle, the second wife (who is also Alayna's older sister). Danielle, in contrast, is very intense, has strong views, and is ambivalent about aspects of her relationship with Carlyn. Whereas Danielle wants to confront and discuss their relationships and family life openly, Carlyn seems to avoid conflict, tries to smooth things over quickly, and often speaks about resolving problems through prayer and reliance on their religious faith. Differences in their personalities seem to create some tension between Danielle and Carlyn.

Some wives claim that they are very friendly and supportive of one another; indeed, they may be crucial to one another's social life.

Family 9

Joyce, the first wife, is an outgoing and warm person. She says that she has worked hard to welcome Clara and Marjorie as plural wives; they agreed that she has been very supportive of them. Clara expressed appreciation for Joyce's continuing friendship, and the two women get along well. Clara told how stressed she was at one point, with two young children to care for, working outside the home and having to spend time with her family when her father died suddenly. When she came home, Joyce and her daughter gave her a special gift. They had made a quilt for Clara out of fabric she had previously purchased but never had the time to make into a quilt herself. She was overwhelmed and appreciative of Joyce's support and friendship.

Family 10

The eight wives admitted that their relationships with one another are complex and varied. In general, however, they claim to be individually enriched by being together in a family. They have learned to recognize each other's and their own individual strengths and weaknesses and to accommodate and cope with them. Indeed, they believe that each of them has become a better person through their dealings with one another. And they emphasize that every wife makes a different contribution to the family, is a unique individual, and that they all need to work together and love one another and all their children. They also pointed out that their sister-wives are their social friends, to some extent their only friends, and that they are an important source of social support for one another.

Anita, the first wife, who now lives alone, said that she is lonely for companionship and recalls the 10 wonderful years that she and Joanne lived together. They were friends, enjoyed jointly managing their home, and provided important mutual social support. Joanne chimed in, agreeing, saying that Anita was a special person to all of the wives – a leader, but a warm, supportive, and helpful sister wife. Everyone agreed.

Age, prior relationships between wives, interests, and personality sometimes combine to affect how well wives get along.

Family 6

Hilda, the first wife, is a strong and articulate woman who noted that she has different relationships with the seven other wives. With one, she shares common values about practical matters; with another, she has emotionally compatible feelings; and in another wife she finds a good friend and companion. Holly, the fifth wife, chimed in, saying that Hilda was like a mother to her when she joined the family. Young and unskilled in home management, raised in a dysfunctional family, and unsure of herself, she was taken under Hilda's wing, taught how to run a home, encouraged, and helped to eventually feel good about herself. "The time I lived with Hilda," Holly said, "were the best years of my life."

In contrast, Nina and Andrea, the second and third wives, described the hard time they had with Hilda when they joined the family. She was too harsh and unrelenting in her expectations regarding home management, and it took quite a while for them to become independent and free of her criticism and dogmatic views.

The four wives who live in a compound area visit with each other daily, so much so, they said, that they spend more time with one another than with Seymour. Although they acknowledge that they occasionally have differences of opinion with one another, they claim to respect those differences, and that "What the Lord wants will hold us together."

Family 5

Rose, the fourth wife, who is much younger than the others, was describing the serious personal difficulties she faces in coping with plural family life. She is insecure about her own status and ability to manage things and feels inferior to the other wives. Being much younger than the others, she said, "I'll never catch up with them," that is, achieve a level of maturity in plural family living comparable to that of the other wives. She is also struggling to educate her children in the ways of fundamentalism at the same time that they are being exposed to enormous social pressures from the majority monogamous culture. So this is a hard time in her life.

Barbara, the third wife, and Rose's older sister, was very warm and supportive as Rose vented her insecurities. She said that she respects Rose's feelings, has been trying to help her, realizes that her younger sister's problems are very different from the ones she faced, and was positive and optimistic about Rose's ability to work things out. But Valerie, the second wife, was not as interpersonally supportive. She stated that Rose's problems would best be resolved by gaining a proper religious testimony, clarifying her relationships with God, and praying and studying harder. Her demeanor was friendly but not wholly sympathetic with Rose's obvious emotional stress. Thus the two senior wives seemed to have different interpersonal relationships with Rose.

Variations in relationships between wives are also mentioned in accounts by other modern plural wives. On the positive side, one wife has stated that "it is a joy to have a companion with whom to share sorrow and happiness, sickness and health, to have in times of distress someone to lean upon and to turn to for assistance; when sick to know that your children are receiving a mother's loving care" (Bradley, 1990, p. 26). And in her autobiography Lorraine Bronson (n.d.) remarks that she and a second wife got along well throughout their marriages. She attributes their compatibility to their common background and upbringing, and to their mutual determination to make things in the family work. Although they had disagreements, they were short lived.

On the negative side, Melissa Merrill had a stormy relationship with her co-wife:

> Many . . . nights I would walk the streets to and from work, crying. At other times I would take Elizabeth [her child] in the buggy and I would walk and cry. I was so worn out and trying so hard to make Hazel [the second wife] love me. She had my husband, she had free hours with the children that I did not have with mine, she was, to the outside world, the wife while I was the sister-in-law. She was the sole authority on child rearing in the home. What more did she want from me? What did she expect? I tried desperately to keep peace between us. I would write her notes and tell her that I loved her and begged her to help me do the right things. My only response would be an outburst in which she would say she hated me. (Merrill, 1975, p. 78)

Positive and negative feelings were common among 19th-century Mormon women as well. On the negative side, in oral histories of the children of 19th-century wives, we find the following comments:

> Mother and Auntie were not close at all. . . . I just always felt like they didn't want to be close and forgive, no matter what. . . . I have sat at church more than once with Mother on one side and with Auntie on the other side of me. They didn't speak. (Embry, 1987, p. 142)

> Mother was overly sensitive. I think she spent half of her life crying. She could never stand up for her rights and Aunt Olive took advantage of her. I can remember her crying and crying. . . . I think polygamy helped to make Mother sensitive but she was sensitive anyway. She used to imagine slights and be so hurt over everything. (Embry, 1987, p. 143)

Ann Eliza Young (1908), a wife of Brigham Young who became very hostile about polygamy, recounted several cases of conflict between wives: her uncle's first wife hated his younger wife and never spoke to her, even though they lived in the same dwelling; a first wife in another family was so upset with the second wife that she threw bricks through the windows of the second wife's home. In another case there was "unadulterated hatred" between two wives. One boasted, "I haven't spoken to Annie for thirty years and don't expect to speak to her for thirty more if I live that long" (Young, 1954, p. 203).

But as in the present, many 19th-century wives had harmonious and positive relationships, albeit sometimes reflecting a bit of ambivalence: "The wives were friendly and kind to each other. They were always helping each other, sending food, helping with the sewing and they took a deep and real interest in each other's children, but there was an undercurrent of feeling between them that . . . a child of twelve could detect" (Embry, 1987, p. 139).

In other cases, relationships were very positive: In one family the wives "were never happy when separated." In another case, "My aunt . . . and my mother were the closest of friends. They shared the same faith, the same trust, the same hopes and the same husband. Significantly, they [also] shared the same frustrations, the same poverty, the same loneliness, the same widowhood" (Embry, 1987, p. 140). Another wife stated, "To me it is a joy to know that we laid the foundation of a life to come while we lived in that plural marriage, that we three [wives] who loved each other more than sisters, children of one mother love, will go hand in hand together down all eternity" (Embry, 1987, p. 141).

In some cases, because of differences in age, 19th-century wives had almost a mother–daughter relationship with one another. "I loved Sister Woods," said one plural wife; "she was like a mother to me and she died in my arms" (Embry, 1987, p. 139). Another wife told her son, "I was more like one of her own daughters instead of sharing her husband because I was so young" and was glad to have an older person teach her homemaking (Embry, 1987, p. 140). One woman who became a polygynous wife at the age of 16, found the first wife kind and supportive and even referred to her as "Mother" (Eaton-Gadsby and Dushku, 1978).

In some cases, wives bonded together in support of relationships during times of illness, death, and family catastrophes:

> When she was sick I went right into her house and stayed with her and many is the night I've gone to stay with her when she has been sick or when he was away. (Young, 1954, p. 220)

> Whenever Mother was confined with a new baby, the first one there to take care of her and look after her was Dad's other wife, . . . and vice versa. . . . For years Josephine [the first wife] was somewhat frail in health and it was necessary that Flora should assume the responsibility of performing some of the heavier tasks. . . . [S]he accepted conditions in a practical cheerful spirit and did whatever was necessary in a prompt, thorough manner. (Embry, 1987, p. 147)

And sometimes personality qualities seemed to produce warm relationships between wives: "My mother always said that Aunt Phoebus had a lovely disposition. They never quarreled or had words" (Embry, 1987, p. 143).

In summary, there is a range of interpersonal relationships and compatibilities between plural wives – from close and positive bonds to negative and disruptive ones. And within a family different wives enjoy different types of relationships with one another.

Resolving conflicts

How do wives resolve conflicts with one another? Do they settle things by themselves, or does the husband intervene? Do other wives help resolve disagreements? We found no universal procedure across families for settling disputes between wives. It all depends on the nature of the conflict, the personalities of the parties, and general family norms.

In several families, the wives try to work out minor problems between themselves, without involving the husband or other wives. If a conflict is serious, the husband may enter in as a mediator or arbitrator.

Family 1
Joan, Norma, Charlotte, and Cynthia agree that they work out most problems by themselves, without Hal's involvement. But sometimes they privately discuss their conflict with Hal, using him as a sounding board and adviser. Even then he tries not to get actively involved in the dispute but is a "behind-the-scenes" adviser.

Family 2
Judith, Rebecca, Emily, and Phyllis agree that they work out most conflicts by themselves. If that doesn't succeed or a problem is very important, they bring it to David's attention. But they do so as a last resort. David concurred, saying that this approach to settling disagreements has worked well for them over the years. Somewhat ruefully, he went on to say that it has been so successful that he sometimes feels left out of family matters.

To the chagrin of Judith, Rebecca, and Emily, the fourth wife, Phyllis, sometimes tells David about a conflict before she and the other wife have had a chance to settle matters themselves. Phyllis admits that she sometimes does this but finds it personally difficult to talk about conflicts directly with the other wives and prefers to deal with David. They claim that this is not a serious issue in the family, and they are working on it, but it occasionally creates some tensions.

Family 6

The eight wives in this family also try to resolve disputes by themselves and only bring in Seymour when absolutely necessary. He strongly endorses this mode of conflict resolution. Seymour also pointed out that a husband must be careful when a conflict is brought to his attention. Should he encourage wives to work things out themselves? Should he intervene directly, and if so, how? Above all, Seymour believes that a husband must avoid becoming a messenger between wives, or else the problem may become magnified and family unity seriously disturbed.

When conflicts arise, some wives may seek advice from another wife in the family or consult with their own mother or another senior woman. And when nothing works, some wives appeal to an elder in the church, or even the religious leader of the group. Indeed, the leader of the urban group told us that he spends a great deal of time counseling people on all sorts of issues, including unresolved problems between co-wives. Even that drastic step does not always suffice.

Family 14

Sally claims that she tried every means available to work out conflicts between her and Molly about childrearing, management of their home, and relationships with Harvey. Discussing matters with Molly didn't help. They each then began complaining to Harvey about one another, but he did little to help. Sally finally sought the religious leader's assistance, and even his guidance failed to ameliorate their conflicts. Eventually, Sally obtained a divorce and left the family.

Another important mode of resolving family conflicts is prayer.

Family 10

Naomi said that sometimes she prays to the Lord to help resolve problems with another wife. Dorothy agreed, adding that prayer helps overcome personal weaknesses that may have given rise to conflict with another wife. Joanne chimed in, saying that prayer also reminds her of the religious importance of plural living and the need to work through conflicts in order to fulfill her religious commitments and obligations.

Needless to say, there are occasions when conflicts between wives are not resolved by any of these methods. In some cases, wives who cannot get along may live apart and have as little to do with one another as possible. Others simply live with continuing tensions between them. Still others may leave the family. In general, however, wives try to work things out by any of several means – praying, resolving issues between themselves, calling on their husband to help out, appealing for advice and counsel from other wives and their relatives or, as a last resort, appealing to a church leader for assistance. Underlying their motivation to resolve disputes is a strong religious belief in the importance of plural marriages.

Summary

This chapter examined home management, childrearing and child care, and general interpersonal relationships among wives in plural families. Managing homes and raising and caring for children are central responsibilities of women in the present-day fundamentalist culture, as they are in the mainstream monogamous Mormon culture and, indeed, in American society at large. For fundamentalists, however, these responsibilities also have religious overtones, as women have "stewardship" responsibilities to create a proper home environment for their husband and children.

Homes are managed in several ways. When wives live in separate dwellings – a dyadic mode – they by and large care for their own home as they see fit. But they often share some tasks, such as planning and preparing joint meals for holidays and other occasions. When wives share a dwelling, they use any of several management systems – cooperating in household chores, taking turns for various tasks, and having temporary or permanent separate responsibilities. Even in communal home management patterns, however, wives usually take care of their own bedrooms and personal items, in a dyadic manner. Positive feelings between wives in managing homes are not unusual. Indeed, sharing household responsibilities with other wives can be a satisfactory arrangement, freeing them up from or giving them someone to share in ever-present chores. In other cases, tension and conflict can be serious, especially if wives have different management styles, feel that others aren't holding up their end of the tasks, or are failing to meet their responsibilities. And conflict between wives about household management is sometimes associated with other aspects of family upheaval.

Wives in modern plural families also often have a lot to do with one another's children – disciplining them, caring for children of working wives, spending time together as a family. In many instances, there is cooperation, warmth and love, and consensual guidelines about raising and disciplining children. In other cases, wives disagree about how their children are treated by another wife, how other wives' children behave, or what rights and responsibilities wives should have toward one another's children, and the result is serious conflict.

Issues of home management and child care are important areas of day-to-day relationships between wives. Working out acceptable approaches is not easy because these issues touch on important aspects of plural family life; indeed, these are crucial aspects of life in American society at large. First, for fundamentalists, homes and children not only involve ingrained cultural values about gender roles and parenthood, but they also bear directly on theological principles associated with women's roles and the importance of children as a mark of religiosity. Second, because so many present-day Mormon fundamentalists are converts, they have little experience in living communally and must figure out in a trial-and-error fashion how to deal with these complex issues.

Relationships between wives also depend on compatibilities and incompatibilities with respect to personality, age and status, and other factors. Some wives are quite compatible and are good friends – enjoying one another's company, being a source of social support, having common interests and backgrounds. And some wives enjoy an almost mother–daughter relationship, with an older wife helping and nurturing a younger wife in the ways of plural family living. But there also are many cases of incompatibility – wives not liking one another, seeing life differently, feeling that a co-wife is insensitive or selfish.

In resolving their disputes and conflicts, wives commonly work matters out between themselves. In many families, husbands are only apprised of conflicts when wives cannot settle matters themselves, or when an issue is very important. Wives also sometimes seek the advice of other wives, their mothers, or, as a last resort, church elders or the religious leader of the group. Prayer and religious values, especially a belief in the importance of plural marriage, help some wives settle their disagreements with one another.

In general, interpersonal relationships between wives are not that different from those between relatives, friends, or acquaintances in society at large. At the same time, there are some major differences. Wives in plural families are usually "stuck" with one another in close and ongoing relationships that touch on many facets of their lives. They cannot easily escape from one another, ignore one another, or lead separate lives. Their lives are tightly intertwined. Because many participants are inexperienced in dealing with relationships in this unique form of family structure, personal incompatibilities and compatibilities are sometimes magnified and spill over into other parts of daily life.

18

Family structure

The preceding chapters have touched on various aspects of plural family structure. It is time now to look at three interrelated aspects of fundamentalist religious and social ideology that apply to family functioning: the patriarchal status of husbands, the emphasis on family unity, and gender-specific roles of men and women. Following a brief discussion of these principles, we illustrate their application in three families. One stable and smoothly functioning older family operates according to a clearly formulated "theory" about plural family life. The second family is young and growing and has not yet developed a consistent approach to family structure and function; its members are continually experimenting and searching for ways to live this challenging lifestyle. We then present a composite case study of several nonviable families. This profile is based on the experiences of three wives who quit their marriages after years of struggling unsatisfactorily with plural family life.

Religious and cultural values regarding family structure

The father/husband as patriarch and family leader

The historical, theological, and cultural ideology of 19th-century Mormonism and contemporary fundamentalism emphasizes a patriarchal and polygynous family structure in the present life and in the afterlife. This doctrine is based on the belief that God is a patriarchal figure modeled after the God of the Old Testament; and that any man can achieve some level of "godliness" in the afterlife and literally become a "god" or "king" in his own "universe," depending on how he lives his earthly life. (Although this view focuses on a male's potential status in the hereafter, wives can also become "queens" to their husbands in the eternal life.) Mormon theology also states that only "righteous men" should be the patriarchal fathers of many children and the husband of many wives; they are the ones who will have their own family "universe" in the hereafter.

Under this principle, a man must assume major religious and social responsibilities in his family and community. He is expected to be active in the church and serve as a pinnacle of religious wisdom and righteousness. He is to marry honorable and "good" women as plural wives and mothers of his children. A husband is responsible for teaching his wives and children important religious values, resolving problems and conflicts in the family, acting fairly to all wives and children, and being involved in every aspect of family affairs as teacher, counselor, facilitator, arbiter, and decision maker. In sum, a husband/father is expected to provide leadership that will produce a unified, harmonious, productive, and smoothly functioning family in which all wives and children love one another and work together to satisfy God's principles on earth. In theory, then, the authority a husband/father exercises in modern Mormon fundamentalist families is significant and pervasive, if not absolute, as long as he behaves within the bounds of theological principles and respects and defers to church authorities.

Gender distinctions: The role of wives and mothers

Women also have important responsibilities in fundamentalist families. In addition to supporting their husband's religious and family authority and encouraging him to meet his religious obligations, wives must manage day-to-day life in their homes, have as many children as is reasonable for their personal and family status, and be responsible teachers and caregivers to their children.

The principles of patriarchy and gender roles are exemplified in many statements by 19th-century Mormon leaders – sometimes in a strident and dogmatic tone. Regarding patriarchy, Brigham Young said: "Let the wives and children say Amen to what he [a husband/father] says and be subject to his dictates, instead of their dictating to the man, instead of their trying to govern him" (Warenski, 1978, p. 161). For their part, women recognized "that a woman, be she ever so smart, cannot know more than her husband if he magnifies his priesthood. . . . God never in any age of the world endowed women with knowledge above the man" and that "polygamy is predicated on the assumption that a man is superior to a woman. . . . Mormon tradition follows that of the early Hebrews. It teaches woman to honor and obey her husband and look upon him as her lord and master" (Young, 1954, p. 280).

A poem entitled "The Wife I Want" in the December 1893 issue of the Mormon magazine *Young Woman's Journal* depicted the ideal good wife as religious, honest, and kind to everyone. But she should also "reserve her sweetest smiles and kindest acts" for her husband. In addition, she should love and care for children, make a proper home for her family, care for her own physical and mental well-being, and her husband should be "the ONE man on the earth whom she is constantly studying and trying to please, and for whom she is willing to forsake kindred, home, country and everything except God and what pertains to celestial glory." Although some letters and comments praised this poem, one woman wrote, "The husband I would not have is the man who wrote *The wife I want*."[1]

Family unity

A third ideal of fundamentalist theology and social structure is that a husband and his wives and children should form a harmonious and well-integrated family unit, in which the husband/father is fair and sensitive to everyone's needs; and wives love, respect, and support their husband, one another, and all children in the family. Some participants use different metaphors to to express the idea that plural families should strive to become unified, cohesive, and stable.

Family 1
Hal said that during tranquil times his family is like a stable atom. He is the nucleus at the center of the atom, and his wives are the electrons that revolve around him in a predictable, orderly, and stable fashion. But when a new wife joins the family, the "family atomic structure" is disrupted, and it takes a while for the system to reach a new stability.

Family 9
John used the analogy of a wheel to describe the ideal plural family. The husband is the hub, and the wives are the spokes. Together they make for a well-functioning wheel; indeed, adding new wives as spokes increases the strength of the wheel.

Although there is obviously much more to fundamentalist Mormon religious doctrine, we have highlighted only those aspects that are central to the structure of contemporary plural families. The following sections describe the patriarchal values, gender roles, and family unity in three families that adhere to these values in different ways – and with varying degrees of success. Since the fundamentalist culture is relatively young and many of its members have had limited experience with plural family life, these cases also show that families experiment and try out different lifestyles as they strive to attain their cultural and religious goals.

The first family is a stable, well-established, and smoothly functioning unit. Gender roles are clear, a strong patriarchal system is in place, and the family is tightly unified. It is based in the rural Redrock community, and its members belong to the United Fundamentalist Church. Most family members grew up in plural families or in the fundamentalist movement and are therefore experienced in its ways. The second family belongs to the Church of Latter-day Apostles, headquartered around Metropolitan City. Its members are all converts to fundamentalism and are relatively young. They are continuously experimenting and struggling to figure out how to implement the religious principles to which they fervently adhere. The third case is a composite of several dysfunctional families from the urban group. Our portrayal is based on accounts by wives who left their families after several years of interpersonal conflict and upheaval with their husband and co-wives.

A stable and well-established family (family 4)

Harry and his five wives – Anna, Ruth, Belle, Eve, and Shirley – are an older and stable plural family in the Redrock community. They have an explicit and clearly defined family philosophy that bonds Harry and his wives with their 65 children (37 sons and 38 daughters) and more than 300 grandchildren and great-grandchildren. All of the wives except the youngest, Eve, are beyond childbearing years, so the family is only growing slowly; however, the number of grandchildren and great-grandchildren climbs steadily.

Much of the family's stable organization derives from Harry's leadership. At present in his late 60s, Harry has the aura of a biblical patriarch. Tall, handsome, self-assured, intelligent, and articulate, Harry conveys a sense of charisma, grace, and gentility, coupled with strong beliefs and confidence in who he is and what he believes. At ease in a variety of situations, Harry commands attention within the family, in the community, and among many outsiders with whom he has contact.

Harry's father was a leader in the early modern fundamentalist movement. A man of strength and determination, he was a founder of the rural community and a forceful leader in its early and precarious days. As the oldest son, Harry became family leader when his parents died, even though he was quite young. Harry essentially was a parent to his younger brothers and sisters, and to this day they acknowledge the important role he played in their early years. Several of Harry's brothers and relatives hold key civil and religious positions, and the family is prominent in the community. Harry decided years ago not to pursue official positions in the community, stating that he wanted to devote all of his energy to his family.

Harry married Anna when he was 18 and she was 16, and less than a year later, married Ruth, Anna's sister, when she was 15 years old. Anna and Ruth were daughters of a leader in the community and like Harry grew up in the fundamentalist movement. These couples recently celebrated their 50th wedding anniversaries.

Harry and Belle were married about 10 years later, when he was about 29 and she was 21. Belle's parents were converts to the fundamentalist movement when she was a very young girl. Harry and Eve, the fourth wife, who was a daughter of another early community leader, were married 17 years later, when he was about 45 and she was 19. Harry and Shirley were married about two years later. A long-term convert to the movement, Shirley was 39 and a recent widow.

Harry is a college graduate, served as a teacher and principal in the local school, participated in many business ventures over the years, and at present devotes himself to educational activities in the local community. Harry travels extensively from his home base in Redrock to Metropolitan City, as well as to other places. He is always on the go and seemingly never fatigued, in spite of a heart attack suffered a few years ago. Always involved in family and community affairs, including a major lawsuit facing the community, Harry is bright and quick to pick up on topics, speaks easily with charm and enthusiasm, and displays self-confidence and presence. Within his family and in the community, he quickly becomes the center of attention, offering an easy smile and a kind word to everyone. He is clearly adept at making people feel that he is interested in each and every one of them. A successful community leader, Harry is also the hub and heart of his large family, setting its directions and influencing the lives of each of his wives and children.

Anna has been a housewife for most of her married life and had 17 children (2 died). Ruth, mother of 19 children (3 died), worked as a teacher for many years. Belle was a nurse for a number of years, during which time she bore 14 children (1 died). Eve, the youngest wife, has been a housewife for most of the time and has had 12 children (1 died). Finally, Shirley teaches art in the public school system and has 3 children.

We spent many hours and days with the family – we lived in their homes on several occasions, and they visited ours; we ate in restaurants together, took long car trips, and talked at length. In so doing we observed many aspects of their family life. It quickly became quite evident that Harry is an ever-present guiding force in his family and that he has a strong, well-articulated, and highly developed "theory" of family structure that he acts on every day.

Although he believes in and practices fundamentalist Mormon religious doctrine, Harry emphasizes strong family organization as the day-to-day underpinning of his religious values. Conversely, he believes that a patriarchal structure is the anchor of a healthy plural family – so much so, he says, that it is even more important than plural marriage itself.

One central principle Harry follows is to regularly take part in all aspects of family life. He is not a distant, remote, or detached figure. Instead, he participates in the lives of every family member and is viewed and portrays himself as a family patriarch. Harry achieves this in many ways. For example, his position as family leader is reinforced by the title everyone uses in referring to him: "Father" – with a capital "F" implied! No one refers to him as "dad," "pop," or "daddy." Although the wives call him by name, they usually use the term "Father" when referring to him in the presence of children. He even refers to himself in the same way, in the third person, using such phrases as "Father believes" and "Father asks you." He consciously decided years ago to be called "Father" in order to highlight the patriarchal structure of the family and his role as family leader.

The patriarchal principle is played out in many settings and activities. Harry often speaks on the theme of a father's role as family leader and teacher, and as one worthy of loyalty and respect from family members. In various settings Harry also calls on his sons to assume patriarchal roles in their own families, and to do so in an honest, fair, and moral way.

Harry's role as family patriarch is clear in the monthly meeting he holds with all his sons. They and their families gather for a weekend of discussions, religious observances, and social activities. A main theme of the meetings has to do with the principle of patriarchy; other themes emphasize family unity, the gender roles of males and females, and proper moral behavior.

Harry is always careful to give each family member some personal attention. Even if it is for a brief period, he talks personally with wives, sons, and daughters; asks them about their lives; provides guidance and advice; follows up on earlier conversations; and tries to maintain contact with and involvement in each of their lives. Our impression is that everyone in the family with whom he personally consults is pleased and awed by his attention and is always respectful, deferent, and attentive toward him.

Years ago, Harry decided that the family would not celebrate Christmas because it had become too commercial. Instead, they now celebrate "Father's birthday" during the summer – which highlights his patriarchal role and also serves to bond family members together.

The way children are named also reinforces the patriarchal structure of the family. In recent years, all newborn sons were given his first name as their middle name in order, as he put it, "to establish their identity as a part of Father." His first son also has his name and the designation "Junior."

Time and again, we observed Harry at the center of attention in family gatherings, at mealtimes, and in the most informal situations. Whenever he spoke, all eyes were on him, and everyone paid attention – whether he was serious or joking. And he tended to guide the flow of conversations and discussions, and everyone always seemed pleased to be with him, to listen to him, or have a conversation with him.

Harry isn't the only proponent of his patriarchal role. Eve, for example, emphasized the fundamental religious justification of treating him as the family leader and actively instructed her children in the principle.

On several occasions when we spoke with older sons, it was clear that they held him in awe and reverence and had adopted many religious and political views that he had expressed to us in other settings. In some cases, they even used verbatim points and phrases that he held about social, political, and religious matters.

When a two-year-old grandchild died suddenly, Father, as family patriarch, gave the baby a blessing to be released from this world. He then took over responsibility for funeral arrangements and for transport of the deceased baby from Metropolitan City to the burial site in Redrock. He continued to play a strong and central role in managing subsequent events, including the funeral oration.

On many occasions when we were with Harry in his urban or rural home, he received numerous calls and visits from his sons. Some sons called while on the road in their long-distance trucking business; others called from other places. They always seemed to be reporting or following up on a work- or family-related matter, to which he gave advice or suggestions.

On one of these occasions, Harry asked one of his sons to call and asked another son to come over immediately. The son who had been summoned arrived within minutes. Harry put his arm around his son's shoulder, whispered briefly into his ear, and the young man immediately drove away. We later learned that Harry wanted the son to fix the battery on the family bus; the son had dropped everything else he was doing and worked on the problem for several hours. There was no hesitation, recalcitrance, delay, or procrastination by the young man.

On another occasion, we traveled for several hours with one of the family's married sons. He spoke of his enormous respect for Harry, his effective leadership in the family, and his personal strength. He described a time when Harry went on a 40-day food fast in order to lose weight. Although everyone worried about him and he was quite weak at times, they had faith in their father's judgment and mental and physical strength and knew that he would come through this trial.

Harry's sons are very loyal to him. They have helped him out financially in recent years, buy him a new car every couple of years, supported him on trips to Israel and Europe, take care of some bills, and occasionally collect a pool of money to give to Harry.

The patriarchal structure of the family and the roles of wives and children are also evident in other settings.

We were invited on several occasions to have meals with different wives and their children, sometimes with Harry present and sometimes without him. When Harry attended, he was the center of attention and guided conversations, and everyone, children and wives alike, followed his lead. The wife and her daughters did all the cooking, serving, and cleanup.

Another time, we were enjoying a light snack in Ruth's living room with about 20 children and grandchildren. The girls were busily serving the food and cleaning up afterward, all under Ruth's supervision. During the gathering, which was casual and lighthearted, all eyes were constantly on Harry, with everyone hanging on his every word. When something was needed – a drink, napkin, or more food for someone – he would tell one of the girls, and she invariably jumped up and took care of the request immediately.

When we were done with refreshments at another informal gathering, Harry said in a lighthearted way, "Which girl would like to have the 'honor' of collecting the dishes from everyone?" Although he joked about it, there was no doubt that this was an order, and several young girls hastened to the task without a moment's delay. On other occasions, we observed Harry politely and delicately ask a child or grandchild to do something, whereupon it was done without question, hesitation, or resistance.

Once we were having breakfast in Ruth's home with Harry and several of their older children. Harry sat at the head of the table, Ruth was at his right, and we and the children sat around the table. Harry guided the conversation, the children or Ruth rarely spoke unless spoken to, and their comments were brief and deferential. Everyone laughed and showed pleasure when he or others made jokes or light comments, but the children never spontaneously initiated any line of conversation.

Two other occasions make clear Harry's patriarchal role in the family. Both incidents involved dinners we participated in at Belle's home with her children and their families. Harry attended on one occasion, but was absent the other time.

On the first occasion, dinner was delayed until Harry arrived, at which time he gave a blessing and encouraged everyone to eat so that they would be on time for a later meeting. The older members of the family sat at one table and the younger ones sat at another table. Harry sat at one end of the table, and Belle sat at the other end. Although the dinner conversation was wide-ranging and light, Harry by and large controlled it, with most members of the family quiet unless spoken to directly and everyone following his lead.

The situation was quite different when we were at Belle's home when Harry was not present. She sat at the center of the table, arranged the seating, carved the turkey, and supervised all arrangements. The conversation was lively, spontaneous, and freewheeling. She and her children enjoyed one another's company, and everyone participated in the conversation whenever they felt so inclined.

But the patriarchal structure of the family is not solely formal or serious. From years of contact with this family, even before the present project, Harry has been a warm and outgoing man who easily expresses support and fondness to his family members and works to maintain ties with every one of his children.

In addition to emphasizing religious and moral issues in monthly meetings with his sons, Harry encourages them to spend time with their children, raise their self-esteem, and show them warmth and affection, as well as teach them proper values. He openly discusses the idea that a patriarchal family structure is enhanced by expressions of love and concern for each member of his family. And we observed him putting this idea into practice in a natural way. He easily gives family members hugs and kisses, is warm and ready to cuddle young children and grandchildren, and once even showed us around the rural community in a car full of infants and toddlers – interspersing the tour with good-natured attention to the little ones.

During a tour of Redrock, we stopped at the town cafeteria. After greeting several townspeople, Harry led us to a table where several of his sons were talking about business and social things. Everyone seemed very pleased to see him, he greeted each son with a handshake or hug, had brief private talks with some of them, arranged for the young children to have ice cream, and quickly became the center of attention. It was all light and sociable, and everyone seemed to have a good time.

Harry's patriarchal status was dramatically illustrated when he had a serious heart attack and was hospitalized in a nearby larger town. Hundreds of people visited him, including many of his sons who redirected their travel in order to see him. He mentioned that one of his daughters and other relatives were nurses in the hospital and that he received very special attention. His five wives took turns spending days with him and, as described earlier, when recuperating, he stayed at each wife's home on alternating nights in order to fulfill his responsibilities to each of them. This was a time of great anxiety in the family, and everyone watched his progress with concern and hope. Knowing everyone's interest and fears, Harry was always optimistic, showed determination and strength, and soon resumed his day-to-day patriarchal role and demeanor.

The patriarchal structure of the family both serves and is served by a strong sense of family unity. Harry firmly believes in and attempts to teach the idea that the whole family is an integral unit and that his patriarchy is a vehicle for achieving that goal. Because they are all tied to him, they have bonds and responsibilities to one another, and he strives to abide by this principle on an everyday basis.

Years ago Harry insisted that his wives live in proximity to one another, so that they and all of the children would be friends and have a sense of bonding and responsibility toward one another. Four of the wives and their children live in a compound area; his first wife, Anna, lives about a mile away.

Harry emphasizes to his children that all brothers and sisters are part of a single family and that they should not refer to or even think about siblings of a different mother as "half" brothers and sisters. They are all true brothers and sisters, he says.

When we were touring Redrock on one visit, we made many stops, at which time we and the dozen or so young children with us got out of the car to have a view or visit inside a building. At one point, we discovered that we had left a three- or four-year-old boy behind at our last stop. Harry turned on the CB in his car, asking, "Is anyone out there?" Immediately, several sons reported in, saying, "Yes Father, this is _____; I am here." Harry described the problem, and by the time we returned to our last stop, several sons were at the scene, with the rescued youngster. On reflection, we realized that some of Harry's sons had left their CBs on and apparently were part of a communication network in which family members were readily available to one another. We subsequently learned that sons who were active in the family's long-haul trucking business had their own radio channel, so that brothers could be in touch with one another on the road – to provide help when needed, to meet up if possible, or simply to communicate.

A sense of family unity and responsibility begins early, as younger members of the family are expected to be responsible for one another:

Time and again, we observed young girls and boys taking care of their infant and toddler sisters and brothers – regardless of who the child's mother was. Although it was usually the responsibility of girls, boys also took care of the little ones.

As we were leaving Anna's home, some of the toddlers of the fifth wife, Eve, who had been with us, wanted to stay and play there. Harry agreed but instructed one of Anna's teenage sons to look after the youngsters and be sure that they returned home safely. We had no doubt that Harry's instructions would be followed – both patriarchy and family unity were at work! We saw this pattern over and over, with young children under the supervision of older children who took care of them, disciplined them, and worried about their well-being – regardless of which mother's children were involved. Older children assumed responsibility for youngsters without hesitating, and the children they supervised responded readily to their caretakers. Younger and older children seemed to know and accept one another and their roles.

The unity of the family is also reflected in the principle that family members assist one another as they are called upon to do so by Harry, a wife, or one another.

On arriving at the family compound, we were met by Arnold, one of the older sons in the family, who had been assigned to serve as our tour guide pending Harry's arrival. As part of the tour, he showed us a warehouse stocked with used furniture that another brother owned, pointing out that several brothers in the family had helped build the warehouse and that they often assisted one another in similar tasks, or in building one another's homes. He described this pattern of mutual assistance in a matter-of-fact way.

We also learned from Arnold that several brothers in the family worked cooperatively in a family long-distance trucking business. Although two brothers are the principals in the business, others work with them and share or exchange routes.

On this tour we also visited the main meetinghouse in the community (see chapter 4). Because the brothers in the family were often not home long enough to offer their volunteer labor as the building was being constructed, they decided to financially support Arnold, who now works full time on the building and represents the family's contribution to the project.

One son, Joshua, also described the way his brothers help one another in business and personal matters. For example, those who are truckers are in frequent radio contact with one another, try to travel together on the road, and often plan to meet at truck stops or in cities where they deliver goods. Joshua also felt a strong sense of mutual trust and reliance on his brothers, noting, for example, that one of them loaned him several thousand dollars without hesitating and never even followed up to inquire about being reimbursed. Joshua said that his brothers would give each other almost anything without question, help each other build their homes, give work to one another, and operate as a strong support group.

Another interesting example of unity occurred during the weekend of the family meetings, when some sons invited us to join them driving over the sand dunes on recreational vehicles – dune buggies. About 10 vehicles manned by younger and older sons were in the party. They were very solicitous and helpful to us, taking photographs, teaching us how to drive, and enjoying watching us gradually learn how to operate and maneuver these vehicles over some challenging (at least for us!) terrain. They seemed to have a strong spirit of bonding and friendship among themselves, praising one another, competing on tricks, racing one another, and easily laughing and joking. Riding the dune buggies was something they did often when they were together, perhaps as a counterpoint to the rather serious meetings and church events that were central to the weekend. There was also an organizational structure to the whole activity. One of the sons, a principal in the family trucking business, also seemed to be in charge of the whole adventure – leading the way, deciding where to go, monitoring the time. Specific brothers were also assigned to take care of each of us, and our mentors were always close by, providing advice, urging us on, being supportive, and in charge of our well-being. Another brother seemed to be responsible for taking pictures. This type of family unity and organization occurred in other situations. Someone was always in charge, others knew who that person was and responded to that person's authority in that situation. As noted earlier, even small children were always monitored by older children, and we often had a sense of tight organization and delegation of authority, responsibility, and family unity.

The concept of family unity and cooperation is also reflected symbolically in a discussion we once had with Harry about sports and competition in sports. Although he acknowledges the value of recreation, Harry is opposed to competitive sports because they pit people against one another and because they deemphasize cooperation. Cooperation is the most important principle of family life, he said, and athletic competition eliminates mutual aid, leads to inequalities, and lowers people's mutual respect for one another. So, he discourages any form of competitive activity among his children.

In summary, family members reflect their unity, responsibilities, and obligations to one another in a variety of formal and informal ways. This value is emphasized among brothers and sisters, younger and older children, and children of all mothers.

Wives and daughters also have an important role in the family structure. Whereas men are encouraged to become patriarchs in their own families and to view Harry as their patriarch, wives and daughters are expected to be homemakers, teach the children religious and patriarchal values, and raise them in a proper way. The wives and girls in the family themselves enunciated these principles on several occasions, and it was clear that they carried them out on a day-to-day basis. Anna, Ruth, Belle, Eve, and Shirley are clearly responsible for and have authority to manage their homes. Their daughters are trained early to become accomplished at domestic responsibilities, and we saw even very young girls displaying considerable competence in domestic tasks.

During the weekend of the monthly family meetings, women and girls prepare all the meals, with only minimal assistance from boys in the family.

Girls of all ages hurry about, delivering and preparing food to feed the more than a hundred family members who will have several meals together, working on tasks befitting their age and experience. When we attended meetings there was no whining or complaining, the wives gave orders that were followed promptly, and events proceeded with efficiency and with an enormous display of focused energy by women and girls of all ages. We saw this pattern repeated in almost every setting and meal.

The time that Harry asked which girl would like to have the "honor" of carrying away his dishes during a social gathering reflected not only his patriarchal role but also the gender roles of children. On the same occasion, at the end of the snack, one of us arose and offered to help collect and wash the dishes. Ruth refused this offer quite firmly, and boys who were listening nearby laughed, saying that "boys don't wash dishes; only girls do." This pattern occurred in every setting where we ate or had refreshments. Girls helped prepare and serve food, collected and cleaned up afterward, and did so with teamwork and competence. Boys were rarely involved in these tasks and instead remained seated with the men.

Usually girls were also the regular caretakers of younger brothers and sisters. Although boys sometimes helped out, it was older girls who more often had responsibility for the little ones in the family.

Boys become involved in male activities at an early age. They spend a lot of time helping their older brothers and relatives build homes, assisting in whatever way they can, and learning about community responsibility and skills. And it is the males who engage in the serious business of the family meetings with Harry, listening to his remarks and teachings, expressing their views and feelings, and becoming indoctrinated into the male role in the family and community.

As part of their gender socialization, boys are expected to be strong and to deal with discomfort in a "manly" way, and boys and girls participate in gender-linked activities.

We were having lunch one afternoon at Eve's home when she and Harry were told that one of her teenage sons had injured his leg when a dune buggy tipped over. He was in serious pain. Harry called for the boy who, when he arrived, described the incident with tears in his eyes. Harry was very firm, offered a bit of comfort or support, but told the boy to act more manly about the incident. Everyone who was present, including Eve, remained silent. Harry later explained that he was trying to instill strength and determination in his son, so that he would learn to cope with adversity in a strong and responsible way.

While we were chatting informally with a few young teenage boys and girls, the boys teased, saying that "girls get to do everything." They went on to claim that Harry always takes the girls to town and buys them gifts, while the boys have to stay home and work. In response, the girls said that they were never allowed to ride on the dune buggies and that boys hardly do any work and only have fun. As the bantering continued, one of the girls said that she works all the time, "mopping floors" and doing other chores around the house. She also said boys were boring because all they ever did was talk about horses or recreational vehicles. Gender roles and interests were not at all ambiguous among these youngsters.

Recall, too, that when Eve was redecorating her home, Harry was barely involved (see chapter 11). In addition, she mentioned that the girls were encouraged to decorate with domestic pictures of furniture, bedspreads, and religious items.

The fundamentalist emphasis on patriarchal structure, unity, clearly defined gender roles is vividly reflected in two unique family observances: the monthly gathering of family members and the annual celebration of Father's birthday.

The monthly gathering of the family

There are now 65 children in the family – 38 sons and 27 daughters. In 1969, when there were considerably fewer children, Harry began to worry that some of them, especially the sons, might begin to drift away and not have the family as a center of gravity in their lives. To prevent that from happening, Harry initiated a monthly meeting of his sons (with auxiliary events for daughters), designed to preserve and strengthen their collective bond and place Father at the center of the family as a unifying force. These monthly meetings have been held without interruption for 25 years. (Harry told us that some of his brothers followed his lead and now hold similar meetings with their sons.)

The monthly gathering involves a full weekend of meetings, social events, church-related activities, and group meals. The sons, several of whom work in the family long-distance trucking company and others who work in construction and related occupations in distant cities and regions, arrange their work schedules so that they can return home on the second Saturday and Sunday of every month. One son, Joshua, told us how strongly he and the others feel about the monthly family meeting. For him it is an uplifting experience and an opportunity to see his family, especially his brothers, many of whom are away from the community because of work. He has only missed a few meetings over the years, even though he sometimes has to travel long distances to be there. And when he is absent, he feels very lonely and isolated. Joshua claims that very few other brothers miss the meetings and that they all try to rearrange their work schedules so that they can make it home every month.

Family members begin arriving for the monthly weekend reunion on Friday evening and Saturday morning. On one occasion, when we arrived with Harry on Friday evening, toddlers, youngsters, and teenagers came from every direction to welcome Harry. He greeted every child with a hug, kiss, handshake, and a personal remark, and they were all happy to see one another. We went into Ruth's home to sit and relax, and over the course of the next hour, the other three wives who lived in the compound came over to greet Harry and us, as did more children in the family. He greeted each wife with affection and respect and was careful to have a word or two with as many family members as possible.

That evening we attended a dance in the community meetinghouse (see chapter 4). Harry enjoyed the dance, warmly exchanged greetings with many friends and family members, and danced with his children and relatives. The focal events of the weekend were the formal meeting of Harry and his sons on Saturday afternoon, the food repast following the meeting, and the breakfast of all men and boys in the family on Sunday morning. Other events described earlier included the visit to the town cafeteria, social gatherings in homes, mealtimes, and the dune buggy adventure.

The meeting of sons. One of us attended parts of two meetings with Harry and his sons; the other of us participated in several meetings over the years. The meeting is held on a Saturday afternoon or evening in a large room, perhaps 20 feet by 50 feet, in the building where Eve, the fourth wife, lives. Sofas and chairs are arranged around the room in a more or less oval configuration. A piano is at one end of the room, and a few photographs, prints, and other items are on the walls. The photographs include a collage of Harry's brothers and his father. A biblical relief map of Israel hangs on another wall.

Most of Harry's 37 sons attend the meeting, with everyone dressed somewhat formally, in a suit, shirt, and tie, or in a shirt and tie. The men are neatly groomed, their hair trimmed and combed, and everyone appears to be in their "Sunday best."

Harry sits near the middle of the long axis of the oval. His chair has armrests and is strikingly different from the folding chairs and ordinary straight chairs and sofas on which everyone else sits. There does not appear to be any order of seating for the sons. We joined one meeting about 45 minutes after it began. (At another meeting that one of us attended, the first portion was a religious sacrament service.)

Harry begins each meeting with a lengthy speech. In one presentation, he focused on the role of fathers, pointing out that he and his father before him wanted their sons to have a better life than they did. He went on to emphasize the role of the father in the family – as leader and teacher; as the final authority in the family; and as someone needing to be gentle but firm, attending to each family member on a personal basis, and serving as a role model. He also emphasized that mothers should teach their children proper religious and moral values, including respect for the patriarchal structure of families. Harry also stated that children should be taught to support their parents, financially if necessary, so that the father in the family can continue his patriarchal work.

At another meeting he emphasized several themes in his opening remarks, one being that the brothers in the family must remain unified – helping, loving and supporting one another. Another theme focused on moral principles, including honesty, civility, and dedication to religious doctrine. Another theme concerned the reality that "Father will not be around forever." Harry mentioned his own recent heart attack and the inevitable frailty of old age. Each of them, he said, has a responsibility to keep the family together, now and when Father is gone. He stressed that each son should be a strong father to his sons – teaching them, spending time with them, allowing them to work side by side with their father. Another consistent theme was the special relationship that each son was to have with his mother, supporting, loving, and respecting her. A final theme he discussed on one occasion was that self-indulgence through material and personal gain was an unworthy goal.

Thus, in his opening statements Harry often touches on some aspect of the importance of the patriarchal structure of the family, the unity of family members, and the role of wives and mothers. Sometimes he also reviews events in the community, such as impending court cases, his current state of health following a heart attack, and other issues of general interest. In these ways Harry not only teaches moral and family values but also brings his sons up to date on community affairs and other aspects of family life.

Following his remarks, Harry asks each of his sons to make a statement about some aspect of their life and present thoughts. At one meeting, he called on them in order, from the youngest to the more senior ones. On another occasion, the sons spoke in the order in which they were seated in the room. In another meeting, he only asked a half dozen sons to speak, perhaps because they were going to celebrate his birthday during the last part of the meeting.

When speaking, each son rose from his seat, gave his remarks, and ended with words to the effect, "I say this in the name of Jesus Christ," following which everyone responded "Amen." (This is a typical practice among Mormons following personal testimonials.)

Whereas Harry is an eloquent and flowing speaker, as are some of his older sons, the younger boys were often shy and halting. They often made stilted, brief, and awkward statements that emphasized any of several themes: appreciation and love for Father, their mother, or the prophet of the church; their desire to be a good person; their attempts to observe the teachings of their parents and the church; their thanks for being able to attend the meeting. Many of the younger boys made their remarks with bowed heads, mumbling, and were evidently embarrassed.

The older sons made similar but lengthier statements and delivered them in a more polished manner. Some of them spoke of the importance of communication among family members and giving help to one another; many expressed gratitude toward Father and their brothers for support they had personally received. They also related experiences to illustrate their feelings. One son described how the principles he had learned in the family helped him when he was out in the working world among people with different values. Another son spoke about his seriously ill child for whom he was praying. Others told about bad influences in the world that they had to resist when they were away from home and mentioned how pleased they were to see their brothers when they were on the road and under pressure from other truckers to behave immorally. One older brother described how much he cared for his brothers and how they had supported him in difficult times; his voice choked and his eyes filled with tears as he spoke. Over and over, sons expressed their appreciation for being at the meeting and seeing their brothers and gave thanks to Father for his leadership, teaching, and support. (Harry also asked us to make statements at the meetings we attended.)

Lasting about two hours, the formal meeting is followed by a relaxed social event, with everyone eating, enjoying refreshments, and socializing informally. The food is brought in by younger daughters in the family – having been prepared by the wives and their daughters. It is set up buffet style on a long table and consists of salads, crackers, cheese, and fruit. The younger boys are first in line, followed by the older brothers. We were invited to sit on each side of Harry, and a plate of food was prepared and brought to us by one of the girls. Perhaps symbolic of his status as Father and ours as guests, our food was served on regular dishes, whereas everyone else ate from paper plates and cups. (A young son also placed a small table in front us so that we could put our plates and drinks on it.) Many sons greeted and chatted with us; those who had not yet seen Harry hugged him or shook hands and had a brief conversation. In observing the flow, we noticed that Harry would discuss, query, offer advice, or render an opinion about a particular problem or issue in each son's life.

We also observed other activities during one or more of the meetings we attended. On Harry's 67th birthday, for example, the girls brought in a large birthday cake. Each son was given a piece, and Harry instructed that each mother also be given some of the cake. At another meeting, we noticed the son who was a principal in the trucking business handing out papers to various other brothers, perhaps paychecks, future assignments, or business-related items. We also observed another son collecting cash from his brothers; this could have been financial support for Father. Following the meal, sons and their families gather at their mother's home, or people socialize in other groupings. The evening usually ends early as family members prepare for church and the large breakfast on the following day, Sunday.

The meeting of sons with Harry reaffirms their religious values, emphasizes the patriarchal and unified structure of the family, and reinforces the social and fraternal bonds between brothers and their families. It is also an occasion to catch up on news and friendships, do some personal and family business, and have a good time. The Saturday meeting is an important anchoring event in the weekend gathering.

The Sunday breakfast. The next day, following morning priesthood meetings at church, sons and daughters and their spouses and children gather at the family compound. A special breakfast or brunch is held for all sons, even toddlers, and for sons-in-laws and special guests (at one breakfast Harry invited the son of the former prophet). Thus this event brings together sons of all ages and also weaves the husbands of the family's daughters into the extended clan.

The breakfast is held in the same room as the previous meeting of sons. On one occasion, a long table with a T at the end extended the length of the room. Harry sat at the center of the T, and we sat on either side of him. Two of his senior sons, invited guests, and one of his sons-in-law also sat at the head of the table. The youngest boys, aged 3 to 5, and boys up to about 11 years old, were seated at two other tables. Altogether there were 100 to 120 men and boys at the breakfast. (On another occasion, the room was set up without the T at the end of the long table. Harry sat at the center of the long table, seated us on either side of him, and put honored guests in adjacent positions.)

The tables were preset with platters of baked potatoes, hard boiled eggs, salads, homemade biscuits and rolls, bowls of gravy, and milk and water. Everyone was dressed in their Sunday finery and, with the exception of those Harry assigned to particular locations, seating was informal. As the men and boys filed into the breakfast room, Harry's presence was unmistakable. In addition to assigning a few special seats, he personally greeted every newcomer, hugging and kissing the youngsters, shaking hands and putting his arm around others, saying a special word or two to some, and showing pleasure in their presence.

When everyone was seated, Harry rose, welcomed them, and then made some formal comments. On one occasion, he first addressed himself to the very young boys, emphasizing the need for them to respect their father, him as Father, and the prophet of the church. He called on them to become leaders, follow the teachings of the church, and assume their responsibilities in the world. Now and then, when some of the little ones talked, cried, or were distracted, he spoke directly but gently to them, saying that they were little men and should pay attention to Father since this was a special time with him. Most responded to his mild admonishment immediately (when one youngster was especially disruptive, his own father at the other table was very upset and embarrassed, and angrily told his son to behave).

On other occasions, Harry talked about boys decorating their rooms with the proper kinds of pictures and decorations, ones that were uplifting, inspirational, and that reflected proper values. He urged them to carry pictures of their fathers and family in their wallets – not immoral things. Although he made some comments urging fathers to spend time with and be role models for their sons, most of Harry's remarks were directed at the boys, to whom he spoke gently but firmly. It was as if he was beginning to educate the very youngest boys in the doctrine of family patriarchy, male responsibilities, family unity, and principles of morality.

The meal began following his introductory remarks. The atmosphere was informal, people talked about a variety of topics, laughed and joked, and seemed to have a good time. During the meal, young girls circulated around the room, clearing empty food platters and pitchers of drinks, replacing them with new ones, and helping the very young boys with their food – all under the supervision and watchful eye of one of Harry's wives. Girls left the room with empty platters and dishes and returned with newly stocked ones, so that everyone had all they wanted to eat. At the end of the meal, Harry again spoke briefly, thanking everyone for attending, wishing them well, expressing his hope for their safe journey home or to their work assignment.

We learned later that more than 100 family members had been fed at breakfast that day and more than three dozen sons the evening before. Ruth, the second wife, is the manager of the whole operation, and her home is the major base. She is responsible for organizing the meal, asking the other wives and their daughters to cook certain things, and supervising daughters from all families in a variety of tasks. Eve and her own and other wives' children are responsible for setting up tables and chairs, doing the place settings, putting out food, and cleaning up. Shirley is responsible for preparing some of the food. (Once she couldn't attend the weekend gathering because she was teaching at a distant site. Nevertheless she baked a large number of biscuits and arranged for them to be delivered in time for the Sunday breakfast.) And Anna bakes bread, which is brought to the site from her home in town by some of the girls. Belle also participates in the preparations but did not help on one occasion because many of her older sons and their families had come home and she spent a great deal of time preparing their meals. Even though the wives had particular assignments, we observed that young girls from all mothers participated jointly in various activities. And none but the smallest girls were excused from jobs; all of them did something. The preparations obviously took days to complete; so it was that we noted the hustle and bustle of girls and wives all day Saturday and on Sunday morning.

During the meal, the women and girls gathered in Ruth's home and in a patio area, both of which are adjacent to the meeting room. Women and children were everywhere, socializing, talking, and helping with the food. Children were playing and laughing; toddlers and infants were crawling, sitting, crying, and playing. It was a busy, cheerful, and crowded scene as the family's daughters and their children interacted with one another and with their sisters-in-law and their children.

When the breakfast was over, the men and boys gathered on the patio with their wives and children. It was quite a spectacle, with everyone in their Sunday clothing and chatting in an animated way. There must have been 200 people on the patio. The women and girls wore attractive pioneer-style dresses with wide collars in gay bright prints or solid materials. Their hair was elaborately groomed in the traditional style of the community – braids looped into buns, deep waves, and tightly combed hair. Their dress and hairstyles were reminiscent of 19th-century pioneer days or of an earlier generation in this century. The men were dressed in dark suits or vests, with white shirts and ties.

The scene was festive, with individuals and families chatting, greeting one another, and enjoying themselves in the summer sun. Amid all the hustle and bustle, Father was everywhere, greeting people, moving from group to group and person to person, offering his good wishes, catching up on someone's activities, and displaying his charm, charisma, and interest in every member of his family with whom he came in contact. After a while, people said their good-byes and drifted off to their homes or afternoon church services.

The array of formal and informal activities during the monthly family reunion illustrates Harry's conscious attempts to put his "theory" of family structure into practice. Patriarchy, family unity, and strict gender roles are evident in a variety of ways: Harry's attention to each family member, his benevolent but firm hand, the mixture of formal and informal events, the blending of sons-in-laws and his daughters into activities, the variety of themes he speaks about, the testimonials of his sons, the attention he gives to even the youngest children.

Harry's birthday provides another occasion to reinforce and celebrate family values and allegiance.

Father's birthday

A major family event during the summer is the celebration of Harry's birthday. Many years ago, Harry decided that his family would not celebrate Christmas, even though the holiday was observed in his parents' home when he was a boy. Christmas had become too commercialized, he said, and had lost its true spirit amid the materialism of society. Furthermore, people were essentially worshipping graven images in the form of trees and decorations, and Santa Claus had almost become a substitute for God. Instead of Christmas, Harry decided to celebrate "Father's birthday" as a major annual event to unify the family and reinforce its patriarchal structure. And it is a major event, indeed, often involving several hundred people – sons and daughters, grandchildren and great-grandchildren, relatives, friends and community dignitaries. At one birthday celebration, we estimated that 400 to 500 people were present.

The birthday event is usually scheduled in the summer during the weekend of the monthly gathering of the family, and it takes place in lieu of the Sunday breakfast or brunch of men and boys. It is held on the large lawn adjacent to one of the homes in the family compound, with activities beginning after the men and boys return from the morning church priesthood services. Preparations for the event are elaborate and involve many of the wives and daughters in the family. As with the large breakfast, Ruth is in charge of food preparations and assignments, and her home is the center of activity. The night and day before, women and girls prepare hundreds of sandwiches and drinks, packaging them in sets so that guests each have several sandwiches. Early the next morning the food is placed on tables set up on the lawn.

Amid all the activity of food preparation, Leah, an energetic and competent teenage daughter of Eve, directed the younger children in setting up chairs and tables on the lawn. She told them where to place chairs and tables, encouraged and praised them, and explained when they did not quite understand what she wanted. Leah was also in charge of the part of the program involving the young children. When all the chairs and tables were in their proper place, she rehearsed the youngsters for their part in the birthday program – lining them up, marching them to the place where they were to stand, and rehearsing them in their songs and readings. Leah did all of this with energy, efficiency, and a commanding demeanor, and the children accepted her authority and readily responded to her directions.

Although the flow of events and the program of the celebration vary from year to year, Harry is always the master of ceremonies. He welcomes everyone, offers his thanks and appreciation to family members and guests, and makes comments before and after the various performances – praising participants, expressing his appreciation for their work, and so on. Harry concludes the formal part of the celebration in a gracious way and invites everyone to eat, drink, and enjoy themselves.

At one of the celebrations we attended, the program began with the very young children and grandchildren coming from behind one of the homes in a line of twos. After assembling in front of the guests, they sang several songs. Next, all of the unmarried daughters in the family sang songs and read poems. Later the small children reappeared, some of them in a miniature automobile that had the same license plate as Harry's new car. This performance symbolized the fact that Harry's sons had chipped in to buy him a new car – something they did every few years. And because he travels a great deal on family and community business, driving long distances at a time, they usually buy him a Lincoln or a Cadillac. With the formal program completed, the guests ate, socialized, and personally wished Harry a happy birthday. As in other settings, he was gracious, mingled widely among family and guests, and treated everyone with respect and warmth.

Gift exchanges are another feature of Father's birthday celebration, for which Harry sets the procedures and ground rules. He gives all his young children and grandchildren a small gift, and they each give him a gift. He and the wives decide what gifts are given to him and what gifts he will give to the children. The wives/mothers coordinate the whole process, so much so that he once jokingly said that sometimes he did not know what gifts he was giving to various children. The gifts are always modest, he affirmed, and their material features are not important. Rather, he developed this procedure as a way of teaching the children to relate to him as the family patriarch and to symbolize his personal interest in each of them. (We also observed some other family members, relatives, and guests giving Harry gifts.)

Once again, this event reveals Harry's deliberate effort to foster a sense of patriarchal structure and unity among his family members. Arranging for his birthday to be celebrated, leading the program, and managing the gift-giving process highlights Harry's role as family patriarch. The fact that the whole family comes together for the observance and that the young children play a central role contributes to a sense of family unity and loyalty. Here, too, gender roles come to the forefront, with the women and girls responsible for food preparation, setting up and cleaning, coordinating gift giving, and managing the logistics of the event.[2]

Although this family is stable, well functioning, and highly organized, it has its share of problems. Recent deaths of a young grandchild and a teenage son were tragic and upsetting, problems of rebellious behavior by some children and grandchildren are hinted at, and differences in wives' willingness to assume their share of joint responsibilities sometimes create strain. We are surely not privy to the personal feelings of many family members, since most of our contacts were primarily with Harry and his wives. So we can assume that some strains exist in this large and complex family of 5 wives, 65 children, many sons- and daughters-in-law, and more than 300 grandchildren and great-grandchildren. (Other aspects of life in this family are described in the preceding chapters.)

Nevertheless the family is a stable and well-functioning unit, in large measure because Harry is a bright, energetic, charismatic, and perceptive man who consciously puts into practice the concepts of patriarchy, family unity, and role and gender responsibilities. In addition, he and his wives have lived in their plural family for many years, and all of them were either born into the fundamentalist movement or grew up in families that had converted to the group. Furthermore, Harry and some of his wives are from prominent families and are part of the network in the community and church hierarchy. All of these personal, background, and experiential factors make this family an exemplar of stable plural family life.

An "experimenting" plural family (Family 3)

William, Carlyn, Danielle, and Alayna belong to the Church of Latter-day Apostles, the urban group of fundamentalist Mormons. They live in a semi-rural area near a small town several miles from Metropolitan City. They are a relatively young family and are still growing. William is in his mid-40s, as is Carlyn; Danielle is in her late 30s, and Alayna, the third wife, is in her early 30s. Carlyn has no children; Danielle has six children and Alayna has six children. The family will probably continue to grow as Danielle and Alayna have additional children. And they all hope to have a new wife in the family someday, so it is likely that the family composition and structure will continue to emerge for quite some time.

William and his wives were all raised in monogamous families and only converted to the fundamentalist group when they were adults. They have no previous roots in the movement, were not raised in the geographical area, and have no familial linkages to other fundamentalists. Although William and Carlyn joined the movement 15 years ago, the family has few close friends in the group and feels somewhat isolated socially.

William grew up in a monogamous Methodist family in a southwestern state, completed an undergraduate college degree, and did some graduate work in social science. William and Carlyn were married when they were in their early 20s. Also raised in a monogamous Christian family, Carlyn completed a high school education. She and William joined the fundamentalist movement about 10 years after they had been married. William and Danielle married shortly after he and Carlyn joined the group. He was about 30 and she was about 25 years old. She had been raised in a regular Mormon family, attended a Mormon university, and received a degree in elementary education. Danielle also served as a Mormon missionary (somewhat unusual for a woman, and a sign of her religiosity). As described in chapter 6, Danielle converted to fundamentalism following several weeks of study with William and his friends; they became attracted to one another during this period and eventually married. The same process unfolded with Alayna, who married William about six months later, when she was about 19 years old. She was introduced to him by Danielle, who was her older sister. We met the family when William and Carlyn had been married for about 20 years and when Danielle and Alayna had been married to William for upward of 10 years.

The family has struggled economically and otherwise for many years. William has held many jobs over the years as a steelmill worker, electrician, and skilled and semiskilled worker. On occasion he has had to work in distant settings, coming home on weekends. Because of a back injury, he has had to convalesce for periods of time and was recently advised to avoid heavy labor. To make ends meet, he, Danielle, Alayna, and all the children recently relocated to his native state, where he hoped to engage in sales work (Carlyn remained at home, caring for and renting the house, continuing to work at her long-term position as a secretary, and helping support the others until they established themselves in the new setting).

Danielle holds a degree in elementary education, has teaching experience, and has taught in the fundamentalist group's own school. She has also conducted training workshops for other teachers in the group school. Alayna has not worked on a regular basis and spends most of her time caring for the family's children and helping manage the family home.

We described the many changes in the family's living arrangements in chapter 10. Suffice it to say that they have struggled over the years to achieve a stable home environment. For financial and other reasons, they have lived in difficult circumstances at one time or another – in tents, trailers, rented basement apartments. They were finally able to purchase a piece of land in a semirural area, on which William and his friends built a large family home. They moved into the home as quickly as they could, even though it was not finished. As a result, they continue to engage in construction, shift internal living arrangements often, and seem to operate in a state of continuous transition.

William, Carlyn, and Danielle are outspoken and highly ideological in their religious beliefs. They often portray many aspects of family life, including relationships with one another, in religious terms, and they speak about fundamentalist doctrine with intensity and sincerity. They are striving to actively apply religious principles in every aspect of their day-to-day life, and frequently explained to us how they were doing so. On several occasions they told us they resolve problems, conflicts, and complexities by invoking religious doctrine and are determined to "live the principle" in this world.

William is bright, intense, and outspoken and constantly presses the family to adhere to religious values by changing aspects of their lifestyle. He has many new plans for remodeling the home, changing the organization of the family, altering children's routines and responsibilities, and restructuring the way the home is managed, and he theorizes about alternative "models" of family life. A central theme underlying many of his proposals is that the family needs to "get organized" in order to better meet the religious values to which they subscribe. As a result, on almost every one of our visits or discussions, we learned about their latest plan for remodeling the home, using the space in a different way, or changing the way they managed the home and their day-to-day lives or how they were working through their relationships with one another. On one occasion, Danielle said to us: "You always catch us when we are doing something different. We always meet with you when we are in a transition period, and I don't remember when you did come to us when we were not in transition."

Carlyn is low-key, does not usually offer strong opinions in group discussions, and tends to espouse religious doctrine as the solution to most family or personal problems. Much of her discussion is oriented toward family unity, patriarchal values, and reliance on religious beliefs in her personal life and family functioning.

Danielle is outspoken, articulate, and intense and plays a central and powerful role in the family. She expresses strong religious beliefs and acknowledges the need for them to experiment and explore alternative lifestyles so as to achieve their religious ideals. She also freely and openly criticizes William for aspects of his leadership and their personal relationship and is open about conflicts and tensions in the family. (As mentioned in earlier chapters, she has strong feelings about William's failure to act properly during their courtship, wedding, and early marriage.) Danielle does not hesitate to discuss and challenge William about religious or family matters, and he usually attends carefully to her remarks.

Alayna, the third wife, is quite different from her sister Danielle, and even Carlyn. She is usually quiet and reserved, rarely enters into discussions, hardly ever expresses strong religious beliefs, and appears to be a contented and placid person. During many of our visits, she focused her attention on her own and other children in the family, did household chores, or simply sat quietly and listened to the discussion. When she does express opinions, she is direct and brief.

In our many contacts with the family, its members openly described themselves as exploring, experimenting, and struggling to figure out how to live in a plural family. They acknowledge that their struggles result from several things: their often precarious financial situation and the fact that they were raised in monogamous families outside the fundamentalist culture, do not have a multigeneration plural family background, are not closely connected with experienced families in the group, and have a growing family that requires new adjustments all the time. So, they admit that they are by and large on their own and have to figure out for themselves how to build a family structure and lifestyle that will work for them. They also collectively agree that it is likely that they will have to experiment for quite some time into the future. William put it succinctly in one discussion: "We are like doctors who receive a license to practice. Sometimes we do it [plural marriage] well and sometimes we make mistakes. It isn't an ironclad contract, but an agreement that we try to fulfill our beliefs as best we can."

Within their seemingly ever-changing lifestyle, William, Carlyn, Danielle, and Alayna are serious about adhering to fundamentalist religious doctrine, and they cast many of their day-to-day decisions in religious terms. Indeed, many of their conversations were laden with doctrinal and theological references, as they explained how they attempt to translate religious concepts into every aspect of their lives.

William is serious and articulate, and often emphasizes the patriarchal family structure, in which he, as husband and father, serves as "the hub of the family wheel." Although Danielle is a strong and vocal influence in family affairs, William is clearly the architect of the family's lifestyle and often talks about different models or metaphors of family life, with patriarchy as a central feature. His metaphors include business organizations, survivalist philosophy, and military organization.

At one time, he portrayed the family as a business organization, stating that they needed to organize themselves in a more efficient and businesslike way. He even used the analogy of the children as "employees" and the wives as "supervisors." Ideally, he said, they need to do strategic planning, hold regular meetings, and provide reinforcement and feedback. And the children need to learn self-sufficiency and responsibility in their jobs – taking care of themselves and their younger siblings. To implement this organizational metaphor, William, Carlyn, Danielle, and Alayna worked out a "theory" of family life based on "problem definition, systems of functioning, and problem-solving principles." They have used this model for several years to deal with disagreements and conflicts. Although often quiet, Alayna elaborated on the model, describing how they might use it to resolve conflicts about the simple matter of doing the dishes after a meal. In another analogy close to the organizational metaphor, William once said that his long-term ideal was to make their home a high-technology center with computers, robotics, and other advanced systems.

On another occasion, he likened their situation to that of survivalists or a military unit who might someday face a major emergency, or a possible conflict with political enemies – at the time, communism. He talked about the need to store large amounts of food, become self-sufficient by growing their own crops, and build a fallout shelter in preparation for any "emergency." William has spent a fair amount of time learning survival techniques and even claims to know how to deliver a child at birth. As part of this philosophy, he encourages the children to play with military toys and engage in games of war, has had identification labels sewn in the children's clothing in case family members are separated, and has asked Joseph Ginat how to obtain gas masks from Israel. William is also a black-belt judo expert and teaches martial arts to some of the children.

As family patriarch, William's general demeanor toward his children appears to be one of distance, detachment, and authority. On one occasion when he was working on a project, we observed William asking his oldest son to get him a tool. His manner was official and brusque, as if he was a military officer speaking to an enlisted man. He behaved similarly at another time when he returned home in the morning, exhausted from working all night. Without a word of greeting on entering the home, he "ordered" some of the older children to bring in the food supplies he had purchased; they responded at once. We rarely saw William hold, hug, or kiss little children; they seldom went to him spontaneously or when they were crying or wanted to be held. If a child needed attention or a problem had to be resolved, he suggested that a mother deal with it. It is possible that William's energies were so devoted to our discussions that we gained an incomplete picture of his relationships with the children. Nevertheless, while interested in and concerned about them and their well-being, William appears to be a somewhat remote, formal, and detached patriarch with respect to his children.

Another aspect of his patriarchal views came to light when William drew a diagram of his long-range hopes for a community in which he and his children and their families would all live near one another. If it ever comes about, he will give each child a 1-acre plot of land around the present home, build roads and improvements, and ensure that everyone lives in a United Order format – raising food together, sharing resources, and functioning as a unified and extended patriarchal family. If possible, he would also like to include some close friends in the plan.

William describes these visions with enthusiasm and hope – recognizing that they are at present only dreams for the future and ideals to be achieved. However, these models reflect William's and his wives' attempts to construct a family system that will enable them to live together in a plural family. And successful or not, and changeable as their life seems to be from time to time, all of their attempts to create a viable approach to plural family life are anchored around the idea of William as family patriarch.

Achieving unity of all family members is also an important goal for William, Carlyn, Danielle, and Alayna. William once said, "This is my family, my children, my wives, and we are a unit serving God." Much of their energy as a family is directed at achieving a coherent and unified lifestyle – from their relationships with one another to managing the mundane affairs to day-to-day life. And they admit to exploring, experimenting, and doing things by trial and error. Some things work; some don't. Some things work for a while, but not permanently. But they are motivated to succeed and keep struggling to find their way toward a unified and coherent plural family.

A key aspect of their search for a unified family has been to live together under one roof in a home of their own. After many years of residing in temporary quarters, they are pleased to be in their own home, even though it is not completely built and needs a great deal of interior work. William paraphrased the comment of a former prophet who said that "one can learn more about family members in one year living under one roof than one can learn in 10,000 years living apart from one another." As part of his dream, William hopes that the family can be self-sufficient, growing their own food on the 4 acres of land surrounding the home and having everyone work the land together as a family. William also hopes that his children and their families can live close to one another in a unified community, as noted earlier.

To achieve unity in their day-to-day life, they have also experimented with a variety of systems for preparing and eating meals, cleaning, and managing the home. At one time, when William and Carlyn worked in a distant location and only came home on weekends, things were relaxed. Danielle and Alayna, sisters and good friends, did things informally – each performed different chores spontaneously, shifted assignments readily, and followed no formal pattern. When they tried the same system with everyone living permanently at home, it didn't work out very well. Then the wives tried to share all jobs or work out ad hoc assignments, without a systematic plan for rotating responsibilities. But that only worked for a while.

At one point, when things were so confused and tensions were mounting, William stepped in and tried to "get the family organized." He redesigned the kitchen to make it more efficient, moving counters and cabinets, redesigning work spaces, and even shifting the location of electrical outlets. It didn't help, and Carlyn, Danielle, and Alayna teased him in our discussions, saying that William simply didn't understand how a kitchen should work, and his solution only added to their confusion. Another thing he did was develop a rigid work schedule for each wife and the children. They designed a chart listing various responsibilities and assigned children to "work teams." With great amusement, the wives noted that this system didn't work either, and they finally had a "revolt," essentially telling William to "mind his own business."

They have continued to try other systems for home management and for training the children to assume some family responsibilities. On one visit, we saw a detailed summer schedule of activities for each child posted on a blackboard in the kitchen. It included when children were to wake up in the morning, have their meals, clean up and work in the fields, and go to bed. The board also contained brief educational statements about technology, preservation of the earth, and so on. Whether this system worked is not known, but it is another example of the family trying to achieve a unified and organized lifestyle. (We also know that at another time they had a system in which the mothers met with all the children in the morning, gave out work and study assignments, and then checked periodically during the day to see how things were going.) They do have a system for managing Sundays that has worked well for many years. One wife cooks and cleans; another wife takes care of the children; the third wife has the day off. William hopes that someday they can observe Saturday as a day of rest, as in the Jewish tradition, and worship on Sundays.

Another aspect of their attempts to achieve family unity centers around the children – their education, socialization, and sleeping and eating arrangements. Here again, they have experimented with different approaches and will probably continue to do so in the future. For one brief period, they allowed the children to sleep anywhere they desired; the result was a fair degree of confusion as children were all over the house, changing places during the night, bickering with one another, and so on. They then shifted to a dormitory arrangement, with all the older children sleeping in one large room, and boys and girls in different sections separated by a curtain. The smaller children slept in one nursery. More recently, children have been sleeping with their own mothers on separate floors of the home.

In addition to sleeping communally, in keeping with the principle of family unity, the children were also given clothing from a common pool. They were taught that they did not "own" their clothing in a literal sense, but had "stewardship" and were expected to care for their garments – changing regularly, putting dirty items in the laundry area, obtaining clean clothing from the pool, and maintaining it in drawers assigned to them. They were also expected to repair the clothing they wore or seek assistance from a mother. If they did not meet these rules of stewardship, their clothing was taken away and they had to ask their mothers for individual items as needed. We do not know how long this system was used.

At one time, they also had strict rules about children's behavior at mealtimes. Adults could speak freely, but children had to raise their hands and be acknowledged before speaking. In effect for about six months, these rules seemed to be working all right. We do not know whether they are still practiced. In addition, they recently adopted some procedures for the children's schooling. Whereas Danielle had been teaching children at home, on a somewhat loose schedule, they are now doing things more systematically. She teaches three days a week at the group's private school, and the children attend on those days. On the other two days she teaches them at home on a regular schedule.

They have even sought to symbolize family unity and a patriarchal organization through seating arrangements at meals. After experimenting with different configurations, they tried a U-shaped arrangement, with William sitting at the center head position, the wives alongside him, and the children in the remaining seats. This didn't work because the children got out of hand. So now Carlyn sits anywhere she desires (she has no children of her own), Danielle sits among her children on one side, and Alayna sits on the other side of the table with her children. They developed these arrangements as a way of ensuring that the whole family will eat together, as a symbol of their unity.

The search for family unity is also reflected in the relationships between William, Carlyn, Danielle, and Alayna. Years ago, William called for regular meetings in which they were to discuss family issues. As noted in an earlier chapter, problems arose, with all the wives feeling, in their own way, that William was treating them too much as a "group" and not as individuals. To work out these and related problems, Carlyn and Danielle took a sensitivity training course at a local university, in which "freedom, fairness, and power" in family life were highlighted. William eventually took the class himself and came to realize that in searching for family unity he had not paid sufficient attention to the wives' individuality and need for freedom. He went on to say that during that time, he had felt superior to the wives, was autocratic and paternalistic, and took away their freedom. Nowadays, although he is still the family patriarch, they try to be more flexible in their decision making and give one another more individual freedom. But as in so many aspects of their life, they continue to explore and experiment with how to relate to one another as individuals, while still striving for cohesion and unity.

For the most part, William, Carlyn, Danielle, and Alayna subscribe to and follow traditional fundamentalist gender roles – he is the family patriarch in principle and the wives manage day-to-day affairs in the home, care for the children, and are supportive of his leadership. For the most part, Danielle and Alayna manage the home, although Danielle also teaches part-time at the group's school and is in charge of home teaching of the family's children. Alayna doesn't work and spends all of her time at home. Carlyn works full-time and is only responsible for helping out at home on a limited basis. In a recent move to another state, Carlyn remained at the family home and continued working, Danielle took care of all the children, and William and Alayna worked outside the home.

Although varying in assignments from time to time, gender responsibilities are clearly defined and practiced. At the same time, they have occasionally blurred role boundaries, with unsatisfactory results, as was the case when William tried to set things right with a kitchen design and a plan for general management of household duties. And when he was at home convalescing for a long period, Danielle saw it as a mixed blessing. Although it was nice to have him around, she said he tried to control family life and routines too much. She felt a loss of freedom and independence as he meddled in "her business." In contrast, Alayna said that it was good to have him home because it gave him an unusual opportunity to be with the children. Carlyn chimed in, saying that his being home helped them become better organized. A spirited discussion followed, with much freewheeling interchange between the wives and William. They were quite open with one another and not at all hesitant about disagreeing or expressing different points of view. But William, referring to Danielle's strong statements, finally said something to the effect that "when all is said and done, I am the family patriarch and you (Danielle) will have to accept that fact." She agreed, but they continued to vigorously debate the issue.

Although she accepts and advocates their different gender roles and religious status, Danielle is a very influential member of the family. And she and William often refer to their mutual acceptance of one another's differences and their freedom to express their views openly to one another. She emphasized that he gives her the freedom to disagree, they are honest with one another, and that they are all making progress in family life and in their relationships with one another. Our observations confirm her statements; they do work hard trying to relate to one another constructively and are genuinely serious about their religious values.

On the whole, this family reflects the situation among many young fundamentalist plural families. Being converts who are inexperienced in polygynous family life, living in difficult financial circumstances, and in a family that is growing rapidly with new children, they struggle to figure out how to manage their complicated lifestyle. As their circumstances change, old systems no longer work, so new solutions for day-to-day living are tried out, and life becomes a series of trial-and-error experiments. The members of this family, and others like them, are very much aware that their life is and will continue to be an "experiment." They know that they are likely to be in a transitional state for a long time and that they will have to continually struggle to figure things out anew. William, Carlyn, Danielle, and Alayna said as much on several occasions, emphasizing their inexperience in plural family life, their need to try things out, and the importance of being flexible and open to alternatives – individually and as a family.

Family structure in disrupted families

We now examine a composite of several plural families who failed to work out a viable lifestyle. Our analysis is based on the experiences of three wives from different families who eventually left their husbands and co-wives (Families 12, 13, and 14, all of which are or were affiliated with the Church of Latter-day Apostles in the Metropolitan City region).

Lauren was the second wife in Family 12. Her monogamous parents converted to the fundamentalist movement when she was a young teenager, and she married Fred when she was 15 years old. Fred and Elaine, his first wife who was about two years older than Lauren, had been married for a short time when Lauren joined the family. After eight years of marriage in which she didn't get along with Elaine and also felt that Fred favored Elaine, Lauren was granted a "release" (divorce) by the fundamentalist church. At the time we met her, about seven years after the divorce, Lauren and her three children no longer had very much contact with the fundamentalist group.

Sally, the first of two wives in Family 14, had been raised in the main Mormon culture; Harvey grew up in a mainstream Christian family. Married when she was 19 and he was 22, they were unable to have children and eventually adopted a son. When Harvey was in military service, Sally became interested in and eventually convinced Harvey that they should join the fundamentalist movement. After doing so, about nine years after they were married, they adopted a second son. Some five years later, Molly joined them as a plural wife; she was about five years younger than Sally. Things were all right for a while but then turned sour – with considerable conflict and competition between Sally and Molly, and favoritism by Harvey toward Molly. After a couple of years of plural marriage, Sally divorced Harvey, left the movement with her two sons, and eventually remarried outside the fundamentalist community. Harvey, Molly, and their children also eventually left the group and relocated to a distant state.

Muriel, the fourth wife in Family 13, was married four times – in a monogamous relationship and in three plural marriages. Raised in a monogamous Christian family, she married and had one child, joined the main Mormon Church in spite of her husband's objections, and they divorced. Somewhat later, she joined the fundamentalist group and subsequently became the second wife of a man who had been married monogamously for 10 years. Three months after their marriage, he was killed in an accident. A few months later, she and her co-wife both married the son of a prominent member of the church. He had been married to his first wife for 15 years and, Molly subsequently discovered, had also secretly married another woman. She stayed in this relationship for about 10 years, eventually divorced her second husband, and a year later became the third wife of a man who had been married to his wives for 25 to 30 years. This fourth marriage lasted about 3 to 4 years, when Molly requested and was granted a release, allegedly because the husband became psychologically and physically handicapped, gossiped about her inappropriately, and eventually evicted her from the home. She still occasionally attends church services in the group, and her daughter is a member of a plural family. (Sometime after our discussions, we learned that Molly joined another family as the fourth wife.) Molly claimed that her marriages failed for many reasons – incompatibility between wives, conflicts between husbands and wives, and disagreements about a variety of issues, examples of which have been presented elsewhere in the book.

Here we wish to focus on aspects of family disruption in these cases that relate to the patriarchal nature of families, family unity, and gender roles and responsibilities. Our data are based solely on interviews with the three former wives; we did not interview or observe them during their marriages, nor did we have any contact with their former husbands or co-wives. Furthermore, we do not suggest that the issues discussed here were the primary or only sources of family disruption, although they certainly seemed to be important factors.

The three women were consistent in claiming that their husbands had failed in their patriarchal and leadership roles, the result being a serious lack of family unity. They had either not assumed proper leadership roles or had behaved in irresponsible and inappropriate ways. Lauren gave many examples and was very vocal about Fred's failure as a just and responsible patriarch. As minor but symbolic examples, she told us that during a late stage of a pregnancy, she was still doing hard garden work while he sat on the porch reading a newspaper and did not help her because it was not what he, as patriarch, felt he should do. Similarly, she claimed that when they celebrated Valentine's Day in his honor as family patriarch, he did not reciprocate. He also expected them to draw his bath, bring his slippers to him, and otherwise treat him as the "king" of the family. But there were many other more important ways in which Lauren alleged that he didn't fulfill his patriarchal responsibilities – a most serious aspect of which was his unfairness and mistreatment of Lauren and his favoritism toward Elaine. Time and again, and in many ways, she claimed that he strongly favored Elaine and denigrated her, as discussed at length in other chapters. He openly told Lauren that he preferred Elaine, ridiculed her skills at household management, openly showed more affection to Elaine, provided her with better furniture, spent more time in Elaine's home, made decisions with Elaine without consulting Lauren, and favored Elaine's children. At the same time, Lauren and Elaine had serious conflicts, which Fred did nothing to resolve or ameliorate. This only added to family disunity. Lauren said that Elaine openly flaunted her favored status in Fred's eyes, joined him in demeaning Lauren's home management skills, boasted about her sexual relationship with Fred, did nothing to encourage him to treat Lauren better, and generally deepened the rifts in the family. And he did nothing to resolve the conflicts between the wives, thereby failing in Lauren's view to meet his patriarchal responsibilities.

The same themes are repeated in the other two dysfunctional families. Muriel claimed that one of her husbands refused to help resolve conflicts about his rotation schedule among wives, saying something to the effect that "I am tired of deciding who I'm going to be with. You girls fight it out and the winner gets me." He was so lax in providing any kind of leadership in other aspects of their life that Muriel said that a "pecking order not unlike that among apes" existed among the wives. She claimed that those wives with stronger and more dominant personalities ran the family, had more resources, and lived in more comfortable homes. The husband gave no guidance and direction, and Muriel stated that there was no structure or unity to the family's day-to-day life. Moreover, she said that he was unfair in the amount of time he spent with the several wives, clearly favoring the dominant ones. These same wives freely overspent their budgets, indirectly taking funds away from Muriel when shortfalls had to be made up. All in all, Muriel felt that this marriage failed in large part because her husband never met his patriarchal responsibilities and did little to foster a sense of unity among the wives.

The details are different but the themes are similar in Sally's complaints about life in her plural family. Her husband Harry showed favoritism toward the second wife – not only in the time he spent with her and his displays of affection but also in his decision to give some of Sally's furniture to the other wife without asking her permission. Moreover, he did nothing to resolve things when the two wives began to openly disagree about a variety of issues – their relationships with him, treatment of their children, finances – but allowed the emotional wounds between the wives to fester. On top of all this, Sally said that he was a very poor manager of family finances and that they were often in financial difficulty because of his mismanagement. Without being specific, she said that he was also dishonest in his financial dealings with others.

In these cases, therefore, three wives who quit their marriages in plural families felt that their husbands had not provided the effective leadership called for by religious values. They accused their husbands of not setting proper family goals, not establishing guidelines for proper relations between wives or between him and the wives, not ameliorating conflicts, and violating principles of fairness and evenhandedness. The result, they claimed, was disunity among wives, fragmentation of their common beliefs in plural family life, and a deterioration of the family in the direction of self-interest and divisiveness. In contrast to the highly stable family described earlier, these cases illustrate that the problems in nonviable families are caused not only by personality differences and interpersonal incompatibility but also by a family structure that had failed to anchor itself in the religious concepts of a patriarchal and unified plural family.

Summary

The present chapter examined the structure of the ideal contemporary Mormon polygynous families in terms of three fundamental social and religious values: patriarchal leadership, a unified and cohesive family, and strict gender roles. To illustrate how these principles play out in day-to-day life, we presented case studies of three types of contemporary plural families.

One family is large and well established and is composed of a husband, 5 wives, 65 children, and more than 300 grandchildren and great grandchildren. Members of the rural community, most family members come from multigeneration polygynous families. Over the years the family has developed a number of rituals and customs under the husband's leadership that strongly reinforce the patriarchal and unified nature of the family, as well as strict gender roles for boys and girls and men and women. Much of their success is a result of the forceful and charismatic leadership of the husband/father, who consciously and skillfully conceives of ways to put these principles into practice in many aspects of the family's life.

We also described the case of a husband, 3 wives, and 12 children who are struggling to develop a viable family structure in accordance with the ideal principles of patriarchy, a unified family, and gender roles. Like many other contemporary plural families in the urban Church of Latter-day Apostles, the adults are converts who grew up in monogamous families. As a result, they have had little experience with plural family life and are constantly experimenting with different ways to achieve their religious goals. Aspects of their life change frequently and are often stressful, as they experiment with alternative ways of doing everyday things – sleeping arrangements, home management, seating patterns at mealtime, and so on. They are quite aware of their situation and accept the fact that change and experimentation will probably be necessary for some time to come as their family evolves and as they face new situations with which they have had little prior experience. Although this family has unique personalities and circumstances, its experiences are similar to those of many contemporary, young, and growing polygynous families – who must experiment, explore, and engage in trial and error to figure out how to live this complex lifestyle in a healthy and viable way.

The third case is a composite of several unsuccessful families. It is based on the experiences of plural wives who have divorced their husbands. Again, many of the participants are unfamiliar with plural family life because they have grown up in monogamous families and are converts to the fundamentalist movement. In these cases, the husbands failed to play out a "proper" patriarchal role, and the husband and wives neglected to work out their varied relationships with one another. The end result was family disunity. Husband and wife roles and co-wife relationships were poorly defined, people trespassed on one another's responsibilities and identities, and the families gradually disintegrated. These cases illustrate how well-established and stable families, emerging and exploring families, and non-viable families cope with religious and social issues of patriarchy, family unity, and gender roles. Chapter 19 summarizes a few other features of family structure in plural families.

19

Parents and children

In this chapter we discuss three qualities of parent–child relationships that relate to family structure and to gender relationships between husbands and wives: fathers' relationships with their children; the naming of newborn children; and the terms of reference children use to refer to their own mother and to other wives in their family.

Fathers and their children

By now it should be clear that plural wives/mothers are central figures in the lives of their children. According to traditional Mormon theology and cultural values (and American values as well), wives/mothers are the main caregivers, teachers, and socializers of children. Mothers in contemporary plural families are closely bonded to their children, become upset when they feel that their children are not being treated fairly by their husband, and are sensitive to how their children are cared for and disciplined by other wives.

The questions of concern here are: How do husbands/fathers relate to and interact with their children? Do they display the same emotional bonding to their offspring as do wives? What role do they play in day-to-day socialization, discipline, and care giving? We cannot fully address these questions since we only have a handful of cases from which to draw information on the relationship between parents and children. Furthermore, we observed fathers interacting with children only infrequently, and then mostly during our discussions. What we describe next must therefore be viewed with caution and is not necessarily representative of plural families in general.

First and foremost, we saw considerable variability in father–child relationships. In some cases, notably in Harry's Family 4, fathers are in contact with, attentive to, and concerned about their children's lives. Although Harry does not seem to deal with the day-to-day care giving of his children, he is an ever-present, awesome, revered, and loved parent, and he is personally attentive to his children, shows warmth and affection, and uses a series of family practices and rituals to remain involved with his children. A similar pattern seems to occur in other families.

Family 1

Many of Joan's and Norma's children were present on our first visit with the family. They freely entered and left the living room where we were sitting, played inside and outside the home, and the very young ones readily went from one mother to the other. They also easily went to Hal, sitting on his lap, kissing and hugging him, asking questions. He was very patient, as were the mothers, in spite of the high energy level and large number of children present. Hal and the wives were calm and easygoing, and he seemed to have a strong emotional bond with his children. At the end of the evening, as Joan assembled her children to take them home (Hal planned to stay in Norma's home that evening), each child kissed Hal good night. Their final exchanges seemed warm and good-natured.

This outward affection between fathers and their children was not typical of most other cases we observed. Fathers generally seemed to treat their children, and to be treated in return, in a distant, cool, and detached way. In some cases, fathers did not know how many children were in the family or how many children each wife had.

Family 10

Barry couldn't recall the exact number of children in the family, and the wives teased him and joked back and forth, finally convincing him that there were 53 children in the family. The same thing happened when we talked about the number of grandchildren. The wives were quite clear on the facts, including which wife had how many children, which children were married, how many grandchildren there were, and other such facts. They were obviously the repository of information about the family demography, whereas Barry was murky on details.

At the same time, Barry spoke of his love for all of his offspring, casting his remarks in the context of religious beliefs about a unified family in the present life and hereafter, and in regard to his patriarchal role. He even went beyond the importance of loving his own children to say, "I need to love all of the children, not only in my own family, but also children outside of my family," meaning that a true patriarch needs to love all of humanity. (Because we only had contact with Barry in group discussions, we had no opportunity to observe day-to-day interactions between him and his children.)

Family 8

Ira has 8 wives and 43 children. He had considerable difficulty remembering the number of children in the family, which child belonged to which mother, whether they were in plural marriages, had left the group, or other facts. At one point, he said, "Sometimes I cannot even remember my own children's names."

In several families we observed aloof and detached relationships between husbands and their children.

Family 3

In chapter 18 we noted that William related to his older children rather formally, asking them to do things in a serious and strict manner. And children always obeyed his requests or commands immediately. We never saw any exchange of kisses, hugs, or joking between William and his children. As we talked with him and the wives, if small children were present they rarely went to him with questions, sat on his lap, or stayed near him. They always went to their mother or another wife. If a child cried or needed something, William might discuss it with a wife, but we rarely saw him interact directly with a child to address its needs. (It is possible that these observations only applied to our discussion settings, in which William was very interested and intense, and that his demeanor with his children was different in other situations. We simply cannot say.)

Family 2

On one visit with David, Judith, Rebecca, Emily, and Phyllis, we sat in Judith's living room. There were many children everywhere – playing outside, in the various rooms of the upstairs and downstairs apartment, coming in and out of the living room. Most of the children were toddlers through preteenagers. As they came and went from the room, or sat with us for a while, they invariably went to their mother or another wife. Only rarely did we see children spontaneously approach or stay near David. When he spoke to them, gave instructions, or chided them for misbehaving, they responded immediately – with deference and respect. But there was very little spontaneous contact, physical or verbal, between David and any of the children.

On another occasion, we arrived by car at one of the family's homes. A couple of David's sons were playing in the driveway. We walked up to and past them, and neither David nor the boys greeted or acknowledged one another. It was as if they were strangers to one another. In several such experiences, we had a feeling that David was someone they respected and responded to, but to whom they showed little spontaneous or informal affection, as was the case for him as well.

Family 5

Constance, the first wife, recounted that she had always referred to her father as "uncle" up to the time she was in the 6th grade – when she first learned that he was her father. Although the family might have done this to avoid prosecution or discrimination, the fact is that Constance's father spent little time with his children and was viewed by them as only a family relative.

Family 6

When we visited one of the family's homes, four children were in the living room. As Seymour introduced us, he asked one of his sons what his name was – he had forgotten. Three other sons who were watching TV did not stand up or acknowledge the presence of their father or us but ignored us until Seymour introduced us.

During our visits to various homes in the family, we encountered many children of all ages. Again and again, Seymour and the children ignored and rarely greeted one another. It was as if he was a visitor and they were strangers to one another. (It must be acknowledged that Seymour has very strong ties with one of his daughters, with whom we met regularly. That daughter claims that Seymour also has close relationships with some of his other children. However, she felt that his basic shyness, the reticence of children toward strangers, family customs regarding greetings, and Seymour forgetting names temporarily resulted in their seeming aloofness.)

We saw wide variations in relationships between fathers and their children in plural families. There were instances of fathers and children having warm, spontaneous, and informal relationships. In most cases, however, we sensed a rather distant, formal and aloof relationship between fathers and children. Because our sample of families is small, and many of our observations occurred in the context of discussions with the husband and wives, it is possible that what we observed is not representative of relationships between fathers and children in other aspects of their day-to-day life.

Choosing children's names

Another topic that arose late in the project and about which we have incomplete information concerns the process used to select names for newborn children. It reflects husband and wife gender roles and, indirectly, their relationships with their children. Several questions arise concerning the selection of children's names in plural families: Who does the choosing – the husband, the wife, or both? Do other wives participate in selecting a newborn's name? Are there customs for selecting the names of children, for example, a first child or a first son?

Some aspects of naming Mormon fundamentalist children and Americans in general are probably similar, although there may well be differences among subgroups. In American society, for example, it is customary for a husband and wife to choose the name of their offspring. Sometimes religious, ethnic, or family traditions enter in, and children are named after living or deceased relatives of the father or mother. Sometimes sons are named after their fathers and grandfathers. And it is probably not uncommon for new parents to be pressured by relatives to choose a certain name or to be questioned about the name that they have in mind. So although it is customary for parents to decide on the names of their children, a variety of factors come into play during the decision-making process.

How does naming a new child work in contemporary Mormon polygynous families? Although our information is limited, it strongly points to two conclusions. First, the decision is made by the husband, wife, or both, and other wives in a plural family have little to say about the matter. Selecting a name for a new child is a dyadic decision, and other wives play no communal role in the matter (although it is possible that co-wives may discuss the matter informally).[1] Second, the way children are named varies from couple to couple. Their approach even changes from one child to another.

The first question is, Who decides on a new child's name – the husband, wife, or both of them together? In keeping with theological and cultural norms, sometimes the husband, as family patriarch, unilaterally assigns names to new children.

Family 24

Sidney always chooses the names of new children in his family. It is his responsibility as family patriarch to do so, he said.

This practice is rare, however. In many cases, mothers play a significant role, although the husband theoretically has veto rights or can make a final decision.

Family 1

Hal says he and each wife jointly choose a new child's name, although he has ultimate patriarchal authority in the matter. The mother of the newborn draws up a list of possible names, and she and Hal discuss it and usually arrive at a mutually acceptable decision. On only one occasion did Hal insist on a particular choice, so his formal authority in choosing a child's name is rarely invoked.

Family 2

David said that he has the patriarchal authority to make a final decision about a child's name, but most often he and the mother jointly arrive at a choice. One procedure they followed for years was for each of them to independently prepare a list of possible names, discuss them, and reach a choice acceptable to both. At another time, David, Rebecca, Emily, and Phyllis decided that a mother would name the girls and David would choose a name for boys.[2] Whatever the procedure, there was always the understanding that David could veto a selection if he disapproved.

Family 6

In this family, a mother draws up a list of possible names for a new child, and Seymour selects one of them. In actuality, they said, the two parents discuss the names and jointly decide on the final choice. There have even been instances in which he didn't especially like a name but agreed to the mother's preference. At the same time, they have always named the first son of every mother after Seymour. This is a long-standing tradition in Seymour's family, and he is the fifth-generation son to carry the name of "Seymour."

Family 8

Ira theoretically may veto the choice of a name for a new child, but rarely invokes his authority in practice. Instead, either he or the mother makes suggestions, the couple discusses possible names, and they usually reach a consensus. Ira claims to be especially sensitive to a mother's desires in the matter. Yet there have been times when Ira unilaterally decided on a child's name. In his presence, Betty, the fourth wife, said that Ira selected the names of the two children she had with him. She said she was surprised and angry at the time and resents it to this day. She didn't object to the names he chose but to the fact that she played no role in the matter. How often this occurred with other wives is not known.

In some families, the naming process changes from time to time, as family circumstances and attitudes evolve.

Family 4

For many years, Harry chose the names of new children in the family. There were occasions when a mother didn't know her newborn's name until he told her what he had decided. He did this when he was a much younger man, when he saw it as his responsibility as family patriarch to name all children. In more recent years, the family has been using a flexible system, perhaps in deference to Eve, who years ago was "shocked" when Harry named a child without discussing it with her. It obviously became a matter of considerable discussion between them. Although we cannot pinpoint the change in practice to that time, the context of our discussion suggested that Harry might have become more flexible following that incident. Thereafter, he and each wife more or less mutually decided on names for new children. In some instances, wives proposed possible names, and he selected one from the list. In other cases, they discussed it and decided together. And in some recent cases, he wasn't especially happy with a name preferred by a mother but nevertheless deferred to her wishes. So they seem to use a variety of approaches, most of which involve negotiations between Harry and a wife.

But Harry continues to insist on some principles. For example, all boys are given his name as their middle name. As he put it, this strengthens their identity with "Father." Then, either a mother chooses the child's first name or she and Harry decide together.

All in all, decisions about naming children in plural families symbolize parental gender roles and, indirectly, parent–child relationships. The central role of husbands/fathers highlights their patriarchal role in families. Sometimes husbands/fathers act on their patriarchal status, either assigning children names by themselves, or they retain formal "veto" power over a wife's choice. More customarily, however, husbands and wives negotiate a new child's name, often with the wife/mother taking the lead and recommending possible names. And, as in many other aspects of modern plural family life, families change the way in which they go about selecting names of newborn children.

Terms of reference

How do children refer to their parents? In American culture, most children probably use any of several terms: "mother," "mom," "mommy," "ma"; "father," "dad," "daddy," "pa," "pop." But what happens in some emerging forms of family structure, such as blended families in which the parents have children from previous marriages? Or in cases in which the partners are not married, or are gay or lesbian? More to the point of this discussion, how do children in plural families refer to their birth mother and to other wives? Are all wives called "mother" or "mom," or is there another designation for other wives?

Although our information is limited, the terms children use to refer to their mother and other wives in plural families symbolize dyadic and communal aspects of parent–child relationships. That is, children in several families call their birth mother "mother" or some variant thereof, and they call other wives "aunt X." In so doing, they acknowledge their unique dyadic familial relationships with their birth mother, and their communal family relationships with other wives.

Family 1

Children are taught to refer to another wife/mother in the family as "aunt X" and to call their own mother "mother," "mom," or other variations, depending on a wife's preferences and the age of her children. The wives noted jokingly that one wife's children are not always proper in this respect, sometimes calling another wife by her name, although they view this in a good-natured way.

They said that it is also customary for children in most families in the group to refer to other wives as "aunt X," although they knew of a few instances in which children use the term "mother X" for another wife and "mother" for their birth mother.

When they changed living arrangements from separate dwellings to pairs of wives sharing homes, some of the younger children were a bit confused about what to call the other wife. For example, some of Cynthia's little ones asked if they were supposed to call Charlotte "mom." They were instructed to refer to her as "aunt Charlotte."

This pattern of calling one's own mother "mother" and other wives "aunt X," or variants thereof, occurs in other families as well (Families 2, 5, 6, 10, 23). Some of the members of these families said that they followed the same practice when they were children and that it is prevalent in many other families (one wife claimed that 90% of the families with whom she has contact use these terms). Similar practices occurred in Mormon pioneer families (Embry, 1987; Embry and Bradley, 1985; Spencer, 1961; Young, 1954).[3]

It is thus customary for children to be taught the distinction between their own mother and other wives in plural families. This practice reflects a distinctive "dyadic" bond between a birth mother and her child. At the same time, other wives are treated as an important part of a child's life, in observance of "communal" family values.

Some families use a different approach, teaching children to use the term "mother" to refer to their birth mother and "mother X" to refer to other wives in a plural family (Families 4, 22). Members of several other families also knew of other cases in which "mother X" is used (Families 1, 8, 10). It was not uncommon for some pioneer families to use this terminology. Some families use the terms "mother X" or "aunt X" interchangeably or in different settings.

Family 8

Betty, the fourth wife, said that the term "mother X" for another wife is a more intimate term than "aunt X" and is sometimes used in an affectionate way on certain occasions. In general, however, children in their family refer to other wives as "aunt X." (There are also instances, she noted, in which older children call another wife by her first name; but this is only done on rare occasions.)[4]

Family 22

Pauline, the second wife, and Florence, the daughter of the first wife, are the same age and were school friends before Pauline married Florence's father. How does Florence refer to Pauline? When they are alone, they refer to each other by first names; when other children or other people are present Florence uses the term "mother Pauline."[5] Pauline also observed that families differ, some using the term "aunt X" and others using "mother X."

How do children of different mothers refer to one another? Although the question only bears indirectly on parent–child relationships and our information is fragmentary, participants in Families 5, 6, and 23 said that all children refer to one another as "brother" or "sister." They are encouraged not to view other wives' children as "half" brothers and sisters but to refer to and treat them as full-fledged family members.

The ideal in 19th-century Mormon plural families was to have all siblings view one another as "true" brothers and sisters (Embry, 1987; Young, 1954). As an example of the ideal, one of Embry's informants recalled:

> I had a friend call me one day, and she said, "Are Gaskell and George Romney your half brothers?" I said, "No, I don't have any half brothers. They all have two eyes and two ears and two arms and two legs. Although I was the youngest, I always felt right at home in any of my brothers' and sisters' homes just as much as I would have in my mother's sons and daughters." (Embry, 1987, p. 170)

However, there were wide variations in relationships between siblings in pioneer families, from very good to very poor, depending on personal compatibility and feelings between wives (Young, 1954; Embry 1987).

Summary

This chapter examined the emotional bonding of parents, especially husbands, to their children, the selection of new children's names, and the terms children use to refer their own mother and to other wives in their family.

Earlier in the book we noted that children and their mother are strongly attached to one another. In keeping with their historical and theological role, women are the primary caretakers of their children, children are a symbol of a woman's religious and social status, and the mutual emotional ties between mothers and children are strong and pervasive. But what about husbands/fathers? Although some fathers displayed warmth and affection toward their children, our general impression is that many men in contemporary Mormon fundamentalist families have somewhat distant and detached relationships with their children. In several families, children showed a blend of awe, respect, and deference toward their father, but we observed little warmth and informality or overt displays of affection between children and their fathers. On the other hand, mothers and their children have more intimate, affectionate, and spontaneous relationships with one another.

Parental gender roles are also reflected in the naming of new children. In most families, the father and mother of a newborn child jointly participate in selecting a name. At the same time, it is customary for the husband/father to at least have "veto power" or final authority for selecting a child's name. The mother may initiate the process, proposing a list of possible names, and even indicate her preference. In some families, the husband chooses from the list she draws up; in other cases, the mother and father discuss and negotiate a final selection; in some instances, the husband defers to his wife's preference. In general, therefore, it is customary for the husband and wife to discuss and negotiate possible names for a new child. But below the surface, the patriarchal power and authority of the husband/father is usually present. In a few rare cases, husbands choose names for a new child without consulting the wife/mother, but this does not happen very often. Some families also follow such principles as naming the first son of each wife after the husband and using the husband's name as a middle name for all sons. (We did not encounter *any* cases in which a mother's name is similarly used.)

We also learned a bit about the way children refer to their own mothers and to other wives in a plural family. Children consistently call their birth mother "mother," "mom," or some variant thereof. Other wives are most often referred to as "aunt X" or "mother X," with the former designation being more prevalent in the families with whom we spoke. Thus children acknowledge their distinctive bond with their birth mother, as well as their special but different familial relationships with other wives in the family.

Taken together, these few items of information about husbands/fathers, wives/mothers and their children fit with our earlier discussions of family structure, gender roles of husbands and wives, and dyadic and communal aspects of contemporary Mormon plural family life.

20

Summing up

We conclude this discussion of polygyny in Mormon families with some reflections on our experiences as researchers, the transactional perspective as a way of studying close relationships, impressions about life in modern polygynous families, and the future of the people and groups with whom we worked.

We began this project more than eight years ago with a sense of awe and wonder. On each of our respective first contacts with plural families, we were amazed to observe a lifestyle that was completely out of the realm of our experience and imagination.[1] Seeing modern American men and women in plural families was almost incomprehensible, even though we understood and intellectually accepted the concept in other cultures and historical periods. Moreover, polygyny has run counter to Western cultural values for hundreds of years. So at first we were amazed, bewildered, confused, and, to be honest, even felt a twinge of disapproval. After all, fundamentalists are violating the law and deviating from powerful cultural norms about what marriage "is supposed to be." And they are doing so in an era when sexism, sexual harassment, and physical, mental, and social abuse of women are being talked about in almost every institution of American society. There we were, seeing a lifestyle in which men are viewed as authoritative patriarchs and women live as co-wives under the apparent control of their husbands. How could people live this way in modern America? How could it be "right" for men to be married to several women at once? How could women accept such a seemingly demeaning status? These and related thoughts ran through our minds when we first met and spent time with members of fundamentalist groups. Interestingly, when we give professional talks on our work, there are invariably members of the audience who express these same thoughts, even though they have never met members of a plural family. The idea of polygyny in present-day America is simply out of the realm of possibility and is often reacted to with a mixture of incomprehensibility and hostility – even outright anger. Indeed, there have been occasions when we have been verbally lambasted for even studying plural families, the implication being that we somehow approve of and are advocating polygyny. Over time, however, and as reflected throughout this book, we saw things in a more balanced way, with women and men both playing important formal and informal roles in their families and communities, and plural family life being one aspect of a fundamentalist culture.

Aside from the question of "why" these people lived in polygyny, we wondered how they managed to survive and cope with the challenges of this extraordinary lifestyle. Questions tumbled out. What is it like for a woman to share her husband with other women? How do husbands deal with several wives and their children? How do they manage their money? What are their living arrangements? And on and on. Many of the issues that are addressed in this book immediately came to the forefront: how do they manage relationships, visitation patterns, celebrations, courting, running households, and so on? In the early days, our minds buzzed with wonderment and we talked about it endlessly with one another and with our wives. It was as if we were on another planet, yet here we were in America, with people who spoke our language, yet were completely different in their marriage and family lifestyles. The whole scene was amazing and incongruous.

As we spent more and more time with Mormon plural families, our wonderment subsided (as did our initial latent feelings of disapproval). We became accustomed to seeing husbands and wives in plural families dealing with one another. We came to better understand their religious commitment to the principle of plural marriage. We gained a broader sense of the history of the fundamentalist movement. We saw them struggle day by day, figuring out how to live constructively in polygynous families. We learned about their commitment and successes, and their ever-present stresses and attempts to cope with the difficulties of their lifestyle. Slowly, we discovered that individuals, children, and families were "real people" – some were congenial, others were shy; some enjoyed a good joke and told interesting stories, others were reserved and cautious; most men and women worked hard and faced many of the same work and family issues that monogamous families experience.

Over time, we also realized that contemporary fundamentalism is an emerging culture on the American landscape. That is to say, Mormon fundamentalism is "a culture in search of itself." The groups and people with whom we worked share some values with society as a whole but also hold fast to theological and cultural values that set them apart from the larger culture. But a culture it is. Or, better said, Mormon fundamentalism is a culture in the process of "becoming."

As we saw that participants in modern Mormon fundamentalism were committed to and firmly believed in what they are doing, we shifted our perspective from what anthropologists call an "etic" perspective to a balanced "etic" and "emic" orientation. That is, instead of attempting to evaluate and understand Mormon fundamentalists solely in terms of *our* cultural frame of reference – an etic orientation – we adopted a combined emic and etic orientation. That is, we attempted to understand what *they* believed about family life, and how *they* were trying to cope with *their* circumstances in order to achieve *their* goals (an emic orientation). Then we linked their perspective with our conceptual and cultural orientation in order to arrive at a combined emic and etic approach.

The transactional approach to studying close relationships

We have concluded that our transactional or contextual philosophical approach to research is an appropriate way – perhaps even the best way for our purposes – to study contemporary plural family life. And we trust that the substance of this book confirms that judgment. Although each aspect of plural family life discussed up to this point warrants a great deal of further study, perhaps in a more analytic fashion than pursued here, we believe we have achieved our main objectives:

1. We developed a holistic and broadly based understanding of how husbands and wives in plural families deal with the challenges of the dyadic and communal aspects of their relationships. By tracking the interplay of dyadic and communal processes in a variety of everyday life experiences, we presented a holistic (but obviously incomplete and imperfect) picture of their lives – much as one might obtain of a symphony or ballet by seeing how various aspects combine to yield a whole. We hope that the results of our work encourage others to search for holistic patterns of everyday life in other types of close relationships.
2. It is possible, and perhaps even necessary, to develop a holistic understanding of close relationships by tracking many different kinds of behavior, including feelings and emotions, the activities in which participants engage, the ways in which they use the physical environment as an aspect of their relationships, and so on. We believe that our work illustrates that understanding close relationships is enhanced to the extent that one taps into many different types of behavior.
3. We are more convinced than ever that close relationships are inseparable from other *social contexts*. That is, each husband–wife dyad in a plural family is embedded in other pairs and the family as a whole, as well as being linked to relatives and kin; the *physical contexts* of homes, places

in homes, objects and other environmental things and locales; and broad *historical and cultural contexts*, that is, the long history of the LDS religion and of modern fundamentalism, theological values, and the broader and often threatening larger American culture and the LDS Church. So it is that any close relationship is embedded in and inseparable from its contexts. Without sensitivity to those contexts, we will, at best, only achieve a fragmentary and superficial appreciation of interpersonal relationships.

4. Our study of contemporary plural families highlights the dynamic nature of any close relationship. Over and over we found that husband–wife and wife–wife relationships in plural families display stability and change throughout their history. In almost every life domain, there were periods of stability and instability, with families experimenting with, holding onto a practice for a while, and changing anew as they coped with evolving circumstances in almost every facet of their day-to-day activities. And they are not unique in this respect. All close relationships are dynamic, and all call for research and theory that are process-oriented and that study stability and change as integral aspects of interpersonal bonds.

Taken together, we are satisfied with our transactional and contextual approach to studying husband–wife and wife–wife relationships in modern plural families and encourage research of this genre on other forms of close relationship. Not that a transactional approach is the end-all, or the single "correct" strategy. What it does offer, however, is a rich, multifaceted, and broad-grained approach to close relationships that complements and enhances analytic, dimensional, and parametric strategies.

Close relationships in plural families: The present and the future

Plural family life is difficult for both husbands and wives. Almost every aspect of family life discussed in this volume reveals the stresses and challenges faced by plural husbands and wives. Conflict, adjustment, compromise, negotiation, competition, and jealousy are frequent in wives' relationships with one another and with their husband. Stresses and strains arise with respect to children, budgets and finances, home furnishings and living arrangements, celebrations, the management of homes, jealousies about one another's relationship with their common husband, and so on.

The challenge is no less difficult for husbands. They are expected to be wise, all-knowing, calm and cool, always available to help resolve conflicts, fair to all wives, and attentive to all family problems. They are also supposed to spend time with each wife and her children, ensure adequate financial support for everyone, and "love" each wife equally. At the same time, men are expected to be active in church affairs and to assume religious responsibilities.

Many participants described life in a plural marriage as an unending struggle; every day is a challenge, and one never completely resolves the conflicts, jealousies, and stresses that inevitably arise. Plural marriage, they say, calls for self-understanding and strength and the ability to be independent, tolerant, accepting, and mature. All of these phrases may seem like platitudes. However, hearing our participants say them with feeling, a sense of commitment, and, on occasion, with tears and breaking voices, made us aware of the depth and intensity of the daily challenges faced by men and women in plural families.

The complexity of contemporary plural family life is the result of an array of internal and external pressures. As discussed in chapter 1, present-day Mormon fundamentalists are exposed to a variety of symbolic and tangible external pressures. Strong and ever-present pressure comes from the main Mormon Church. The Mormon Church and its nine million members are part and parcel of modern America and have struggled for decades to overcome a common stereotype that suggests they are a "strange" people who still practice plural marriage. With fundamentalists all around them and coloring their image in American society, the Mormon Church and its members have worked hard to distance themselves from fundamentalist groups.

As for fundamentalists, they see themselves as being surrounded by a powerful and wealthy Mormon Church whose intentions they believe to be potentially threatening and destructive. In spite of the fact that there have been no mass arrests and attempts at prosecution in recent years, members of Mormon fundamentalist groups have etched in their minds the "persecutions" they suffered only a few decades ago, and they are ever wary of what might happen in the future. (In some respects, having a powerful and visible "enemy" may strengthen the allegiance of members of fundamentalist groups to their own churches and communities.)

American society is also hostile to polygyny, and fundamentalists are quite aware of that fact. Federal and state laws universally reject plural marriages. Furthermore, when polygyny is displayed in the public media – often on talk shows that seem to be interested in prurient and dramatic topics – plural family life is presented as a curiosity, with special attention given to sexual matters. And with few exceptions, the representatives of fundamentalism who are willing to discuss and portray their lifestyle are usually independent practitioners or those representing small groups who seem interested in gaining attention and visibility. The result is continued rejection of plural family arrangements by American society, hostile perceptions by average citizens, and feelings by members of fundamentalist groups that they are isolated, rejected, misunderstood, and even threatened by American society at large.

There are also a host of internal pressures in everyday plural family life; these are the central focus of this book. But the problems faced by husbands and wives in their multifaceted dealings with one another are enormously magnified by that fact that many participants in contemporary Mormon fundamentalist groups are converts. (This is especially the case in the urban group with whom we worked.) Many people join fundamentalist groups after having been raised in monogamous families – frequently as Mormons. Aside from the pressures of being rejected by their parent church, and sometimes by their families, converts must now live a lifestyle with which they have had essentially no experience – and which is antithetical to everything they grew up believing about family life. Over and over, members of plural families told us, and we observed, that their family life is a struggle. They seem to be engaged in an endless process of experimentation, trial and error, and hit and miss, as they try to figure out how to maintain viable families in a lifestyle with which they have had little prior experience.

The larger fundamentalist culture and community is not always able to help individuals and families very much. To be sure, religious leaders, elders, friends, and family counsel members when stresses mount, and they probably help to some extent. But the fact is that there are few widespread cultural norms, rituals, and practices to guide individuals and families in managing day-to-day life and intimate relationships between husbands and wives in American polygynous families. Why not? Because the fundamentalist culture itself is new, especially in regard to plural family life. The 19th-century Mormons openly practiced polygyny for only about 40 years, between 1852 and 1890. Before and after those years, plural marriage was engaged in secretly and by relatively few men and women. And even during the years of open practice, only a small number of families were polygynous. As noted in an earlier chapter, Mormon fundamentalism rose up again in the 1930s, but the groups were small. Only in the last few decades has the number of fundamentalists grown, and there are still only a small number of families who are polygynous. So, there has never been broadly based or multigenerational and culture-wide experience about how to live in plural families. As a result, each family is more or less on its own and must itself figure out how to live this complicated lifestyle.

Taken as a whole, therefore, participants in contemporary plural families face a variety of external and internal challenges, which in the end have produced a culture, families, and individuals "in search of themselves." But many modern American families also face uncertainty, although their circumstances are somewhat different from those of plural families. In their case, the challenge is how to live in blended families, single-parent families, same-gender families, families with unmarried partners, and others. To be sure, all of these family forms are monogamous, but they often involve dynamics that are unique and new to many participants. And cultural guidelines are not always readily at hand to help people cope with the unique stresses and requirements of such relationships. Members of modern plural families and those in newly emerging family forms are similarly inexperienced, and all must experiment and engage in a process of trial and error to figure out how to live in a viable way.

Thus internal and external challenges are integral to *all* close relationships. Social and physical contexts, and cultural and historical contexts, are a crucial aspect of the milieu of every close relationship. As a result, a transactional perspective demands sensitivity to the variety of contexts of close relationships if we are to fully appreciate the dynamics and functioning of any close social bond.

Given all this stress and strain, turmoil and conflict, external and internal pressure, why do people stay in plural families? There were a number of divorces in the families with whom we worked, and divorces were not uncommon in plural families in the 19th century. However, fundamentalist groups are growing, people are not leaving in great numbers, and those with whom we spoke are committed to their lifestyle. Why is this the case? A major reason is that they believe in their religion. Mormon fundamentalists hold fast to 19th-century notions regarding plural marriage, a patriarchal family and religious structure, an afterlife with husbands as "kings" and wives as "queens" governing in their own heavenly universe and surrounded by their children, and other doctrinal teachings. Thus fundamentalists are willing to suffer pressures from the outside world and cope with the internal stresses of plural family life because they believe in the religious righteousness of their lifestyle.

Are there other motives? Do men seek "harems" and an exciting sexual life as a reason for engaging in polygyny? We cannot answer these questions and admit to the possibility that some men and women may have motives above and beyond religious beliefs as a basis for joining the fundamentalist movement. For men, however, any sexual motives must surely pall after a while, as the day-to-day pressures of plural family life cumulate – the financial burdens, the needs of large families, family tensions and conflicts, and so on. From our perspective, plural family life is not especially "romantic" for men. (Indeed, in some ways the widespread occurrence in American society of serial marriages and divorces, repeated cases of cohabitation of unmarried couples, affairs and mistresses, seems much simpler, more "romantic," and less burdensome than a permanent involvement with multiple wives and families!)

And are there other than religious reasons, or additional reasons, for women to enter plural families? Some women seem to convert to fundamentalism because they have "discovered" the true and underlying basis of Mormonism, including plural marriage (Ginat, 1985). Others are divorced women seeking security; still others have children and are alone or are rejected by their families; some are older widows or divorcées who have few options or support systems. In addition to satisfying religious beliefs, plural marriages offer an "instant" support group for many women in precarious social, financial, and interpersonal circumstances. They have the security of a community and family, the support and assistance of other women, someone to care for their children, and a highly structured set of roles with respect to their husband and children. So although plural family life is difficult, it has the potential to provide a structured and secure religious value system and family life for some women who may have lost their way in mainstream society, as well as for those who believe in fundamentalist theology. Needless to say, men and women who grow up in fundamentalist families and communities are socialized into the religious and social values of the movement. For them, it is probably only "natural" to live a plural family lifestyle, even though they must also cope with a variety of internal and external pressures.

The religious underpinnings of modern plural families are evident in many aspects of day-to-day living. For example, adding a new wife to a plural family is not solely up to a husband; theoretically, it must be justified on religious grounds. In the urban community, wives often play an active role – agreeing to the idea, approving a prospective wife, and, in some instances, initiating the idea and seeking out potential wives themselves in order to meet their religious obligations. And permission is not only required of a prospective wife's parents but must be granted by the religious leader of the church, on the basis of the religious worthiness of a man and his family (in the rural community marriages are arranged by the prophet, sometimes with participation by families or couple members). Although these principles are not always followed, they reflect the cultural and religious underpinnings of plural marriages. And wedding ceremonies are religious, with established wives participating and giving their approval and blessing to a new marriage. The regularity of attendance at church services of large numbers of group members further symbolizes the importance of religion in the lives of the Mormon fundamentalists with whom we worked.

Religious values are also evident in the day-to-day life of plural families. In almost every home we visited – and in almost every room in every home

– religious decorations were prominent. Indeed, our sense is that religious decorations are the foundation and cornerstone of home decor. Paintings of religious figures and scenes, photographs, statues, embroideries, and religious sayings were everywhere. In most cases, religious decorations seemed to be far more extensive and visible in the homes of fundamentalist Mormons than in the homes of most Americans of almost any religious background. Also, Mormon fundamentalists use their homes for a variety of religious and family events, such as Sunday dinners before or after church; Christmas, Easter, and other holidays; and daily prayers by family members. Beyond the home, the social life of many plural families is centered around the church – Sunday church services, church-sponsored children's camps and schools, social dances in the church, work projects involving church members, and so on. And friends and work associates are often members of the fundamentalist group to which people belong, reinforcing and sustaining their common cultural and religious beliefs.

In addition, family members often reported praying, appealing to their religious beliefs, seeking succor in religious study, reminding themselves of the importance of plural family life in the hereafter, and calling on church elders to help them cope with the challenges and stresses of everyday family life. Some participants even said that they never would have survived the stresses and strains of plural family life without their strong religious faith. A rationalization? Perhaps it is in some cases. Nevertheless, their self-affirmed religious beliefs carried them through, or at least helped them cope with this challenging lifestyle.

Once again, a reasonable appreciation of Mormon polygyny cannot be achieved without understanding something about its cultural, historical, and religious underpinnings. A transactional perspective assumes that there is *always* some important cultural context(s) – not necessarily religion – undergirding *all* close relationships, and that understanding how relationships are embedded in and inseparable from those contexts is an essential research requirement.

What is the future of Mormon fundamentalism? Generalizations are risky, but here are our speculations.

Family composition and day-to-day life are somewhat different in the urban and rural groups with whom we worked. Because they are geographically isolated and somewhat separate from the culture at large and because they do not actively seek or easily accept converts, families in the United Fundamentalist Church in Redrock are not exposed to as many external pressures as their counterparts in the Church of Latter-day Apostles in the Metropolitan City region. Moreover, many people in the rural community were raised in multigeneration polygynous families, so they have more experience in plural family life than members of the urban community, a large number of whom are converts to Mormon fundamentalism. As a result, we expect members of the rural group to function reasonably well in plural families. In contrast, people in the urban community are exposed daily to mainstream monogamous society and to lifestyles that may appeal to many fundamentalist group members, especially children and young adults. As a counterforce, however, an increasing number of converts to the fundamentalist movement are seeking security, community, a grounding in strong religious values, and escape from the stresses and tensions of modern life.

We also predict that both fundamentalist movements will continue to grow, by virtue of their internal birth rates – which are quite high – and by conversions (especially in the urban community). At the same time, the inexperience of many participants and the challenge of coping with plural family life will be very stressful for some group members. Advances in technology; the likelihood of working alongside people from the mainstream American culture; the inevitable exposure of adults and children to the larger world through education, the mass media, and technology – all may raise questions in the minds of individual fundamentalists about plural family life. Although we anticipate continued growth and participation in plural family life, we also believe that individuals and families will continue to struggle with many of these issues in the foreseeable future.

We also predict that fundamentalist communities and groups will experience a blend of stability and upheaval in the coming years. On the one hand, the urban and rural groups with whom we worked are relatively stable in several respects. They have grown steadily for more than four decades, hold significant financial resources in land and real estate holdings, and have developed institutional infrastructures (for example, the rural community controls the school system, local government, and a variety of community facilities; the urban group has its own school and also operates a number of satellite communities). Whereas it might have been tempting in years past to label these groups as "sects," "cults," and religious "fanatics," the fact is that they are fairly stable and established organizations and communities. In contrast to earlier periods in history, when their very survival was questionable in view of internal and external pressures, today these groups are well established. In our judgment, they are here to stay.

But this is not to say that all will forever be tranquil, or that internal and external threats will not arise again. The urban group has had at least one major internal split in the past several decades. And the rural community continues in a long-standing legal battle with a dissident group about ownership of land and resources. Furthermore, from time to time splinter groups emerge around new leaders who claim that they are the "true" prophets of Mormon fundamentalism. A variety of internal conflicts also seem likely to arise. For example, we recently learned that members of two of our primary families are no longer in the larger group – one family new to the fundamentalist movement, and the other a long-term and previously well-established family. A combination of theological, political, and interpersonal issues seemed to be at the root of these conflicts. These internal splits and the emergence of new groups stem partly from political power struggles and partly from the religious underpinnings of Mormonism. Because of the belief that any individual can commune with God and experience a "revelation," there have historically been many dissident groups splitting off from the main Mormon Church. And that pattern is likely to continue. Thus other founders of new fundamentalist groups or dissidents from existing groups may well announce that they have received a revelation and that they are "the One and Mighty" who has been instructed by God to lead people along a proper path. Some of these new prophets will attract a core of followers and establish their own version of Mormon fundamentalism. This is what happened to several families in the urban group that recently split off to follow a new leader. We expect that this pattern will continue.

It is also not uncommon for new groups to seek out and attract attention from the media, with appearances on TV and radio talk shows, and reports in the print media. Rarely does one see popularized and public accounts of life in well-established groups, although the Public Broadcasting Service occasionally does careful and balanced documentaries on historical Mormonism and present-day fundamentalism. The high public profile of dissident and independent groups can be a source of instability and worry to established groups, because it often revives public hostility toward fundamentalists in general and raises the specter of arrests, prosecution, and other forms of external pressure. Even though there is no sign on the horizon that civil actions are imminent, or even foreseeable, the possibility is always a source of concern to fundamentalists. Because it was only a few decades ago that arrests, raids, and other punitive actions occurred, Mormon fundamentalists are always wary about the future. At the same time, although mass arrests are highly unlikely, we anticipate occasional targeted legal actions against fundamentalist families and individuals in employment cases, adoption cases, specific legislative proposals, and the like.

All in all, therefore, we project continued growth of Mormon fundamentalism and plural family life well into the future. Nevertheless, internal and external pressures will be ever present and more or less serious from time to time, depending on dissident movements, media interest, and potential threats from the larger society.

Recently, one writer called upon contemporary society to ponder seriously alternative family and marriage styles – particularly the forms of plural marriages now on the scene in our own and other cultures (Kilbride

1994). Following a scholarly analysis of various forms of polygamy, Kilbride suggested that different groups in contemporary cultures might benefit from some form of legitimized plural marriage: religious groups such as Mormon fundamentalists, some women already practicing "mansharing" (i.e., women who desire to be part of a larger family of their own choosing, but not the traditional nuclear family), elderly women faced with few available male partners because of gender mortality differences, bisexual men and women, groups in which there is an imbalanced sex ratio, and others seeking to become part of extended families of choice. Whether one agrees with such possibilities or not, they underscore the complex realities of family life in contemporary society and the need to study, discuss, and understand the dynamics and consequences of alternative family forms.

Although each of the various types of monogamous and polygamous family forms that now exist or that we might conceive of is different in many respects from Mormon plural families, they must all cope with some key problems. First, like fundamentalism, many of these family forms are new and strange to their members. Participants often have had little or unsuccessful previous experience with them and therefore must experiment, search, and engage in trial and error to figure out how to achieve a viable life. Second, and central to the thrust of our analysis, all of these new family forms must manage the interplay of dyadic and communal issues that they inevitably face. That is, partners in all of these relationship forms must cope with the unique circumstances of their dyadic relationships in the context of communal relationships with their children, families, parents, friends, co-workers, and others. Thus partners in blended families, for example, must not only develop a viable dyadic relationship with one another, but they must do so in the context of communal relationships involving their children from previous families. The absence of widespread individual and cultural experience to facilitate a constructive interplay of dyadic and communal processes means that members of all these new forms of close relationships face enormous challenges.

In spite of the problems they face, some of these new forms of close relationships – including plural families among contemporary Mormon fundamentalists – are here to stay in American and Western society. They are not likely to "go away"; they are not fads or fancies; they are not aberrations. They will be part of the family life scene well into the future.

We must therefore learn about them, learn from them, and even help people live the lifestyle of their choice. Doing so increases the probability that participants in emerging forms of close relationships will contribute to the well-being and quality of life in American society at large. Not doing so, and viewing these family lifestyles as inherently immoral, wrong, and unacceptable, increases the probability that American society will fragment, with a declining sense of community and civility in our public and private lives.

Final thoughts on understanding close relationships

Our analysis of life in contemporary plural families was guided by a transactional philosophical approach. This perspective calls for an understanding of *multiple aspects of close relationships,* an appreciation of the *social and physical contexts within which relationships are embedded* and from which they are inseparable, and a tracking of the inevitable *changes, twists, and turns that take place in relationships over the short and long term.*

These principles led us to examine many facets of the bonds between husbands and wives in modern plural families, from their feelings and beliefs to the way they live, decorate their homes, manage their money, and so on. And by accepting the principle that close relationships are dynamic, we tried to be sensitive to the unfolding life of plural families as new wives and more children joined a family, and as a variety of everyday circumstances arose to create new challenges for family members.

Also central to our transactional perspective is the principle that husband–wife relationships and wife–wife relationships are intimately joined with and inseparable from one another. Understanding the *dyadic* relationships between any couple in a plural family requires an appreciation of how couples are embedded in, defined by, and part of the *communal* context of other wives and couples in a family.

Putting a transactional perspective into action may also affect choice of research methodology. We have argued elsewhere that any method can be tailored to a transactional strategy (Altman and Rogoff, 1987). We chose an ethnographic and qualitative approach to study plural families and believe that it has met our goals and has been nicely suited to our situation and participants. Our firm belief is that methodology should be tailored to research needs and problems, not vice versa. As such there is no "perfect," "best," or "most definitive" methodological approach to knowledge, what is "best" depends on the goals, contexts, and requirements of a particular avenue of research. Although qualitative and ethnographic methods are uncommon in some social science fields, notably psychology, they are well developed and valuable approaches, as demonstrated by their sophistication and success in other fields, notably anthropology. Thus, scholars studying close relationships should not be timid, defensive, or apologetic about qualitative and ethnographic strategies; indeed, they offer unmatched richness, scope, and depth to often sterile, narrow, and constricted analyses of close relationships.

As a final word, we encourage scholars and participants to be sensitive to the holistic nature of social relationships, to their social and physical contextual qualities, and to the dynamic and evolving features of close relationships. Doing so will enhance our scholarly *understanding* of social and emotional ties between people and will also magnify the opportunities for people to *achieve in "real life"* more satisfying and healthy close relationships with others.

APPENDIX A

Methodology and procedure

We obtained most of the information for this project over a five-year period, from 1987 to 1992, with some supplementary interviews and observations done up to 1994. However, the foundation for the research was established in the early 1970s, when Joseph Ginat was completing graduate studies in anthropology at the University of Utah. Beginning then, and up to the present, Ginat maintained relationships with members of both fundamentalist groups that are the focus of the present book. He also completed a research project in a fundamentalist community (Parker, Ginat, and Smith, 1975). Ginat has visited the urban and rural communities regularly since the 1970s, consulting with their leaders and members on biblical, archeological, and religious history; visiting and living on occasion in the homes of community members; attending and speaking in church and other meetings; hosting leaders and members in his home in Israel; and taking delegations on tours of holy sites in Israel. Given his extensive knowledge of biblical history, theology, and archeology and the fact that he is not an American but an Israeli (and one who was descended from the biblical tribe of Levi – spiritual leaders of biblical times), Ginat has been readily accepted by the fundamentalist communities.

Our collaboration began when Irwin and Gloria Altman visited Israel in 1986 to participate in professional meetings. Joseph and Dalia Ginat hosted the Altmans and, after two weeks of renewing an earlier casual acquaintanceship, we decided to fuse our interests in close relationships, family structure, environment and behavior, and polygyny, and crafted the present project. Expecting the study to involve a 1- to 2-year collaboration, we are now pleased that it required us to work together for 10 years.

As described in chapter 1, our goal was to learn about husband–wife and wife–wife relationships in contemporary Mormon polygynous families. Specifically, we were interested in the way fundamentalist Mormon families achieved or failed to achieve viable multiple husband–wife dyadic relationships in the context of also believing in the importance of positive communal relationships between wives. To address this general question, we developed the following methodological strategy:

1. Using the transactional perspective described in chapter 1, we identified a series of "life domains," described throughout the book, that seemed to be relevant to dyadic and communal relationships in plural families. These tapped social and physical environmental aspects of family life at different life stages, thereby

incorporating a temporal quality. We had preplanned to obtain information about most of these topics. Others emerged spontaneously during our visits, discussions, and observations, and we included them as we went along. For example, we had not planned in advance to gather information about husbands' clothing, celebrations, choosing names of newborn children, or the terms children use to refer to their mother and other wives. Thus to some extent we were reflexive in learning about husband–wife and wife–wife relationships and were open to new types of information that emerged in the course of the project.

2. Our primary information came from face-to-face interviews and discussions with members of contemporary plural families and from observations of homes, communities, activities, and interactions between family members. We also planned in advance to cast our information in the context of 19th-century Mormon history, theology, and plural family life.

3. We also felt that it was important to place contemporary fundamentalist polygyny in the context of the practice of polygyny in other cultures. Therefore we included descriptions of how other polygynous cultures handled courtships, weddings, husband–wife and wife–wife relationships, and the other topics addressed in the book.

The sample of participants

Table 1 shows that we worked with 26 families (and also collected information about their community activities, such as church meetings and dances). The number of interviews and observations varied from family to family, as did the amount of information (reflected in pages of field notes), number of participants, and the time frame over which we worked with families.

The 26 families were not a random sample. Some families satisfied criteria we had in mind in advance; others were introduced to us by someone, or we happened to meet them at a gathering or event.

Several principles guided the selection of families with whom we worked most closely. First, we sought plural families with two or more wives, even though many families in the fundamentalist movement are monogamous (we did interview a few monogamous husbands and wives; some are children of our main participants with whom we spent time, or we met them spontaneously and included information from them in our analyses). Second, we solicited cooperation from plural families who had varied experiences and were at different stages of family life. Thus some families are well established, with members at middle or later ages; others are younger families and still growing. Third, we selected families with members from established and multigeneration plural families, and families with some members who are converts and new to the fundamentalist movement. Fourth, we included families from the urban Church of Latter-day Apostles who have their headquarters in Metropolitan City, and from the United Fundamentalist Church in the rural area around the town of Redrock. (Most families in our sample are from the urban group.) Fifth, we deliberately sought to include relatively stable families and families that had serious conflict and upheavals (we interviewed four women who divorced

Table 1. *Summary of interviews/observations*

Family	No. of interviews/ observations	Pages of field notes	No. of participants[a]	Data collected
1 (P)[b]	14	158	7 (H, 4 W, others)	9/87–11/92
2 (P)	8	104	8 (H, 4 W, others)	7/87–9/92
3 (P)	11	112	4 (H, 3W)	7/87–8/91
4 (P)	49	241	6 (H, 5 W, others)	7/87–9/92
5 (P)	5	81	5 (H, 4 W, others)	7/88–7/90
6 (P)	16	137	8 (H, 5 W, others)	7/87–9/92
7	5	25	6 (H, 3 W, others)	12/87–8/91
8 (P)	14	92	6 (H, 5W)	7/87–8/92
9 (P)	11	85	6 (H, 3 W, others)	6/88–9/92
10 (P)	3	63	9 (H, 8 W, others)	7/88–8/90
11	4	12	4 (H, 2 W, others)	6/88
12 (P)	7	49	3 (W, others)	12/87–8/91
13	3	23	1 (W)	7/87–6/88
14 (P)	8	40	1 (W)	7/87–8/91
15	2	7	1 (W)	9/87–7/88
16	6	32	1 (W)	7/87–8/91
17	1	4	1 (H)	undated–1987
18 (P)	2	34	6 (H, 3 W, others)	7/88–8/90
19	1	3	1 (W)	7/88
20	2	7	2 (H, others)	12/87–9/92
21 community events[c]	11	58		9/87–7/90
22	1	2	1 (W)	1/89
23	1	2	1 (W)	4/87
24	1	3	5 (H, 4W)	7/88
25	1	4	5 (H, W, others)	8/91
26	1	5	1 H	8/91
27	1	2	1 H	8/91
Total	189	1,385	100 (plus others)	

Note: Contacts with some families continued until 1994, with clarifying information obtained on occasion, but with no new field notes included in our analysis. The information in table 1 underestimates the actual number of interviews or observations. However, the number of field note pages is a slight overestimate, since some information about a few families arose in interviews with other families; in such cases, field note pages are counted twice.
[a]H husband; W wife; others include children or members of other families. They are counted as participants if they contributed to discussions in more than a cursory way.
[b]Primary families.
[c]Church services, dances, etc.

their husbands or left a plural family). Sixth, our informants varied in status in the fundamentalist movement, ranging from those in leadership positions to those who are younger but on the rise, to those who are relatively new or not in influential positions. To satisfy systematically this array of criteria would have required a very large sample of families. That was not possible because of restrictions on time and resources, so we did our best to have at least a few cases satisfying some of these ideal principles.

We sought permission from either the church prophet or religious leader, a church or community leader, or a family elder to meet with members of a family. Because Joseph Ginat had long-standing relationships with church leaders and many families in both fundamentalist groups, they willingly agreed to participate in the project. They also introduced us to other potential participants.

In discussions with leaders and families, we described the research, our plans to publish the results, the voluntary nature of their participation, and our intention to do our best to protect their anonymity and confidentiality.

As our contacts with a family evolved, we decided either to continue our interviews and involve them as key or primary participants or to obtain only selective information from them. Our decision was based on their interest in our work and how they fit into our plan to sample different types of families. We worked closely with 12 families as primary participants, with others providing valuable but more selective information. As shown in table 1, primary families in the project, designated by the letter P, account for 148/189, or 78% of our interviews (and 1,196/ 1,385 pages, or 86% of our field notes).

Information-gathering procedures

We learned about plural family life through interviews, observations, participation in family and public events, and some photography of dwellings. We also used a variety of archival sources, including scholarly books and treatises, newspaper and investigative accounts, personal autobiographies, and historical and ethnographic material.

Interviews and observations

Interviews and observations were our primary source of data. Most interviews were arranged in advance, although in a few cases we happened to meet with someone without advance planning. We also observed several aspects of plural family life, especially in homes, church services, social dances, and public settings in communities. For example, we were especially interested in home furnishings and decorations, and some families with whom we worked closely invited us to visit their homes on several occasions and to see living rooms, kitchens, bedrooms, and other spaces. In these cases, our field notes contain descriptions of decorations and furnishings that we saw and asked about, as well as sleeping arrangements and use of space. These visits involved a combination of observations and interviews and were especially useful in our descriptions of environmental aspects of plural family life. In a few cases, we asked and were permitted to photograph various parts of homes.

We also attended church services and social dances and observed the flow of events and interactions between participants in these settings. In the rural community, we visited its large meeting hall, attended social dances, participated in family recreational activities, and spent time in the town cafeteria and in other settings. Through these participant observations and accompanying discussions with our hosts and others, we learned a great deal about various facets of family and community life.

As noted in table 1, we conducted 189 interviews or observations (many interviews also incorporated observations of family homes). The number of interviews or observations per family varied from 1 to 49 (the latter case involved Family 4 in the rural community, with whom we lived for several days and engaged in a continuous series of observations and interviews). Table 1 also indicates that we had discussions with more than 100 members of the families in our sample – mostly husbands and wives, but a few children as well.

We collected most of the information from 1987 to 1992, with some families participating in our research over the full span of those years. (We also conducted a few additional interviews in 1993 and 1994, in order to supplement and clarify earlier information. Actuarial data from these interviews are not counted in the tables of this appendix.)

Format of interviews

Interviews were unstructured; that is, they did not follow a strict order of questions, nor were questions framed in exactly the same words from interview to interview. Interviews were informal conversations, although we did our best to cover the range of topics in which we were interested.

In the early phases of the project, interviews were wide ranging and touched on a variety of topics from our list, with the discussion flowing in whatever direction emerged. We were especially open to issues that participants seemed comfortable discussing. As our pool of information grew and as participants became more comfortable with our questions and better understood the project, interviewing became more selective. With successive interviews with a family, we reviewed our field notes to identify topics about which more information was needed and focused on those during the next meeting. While we were always open to new topics that related to our research goals and that we had not previously thought about, we also did our best to round out information on previously targeted topics.

Participants in meetings

We met with many different configurations of participants – husbands alone, a husband and one or more wives, a husband, wives and some of their children, members of two plural families who were relatives, divorced or separated wives, and so on. We rarely met with a wife or wives alone. Most meetings were prearranged with a husband, and we were not always sure who would participate, although on some occasions we expressed interest in particular participants who could address or follow up on specific issues.

Many of our meetings involved a husband and some or all wives; in some cases, small children were present; in other cases, adult children had been invited and even spontaneously participated in discussions. The most memorable group interview involved a husband who was a community leader, eight wives, several of their married children and spouses, teens and young adults, and a host of toddlers and infants. At least 50 to 70 people attended this family "event," which probably was a special occasion because of Joseph Ginat's presence. Although the numbers of participants on this occasion violated elementary principles of interviewing, we felt that everyone was frank and open over the course of a several-hour discussion, and even younger members of the family participated from time to time.

The flow of meetings

In the initial meeting with a husband, wife, or husband and wives, we introduced ourselves (everyone knew Ginat personally or by reputation; almost no one knew Altman at first except through his affiliation with Ginat), and then described the project – as a study of family structure and relationships between a husband and each wife and between wives, and with an interest in different areas of family life. We also said that we hoped that our findings would be helpful to them in managing their lives and in educating the larger culture about fundamentalism in a way that might result in better understanding of their lifestyle. We stated that we planned to publish our findings in professional articles and in a book, and that we would attempt to ensure their personal confidentiality and anonymity. We also told potential participants that their participation was voluntary, and that we would respect their wishes if they did not want to discuss a topic. Everyone we approached agreed to participate in the study, and in only a few instances did participants decline to discuss certain issues.

In initial meetings, we usually first asked about family demographics – the number of wives in a family, ages of husbands and wives, number of children, when each marriage occurred, and other aspects of family members' backgrounds and history. As the discussion evolved, we then opened up topics from our general list that seemed appropriate and comfortable to pursue. As noted earlier, for subsequent meetings we prepared in advance to pursue topics for which we needed additional information, or that we had not yet discussed. But even then, we did not rigidly control discussions but allowed conversations to flow in as natural a way as possible. Sometimes it took several meetings to fully explore a single topic, with conversations sometimes ranging widely over various subjects.

We also allowed new topics to emerge spontaneously and pursued them if they meshed with our interests. Or we sometimes talked about things that participants wanted to talk about, even though they did not always apply directly to the project. For example, they sometimes discussed their theology at a level of detail that went beyond the scope of our study. Or some participants wanted to learn about our lives and family relationships, about Ginat's life and politics in Israel, or Altman's role and activities at the university. When we told families that our interviews with them were probably completed and that they were free to ask us questions, some probed further about the research, how they might use the findings, and so on.

We also did not plan precisely who would play what interviewing role when we met jointly with family members. Either one of us entered into the discussion when we felt it was appropriate, when a line of conversation needed further probing, or when either of us felt that it was time to move to a new topic. We relied on our joint and separate intuitions and assessments of the situations and moved in and out of roles in an informal way. It never felt awkward or strained to play things out informally or to interrupt or "take over" from one another.

In some instances, our meetings were primarily social, with less direct attention given to systematic interviewing, except as relevant topics emerged. Social contacts occurred in church meetings and dances and when we visited one another's homes for meals or celebrations.

Most of our interviews and meetings occurred primarily during Ginat's visits to the United States, which averaged about once or twice a year and which lasted for at least 7 to 14 days at a time. We did this for several reasons: we wanted to do as much joint interviewing and development of field notes as possible; Ginat's visits were important occasions in both communities and facilitated our participation in a variety of public events; our participants were eager to spend time with him and be involved in the project when he was present; he could freely consult with leaders regarding families with whom we might work; his discussions with leaders and others often provided important information about community affairs and other background issues.

Table 2 indicates that 31% of the field notes of interviews and observations were done by both Altman and Ginat, 41% were done by Ginat alone, and 28% were done by Altman alone. Table 2 also shows that 59% of our pages of field notes involved interviews and observations that we both summarized. The remainder of our field notes were generated from separate interviews and observations or single reports of joint interviews.

Our wives also participated in some meetings, especially with primary participants. These occurred when we lived in the rural community for several days, when some participants were entertained by the Altmans, and in some visits to participants' homes. Our wives sometimes entered into discussions, chatting generally, or pursuing aspects of the research protocol. In one visit to the rural community, they discussed relevant topics with some wives when we were not present.

Time and length of meetings

Meetings varied widely in length – from brief telephone conversations and casual encounters, to several-hour sessions on long car rides or visits in homes. Most meetings lasted from 1 to 3 hours. Because many sessions took place in homes at a meal or during the evening, or at a restaurant, a couple of hours of conversation was quite natural. The length of meetings was not set in advance; they simply played out informally and as circumstances and social norms warranted. The flow and energy of the discussion also influenced how long we met. Sometimes the conversation was absorbing and intense; sometimes it lagged or petered out; sometimes we or the participants had other commitments, and the session had to be curtailed.

Table 2. *Joint and separate interviews and field notes by Altman and Ginat*

Family	Joint interviews, notes	Pages joint field notes	JG interviews, notes alone	IA interviews, notes alone
1	5	95/158	3	6
2	5	99/104	1	2
3	5	89/112	4	2
4	14	121/241	17	18
5	5	81/81	0	0
6	5	89/137	8	3
7	2	16/25	1	1
8	3	44/92	8	3
9	2	44/85	8	1
10	2	41/63	0	1
11	2	6/12	1	1
12	1	8/49	3	3
13	1	16/23	2	0
14	1	12/40	6	1
15	0	0/7	2	0
16	0	0/32	6	0
17	0	0/4	1	0
18	2	34/34	0	0
19	0	0/3	0	1
20	0	0/7	0	1
21	3	20/58	2	6
22	0	0/2	0	1
23	0	0/2	0	1
24	1	3/3	0	0
25	0	0/4	1	0
26	0	0/5	1	0
27	0	0/2	1	0
Total	59 (31%)	818/1,385 (59%)	76 (41%)	52 (28%)

Note: Sometimes interviews or observations were done jointly, but only one of us did field notes. Thus the number of jointly conducted interviews is actually higher than indicated in the table.

Locations of meetings

We met with participants in many places. A main meeting place was family homes, often in the evening or on weekends. People were hospitable and happy to have us visit their homes. It was a convenient and comfortable place for them, and many participants were proud of their homes. Home visits also gave us an opportunity to observe informal aspects of a family's lifestyle, furnishings, and decorations and, in some instances, to tour a home. In one case, we spent several days living with a

family in the Redrock community and participating in family and community activities (Ginat had visited and stayed with this family on many occasions over the
years).

We also had meetings with families or individuals in restaurants, where we were
often hosts and reciprocated in a small way the hospitality they showed us. When
opportunities arose, we also invited some participants to the Altman home – for
breakfast, dinner, or dessert. Sometimes we entertained a husband and one or more
wives; sometimes they brought along children or other family members. On several
occasions, participants and other members of a group visited Israel, were entertained at the Ginat family home, and were taken on tours by him. Visits to our
homes were pleasant occasions, enabled participants to see how we lived, and
strengthened our mutual relationships.

Other meetings occurred on automobile trips, on the telephone, in church, at
community social events, and elsewhere. We attended several church meetings in
each community, were invited to speak in church about events in Israel (Ginat), or
about our research and its goals (Altman and Ginat). We were sometimes invited
to sit on the platform alongside church leaders during church services, attended
social events in both communities, such as dances, and had an opportunity to meet,
talk with, and observe a wide variety of community members. In these public settings we were highly visible to community members, were publicly welcomed by
church leaders, and were able to observe social interactions, community customs
and practices, and gain a sense of aspects of fundamentalist community life.

Recording information

Our basic data consisted of field notes, that is, our narrative accounts of interviews,
discussions, and observations. When we jointly interviewed families or made observations, we each prepared separate field notes, which we later compared for
consistency and reliability (when our notes disagreed, we resolved issues through
discussion). Field notes were dictated onto a tape recorder immediately following
an observation or interview, or within a very short time thereafter. Field notes
recorded the date, participants, and location of the interview or observation and
which of us prepared the notes. They included a free narrative of what occurred
during our contact with participants, as well as our own comments, interpretations,
questions, and notes for future discussions.

A substantial portion of the field notes were generated from memory, because
we did not always make written notes. We *never* tape-recorded interviews or observations. Although Ginat was widely trusted by group members and Altman gradually assumed credibility, Ginat felt that recordings were out of the question and
that even note taking in initial meetings might lead participants to become reticent
or resistant. After all, members of these groups were not familiar with research
practices, had probably never discussed with outsiders the questions we posed, and
had a long and remembered history of persecution and prosecution. Over time,
however, we were able to take some notes during interviews, especially with participants with whom we had several meetings and had come to know well. Our

note taking was done as unobtrusively as possible, on small pads, by jotting down points intermittently.

With notes in hand, or through memory alone, we independently dictated our recollections of meetings onto a tape recorder. In a few very complex and lengthy meetings involving many people, we discussed the session with one another immediately afterward, jotting down important themes, content, topics, and issues that had been discussed. Although we did not produce completely independent field notes on these occasions, a quick discussion increased the likelihood that we would produce a more thorough account of the meeting.

In general, our field notes were consistent with one another. We tended to remember the same content, rarely disagreed on major points, and readily resolved inconsistencies. There were, of course, occasions on which one of us did not record parts of an interview or observation. But it was relatively easy to acknowledge what had been left out after seeing the other's account. We did not do quantitative reliability checks on our field notes but concluded that we were sufficiently consistent to proceed without formal analyses. Furthermore, our consistency with one another increased throughout the project because successive interviews were usually targeted to specific issues and topics that we had agreed to pursue in advance of a session. Moreover, we had begun to code and organize our data in preparation for the analysis stages of the project, so we were more focused as the research progressed. And because we had learned so much about each family, it became easier to integrate new information about them into what we already knew. In general, therefore, we are confident that our data collection and recording procedures had sufficient checks and balance to make our field notes accurate accounts of our observations and interviews.

As indicated in table 1, the 189 interviews or observations with more than 100 participants in 26 families resulted in 1,385 double-spaced typed manuscript pages of field notes. These field notes constituted the primary data of our analysis (supplemented, as noted earlier, by published research, biographical, and other analyses of 19th-century and present-day Mormon plural families, and by ethnographic reports of other polygynous cultures).

Processing field notes

We first coded field notes according to the categories of information described earlier, for example, adding a wife, courtship, weddings, and so on. This was a relatively straightforward task. The field notes were then regrouped by category for each family. That is, we put all information about a topic in one place, family by family. For example, all the information we had accumulated about courtship was clustered together, family by family. The regrouping of information was done "manually." That is, we worked from the field notes, redictating information contained in them on a given topic to make the material more succinct. In so doing we integrated our separate field notes to produce a single account of the material. The original field notes were "raw data," were not always well organized, and the same point may have been discussed with a different slant by each of us. The redictated summaries for each topic per family extracted key issues, brought to light the central substance, clarified descriptions, and integrated our independent narratives. In preparing summaries, we tried to remain true to the content of the field notes, did not include inferences or interpretations, but focused on the central content of the field notes, point by point. Finally, the summaries of information on each topic per family were linked to pages in the field notes, which made it possible to move back and forth between the summaries and the field notes.

The summaries on each topic constituted the refined data base we used to synthesize information and write up the results described in each chapter of the book. The basic content and organization of chapters derive from our conceptual framework regarding dyadic and communal aspects of life in contemporary Mormon polygynous families.

Commentary on our research methodology

We consciously used a methodological strategy that was multifaceted, selective, reflexive, and sensitive to our participants' perspectives. In retrospect, we are satisfied with our approach but also acknowledge its limitations and deviations from some traditional social science strategies.

Our methodology was multifaceted in that we tapped into a variety of aspects of the life of present-day plural families and also used a variety of sources of information. Thus we drew on ethnographic reports of life in approximately 50 polygynous cultures, studies of 19th-century Mormon polygyny, biographical and autobiographical accounts of present-day and 19th-century participants in Mormon plural families, newspaper and magazine stories and reports, and the like.

Our research strategy was selective in being "broad" in some respects and "deep" in others. We decided at the outset to examine a broad range of life experiences in plural families in order to develop a holistic picture of husband–wife and wife–wife relationships. At the same time we decided in advance to work closely and in depth with a small number of families and to obtain more limited information from others. Thus for some families we tapped broadly and deeply into many aspects of their family life; for others, we gathered selective information to test the generalizability of what we learned from our primary families.

Doing intensive work with many families would have been ideal, but it simply was not possible because of time and resource restrictions. And although a normative study of a few aspects of family life on a large sample would also have been appropriate, we elected to focus on a small sample of families and learn about them in depth. Thus we adopted a case study strategy, rather than a large sample analysis.

We were also selective in data collection methods, using open-ended interviews and informal observations, explicitly ruling out standardized and highly structured questionnaires or interviews. Given the participants' history of perceived persecution and prosecution, we decided that they might feel threatened by highly structured methods. In addition, we wanted to be open to a range of topics and different facets of family life that we might not have anticipated in advance; a structured approach would rule out that possibility.

There are obvious tradeoffs in our selective research strategy – a nonrepresentative sample of families, incomplete and potentially biased information, uncertain reliability and validity of the data as a result of open-ended procedures, and not easily replicable information. In spite of these potential problems, we believe that our results offer a unique perspective on the life of plural family members, and that it is one that would have not emerged had we used a large sample survey or structured interview or questionnaire procedures. Furthermore, we attempted to address the same issues with several families and with the same family on multiple occasions, as a way of corroborating findings. So doing, and using a variety of historical, archival, and ethnographic materials, helped round out and place our findings in perspective.

Our research methodology was also reflexive in that, contrary to much social science research, we did not specify in advance a fixed study design, procedures, and sample and then follow them rigidly throughout the project. Thus we did not select a full set of families to work with at the outset but added families as the research progressed, as our network of contacts evolved, and as we learned about different types of families.

Being open to new and unanticipated topics regarding plural family life was another way in which our methodology was reflexive. In some cases we were able to pursue new issues in some detail, such as the management of a husband's clothing or celebrations. In other cases, new topics – such as the terms children used to refer to their own mother and other wives and the procedures for naming newborn children – emerged late in data collection, so that we only have fragmentary information about them.

Another aspect of our reflexive methodology relates to when we stopped collecting information on a given topic. For some topics (e.g., weddings and courtship), it became evident after a few interviews with several families that practices were quite consistent across families. So we did not discuss every aspect of these topics with all or many families. For other topics (e.g., husband–wife and wife–wife relationships), there was so much variation and so many facets to these relationships that we discussed them repeatedly with the same families and with as many different families as possible. Deciding when to continue or cease collecting information on an issue or from a family was partly based on our summaries and reflections on field notes, and on our intuitions about what we had learned.

Finally, our methodological strategy was attuned to the lives, settings, and social contexts of the participants. As discussed elsewhere, the practice of polygyny and cohabitation are legal felonies in Utah; there is a long history of prosecution of Mormon polygynists; people have lost their jobs for practicing plural marriages; there are court suits and legislative proposals that may affect them negatively. And there is ever present actual and perceived animosity by the main LDS Church toward fundamentalists, and curiosity, criticism, and lack of understanding by the culture at large. In addition, conflicts and dissension occur within and between some polygynous groups, and there are independent polygynists who seek attention through newspapers, magazines, and radio and television talk shows.

These historical and present realities create a sense of suspicion, caution, and reticence among many fundamentalists, most of whom wish to practice their religion quietly and out of the limelight. Given their feelings and background, we decided that it would have been insensitive, foolhardy, and nonproductive to use tape recorders, checklists, highly structured surveys or interviews, and other standard social science instruments.

We also viewed members of the families with whom we worked as participants, collaborators, and partners in our quest for an understanding of dyadic and communal aspects of contemporary plural family life. They were not "under the microscope," "subjects," "informants," or "objects" from whom we were detached. They were "real" people with whom we collaborated and through whose minds and experiences we tried to understand the dynamics of plural family life. We did not want our goals, methods, and values as social scientists to be superordinate to or exploitive of these families – nor were we willing to sacrifice or subordinate our research goals to the needs of participants. Instead, we sought an application of scholarly concepts and methods that were appropriate to the circumstances and orientations of those with whom we collaboratively worked and that would also be amenable to some level of scholarly analysis and contribute to theory and knowledge about family and interpersonal relationships – a delicate balance of aspirations, to say the least! Whether or not we have achieved such a rapprochement is for readers, critics, colleagues, and history to determine.

Demographics of Mormon polygyny

This appendix presents some facts and figures about the families who participated in our project, including the number of wives in plural families, age of marriage of husbands and wives, sororal marriages (sisters married to the same husband), number of children in families, divorce rates, and men's and women's occupations. We also present comparative data for 19th-century Mormon plural families.

These seemingly straightforward demographic topics are more difficult to study than meets the eye – and for different reasons for the pioneer and contemporary eras of Mormon polygyny. For example, we found no published demographic analyses of present-day groups. Elders of the groups with whom we worked said that detailed demographic records are not maintained. Furthermore, our sample of families is quite small and is not randomly selected or representative of the total population of families in fundamentalist groups. What we present, therefore, is based on a combination of estimates by contemporary scholars and observers, our discussions with fundamentalist leaders, and information from the families with whom we worked. The complete facts are also not available for 19th-century Mormons. Records of marriages, births, and divorces were not always kept or were incomplete during the pioneer era, especially because of attempts to maintain secrecy about plural marriages. Once the Mormons settled in Utah in 1847, and prior to the Manifesto of 1890, good records were maintained. Before and after that period, however, the data are less comprehensive.[1] Nevertheless, we are able to draw on several scholarly analyses of aspects of the demography of 19th-century plural families.

Frequency of plural marriage and number of wives

What proportion of pioneer and contemporary Mormon fundamentalist families are plural families? Arrington and Bitton (1979) estimated that a maximum of 5% of men and 12% of women in the pioneer era participated in plural marriages. However, Embry (1987) concluded that there were wide geographical variations in rates of polygynous marriages in the 19th century – from 5% to 67% of marriages in different communities.

The proportion of Mormons in plural marriages appears to have successively declined over the decades following a large number of such marriages from 1856 to 1857, a period of religious fervor known as the Mormon Reformation (Ivins, 1956; Van Wagoner, 1989). Using data on 6,000 families, Ivins (1956) concluded that about 15 to 20% of Mormon families had been polygynous at one time or another. In another analysis, Smith and Kunz (1976) found that 28% of a sample of 19th-century Mormon families were polygynous. Thus available information suggests that a relatively small proportion of 19th-century Mormon families were polygynous – perhaps 15 to 25% – with variations over time and across communities and regions.

What about the number of wives in Mormon pioneer plural families? In general, the data are consistent from study to study and suggest that the great majority of plural families had only two wives, with the number tapering off rapidly thereafter. From her oral history study of the children of original pioneer polygynists Embry (1987, p. 34) concluded that "Mormon men did not collect harems. About 60 percent of the men married only one plural wife. Approximately 20 percent had three wives" and 20 percent had four or more wives.

Similarly, Ivins (1956) concluded from an analysis of about 1,800 cases that approximately 67% of the men practicing polygamy had only two wives, another 20% had three wives, and the remainder had four or more wives. Comparable figures were obtained by Smith and Kunz (1976) from a sample of 6,000 pioneer families.[2]

How do these figures compare with present-day Mormon fundamentalists? As noted previously, we know of no demographic analyses of contemporary fundamentalist groups. Furthermore, leaders in both communities stated that there are no comprehensive census reports about their groups. The leader of the urban Church of Latter-day Apostles provided us with some figures suggesting that about 40% of the families in that group are polygynous (although on another occasion he and a senior elder independently estimated a 20% rate of plural marriage). The only information we have about the rural United Fundamentalist Church came from a senior elder in the community, who estimated that about 30% of the families in that group involved plural marriages.

Our information about the number of wives in contemporary plural families is also very slim. A senior elder in the Church of Latter-day Apostles told us that a survey done in the middle 1980s found that 78% of polygynous families had only two wives; in a separate discussion another elder estimated the number of two-wife families to be about 50%. We have no information on this question for the rural United Fundamentalist Church. The limited data available to us are consistent with pioneer statistics, which show the largest proportion of Mormon plural families to have only two wives, both historically and at present.

Tables 3 and 4 indicate that about one-third of the families with whom we worked have two wives; two-fifths have three or four wives; and the remainder have five or more wives. So our sample underrepresents two-wife 19th-century and contemporary Mormon polygynous families and overrepresents the others.

Some indirect information on the incidence of plural marriage in contemporary groups may be gleaned from the marital status of children of marriageable age in some of our families, especially those families with high status in their communities. In Family 4, for example, Harry and his 5 wives have 65 children (38 sons and 27

Table 3. *Number of wives and children in plural families*

Family	No. of wives	No. of children	No. of wives still of childbearing age
1	4	24	3
2	4	21	3
3	3	12	2
4	5	65	1
5	4	31	1
6	7	58	0
7	3	13	2
8	9	43	0
9	3	8	2
10	8	53–56	up to 4
11	4	30	1–2
12	2	8	*b*
13	3*a*	—	*b*
14	2	4	*b*
15	2	—	*b*
16	5	49	0
17	3	—	—
18	4	10	0
19	1	—	—
20	1	—	—
21*c*	—	—	—
22	2	—	2
23	—	—	0
24	5	59	1
25	2	5	1
26	2	18	—
27	2	—	2

Note: Mean number children in plural families = 28.5; median number children = 21.0; mean number wives = 3.6; and median number wives = 3.0. Dash = information not available.
*a*Participant married three times into plural families; data are for most recent family.
*b*Participant divorced; no information available about other wife (wives) or family status.
*c*Information in this category refers to community-wide activities, such as church services, social events, and so on.

daughters). Their children range in age from a few infants, toddlers, and small children, to men and women in their 30s and 40s. Only four of the 38 sons – slightly less than 10% – have more than one wife; and all four are two-wife plural families. These sons are in their 30s or 40s. At least half of the total number of 38 sons in the family are of marriageable age, and many are married (at least 40 of the 65 children in the family are married). And 15 out of 17 married daughters live in plural families. Thus, consistent with pioneer data, only a few sons in this

Table 4. *Number of wives in plural families*

No. of wives	Frequency	Percentage
2	7	30.4
3	5	21.7
4	5	21.7
5	3	13.0
6+	3	13.0

family in the rural community practice plural marriage at present. At the same time, most of the married daughters are members of polygynous families.

In Family 6, Seymour, an elder in the urban community, and his 8 wives have 58 children (29 sons and 29 daughters). More than half of the children are married, with 3 of 10 married sons having plural wives. (At another time Seymour stated that 5 of his sons have plural wives.) We do not have information on the number of wives each son married. In addition, 18 of 20 married daughters are plural wives. Thus most married daughters in this family are in plural families, whereas a smaller proportion of sons had plural wives at the time of our interviews. Given the fact that many of the sons in the family are or will soon be of marriageable age, it is possible that additional plural marriages may occur. (As an aside, Seymour also told us that only 4 of his own approximately 20 brothers had married more than one wife, a figure consistent with Mormon pioneer data.)

In Family 8, Ira, husband of 8 wives and father of 43 children (23 are his birth children and 20 are children of wives who were previously widowed or divorced), told us that only 3 of his 15 birth sons have plural wives at present. And all but 2 of his many daughters who are married (we do not know the number) are wives in plural families. Once again, these bits of information are consistent with the idea that only a small proportion of men engage in plural marriages, although a high proportion of daughters from high-status families become plural wives.

Although our data about the number of plural marriages and the numbers of wives in such marriages are fragmentary, they are reasonably consistent with pioneer data and information from other cultures reported in chapter 2.

Sororal marriages

We noted in chapter 2 that sororal marriages are not uncommon in other polygynous cultures. Embry (1987) reported that 25% of the 19th-century Mormon plural families in her sample had wives who were sisters. She also referred to an earlier analysis by Young (1954) indicating that 20% of a sample of pioneer families included sisters who had married the same husband. Burgess-Olson (1978), cited in Foster (1981, p. 213), stated that 31% of 19th-century Mormon plural marriages contained at least one pair of sisters. On the other hand, Ivins (1956) found only a 10% rate of sororal marriages.

We know of sororal marriages in six of our families, for a 25% rate, which is consistent with pioneer data. Because we did not have information about all families, it is possible that the incidence of sisters marrying the same husband is even higher. Four of our families have two sisters as co-wives; in another family, three of four wives are sisters; in yet another family, five of eight wives are sisters. (In some cases wives may have been only half-sisters, i.e., daughters of the same father but of different plural mothers.)

Age of marriage of husbands and wives

Many critics in the 19th century, and even today, argued that Mormon polygyny involves "old men" marrying "young girls." The fact is that the marriage age in pioneer and present-day Mormon plural families is a complex matter and simplistic conclusions are not appropriate. Fortunately, several analyses of 19th-century Mormon pioneers shed some light on the question.

By and large, it seems that first marriages occurred when men and women were in their teens or early 20s. A first plural marriage usually occurred some years later, although the husband tended to marry a woman close to the age of his first wife when he married her. Thus there was a greater age gap between the husband and wife on a second marriage. This pattern recurred in successive marriages, with a greater and greater age gap between the husband and successive wives. However, some analyses indicate that most pioneer plural marriages were completed by the time a man had reached the age of 40. And since most pioneer plural families had only two wives, as noted earlier, the idea of "old men" marrying "young girls" was rare.

Ivins (1956) concluded from an analysis of 1,200 pioneer polygynous families that "the composite polygamist was first married at the age of twenty three to a girl of twenty. Thirteen years later he took a plural wife, choosing a twenty-two year old girl [when he was thirty six] . . . If, however, he took a third wife, he waited four years, then selected another girl of twenty two [when he was forty]" (Ivins, 1956, p. 234).

In a further breakdown, Ivins (1956) found that 38% of all wives were in their teens, and 29% were between 20 and 25 years of age when they married. Thus two-thirds of women were at or below the age of 25 when they married; 30% were over 30 years of age. Furthermore, 10% of the men married their last wives while in their 20s, and more than half completed their plural marriages before reaching the age of 40. However, the fact that somewhat less than 20% of the men continued to marry additional wives after their 50s suggests that the age gap between husbands and new wives probably continued to widen in larger plural families. Smith and Kunz (1976) reported comparable results in a sample of 6,000 pioneer families. The marriage age of first wives was about 20 years, that of second wives was about 22 years, and third wives married on average when they were 23 years old. Husbands married their later wives when they were in their 30s and 40s.

In an analysis of marriage ages in one region, Logue (1984) reported that Mormon pioneer men were about 24 years old when they married their first wife, 38 when they married a second time, 41 when they married a third wife, and 44 when they married a fourth time. Thus men waited over a decade before entering plural marriage, and then married successive wives fairly soon thereafter. (Logue did not present information about ages of wives at successive marriages.)

In an extensive oral history study of the surviving children of late-19th-century polygynous families, Embry (1987) found that husbands were in their early 20s in first marriages (28% were 15 to 20 years of age, and 59% were between 20 and 25 years of age), and first wives were in their teens (74% were between 15 and 20 years old, 25% were 21 to 25). When the husband married a second wife, he was between 26 and 35 years old (57%) and she was 15 to 19 years of age (57% were between 15 and 20, and 28% were between 21 and 25). For third wives, the variability of men's ages increased. Embry stated that the husband was usually in his late 30s (22% of the men were 31 to 35, 28% were 36 to 40, 16% were 41 to 45, 12% were 46 to 50 years of age). For fourth wives, men's ages gradually increased, with two-thirds being in the range of 36 to 50 years of age. At the same time, successive wives' ages were more or less comparable to the age of the first wife when the husband married her, as is consistent with other data, although there were cases of men marrying older wives as their fourth wife (e.g., 17% of the men married fourth wives who were 31 to 40; some of these may have been widows or divorcées).

Embry's data show an increasing disparity between the ages of husbands and successive wives. Thus 72% of husbands and wives in first marriages were within 0 to 5 years of the same age. This reduced to 20%, 7%, and 0% for second, third, and fourth wives, respectively. Thus 43% of second wives were 11 to 12 years younger than their husband; 46% of third wives were 16 to 25 years younger than their husbands, and 33% of fourth wives were 21 to 30 years younger than their husbands.

Finally, Embry (1987) noted that about 60% of men married a second wife 6 to 15 years after their first marriage, with about 23% marrying somewhat earlier. However, successive marriages occurred more rapidly, with 57% of third marriages and 77% of fourth marriages occurring within 2 to 10 years after prior marriages. Thus, as noted earlier, there usually was a delay of several years before a man married a second wife, but subsequent marriages occurred more quickly.

In general, therefore, ages of first marriages by 19th-century Mormon polygynists involved men and women in their early 20s and late teens. On each successive marriage, the wives continued to be about the same age as the wife in the first marriage, with the husband being older and the age gap between husbands and successive wives widening. Given these data, it is probable that some older men in the pioneer era married very young women, but it was by no means a standard or widespread practice, especially since most plural marriages only involved two wives.

What about our sample of contemporary fundamentalists? In general, the ages of marriages of husbands and wives in our families are similar to the data reported for 19th-century plural families. But there are several reasons to be cautious about drawing definitive conclusions from our sample. We are dealing with only a small number of families, and our sample is not representative or random, as noted in appendix A.

What we do know is, first, husbands in our families were in their early 20s when they married their first wife (mean and median = 21 years of age); first wives were in their late teens (mean = 18, median = 17 years of age), with a gap of 3 to 4 years in their ages (tables 5 and 6). Second and third plural marriages occurred when husbands were in their early 30s and new wives were in their early 20s or late teens. Thus marriages to second and third wives occurred when a husband was about 10 to 13 years older than when he married his first wife. The second and third wives were a few years older than the first wife when she married. However, the average age gap of about 3 to 4 years between husbands and first wives increased to 10 to 14 years in second and third marriages, respectively.

This pattern continues for fourth, fifth, and sixth wives – with the husband in his late 30s to early 40s, and new wives averaging in their early to mid-20s, with an age gap of 16 to 18 years, depending on how one calculates the difference (note that since the number of fourth to sixth and later marriages is small, these are not firm estimates). Thus husbands' ages at successive marriages increase disproportionately to wives' ages, although in successive marriages women appear to be older than in earlier marriages.

These figures are more or less consistent with Mormon pioneer marriage patterns. That is, husbands and first wives are young and relatively close in age when they marry; and there is usually a several-year delay before a second marriage occurs, followed by successive marriages over shorter time spans. With successive marriages, the gap between husbands' and wives' ages increases, with new wives in their 20s, on average, and the husband's age extending from the 20s to 30s to 40s and beyond.

The preceding statements are only tentative, because they are based on a small sample of cases and because there is a great deal of variability in the marriage ages of husbands and wives – as shown in the last column of table 5 and in the listing of ages in table 6. For example, table 5 shows that husbands' ages in their third marriages range from 23 to 47 years, and third wives' ages range from 15 to 36 years. Thus average ages in our sample need to be viewed with some caution.

As for the question of "old men" marrying "young girls," the average age of women in second and later marriages is in the 20s, with husbands in their 30s to 40s, and some in their 50s (table 5). The tabulations in tables 6 and 7 indicate that 55% (28/51) of wives in our sample were married when they were teenagers, with 28% (14/51) of wives in their 20s, and 18% (9/51) in their 30s or beyond. A further breakdown in table 8 shows that 25% of teenage marriages of wives were first marriages, and an additional 50% were second and third marriages. Thus, although a high proportion of plural marriages in our sample involved teenage wives, 25% occurred in first marriages, when husbands were also young, and 50% occurred in second and third marriages, when husbands averaged in their early 30s. At the same time, some marriages involved older husbands and younger women, as in the following cases: a 45-year-old man married a 19-year-old woman; a man in his early 40s married a 15-year-old; a 47-year-old man married a 17-year-old woman; three men in their early 40s married women of 17, 18, and 20 years of age. We

Table 5. *Husband's and wife's ages at marriage*

Wife's marriage order	Husband's age			Wife's age			Age gap of husband and wife		Age range	
	Mean	Median	No. cases	Mean	Median	No. cases	Mean	Median	Husband	Wife
1	21.1	21.0	11	17.9	17.0	9	3.2	4.0	18–25	16–20
2	32.3	31.0	12	22.3	19.0	12	10.0	12.0	19–47	15–44
3	34.0	31.5	10	20.5	18.0	11	13.5	13.5	23–47	15–36
4	40.5	38.5	8	23.1	20.0	8	17.4	18.5	27–56	18–36
5	42.4	40.0	5	25.7	24.0	6	16.7	16.0	35–53	18–39
6	43.5	43.5	2	26.5	26.5	2	17.0	17.0	42–45	17–36
7	48.5	48.5	2	26.0	26.0	2	22.5	22.5	45–52	22–30
8	52.5	52.5	2	42.0	42.0	2	10.5	10.5	45–60	35–49

Table 6. Husband's and wife's age at marriage

Wife's marriage order	Husband's age at marriage
1	18, 19, 19, 20, 21, 21, 21, 22, 23, 24, 25
2	19, 20, 21, 28, 29, 31, 31, 32, 40, 44, 45, 47
3	23, 23, 28, 31, 31, 32, 33, 45, 47, 47
4	27, 34, 35, 37, 40, 45, 50, 56
5	35, 37, 40, 47, 53
6	42, 45
7	45, 52
8	45, 60

Wife's marriage order	Wife's age at marriage
1	16, 17, 17, 17, 17, 18, 19, 20, 20
2	15, 15, 16, 18, 19, 19, 22, 23, 26, 28, 44
3	15, 17, 17, 18, 18, 18, 19, 19, 21, 27, 36
4	18, 18, 19, 19, 21, 27, 27, 36
5	18, 19, 20, 28, 30, 39
6	17, 36
7	22, 30
8	35, 49

Table 7. Husbands and wives in different age groups at marriage

Wife's age at marriage	No. of cases	Percentage
15–19	28	54.9
20–24	8	15.7
25–29	6	11.8
30–39	7	13.7
40s and up	2	3.9

Husband's age at marriage	No. of cases	Percentage
15–19	4	7.7
20–24	11	21.2
25–29	5	9.6
30–39	12	23.1
40s and up	20	38.5

found five cases of men in their 40s marrying teenage brides, and three cases of men in their 50s marrying women in their 20s. All other cases in our sample involved smaller age gaps between husbands and wives. Although men's ages at successive marriages increased from their 20s to 30s to 40s, and women's ages

Table 8. *Teenage wives and order of marriage*

Wife's order	No. of cases	Percentage
First	7	25.0
Second	6	21.4
Third	8	28.6
Fourth	4	14.3
Fifth	2	7.1
Sixth	1	3.6
Seventh	0	0
Eighth	0	0

increased from teens to their 20s in successive marriages, the data do not indicate a pervasive pattern of older men marrying much younger women.

Another facet of marital demography concerns the ages of subsequent marriages by divorced and widowed women. We know of five previously widowed wives and eight divorced wives who married into seven families in our sample. The average age of these women when they married into one of our plural families was about 33, and their new husbands' age averaged 41. On average, they were the fourth wife in the new marriage, with about half being the second or third wife and half being fourth to eighth wives. So ages of marriage of husbands and wives described previously also need to be viewed in the light of marriages involving widowed or divorced wives.

Divorce rate

We know that there were many stresses in 19th-century plural marriages and that present-day fundamentalists also experience tensions and difficulties in their lives. To what extent do plural marriages fail and result in divorce?

Campbell and Campbell (1978) and Quinn (1973) concluded that divorce rates in 19th-century Mormon plural families were high. They noted that Brigham Young granted 1,645 divorces during his almost 30-year presidency, many of which involved church leaders. Extrapolating these figures up to 1890, when the Mormon Church first spoke out against plural marriage, Campbell and Campbell inferred that the incidence of divorce among Mormons exceeded the national rate. In another study cited in Van Wagoner (1989) and Foster (1982), Quinn (1973) analyzed divorce rates among Mormon Church leaders between 1832 and 1932. Fifty-four percent (39/72) of church leaders were involved in 81 marital rifts (i.e., conflict arose in 21% of their 391 marriages). These conflicts resulted in 54 divorces, 26 separations, and 1 annulment. A study by Kunz that is cited in Embry (1987) concluded that the divorce rate in 19th-century plural marriages was three times that of monogamous families. In a more informal analysis, Young (1954) concluded that one-fourth of the 175 pioneer plural families he studied had serious marital conflict. These data have led some commentators to conclude that divorce rates were fairly high among pioneer Mormon polygynists.

But others disagree, stating that divorces in polygynous and monogamous marriages are not comparable. Plural marriages outside the civil system did not have the underpinning of secular law; there were many forms of marriage in the early days of the Mormon religion, including spiritual wifery, proxy relationships, marriages without full conjugal relationships or cohabitation, and so on. How are these to be counted? Furthermore, Embry (1987) refers to studies indicating that the highest rates of divorce in plural families occurred in the earlier years of Mormonism and that plural marriages were much more stable thereafter (in contrast, the national divorce rate showed an opposite pattern, increasing dramatically toward the latter part of the 19th century). So although absolute comparisons are difficult to make, there is no question that significant numbers of divorces or marital rifts occurred in 19th-century Mormon plural families.

The existence of serious problems in some marriages is reflected in comments by Brigham Young and other church leaders – some discouraging divorces and calling for men and women to work things out, and others giving women the freedom to be released from poor relationships. In 1858 Brigham Young publicly stated: "It is not right for the brethren to divorce their wives the way they do. I am determined that if men don't stop divorcing their wives, I shall stop sealing [performing marriages]" (Van Wagoner, 1989, p. 92). Brigham Young also stated that a woman should "stay with her husband as long as she could bear with him, but if life became too burdensome, then leave and get a divorce." Furthermore, "when a woman becomes alienated in her feelings and affections from her husband, it is his duty to give her a bill and set her free . . . [it] would be a fornication for a man to cohabit with his wife after she had thus become alienated from him" (Van Wagoner, 1989 p. 93).

According to Foster (1981), the early Mormon Church discouraged divorces, putting pressure on men and women to stay in marriages, giving women the freedom to institute divorce proceedings and being liberal in granting divorces to them, and making it easy and not a stigma for divorced women to remarry. Indeed, some divorces were granted "if the woman Preferred – a man higher in [religious] authority and he is willing to take her. And her husband gives her up – there is no Bill of divorce required in the case it is right in the sight of God" (from a sermon by Brigham Young, 1861, cited in Foster, 1981, p. 162).

What about divorce among present-day Mormon fundamentalists? We were told that they do not keep such records or that the information is incomplete or not readily accessible. (The leader of the urban Church of Latter-day Apostles informally recalled only 3 to 4 divorces in the whole congregation during the last year we were collecting information; these were initiated by wives who felt they had not been treated properly by their husbands.)

We do have some information about divorces from our sample of families (see table 9): 12/20 families in our sample experienced some form of divorce or separation – either a wife joined a family after leaving another family, or a wife left one of our families. Thus half of our families experienced at least one divorce. When one looks at the proportion of marriages that resulted in divorce, the incidence is

Table 9. *Separation and divorce among husbands and wives*

Family 1	First wife left family earlier; one of present wives was divorced from another plural family
Family 2	No separations/divorces
Family 3	No separations/divorces
Family 4	No separations/divorces
Family 5	No separations/divorces
Family 6	One wife left husband
Family 7	One wife was divorced/separated from another plural family
Family 8	One wife left husband; 2 wives were divorced from other families
Family 9	No separations/divorces
Family 10	Two wives divorced/separated from other plural families
Family 11	No separations/divorces
Family 12	One wife separated/divorced from husband
Family 13	Informant divorced from three marriages; widowed in one
Family 14	Informant divorced from husband
Family 15	Informant divorced from husband
Family 16	First wife left family earlier
Family 17	One wife left divorced/separated from husband
Family 18	One wife left husband; one wife divorced another husband
Family 19	No information
Family 20	No information
Family 21	No information
Family 22	No divorces/separations
Family 23	No information
Family 24	No information
Family 25	No information
Family 26	No information
Family 27	No separations/divorces

Note: The sample consisted of 20 families. Twelve of these (60%) experienced a divorce or separation, of which 7 (35%) experienced one divorce or separation and 5 (25%) experienced more than one divorce or separation. Eight (40%) experienced no divorce or separation.

low: only 13% of the 84 marriages we have information on resulted in divorce. But these figures are probably underestimates, since some of our families may have divorces in the future (we recently learned of one case in which several wives in a family all left their husband at the same time).

Number of children in plural families

It should come as no surprise that 19th-century and modern plural families have large numbers of children. In keeping with their religious beliefs, couples have as many offspring as possible. Data from genealogical records supports this expectation. Ivins (1956) found that 25% of pioneer Mormon plural families had 20 or more children, 50% had 15 or more offspring, and 80% had 10 or more children. Embry (1987) reported that 74% of the families in her sample had between 11 and 25 children, with 19% having 26 to 35 children.

As for the average number of children per wife, archival records indicate that the figures were about the same for plural and monogamous wives in the 19th century. However, some studies show that plural wives gave birth to a somewhat smaller number of children than their monogamous counterparts. Ivins (1956) found that individual wives in plural families had about 6 children on average, whereas monogamous Mormon wives of the era each had about 8 children. On the other hand, Smith and Kunz (1976) found similar birthrates among women in monogamous and polygynous families (7.8 and 7.5 children on average, respectively). They qualified these data, however, showing higher fertility rates among first wives and in two-wife families, in comparison with three-wife families. Embry (1987), while reporting somewhat lower birthrates for plural wives, confirmed that first wives had higher fertility rates than subsequent wives. As a whole, the evidence indicates that 19th-century Mormon plural families had large numbers of children and that first wives tended to have higher fertility rates than later wives. At the same time, individual plural wives tended to have the same or an even smaller number of children than monogamous wives of the era.[3]

Before examining the figures for our sample of families, it important to remember the selective nature of the families with whom we worked. The number of children we counted are probably underestimates because several of our families are young and still growing. Established and new wives are likely to have additional children for several years to come.

Tables 3, 10, and 11 present information on number of children per family, number of children per wife, and number of children for first and later wives. In the 18 families about whom we have comprehensive information, there is an average of more than 20 children per family (the mean = 28.5 and the median = 21.0 children). However, there is a great range of family sizes, with several families having 12 or fewer children and several having 43 to 65 children. As a result, the "average" is based on a wide distribution of family sizes that are not tightly clustered around the mean or median. In spite of the great range in numbers of children, families in our sample are roughly comparable as a group to pioneer families described previously.

Considered in the aggregate, 35% of wives have 4 to 6 children, and 25% have 7 to 10 children (table 10). Thus about 60% of the wives in our families have 4 to 10 children. Smaller numbers of wives have 11 to 19 children (18%) and 1 to 3 children (18%), with only a few wives having no children. Once again, these data are roughly comparable to fertility rates of wives in 19th-century Mormon plural families.

Table 11 presents information about the number of children of first, second, and later wives. There is little difference between wives and considerable variability within and across first, second, and other wives. However, it is interesting to note that two first wives and one second wife have 14 to 19 children each, and only one subsequent wife, a third wife, has as many as 14 children. But this might change as newer and younger wives in growing families continue to have children. In any

Table 10. *Number of children per wife in plural families*

No. of children	No. of wives	Percentage	Aggregated percentage
0	2	3.3	3.3
1	5	8.3	
2	2	3.3	18.3
3	4	6.7	
4	8	13.3	
5	6	10.0	35.0
6	7	11.7	
7	2	3.3	
8	5	8.3	25.0
9	4	6.7	
10	4	6.7	
11	5	8.3	
12	2	3.3	
13	0	0	
14	2	3.3	
15	0	0	18.3
16	0	0	
17	1	1.7	
18	0	0	
19	1	1.7	

case, unlike pioneer first wives, those in our sample do not, on average, have more children than later wives – although a few first, second, and third wives have very large numbers of children.

Converts and "native" fundamentalists

An interesting question concerns the number of husbands and wives in our families who were born into or grew up in the fundamentalist movement and the number who are converts. A related question concerns the number of families composed of all "natives," all converts, or mixed converts and members born or raised in the movement.[4] Again, our data are incomplete but may be somewhat informative. Table 12 shows that 63% (10/16) of the husbands about whom we have information were born or raised in the fundamentalist movement; the others are converts. The data are roughly comparable for wives, with 58% (34/59) born or raised in the fundamentalist movement and 42% (25/59) being converts. Thus somewhat more than half of the husbands and wives in our sample have had prior experience in plural families.

Table 11. *Wife's marriage order and number of children*

Wife's marriage order	No. of children per wife																		
	0	1	2	3	4	5	6	7	8	9	10	11	12	13	14	15	16	17	19
1	1		1	1	4	1	1		3	1	1				1			1	
2	1	1	1	2	1		2	2		2	1								1
3		2		1	1	1	1		2		1		1		1				
4					1	4				1									
5		1					1					5							
6		1					1												
7					1								1						
8							1				1								

Wife No.	Children per wife and order of marriage			
	No. children/No. wives	Mean	Median	Range
1	106/16	6.7	5.5	0–17
2	86/14	6.2	6.0	0–19
3	72/11	6.5	5.5	1–14
4	33/ 6	5.5	5.0	4–9
5	62/ 7	8.9	11.0	1–11
6	7/ 2	3.5	3.5	1–6
7	16/ 2	8.0	8.0	4–12
8	16/ 2	8.0	8.0	6–10

In 62% (8/13) of the families about whom we have information, some wives were born or raised in the fundamentalist movement and some are converts; thus many families are "mixed" in this respect. Fewer families are composed of wives who were either all born or raised in the fundamentalist movement (3/13), or who are all converts (2/13). In the three families in which all wives are "natives" in the movement, the husbands are, too; similarly, the husband is a convert in one family in which all wives are converts.

Work and occupations

In 19th-century America the industrial revolution created many manufacturing and spin-off jobs in and around cities, especially in the Northeast. Farming and agriculture were prevalent in the South and Midwest, with a high proportion of people living in rural areas and working on family farms. Parts of those regions and the western United States were still a frontier, with cheap and readily available land, and with agriculture and ranching as primary occupations. A rural and somewhat isolated existence was even more evident in Utah and the surrounding region. The economics of Utah was fragile, people worked hard to survive and maintain their

Table 12. *Husbands and wives born or raised or converts to fundamentalism*

Family	Converts		Born or raised		Comment
	Wife	Husband	Wife	Husband	
1	3	0	1	1	
2	0	0	4	1	
3	3	1	0	0	
4	1	0	4	1	
5	0	0	4	1	
6	2	0	6	1	
7	1	1	2	0	
8	2	0	?	1	6 other wives not known
9	2	1	1	0	
10	3	1	5	0	
11	0	0	4	1	
12	?	0	1	1	1 other wife not known
14	1	1	?	0	1 other wife not known
15	1	?	?	?	2–4 other wives/husband not known
18	3	1	1	0	
22	2	?	0	?	Husband not known
24	?	0	?	1	5 wives not known
26	1	0	1	1	
Total	25	6	34	10	
	(42.3)	(37.5)	(57.6)	(62.5)	

Note: Figures in parentheses are percentages.

families, there was only a small local industrial base, and farming and ranching were major occupations, along with auxiliary service occupations. Establishing agricultural viability was a prime goal, since the region was isolated from major supply sources in the East, and since the Mormon pioneers wished to achieve independence and self-sufficiency. Given the challenges of economic survival, people were flexible about the work they did and often changed occupations out of necessity or as opportunities arose. They also did not always work steadily in the same jobs over a lifetime but changed jobs as circumstances dictated. In this environment, women were central to a family's economic viability. They worked on family farms or in family businesses and held jobs in the community. Because some husbands were away for long periods of time on Mormon Church business, wives often assumed complete responsibility for family farms or businesses and often supported their families by themselves.

Embry (1987), citing from Young's (1954) analysis of a sample of 19th-century Mormon plural families, reported that 80% of the men had "proprietary" occupations (farming, ranching, manufacturing, merchandising, freighting), with roughly two-thirds engaged in ranching or farming as their major source of income.

The others worked in manufacturing, merchandising, skilled craft, and professional occupations. Embry (1987) found roughly comparable data in research by Burgess-Olsen (1978) and in her own sample of polygynous and monogamous families of the era (albeit with somewhat more men engaged in professional occupations).

Embry (1987, p. 92) reported that a fair number of men in her sample held more than one job at the same time: "The typical nineteenth century frontiersman, whether Mormon or non-Mormon, whether monogamous or polygamous, had a variety of occupations. . . . [H]e would travel, working on ranches, in mines, or freighting goods. After marriage he might purchase a farm. . . . When a farm did not produce a large enough income, he would supplement it with freighting, mining, or railroad work."

What about women? The idea of a woman's place being in the home was an entrenched value of 19th-century Victorian America and of Mormons. In rural settings, this also often included women managing gardens and some domestic animals and assisting in ranching and agricultural activities. Among Mormons of the era, this often went beyond women being "assistants" to men. They often ran and managed these enterprises by themselves, because men were often away for long periods on church business or were spending extended periods of time with plural wives in distant locations. For the many women who had to be self-supporting, it was often necessary to work outside the home. Embry (1987) found that 20% of polygynous wives in her sample worked outside the home at some time in their marriages, but few did so on a regular basis. Almost half worked at home selling farm products, housing boarders, and washing clothes for others. Comparable but somewhat lower numbers of monogamous Mormon women engaged in similar types of wage-earning work. Thus two-thirds of pioneer polygamous women worked at one time or another, in and out of their homes – but not continuously – to contribute to the family's economic viability.

Embry's data also indicate that few polygynous or monogamous wives in 19th-century Mormon families received *no* financial support from their husbands (9–10%), or were totally supported financially by their husbands (0%). Thus while men were the primary sources of family support in these families, women contributed in significant ways to family economics.

We had information about the occupations of 20 husbands and 50 wives in our sample. Our sense is that most families in our sample are in the middle to lower-middle occupational classes, with a few in somewhat higher or lower socioeconomic strata. Our impression is that many other contemporary Mormon fundamentalist families are similarly situated. Furthermore, because many of our families are struggling to make financial ends meet, it is customary for some or all wives to work on a regular or intermittent basis. Thus 19th-century and present-day Mormon fundamentalists are similar in their overall economic status, as well as in the extent to which husbands and wives work to help support families. In contrast to pioneer men and women, however, people in our sample tend to work in more industrialized, technical, managerial, and sales occupations, not primarily in agriculture and ranching – although some do so, and others farm or raise animals on a small scale or on a part-time basis.

A few men in our sample have their own business – an automobile body repair shop, a lumber yard, a trucking firm, a small clothing factory. Other men have worked at one time or another as a supervisor in a small construction business, school principal, security and safety administrator, town official, and the like. Still other men are in professions or skilled and semiskilled occupations, such as public or private school teacher, cabinet maker, factory worker, home construction worker, long-distance truck driver, and engineering technician.

Like men in the Mormon pioneer era, contemporary fundamentalist husbands are often the major family provider, and they work continuously over the course of their careers. Except for those who are retired or temporarily unemployed, men in our sample work steadily and on a full-time basis. In addition, some men have more than one job, at least on occasion. Thus a few have small farm plots while working elsewhere; one man is both a town official and owner of a small factory; another man does both home remodeling and part-time sales. Also like their 19th-century counterparts, men in present-day plural families often change jobs, probably as a result of economic need or opportunity. For example, one man worked in a small home remodeling company, then bought and sold used furniture, and now buys, remodels, and sells homes. Another man taught school for a while and then engaged in a variety of small business ventures. Other men worked at one time or another in home construction, manufacturing, and sales. Another man dabbled in a variety of occupations including farming, handicrafts, shoemaking, and teaching. In sum, men in our sample of families have worked in numerous professional, managerial, business, skilled, and semiskilled occupations. They are major providers of family income, work steadily and continuously if possible, sometimes hold more than one job at a time, and not infrequently change occupations as circumstances warrant. Overall, their work profile is probably similar to that of many men in present-day American society.

As for wives, in 13 of the 16 families about whom we have information, at least one wife in every family has a steady and long-term job. And 29 of 50 wives in these families work in more or less full-time jobs on a regular basis. These data contrast with the pattern in 19th-century families, where women worked intermittently. But they are quite in line with present-day American society, where more and more families have two wage earners.

Several plural wives work in office jobs as receptionists, secretaries, clerks and typists, administrative assistants, telephone operators, and the like (a couple hold supervisory positions). Other women have professional positions as elementary school teachers (one wife teaches high school art) and nurses. Other occupations include factory work, baby sitting, house cleaning, sales, and realty. Two wives in our sample have their own business – one runs a health food shop and the other a seasonal sales business.

A high proportion of wives have full- or part-time jobs. For example, 4 of 4 wives in one family work, 3 of 4 wives in two families work, 2 of 3 wives in two families work, 2 of 4 wives in two families work, and at least 4 of 8 wives in one family work. The wives not working for pay often care for the children of employed co-wives.

Thus women in contemporary plural families work full-time and part-time, regularly and intermittently, and in a variety of occupations comparable to those of monogamous women in present-day American society. Like many American families, plural families often rely on multiple wage earners in to make financial ends meet. At the same time, contemporary plural wives are responsible for fulfilling traditional gender roles of managing homes and caring for children. In some large plural families, where husbands are only present periodically, wives may be responsible for managing many "men's jobs around the house," such as home and auto repairs, yard care, and snow removal. The challenges of work and home are considerable for wives in contemporary polygynous families, perhaps even greater than for many women in American society.

Notes

Chapter 1

1. Kilbride (1994) describes a variety of other de facto polygamous arrangements on the contemporary scene, including "man sharing" in which two or more women knowingly have close relationships with a man but do not marry him, extramarital polygamy by men and women, same-gender and mixed-gender triadic and group relationships, and others.

2. An emerging body of research and theory in psychology and anthropology has been exploring an "evolutionary" approach to aspects of human social behavior – including mating and sexual selection, family structure, parental behavior, and polygamy. Rooted in Darwinian thinking, this work postulates that over the course of evolution humans and other species have developed characteristics and capabilities that improve the chances of survival. In the realm of sexual selection and mating, evolutionary psychologists and anthropologists hypothesize that men and women have propensities to act in ways that ensure reproductive success and the survival of their offspring. Buss (1994) cites data indicating that males seek access to a wide variety of women as sexual partners, prefer women who are attractive and healthy (young women with clear skin, full lips, and good muscle tone, who have certain physical features, for example, certain waist–hip ratios, who are ideally sexually loyal, etc.). Some evolutionary theorists therefore hypothesisize that polygyny is a desired state of affairs for men, since it increases their reproductive potential. For women, whose investment in childbearing and child survival is very high, evolution is thought to have resulted in their preference for men who have resources and status, who are likely to be long-term and committed partners and parents, and who are stable, intelligent, healthy, and strong. Some theorists see polygyny as often satisfying these goals for women. The literature on evolutionary approaches to human social behavior is growing. For more details, see, for example, Betzig (1986); Betzig, Mulder, and Turke (1988); and Buss (1994, 1995).

   Evolutionary concerns have to do with the *why* of human social behavior, the underlying foundations of men's and women's orientations to sexual selection, mating and procreation, and the plausibility of an evolutionary orientation to account for complex social processes. We encourage this line of theory and research but consider it tangential to our analysis of husband–wife and wife–

wife relationships in contemporary polygynous families. Our focus is not so much on why Mormon fundamentalists *ultimately* practice plural marriage as it is on how they practice plural marriage, how they cope or fail to cope with the challenges of their unusual lifestyle in present-day American society, how they function in a range of everyday life activities. Therefore an evolutionary approach does not apply to our present analysis, although it conceivably may be informative in the future.

3. *Trait* worldviews focus on the person as the basic unit of analysis and assume that intrinsic qualities or "essences" of people – e.g., classical instinct and traditional personality theories – are the primary determinants of psychological functioning. Although environmental variables can affect psychological processes, trait approaches assume that the operation of a psychological quality is more or less independent of external contexts. Trait approaches also assume stability of personal characteristics, and they portray change as following a predetermined timetable and course. *Interactional* worldviews, which predominate in contemporary psychology, treat psychological qualities and environmental factors as independent entities that interact to affect psychological functioning. These approaches examine the separate and interacting effects of independently defined person and environment variables on psychological outcomes, and analytically search for the elements, dimensions, and building blocks that constitute the phenomenon of interest. Time is separate from psychological processes, and change results from the interaction of independent personal and environmental entities. Time is a location or means of marking the state of a phenomenon, with change being the difference between states at different times. Actual processes of change are not examined directly but are inferred from differences in states at two or more times. *Organismic* approaches emphasize the study of holistic, integrated systems, not the analysis of parts or elements that make up a phenomenon. Changes in one part of an organismic whole may reverberate in complex ways throughout a system and lead to a complex interplay of elements, subsystems, and relationships. Organismic worldviews consider the whole to be the proper unit of analysis of psychological phenomena, with the whole possessing distinctive properties that are not directly derived from the properties of its elements. In the organismic view, systems are in dynamic change, often in preestablished stages toward some long-range ideal. Although they focus on the whole, organismic approaches also assume that a whole can be broken down into separate constituent parts. *Transactional* approaches assume that psychological phenomena are holistic events composed of inseparable and mutually definable psychological processes and physical and social environments. Whereas organismic orientations treat systems as composed of independent elements whose relationships yield the whole, transactional approaches consider the whole to be composed of inseparable aspects that immediately and simultaneously define the whole. Transactional approaches also include temporal factors and change as central aspects of all psychological events, and are central parts of the definition and qualities of a psychological phenomenon.

4. Here is a technical statement on this theme: "the unit of psychological analysis is holistic entities such as events involving persons, psychological processes, and

environments. The transactional whole is not composed of separate elements but is a confluence of inseparable factors that depend on one another for their very definition and meaning . . . there are no separate elements or sets of discrete relationships into which the system is ultimately divisible. Instead, the whole is composed of inseparable aspects that simultaneously and conjointly define the whole . . . there are no separate actors in an event; instead, there are acting relationships, such that the actions of one person can only be described and understood in relation to the actions of the other persons, and in relation to the situational and temporal circumstances in which the actors are involved. Furthermore, the aspects of an event are mutually defining and lend meaning to one another, since the same actor in a different setting (or the same setting with different actors) would yield a different confluence of people in contexts . . . the transactional world view does not deal with the relationship *between elements,* . . . instead, a transactional approach assumes that the *aspects* of a system, that is, person and context, coexist and jointly define one another and contribute to the meaning and nature of a holistic event" (Altman and Rogoff, 1987, p. 24).

5. For a technical discussion of dialectics as applied to social and psychological processes, see Altman, Vinsel, and Brown (1981); Baxter (1988); Baxter and Montgomery (1996); and Werner and Baxter (1994).

6. Our full technical analyses include other features of linear and cyclical change: *sequencing* or the order in which events unfold and the degree to which the actions of couple members are coordinated; *pace,* or how quickly events proceed per unit of time; *amplitude,* or intensity of events; *rhythm,* or the relative smoothness and regularity of the pace/scale/amplitude/sequence features. These and other temporal properties of relationships were not easy to study or systematically assess in plural family relationships. For further information on these and other features of time and change, see Kelly and McGrath (1988); McGrath and Kelly (1986); Werner, Altman, and Oxley (1985); Werner and Baxter (1994); and Werner and Haggard (1985).

Chapter 2

1. Emma remained recalcitrant and even burned the revelation statement, with his permission, not knowing that others had copied it. Her resistance continued, and after his death she joined with dissidents who formed the Reorganized Church of Jesus Christ of Latter Day Saints, which renounced polygyny. However, she never publicly admitted that Joseph had practiced plural marriage. In spite of her continued resistance and knowledge of his actions following the revelation, Joseph Smith continued to marry new wives.

2. Several questions come to mind about Joseph Smith's plural marriages. How many wives did he have? What kind of relationship did he have with these wives – spiritual or physical? The answers to these questions are complex, and scholars have debated them at length. Van Wagoner (1989, p. 27) summarized the situation as follows: "The exact number of women sealed to Joseph Smith during his lifetime is difficult to assess. Assistant church historian Andrew Jenson doc-

umented twenty-seven from statements of the women themselves or witnesses to the ceremony. . . . D. Michael Quinn (1973) identifies thirty-four, Fawn Brodie (1975) and Daniel Bachman (1975) both name forty-eight, while Stanley S. Ivins . . . put forth eighty-four women as possible wives of the prophet. None of these studies undertakes the near-impossible task of determining if these women were connubial wives, eternal or 'celestial' wives, or merely linked by name to Smith. In addition the numbers do not reflect the hundreds of women – such as Josephine Bonaparte, Madam Victor Hugo, St. Therese, St. Helene . . . , and Matilda (empress of Germany) – who were sealed to him by proxy after his death." Scholars also generally agree that Joseph Smith rarely practiced polygyny during the 1830s in Ohio and Missouri but that he began to marry women at a rapid rate and over a short period of time during the Nauvoo era in the early 1840s.

Another question concerns the relationships between Joseph Smith and his plural wives: Were they spiritual, conjugal, or physical? Again, the issue is complex. On the basis of reports of wives themselves, informed followers, and former followers, Foster (1981) concluded that "many" of Joseph Smith's plural wives had a physical relationship with him. Arrington and Bitton (1979), while uncertain about numbers, believed that some wives lived conjugally with Joseph Smith, although a number of others were married to him only in a spiritual and theological sense.

3. Guinn and Scherr (1987) noted that 12 Mormon polygyny cases reached the U.S,. Supreme Court during a 15-year period in the late 1800s. Of these, the Court decided only three cases in favor of the Mormons and rendered 16 opinions aimed at eliminating polygyny.

4. Van Wagoner (1989) also stated, however, that in the last years of his leadership Brigham Young had begun to doubt the wisdom of plural marriages, since there were many cases of marital dissatisfaction, the expected millennium of the 1850s had not occurred, and the political price was becoming heavier and heavier.

5. Cannon (1983) stated that Woodruff appointed five men strongly committed to polygyny as church apostles. And Van Wagoner (1989) noted that there were approximately 250 church-approved plural marriages between 1890 and 1904, with a significant increase in plural marriages after Utah became a state in 1896. (For a year-by-year count of plural marriages between 1890 and 1910 see Hardy, 1992.)

6. Murdock (1967) also reported the levirate practice (where a widow marries the brother of her deceased husband) in 69% (127/185) of societies, and sororal polygyny (where a man marries two or more biological sisters) in 44% (84/193) of societies.

7. A series of analyses reveal the following: polygyny occurred in 2% to 36% of marriages in 15 African countries in 1966–1977, the average being about 25% (Welch and Glick, 1981). Dorjahn (1959) reported that an average of 35% of men in a sample of sub-Saharan societies had more than one wife. Goody (1976) found polygyny in about 35% of marriages in African cultures, with much lower rates in Egypt (4%) and Algeria (3%). Similarly, among Israel Bedouins in the Negev Marx (1987) observed that only about 7% of the men had more than one wife. Among the !Kung bushmen of southern Africa, Marshall (1976) found

that 10% of the men practiced polygyny. The following rates of polygyny were reported in other African cultures and communities: 27% in a community in Ghana (Hagan, 1983); about 50% in two communities in the Niger Delta (Leis, 1974); and 20% in a district in northern Uganda (Curley, 1973). Geertz (1961) stated that polygyny was relatively rare in Javanese culture, with only 2% of new marriages in 1953 being polygynous. Without citing statistics, Strathern (1972) stated that the great majority of marriages in the Hagen culture of New Guinea were monogamous. Ryan (1969) indicated that about 33% of the men in Mendi, New Guinea, were polygynous; O'Brien (1969) reported polygyny rates of about 25% in another New Guinea culture; Langness (1969) observed a polygyny rate of about 25 to 30% among the Bena Bena of New Guinea; and Strathern and Strathern (1969) stated that about 25% of marriages in the Melpa culture of New Guinea were polygynous.

8. Two wives was the norm among the Sioux Indians in traditional times (Hassrick, 1964), with sororal marriages quite a common occurrence. In the small number of polygynous families among the !Kung (Marshall, 1976), two wives was common. Clignet (1970) reported that 80% of polygynous marriages among the Aboure of Africa involved two wives; among the Highlanders (O'Brien, 1969), the Mendi (Ryan, 1969), and the Hagen of New Guinea (Strathern, 1972), the great preponderance of plural marriages also involved two wives.

Chapter 3

1. Lorin Woolley led the group until his death in 1934, when he was succeeded for a short time by Leslie Broadbent, a council member he had appointed. At Broadbent's passing, John Y. Barlow became prophet (Van Wagoner, 1989). He was succeeded by Joseph Musser, who had recorded and published Woolley's account of the 1886 events involving John Taylor. We were also told by a senior elder that only Joseph Musser had received the full priestly ordinances from Lorin Woolley and that Musser, not Barlow, should have become the group's leader. Our informant believed that the eventual schism between the Barlow and Musser factions resulted from disagreements about the proper line of succession for the group's leadership. On the other hand, another early participant and Bradley (1993) noted that Barlow was the senior member of the council and that he probably was the appropriate successor.

2. *Truth* magazine was alleged to be "obscene, lewd, lascivious, indecent and immoral in that sexual offenses against society, to wit, plural marriages, were to be and were advocated and urged, thereby tending to deprave and corrupt the morals of those whose minds were and are open to such influences, and into whose hands said *Truth* might fall" (Van Wagoner, 1989, p. 190).

3. Baer (1988) stated that the group apparently functioned as a single organization with two councils for the next few years. When Musser died, however, the split became formal, and each group went its own way, with its own leader, governing council and membership.

4. Bronson (n.d.) stated that only 5 members of the original council remained loyal.

Bradlee and Van Atta (1981) claimed that "only" a thousand members remained loyal to the Musser–Allred group. An elder in the movement told us that only 8 men and their families remained with Musser, constituting about 50 people. He stated that most of the people went with the Short Creek group and that many families and friendships were split up by the schism. In some cases animosities continued for years.

5. Driggs (1990) stated that the Arizona authorities kept the leaders of the Mormon Church informed of their plans in advance, and the *Deseret News*, a Mormon Church newspaper in Salt Lake City, later supported the raid in an editorial. However, Utah's governor at the time, a non-Mormon and freewheeling personality, J. Bracken Lee, refused to publicly support the raid (Bradlee and Van Atta, 1981).

6. Legal actions were also initiated on the Utah side of the Short Creek community. In one case eight children in the Black family were declared wards of the state on the grounds of parental neglect (Bradley, 1993; Driggs, 1990). The conviction was upheld by the Utah Supreme Court, and denied review by the U.S. Supreme Court. The children were eventually returned to their parents when the mother agreed not to teach or live in plural marriage in the future.

7. These figures are based on estimates by others and discussions we had with church elders. We know of no formal census of AUB membership.

8. In 1992 the Rulon Allred family brought a civil suit against Rena Chynoweth (who was not convicted of Allred's assassination but who subsequently admitted that she had killed him). The Allreds' case was upheld and they were awarded $54 million. Although Chynoweth had no resources, the Allreds viewed the successful legal action as symbolic vindication and condemnation of Rulon's assassin.

9. Van Wagoner (1989) also described another dissident, John Bryant, a convert to Mormonism, who later joined the AUB and subsequently established his own group – resulting from a personal revelation that he was the "right person" to fulfill the religious principles of the fundamentalist movement.

10. Kingston was a member of the original Lorin Woolley group in the late 1920s. He claimed to be the proper successor to the man who succeeded Lorin Woolley and who died shortly thereafter. Kingston's leadership claim was rejected, and he quit to establish his own group (Baer, 1988).

11. Apparently there have been 100 dissident Mormon groups over the history of the church, most of which failed to survive over the long run (Baer, 1988).

Chapter 4

1. Because no census information is available, this is only an estimate gleaned from participants in our study and from various published sources.

2. In some families, groups of girls get together on Sunday morning and help comb one another's hair in preparation for church and family activities.

Chapter 5

1. To be sure, many other considerations enter into adding a wife to a contemporary fundamentalist family. These include the economic status of participants, the desire by some families to have affiliations by marriage with one another, the fostering of political-religious power blocs within a community, and a desire to provide widows and divorced women social and economic security. Religious values, however, are the underpinning of polygyny among contemporary Mormon fundamentalists.

2. The discussion to follow applies primarily to the urban group of fundamentalists. In the rural group, discussed later, marriages are arranged by the prophet. Thus the decision to add a wife to a family is often in his hands, although participants and families may play an informal role.

3. Practical factors also played a role in 19th-century marriages, as they undoubtedly do among modern fundamentalists. Young (1954) raised the possibility that additional wives and children were a good source of labor in pioneer times, as they are in other low-technology polygynous cultures, and suggested that this might have been appealing to some men and their wives. Goodson (1976) also stated that some 19th-century Mormon men married their domestic servants, governesses, and seamstresses as plural wives to help maintain their households. In a somewhat satirical vein, Mehr (1985) commented that some pioneer men might have married their domestic servants in order to avoid paying them a salary!

Chapter 6

1. In other cultures, prospective partners first chose one another in a variety of settings, including funerals (Tiwi, Australia: Goodale, 1971); formal visits by males to neighboring settlements (Dassantech, Ethiopia: Almagor, 1983; Mundurucu, Brazil: Murphy and Murphy, 1974); a male sleeping near a partner in her dwelling or compound (Hottentots, Africa: Freeman, 1968). In many cases parents and kin played crucial roles in later phases of courtship.

2. We did not find any detailed ethnographic accounts of the communal role of established wives in courtships in other cultures. Whether they actually participated or whether their roles were simply not described by anthropologists is an open question.

3. Young's analyses are based on the records of 175 19th-century plural families, as well as Hulett's (1943) interviews in the 1930s with members of pioneer polygynous families. Embry's analyses are based on oral history data collected from 250 children of pioneer Mormon polygynists.

Chapter 7

1. Ginat (personal observation) also noted that some young lovers "arrange" an abduction themselves because they wish to marry one another. In collaboration

with friends and a respected elder who shelters the girl, pressure is put on her father to accede to the match, which he often does. This pretense of an "abduction" in what is really an "elopement" preserves the cultural norms of traditional Bedouin marriages.

2. Nineteenth-century Mormon weddings apparently were also rather simple. Young (1954, p. 142) stated: "By ordinary Christian standards there was no glamour in this ceremony. . . . The bride and groom kneel before a simple altar. There are no crucifix, candles, or other paraphernalia of the usual Christian sort."

3. Among 19th-century Mormon pioneers, an established wife was expected to "accompany her husband and the prospective wife to the temple for the sealing [marriage]" (Young, 1954, p. 141), but this ideal was not always met: "Travel was hard, distances were long, and it was often necessary for someone to remain to care for the household and children. In some families – especially where the first wife's consent was not given at all or reluctantly given – there was no motivation to go along" (Young 1954, p. 142). With increasing federal pressure and arrests, it became dangerous for wives to attend their husbands' weddings (Young, 1954; Goodson, 1976). If wives didn't attend weddings, they wouldn't have to testify in court that they had witnessed or participated in a plural marriage.

4. In marriages at a sacred altar in the 19th century, "the participants [were] clothed in their official underwear, a full length union suit over which [was] worn a loose white cotton or linen robe" (Young, 1954, p. 142).

Chapter 8

1. We found few descriptions of Mormon honeymoons in the 19th century. Post-wedding honeymoons were probably rare at the time, especially in plural families, in view of the challenges of that era, especially trying to build a new community in a harsh environment and avoid pressure from the federal government for practicing polygyny.

Chapter 10

1. We substantiated Murdock's conclusion in a tally of information from 205 cultures drawn from the *Atlas of World Cultures* (Murdock, 1981). Plural wives lived dyadically in 65% (96/148) of polygynous cultures, and wives who were also sisters lived communally in 82% (48/57) of cultures practicing sororal polygyny.

2. This pattern of wives having independent homes but sharing communally some public spaces also occurs among the Kikuyu (Kenyatta, 1973), Lodabaga (Goody, 1958), Shampla (Winans, 1964), Fulani (Stenning, 1958), Nuer (Evans-Pritchard, 1951), and Hottentots of Africa (Freeman, 1968) and the Javanese (Geertz, 1961), to name a few.

3. A roughly similar pattern of living with parents or in-laws until a first child is born occurs among the wives of the Nuer (Evans-Pritchard, 1951), Mende (Little, 1951), Lobedu (Crige, 1964), and Lodagaba of Africa (Goody, 1958). A reverse pattern also sometimes occurs; that is, a new couple lives with the parents of the bride for a period of time before having its own dwelling, as is the case among the Lango (Curley, 1973) and the Hottentots (Freeman, 1968).

4. Embry's data do not seem to distinguish between dyadic sharing of a home, that is, between two essentially separate apartments in the same structure versus sharing dining, living, kitchen, and other facilities. Thus communal living may have been even less frequent than the figure stated above.

5. Although highly communal, there were dyadic aspects to this configuration. For example, wives did their own laundry and ironing according to a weekly schedule and were responsible for cleaning their own private "apartments" (bedrooms and sitting areas).

6. In her autobiography, Melissa Merrill (1975), a contemporary plural wife, noted that she changed residences 38 times during her marriage. Although we did not obtain specific data on this point from all families in our sample, Sally, the first wife in Family 14, said that she changed homes at least 8 times in 10 years. From our case reports it is clear that others also moved frequently.

7. We had little information on the rural group's changes in living arrangements. Our impression, however, is that a lifelong pattern of communal living is more customary in the rural community. This is partly due to the fact that the religious group owns a great deal of land and permits members to build homes on the land and dwellings may be larger and more suited to a plural family.

Chapter 11

1. As an aside, in one discussion with Family 1 the wives asked *our* wives how they managed to have any solitude when they had to deal with *us* every single night! They thought that monogamous life would be especially difficult in this respect, and they felt that our wives were faced with a difficult challenge of never being alone. They considered their situation to be better because they did not see their husband every single day. We had a good-natured discussion about the issue, noting that even though we were together every day, we often did separate things at home in the evening. They still seemed perplexed about our lifestyle!

2. The interested reader may consult Csikszentmihalyi and Rochberg-Halton (1981) and Belk (1992) regarding research on attachments to personal objects.

Chapter 12

1. Although little has been written about husbands and homes in 19th-century Mormon plural families, what exists is consistent with our contemporary data. The home was a woman's domain, with husbands moving about from home to home, probably taking little part in managing or decorating them. Furthermore,

men were often away on business or church missions for long periods, were in flight or hiding from the authorities, and often were responsible for families widely separated from one another.

Embry (1987) sheds some light on the issue, noting that 80% of the men in her sample of turn-of-the-century Mormon polygynous husbands did not reside at any particular wife's home; they rotated more or less equally among homes. But one in five did tend to favor certain homes, often because they preferred a particular wife. One informant stated that her father often stayed at her mother's home because "my mother had a home. It was always comfortable, and food and everything was always ready. I don't know about the other home" (Embry, 1987, p. 83). Another informant stated that her father tended to stay at her mother's home often because "I don't think he felt welcome" at the second wife's home. "He used to go there, but he would never stay long. They were different people" (Embry, 1987, p. 83). In other families, men treated the first wife's home as the "family headquarters": "The second wife occasionally tried to get him to build a barn at her house or set out an orchard or a garden, but he always refused saying he wanted everything at one place" (Young, 1954, p. 198).

Young also describes a number of cases in which official entertaining always occurred at the home of the first wife. In another family even the husband's laundry and mending was always done at the headquarters home. But liking a particular home or wife was not always the primary or sole reason for a husband to live more often in one place. Fear of prosecution, business obligations, health, or other factors sometimes played a role. Embry (1987) reported the case of a husband who lived with one wife in Mexico for 15 years because of the threat of arrest, rarely seeing his other wife. When the first wife died, however, he returned to live with the second wife, presumably because he was no longer living in a plural marriage. In other cases, a husband might live with a particular wife because only one wife was the "legal wife" and the church allegedly pressed him to live with her following the Manifesto of 1890 (Embry, 1987).

2. We visited children's rooms on touring homes, but did not spend as much time in their rooms, as in other parts of homes or in wives' bedrooms. In addition, we did not always have exact information about the ages of children in various rooms, so who decorated particular rooms – a parent or a child – is often not known. Thus our discussion is only exploratory and suggestive.

3. We visited 45 children's rooms in seven families, including those of 21 girls and 24 boys of all ages (some rooms had more than one child). Our visits were brief and we were unable to make detailed observations. We estimated differences in overall volume of decorating between genders within a family (not across families or among boys and girls in general) and tried to recall the types of items that were salient in rooms.

Chapter 13

1. Fixed visitation patterns also occur among the Dakar (Falade, 1963), Lango (Curley, 1973), and Tonga of Africa and the Tanla of Madagascar (Stephens, 1963).

2. There are exceptions to this general practice, but they are rare and often only temporary. In Family 14, for example, Harvey, Sally, and Molly lived together for a short period in a very small home. They tried out several different rotation and sleeping arrangements, including both wives sharing a single bedroom and Harry sleeping in another room. In this arrangement, which lasted for only a short time, each wife visited him on a rotating basis. Eventually the wives had their own rooms or homes, and Harvey visited them.

3. It is not possible to pinpoint exactly the extent to which pioneer plural families followed rigid, laissez-faire, or flexible rotation systems. We do know, however, that most rotation patterns of the era were systematic, following either a rigid or flexible pattern. In support of the idea that husbands were fair and responsible, Young (1954) and Embry (1987) indicate that many polygynous husbands of the era spent time with their wives on a regular basis – although the length of intervals between visits varied quite a bit. An examination of 50 family records showed that "in slightly more than a quarter of families the husband spent alternate days with each wife, about the same proportion took them week-about, and the same percentage were irregular, that is, had no fixed schedule. The balance [a quarter] were scattered into two-day, three-day, and fortnightly arrangements. A few fell into special groupings, such as, seasonal variations where the families were widely scattered in the summer time but might be living in the same village during the winter, or where a plural wife's long absence on the Underground would require considerable change in former regularities" (Young, 1954, p. 178).

   In an analysis of 156 families Embry (1987, p. 81) found an even higher rate of systematic rotation practices: "27% of the husbands changed homes nightly, 21% moved every week, only 8% had no routine, and 21% stayed primarily with one wife. The rest visited either once every three days or rotated monthly."

4. Cairncross (1974) described a rotation process used by John of Leyden, leader of a polygynous Protestant sect in the 1500s, that reflected his control of the rotation process. At dinner time he and his wives sat at "a table on which he wrote the queens' [wives] names in order of precedence. And he had a whole board in front of each name to hold a stick. The queen who found the stick thus inserted in front of her dinner knew that she had been chosen to spend the night with the King [John]. But she was allowed to pass on the honor to a fellow queen if she was indisposed" (p. 19).

5. Husbands in the Lango culture of Africa do a similar thing (Curley, 1973). They rotate among their wives for three to four consecutive nights at a time but also visit every wife a few times each day.

Chapter 14

1. However, women often have jewelry and valuables that they personally own. And they may receive inheritance money from their natal family, which they can use to buy their own animals and land – and which is strictly under their control (Ginat, 1982).

2. Sometimes, husbands distributed resources on a proportionate basis according

to number of children; in some cases allocations were equal regardless of family size. In other instances, wives received resources in accordance with their status, usually as first versus later wives. And in some families the first wife had the choice of items and the remainder was distributed to other wives (Embry, 1987).

Chapter 16

1. The ethnographic literature does not usually distinguish between wife–wife feelings associated with the husband and those involving interpersonal compatibility of wives, resources, children, or day-to-day issues. As a result, the ethnographic material presented here addresses all aspects of wife–wife relationships, some of which may apply to chapter 17.

2. Moreover, in some cultures co-wives sometimes have formal roles that may smooth out their day-to-day communal relationships with one another. A senior wife among the Bete of Africa, for example, assigns work, supervises the care of all children in the plural family, controls presents given to wives by the husband, eats before and separately from other wives, and even decides which wife will sleep with the husband (Clignet, 1970). In other cases, a senior wife's authority is more limited. Among the Fulani of Africa (Stenning, 1958, 1971), the first wife may milk the husband's cattle before the other wives, appoint milking rights to the other wives, has her bed set up first in a pastoral camp, and may generally be deferred to by junior wives. In some cultures, such as the !Kung of Africa, a first wife theoretically has authority over other wives, but her status is sometimes only symbolic (Marshall, 1976).

   Which wife is senior and the range of her authority varies from culture to culture. In many cultures the first wife is senior; in other cases it may be a different wife. The "chief wife" among the Lobedu of Africa is the daughter of the husband's mother's brother, and it is she who bears the family's official heir – although she has no day-to-day authority over other wives (Crige, 1964). In some cultures a senior wife may have culturally prescribed priorities in relation to the husband. Senior wives among the Lango (Curley, 1973) and Tonga of Africa (Stephens, 1963) have some combination of more access and time with the husband, are freer to express opinions, and have more influence than other wives. Yet they do not directly control the day-to-day activities of their co-wives. Senior wives have a similar status among the Pedi (Kuper, 1980) and Nyakyusa of Africa (Radcliffe-Brown, 1950). In other cultures, such as the Hagen of New Guinea (Strathern, 1972), wives theoretically have equal status in respect to resources, the husband, and various aspects of day-to-day life. In summary, many cultures have prescribed role relationships among co-wives that may serve to reduce competition, jealousy, hostility, and conflicts.

3. On the other hand, there were cases in which wives, especially senior wives, objected to being treated equally to other wives: "My father expressed to both families very often that when he was a boy and where there was polygamy, there was always a favorite wife. That was the older wife. . . . He determined in his marriages that he would have strict equality. I suspect that caused more

friction than the old system that my mother had thought would exist when she agreed to polygamy. She thought she would be the queen bee as it were instead of strict equality" (Embry, 1987, p. 129).

In another case, the first wife of Orson Pratt, the original spokesperson for the establishment of polygamy in the Mormon Church, was not very happy about the whole process: "She insisted that the first wife should be it, and resented her husband's affection toward his other wives. 'Here was my husband, gray headed, taking to his bed young girls in mockery of marriage. Of course there could be no joy for him in such an intercourse except the indulgence of his fanaticism and of something else, perhaps, which I hesitate to mention.' " She also said: "By and by he told me that he intended to put these five women [his other wives] on an exact equality with me," by spending "a week with one, a week with another, and so on, and that I should have the sixth week! I told him plainly that I wouldn't endure it. I said, 'If you take five weeks with your other women you can take the sixth with them also' " (Van Wagoner, 1989, p. 100).

4. In her autobiography, Melissa Merrill (1975) says her husband praised her sister-wife and demeaned her, gave the other wife special gifts, spent more time with and openly displayed more affection to the other wife, paid more attention to the other wife's children, spent time away with the other wife, and so on.

Chapter 17

1. Years ago, one of us observed another highly communal approach in a family with seven wives who shared a dwelling. They rotated responsibilities every week as follows: two wives cooked, two did the laundry, two did other work at home and purchased groceries. In any given week one wife was free of all household chores.

Chapter 18

1. The superiority of men over women was sometimes reacted to strongly by critics, who teased, ridiculed, and sometimes viciously attacked the fledgling Mormon culture. Ann Eliza Young (1908), an embittered wife of Brigham Young, said that one Mormon leader of the 19th century treated his wives as property and even described them as "my heifers," or "my cows," thereby reflecting women's inferiority and suggesting that they had the status of animals. Several authors (Bitton and Bunker, 1978; Cannon, 1974; Sheldon, 1976) have noted that critics and satirists attacked Mormon men, portraying them as wife and women abusers who "purchased" women as if they were slaves, examined their bodies at "markets," forced women out of their homes when they didn't obey men, physically mistreated wives, lacked morality, and contributed to the downfall of the family and the human social order of the times.

On the other side, women were also criticized and satirized for participating in polygyny. In one bit of satire, Mark Twain said: "With the gushing self-sufficiency of youth I was feverish to plunge headlong and achieve a great reform here until I saw the Mormon women. Then I was touched. My heart was wiser than my head. It warmed toward these poor, ungainly, and pathetically 'homely' creatures, and as I turned to hide the generous moisture in my eyes, I said, 'no – the man that marries one of them has done an act of Christian charity which entitles him to the kindly applause of mankind, not their harsh censure – and the man that marries sixty of them has done a deed of open-handed generosity so sublime that the nation should stand uncovered in his presence and worship in silence' " (Sheldon, 1976, p. 116).

And Mormon women were sometimes characterized as lustful and oversexed, fighting with one another, flirtatious, acquisitive, and ill-tempered, as if they deserved to live in the evils of polygamy (Bitton and Bunker, 1978).

2. We recently learned of two new family activities designed to foster family cohesion. A few years ago, Harry decided to meet several mornings a week for breakfast with all of his unmarried children. They pray, sing a few songs, and talk about various matters. Harry sees this as a way to maintain contact with those of his children who are still living at home. He also told us of a new community-wide event, in which families are designated by the church leadership to put on some type of "show" for the community as a whole. For their contribution, Harry's children – mostly the unmarried ones – have adapted a pioneer play-musical and have been working at building stage sets, rehearsing, practicing songs, and making costumes for an upcoming performance. Between scenes, the very young children from throughout the family will do short dances, and the play will culminate with the whole family – children, spouses, grandchildren, and great-grandchildren, some 400 family members in all – coming up on the stage as a symbol of their unity, harmony, and cooperation.

Chapter 19

1. We found little in the literature about the naming of children among Mormon pioneers. However, Embry (1987) described a case in which two wives argued about which child in the family should bear the name of their grandfather – who happened to be Joseph Smith, the founder of the church.

2. We came across a similar procedure reportedly used by Brigham Young. Cornwall (1978) quoted from a daughter of Brigham Young, who said that as a rule he named the boys and the child's mother named the girls.

3. The term "aunt X" is appropriate in a number of historical and contemporary cases, since some wives in plural families are biological sisters. Moreover, several participants noted that these terms were customary during earlier years when the civil authorities were actively arresting and prosecuting Mormon polygynists. The term "aunt" was a way of acknowledging a close relationship between a wife and a co-wife's child but did not directly implicate anyone as a member of a plural family. As an aside, during the years of active arrests and prosecution, children sometimes used their mother's family name when registering in schools.

And in some cases, we were told, children were taught to call their father "uncle" in public settings in order to hide their identity as members of plural families. In her autobiography of life in a modern plural family during an era of prosecution, Dorothy Solomon (1984), daughter of a former prophet, said children in the family were registered in school under the family name, but with different combinations of her father's first and middle names and initials. And children in the family called him "uncle" in public situations. These practices are rare nowadays.

4. Logue (1984) reported an unusual case in a pioneer Mormon plural family in which the second wife's children called the first wife "ma"; the first wife's children called the second wife "aunt" and referred to the third wife by her given name. A complex set of terms of reference indeed!

5. Embry (1987) described a similar pioneer case in which children who were close in age to a wife referred to her as "sister X" or called her by name.

Chapter 20

1. Although Joseph Ginat had been associated with the fundamentalist groups for several years prior to this project, Irwin Altman had not had any previous contact with them.

Appendix B

1. The problem is compounded by the fact that the concept of plural marriage was not precisely defined in Mormon theology in its formative years. There were marriages for "time" (on earth) and marriages for "time and eternity" (earth and heaven), "spiritual wife" marriages between a man and a married woman, and "proxy husband" marriage in which a man "cared for" another man's wife when he was away on an extended mission for the church. Some of these relationships were formalized in religious ceremonies, others were not; some may have been physically consummated, others were not; some may have resulted in children, others did not. So the demographics of 19th-century Mormon polygyny is a complicated matter.

2. Yet there were some dramatic examples of men, especially church leaders, who had very large numbers of wives and children. Brigham Young, church leader from 1844 to 1879, allegedly had 27 wives and was sealed to twice that many living women and to at least 150 other women who had previously died (Ivins, 1956). And Heber Kimball, a church leader close to Brigham Young, had 43 wives (Van Wagoner, 1989). Another church leader, Franklin Richards, had 11 wives. Church leaders John Lee and Parley Pratt had 19 and 10 wives, respectively (Goodson, 1976). It is important to note, however, that some of these marriages involved older women and widows who entered plural marriages for security and support. Thus Brigham Young married several of Joseph Smith's widows following his assassination. This practice derived, in part, from the bib-

lical principle that a man was to marry his brother's widows in order to care for them. Furthermore, many of these marriages were "for time only," for in the hereafter the wife was her original husband's wife.

3. The lower fertility rates for polygynous wives, especially later wives, may have been due to the long absences of men away from home on church business (especially as they gained seniority in the church hierarchy), the waning physical vitality and health of older husbands, marriages to older widowed or divorced women, and the like.

4. We classified people as "natives" if they were born into a fundamentalist family or if their parents converted to the fundamentalist group up to the time that they were about 15 years of age. For many such families, commitment to fundamentalism often involved several years of prior deliberation and discussion, so that children had some idea of plural family life before their families joined the movement. We categorized anyone joining the group after age 15 as a "convert."

References

Almagor, U. (1983). Alternation endogamy in the Dassanetch generation-set system. *Ethnology, 22,* 93–108.

Altman, I. (1975). *Environment and social behavior: Privacy, personal space, territory, and crowding.* Monterey, CA: Brooks/Cole. (Reprinted by Irvington Press, New York, 1981)

Altman, I. (1977). Privacy regulation: Culturally universal or culturally specific? *Journal of Social Issues, 33.* (3), 79–109.

Altman, I. (1990). Toward a transactional perspective: A personal journey. In I. Altman and K. Christensen (Eds.), *Environment and behavior studies: Emergence of intellectual traditions.* Vol. 11 of *Human behavior and environment: Advances in theory and research* (pp. 225–256). New York: Plenum.

Altman, I., Brown, B. B., Staples, B., & Werner, C. M. (1992). A transactional approach to close relationships: Courtship, weddings and placemaking. In B. Walsh, K. Craik, and R. Price (Eds.), *Person-environment psychology: Contemporary models and perspectives* (pp. 193–241). Hillsdale, NJ: Erlbaum.

Altman, I., & Chemers, M. M. (1989). *Culture and environment.* New York: Cambridge University Press.

Altman, I., & Gauvain, M. (1981). A cross-cultural and dialectic analysis of homes. In L. S. Liben, A. H. Patterson, & N. Newcombe (Eds.), *Spatial representation and behavior across the life span* (pp. 283–320). New York: Academic Press.

Altman, I., & Low, S. M. (Eds.). (1992). *Place attachment.* Vol. 12 of *Human behavior and environment: Advances in theory and research.* New York: Plenum.

Altman, I., Nelson, P., & Lett, E. (1972). The ecology of home environments. *Catalog of Selected Documents in Psychology.* Washington, DC: American Psychological Association.

Altman, I., & Rogoff, B. (1987). World views in psychology: Trait, interactional, organismic, and transactional perspectives. In D. Stokols & I. Altman (Eds.), *Handbook of environmental psychology* (Vol. 1, pp. 1–40). New York: Wiley.

Altman, I., & Taylor, D. A. (1973). *Social penetration: The development of interpersonal relationships.* New York: Holt, Rinehart & Winston. (Reprinted by Irvington Press, 1981)

Altman, I., Vinsel, A., & Brown, B. B. (1981). Dialectic conceptions in social psychology: An application to social penetration and privacy regulation. In L. Berkowitz (Ed.), *Advances in experimental social psychology* (Vol. 14, pp. 107–160). New York: Academic Press.

Altman, I., & Werner, C. M. (Eds.). (1985). *Home environments.* Vol. 8 of *Human behavior and environment: Advances in theory and research.* New York: Plenum.

Anderson, J. R. (1957). Polygamy in Utah. *Utah Law Review, 5,* 381–389.

Arrington, L. J., & Bitton, D. (1979). *The Mormon experience: A history of the Latter-day Saints.* New York: Knopf.

Asante-Darko, N., & Van Der Geest, S. (1983). Male chauvinism: Men and women in Ghanaian highlife songs. In C. Oppong (Ed.), *Female and male in West Africa* (pp. 242–255). London: Allen & Unwin.

Baer, H. A. (1988). *Recreating utopia in the desert: A sectarian challenge to modern Mormonism.* Albany: State University of New York Press.

Bailey, B. L. (1988). *From front porch to back seat: Courtship in twentieth-century America.* Baltimore, MD.: Johns Hopkins University Press.

Barker, R. G. (1968). *Ecological psychology: Concepts and methods for studying the environment of human behavior.* Stanford, CA: Stanford University Press.

Baxter, L. A. (1988). A dialectical perspective on communication strategies in relationship development. In S. Duck (Ed.), *Handbook of personal relationships* (pp. 257–273). New York: Wiley.

Baxter, L. A., & Montgomery, B. M. (1996). *Relational dialectics: A dialogic approach.* New York: Guilford.

Belk, R. W. (1992). Attachment to possessions. In I. Altman and S. M. Low (Eds.), *Place attachment.* Vol. 12 of *Human behavior and environment: Advances in theory and research* (pp. 37–62). New York: Plenum.

Betzig, L. L. (1986). *Despotism and differential reproduction: A Darwinian view of history.* New York: Aldine.

Betzig, L. L., Mulder, M. B., & Turke, P. (1988). *Human reproductive behavior: A Darwinian perspective.* Cambridge, England: Cambridge University Press.

Bitton, R. (1987). Polygamist leader passes on. *Sunstone, 11,* 48.

Bitton, D., & Bunker, G. L. (1978). Double jeopardy: Visual images of Mormon women to 1914. *Utah Historical Quarterly, 46,* 184–202.

Brabin, L. (1984). Polygamy: An indicator of nutritional stress in African agricultural societies. *Africa, 54,* 31–45.

Bradlee, B. J., Jr., & Van Atta, D. (1981). *Prophet of blood: The untold story of Ervil LeBaron and the Lambs of God.* New York: Putnam.

Bradley, M. S. (1990). Changed faces: The official LDS position on polygamy, 1890–1990. *Sunstone, 14,* 26–33.

Bradley, M. S. (1990). The women of fundamentalism: Short Creek, 1953. *Dialogue, 23,* 15–37.

Bradley, M. S. (1993). *Kidnapped from that land: The government raids on the Short Creek polygamists.* Salt Lake City: University of Utah Press.

Bronson, L. A. (n.d.). *Winnie.* Privately published.

Brooks, J. (1934). A close-up of polygamy. *Harpers Magazine,* February 1934, 299–307.

Brown, B. B. (1987). Territoriality. In D. Stokols & I. Altman (Eds.), *Handbook of environmental psychology* (pp. 505–532). New York: Wiley.

Burgess-Olson, V. (Ed.) (1978). *Sister saints*. Provo, UT: Brigham Young University Press.

Buss, D. M. (1994). *The evolution of desire: Strategies of human mating*. New York: Basic Books.

Buss, D. M. (1995). Psychological sex differences: Origins through sexual selection. *American Psychologist, 50*, 164–168.

Cairncross, J. (1974). *After polygamy was made a sin: The social history of Christian polygamy*. London: Routledge and Kegan Paul.

Campbell, E. E., & Campbell, B. L. (1978). Divorce among Mormon polygamists: Extent and explanations. *Utah Historical Society, 46*, 4–23.

Cannon, C. A. (1974). The awesome power of sex: The polemical campaign against Mormon polygamy. *Pacific Historical Review, 43*, 61–82.

Cannon, K. L. (1983). After the Manifesto: Mormon polygamy, 1890–1906. *Sunstone, 8*, 27–41.

Clignet, R. (1970). *Many wives, many powers: Authority and power in polygamous families*. Evanston, IL: Northwestern University Press.

Clignet, R., & Sween, J. A. (1981). For a revisionist theory of human polygyny. *Signs, 6*, 445–468.

Coontz, S. (1988). *The social origins of private life: A history of American families 1600–1900*. London: Verso.

Cornwall, R. F. (1978). Susa Y. Gates. In V. Burgess-Olson (Ed.), *Sister saints* (pp. 63–93). Provo, UT: Brigham Young University Press.

Crige, E. J. (1964). Property, cross cousin marriage, and the family cycle among the Lobedu. In R. F. Gray and P. H. Gulliver (Eds.), *The family estate in Africa* (pp. 155–197). London: Routledge and Kegan Paul.

Curley, R. T. (1973). *Elders, shades, and women: Ceremonial change in Lango, Uganda*. Berkeley, CA: University of California Press.

Csikszentmihalyi, M., & Rochberg-Halton, E. (1981). *The meaning of things: Domestic symbols and the self*. New York: Cambridge University Press.

Dewey, J., & Bentley, A. (1949). *Knowing and the known*. Boston: Beacon.

Dorjahn, V. R. (1959). The factor of polygyny in African demography. In W. R. Bascom & M. J. Herskovits (Eds.), *Continuity and change in African cultures* (pp. 87–112). Chicago: University of Chicago Press.

Dovey, K. (1985). Home and homelessness. In I. Altman & C. M. Werner (Eds.), *Home environments*. Vol. 8. of *Human behavior and environment: Advances in theory and research* (pp. 33–64). New York: Plenum.

Dredge, N. T. (1976). Victims of the conflict. In C. L. Bushman (Ed.), *Mormon sisters: Women in early Utah* (pp. 134–155). Cambridge, MA: Emmeline Press.

Driggs, K. (1990). After the Manifesto: Modern polygamy and fundamentalist Mormons. *Journal of Church and State, 32*, 367–389.

Driggs, K. (1991). Utah Supreme Court decides polygamist adoption case. *Sunstone, 15*, 67–68.

Driggs, K. (1988). The persecutions begin: Defining cohabitation in 1885. *Dialogue: A Journal of Mormon Thought, 21*, 109–125.

Dunfey, J. (1984). "Living the principle" of plural marriage: Mormon women, utopia, and female sexuality in the 19th century. *Feminist Studies, 10*, 523–536.

Dupire, M. (1963). The position of women in a pastoral society. In D. Paulme

(Ed.), *Women of Tropical Africa* (pp. 47–92). Berkeley, CA: University of California Press.

Dyer, R. G. (1977). The evolution of serial and judicial attitudes toward polygamy, *Utah Bar Journal, 5*, 35–45.

Eaton-Gadsby, P. R. & Dushku, J. R. (1978). Emmeline B. Wells. In V. Burgess-Olson (Ed.), *Sister saints* (pp. 457–478). Provo, UT: Brigham Young University Press.

Embry, J. L. (1984). Effects of polygamy on Mormon women. *Frontiers, 3*, 56–61.

Embry, J. L. (1987). *Mormon polygamous families: Life in the principle.* Salt Lake City, UT: University of Utah Press.

Embry, J. L., & Bradley, M. S. (1985). Mothers and daughters in polygamy. *Dialogue: A Journal of Mormon Thought, 18*, 99–107.

Evans-Pritchard, E. E. (1951). *Kinship and marriage among the Nuer.* Oxford: Clarendon Press.

Falade, S. (1963). Women of Dakar and the surrounding urban area. In D. Paulme (Ed.), *Women of tropical Africa* (pp. 217–229). Berkeley, CA: University of California Press.

Faux, S. (1983). Genetic self-interest and Mormon polygyny: A sociobiological perspective of the doctrinal development of polygyny. *Sunstone, 8*, 37–40.

Feeley-Harnik, G. (1980). The Sakalava house (Madagascar). *Anthropos: International Review of Ethnology and Linguistics. 1*, 27–41.

Forde, D. (1950). Double descent among the Yako. In A. R. Radcliffe-Brown & D. Forde (Eds.), *African systems of kinship and marriage* (pp. 285–332). London: Oxford University Press.

Fortes, M. (1950). Kinship and marriage among the Ashanti. In A. R. Radcliffe-Brown & D. Forde (Eds.), *African systems of kinship and marriage* (pp. 252–284). London: Oxford University Press.

Foster, L. (1981). *Religion and sexuality: Three American communal experiments of the 19th century.* New York: Oxford University Press.

Foster, L. (1982). Polygamy and the frontier: Mormon women in early Utah. *Utah Historical Quarterly, 50*, 268–289.

Foster, L. (1991). *Women, family and utopia: Communal experiments of the Shakers, the Oneida community, and the Mormons.* Syracuse, NY: Syracuse University Press.

Franck, K. A., & Ahrentzen, S. (1989). *New households new housing.* New York: Van Nostrand Reinhold.

Freeman, L. C. (1968). Marriage without love: Mate selection in Nonwestern societies. In R. F. Winch & L. W. Goodman (Eds.), *Selected studies in marriage and the family* (pp. 456–468). New York: Holt, Rinehart & Winston.

Fried, M. N., & Fried, M. H. (1980). *Transitions: Four rituals in eight cultures.* New York: Norton.

Gauvain, M., Altman, I., & Fahim, H. (1983). Homes and social change: A cross-cultural analysis. In N. R. Feimer & E. S. Geller (Eds.), *Environmental psychology: Directions and perspectives* (pp. 80–118). New York: Praeger.

Geertz, H. (1961). *The Javanese family.* Glencoe, IL: The Free Press.

Ginat, J. (1982). *Women in Muslim rural society: Status and role in family and community.* New Brunswick, NJ: Transaction Books.

Ginat, J. (1985). Women in the polygynous Mormon society. In G. Volger and K. Welch (Eds.), *Die Braut. Ethnologica* (pp. 210–216). Köln, Germany.

Ginsburg, G. P. (1980). Situated action: An emerging paradigm. In L. Wheeler (Ed.), *Review of personality and social psychology* (pp. 295–325). Newbury Park, CA: Sage.

Gluckman, M. (1950). Kinship and marriage among the Lozi of Northern Rhodesia and the Zulu of Natal. In A. R. Radcliffe-Brown & D. Forde (Eds.), *African systems of kinship and marriage* (pp. 166–206). London: Oxford University Press.

Goodale, J. C. (1971). *Tiwi wives: A study of the women of Melville Island North Australia.* Seattle: University of Washington Press.

Goodson, S. S. (1976). Plural wives. In C. L. Bushman (Ed.), *Mormon Sisters: Women in early Utah* (pp. 89–111). Cambridge, MA: Emmeline Press.

Goody, J. R. (1976). *Production and reproduction: A comparative study of the domestic domain.* Cambridge, England: Cambridge University Press.

Goody, J. R. (1958). The fission of domestic groups among the Lodagaba. In J. R. Goody (Ed.), *The developmental cycle and domestic groups* (pp. 53–91). Cambridge, England: Cambridge University Press.

Guinn, R. D., & Scherr, G. C. (1987). The Mormon polygamy cases. *Sunstone, 11* (5), 8–17.

Hagan, G. P. (1983). Marriage, divorce and polygyny in Winneba. In C. Oppong (Ed.), *Female and male in West Africa* (pp. 192–205). London: Allen & Unwin.

Hardy, B. C. (1992). *Solemn covenant: The Mormon polygamist passage.* Urbana, IL: University of Illinois Press.

Hassrick, R. B. (1964). *The Sioux: Life and customs of a warrior society.* Norman, OK: University of Oklahoma Press.

Hawes, J. M., & Nybakken, E. I. (Eds.), (1991). *American families: A research guide and historical handbook.* New York: Greenwood.

Hulett, Jr., J. E. (1943). The social role of the Mormon polygamist male. *American Sociological Review, 8,* 279–287.

Iversen, J. (1984). Feminist implications of Mormon polygamy. *Feminist Studies, 10,* 505–522.

Ivins, S. S. (1956). Notes on Mormon polygamy. *Western Humanities Review, 10,* 229–239.

Kelly, J. R., & McGrath, J. E. (1988). *On time and method.* Newbury Park, CA: Sage.

Kemper, S. (1980). Polygamy and monogamy in Kandyan Sri Lanka. *Journal of Comparative Family Studies, 11,* 299–324.

Kenyatta, J. (1973). Marriage system. In E. P. Skinner (Ed.), *Peoples and cultures of Africa* (pp. 280–296). Garden City, NY: Natural History Press.

Kern, L. J. (1981). *An ordered love: Sex roles and sexuality in Victorian utopias – the Shakers, the Mormons, and the Oneida community.* Chapel Hill, NC: University of North Carolina Press.

Kilbride, P. L. (1994). *Plural marriage for our times: A reinvented option?* Westport, CT: Bergin & Garvey.

Kilbride, P. L., & Kilbride, J. C. (1990). *Changing family life in East Africa: Women and children at risk.* University Park, PA: Pennsylvania State University Press.

Kuper, H. (1950). Kinship among the Swazi. In A. R. Radcliffe-Brown and D. Forde (Eds.), *African systems of kinship and marriage* (pp. 86–110). London: Oxford University Press.

Kuper, A. (1980). Symbolic dimensions of the Southern Bantu homestead. *Africa, 50,* 8–24.

Kuper, H. (1963). *The Swazi: A South African kingdom.* New York: Holt, Rinehart.

Lamphere, L. (1974). Strategies, cooperation, and conflict among women in domestic groups. In M. Z. Rosaldo and L. Lamphere (Eds.), *Women, culture, and society* (pp. 107–112). Stanford, CA: Stanford University Press.

Langness, L. L. (1969). Marriage in Bena Bena. In R. M. Glasse and M. J. Meggitt (Eds.), *Pigs, pearl shells, and women* (pp. 38–55). Englewood Cliffs, NJ: Prentice-Hall.

Lee, R. E. (1984). *The Dobe Kung.* New York: CBS College Publishing.

Leis, N. B. (1974). Women in groups: Ijaw womens associations. In M. Z. Rosaldo & L. Lamphere (Eds.), *Women, culture, and society* (pp. 223–242). Stanford, CA: Stanford University Press.

LeVine, R. A. (1964). The Gusii family. In R. F. Gray and P. H. Gulliver (Eds.), *The family estate in Africa* (pp. 63–82). London: Routledge and Kegan Paul.

LeVine, R. A., & LeVine, B. B. (1963). Nyansongo: A Gusii community in Kenya. In B. B. Whiting (Ed.), *Six cultures: Studies of child rearing* (pp. 15–202). New York: Wiley.

Little, K. L. (1951). *The Mende of Sierra Leone.* London: Routledge and Kegan Paul.

Logue, L. (1984). Time of marriage: Monogamy and polygamy in a Utah town. *Journal of Mormon History, 11,* 3–26.

Low S. M., & Chambers E. (Eds.). (1989). *Housing, culture and design: A comparative perspective.* Philadelphia, PA: University of Pennsylvania Press.

Mair, L. (1977). *Marriage.* London: Scholar Press.

Marshall, L. (1961). Sharing, talking and giving: Relief of social tensions among Kung Bushmen. *Africa, 32,* 221–252.

Marshall, L. (1976). *The !Kung of Nyae Nyae.* Cambridge, MA: Harvard University Press.

Marx, E. (1967). *Bedouin of the Negev.* Manchester, England: Manchester University Press.

Marx, E. (1987). Relations between spouses among the Negev Bedouin. *Ethnos, 1–2,* 156–179.

May, D. (1992). A demographic portrait of the Mormons, 1830–1980. In D. M. Quinn (Ed.), *The new Mormon history* (pp. 121–135). Salt Lake City, UT: Signature Books.

McGrath, J. E., & Kelly, J. R. (1986). *Time and human interaction.* New York: Guilford.

Mehr, K. (1985). Women's response to plural marriage. *Dialogue: A Journal of Mormon Thought, 18,* 84–97.

Merrill, M. (1975). *Polygamist's wife.* Salt Lake City, UT: Olympus.

Murdock, J. P. (1980). The Tenino Indians. *Ethnology, 19,* 129–150.

Murdock, G. P. (1967). *Social structure.* New York: Macmillan.

Murdock, G. P. (1981). *Atlas of world cultures.* Pittsburgh, PA: University of Pittsburgh Press.

Murphy, Y., & Murphy, R. F. (1974). *Women of the forest.* New York: Columbia University Press.

Newell, L. K., & Avery, V. T. (1984). *Mormon enigma: Emma Hale Smith.* Garden City, NY: Doubleday.

O'Brien, D. (1969). In R. M. Glasse and M. J. Meggitt (Eds.), *Pigs, pearl shells, and women: Marriage in the New Guinea Highlands* (pp. 198–234). Englewood Cliffs, NJ: Prentice-Hall.

O'Connell, M. C. (1982). Spirit possession and role stress among the Xesibe of Eastern Transkei. *Ethnology, 21,* 21–38.

Ottenheimer, M., & Ottenheimer, H. (1979). Matrilocal residence and nonsororal polygamy: A case from the Comoro Islands. *Journal of Anthropological Research, 35,* 328–335.

Otto, R. M. (1991). "Wait till your mothers get home": Assessing the rights of polygamists as custodial and adoptive parents. *Utah Law Review, 4,* 881–931.

Parker, S., Ginat, J., & Smith, J. (1975). Father absence and cross-sex identity: The puberty rites controversy revisited. *American Ethnologist, 2,* 687–706.

Pepper, S. C. (1942). *World hypotheses: A study in evidence.* Berkeley, CA: University of California Press.

Pepper, S. C. (1967). *Concept and quality: A world hypothesis.* La Salle, IL: Open Court.

Peters, E. L. (1965). Aspects of the family among the Bedouins of Cyrenica. In M. F. Nimkoff (Ed.), *Comparative family systems.* Boston, MA: Houghton Mifflin.

Prussin, L. (1989). The architecture of nomadism: Gabra placemaking and culture. In S. M. Low & E. Chambers (Eds.), *Housing, culture and design: A comparative perspective* (pp. 141–164). Philadelphia, PA: University of Pennsylvania Press.

Quinn, D. M. (1973). *Organizational development and social origins of the Mormon hierarchy: 1832–1932.* Unpublished master's thesis, University of Utah, Salt Lake City.

Quinn, D. M. (1985). LDS church authority and new plural marriages, 1890–1904. *Dialogue: A Journal of Mormon Thought, 18,* 9–105.

Radcliffe-Brown, A. R. (1950). Introduction. In A. R. Radcliffe-Brown & D. Forde (Eds.), *African systems of kinship and marriage* (pp. 1–85). London: Oxford University Press.

Rasmussen, S. J. (1987). Interpreting androgynous women: Female aging and personhood among the Kel Ewey Tuareg. *Ethnology, 26,* 17–30.

Rothman, E. K. (1984). *Hands and hearts: A history of courtship in America.* New York: Basic Books.

Ryan, D. (1969). Marriage in Mendi. In R. M. Glasse & M. J. Meggitt (Eds.), *Pigs, pearl shells, and women: Marriage in the New Guinea Highlands* (pp. 159–175). Englewood Cliffs, NJ: Prentice-Hall.

Sheldon, C. H. (1976). Mormon haters. In C. L. Bushman (Ed.), *Mormon sisters: Women in early Utah* (pp. 113–131). Cambridge, MA: Emmeline Press.

Smith, J. E., & Kunz, P. R. (1976). Polygyny and fertility in 19th century America. *Population Studies, 30,* 465–480.

Solomon, D. A. (1984). *In my father's house.* New York: Franklin Watts.

Spencer, C. Y. (1961). *Brigham Young at home.* Salt Lake City, UT: Deseret Book Company.

Stenning, D. J. (1958). Household viability among the pastoral Fulani. In J. Goody (Ed.), *The development cycle in domestic groups* (pp. 92–119). Cambridge, England: Cambridge University Press.

Stenning, D. J. (1971). Household variability among the pastoral Fulani. In Y. A. Cohen (Ed.), *Man in adaptation: The institutional framework* (pp. 49–68). Aldine: Chicago.

Stephens, W. (1963). *The family in a cross-cultural perspective.* New York: Holt, Rinehart & Winston.

Stone, L. (1977). *The family, sex and marriage in England, 1500–1800.* New York: Harper & Row.

Strathern, M. (1972). *Women in between: Female roles in a male world: Mount Hagen, New Guinea.* London and New York: Seminar Press.

Strathern, A., & Strathern, M. (1969). Marriage in Melpa. In R. M. Glasse & M. J. Meggitt (Eds.), *Pigs, pearl shells, and women: Marriage in the New Guinea Highlands* (pp. 138–158). Englewood Cliffs, NJ: Prentice-Hall.

Talle, A. (1987). Women as heads of houses: The organization of production and the role of women among pastoral Maasai in Kenya. *Ethnos, 1–2,* 50–80.

Tanner, A. (1983). *A Mormon Mother.* Salt Lake City, UT: Tanner Trustfund.

Taylor, S. W. (1972). The second coming of Santa Claus: Christmas in a polygamist family. *Dialogue, 7,* 7–10.

Van Wagoner, R. S. (1989). *Mormon polygamy: A history* (2nd ed.). Salt Lake City, UT: Signature Books.

Ware, H. (1979). Polygamy: Women's views in a transitional society, Nigeria, 1975. *Journal of Marriage and Family, 41,* 185–195.

Warenski, M. (1978). *Patriarchs and politics: The plight of the Mormon woman.* New York: McGraw-Hill.

Watt, B. F. (1978). Bathsheba Smith. In V. Burgess-Olson (ed.), *Sister saints* (pp. 203–221). Provo, UT: Brigham Young University Press.

Welch, C. E., & Glick, P. C. (1981). The incidence of polygamy in contemporary Africa: A research note. *Journal of Marriage and the Family, 43,* 191–193.

Werner, C. M., Altman, I., & Oxley, D. (1985). Temporal aspects of homes: A transactional perspective. In I. Altman and C. M. Werner (Eds.), *Home environments.* Vol. 8 of *Human behavior and environment: Advances in theory and research* (pp. 1–32). New York: Plenum.

Werner, C. M., & Baxter, L. A. (1994). Temporal qualities of relationships: Organismic, transactional, and dialectical views. In M. L. Knapp and G. R. Miller (Eds.), *Handbook of interpersonal communication* (2nd ed.) (pp. 323–379). Beverly Hills, CA: Sage.

Werner, C. M., & Haggard, L. M. (1985). Temporal qualities of interpersonal relationships. In G. R. Miller and M. L. Knapp (Eds.), *Handbook of interpersonal communication* (pp. 59–99). Beverly Hills, CA: Sage.

Wicker, A. W. (1982). *An introduction to ecological psychology.* New York: Cambridge University Press.

Wicker, A. W. (1987). An expanded conceptual framework for analyzing behavior settings. In D. Stokols and I. Altman (Eds.), *Handbook of environmental psychology* (pp. 613–654). New York: Wiley.

Wilson, M. (1950). Nyakyusa kinship. In A. R. Radcliffe-Brown & D. Forde (Eds.), *African systems of kinship and marriage* (pp. 111–139). London: Oxford University Press.

Winans, E. V. (1964). The Shambla family. In R. F. Gray and P. H. Gulliver (Eds.), *The family estate in Africa* (pp. 35–62). London: Routledge and Kegan Paul.

Young, A. E. (1908). *Life in Mormon bondage.* Philadelphia: Aldine.

Young, K. (1954). *Isn't one wife enough?* New York: Holt, Rinehart & Winston.

Index